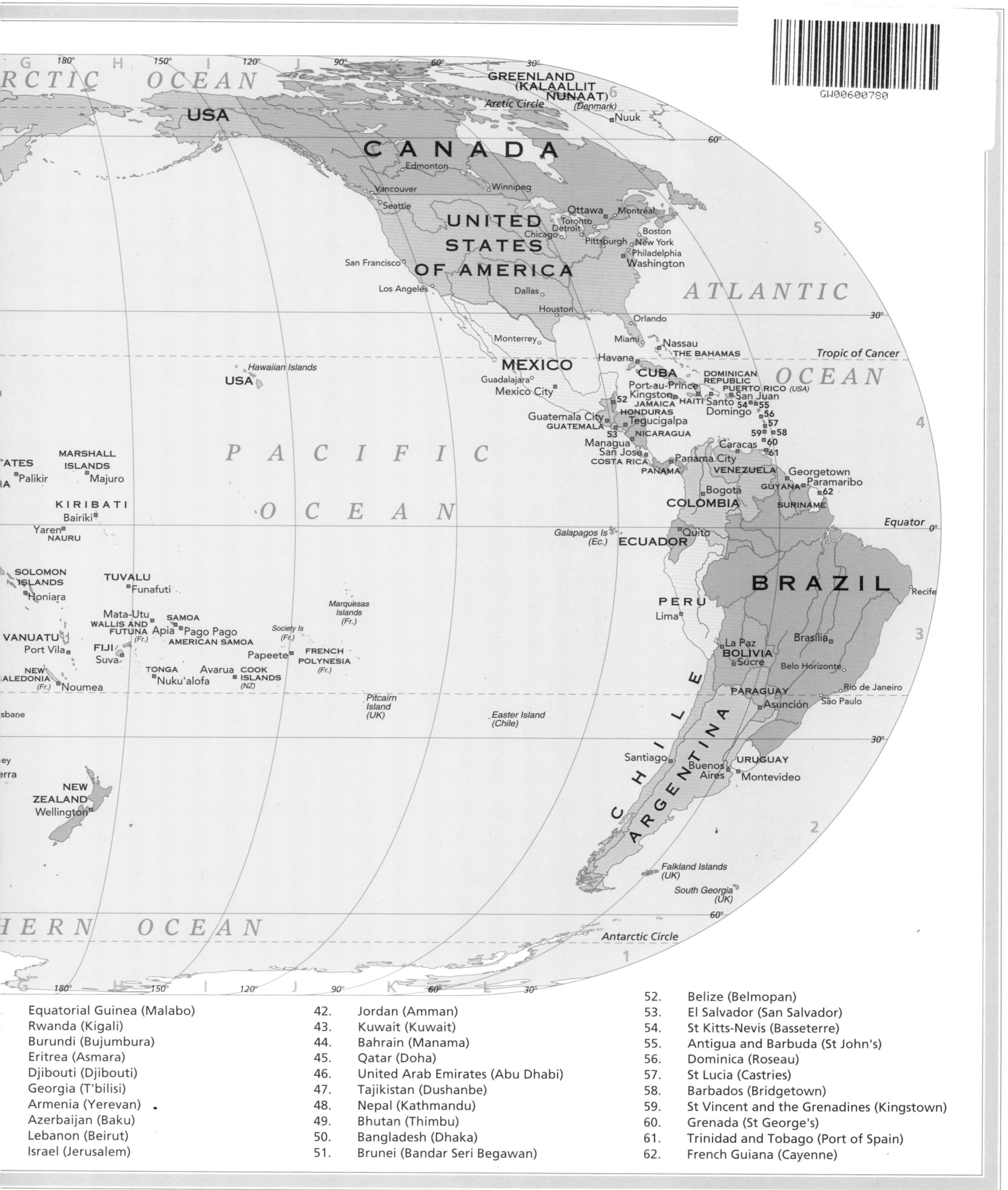

Equatorial Guinea (Malabo)
Rwanda (Kigali)
Burundi (Bujumbura)
Eritrea (Asmara)
Djibouti (Djibouti)
Georgia (T'bilisi)
Armenia (Yerevan)
Azerbaijan (Baku)
Lebanon (Beirut)
Israel (Jerusalem)

42. Jordan (Amman)
43. Kuwait (Kuwait)
44. Bahrain (Manama)
45. Qatar (Doha)
46. United Arab Emirates (Abu Dhabi)
47. Tajikistan (Dushanbe)
48. Nepal (Kathmandu)
49. Bhutan (Thimbu)
50. Bangladesh (Dhaka)
51. Brunei (Bandar Seri Begawan)

52. Belize (Belmopan)
53. El Salvador (San Salvador)
54. St Kitts-Nevis (Basseterre)
55. Antigua and Barbuda (St John's)
56. Dominica (Roseau)
57. St Lucia (Castries)
58. Barbados (Bridgetown)
59. St Vincent and the Grenadines (Kingstown)
60. Grenada (St George's)
61. Trinidad and Tobago (Port of Spain)
62. French Guiana (Cayenne)

Eckert IV projection

fifth edition

Longman
Atlas

Malcolm Stacey
Brian Ralph

PEARSON
Longman

Sydney, Melbourne, Brisbane, Perth and
associated companies around the world

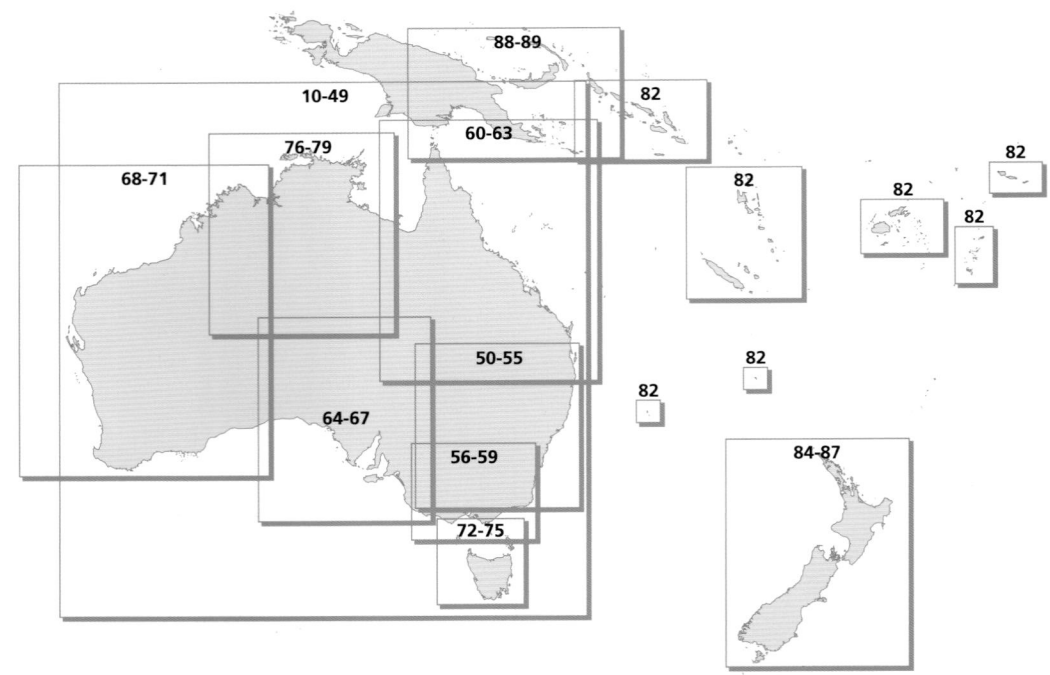

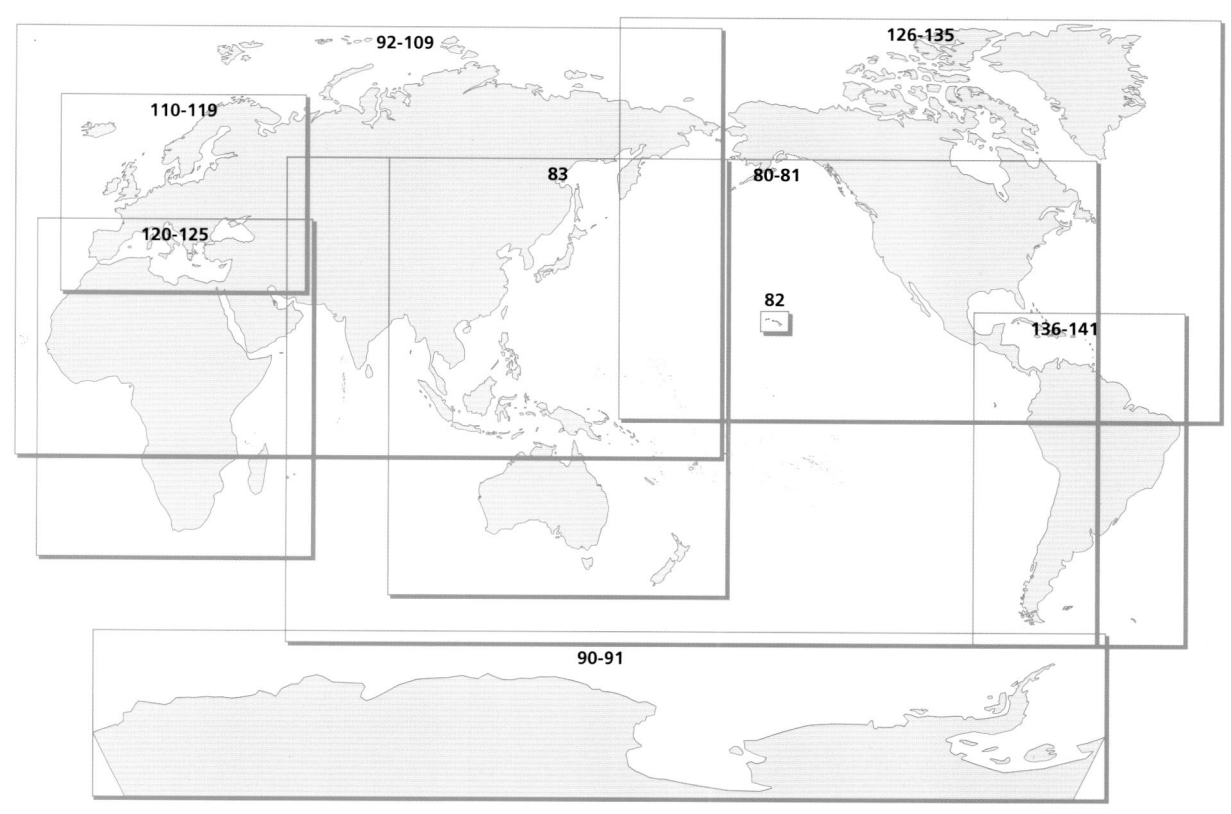

1 MAP SYMBOLS

Symbols are used on a map to show the location of features such as roads, rivers and towns. The meaning of each symbol used on a map is explained in the **key**.

Map symbols often look like the features they represent. The colour of a symbol may also provide a clue to its meaning. The importance of a feature might be shown by the size of the symbol itself or the size of the printing next to the symbol.

Some examples of the symbols used in this atlas are shown below:

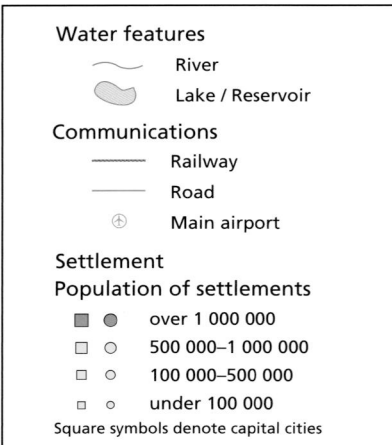

Water features
~ River
Lake / Reservoir
Communications
—— Railway
—— Road
⊕ Main airport
Settlement
Population of settlements
■ ● over 1 000 000
□ ○ 500 000–1 000 000
□ ○ 100 000–500 000
□ ○ under 100 000
Square symbols denote capital cities

2 DIRECTION

Direction is important in atlas work because it tells us where one place is in relation to other places. The easiest way of explaining the direction of one place from another is to use the **points of the compass** shown in the diagram below.

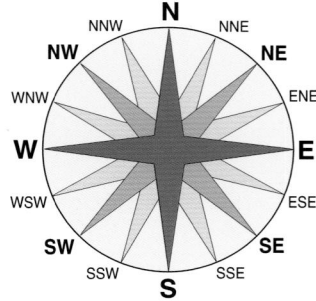

North, south, east and west are called the **cardinal points** of the compass. The other points are called **intermediate points.** Many maps have a **north point** to show us where north is. If a map does not have a north point then north is at the top of the map.

3 TYPES OF ATLAS MAPS

The countries of South-East Asia

Settlement maps are used to give you an idea of the size and location of the countries and cities in each continent. Coloured squares denote a capital city. Coloured circles denote other cities and towns. These maps are also often called political maps.
See pages 110, 136, and 142-143 for further examples of this type of map.

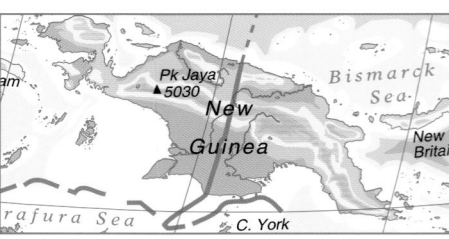
Physical map of New Guinea

Physical maps are used to show oceans, seas, rivers, lakes, the height of the land and the names of major landforms. Please see page 8 for more information about land height, relief, colour layers and spot heights.
See pages 11 and 94-95 for further examples of this type of map.

Reference map of Southern Greece

Reference maps bring together the information provided in settlement maps and physical maps. They show the relief and physical features of a region, as well as country borders, major cities and towns, main roads, railways and main airports.
See pages 52 and 98 for further examples of this type of map.

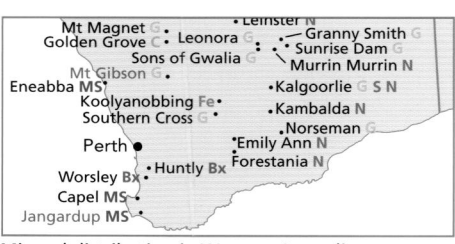
Mineral distribution in Western Australia

Simple distribution maps use different colours, symbols or shading to show the location and distribution (spread) of a particular natural or human feature in an area. In this map on the left, different symbols have been used to show the location of different minerals in Australia.
See pages 20 and 49 for further examples of this type of map.

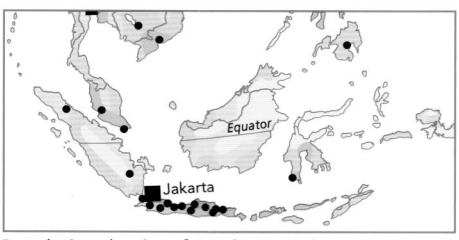
Population density of South-East Asia

Density maps use dots, colours or shading to show a feature's location and density (how close together or how far apart it is). In this map on the left, colours are used to show population density. The darker the colour, the greater the number of people in that area.
See pages 42 and 43 for further examples of this type of map.

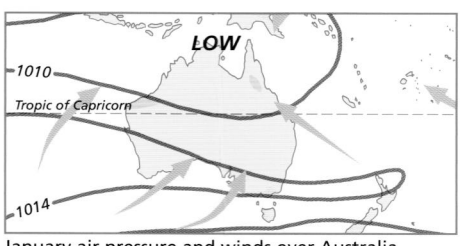
January air pressure and winds over Australia

Isoline maps use thin lines on a map to show the distribution (spread) of a feature. An isoline is a line which passes through places which have the same value or quantity. Isolines may show features such as rainfall, air pressure, temperature and the height of the land. The value of each line is usually written on it.
See pages 16 and 101 for further examples of this type of map.

1 SCALE

To draw a map of any part of the world, the area must be reduced in size, or 'scaled down', so that it will fit onto an atlas page. The scale of a map will tell you by *how much* an area has been reduced in size.

The scale of a map can also be used to work out the real distance between two or more places, or the real size of an area, shown on a map. The **scale** of a map tells us *the relationship between distances on the map and distances on the ground in real life*.

Scale can be shown in a number of ways:
a in words
   e.g. 'one centimetre to one kilometre' (This means that one centimetre on the map represents one kilometre on the ground.)
   e.g. 'one centimetre to one metre' (This means that one centimetre on the map represents one metre on the ground.)
b in numbers
   e.g. '1:100 000' or '1/100 000' (This means that one centimetre on the map represents 100 000 centimetres, or one kilometre, on the ground.)
   e.g. '1:25 000' or '1/25 000' (This means that one centimetre on the map represents 25 000 centimetres, or 250 metres, on the ground.)
   e.g. '1:100' or '1/100' (This means that one centimetre on the map represents 100 centimetres, or one metre, on the ground.)
c as a line scale
   e.g.

```
0        200      400      600        800 km
```

2 MAP SCALE AND MAP INFORMATION

Every map provides you with some sort of information about a place. The scale of the map, however, will also determine *how much* and *what type* of information can be shown. As the area shown on the map becomes larger and larger, the amount of detail and the accuracy of the map become less and less. Look at the examples below:

Example 1: Hobart, Capital City of Tasmania, Scale 1:2 500 000
At this scale you can see that the city of Hobart is located on the western side of a river mouth, protected from the open sea by several islands and peninsulas.

Example 2: Tasmania, Scale 1:20 000 000
At this scale detailed information about Hobart is lost, but you can discover two new facts:
a Tasmania is an island, separated from mainland Australia by a body of water known as Bass Strait
b Hobart is located in the south-east corner of this island.

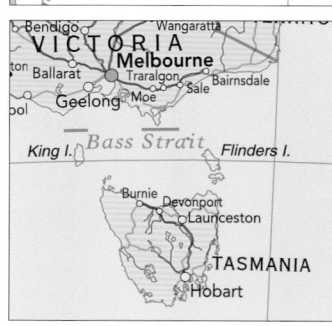

3 USING THE SCALE TO MEASURE DISTANCE

When a map does not have any distances printed on it, you can use the scale of the map to work out how far it is from one place to another. The easiest scale to use is the **line scale**. You must find out how far apart the places are on the map and then see what this distance represents on the line scale.

To measure the straight line distance between two places on a map:
a place the edge of a sheet of paper on the two points on the map,
b mark off the distance between the two points onto the paper,
c place the paper on the line scale,
d read off the distance on the scale.

STEP 1: To find the distance between Adelaide and Wagga Wagga, for example, line up the paper between the two places and mark off the distance.

STEP 2: Compare this distance with the marks on the line scale. The straight-line distance between Adelaide and Wagga Wagga is about 800 kilometres.

```
0      200    400    600    800    1000 km
```
Adelaide   Wagga Wagga

To measure the distance between two places when there are bends or curves:
a place the edge of a sheet of paper on the map and mark off the starting point on the paper,
b now move the paper so that its edge follows the bends and curves on the map (Hint: Use the tip of your pencil to pin the edge of the paper to the curve as you pivot the paper around each curve),
c mark off the end point on your sheet of paper,
d place the paper on the line scale,
e read off the distance on the scale.

To find the distance by road between Mildura and Goulburn, for example, mark off the start point, then twist the paper to follow the curve of the road through Hay and Wagga Wagga. The distance is about 720 kilometres.

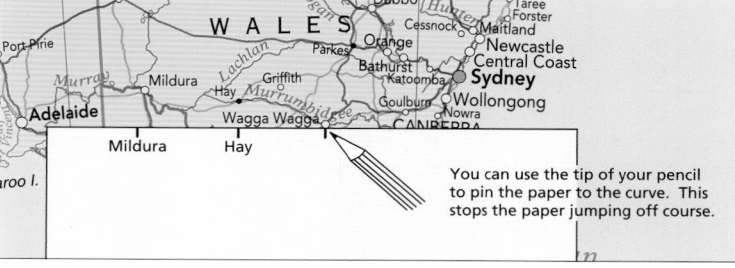

You can use the tip of your pencil to pin the paper to the curve. This stops the paper jumping off course.

There are several different ways of finding places on a map. In this atlas we use two different methods:

a **letters and numbers** around the edge of the map
b **lines of latitude and longitude** drawn on the map.

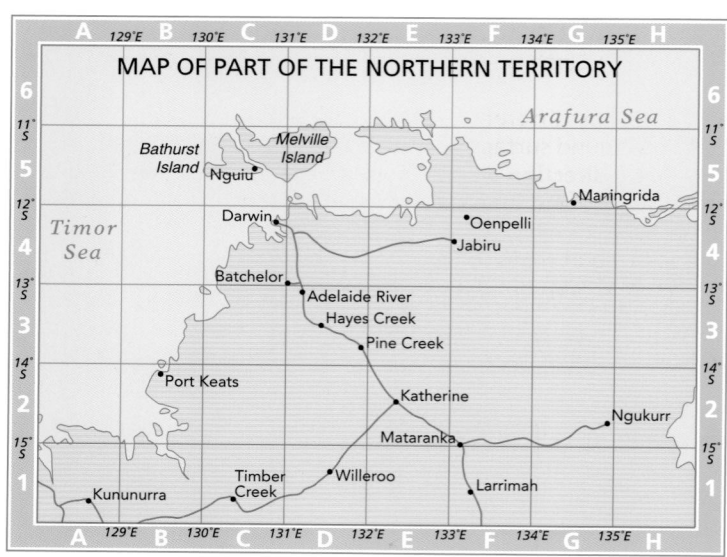

MAP OF PART OF THE NORTHERN TERRITORY

1 LETTERS AND NUMBERS

To use the letters and numbers to find a place :

a look up the name of the place in the index at the back of the atlas,
b find the page number and the area reference, e.g. page10, **E2**,
c go to the correct page in the atlas,
d find **E** in the border below the map,
e find **2** in the border up the side of the map,
f follow the letter up and follow the number across until you find the correct square, **E2**,
g search the square for the place you are looking for.

Look at the Northern Territory map on the right. Katherine is in square **E2**, Darwin in **C4**, Adelaide River in **D3** and Larrimah in **F1**.

2 LATITUDE

Lines of latitude are imaginary lines which run in an east–west direction around the world. They are also known as **parallels of latitude** because they run parallel to each other in a series of shrinking circles from the equator to the poles. Latitude is measured in **degrees** (°).

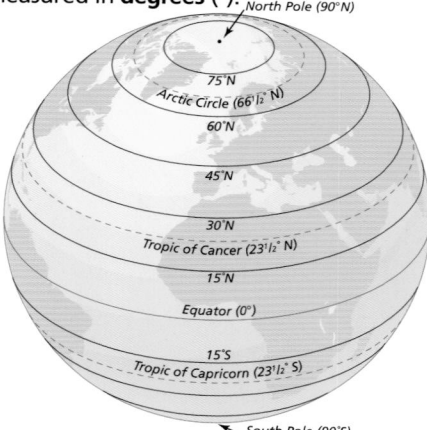

The most important line of latitude in the world is the **equator**. The equator is at 0° latitude, while the **North Pole** is at latitude 90° north and the **South Pole** is at latitude 90° south.

All lines of latitude are given a number between 0° and 90° either **north (N)** or **south (S)** of the equator. Some well-known lines of latitude include:
• the Arctic Circle (latitude 66½°N)
• the Tropic of Cancer (latitude 23½°N)
• the Tropic of Capricorn (latitude 23½°S)
• the Antarctic Circle (latitude 66½°S).

The equator is used to divide the Earth into two halves. The northern half is called the **northern hemisphere**. The southern half is called the **southern hemisphere**.

3 LONGITUDE

Lines of longitude are imaginary lines which run in a north–south direction from the North Pole to the South Pole in large circles of the same size. These lines are also known as **meridians of longitude**. They are also measured in **degrees** (°).

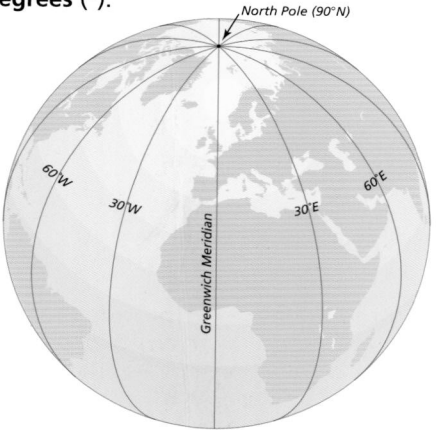

The most important line of longitude in the world is the **prime meridian** or **Greenwich meridian**, which is at 0° longitude. Exactly opposite this meridian on the other side of the Earth is longitude 180°, often called the **International Date Line**.

All lines of longitude are given a number between 0° and 180° either **east (E)** or **west (W)** of the Greenwich meridian.

The Greenwich meridian (0°) and the International Date Line (180°) can be used to divide the Earth into two halves. The half to the west of the Greenwich meridian is called the **western hemisphere**. The half to the east of the Greenwich meridian is called the **eastern hemisphere**.

4 FINDING PLACES

When lines of latitude and longitude are drawn on a map they form a grid, which looks like a pattern of squares. We can use this grid to find places on a map. **Latitude is always given before longitude.**

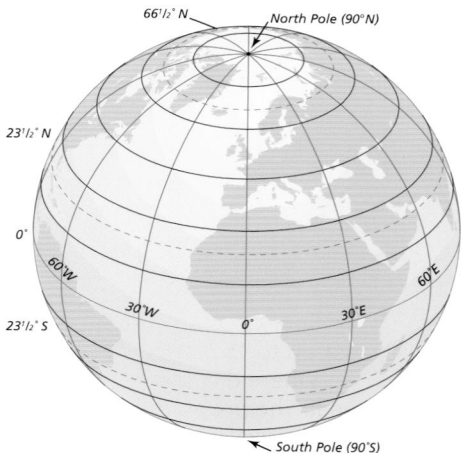

On the Northern Territory map (above), Batchelor is very easy to find because it is almost exactly at latitude 13° south (13°S) and longitude 131° east (131°E). Similarly, Mataranka is very close to latitude 15°S and longitude 133°E (15°S 133°E).

However, we often need to be more accurate than this. Each degree of latitude and longitude can be subdivided into 60 equal parts called **minutes** ('). A place halfway between latitude 33° and 34° would therefore be at latitude 33°30'. A place one-quarter of the way between 33° and 34° would be at 33°15'. On the Northern Territory map, Katherine is about halfway between 14°S and 15°S, and about one-quarter of the way between 132°E and 133°E. Its location is therefore approximately 14°30'S 132°15'E.

We all know that the Earth is a *sphere* and that atlas maps are *flat*. Map makers have invented different ways of drawing the curved surface of the Earth on a flat piece of paper. These different ways of drawing the Earth are called **map projections**.

There are many different types of map projection but none of them is perfect. This is because every map projection has to stretch or squash the round surface of the Earth to make it fit onto a flat piece of paper. As a result, no map projection can ever show correct **shape, area, direction and distance** all at the same time. To draw any one of these four things accurately, the other three end up being distorted and inaccurate to some extent.

When looking at maps in an atlas it is important to remember that each map projection has its advantages and disadvantages. The main types of map projection are shown below, and four world map projections are compared on the inside back cover.

1 CYLINDRICAL PROJECTIONS

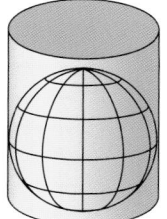 

Cylindrical projections are constructed by projecting the surface of a globe (the Earth) onto a **cylinder** which just touches the outside edges of the globe.

Some examples of cylindrical projections are:

Mercator
South-East Asia pp. 98–99

Mercator is a cylindrical projection. It is useful for areas up to 15° north or south of the equator, where distortion of shape is minimal. The projection is useful for navigation as directions can be plotted as straight lines.

Eckert IV
World pp. 144–145

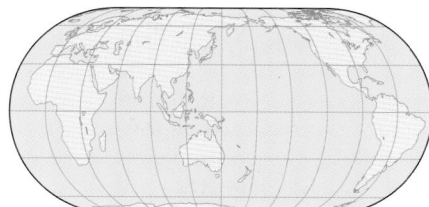

Eckert IV is an equal-area projection. Equal-area projections are useful for world thematic maps where it is important to show the correct relative sizes of continental areas. Eckert IV has a straight central meridian but all others are curved, which helps suggest the spherical nature of the earth.

2 CONIC PROJECTIONS

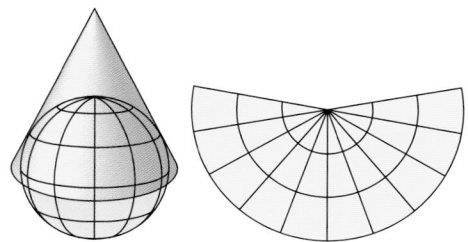

Conic projections are constructed by projecting the surface of a globe (the Earth) onto a **cone** which just touches the outside edges of the globe.

Some examples of conic projections are:

Conic Equidistant
Russian Federation pp. 118–119

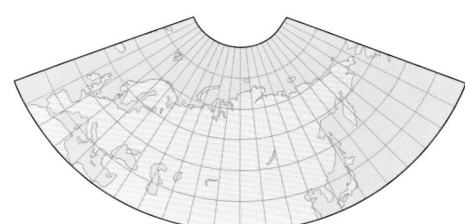

Conic projections are best suited for areas between 30° and 60° north and south of the equator with longer east–west extent than north–south extent, such as the Russian Federation. The meridians are straight and spaced at equal intervals.

Chamberlin Trimetric
North America p. 126

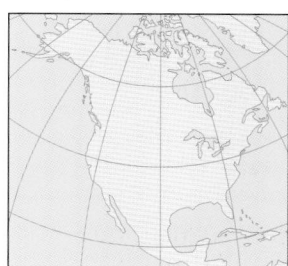

Chamberlin Trimetric is an equidistant projection. It shows correct distances from approximately three points. It is used for areas with greater north–south than east–west extent, such as North America.

3 AZIMUTHAL PROJECTIONS

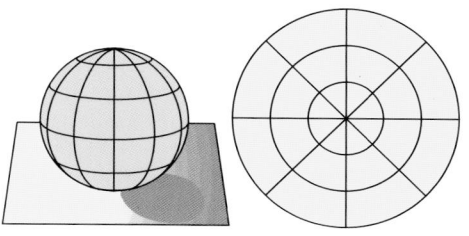

Azimuthal projections are constructed by projecting the surface of a globe (the Earth) onto a **flat surface** which just touches the globe at one point only.

Some examples of azimuthal projections are:

Lambert Azimuthal Equal Area
Australia p. 10

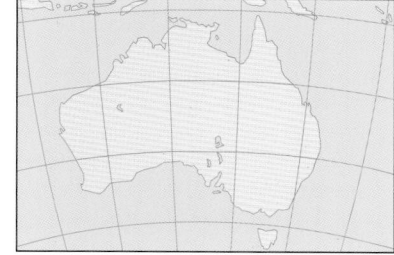

Lambert's projection is useful for areas which have similar east–west and north–south dimensions, such as Australia.

Polar Stereographic
Antarctica pp. 90–91

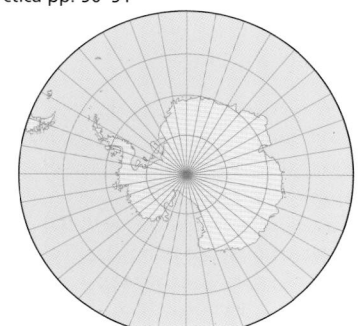

This projection is a good choice for showing travel routes from a central point, as points on the map are in constant relative position and distance from the centre.

1 CLIMATIC STATISTICS AND TABLES

Throughout this atlas there are sets of **climatic statistics** (numbers showing temperatures and rainfall) for many different places. These statistics are set out in **climatic tables** like the one below for Albany, Western Australia:

Albany (68 m)	Jan	Feb	Mar	Apr	May	Jun	Jul	Aug	Sep	Oct	Nov	Dec
Temperature, max. (°C)	25	25	24	22	19	17	16	16	17	19	21	23
Temperature, min. (°C)	14	14	13	12	10	8	7	7	8	9	11	12
Rainfall (mm)	28	25	29	66	102	104	126	104	81	80	46	24

a On the top line in the table are the name of the place, its altitude (height above sea level) and the months of the year.
b On the next two lines is information about the average maximum (highest) and minimum (lowest) temperatures for each month.
c On the bottom line is information about the average amount of rainfall for each month.

We can use this information to draw climatic graphs and understand what the climate is like in these places.

2 CLIMATIC GRAPHS

A **climatic graph** is a graph of the average temperatures and average rainfall of a place for the twelve months of the year. Look at this example of a climatic graph for Albany, which has been drawn from the climatic table shown above:

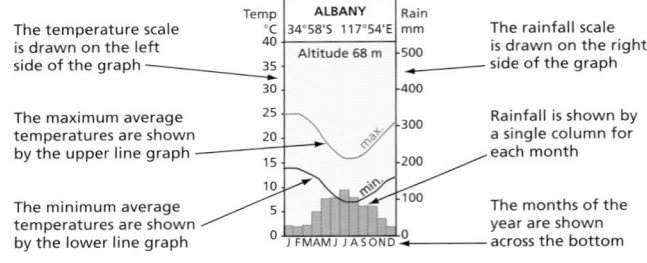

3 UNDERSTANDING CLIMATIC GRAPHS

a Temperature lines which are almost flat show that this place is close to the equator and that it has even temperatures all year.
b Temperature lines which have a large dip (∨) during one half of the year and a large bump (∧) during the other half of the year show that this place has a definite winter and summer season.
c If the winter (∨) is during June, July and August then this place is in the southern hemisphere.
d If the summer (∧) is during June, July and August then this place is in the northern hemisphere.
e The grouping together of a number of high rainfall columns shows that this place has a distinct wet season.
f The grouping together of a number of low rainfall columns shows that this place has a distinct dry season.
g If all the rainfall columns are high then this place is wet all year.
h If all the rainfall columns are quite low (or non-existent) then this place is very dry all year.

The climatic graph for Albany is an example of **b, c, e,** and **f**.

4 UNDERSTANDING RELIEF

When we talk about the **relief** of an area we are talking about the height of the land, or to be more accurate, *differences in the height of the land*. In this atlas, differences in the height of the land are shown by:
a **colour layers**, where different colours are used to show the different heights
b **spot heights**, where dots or triangles, with numbers beside them, show the location and height of places on the map.

5 COLOUR LAYERS

Maps which use colour layers to show the relief of an area will always have a **relief scale** nearby to explain what each colour means. Look at this relief scale and the explanation beside it:

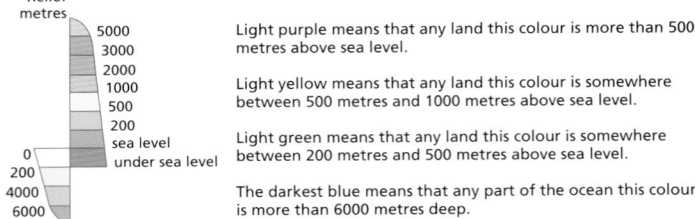

Light purple means that any land this colour is more than 5000 metres above sea level.

Light yellow means that any land this colour is somewhere between 500 metres and 1000 metres above sea level.

Light green means that any land this colour is somewhere between 200 metres and 500 metres above sea level.

The darkest blue means that any part of the ocean this colour is more than 6000 metres deep.

6 SPOT HEIGHTS

Many maps use spot heights to show the highest mountains in an area. Look at this example from a map of the island of New Guinea:

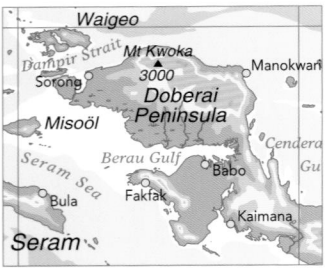

Doberai Peninsula, New Guinea

3000 ▲ Mountain height (in metres)

The Doberai Peninsula is located on the north-western end of New Guinea. This map tells us that the highest mountain on this peninsula is Mt Kwoka, which is 3000 metres high.

If we combine our knowledge of spot heights with our knowledge about colour layers, we can also say that:
a the Doberai Peninsula has a large mountain area in the north-east
b this mountain area covers nearly half the peninsula
c Mt Kwoka is located at the north-western end of this mountain range.

7 PUTTING IT ALL TOGETHER

The next step in developing our skills is to try to imagine what an area would look like in real life. Here is an example of what the Doberai Peninsula would look like if we were in a high-flying aeroplane south of the town of Babo, and it was a very clear day:

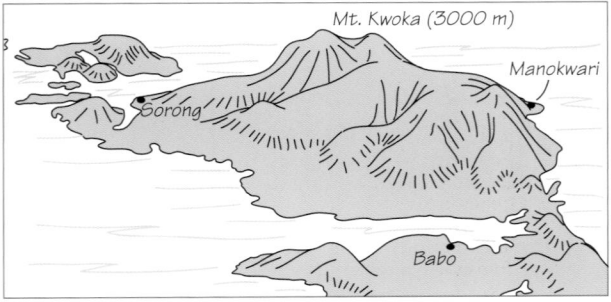

Field sketch of Doberai Peninsula

This extract from the conventional 'false colour' Landsat image of Adelaide (p. 66) shows the city and its surrounding urban area of houses, gardens and parks **C9** as a mix of blue-greys and reds, coastal mangroves **B11** and forested hills **E9** as dark reds, and farming areas **C13** as a patchwork of reds, greens, blues and yellows.

One of the recent trends in Landsat imagery has been to alter its conventional false colours to give a more natural colour image. In this 'natural colour' image of the same area as shown above, Adelaide's urban areas show up as mauve and green, forests and mangroves as dark green, and farmlands as a patchwork of colours.

1 SATELLITE REMOTE SENSING

A large number of specialised satellites currently orbit the Earth, sending back a mass of useful information for a wide variety of purposes. These satellites are fitted with cameras, scanners and/or sensors to obtain data for scientific research, observation and analysis of the world's atmosphere, oceans and continents.

Unlike cameras which use visible light to produce photographs, satellite scanners and sensors can make scientific measurements and detect different types of electromagnetic radiation including X-ray, ultraviolet, visible, infrared and microwave. This information is recorded in digital form, transmitted back to the Earth and may then be processed into images or 'pictures'.

2 SATELLITE IMAGES IN THIS ATLAS

A wide variety of satellite images and photographs has been used in this atlas to help explain different topics and themes. You may wish to examine some of the following examples:

a   Colour-enhanced NOAA-15 satellite image of Cyclone Vance (p. 26)
b   Infrared satellite image of Australian weather patterns (p. 16)
c   Landsat 'false colour' image of the Great Barrier Reef (p. 61)
d   Landsat 'natural colour' image of Brisbane (p. 62)
e   NOAA satellite images of Australian ocean currents (p. 24)
f   NOAA NDVI satellite image of Tasmanian vegetation (p. 73)
g   NOAA visual/infrared composite image of Asian fires (p. 100)
h   NASA ozone spectrometer image of fire pollution (p. 100)

3 UNDERSTANDING LANDSAT IMAGES

One of the most often used satellite images is the Landsat image. These have been specifically designed to provide data about the Earth's surface and its resources. Landsat 7, the most recent of the Landsat satellites, was launched in April 1999. It orbits the earth at an altitude of 705 km, scans a 185 km wide strip each orbit, and provides coverage of the entire globe once every 16 days.

Landsat 7 has sensors which can record data in the visible, near-infrared, middle and thermal infrared wave bands. This data is translated into black-and-white or colour images which, because they are not photographs, are called 'false colour' images. These are used in land use, mapping, agricultural, forestry, geological, water resource, marine resource and environmental studies.

In a conventional 'false colour' Landsat image, the following colours indicate the following features:

White–cream	Bare ground, sand areas, salt areas, clouds
Yellow	Areas with little vegetation cover, heavily grazed areas, desert sand dunes
Pink–red	Early growth in crops and grasslands
Red	Healthy green vegetation, growing crops, rainforest (deep red), mangroves (red–brown)
Brown	Woodland, bare rock areas
Light green	Moist ploughed fields, poor grazing lands
Dark green	Forests or scrub, clear shallow water, muddy flood waters
Blue–light blue	Arid scrubland, very shallow water
Blue–grey	Urban areas, concrete, houses, river flood plains
Dark blue–black	Ocean, deep clear water, shadows from clouds

A   120°   B   130°   C   140°   D   150°   E

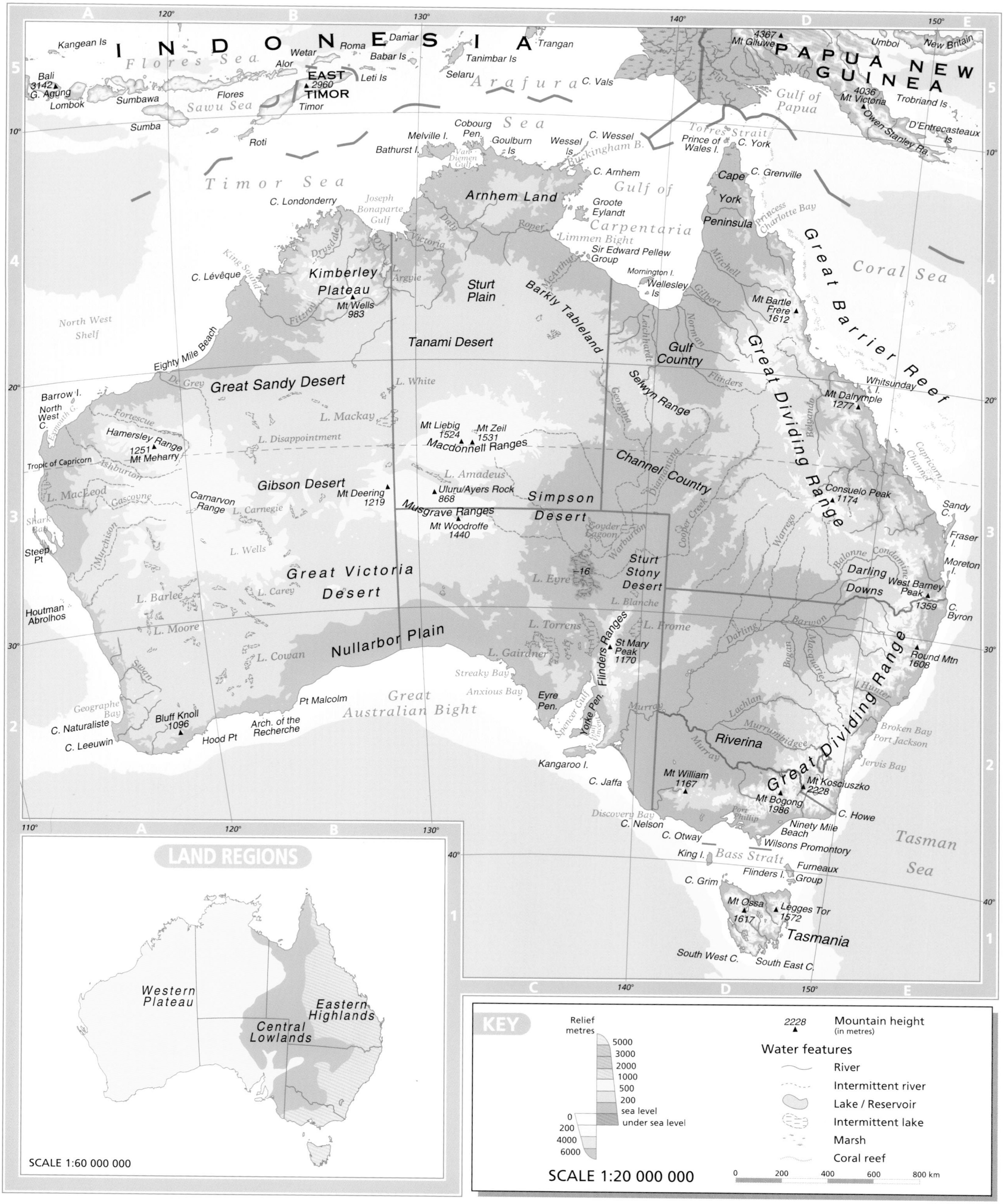

I N D O N E S I A

Kangean Is

Flores   Sea

Bali
3142▲
G. Agung
Lombok

Wetar   Roma   Damar

Sumbawa   Alor

Flores

Sawu Sea

Sumba   Roti

Babar Is   Trangan

Leti Is

**EAST
TIMOR**
2960▲

Timor

Arafura   C. Vals

4367▲
Mt Giluwe

P A P U A   N E W
G U I N E A

Umboi   New Britain

4036▲
Mt Victoria   Trobriand Is

D'Entrecasteaux
Is

Timor   Sea

C. Londonderry

*Joseph
Bonaparte
Gulf*

Melville I.

Bathurst I.

Cobourg
Pen.

*Van
Diemen
Gulf*

Goulburn
Is

Wessel
Is

C. Wessel

Buckingham B.

Torres Strait

*Gulf of
Papua*

Owen Stanley Ra.

10°   Tanimbar Is

Selaru

Prince of
Wales I.   C. York

10°

Gulf of

Arnhem Land

Groote
Eylandt

Sir Edward Pellew
Group

Limmen Bight

Mornington I.
Wellesley
Is

C. Arnhem

Roper

C. Wessel

Cape
York
Peninsula

C. Grenville

*Princess
Charlotte Bay*

Great Barrier Reef

Coral   Sea

C. Lévêque

King Sound

Kimberley
Plateau

Mt Wells
983▲

L.
Argyle

Sturt
Plain

Daly

Victoria

Barkly Tableland

McArthur

Gulf
Country

Leichhardt

Gilbert   *Norman*

Mitchell

Mt Bartle
Frere
1612▲

*North West
Shelf*

Fitzroy

De Grey

Eighty Mile Beach

Great Sandy Desert

Tanami Desert

L. White

Flinders

Selwyn Range

Great Dividing Range

Whitsunday
I.

20°   Barrow I.
North
West
C.

Fortescue

Ashburton

Exmouth G.

Hamersley Range
1251▲
Mt Meharry

L. Mackay

L. Disappointment

Mt Liebig
1524▲   Mt Zeil
1531▲
Macdonnell Ranges

Georgina

Channel Country

Diamantina

Mt Dalrymple
1277▲   20°

Tropic of Capricorn

Murchison

Gascoyne

L. MacLeod

Gibson Desert

Carnarvon
Range   L. Carnegie

Mt Deering
1219▲

L. Amadeus

Uluru/Ayers Rock
868▲

Simpson
Desert

Cooper Creek

Consuelo Peak
1174▲

Sandy
C.

Fraser
I.

*Capricorn
Channel*

Shark
Bay

Steep
Pt

L. Wells

Musgrave Ranges

Mt Woodroffe
1440▲

Warburton

Coyder
Lagoon

Sturt
Stony
Desert

Warrego

Balonne

Condamine

Darling
Downs

West Barney
Peak
1359▲

Moreton
I.

C. Byron

Great Victoria
Desert

L. Barlee

L. Carey

L. Eyre   -16

L. Blanche

Barwon

Darling

Round Mtn
1608▲

Houtman
Abrolhos

Swan

L. Moore

L. Cowan

L. Torrens

L. Frome

Bogan

Lachlan

Macquarie

Great Dividing Range

30°   L. Gairdner

Nullarbor Plain

Flinders Ranges

St Mary
Peak
1170▲

Murrumbidgee

Hunter

30°

*Geographe
Bay*

C. Naturaliste

C. Leeuwin

Bluff Knoll
>1096

Hood Pt

Arch. of the
Recherche

Pt Malcolm

*Great
Australian Bight*

Streaky Bay

Anxious Bay

Eyre
Pen.

Spencer Gulf

Yorke Pen.

Murray

Murray

Riverina

Jervis Bay

Broken Bay
Port Jackson

Kangaroo I.

C. Jaffa

Mt William
1167▲

Mt Bogong
1986▲

Mt Kosciuszko
2228▲

Great Dividing Range

C. Howe

*Tasman
Sea*

Discovery Bay
C. Nelson

C. Otway

Ninety Mile
Beach

Wilsons Promontory

*Port
Phillip*

40°   King I.   *Bass Strait*

Flinders I.

Furneaux
Group

40°

C. Grim

Mt Ossa
1617▲   Legges Tor
1572▲

Tasmania

South West C.   South East C.

110°   120°   130°

A   120°   B   130°

LAND REGIONS

Western
Plateau

Eastern
Highlands

Central
Lowlands

SCALE 1:60 000 000

C   140°   D   150°   E

KEY

Relief
metres

5000
3000
2000
1000
500
200
sea level
0   under sea level
200
4000
6000

2228
▲   Mountain height
(in metres)

Water features

— — —   River

- - - -   Intermittent river

Lake / Reservoir

Intermittent lake

Marsh

Coral reef

SCALE 1:20 000 000

0   200   400   600   800 km

Lambert Azimuthal Equal Area projection

1 JANUARY AVERAGE TEMPERATURE

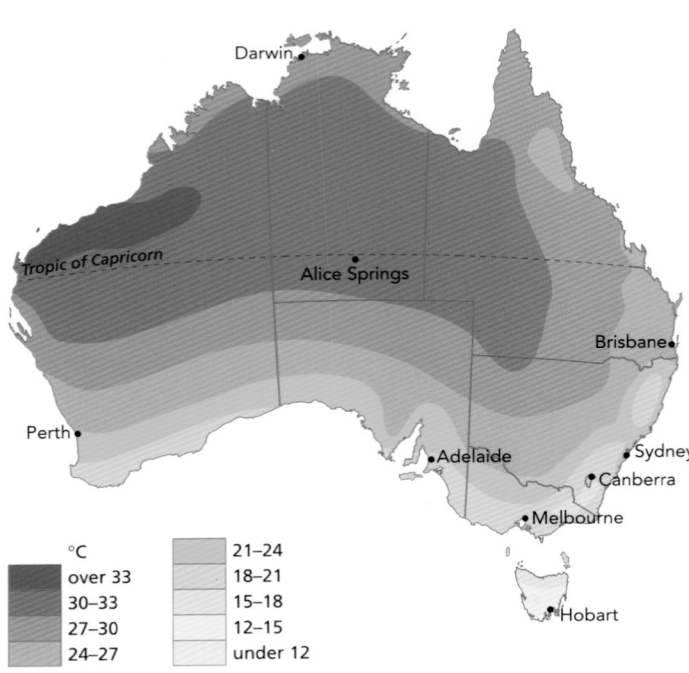

°C
over 33
30–33
27–30
24–27

21–24
18–21
15–18
12–15
under 12

Combining of information about daily maximum temperatures and daily minimum temperatures creates this map of the 'average' temperatures for January. This map also shows how temperatures are usually much higher in inland Australia than around the coast.

2 JULY AVERAGE TEMPERATURE

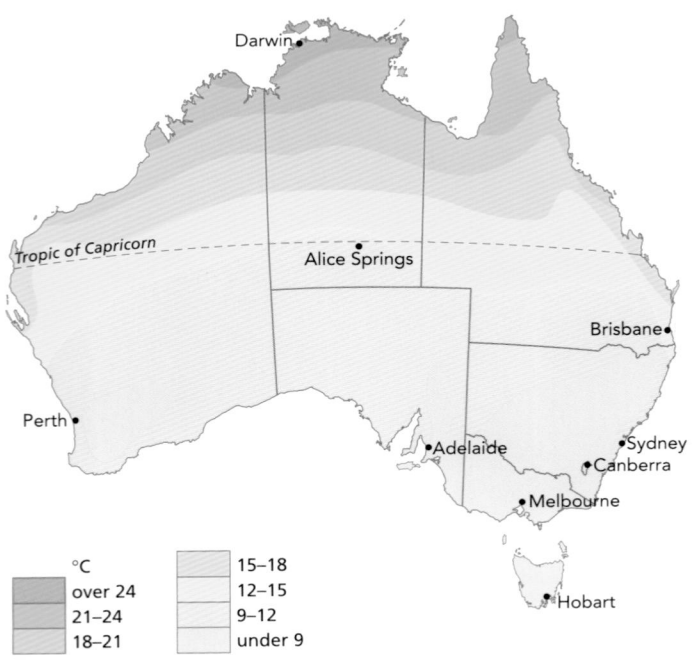

°C
over 24
21–24
18–21

15–18
12–15
9–12
under 9

Combining of information about daily maximum temperatures and daily minimum temperatures creates this map of the 'average' temperatures for July. This map also shows how temperatures decrease as you move south, away from the equator.

3 JANUARY AVERAGE RAINFALL

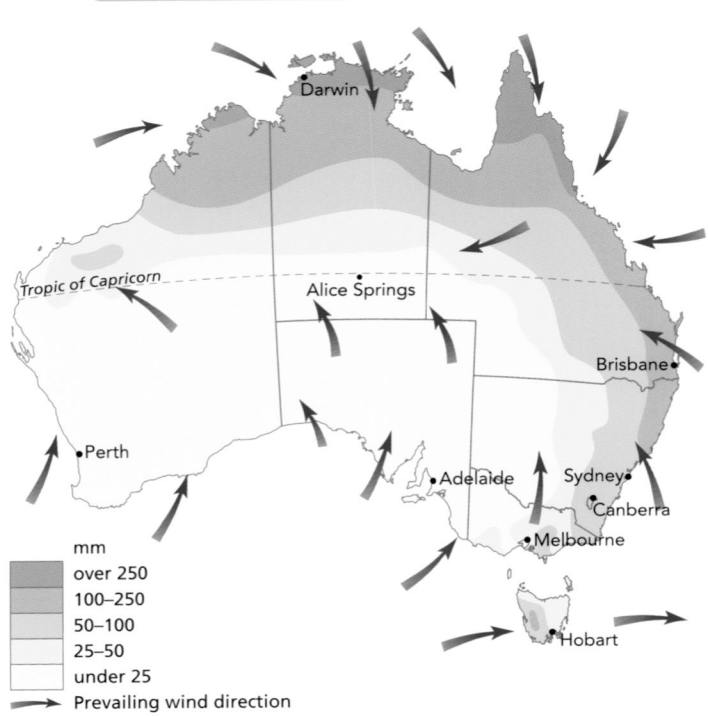

mm
over 250
100–250
50–100
25–50
under 25
➤ Prevailing wind direction

Rain and wind information over many years has been combined on this map to show the 'average' rainfall for January and the most frequent direction of winds at this time. Summer is a time of heavy rains in northern Australia because of the onshore monsoon winds.

4 JULY AVERAGE RAINFALL

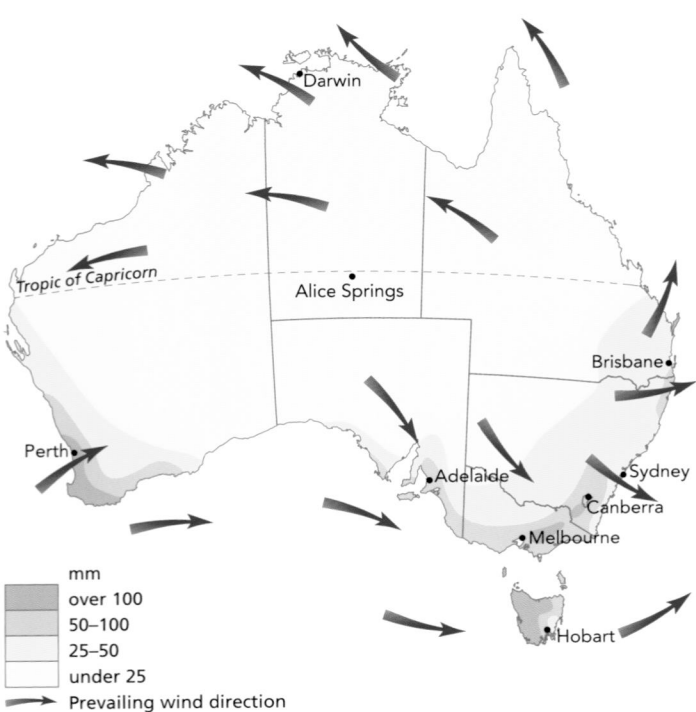

mm
over 100
50–100
25–50
under 25
➤ Prevailing wind direction

Combining of rain and wind information on this map shows that winter is a time of rain in south-west and south-east Australia, but that northern Australia is quite dry. The rain in the south is often caused by the movement of cold fronts from west to east.

SCALE 1:45 000 000

Lambert Azimuthal Equal Area projection

1 AVERAGE ANNUAL TEMPERATURE

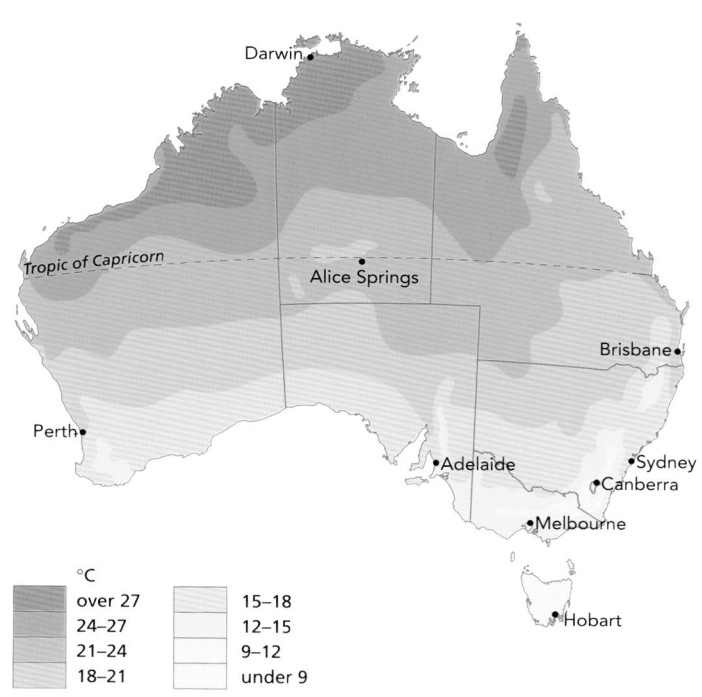

°C
over 27	15–18
24–27	12–15
21–24	9–12
18–21	under 9

Combining of maximum and minimum temperatures throughout the year creates this map of 'average' annual temperatures. This map also shows how temperatures can be affected by landforms. For example, it is cooler in the south-east because of the highlands.

2 HEAT DISCOMFORT

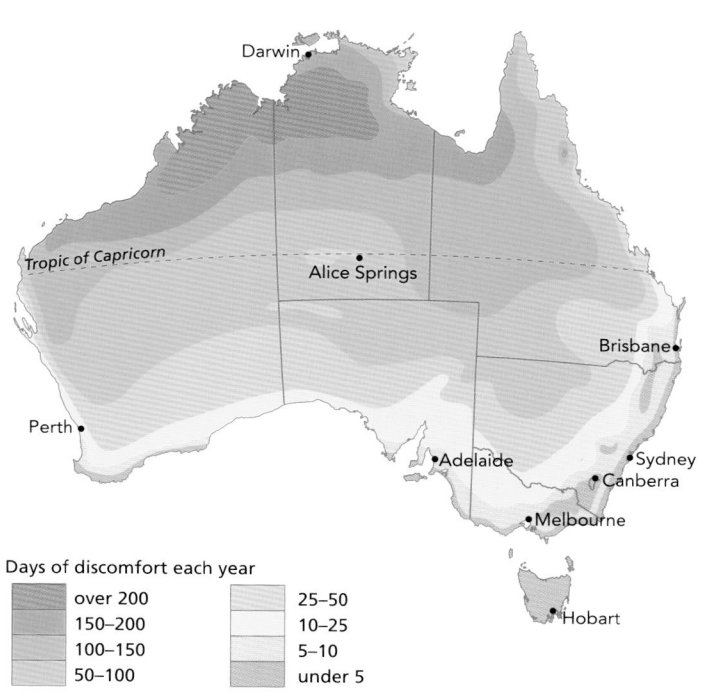

Days of discomfort each year
over 200	25–50
150–200	10–25
100–150	5–10
50–100	under 5

A combination of high temperatures and high humidity can cause people great physical discomfort. This map shows the average number of days of discomfort which can be expected each year. Northern Australia is the most uncomfortable place in which to live.

3 AVERAGE ANNUAL RAINFALL

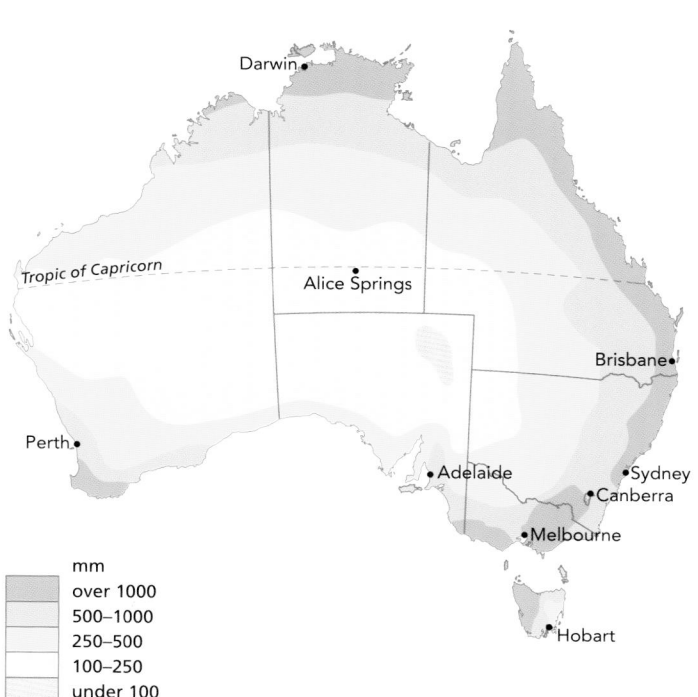

mm
- over 1000
- 500–1000
- 250–500
- 100–250
- under 100

Although this map does not show Australia's distinctive summer and winter rainfall pattern, it does show clearly that coastal areas generally have far more rain than inland Australia. The areas of highest rainfall are where winds blow consistently onshore.

4 RAINY DAYS

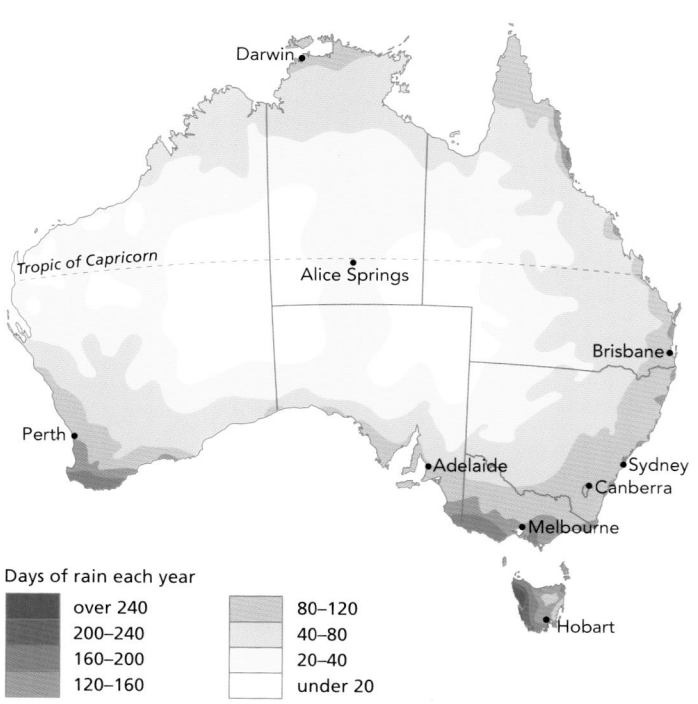

Days of rain each year
over 240	80–120
200–240	40–80
160–200	20–40
120–160	under 20

This map shows how many days of rain can be expected during the year in different parts of Australia. Tasmania is the rainiest state, with its west coast experiencing more than 240 days of rain each year. Inland Australia has the lowest number of rainy days.

SCALE 1:45 000 000

Lambert Azimuthal Equal Area projection

1 CLIMATIC REGIONS

Australia's climatic regions are a result of the interaction of factors such as latitude, landforms, ocean currents and the size of the continent.

Tropical—wet summers
Summers hot to very hot, humid, heavy to very heavy rain.
Winters mild to warm, little or no rain.

Subtropical—wet summers
Summers hot, humid, heavy rain.
Winters mild, moderate rain.

Temperate—uniform rainfall
Summers warm to hot, moderate rain.
Winters cool to cold, moderate rain.

Temperate—wet winters
Summers warm to hot with little rain.
Winters cool to mild, moderate to heavy rain.

Subtropical—arid
Summers hot to extremely hot, some irregular rain, very dry.
Winters mild to warm, little rain, very dry.

Subtropical/Warm Temperate—arid
Summers hot to extremely hot, some irregular rain, very dry.
Winters cool to mild, some irregular rain, very dry.

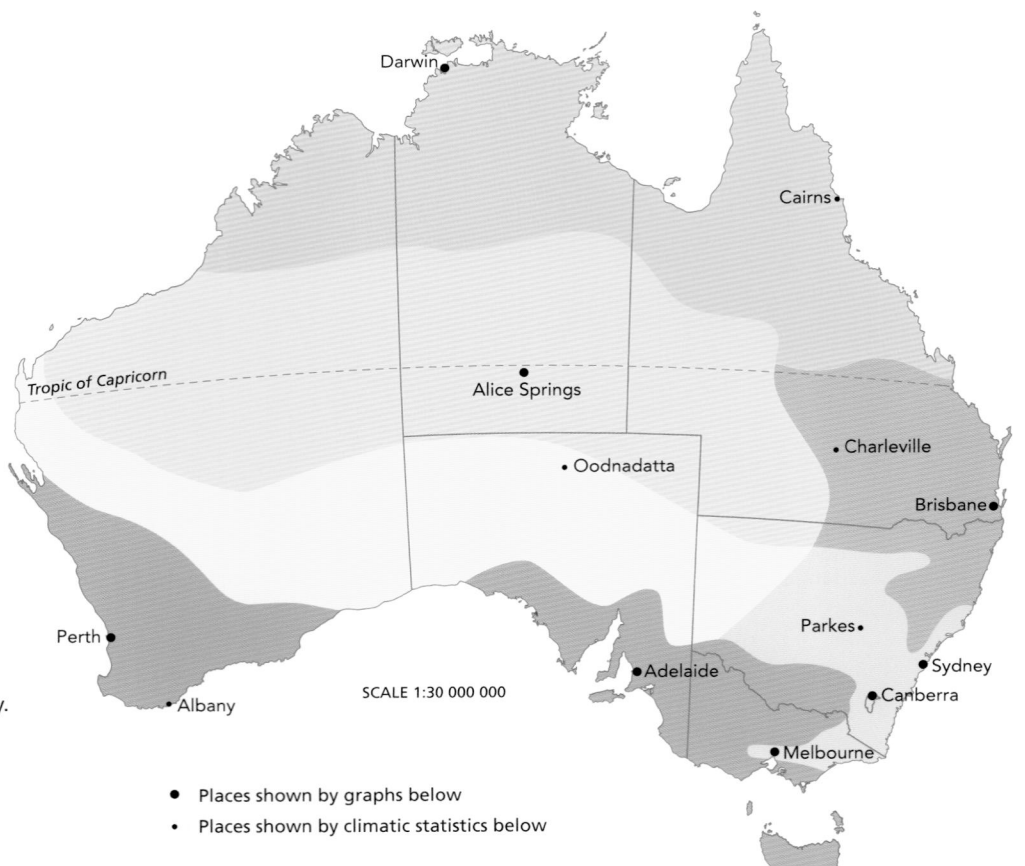

SCALE 1:30 000 000

● Places shown by graphs below
● Places shown by climatic statistics below

2 CLIMATIC GRAPHS

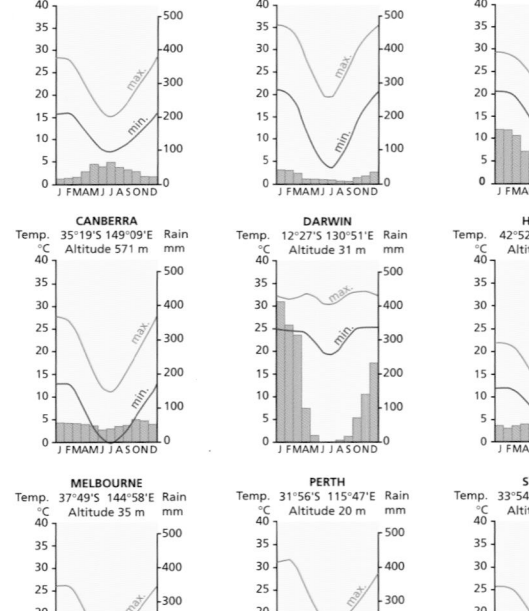

3 CLIMATIC STATISTICS

Albany (68 m)	Jan	Feb	Mar	Apr	May	Jun	Jul	Aug	Sept	Oct	Nov	Dec
Temperature, max. (°C)	25	25	24	22	19	17	16	16	17	19	21	23
Temperature, min. (°C)	14	14	13	12	10	8	7	7	8	9	11	12
Rainfall (mm)	28	25	29	66	102	104	126	104	81	80	46	24

Cairns (2 m)	Jan	Feb	Mar	Apr	May	Jun	Jul	Aug	Sept	Oct	Nov	Dec
Temperature, max. (°C)	32	32	31	29	28	26	26	26	28	30	31	32
Temperature, min. (°C)	24	23	23	21	19	17	16	16	18	20	21	23
Rainfall (mm)	419	422	460	264	111	73	39	42	44	50	98	203

Charleville (293 m)	Jan	Feb	Mar	Apr	May	Jun	Jul	Aug	Sept	Oct	Nov	Dec
Temperature, max. (°C)	36	35	33	29	24	20	20	23	27	31	34	36
Temperature, min. (°C)	21	21	18	13	8	6	4	6	9	14	18	20
Rainfall (mm)	67	69	63	35	31	32	30	19	21	35	40	56

Oodnadatta (116 m)	Jan	Feb	Mar	Apr	May	Jun	Jul	Aug	Sept	Oct	Nov	Dec
Temperature, max. (°C)	37	36	34	28	23	20	20	22	26	30	34	36
Temperature, min. (°C)	23	22	19	14	10	7	6	7	11	15	18	21
Rainfall (mm)	28	29	14	11	15	12	10	9	10	13	11	14

Parkes (324 m)	Jan	Feb	Mar	Apr	May	Jun	Jul	Aug	Sept	Oct	Nov	Dec
Temperature, max. (°C)	32	31	28	23	19	15	14	16	19	24	28	31
Temperature, min. (°C)	18	18	15	11	8	5	4	5	7	10	13	16
Rainfall (mm)	61	47	48	43	49	49	49	49	41	52	46	51

Lambert Azimuthal Equal Area projection

1 TEMPERATURE AND HEAT STRESS

Humans are increasing the concentration of greenhouse gases in the atmosphere, trapping more of the sun's energy. As a result, the lower atmosphere and the oceans are becoming warmer, and ice sheets and glaciers are melting. Using 1961–90 values as 'normal', scientists predict that by 2100 the Earth will warm by 1.4°C to 5.8°C and sea levels will rise by between 9 and 88 centimetres.

Most of Australia may warm 0.4°C to 2.0°C by 2030, with slightly less warming near the coast. This would likely result in more evaporation, more hot days above 35°C, and fewer cold days.

Coral reefs bleach and die as ocean water warms and becomes more acid

Southward spread of diseases spread by mosquitoes, e.g. malaria

Stronger, more frequent tropical cyclones move further south. Increase in coastal flooding, beach erosion and property damage

More extremely hot days cause greater electricity demand for cooling and increased deaths from heat stress

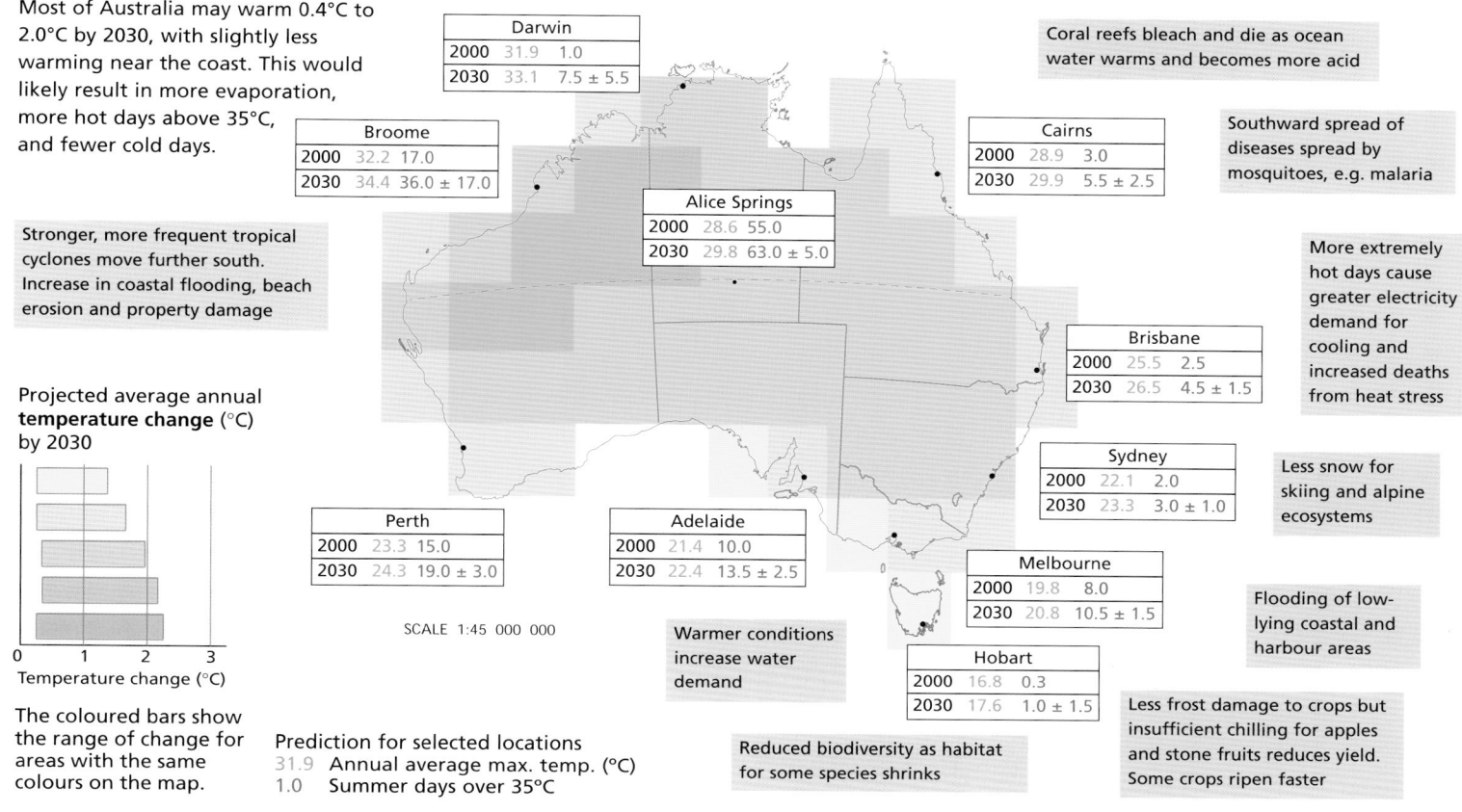

Darwin		
2000	31.9	1.0
2030	33.1	7.5 ± 5.5

Broome		
2000	32.2	17.0
2030	34.4	36.0 ± 17.0

Cairns		
2000	28.9	3.0
2030	29.9	5.5 ± 2.5

Alice Springs		
2000	28.6	55.0
2030	29.8	63.0 ± 5.0

Brisbane		
2000	25.5	2.5
2030	26.5	4.5 ± 1.5

Sydney		
2000	22.1	2.0
2030	23.3	3.0 ± 1.0

Perth		
2000	23.3	15.0
2030	24.3	19.0 ± 3.0

Adelaide		
2000	21.4	10.0
2030	22.4	13.5 ± 2.5

Melbourne		
2000	19.8	8.0
2030	20.8	10.5 ± 1.5

Hobart		
2000	16.8	0.3
2030	17.6	1.0 ± 1.5

Less snow for skiing and alpine ecosystems

Flooding of low-lying coastal and harbour areas

Projected average annual **temperature change** (°C) by 2030

Temperature change (°C)

The coloured bars show the range of change for areas with the same colours on the map.

SCALE 1:45 000 000

Prediction for selected locations
31.9 Annual average max. temp. (°C)
1.0 Summer days over 35°C

Warmer conditions increase water demand

Reduced biodiversity as habitat for some species shrinks

Less frost damage to crops but insufficient chilling for apples and stone fruits reduces yield. Some crops ripen faster

2 RAINFALL AND MOISTURE STRESS

Most of Australia will receive less rainfall, particularly in the south, mainly in winter/spring. The trend to less rainfall and greater evaporation will mean that less water will be available in the soil and in vegetation, rivers, lakes, wetlands and dams than at present. The moisture balance (rainfall minus potential evaporation) is an indication of the projected increasing moisture stress.

Less water available for cities and towns

Greater risk of forest and grassland fire

Reduction in irrigation water and irrigated crop yields

Less water for natural ecosystems reduces biodiversity

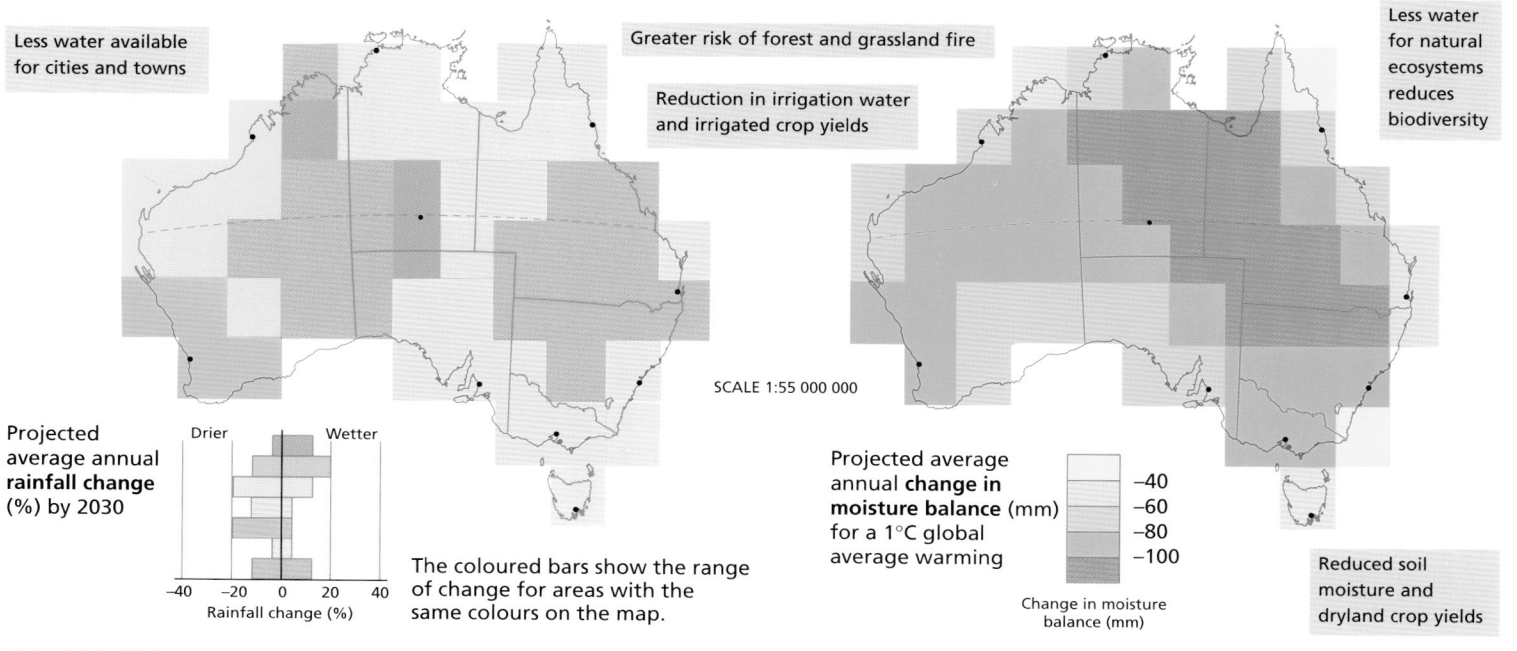

Projected average annual **rainfall change** (%) by 2030

Drier | Wetter

Rainfall change (%)

The coloured bars show the range of change for areas with the same colours on the map.

Projected average annual **change in moisture balance** (mm) for a 1°C global average warming

	−40
	−60
	−80
	−100

Change in moisture balance (mm)

SCALE 1:55 000 000

Reduced soil moisture and dryland crop yields

1 TYPICAL SUMMER PATTERN

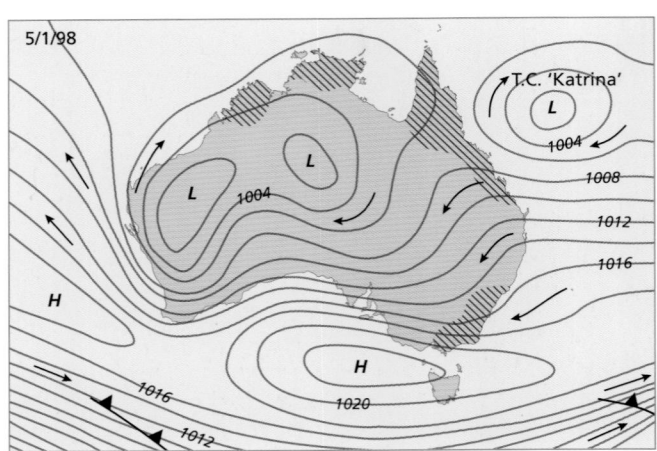

WEATHER MAP KEY

Pressure in hectopascals (hPa)

Isobar
1004

Cold front ▲▲

Wind direction →

Rainfall ░

Australia's summer weather pattern usually has equatorial low pressure systems over northern Australia, subtropical high pressure systems over the ocean just to the south of Australia, and cold fronts which extend up from the far south towards these high pressure systems.
(a) The 'lows' bring cloudy, unsettled weather and heavy rain.
(b) The 'highs' are usually associated with fine, settled weather.
(c) The cold fronts bring cloudy conditions and a chance of rain.

2 TYPICAL WINTER PATTERN

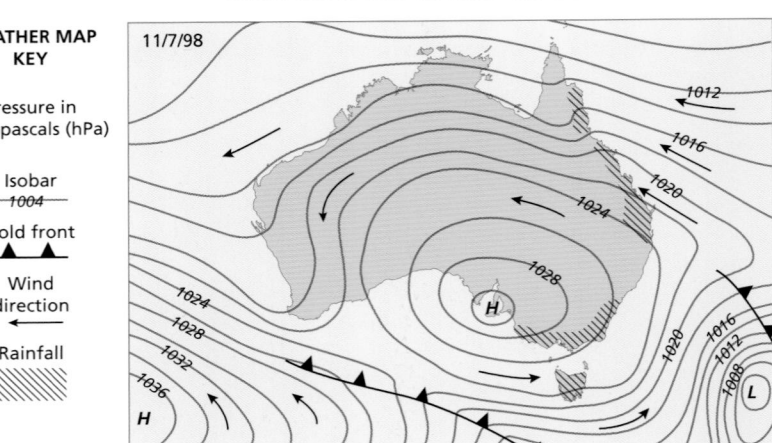

Australia's winter weather pattern usually has subtropical high pressure systems over mainland Australia, subpolar low pressure systems to the south of Australia, and cold fronts which extend up from the subpolar lows towards the high pressure systems.
(a) The 'highs' are usually associated with fine, settled weather.
(b) The cold fronts and their related low pressure systems bring cold weather, clouds and rain to southern Australia.

3 SUMMER SATELLITE IMAGE

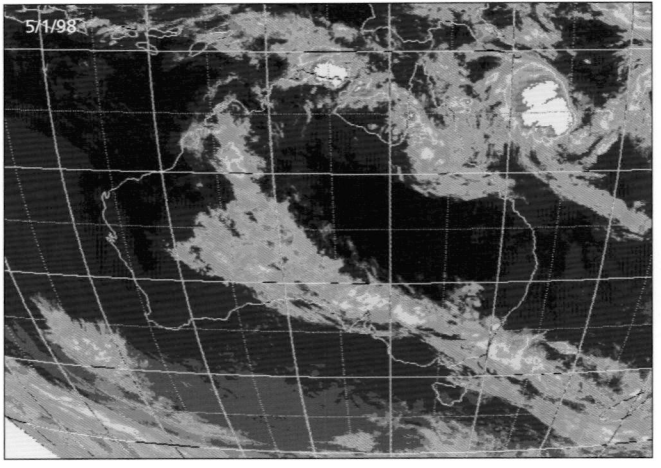

TEMPERATURE SCALE FOR INFRARED SATELLITE IMAGES

26°C
19°C
12°C
5°C
-2°C
-9°C
-16°C
-23°C
-30°C
-37°C
-44°C
-51°C
-58°C
-65°C
-72°C

4 WINTER SATELLITE IMAGE

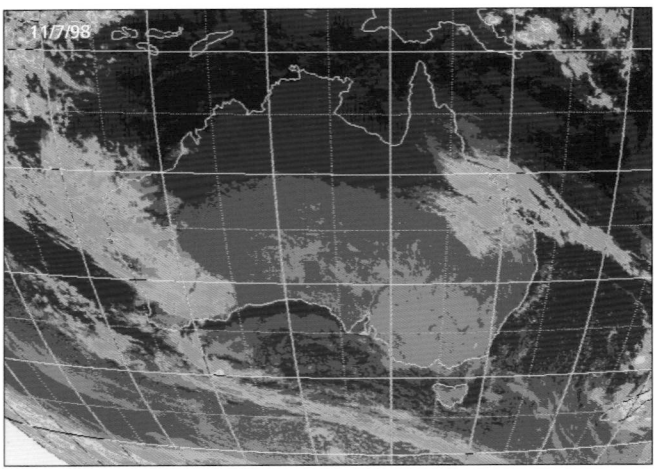

5 FORECASTING THE WEATHER

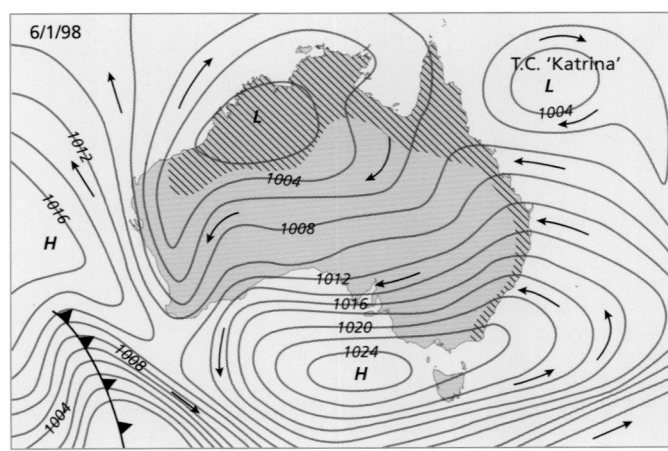

Forecasting the weather can often be quite difficult, but you can make a reasonable weather forecast if you remember these facts:
(a) During summer, low pressure systems and tropical cyclones over northern Australia generally tend to stay in the one area for several days, bringing very unsettled weather and light, moderate or heavy rain.
(b) During both summer and winter, high pressure systems move from west to east across Australia bringing fine, settled weather. They may move quickly to the east, or may remain almost stationary for several days.
(c) During both summer and winter, cold fronts move from west to east across the south of Australia bringing clouds and possible rain.
(d) Whenever winds blow from the ocean onto the land there could be rain.

Map 5 is the forecast map, or expected weather pattern, one day after Map 1. The tropical cyclone should remain almost stationary. The two low pressure systems over north-western Australia could merge into one. The high could start to move east. A cold front could come up from the south-west. Rain might fall around the cyclone, low system or wherever winds blow onshore.

1 SURFACE WATER DRAINAGE DIVISIONS

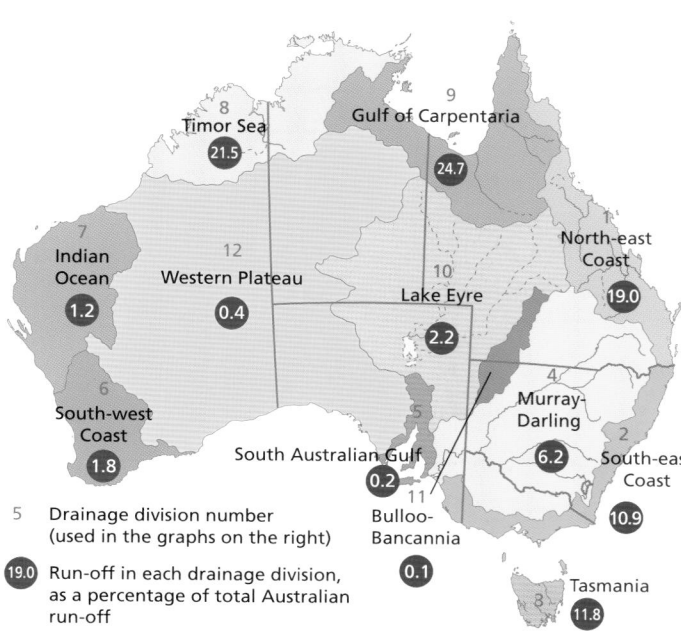

5   Drainage division number (used in the graphs on the right)

19.0   Run-off in each drainage division, as a percentage of total Australian run-off

Rainfall and run-off in Australia are both very low and unevenly spread. One-quarter of the continent, mostly north of the Tropic of Capricorn, provides three-quarters of total annual run-off. Most rivers are short coastal streams, and many inland rivers only flow after heavy rain. Only the Murray–Darling is a major river by world standards.

2 AVAILABILITY OF WATER

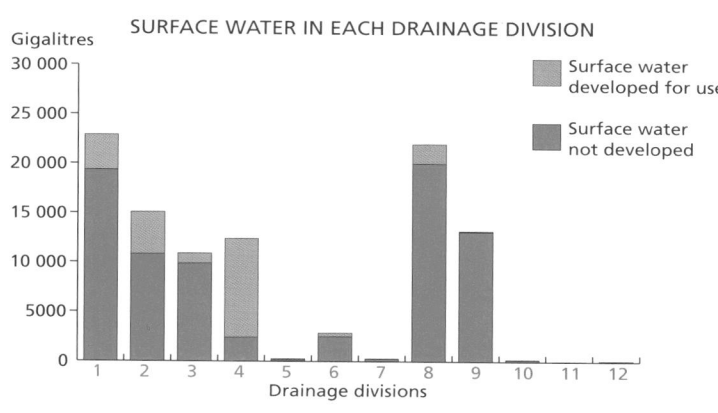

SURFACE WATER IN EACH DRAINAGE DIVISION

- Surface water developed for use
- Surface water not developed

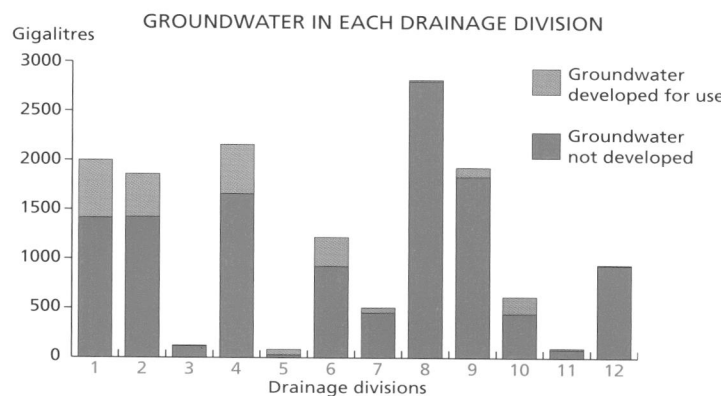

GROUNDWATER IN EACH DRAINAGE DIVISION

- Groundwater developed for use
- Groundwater not developed

3 USE OF WATER RESOURCES

Water is Australia's most valuable resource. More surface water is stored in giant dams per head of population than in any other country. Most is used for irrigation, notably in the Murray–Darling Basin.

Groundwater (water that soaks into underground rock layers) is the main source of water for 60 per cent of the country, especially in arid areas. Its quality and quantity is declining in some areas because more is being used by people than is being replaced by water soaking into the ground in higher rainfall areas.

   Great Artesian Basin

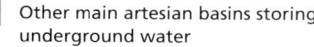   Other main artesian basins storing underground water

Main water storage dams (capacity in gigalitres)

—   over 5000

—   2000–5000

—   1000–2000

•   100–1000

   Irrigation areas using surface water

   Irrigation areas using groundwater

SCALE 1:30 000 000

Lambert Azimuthal Equal Area projection

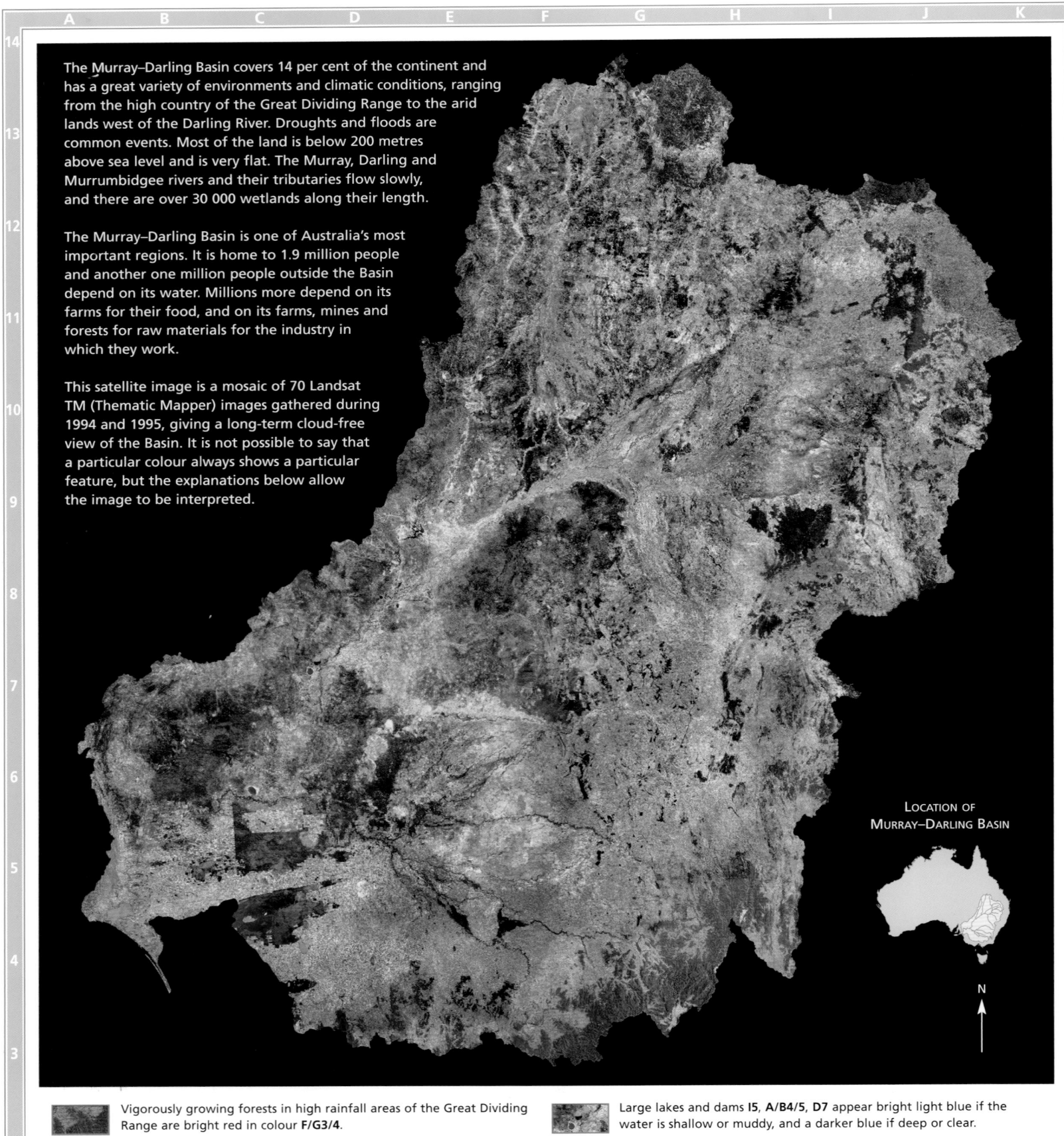

The Murray–Darling Basin covers 14 per cent of the continent and has a great variety of environments and climatic conditions, ranging from the high country of the Great Dividing Range to the arid lands west of the Darling River. Droughts and floods are common events. Most of the land is below 200 metres above sea level and is very flat. The Murray, Darling and Murrumbidgee rivers and their tributaries flow slowly, and there are over 30 000 wetlands along their length.

The Murray–Darling Basin is one of Australia's most important regions. It is home to 1.9 million people and another one million people outside the Basin depend on its water. Millions more depend on its farms for their food, and on its farms, mines and forests for raw materials for the industry in which they work.

This satellite image is a mosaic of 70 Landsat TM (Thematic Mapper) images gathered during 1994 and 1995, giving a long-term cloud-free view of the Basin. It is not possible to say that a particular colour always shows a particular feature, but the explanations below allow the image to be interpreted.

LOCATION OF
MURRAY–DARLING BASIN

N

Vigorously growing forests in high rainfall areas of the Great Dividing Range are bright red in colour **F/G3/4**.

Woody forest stands out as a brown colour **H/I9**. Woody shrub lands show up as brownish colours **D6**.

Recently flooded or moist river plains with their lush vegetation growth appear as red to pink **G/H9**.

Irrigation areas with vigorously growing crops and pastures, e.g. Shepparton **E/F4**, stand out as bright red, while grapes, fruit and vegetables in the Murray Irrigation Area **F5** show up as dull red.

Large lakes and dams **I5**, **A/B4/5**, **D7** appear bright light blue if the water is shallow or muddy, and a darker blue if deep or clear.

Bluish colours may indicate dryland crops and pastures on black or dark soils, e.g. on the Darling Downs **J11/12**.

Dry, bare or sandy areas in the west of the Basin, such as north of Wilcannia **E8/9**, show up as a whitish colour.

Dryland crops and pastures grown on brown/red soils appear as yellow-greenish colours **F6**, and as yellowish colours if on light sandy soils in drier areas **D5**.

SCALE 1:6 500 000   0   50   100   150   200 km

1 AGRICULTURAL HEARTLAND

Water is the key to wealth of the Basin. In an area of low rainfall and low run-off, approximately 85 per cent of its surface water has been developed for agricultural use. It has more than 70 per cent of Australia's irrigated land, 50 per cent of the land used to grow crops, 40 per cent of all farms, and supplies more than 40 per cent of the value of Australian agricultural production. Its water resource is so valuable that the Australian Government and the governments of four states and one territory have combined to manage its use and development. Lack of knowledge and overuse of the Basin's fragile environment have degraded large areas and now threaten its future as one of Australia's most important regions.

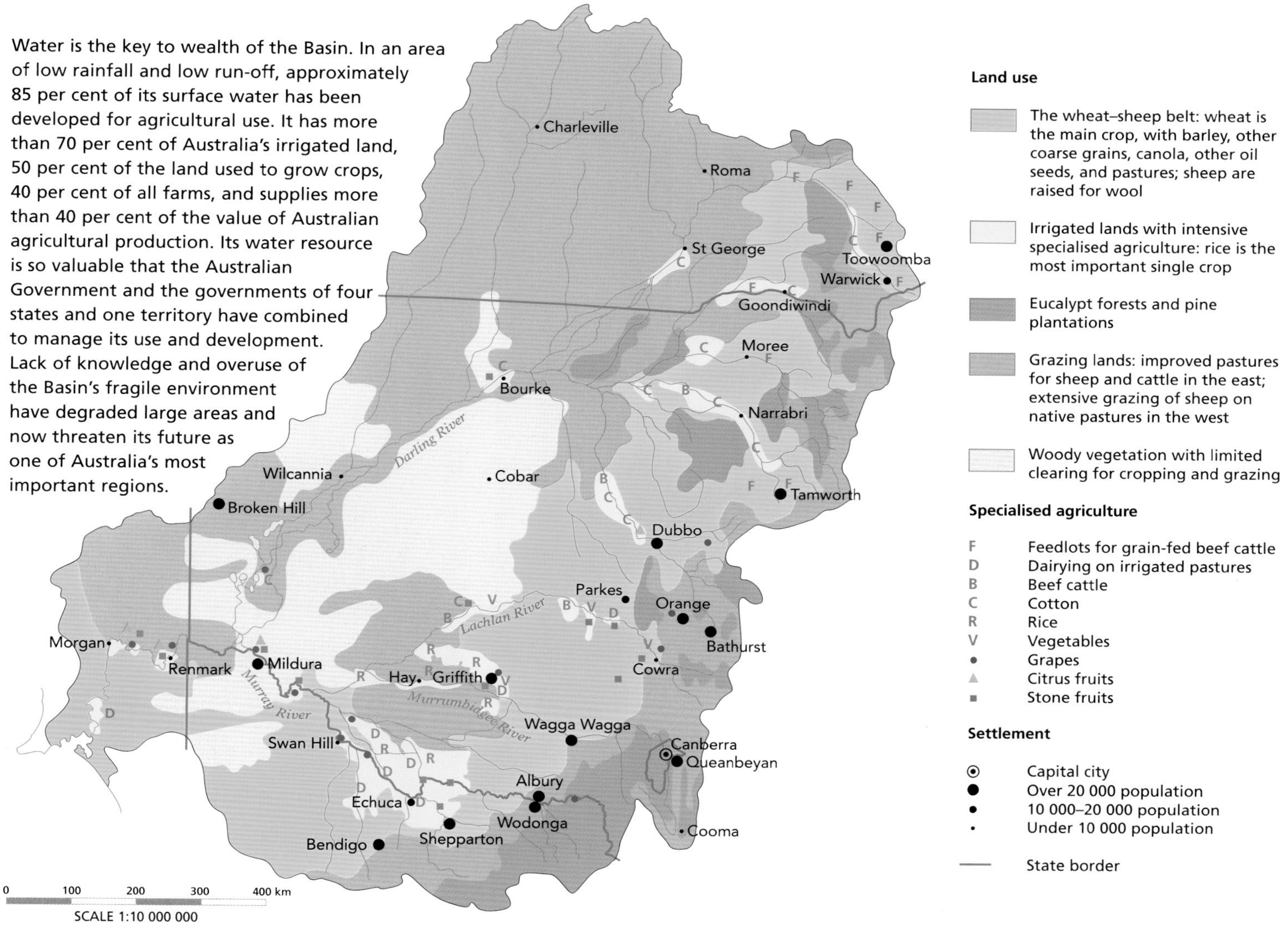

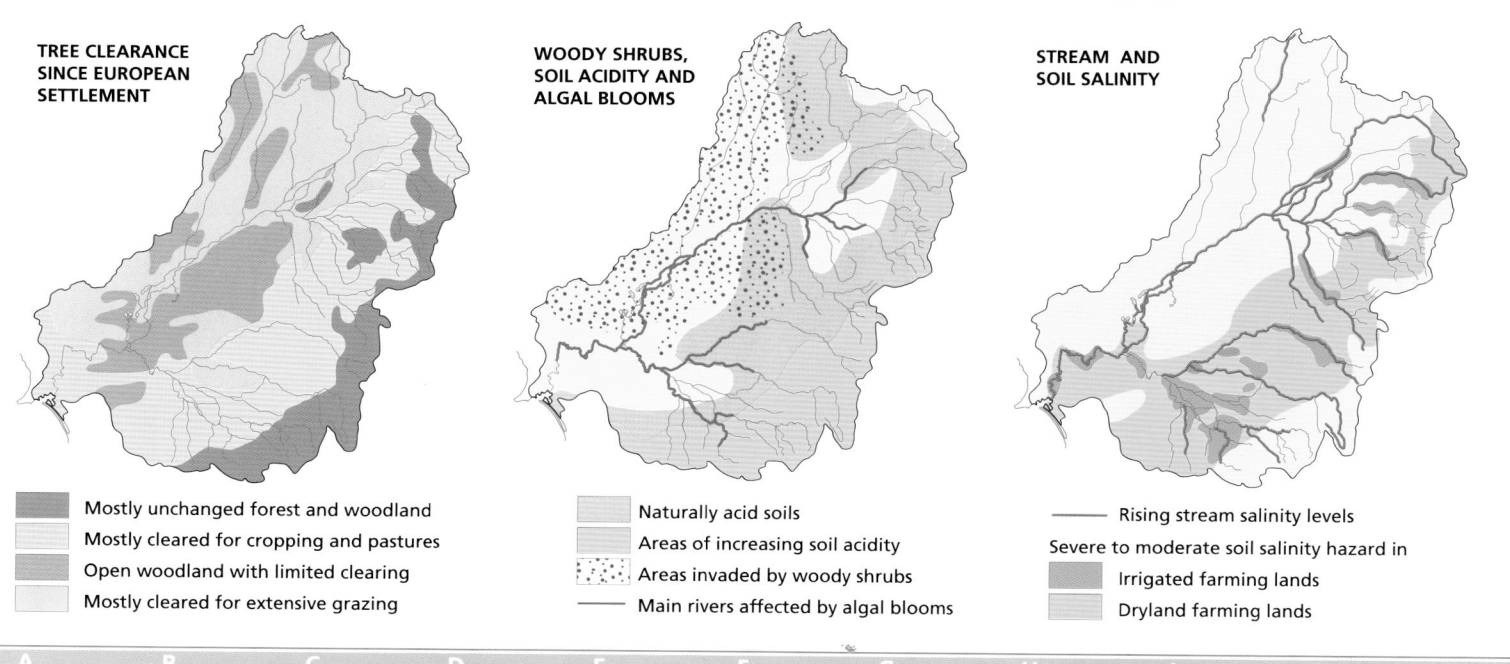

Land use

The wheat–sheep belt: wheat is the main crop, with barley, other coarse grains, canola, other oil seeds, and pastures; sheep are raised for wool

Irrigated lands with intensive specialised agriculture: rice is the most important single crop

Eucalypt forests and pine plantations

Grazing lands: improved pastures for sheep and cattle in the east; extensive grazing of sheep on native pastures in the west

Woody vegetation with limited clearing for cropping and grazing

Specialised agriculture

F Feedlots for grain-fed beef cattle
D Dairying on irrigated pastures
B Beef cattle
C Cotton
R Rice
V Vegetables
• Grapes
▲ Citrus fruits
■ Stone fruits

Settlement

⊙ Capital city
● Over 20 000 population
● 10 000–20 000 population
• Under 10 000 population

— State border

Charleville
Roma
St George
Toowoomba
Warwick
Goondiwindi
Moree
Bourke
Narrabri
Wilcannia
Cobar
Broken Hill
Tamworth
Dubbo
Parkes
Orange
Bathurst
Cowra
Morgan
Renmark
Mildura
Hay
Griffith
Canberra
Queanbeyan
Swan Hill
Wagga Wagga
Albury
Echuca
Wodonga
Cooma
Bendigo
Shepparton

Darling River
Lachlan River
Murray River
Murrumbidgee River

0 100 200 300 400 km

SCALE 1:10 000 000

2 THREATS TO PRODUCTIVITY AND THE ENVIRONMENT

TREE CLEARANCE SINCE EUROPEAN SETTLEMENT

WOODY SHRUBS, SOIL ACIDITY AND ALGAL BLOOMS

STREAM AND SOIL SALINITY

Mostly unchanged forest and woodland
Mostly cleared for cropping and pastures
Open woodland with limited clearing
Mostly cleared for extensive grazing

Naturally acid soils
Areas of increasing soil acidity
Areas invaded by woody shrubs
Main rivers affected by algal blooms

Rising stream salinity levels
Severe to moderate soil salinity hazard in
Irrigated farming lands
Dryland farming lands

1 VEGETATION

European farming practices have greatly changed the vegetation of Australia since 1788. About half of our natural forests have been thinned out or cleared, 35 per cent of our woodlands have been significantly thinned out or cleared, while grasslands have more than doubled in area.

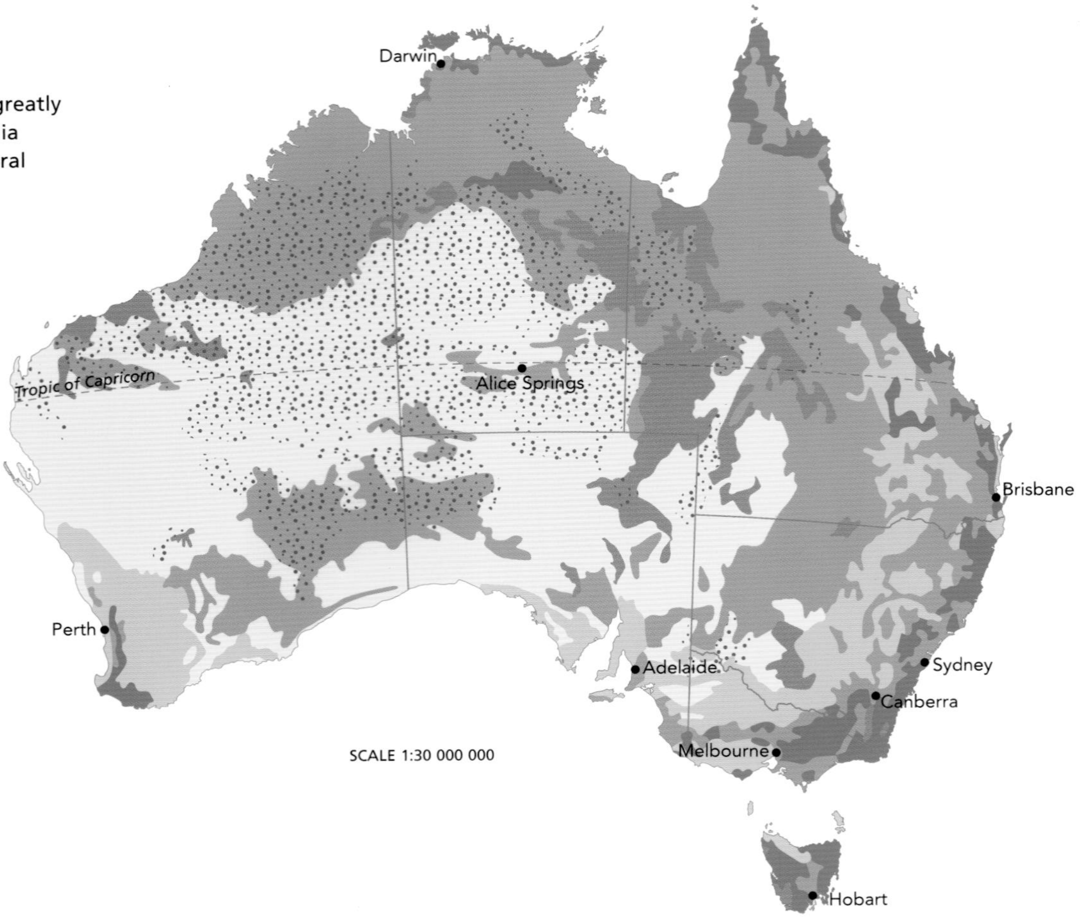

Legend:
- Forest
- Woodland
- Shrubland
- Grassland
- Pasture and cropping
- Spinifex

Darwin

Tropic of Capricorn

Alice Springs

Brisbane

Perth

Adelaide

Sydney

Canberra

Melbourne

SCALE 1:30 000 000

Hobart

2 BIODIVERSITY

Biodiversity is the great variety of all living things and the ecosystems of which they are a part. This map uses Geographic Information System–based (GIS-based) modelling techniques to show Australia's biophysical naturalness—the extent to which the natural environment has been disturbed since European settlement.

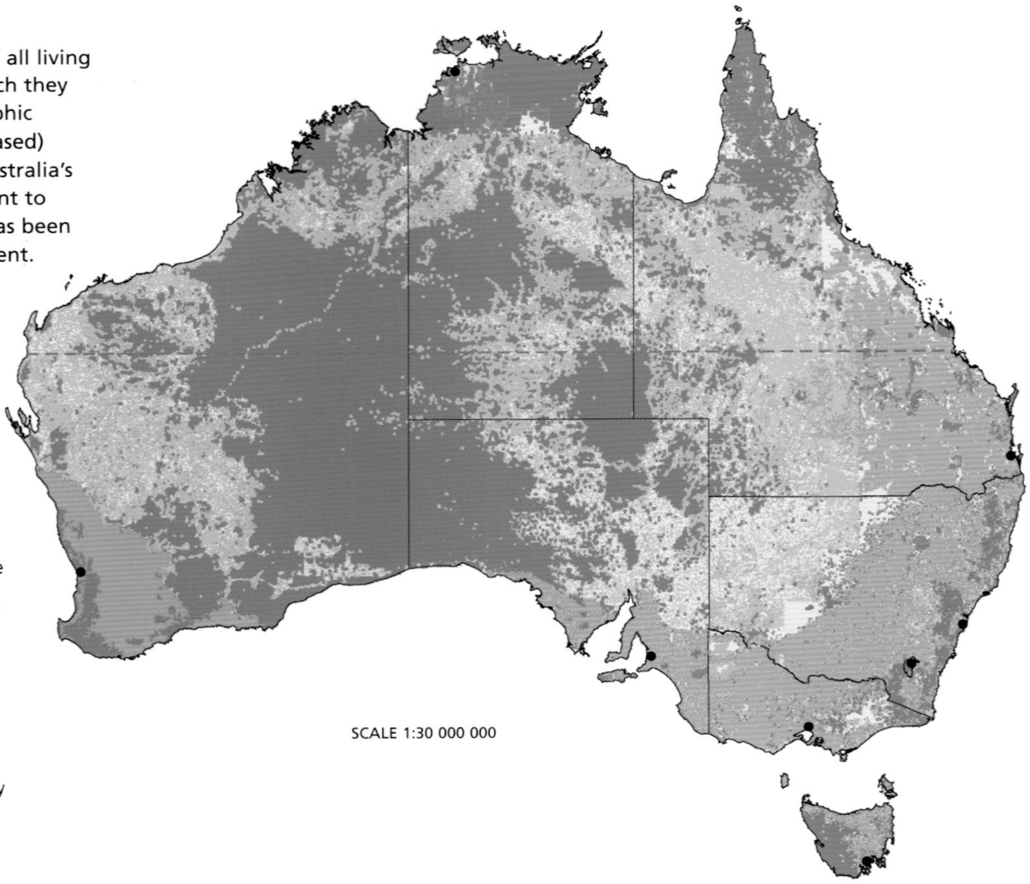

Legend:
- 0 Cleared land
- 1 High disturbance
- 2 Moderate to high disturbance
- 3 Low to moderate disturbance
- 4 Low disturbance
- 5 Natural

SCALE 1:30 000 000

Numbers in key refer to the Biodiversity transect in 21.2, opposite.

1 AGRICULTURAL LAND USE

Agricultural land use in Australia is influenced
by physical factors such as climate, soils and
landforms, and by human factors such
as agricultural practices, economic
costs and market opportunities.

Please note that many small
differences in land use have
not been plotted on this map
to make sure it can be more
easily understood.

- Dairy cattle
- Dairy cattle and beef cattle
- Beef cattle
- Sheep and beef cattle
- Sheep
- Sheep and cereal grains
- Cereal grains
- Sugar cane
- Cotton
- Intensive cropping
- Little or no agricultural activity
  (too arid, too mountainous,
  national parks, not used for agriculture)
- - - - - Transect line (see diagram below)

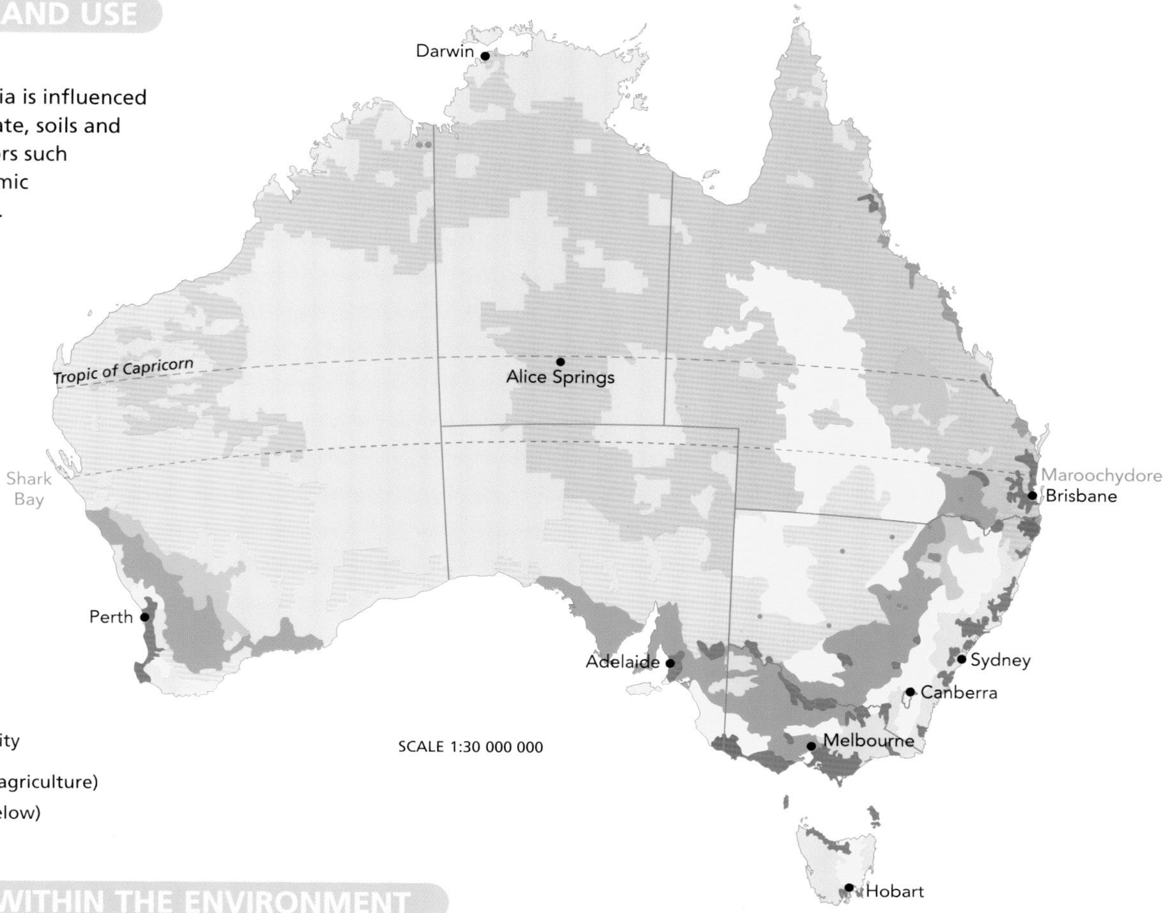

SCALE 1:30 000 000

Darwin
Tropic of Capricorn
Alice Springs
Shark Bay
Maroochydore
Brisbane
Perth
Adelaide
Sydney
Canberra
Melbourne
Hobart

2 RELATIONSHIPS WITHIN THE ENVIRONMENT

This transect diagram shows some generalised relationships between biophysical and human features at latitude 26°40' south,
from Shark Bay on the west coast to Maroochydore on the east coast. Please refer to the map above for their location.

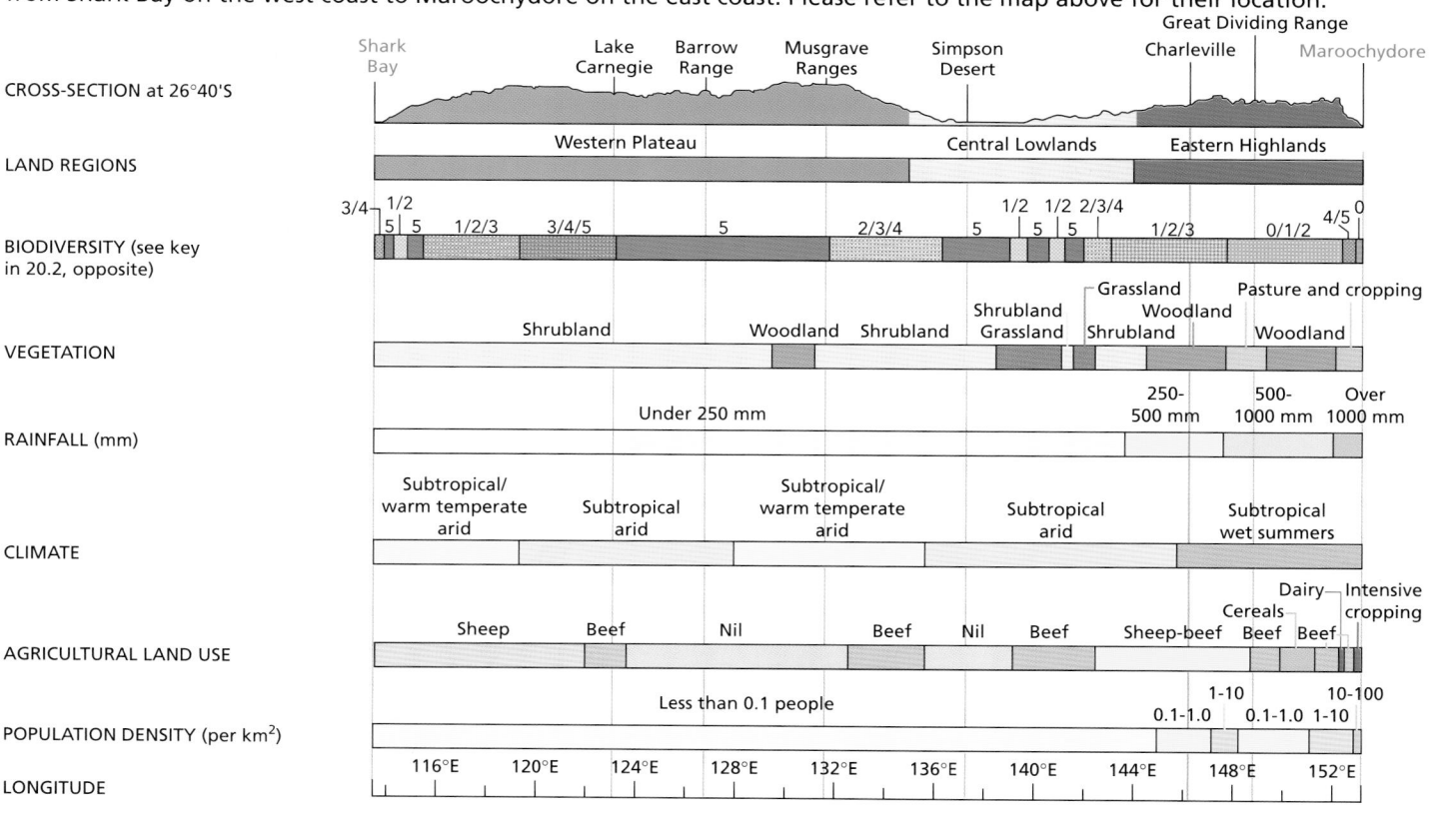

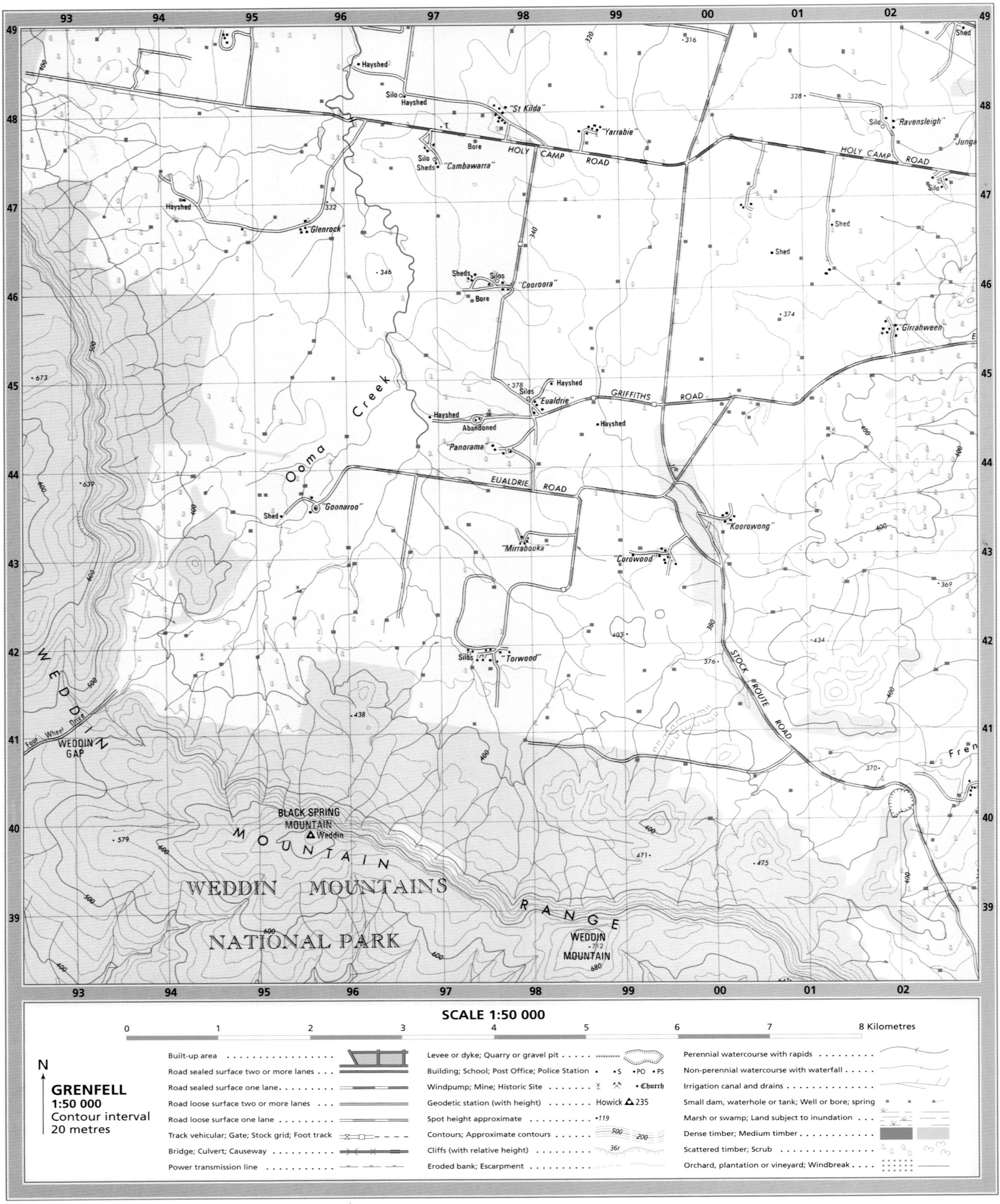

Map labels (selected):

"St Kilda"
"Yarrabie"
Silo · "Ravensleigh"
"Junga
HOLY CAMP ROAD
Hayshed
Silo
Bore
"Cambawarra"
Silo Sheds
HOLY CAMP ROAD
Silo
Hayshed
·332
·346
Glenrock
Sheds Silos
"Cooroora"
Bore
Shed
Shed
·374
Girrahween
·378 Silos
Hayshed
"Eualdrie"
GRIFFITHS ROAD
Hayshed
Hayshed
Abandoned
"Panorama"
EUALDRIE ROAD
·673
Shed "Goonaroo"
"Mirrabooka"
"Corowood"
"Koorawong"
·639
·369
"Torwood"
Silos
·403
·434
·380
376
·438
STOCK ROUTE ROAD
370·
Fren
·579
WEDDIN GAP
Four Wheel Drive
WEDDIN
BLACK SPRING MOUNTAIN
△ Weddin
·471
·475
MOUNTAIN
WEDDIN MOUNTAINS
RANGE
NATIONAL PARK
WEDDIN MOUNTAIN
·680
Ooma Creek

SCALE 1:50 000

0 1 2 3 4 5 6 7 8 Kilometres

N

GRENFELL
1:50 000
Contour interval
20 metres

Built-up area	Levee or dyke; Quarry or gravel pit
Road sealed surface two or more lanes	Building; School; Post Office; Police Station · S · PO · PS
Road sealed surface one lane	Windpump; Mine; Historic Site
Road loose surface two or more lanes	Geodetic station (with height) Howick △ 235
Road loose surface one lane	Spot height approximate ·119
Track vehicular; Gate; Stock grid; Foot track	Contours; Approximate contours 500 200
Bridge; Culvert; Causeway	Cliffs (with relative height) 36r
Power transmission line	Eroded bank; Escarpment

Perennial watercourse with rapids
Non-perennial watercourse with waterfall
Irrigation canal and drains
Small dam, waterhole or tank; Well or bore; spring
Marsh or swamp; Land subject to inundation
Dense timber; Medium timber
Scattered timber; Scrub
Orchard, plantation or vineyard; Windbreak

Church

1 SUGAR CANE FARMING

MURWILLUMBAH, NSW

0   500 m

APPROX. SCALE 1:25 000

2 IRRIGATION FARMING

GRIFFITH, NSW

0   1 km

APPROX. SCALE 1:50 000

3 WHEAT–SHEEP FARMING

This aerial photo
shows part of the
topographic map on
the left (page 22).

GRENFELL, NSW

0   1 km

APPROX. SCALE 1:50 000

4 EXTENSIVE SHEEP FARMING

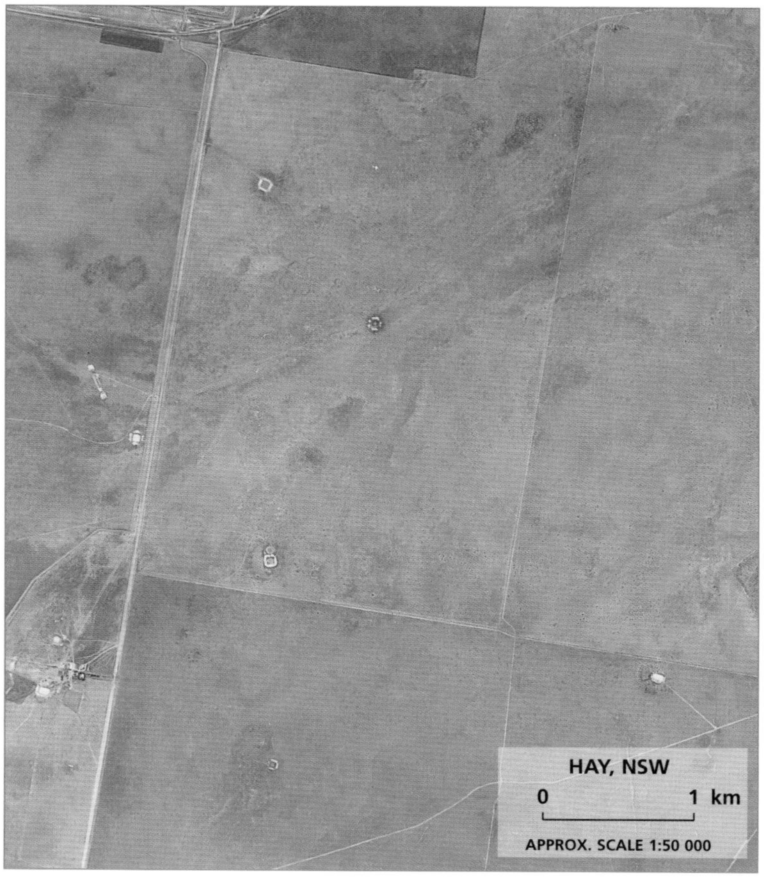

HAY, NSW

0   1 km

APPROX. SCALE 1:50 000

1 OCEAN CURRENTS

Australia's ocean temperatures vary from tropical (25°C to 31°C) to subpolar (4°C to 10°C), with major warm ocean currents flowing south, bringing warm water to both east and west coasts.

These warm currents have considerable influence on climate, settlement and human activity.

Where winds blow onshore across warm ocean currents, the winds are moist and conditions are warmer and wetter than they would be otherwise.

Warm oceans are low in fish nutrient and fish numbers, in comparison with cold oceans.

As a result, despite Australia having one of the world's largest Exclusive Economic Zones (a 200 nautical mile wide zone whose resources it must manage and conserve), its fish production is insignificant by world standards.

The NOAA satellite images below graphically show the Leeuwin Current off the coast of Western Australia and the East Australian Current off the coast of eastern Australia.

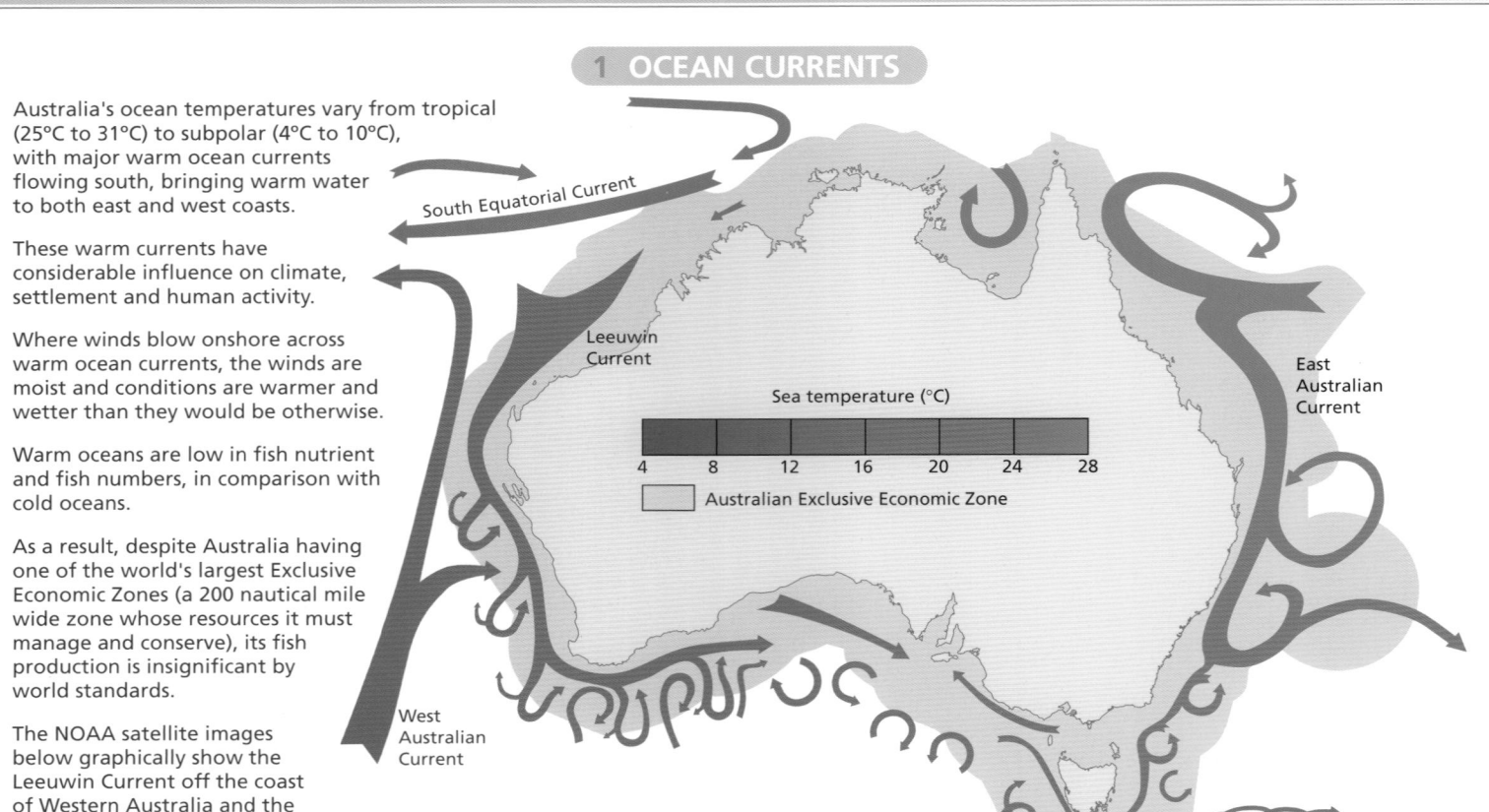

South Equatorial Current

Leeuwin Current

East Australian Current

Sea temperature (°C)

4   8   12   16   20   24   28

Australian Exclusive Economic Zone

West Australian Current

Antarctic Circumpolar Current

2 NOAA SATELLITE IMAGES OF AUSTRALIAN OCEAN CURRENTS

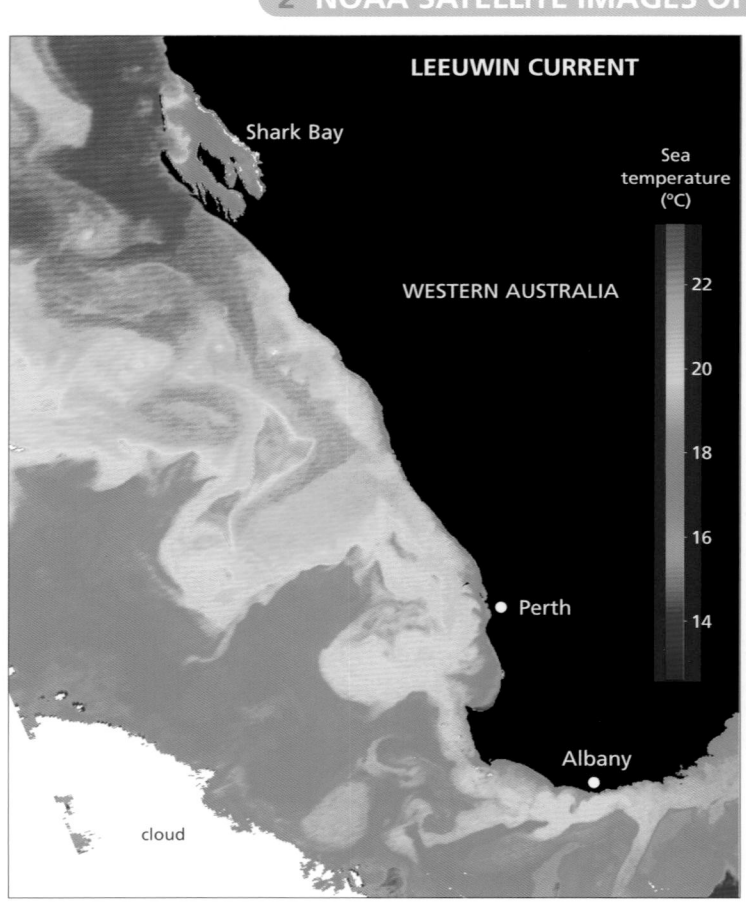

LEEUWIN CURRENT

Shark Bay

Sea temperature (°C)

WESTERN AUSTRALIA

22

20

18

16

14

● Perth

Albany

cloud

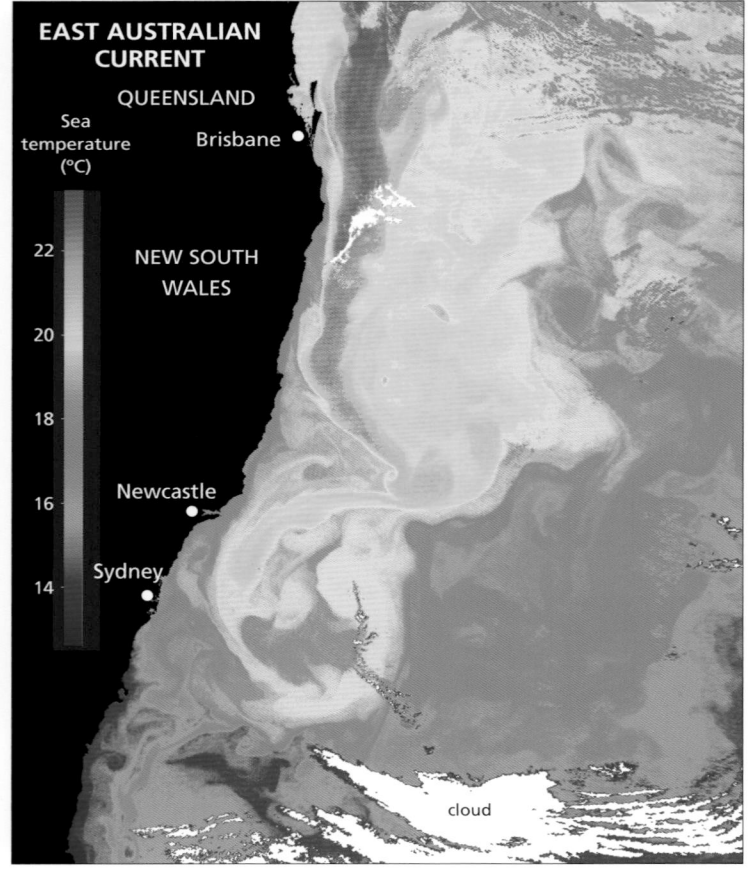

EAST AUSTRALIAN CURRENT

QUEENSLAND

Sea temperature (°C)

Brisbane ●

22

NEW SOUTH WALES

20

18

Newcastle ●

16

Sydney ●

14

cloud

1 AIR AND WATER CIRCULATION IN THE PACIFIC OCEAN

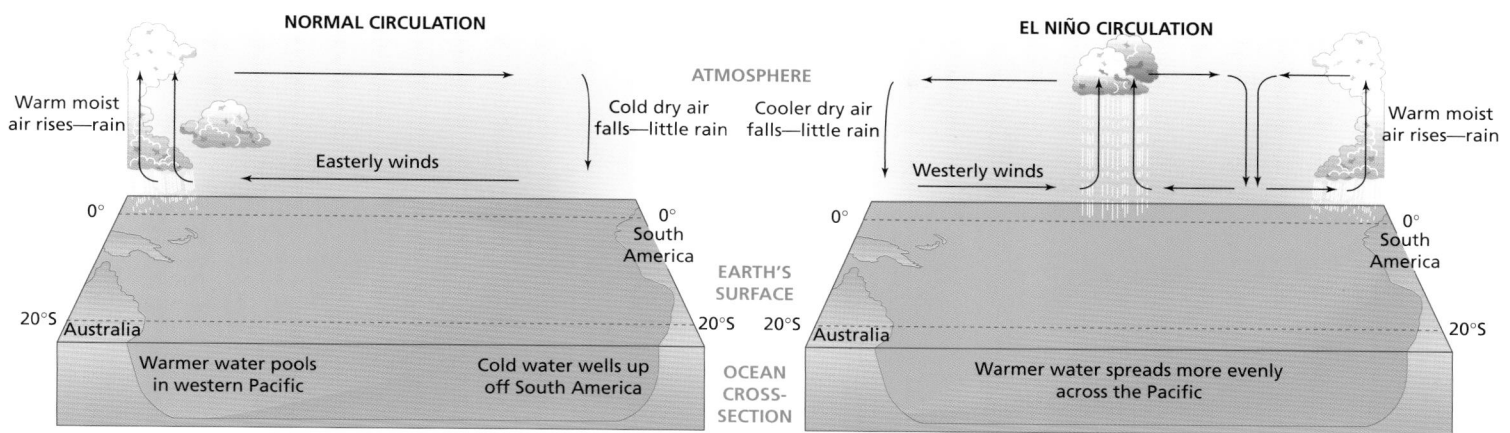

NORMAL CIRCULATION

ATMOSPHERE

Warm moist air rises—rain

Cold dry air falls—little rain

Easterly winds

0°

0° South America

EARTH'S SURFACE

20°S Australia   20°S

OCEAN CROSS-SECTION

Warmer water pools in western Pacific

Cold water wells up off South America

EL NIÑO CIRCULATION

Cooler dry air falls—little rain

Warm moist air rises—rain

Westerly winds

0°

0° South America

20°S Australia   20°S

Warmer water spreads more evenly across the Pacific

The usual situation is that the easterly winds push warm tropical surface waters across to the western Pacific. These form a pool of warmer water to the north-east of Australia. The moist easterly onshore winds bring 'normal' rainfall to north-eastern Australia.

Every three to seven years the easterly winds weaken and even reverse their direction. Warm water is pushed to the east, forming a pool of water 4°C to 5°C warmer than normal off South America. This is an El Niño event. The offshore westerly winds bring drought to the western Pacific.

2 NORMAL AND EL NIÑO SEA SURFACE TEMPERATURES

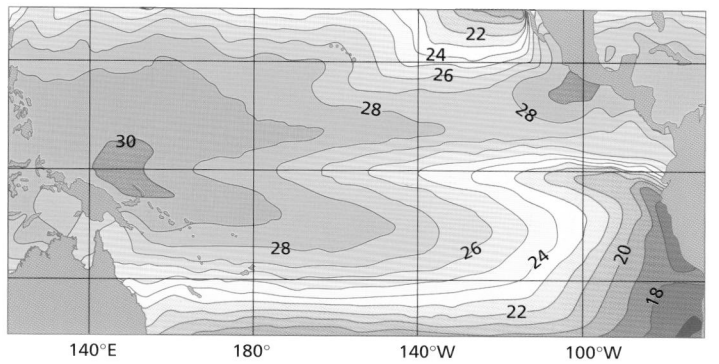

SEA SURFACE TEMPERATURES, SEPT–NOV 1996 (°C)

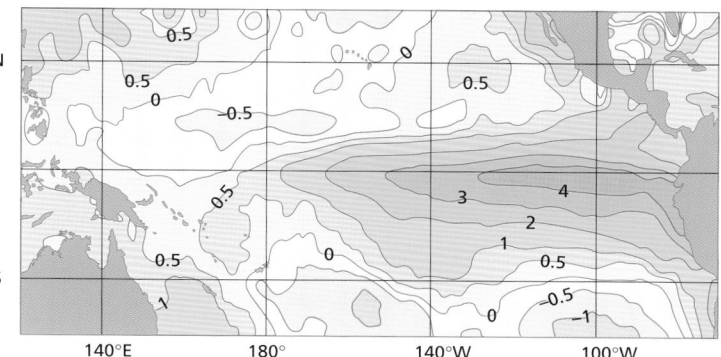

SEA SURFACE TEMPERATURE ANOMALIES, DEC 1997–FEB 1998 (°C)

The sea surface temperature map above shows the usual situation with a pool of warmer water north of Australia. The sea surface temperature anomalies map (right) shows an El Niño pool of water off the coast of South America, up to 4°C warmer than normal.

El Niño was the term fishermen used to describe the pool of warmer water off the coast of South America. However, it now refers to the change in wind patterns, the abnormal warming of the eastern Pacific Ocean, and the changes in temperatures and rainfall which result.

3 THE SOUTHERN OSCILLATION INDEX, EL NIÑO AND LA NIÑA

VARIATIONS IN THE SOUTHERN OSCILLATION INDEX (SOI)

Monthly SOI

5-month mean

El NIÑO Drought

Good rains LA NIÑA

El NIÑO Drought

Drought breaks

Good rains LA NIÑA

Heavy rains and floods in Eastern Australia

Jan 1994   Jan 1995   Jan 1996   Jan 1997   Jan 1998   Jan 1999

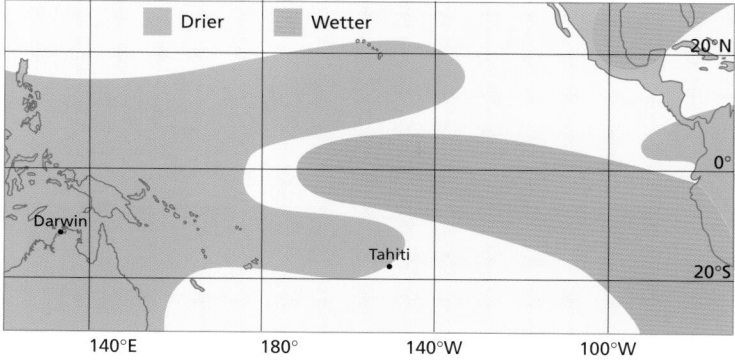

THE IMPACT OF EL NIÑO

Drier   Wetter

20°N

0°

Darwin

Tahiti

20°S

140°E   180°   140°W   100°W

The SOI shows the link between El Niño, La Niña and air pressure. It measures the difference in air pressure in the Pacific between Tahiti and Darwin. If the SOI is negative there may be an El Niño. If the SOI is positive there may be a La Niña.

In an El Niño, winds in the western Pacific blow offshore, resulting in drier weather or even severe drought. In a La Niña, easterly onshore winds are even stronger than normal, resulting in much wetter conditions than normal in Australia and the western Pacific.

1 RISK OF TROPICAL CYCLONES

Tropical cyclones form over warm tropical ocean waters to the north-east and north-west of Australia, usually between November and May each year. They are like a giant whirlwind of high-speed winds and cloud swirling around an 'eye' of intense low pressure. Australia experiences on average about 9 or 10 tropical cyclones each year. They bring very destructive winds, torrential rain and storm surges along the coast. Tropical cyclones are also known as **hurricanes** in North America and **typhoons** in Asia.

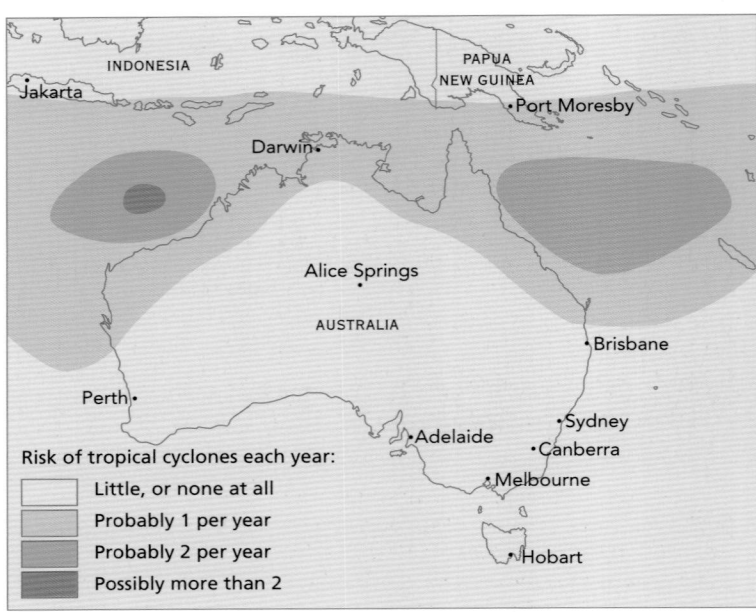

Risk of tropical cyclones each year:

- Little, or none at all
- Probably 1 per year
- Probably 2 per year
- Possibly more than 2

In a study of tropical cyclones in the Australian region, the Bureau of Meteorology found that the area shown as 'Possibly more than 2' had more than 75 tropical cyclones in a 30-year period!

2 SATELLITE IMAGE—CYCLONE VANCE

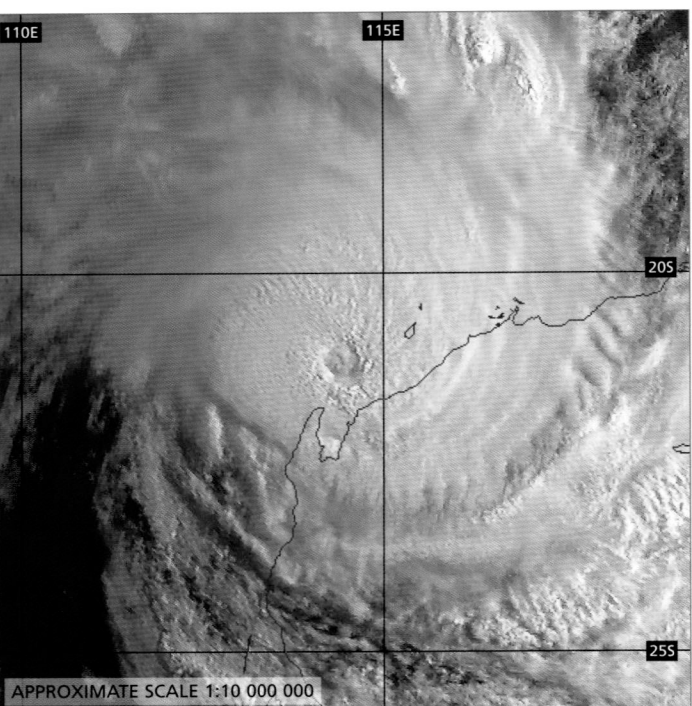

APPROXIMATE SCALE 1:10 000 000

The massive size of Tropical Cyclone Vance can be seen in this colour-enhanced NOAA-15 image taken at 8.34 a.m. local time on 22 March 1999, as the cyclone approached the Australian coast from the north. The weather map (27.3 opposite) shows the pattern of air pressure at about this time. Note the typical southern hemisphere pattern of cloud spiralling into the centre in a clockwise direction. In the northern hemisphere the wind and cloud movement is in an anticlockwise direction.

3 TROPICAL CYCLONES, 2001–03

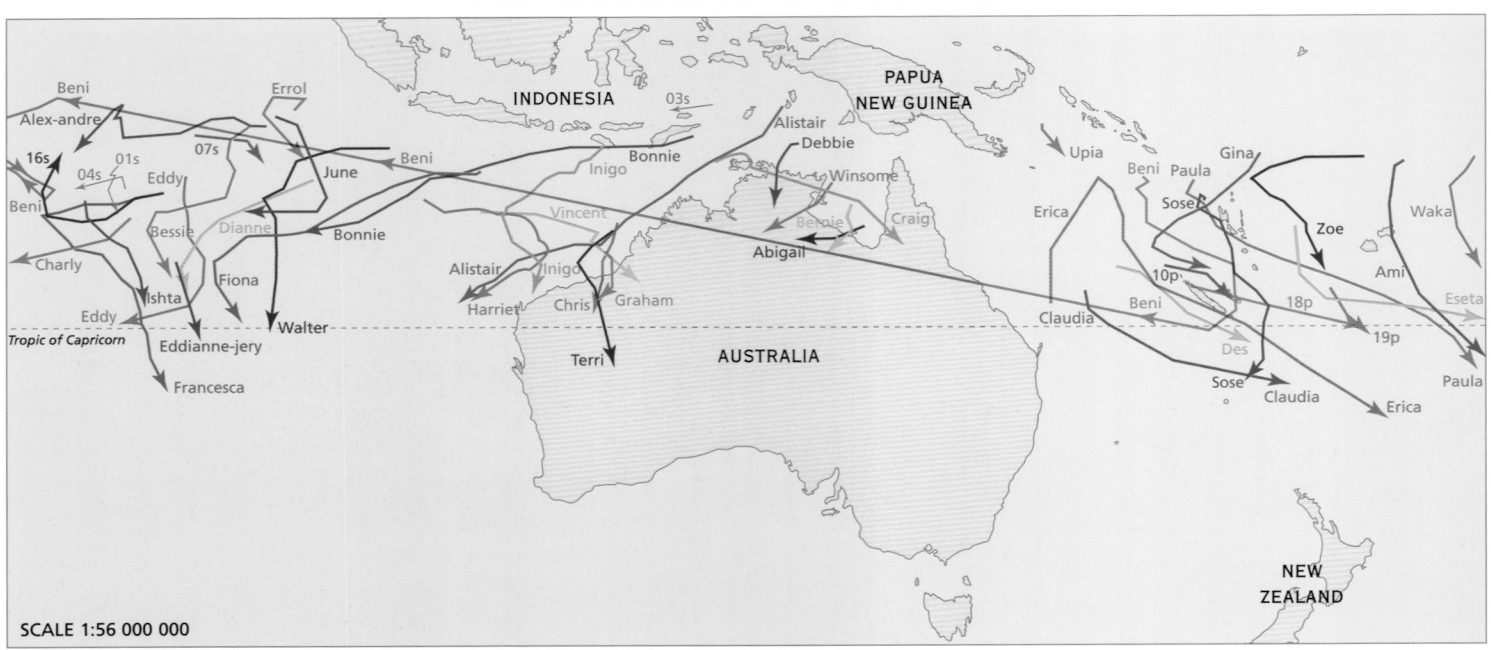

SCALE 1:56 000 000

This map shows the paths of major tropical cyclones that affected Australia and its Oceanic neighbours during 2001, 2002 and 2003. Many of these cyclones have developed in the two 'hot spots' out in the Indian Ocean and Coral Sea. Most cyclones last from 5 to 10 days and lose their intensity and destructive force as they move further south or move inland over the large Australian land mass.

1 PATH OF CYCLONE VANCE

Tropical Cyclone Vance was one of the strongest cyclones in recorded history ever to strike mainland Australia. It left a trail of havoc and destruction behind it, including destroyed homes and property, environmental damage and extensive inland flooding.

Cyclone Vance began as a low pressure system in the Timor Sea near Darwin on 16 March 1999. It crossed the Western Australian coast between Exmouth and Onslow as a category 5 cyclone around midday on 22 March, when a record wind speed for the Australian mainland of 267 km/hour was measured at Learmonth. Once over land it quickly lost force, but was still classified as a category 1 cyclone two nights later when it moved out into the Great Australian Bight.

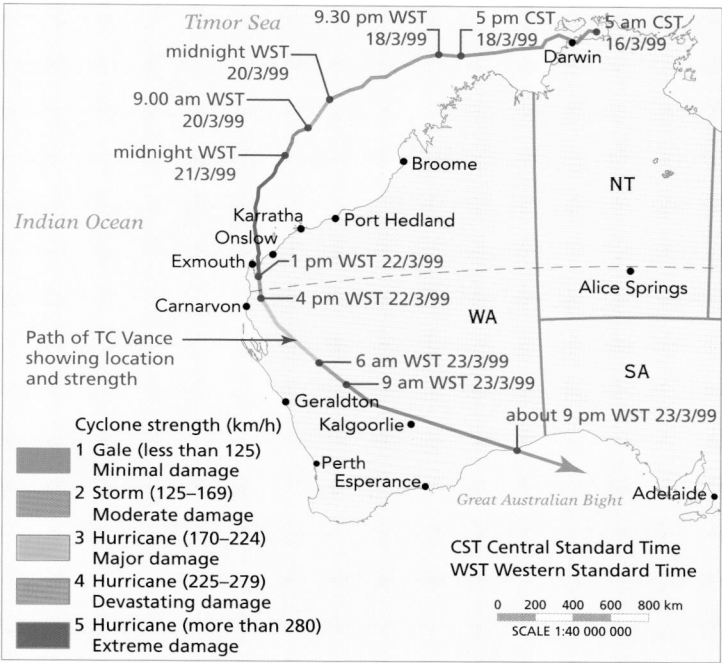

2 RAINFALL INTENSITY IMAGE

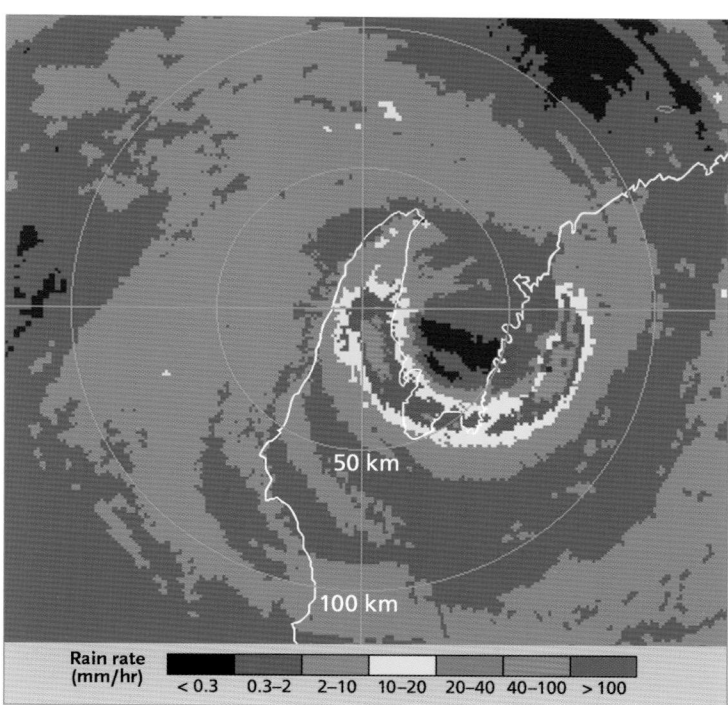

This weather radar image of rainfall intensity, taken on 22 March at 11.20 a.m. local time, shows the Learmonth radar station as a brown dot, the Western Australian coastline as a fine white line and the eye of the cyclone as a purple-black circular shape centred over the waters of Exmouth Gulf, to the east (right) of the radar station. The intensity of rainfall is shown by the different colours.

3 WEATHER MAP, 22 MARCH 1999

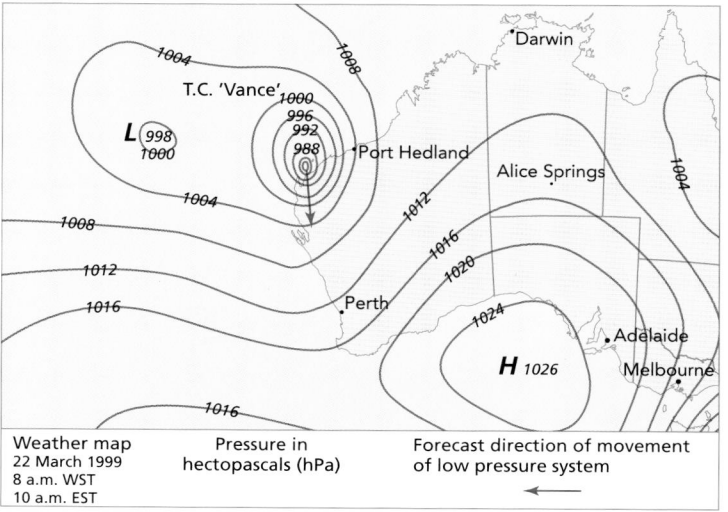

This weather map shows the pattern of air pressure at about the same time as the satellite image (26.2 on the opposite page) was taken. The cyclone is shown just north of Exmouth Gulf and the towns of Exmouth and Onslow in Western Australia.

4 RAINFALL, 22–5 MARCH 1999

This map shows the amount of rain that fell across Western Australia in four days from 22 to 25 March as Tropical Cyclone Vance crossed the coast at Exmouth Gulf and moved in a south-easterly direction towards the Great Australian Bight. There was extensive flooding from the coast to Kalgoorlie.

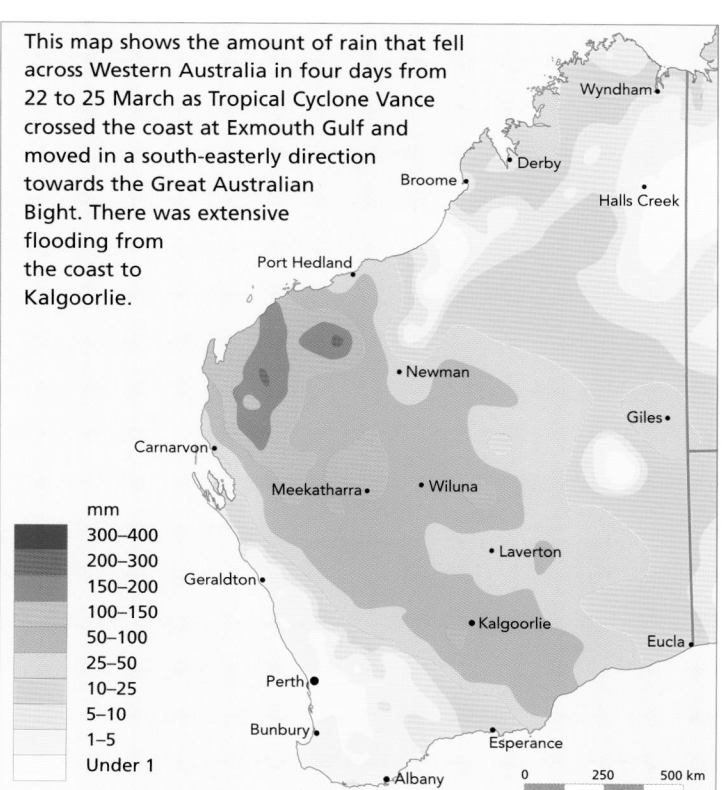

1 FLASH FLOODS

Flash floods are rapid, often violent floods which may last from a few hours to a day. Long-term flooding in mountain and coastal areas may last for up to a week but in inland areas it can last for several months.

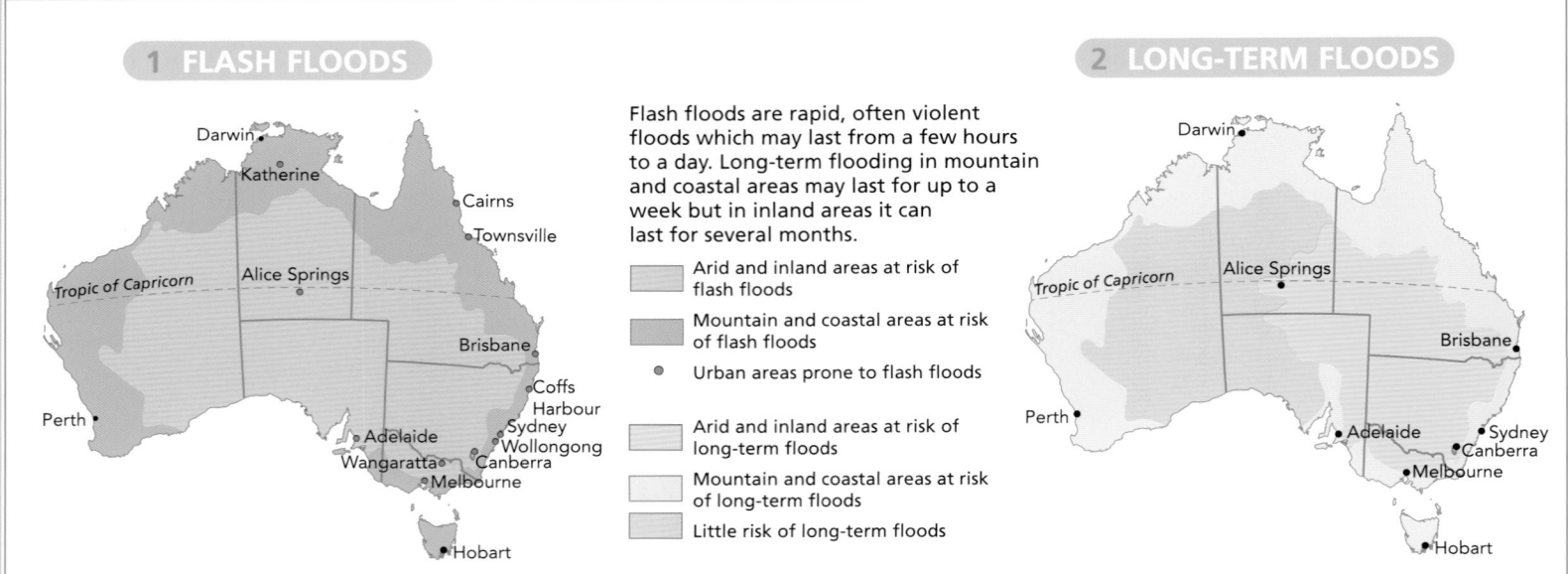

- Arid and inland areas at risk of flash floods
- Mountain and coastal areas at risk of flash floods
- ● Urban areas prone to flash floods

- Arid and inland areas at risk of long-term floods
- Mountain and coastal areas at risk of long-term floods
- Little risk of long-term floods

2 LONG-TERM FLOODS

3 LAKE EYRE BASIN FLOODS, 2000

The Lake Eyre drainage basin covers one-sixth of Australia. It is mostly arid with annual rainfall below 200 mm. Its rivers only flow occasionally after heavy rains in the north, across land with an average gradient of just 16 centimetres per kilometre. Their water spreads out slowly in a vast network of channels called the Channel Country, usually disappearing by evaporation and absorption into the desert sands, and seldom reaching Lake Eyre—which completely filled only three times in the 20th century.

The two false colour Landsat 7 images show the impact of a rare long-term flood reaching Lake Eyre. The 1 January 2000 image shows moist patches on the dry salt surface (bright blue) of Lake Eyre North (**B4**) and South (**C1**). The 6 April 2000 image shows water flooding from both mouths of Warburton Creek (**G6** and **H6**), and from Lake Eyre North into Lake Eyre South. The flood on Cooper Creek (**J4/5**) has not yet arrived. By late May 2000, 85 per cent of Lake Eyre's surface was flooded.

0   20   40 km

APPROXIMATE SCALE 1:1 650 000

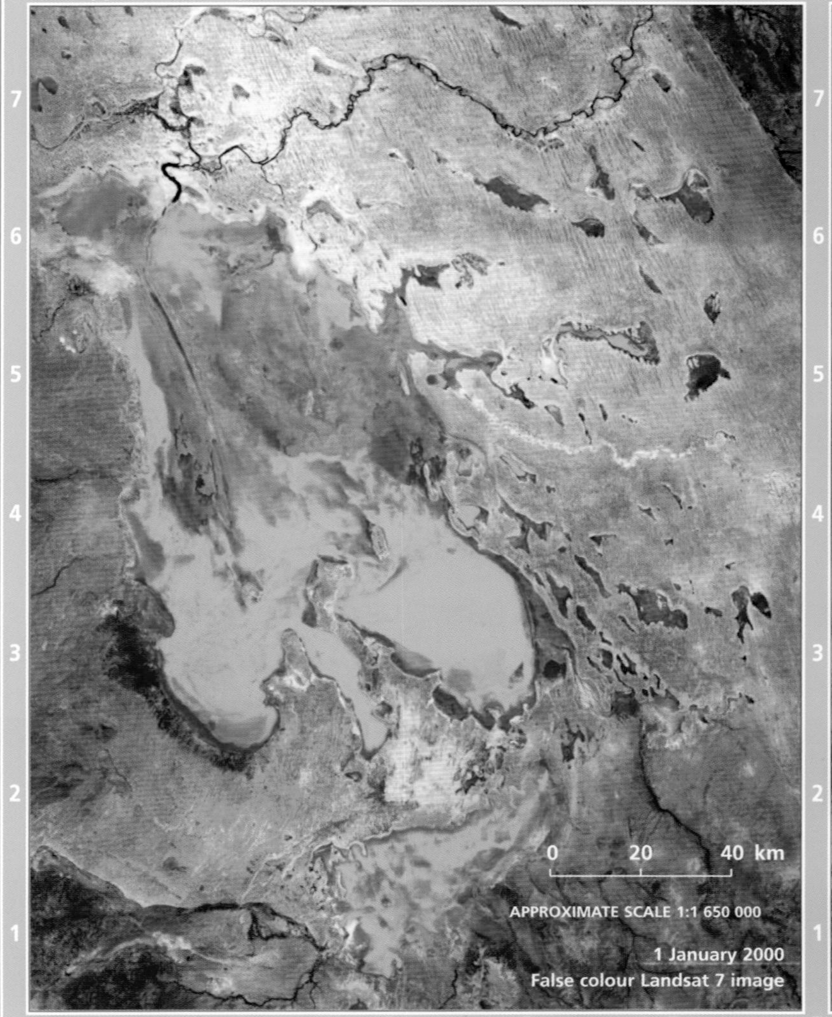

1 January 2000
False colour Landsat 7 image

0   20   40 km

APPROXIMATE SCALE 1:1 650 000

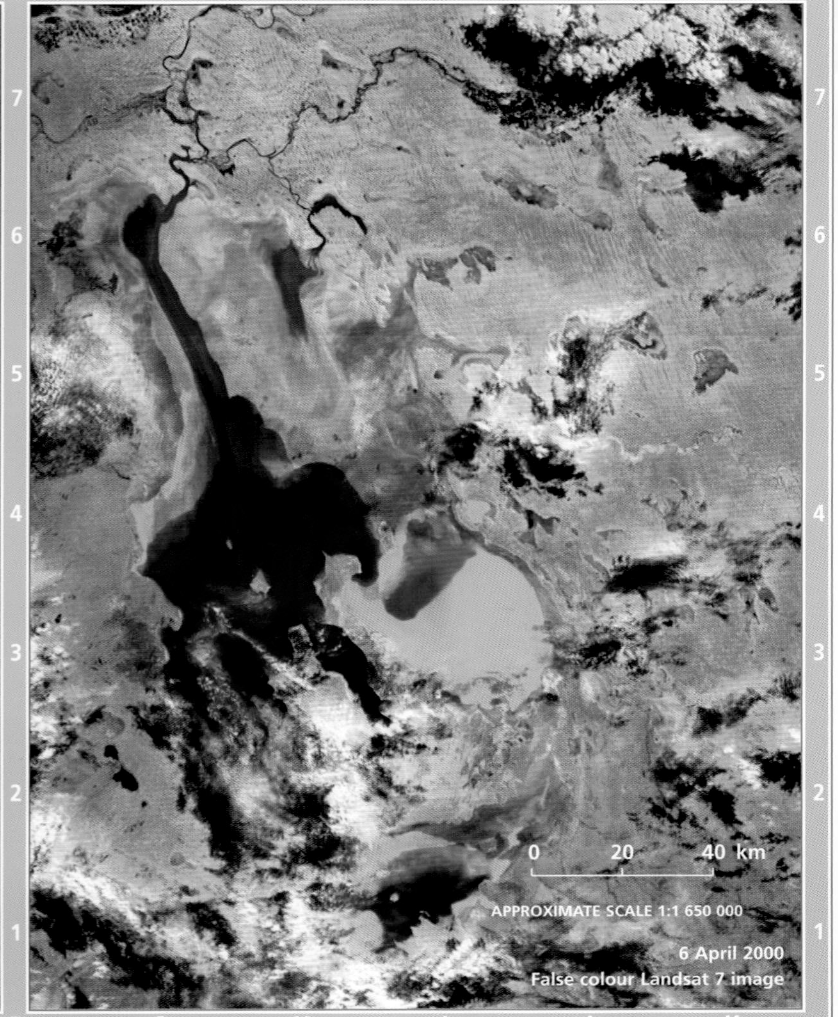

6 April 2000
False colour Landsat 7 image

1 RAIN AND FLOOD EVENT, 2000

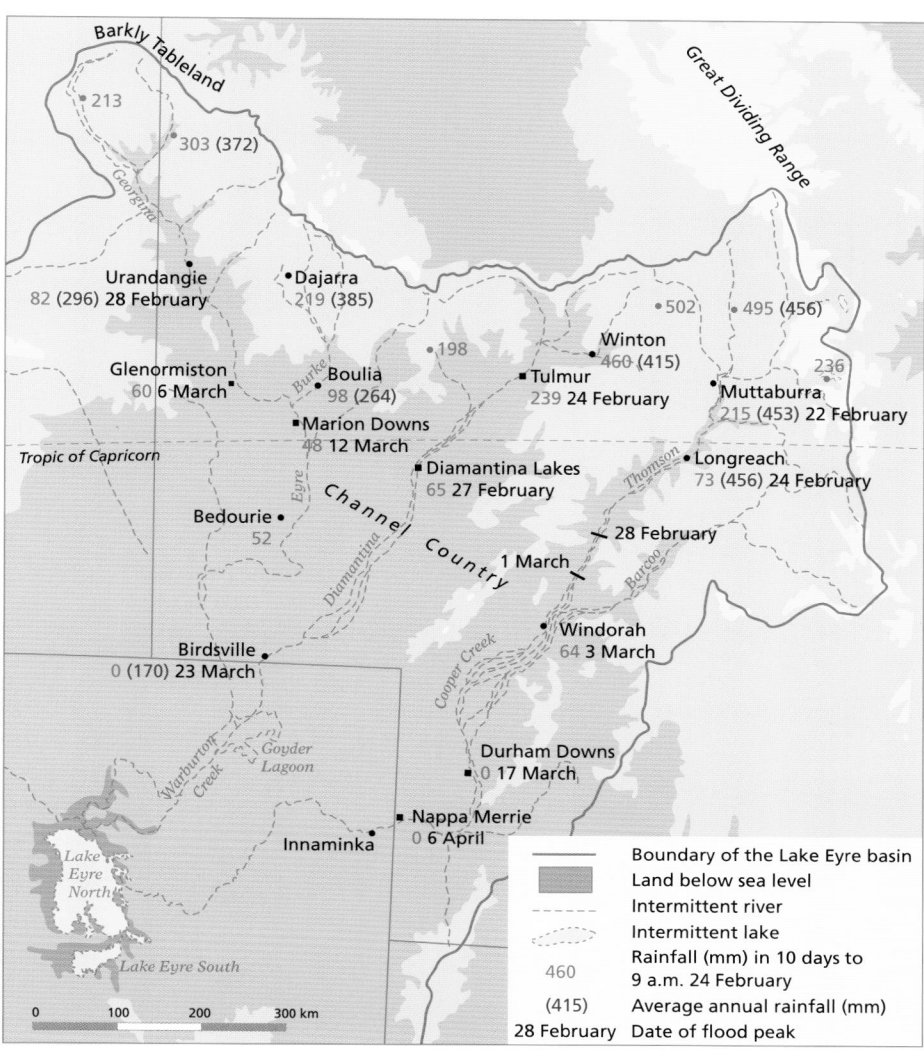

Barkly Tableland

Great Dividing Range

213

303 (372)

Georgina

Urandangie
82 (296) 28 February

Dajarra
219 (385)

502

495 (456)

198

Winton
460 (415)

236

Glenormiston
60 6 March

Boulia
98 (264)

Burke

Tulmur
239 24 February

Muttaburra
215 (453) 22 February

Marion Downs
48 12 March

Tropic of Capricorn

Eyre

Channel Country

Diamantina Lakes
65 27 February

Thomson

Longreach
73 (456) 24 February

28 February

Bedourie
52

Diamantina

1 March

Barcoo

Windorah
64 3 March

Birdsville
0 (170) 23 March

Cooper Creek

Durham Downs
0 17 March

Warburton Creek

Goyder Lagoon

Nappa Merrie
0 6 April

Lake Eyre North

Innaminka

Lake Eyre South

———	Boundary of the Lake Eyre basin
	Land below sea level
– – –	Intermittent river
	Intermittent lake
460	Rainfall (mm) in 10 days to 9 a.m. 24 February
(415)	Average annual rainfall (mm)
28 February	Date of flood peak

0   100   200   300 km

Unusually heavy rain in the headwaters of Cooper Creek and the Diamantina and Georgina rivers in 10 days to 24 February 2000 sent floods slowly across the Channel Country towards Lake Eyre, creating a vast inland sea and isolating townships and properties for months.

2 LAKE EYRE BASIN

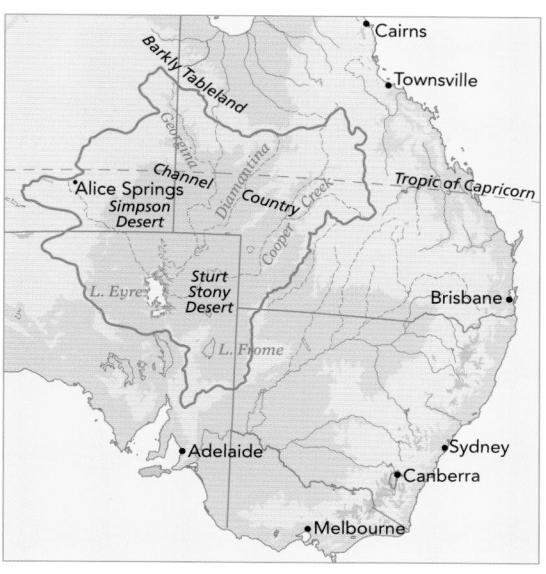

Barkly Tableland

Georgina

Cairns

Townsville

Channel Country

Diamantina

Cooper Creek

Tropic of Capricorn

Alice Springs
Simpson Desert

Sturt Stony Desert

L. Eyre

Brisbane

L. Frome

Adelaide

Sydney

Canberra

Melbourne

3 TOTAL RAINFALL

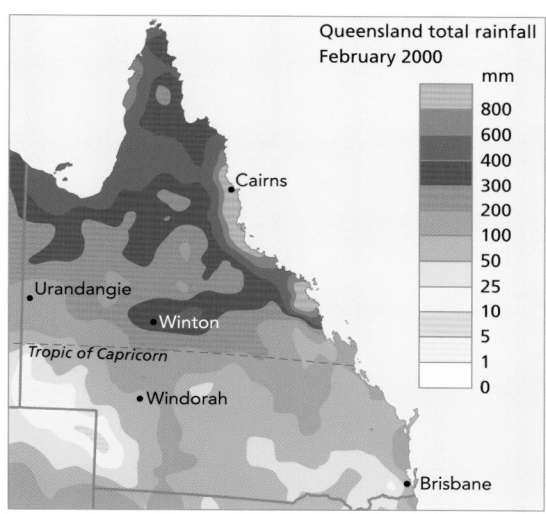

Queensland total rainfall
February 2000

mm
800
600
400
300
200
100
50
25
10
5
1
0

Cairns

Urandangie

Winton

Tropic of Capricorn

Windorah

Brisbane

4 COOPER CREEK FLOOD HYDROGRAPH

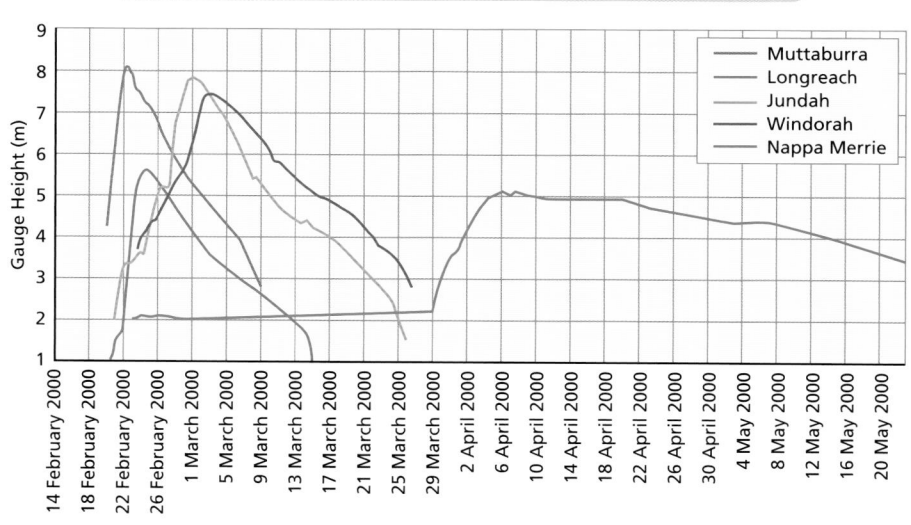

——	Muttaburra
——	Longreach
——	Jundah
——	Windorah
——	Nappa Merrie

Gauge Height (m)

9
8
7
6
5
4
3
2
1

14 February 2000
18 February 2000
22 February 2000
26 February 2000
1 March 2000
5 March 2000
9 March 2000
13 March 2000
17 March 2000
21 March 2000
25 March 2000
29 March 2000
2 April 2000
6 April 2000
10 April 2000
14 April 2000
18 April 2000
22 April 2000
26 April 2000
30 April 2000
4 May 2000
8 May 2000
12 May 2000
16 May 2000
20 May 2000

5 RAINFALL ANOMALIES

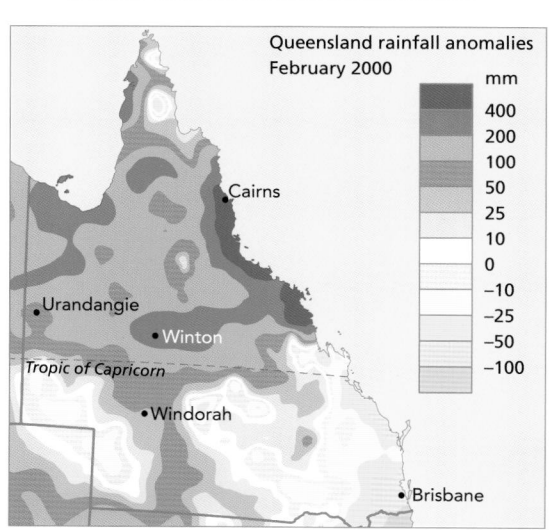

Queensland rainfall anomalies
February 2000

mm
400
200
100
50
25
10
0
−10
−25
−50
−100

Cairns

Urandangie

Winton

Tropic of Capricorn

Windorah

Brisbane

1 RISK OF BUSHFIRES

Bushfires—fires burning out of control in forests and grasslands—are a natural and essential part of the Australian environment. Most are started by lightning or people, and the risk increases in the dry season and during long droughts. Australia has one of the highest bushfire risks in the world.

Extreme
High
Moderate
Low

SCALE 1:55 000 000

2 BUSHFIRE SEASONS

Winter and spring
Spring and summer
Summer
Summer and autumn

3 CANBERRA BUSHFIRES, JANUARY 2003

About 10 per cent of Australia, mostly in the south-east, was blackened by fire in summer 2002–03—one of the worst ever bushfire seasons. Record drought and higher than normal temperatures dried the air, vegetation and soil. Lightning strikes in dry storms on 8 January 2003 created a massive fire front which burned almost unchecked for 59 days in inaccessible country, from the Blue Mountains south to the Victorian high country. The two natural colour Landsat 7 images show the impact of the fires that roared out of the Brindabella Ranges into Canberra on 17–18 January 2003. The 7 November 2002 image shows healthy vegetation, while the 26 January 2003 image reveals dark red-brown burn scars and smoke from fires still burning in the south.

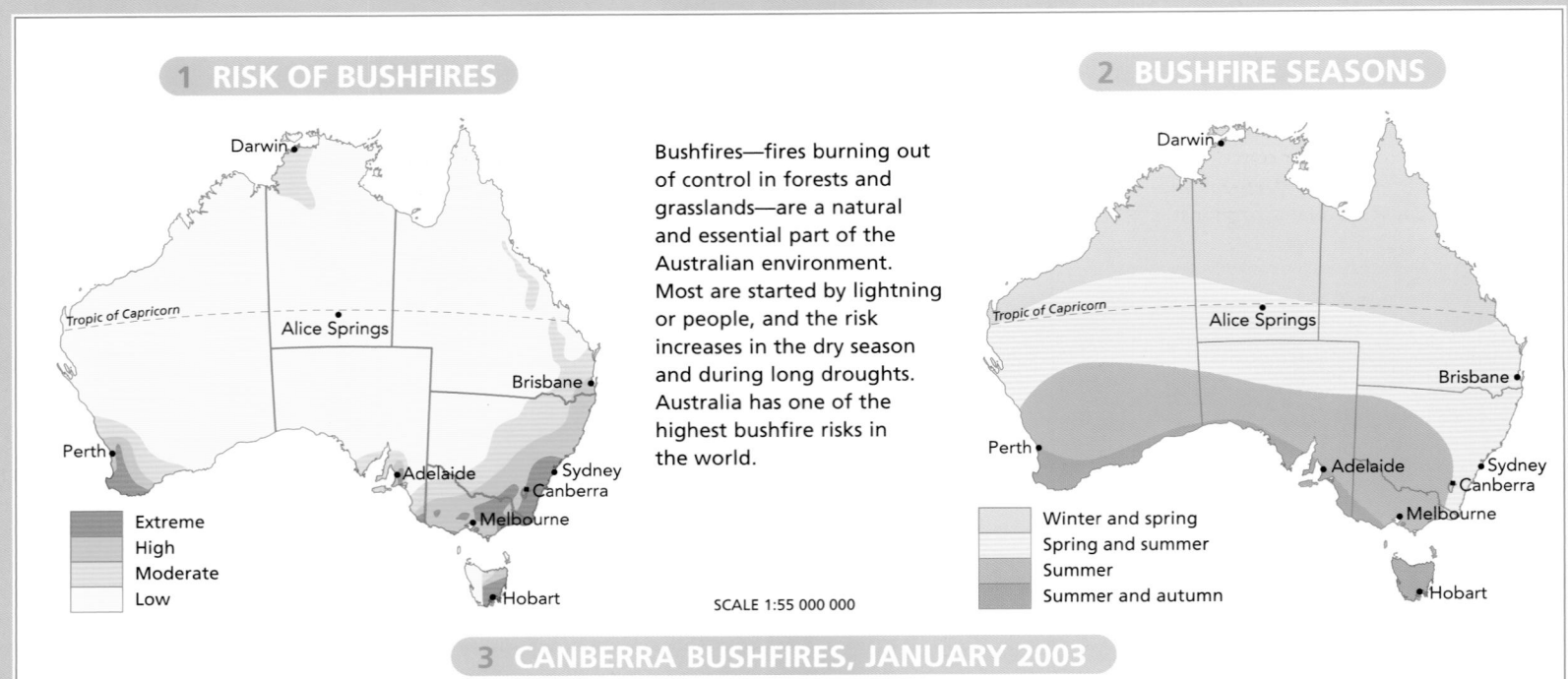

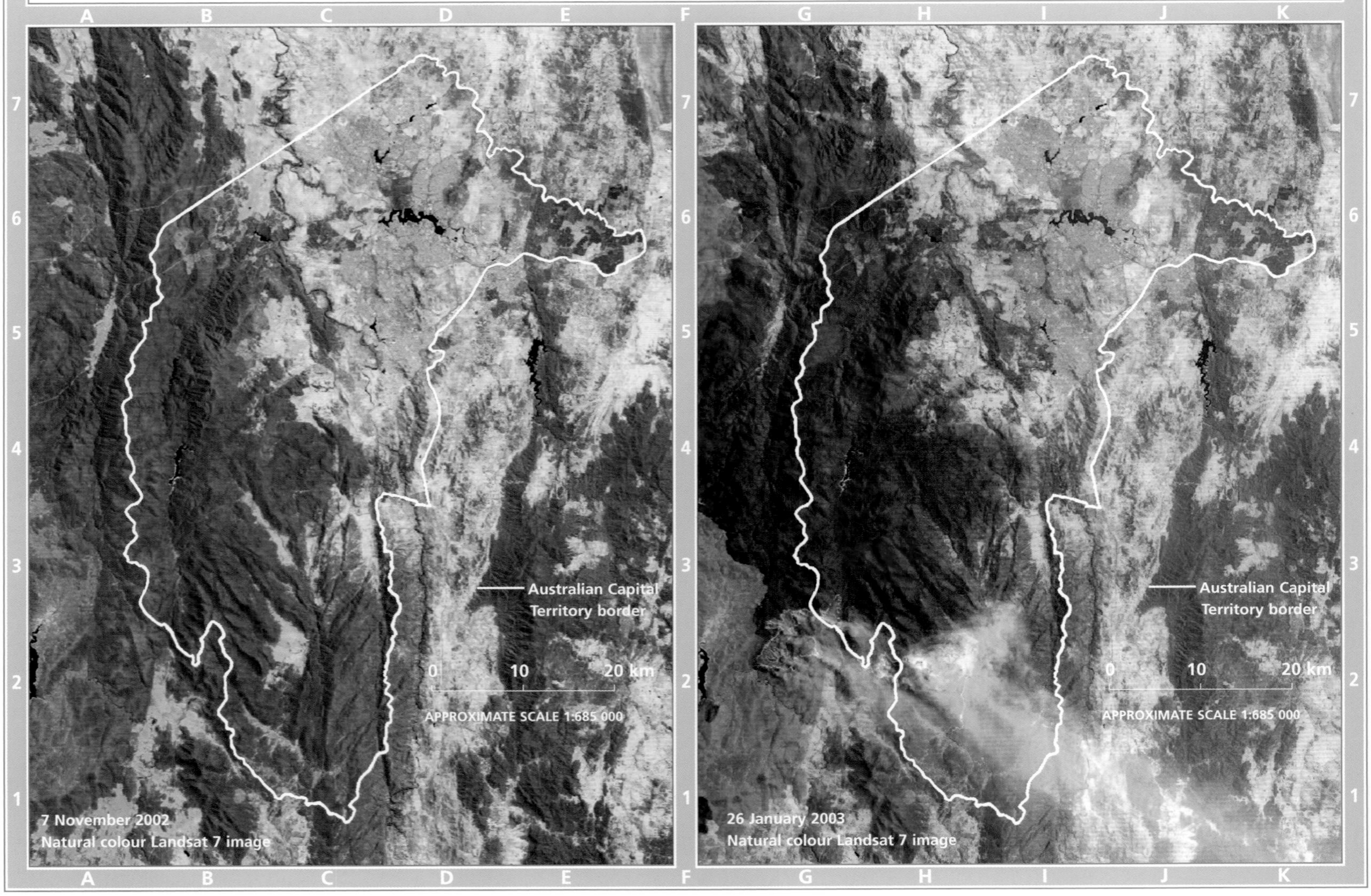

Australian Capital Territory border

0   10   20 km

APPROXIMATE SCALE 1:685 000

7 November 2002
Natural colour Landsat 7 image

Australian Capital Territory border

0   10   20 km

APPROXIMATE SCALE 1:685 000

26 January 2003
Natural colour Landsat 7 image

1 EXTREME CLIMATIC CONDITIONS IN SOUTH-EASTERN AUSTRALIA

There is a strong link between climate, weather and bushfire danger. The 2002–03 drought was particularly severe. Large areas of the south-east received less than 40 per cent of average rainfall in the six months to 31 January 2003. Above normal daytime maximum temperatures caused high evaporation rates and extreme moisture stress, increasing already high fuel levels. Then in late January 2003 extreme conditions forced temperatures up to 6°C above normal across most of NSW.

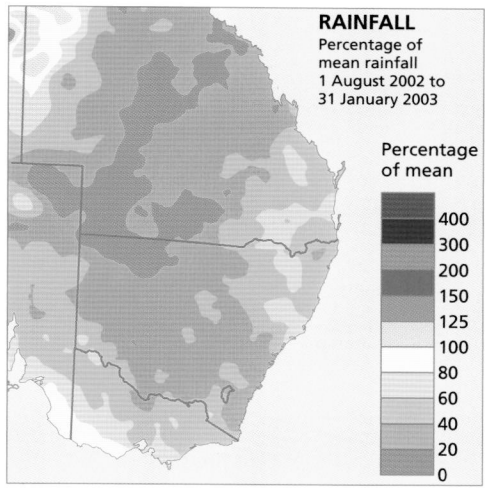

RAINFALL
Percentage of
mean rainfall
1 August 2002 to
31 January 2003

Percentage
of mean

400
300
200
150
125
100
80
60
40
20
0

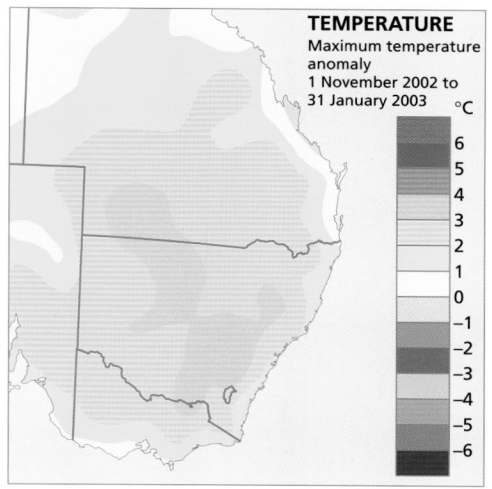

TEMPERATURE
Maximum temperature
anomaly
1 November 2002 to
31 January 2003   °C

6
5
4
3
2
1
0
-1
-2
-3
-4
-5
-6

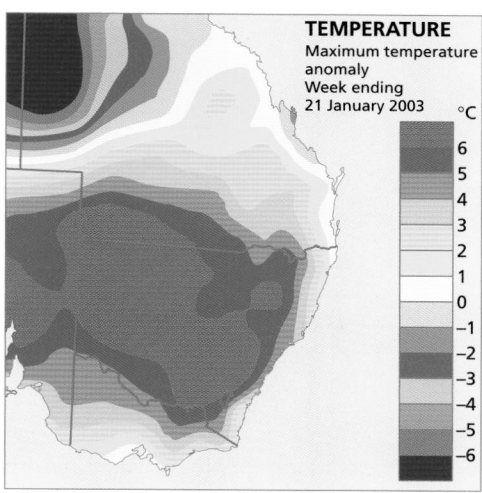

TEMPERATURE
Maximum temperature
anomaly
Week ending
21 January 2003   °C

6
5
4
3
2
1
0
-1
-2
-3
-4
-5
-6

2 THE ADVANCE OF THE FIRESTORM

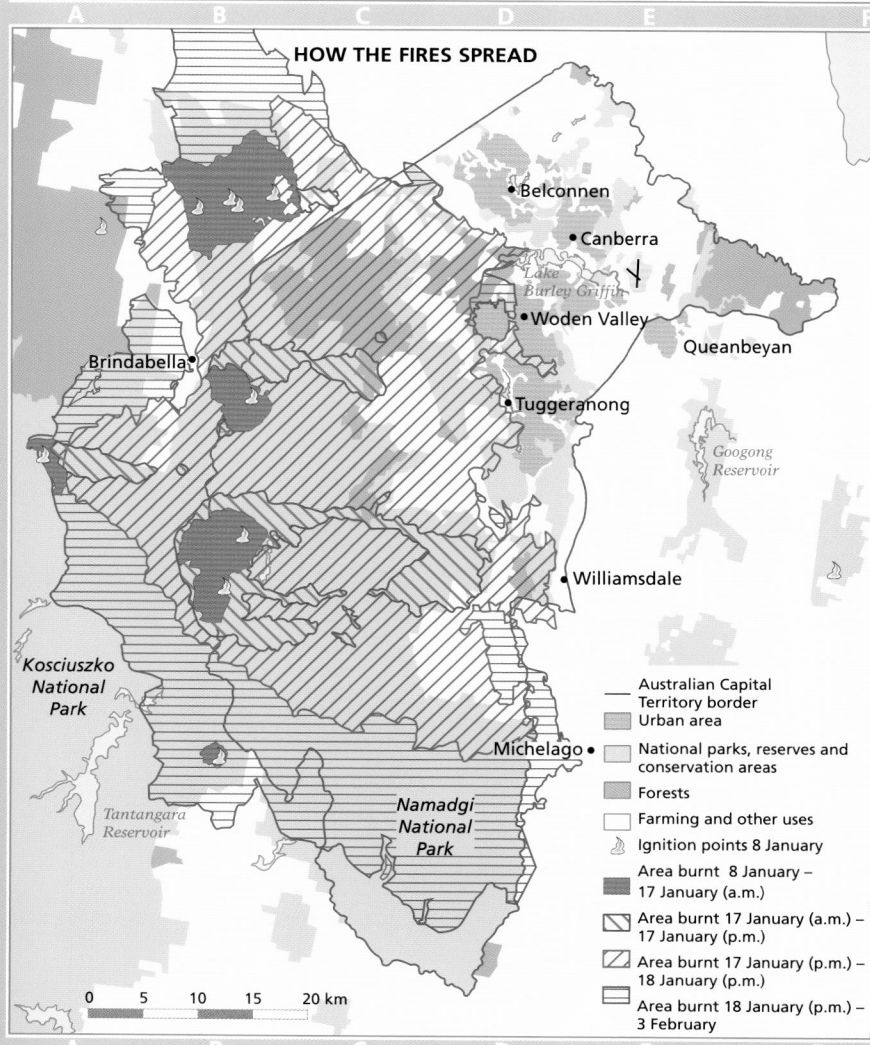

HOW THE FIRES SPREAD

Belconnen
Canberra
Lake Burley Griffin
Woden Valley
Queanbeyan
Brindabella
Tuggeranong
Googong Reservoir
Williamsdale
Kosciuszko National Park
Michelago
Namadgi National Park
Tantangara Reservoir

— Australian Capital Territory border
Urban area
National parks, reserves and conservation areas
Forests
Farming and other uses
Ignition points 8 January
Area burnt 8 January – 17 January (a.m.)
Area burnt 17 January (a.m.) – 17 January (p.m.)
Area burnt 17 January (p.m.) – 18 January (p.m.)
Area burnt 18 January (p.m.) – 3 February

0   5   10   15   20 km

The firestorm that raced into Canberra's western suburbs began with lightning strikes on 8 January 2003. After burning in inaccessible country in the Brindabella Ranges for nine days, the fire fronts joined and raced east towards Canberra on 17 January 2003. They were driven by strong north-westerly winds pushing superheated bone-dry air from central Australia ahead of a rapidly advancing cold front. Temperatures ranged from 47°C in Bourke to 40°C on the coast at Batemans Bay.

On 18 January 2003 conditions were out of control. The firestorm blasted into the suburbs, exploding rather than burning property, with a convection column over 3000 metres high. When it was over, more than 500 homes were destroyed and four people killed, with a damages bill of almost one billion dollars. The continuing social and human cost will eventually be far greater.

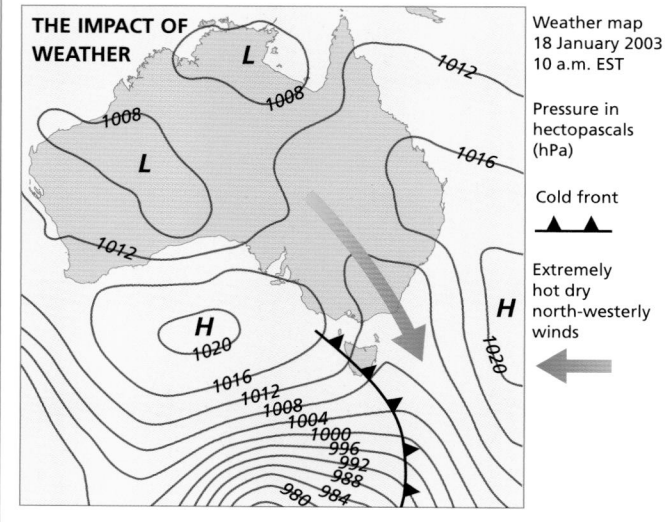

THE IMPACT OF WEATHER

L
1008
1008
1012
L
1016
1012
H
1020
1016
1012
1008
1004
1000
996
992
988
980
984
H
1020

Weather map
18 January 2003
10 a.m. EST

Pressure in hectopascals (hPa)

Cold front

Extremely hot dry north-westerly winds

Australia is the driest inhabited continent on Earth, and drought is part of its natural cycle. Drought is a prolonged dry period when lower than normal water supplies impact on users' needs. Drought is not just a lack of rainfall, known as a meteorological drought. It is also a lack of soil moisture—called an agricultural drought because crops and pasture struggle to grow in dry soil—and reduced stream flow and dam storage, known as a hydrological drought. These three forms of drought last for varying lengths of time and have different recovery periods.

1 RAINFALL VARIABILITY

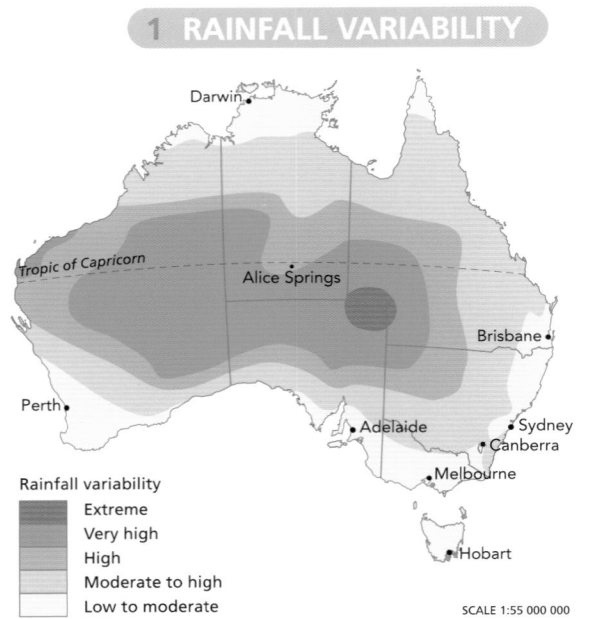

Rainfall variability
- Extreme
- Very high
- High
- Moderate to high
- Low to moderate

SCALE 1:55 000 000

2 RISK OF DROUGHT

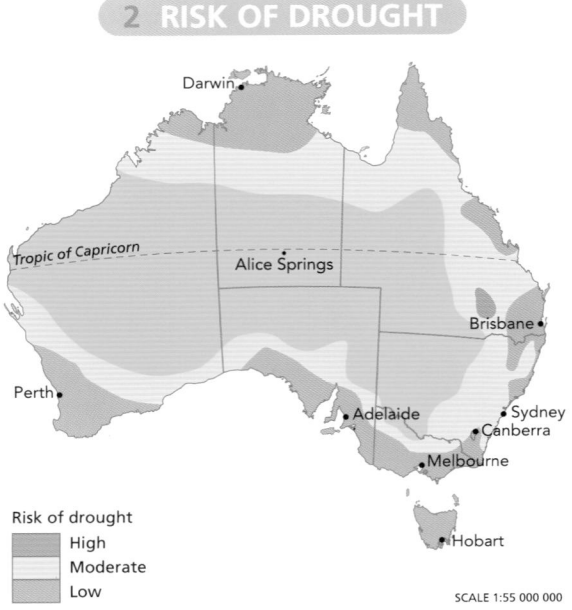

Risk of drought
- High
- Moderate
- Low

SCALE 1:55 000 000

Drought is directly linked to the variability of rainfall, i.e. the extent to which rainfall is above or below normal. Australia's high rainfall variability is related to its position in the mid-latitudes, irregular tropical cyclones, and the impact of El Niño, which has been associated with most of the major droughts of the last 100 years.

Risk of drought or water deficit is measured by the possibility of receiving below normal rainfall, and the likely rate at which moisture will be evaporated from the soil and from wetlands, lakes, rivers and dams. High temperatures, cloudless skies and strong winds all increase evaporation rates.

3 VEGETATION HEALTH AND THE 2002–03 DROUGHT

Vegetation health is directly related to water availability and temperature, and is an important indicator of drought. Information from the USA's NOAA meteorological satellites is used to develop Normalised Difference Vegetation Index (NDVI) maps to show the health of green vegetation and the stress caused by water shortage. Drought regions with vegetation under stress and in poor health are shown in red. These two NDVI vegetation health maps 12 months apart clearly show the variability of Australian rainfall, the extent of the 2002–03 drought, and its impact on vegetation health.

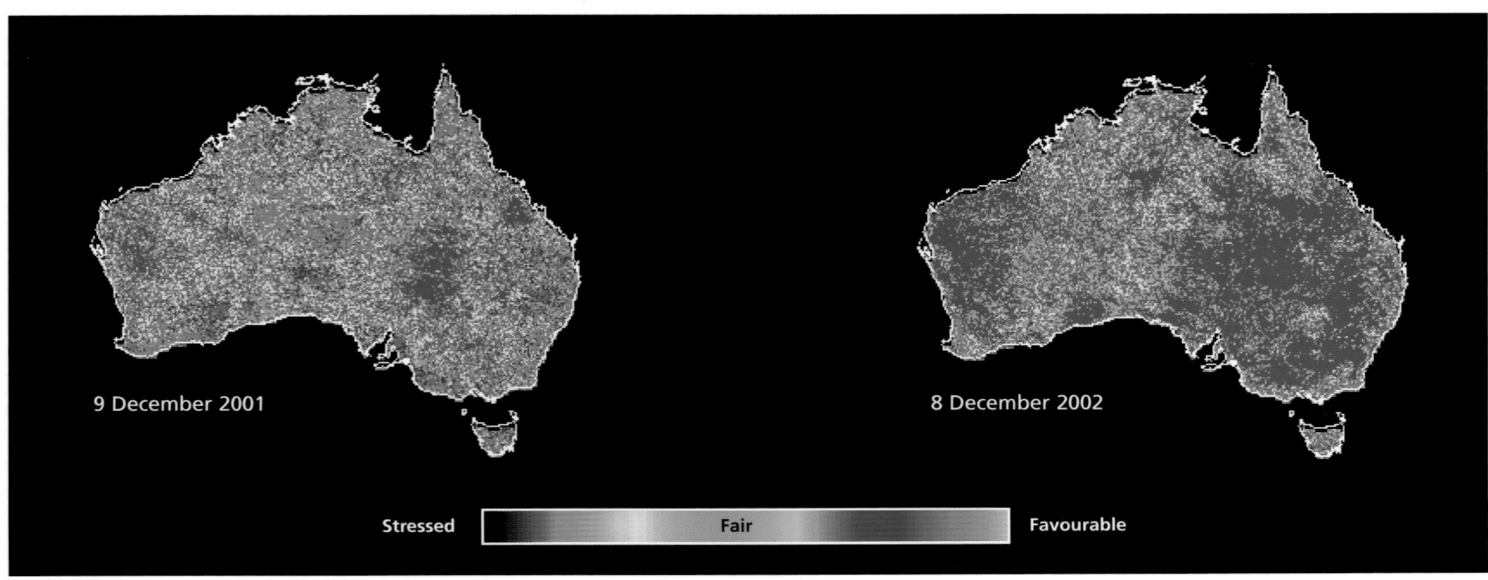

9 December 2001 | 8 December 2002

Stressed — Fair — Favourable

In 2002–03 Australia experienced one of its most extensive and severe droughts on record. The drought was closely linked to an El Niño event in the tropical Pacific Ocean which altered the weather patterns in the Australian region. It was particularly severe because higher than average temperatures increased evaporation rates from soil, vegetation and surface water. The 11-month meteorological drought which began in March 2002 started to wane over most of the continent in February 2003. Its agricultural, hydrological and human impact lasted much longer.

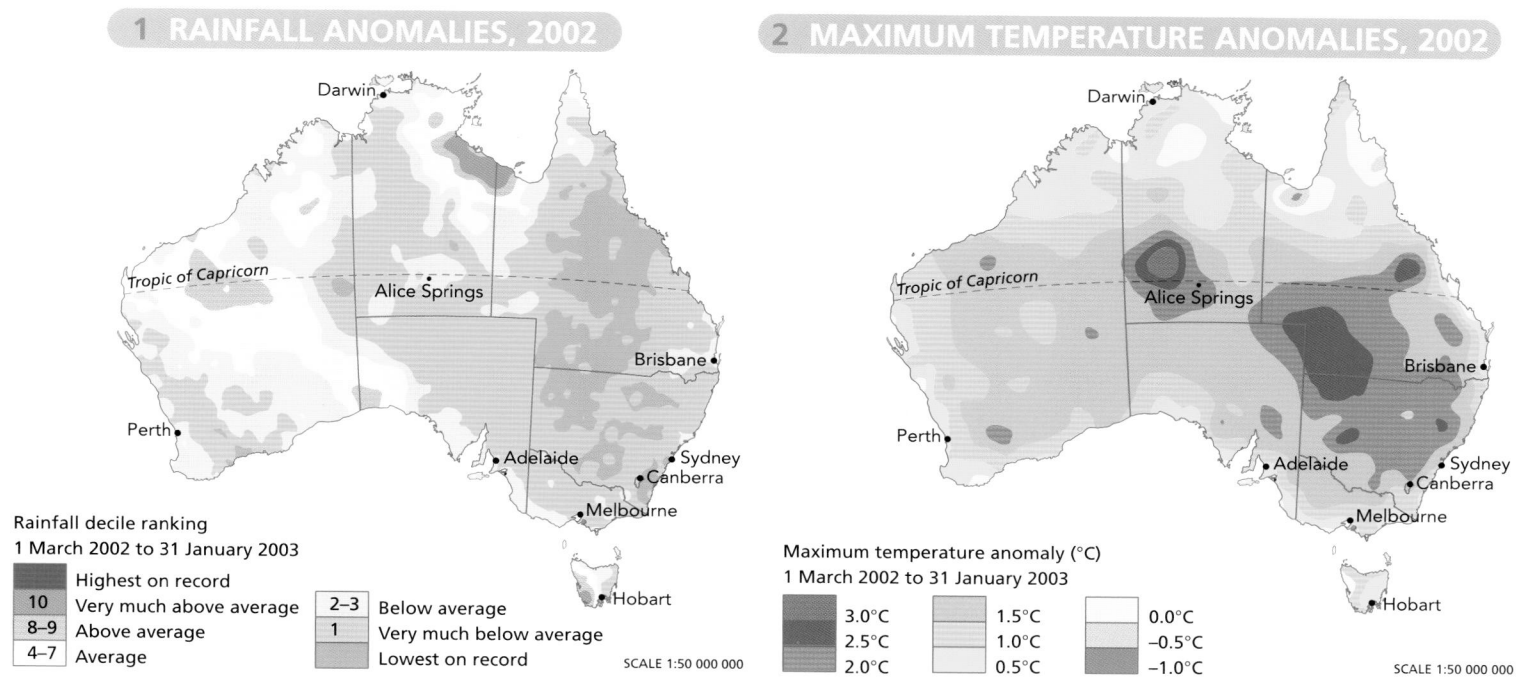

1 RAINFALL ANOMALIES, 2002

Rainfall decile ranking
1 March 2002 to 31 January 2003

- Highest on record
- 10 Very much above average
- 8–9 Above average
- 4–7 Average
- 2–3 Below average
- 1 Very much below average
- Lowest on record

SCALE 1:50 000 000

2 MAXIMUM TEMPERATURE ANOMALIES, 2002

Maximum temperature anomaly (°C)
1 March 2002 to 31 January 2003

- 3.0°C
- 2.5°C
- 2.0°C
- 1.5°C
- 1.0°C
- 0.5°C
- 0.0°C
- −0.5°C
- −1.0°C

SCALE 1:50 000 000

Most of Australia experienced below normal rainfall in the 11 months from March 2002 to January 2003. Ninety per cent of the country received rainfall below the long-term median, with 56 per cent of the country in the lowest 10 per cent of recorded rainfalls—i.e. decile 1, with a serious to severe rainfall deficiency.

Australia-wide autumn, winter and spring average daytime temperatures in 2002 were the highest on record. The maximum temperature anomaly in the 11-month dry period from March 2002 to January 2003 was +1.51°C, 0.61°C above the previous March–January record, greatly increasing evaporation rates during an already extremely dry period.

3 DROUGHT, EL NIÑO AND GLOBAL WARMING

The 2002–03 drought was mainly due to El Niño conditions bringing more stable weather patterns over Australia, reducing the inflow of moist tropical air. Average maximum temperatures were more than 1.0°C higher than during previous droughts, increasing evaporation rates and the severity of the drought. Meteorologists are concerned that record temperatures were caused by the combination of higher daytime El Niño temperatures and human-induced global warming. If so, global warming is likely to make future droughts even hotter and more severe.

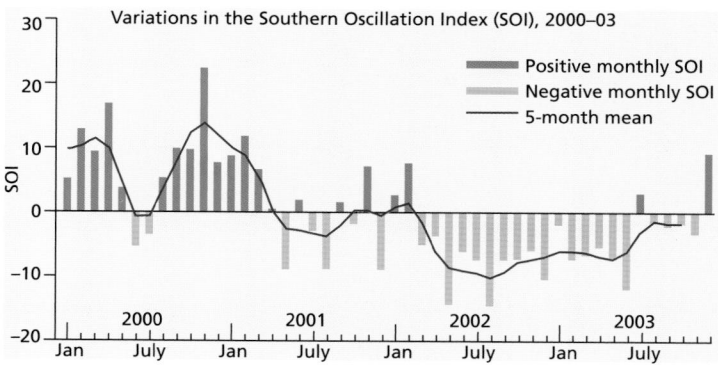

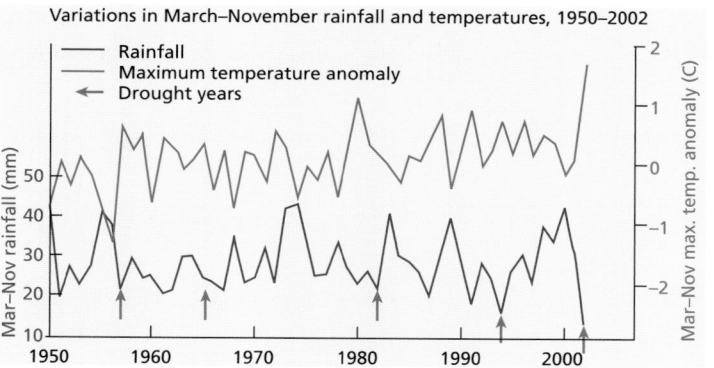

The SOI graphs changes in air pressure across the Pacific Ocean between Darwin and Tahiti, and shows the changes between El Niño and La Niña events (see page 25 for an explanation). Note how the negative SOI—an El Niño—corresponds with the 2002–03 drought, with the SOI returning closer to zero and more normal rainfall patterns in autumn 2003.

This graph plots average monthly rainfall (the blue line) and variations from average daily maximum temperature (the red line) for March–November. Average daily maximum temperature anomalies for these months have increased at the same rate as increases expected due to global warming —a possible indicator of the increasing severity of future droughts.

1 EARTHQUAKES IN AUSTRALIA

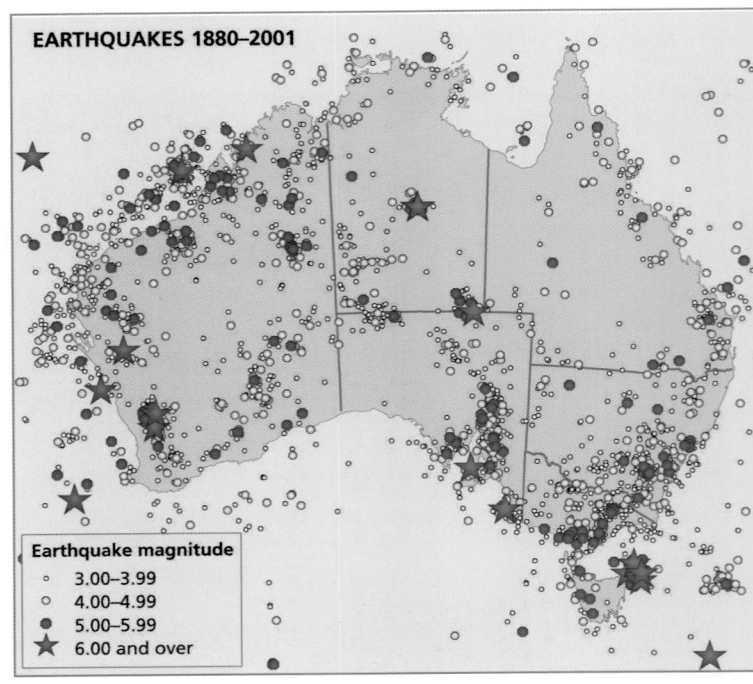

EARTHQUAKES 1880–2001

Earthquake magnitude
- ○ 3.00–3.99
- ○ 4.00–4.99
- ● 5.00–5.99
- ★ 6.00 and over

On average each year Australia experiences 200 earthquakes greater than M2.5 on the Richter scale—the smallest earthquakes humans feel—and one, greater than M5.0, capable of causing damage. The maps on this page show that while Australia experiences earthquakes, its position away from the edge of the Indo-Australian Plate ensures that its earthquake risk is low to very low in comparison with our near neighbours.

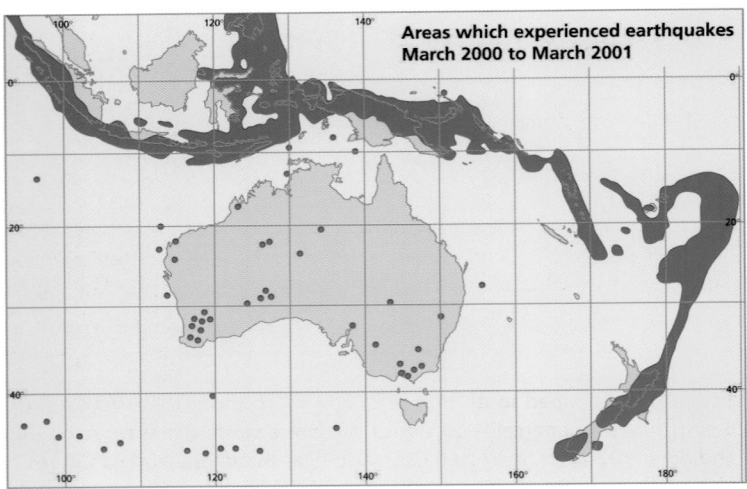

Areas which experienced earthquakes March 2000 to March 2001

2 PLATE BOUNDARIES, EARTHQUAKES AND VOLCANOES

Australia is on the vast Indo-Australian Plate, which is moving north-east to collide with the Pacific, Philippine and Eurasian plates. To the east, the Pacific Plate is moving north-west and colliding with the Indo-Australian Plate. At the plate boundaries the Earth's crust is a complex zone of fractured plates and micro-plates moving at different speeds towards, apart from, and past each other, pushing up the ocean floor to build island chains, subducting to form deep ocean trenches, and creating one of the world's most active earthquake and volcano belts.

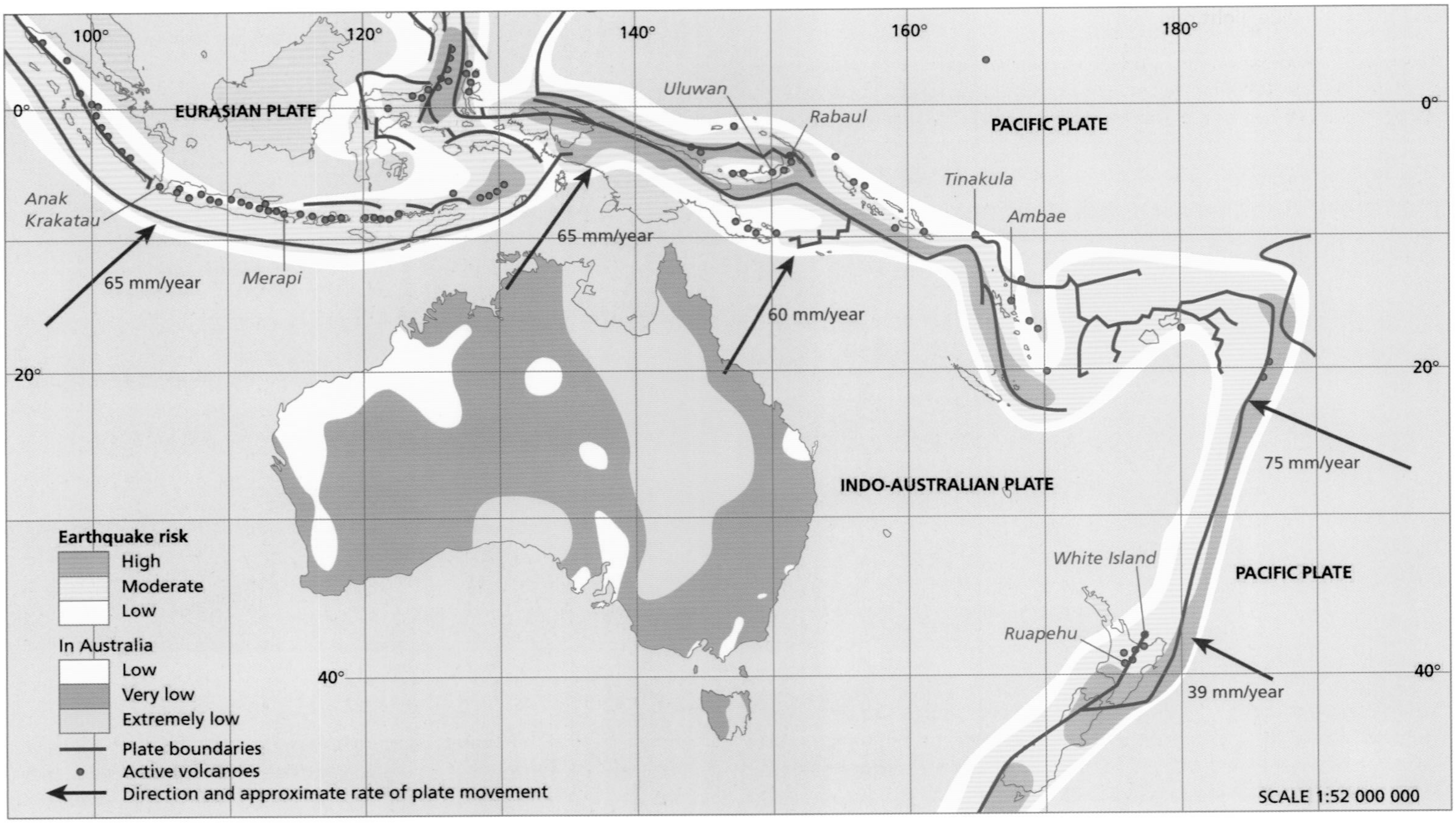

EURASIAN PLATE

Uluwan

Rabaul

PACIFIC PLATE

Tinakula

Ambae

Anak Krakatau

65 mm/year

Merapi

65 mm/year

60 mm/year

INDO-AUSTRALIAN PLATE

75 mm/year

Earthquake risk
- High
- Moderate
- Low

In Australia
- Low
- Very low
- Extremely low

White Island

PACIFIC PLATE

Ruapehu

39 mm/year

— Plate boundaries
• Active volcanoes
← Direction and approximate rate of plate movement

SCALE 1:52 000 000

1 SEVERE STORMS

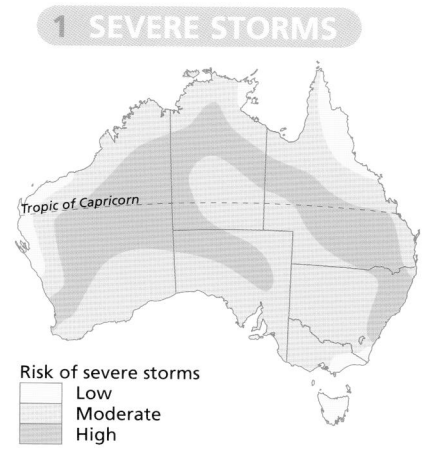

Tropic of Capricorn

Risk of severe storms
- Low
- Moderate
- High

Severe storms cause local damage with wind gusts to 90 kilometres per hour, lightning, large hailstones, heavy rain and flash floods.

2 EXTREME WINDS

December–March

November–March

Tropic of Capricorn

October–February

June–September

September–December

August–December

June–November

Risk of extreme winds

All months

Extreme winds are most frequent during summer and autumn in the north, and during winter and spring in the south.

3 TORNADOES

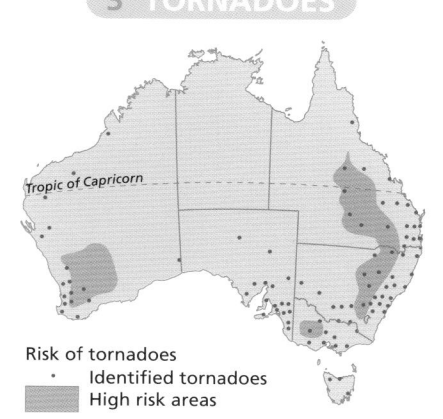

Tropic of Capricorn

Risk of tornadoes
- · Identified tornadoes
- High risk areas

Tornadoes are probably the most violent and destructive of all weather hazards. Winds may exceed 400 km/hour.

4 THE SYDNEY SEVERE HAILSTORM, 14 APRIL 1999

The storm developed south of Sydney and moved north and out to sea. By 6 p.m. it was a 'supercell'—an unusually severe storm with very strong up and down draughts. It crossed over land near Bundeena and continued along the coast before it weakened near Gosford about 10 p.m.

In Sydney's coastal suburbs high winds, torrential rain and hailstones to 13 centimetres in diameter damaged more than 22 000 homes and 63 000 cars, causing Australia's largest natural disaster insurance bill—A$1.7 billion— and total losses of A$2.3 billion. One person was killed by lightning.

Images from the weather radar south-west of Helensburgh provide graphic detail of the storm's intensity and movement. Red indicates intense rain and hail; dark blue, light rain.

The horizontal radar image opposite shows the storm at its most severe with an intense 10-kilometre core. Note the outline of the coast and harbour. Suburb names are abbreviated and 'YSSY' is Sydney airport.

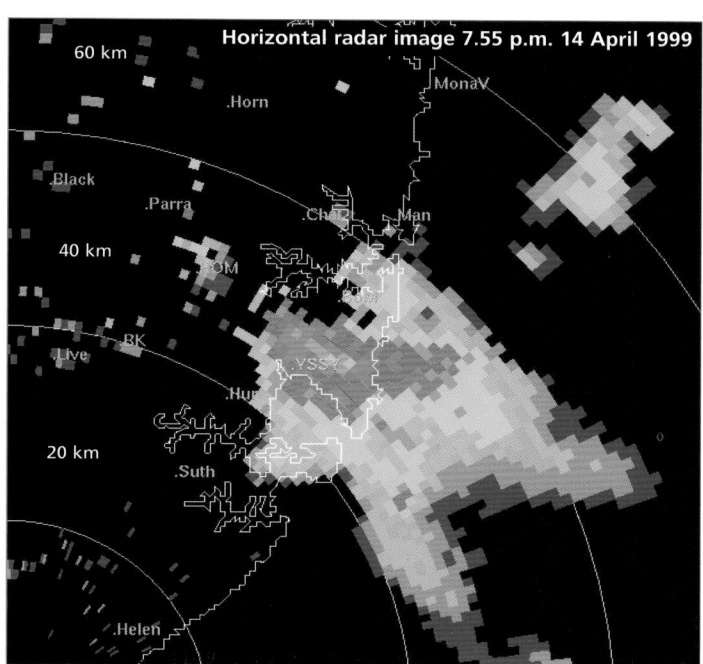

Horizontal radar image 7.55 p.m. 14 April 1999

The vertical radar image below is a cross-section through the storm at 7.55 p.m. when it was over 12 kilometres high. Below the intense centre is a blue area of powerful up draughts which prevented rain and hail falling, increasing the size of hailstones and the damage caused in the core.

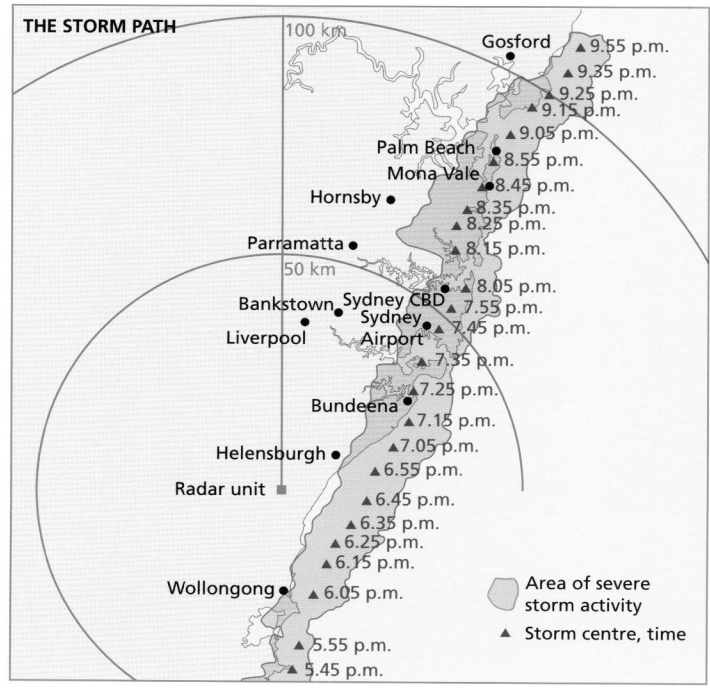

THE STORM PATH

100 km

Gosford ▲9.55 p.m.
▲9.35 p.m.
▲9.25 p.m.
▲9.15 p.m.
▲9.05 p.m.
Palm Beach ▲8.55 p.m.
Mona Vale ▲8.45 p.m.
Hornsby ● ▲8.35 p.m.
▲8.25 p.m.
Parramatta ● ▲8.15 p.m.

50 km

▲8.05 p.m.
Bankstown Sydney CBD ▲7.55 p.m.
● Sydney ▲7.45 p.m.
Liverpool ● Airport
▲7.35 p.m.
▲7.25 p.m.
Bundeena ▲7.15 p.m.
▲7.05 p.m.
Helensburgh ● ▲6.55 p.m.
▲6.45 p.m.
Radar unit ■ ▲6.35 p.m.
▲6.25 p.m.
▲6.15 p.m.
Wollongong ● ▲6.05 p.m.

- ⬡ Area of severe storm activity
- ▲ Storm centre, time

▲5.55 p.m.
▲5.45 p.m.

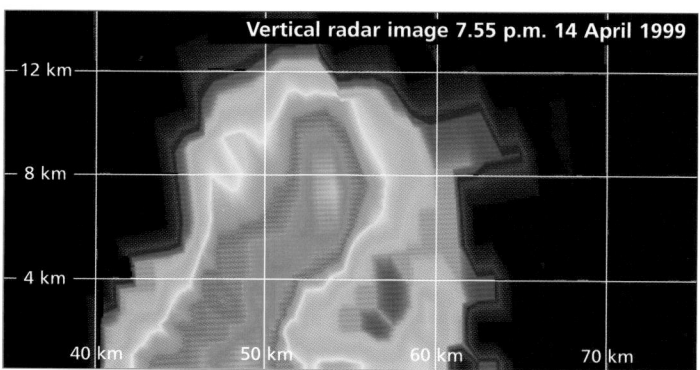

Vertical radar image 7.55 p.m. 14 April 1999

12 km
8 km
4 km

40 km   50 km   60 km   70 km

1 EROSION BY WATER

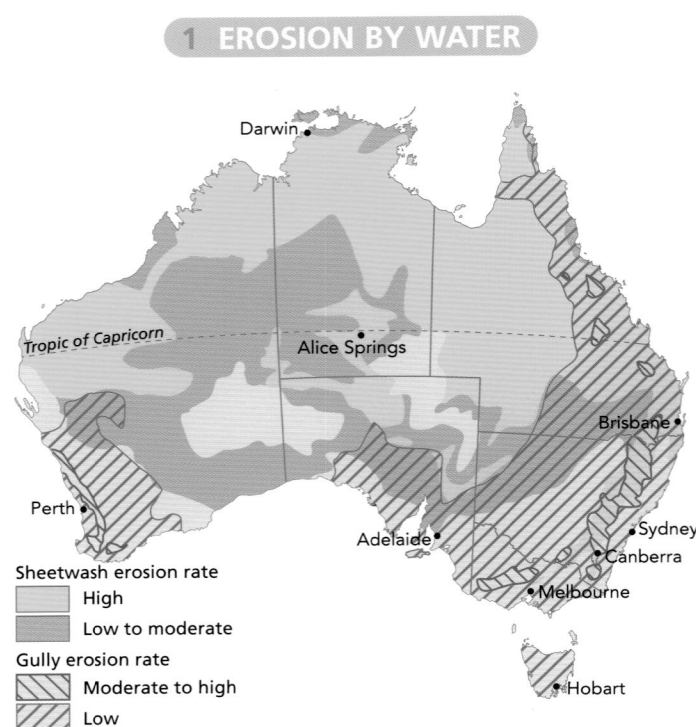

Sheetwash erosion rate
High
Low to moderate

Gully erosion rate
Moderate to high
Low

Erosion by water, either surface sheetwash or gully erosion, is most severe on sloping land where cropping or overgrazing by animals has left the soil unprotected by vegetation and exposed to the full force of raindrops and surface run-off.

2 EROSION BY WIND

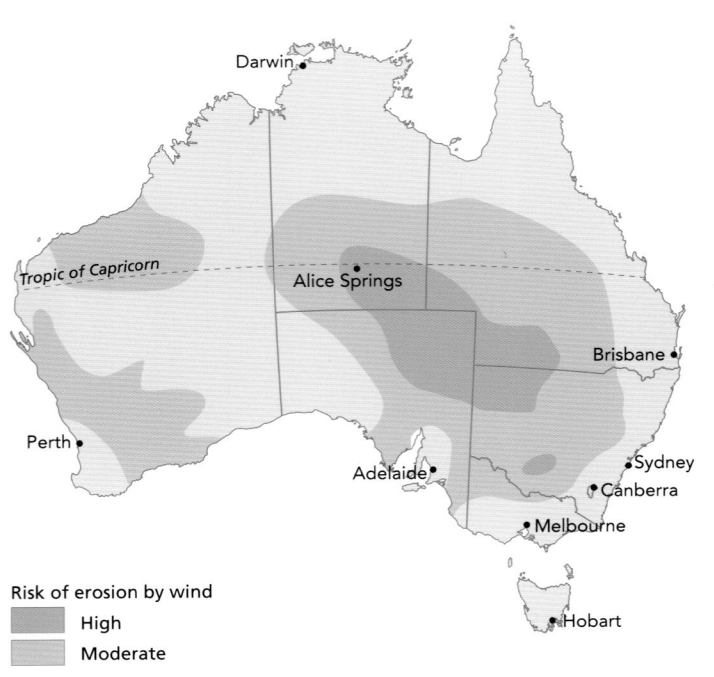

Risk of erosion by wind
High
Moderate

Erosion by wind is more common in semi-arid areas where the soil is dry and sandy, and in farming lands where the protective cover of vegetation has been removed by cropping or overgrazing and the soil exposed, particularly during drought seasons.

3 SOIL SALINITY

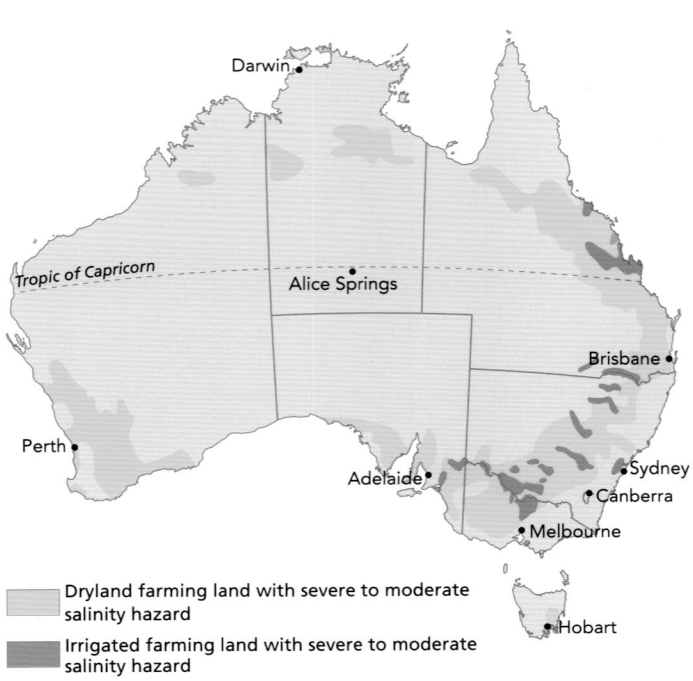

Dryland farming land with severe to moderate salinity hazard

Irrigated farming land with severe to moderate salinity hazard

The removal of trees and the use of water to irrigate crops and pastures have raised the water table and brought salt close to the surface. The productivity of 5.7 million hectares of farming land is already destroyed or at risk—our greatest environmental hazard.

4 ACID SOILS AND WOODY SHRUBS

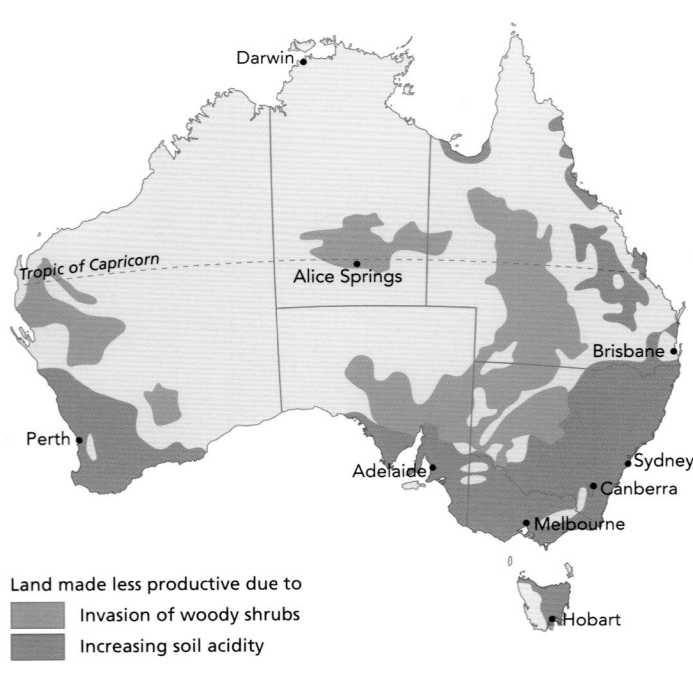

Land made less productive due to
Invasion of woody shrubs
Increasing soil acidity

In moist areas with naturally acid soils, the use of fertilisers and certain pastures and crops has increased soil acidity. In drier lands, overgrazing of pasture grasses has been followed by a dense invasion of woody native shrubs which are inedible to livestock.

SCALE 1:45 000 000

Lambert Azimuthal Equal Area projection

1 DESERTIFICATION

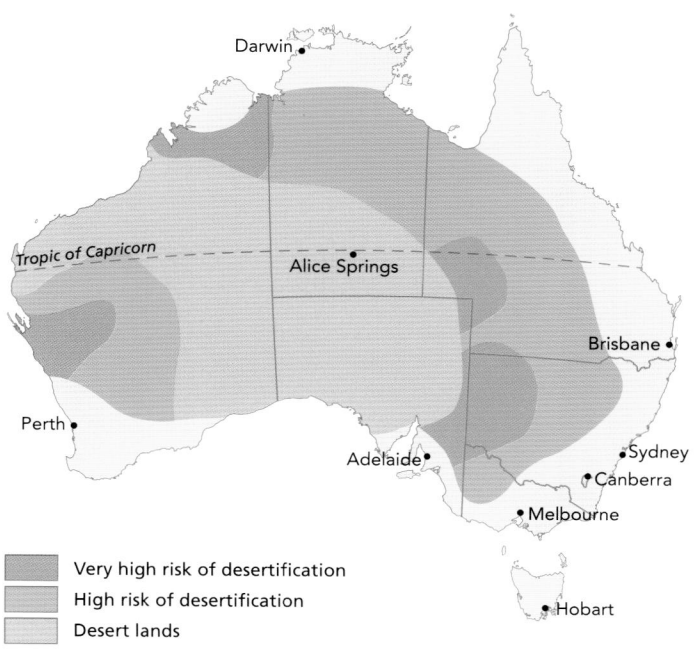

Very high risk of desertification
High risk of desertification
Desert lands

Desertification is the spread of deserts by human activities such as overgrazing during a time of drought. Vegetation cover is reduced and soil erosion increases. Fifty-three per cent of Australia's arid grazing lands have a very high to high risk of desertification.

2 FORESTS AND COASTS

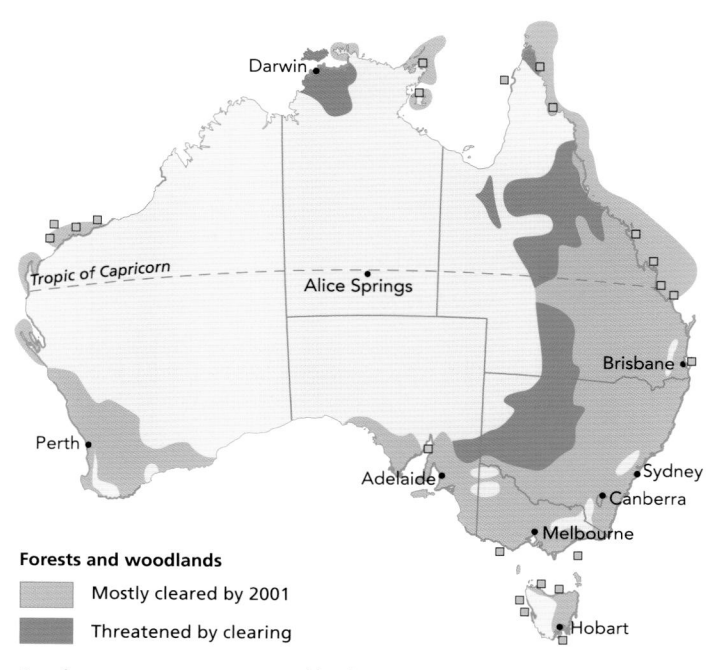

Forests and woodlands

Mostly cleared by 2001
Threatened by clearing

Development pressure on coastal lands
Urban, industrial, recreation and tourism
Mining and petroleum search and production
Coral reefs under threat

3 RABBITS AND CANE TOADS

Distribution of rabbits
Distribution of cane toads

Rabbits were introduced in 1858. They eat crops and pastures and dig warrens, causing severe soil erosion. Cane toads were introduced in 1935 to try to control cane beetles. They have spread rapidly, eating insects and small native animals.

4 FERAL PIGS AND GOATS

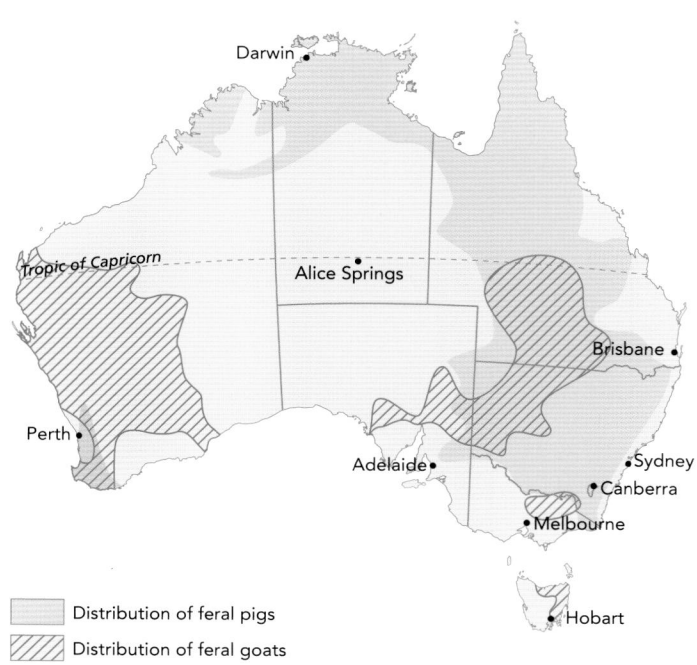

Distribution of feral pigs
Distribution of feral goats

Feral pigs and goats eat and destroy native vegetation and crops and pastures. Pigs also prey on lambs and native animals. Both cause considerable soil erosion and reduce the productivity of the land.

1 EARLY COLONISATION

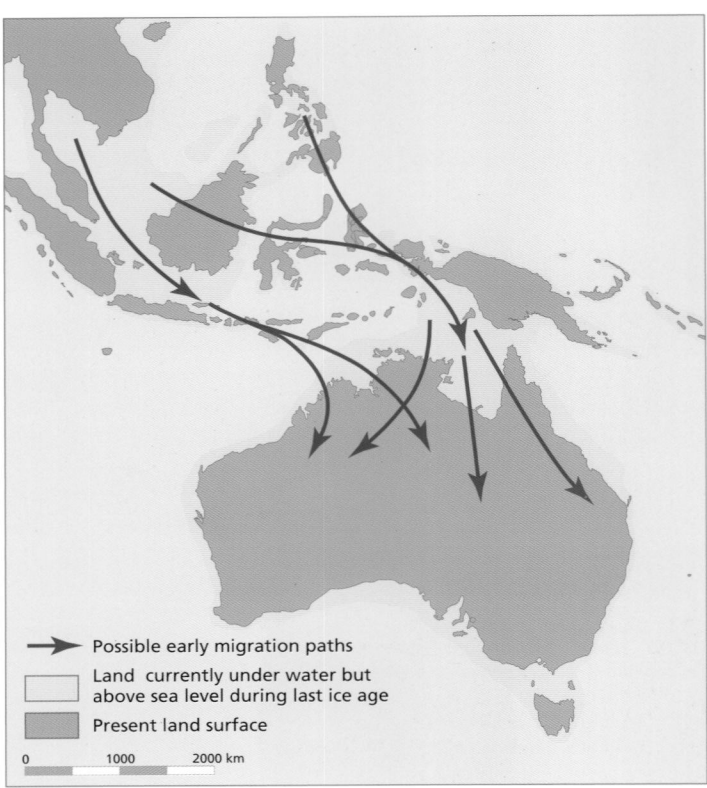

→ Possible early migration paths

☐ Land currently under water but above sea level during last ice age

▦ Present land surface

0   1000   2000 km

Aboriginal and Torres Strait Islander peoples are Australia's Indigenous inhabitants. Aboriginal peoples lived across all of mainland Australia and its islands with the exception of the Torres Strait Islands, which were occupied by Torres Strait Islanders.

From a scientific point of view, the ancestors of the Aboriginal peoples came to Australia from the islands to our north or north-west more than 50 000 years ago. The movement of these people would have been greatly assisted during the last ice age, 25 000 to 10 000 years ago, because the sea was more than 100 metres below its present level. They could have walked across the exposed sea floor or sailed across the shallow seas in rafts or other craft.

Various theories have been put forward as to the colonisation of Australia by our Indigenous peoples. One theory suggests that people moved around the coastline and then into the interior of the continent. Another suggests movement down the eastern half of the continent and then across to the west. Another theory suggests a general movement of people from north to south, right across the continent.

Most Aboriginal peoples believe that they were born of the land and have always been in Australia. Torres Strait Islanders, who have many cultural similarities with the peoples of Papua New Guinea and the Pacific, may have occupied their traditional lands and seas in the Torres Strait Islands more than 10 000 years ago.

It is estimated that at the time of European settlement in 1788 there were between 300 000 and one million Aboriginal and Torres Strait Islander people in Australia. There were more than 500 separate groups of people, many with several subgroups, and about 250 different languages.

2 LIKELY POPULATION DISTRIBUTION, 1788

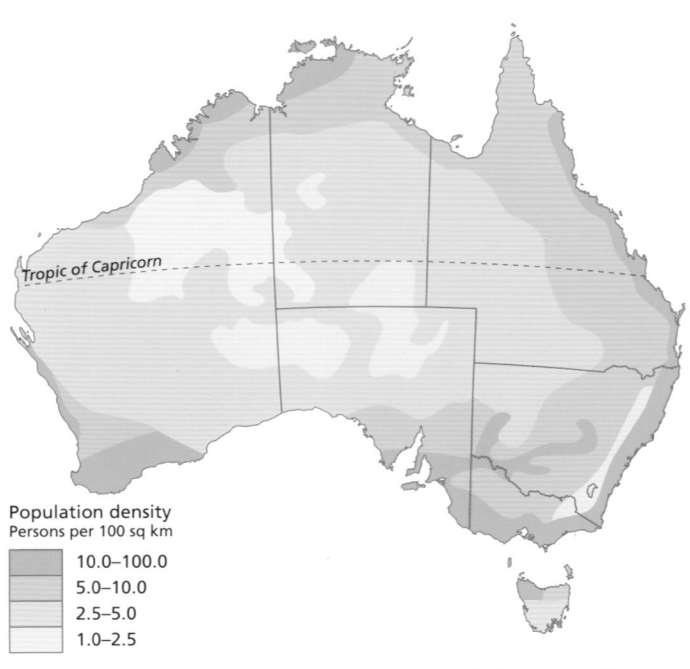

Population density
Persons per 100 sq km

▦ 10.0–100.0
▦ 5.0–10.0
▦ 2.5–5.0
▦ 1.0–2.5

SCALE 1:45 000 000

Aboriginal peoples moved around their land in a seasonal cycle based on the availability of resources. The highest population densities were around the coast and along the major inland rivers.

3 ART AND ARCHAEOLOGICAL SITES

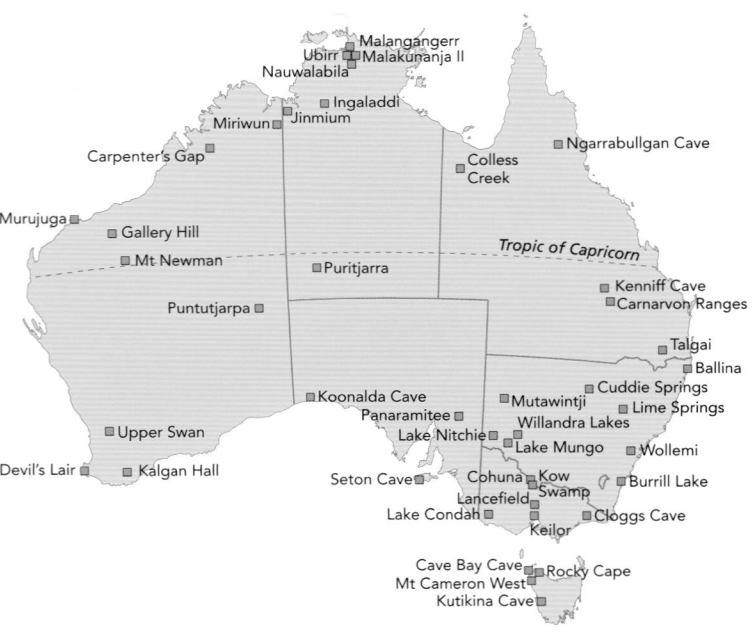

SCALE 1:45 000 000

This map shows a selection of some of the significant Aboriginal art and archaeological sites across Australia. Malakunanja II, for example, has stone artefacts dating back more than 50 000 years.

1 INDIGENOUS REGIONS

Evidence shows that Aboriginal peoples have been in Australia for more than 50 000 to 60 000 years. Over this very long period of time, regional differences in languages, cultures and social organisation developed across the continent.

The map on the right shows 18 broad Aboriginal and Torres Strait Islander language regions. Although these regions loosely correspond with Australia's major water catchment basins, they also take into account the characteristics and relationships which existed within and between the different Indigenous peoples, for example, differences in language, weapons, art styles, body decoration, initiation procedures and burial procedures.

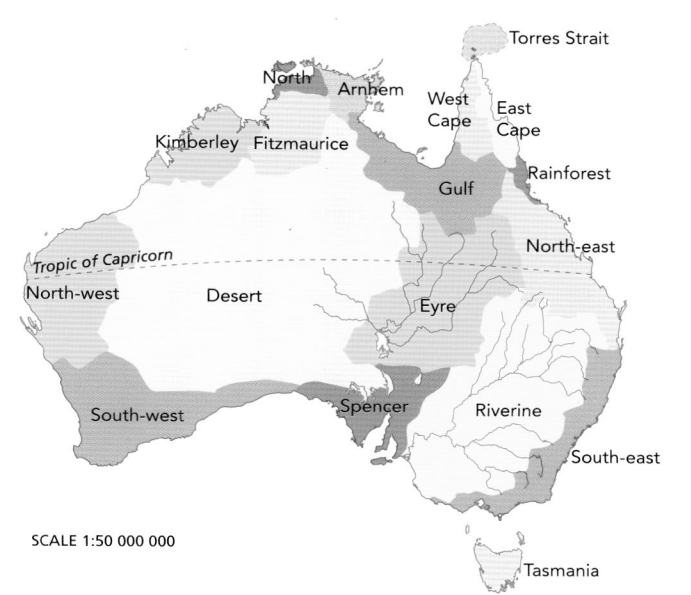

SCALE 1:50 000 000

2 INDIGENOUS LANGUAGE GROUPS

This map shows the main language groups within each Indigenous region. Each group had its own land, language/dialect, culture and spiritual beliefs.

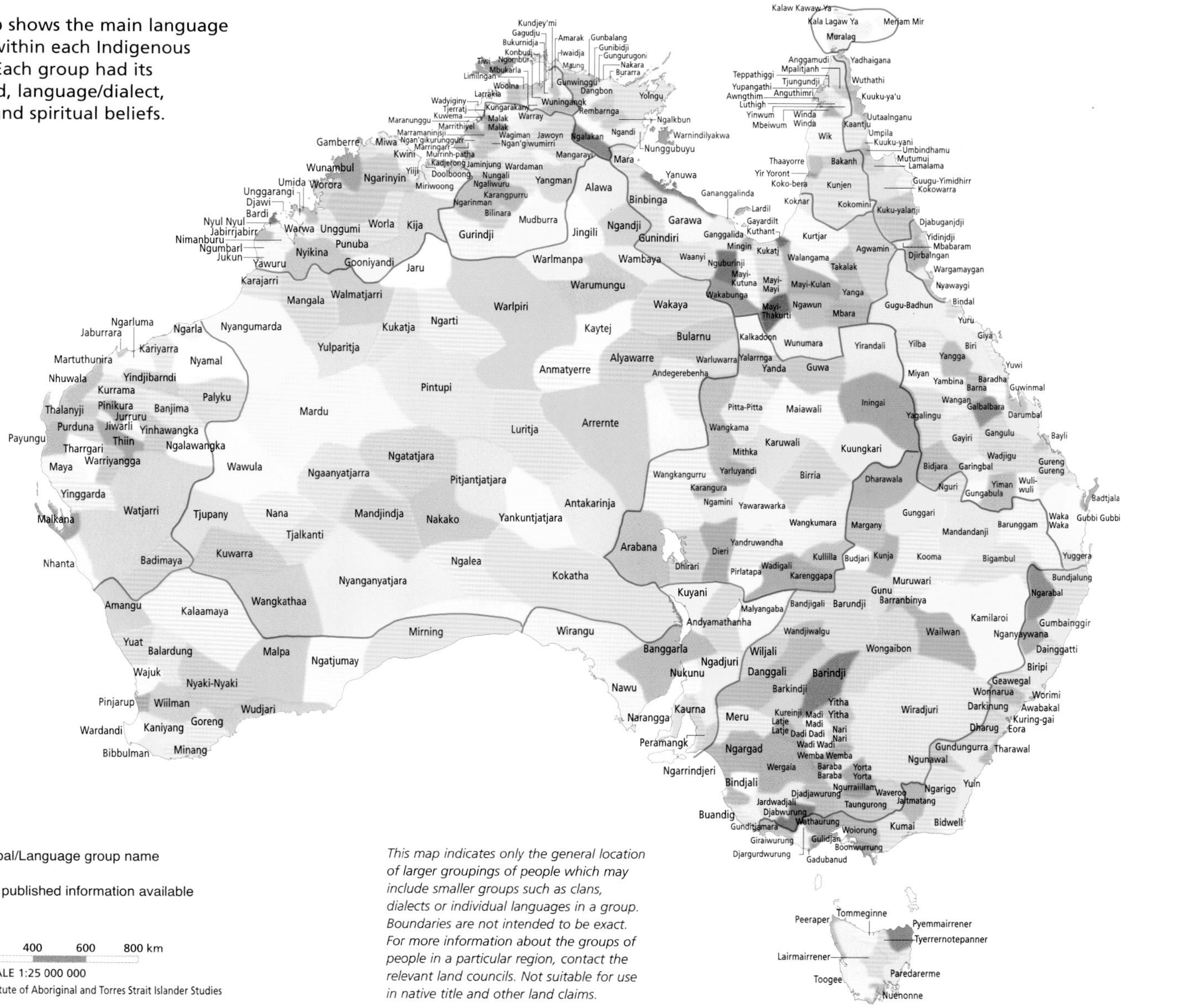

| Malpa | Tribal/Language group name |
| | No published information available |

0   200   400   600   800 km

SCALE 1:25 000 000

© Australian Institute of Aboriginal and Torres Strait Islander Studies

This map indicates only the general location of larger groupings of people which may include smaller groups such as clans, dialects or individual languages in a group. Boundaries are not intended to be exact. For more information about the groups of people in a particular region, contact the relevant land councils. Not suitable for use in native title and other land claims.

1 EARLY SEA EXPLORATION

The first non-Indigenous people to visit Australia are believed to have been the Macassans in the 1400s. The first definite recorded European sighting of Australia was in 1606.

1. Jansz (Dutch) 1606
2. Torres (Portuguese) 1606
3. Hartog (Dutch) 1616
4. Houtman (Dutch) 1619
5. Carstensz, Van Colster (Dutch) 1623
6. Thijssen, Nuyts (Dutch) 1627
7. De Witt (Dutch) 1628
8. Tasman (Dutch) 1642
9. Tasman (Dutch) 1644
10. Cook (English) 1770
11. Bass (English) 1797–98
12. Bass, Flinders (English) 1798–99
13. Flinders (English) 1801–03
14. Baudin (French) 1802

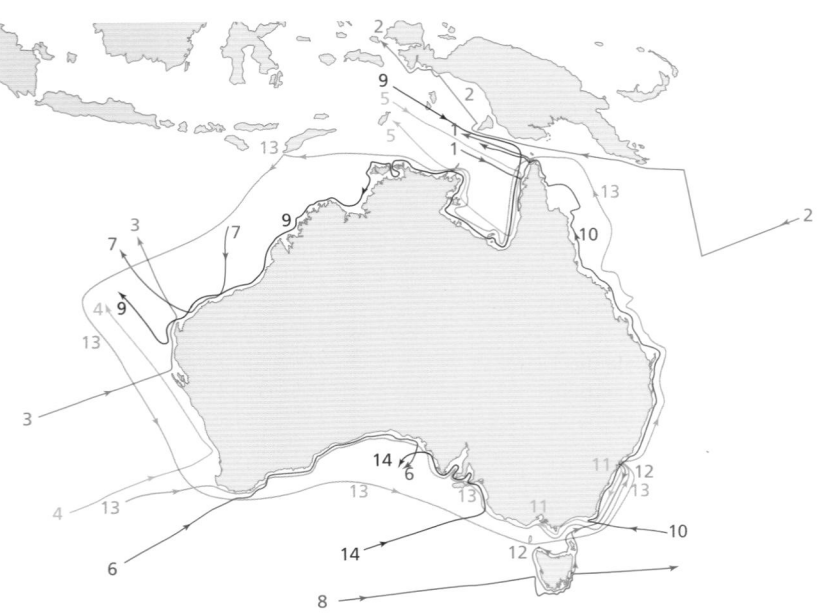

2 LAND EXPLORATION, 1788–1859

After Sydney was established in 1788, most interest focused on finding a way over the Blue Mountains to the west. The explorers often followed the inland rivers as they searched for new farming land.

1. Laycock 1807
2. Blaxland, Wentworth, Lawson 1813
3. Oxley 1817
4. Oxley 1818
5. Hume, Hovell 1824
6. Cunningham 1827
7. Sturt 1829–30
8. Bannister 1830–31
9. Mitchell 1835
10. Mitchell 1836
11. Grey 1839
12. Strzelecki 1840
13. Eyre 1840–41
14. Leichhardt 1844–45
15. Sturt 1844–46
16. Mitchell 1846
17. Kennedy 1847
18. Roe 1848
19. Kennedy 1848
20. A.C. Gregory 1855–56
21. F.T. Gregory 1858

3 LAND EXPLORATION, 1860–1900

By the late 1850s, the European settlers were keen to find extra pastoral land in northern and western Australia. This eventually led to explorers crossing the continent from south to north, west to east and east to west.

1. Burke, Wills 1860–61
2. Stuart 1860–62
3. McKinlay 1861–62
4. Landsborough 1861–62
5. F.T. Gregory 1861
6. Jardine Brothers 1864–65
7. J. Forrest 1869
8. J. Forrest 1870
9. A. Forrest 1871
10. Warburton 1873
11. J. Forrest 1874
12. Giles 1875
13. Giles 1876
14. A. Forrest 1879
15. Carnegie 1896

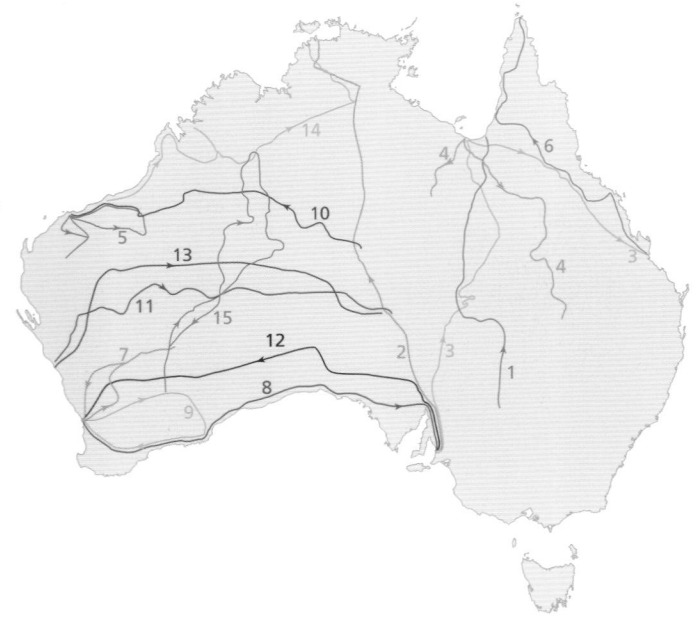

1 SPREAD OF EUROPEAN SETTLEMENT

European settlement of Australia began with the establishment of Sydney in 1788, followed by settlements at Hobart (1804) and Launceston (1806).

The 1820s and 1830s saw the spread of European settlers west of the Blue Mountains, and the establishment of settlements at Brisbane, Perth, Melbourne and Adelaide. By the 1850s there was extensive settlement of much of the fertile agricultural lands of south-east and south-west Australia.

The 1860s saw the extension of agricultural settlement up through central Queensland. Further expansion of settlement after 1870 was hindered by the harsh natural environment of inland Australia.

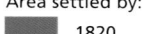
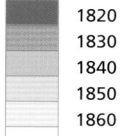

Area settled by:
- 1820
- 1830
- 1840
- 1850
- 1860
- After 1860

Few permanent settlers

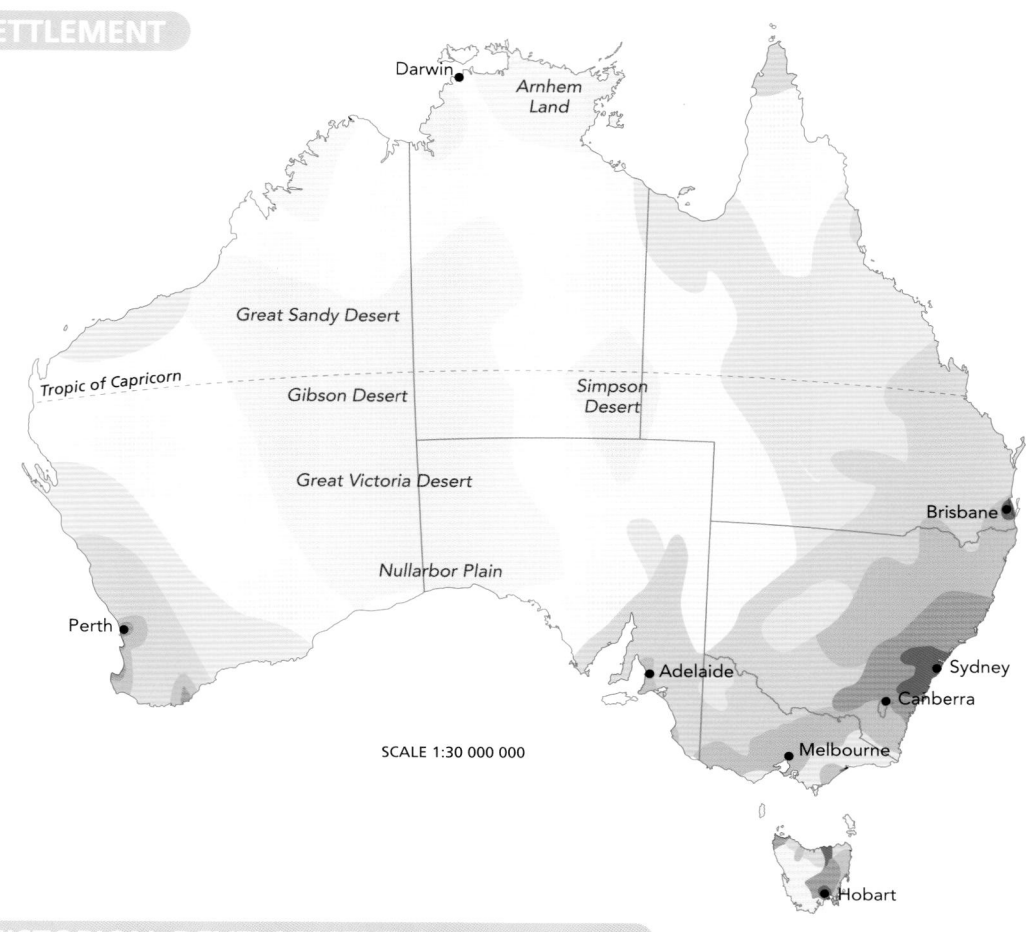

SCALE 1:30 000 000

2 HISTORICAL DEVELOPMENT OF THE STATES

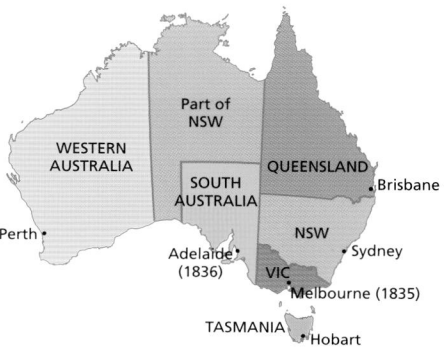

A. 1786–1824

1786	'New South Wales' claimed by England as far west as longitude 135°E ('New South Wales' included both mainland Australia plus Tasmania and New Zealand)
1788	Sydney established
1804	Hobart established
1824	Moreton Bay (Brisbane) established

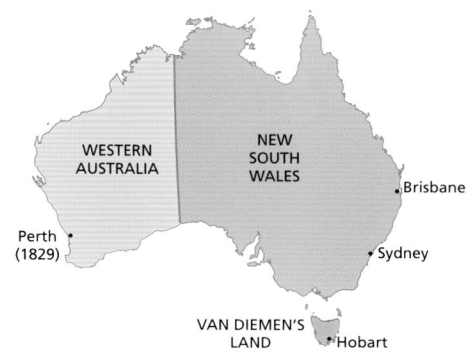

B. 1825–34

1825	New South Wales boundary extended west to longitude 129°E
1825	Van Diemen's Land (now Tasmania) made a separate colony from NSW
1829	Western Australia becomes a colony
1829	Perth established

C. 1835–60

1835	Melbourne established
1836	South Australia proclaimed as a province
1836	Adelaide established
1840	New Zealand becomes a separate colony
1851	Victoria becomes a separate colony
1855	Name 'Tasmania' replaces 'Van Diemen's Land'
1859	Queensland becomes a separate colony

D. 1861–PRESENT

1861	South Australian border is extended west to WA
1862	Queensland border is extended west to 138°E
1863	Northern Territory established (under the control of SA)
1869	Palmerston (Darwin) established
1901	All colonies become states
1911	Australian Capital Territory and Canberra established
1911	NT transferred to Federal Government control
1978	NT obtains self-government
1988	ACT obtains self-government

1 POPULATION DISTRIBUTION, 2001

This dot map shows that Australia has a very uneven population distribution. Information obtained through the 2001 Census also tells us that in 2001:

- 85 per cent of all people lived within 50 kilometres of the coastline, mostly in two narrow coastal strips, from the Sunshine Coast north of Brisbane to Adelaide, including Tasmania, and from Perth to Albany in the south-west.
- 13 per cent of all people lived in the main inland agricultural zone in the south-east and south-west of the continent.
- 87 per cent of all people lived in 713 urban centres with populations over 1000.
- 65 per cent of all people lived in Australia's capital cities—40 per cent in Sydney and Melbourne—which experienced 66 per cent of all population growth from 1996 to 2001.
- The centre of Australia's population was 55 kilometres east of Ivanhoe in western New South Wales, and was moving north at about 1 kilometre a year.

Each dot represents 1000 people.

SCALE 1:30 000 000

2 AUSTRALIANS TODAY

A. POPULATION GROWTH, 1870–2030
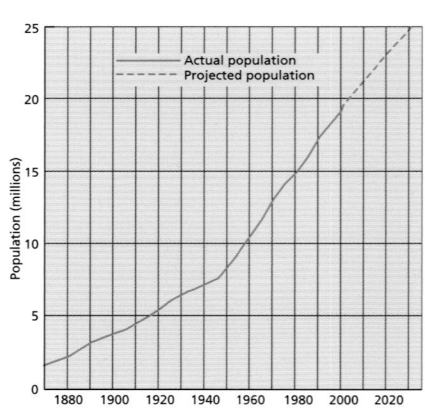

B. STATE POPULATIONS, 2001
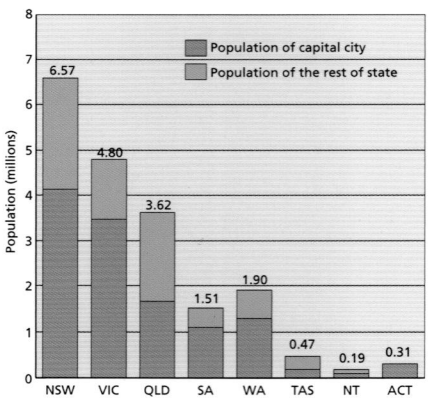

C. GROWTH OF CAPITAL CITIES, 1940–2020
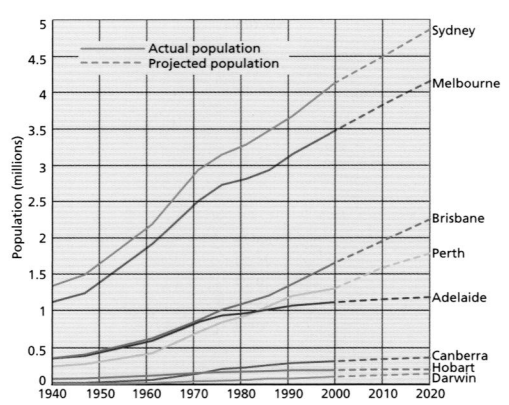

D. COUNTRIES OF BIRTH, 2001
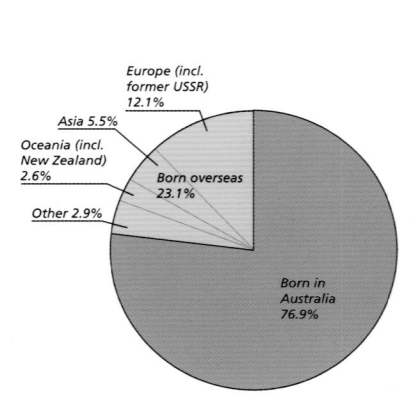

E. BIRTHPLACE OF NEW SETTLERS
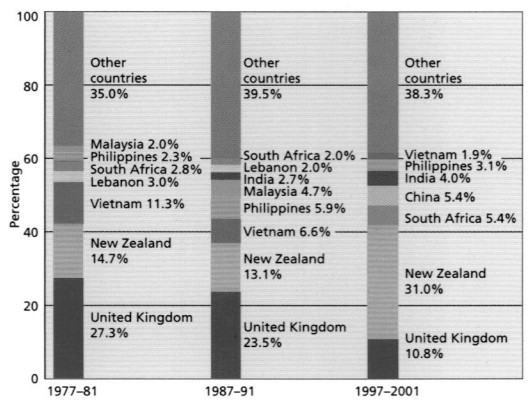

F. URBAN/RURAL POPULATION
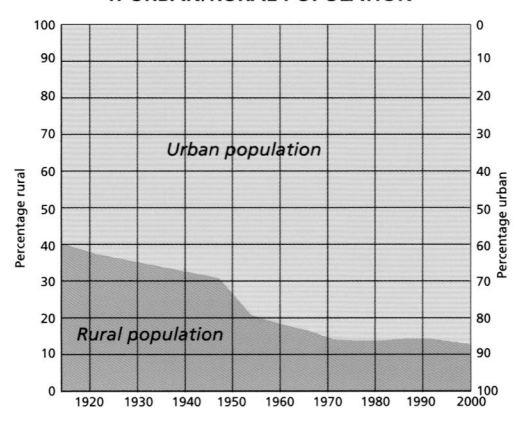

Lambert Azimuthal Equal Area projection

1 POPULATION DENSITY, 2001

This choropleth map shows Australia's population in a different way from the dot map on the opposite page.

The map shows the density of Australia's population—the number of people living in each square kilometre of land—by the use of shading in different colours. It provides a clear visual impression of where most people live in Australia.

Australia's average population density in June 2001 was 2.5 persons per square kilometre. However, there are great differences in population density from region to region across Australia.

In 2001 population density varied from over 5000 persons per square kilometre in inner suburbs of Sydney and Melbourne—the highest was 8400 persons per square kilometre in inner Sydney City—to an average of less than 0.1 persons per square kilometre in vast areas of arid Australia.

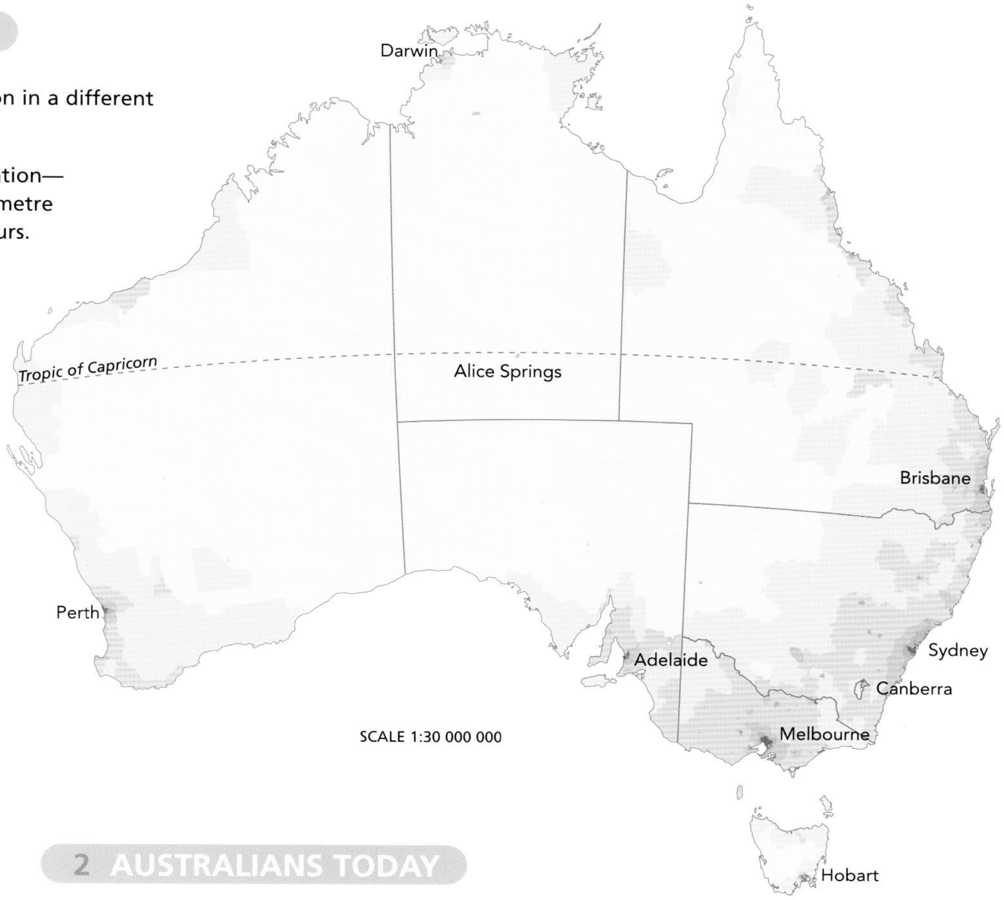

Persons per sq km
- Over 1000.0
- 100.0–1000.0
- 10.0–100.0
- 1.0–10.0
- 0.1–1.0
- Less than 0.1

SCALE 1:30 000 000

2 AUSTRALIANS TODAY

A. AGE/SEX STRUCTURE, 2001

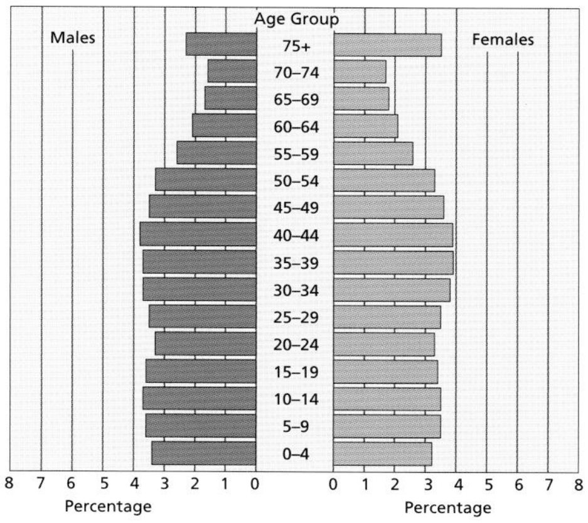

B. AGE GROUP COMPARISONS, 1921–2041

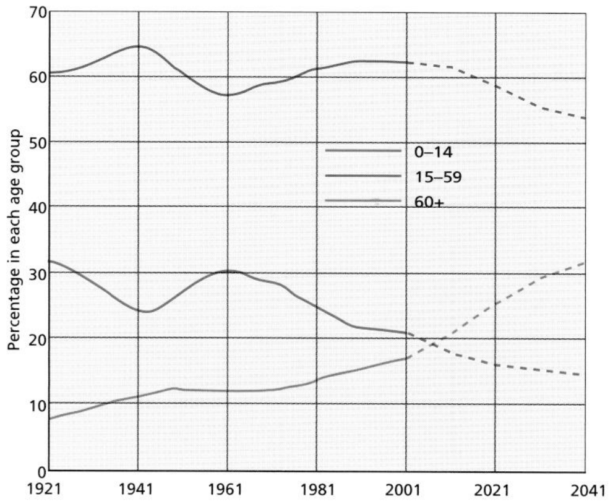

C. LIFE EXPECTANCY AT BIRTH

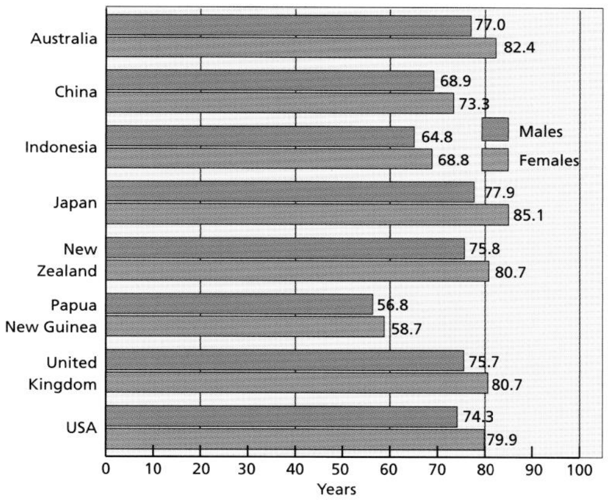

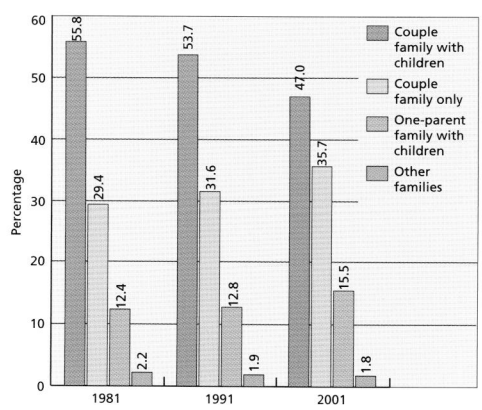

D. FAMILIES

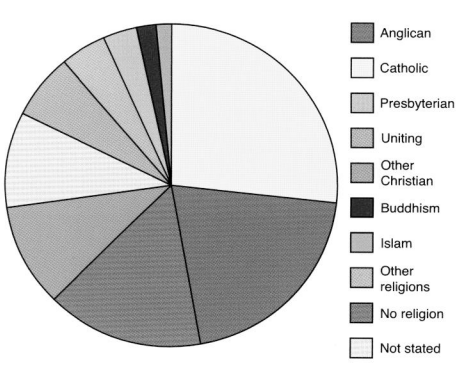

E. RELIGION

F. EMPLOYMENT BY INDUSTRY

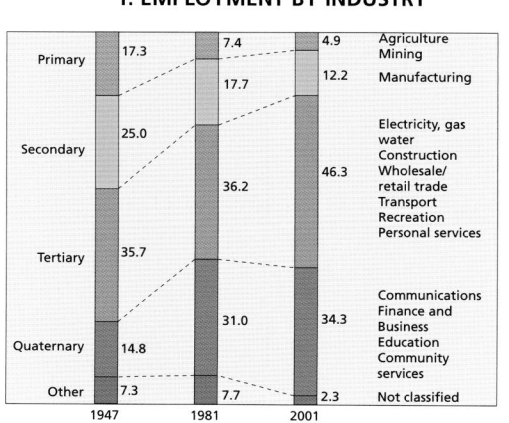

1 INDIGENOUS POPULATION DISTRIBUTION, 2001

Australia's Aboriginal and Torres Strait Islander population in 2001 was 460 000 people, or 2.4 per cent of the total population. While most Australians live along the east and south-west coasts, this dot map shows that Indigenous people are much more widely spread. Whereas 90 per cent of Australia's total population live in just 2.2 per cent of the continent, 90 per cent of our Indigenous population are spread across 23 per cent of the continent. While more than two-thirds of Indigenous people live in urban centres:

- Indigenous people are much more likely to live in remote areas of Australia than non-Indigenous people
- Indigenous people have much lower rates of urbanisation than non-Indigenous people.

Each dot represents 100 people.
Figures in brackets represent the Indigenous population of urban areas with large numbers of Indigenous people at the 2001 Census.

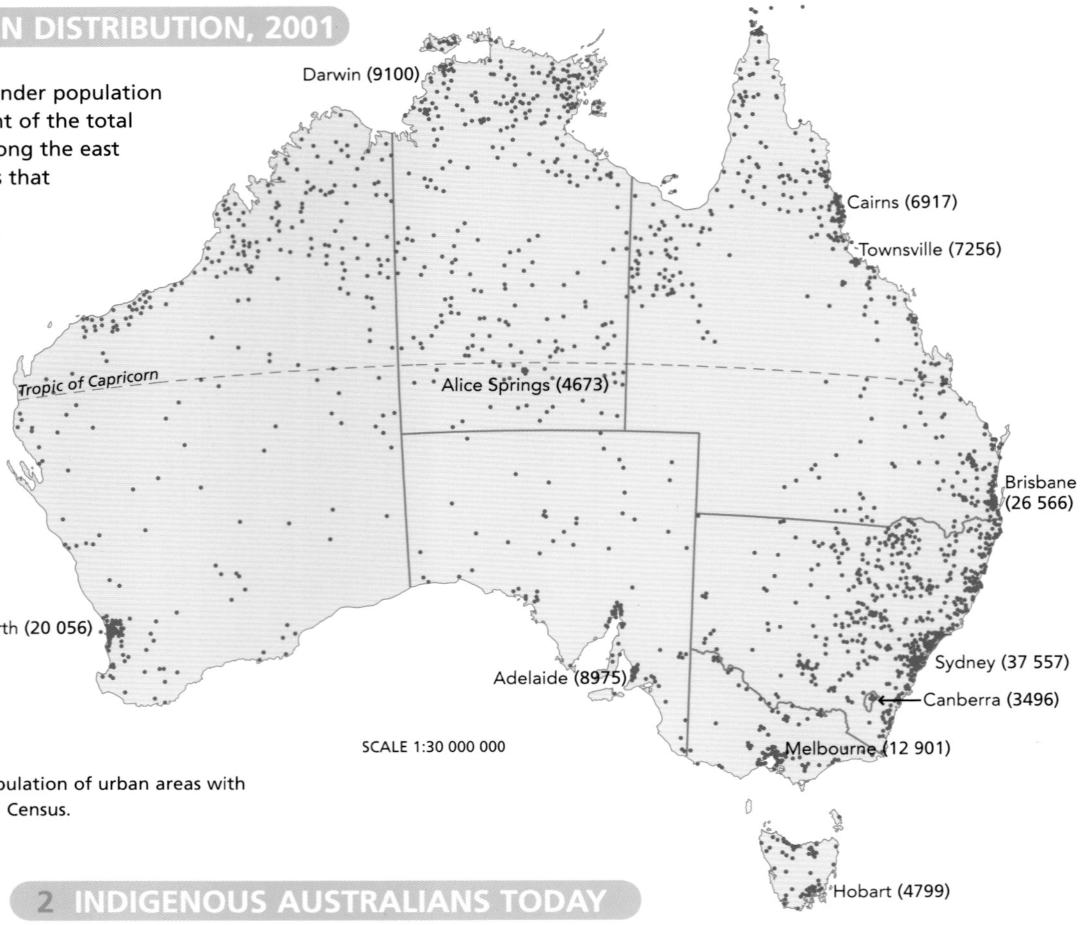

Darwin (9100)
Cairns (6917)
Townsville (7256)
Tropic of Capricorn
Alice Springs (4673)
Brisbane (26 566)
Perth (20 056)
Adelaide (8975)
Sydney (37 557)
Canberra (3496)
SCALE 1:30 000 000
Melbourne (12 901)
Hobart (4799)

2 INDIGENOUS AUSTRALIANS TODAY

A. POPULATION CHANGE, 1788–2001

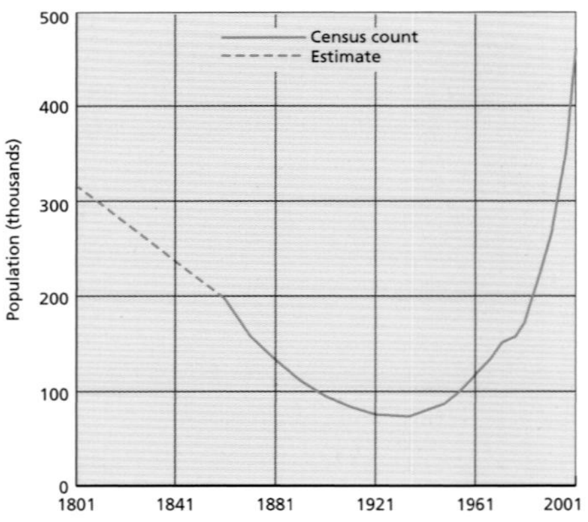

Population (thousands)
— Census count
--- Estimate

1801 1841 1881 1921 1961 2001

B. AGE/SEX STRUCTURE, 2001

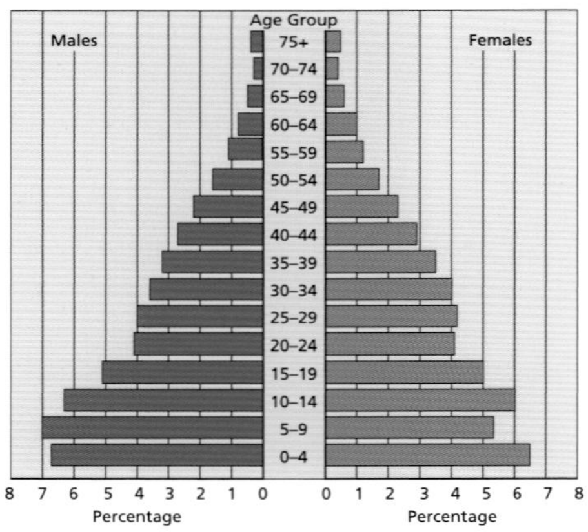

Age Group
Males — Females
75+
70–74
65–69
60–64
55–59
50–54
45–49
40–44
35–39
30–34
25–29
20–24
15–19
10–14
5–9
0–4
8 7 6 5 4 3 2 1 0   0 1 2 3 4 5 6 7 8
Percentage   Percentage

C. AGE GROUP COMPARISONS, 2001

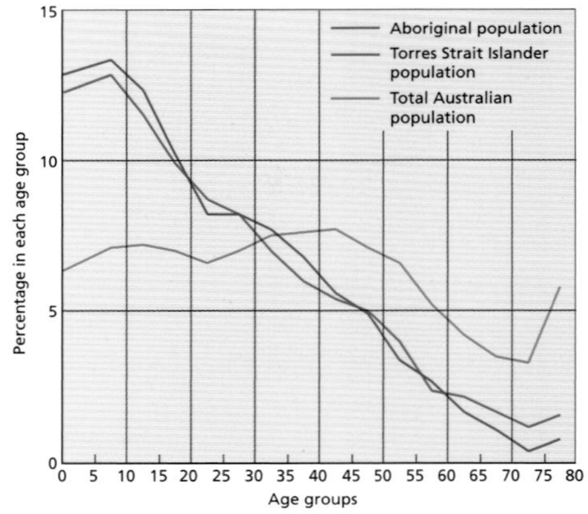

Percentage in each age group
— Aboriginal population
— Torres Strait Islander population
— Total Australian population

0 5 10 15 20 25 30 35 40 45 50 55 60 65 70 75 80
Age groups

D. PROPORTION OF POPULATION, 2001

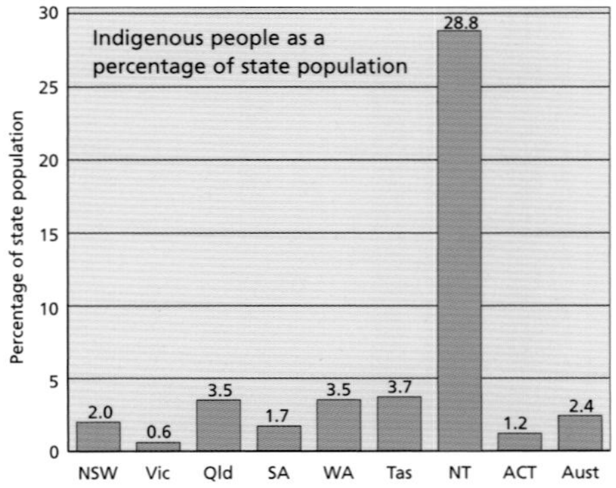

Indigenous people as a percentage of state population

Percentage of state population

NSW	Vic	Qld	SA	WA	Tas	NT	ACT	Aust
2.0	0.6	3.5	1.7	3.5	3.7	28.8	1.2	2.4

E. DISTRIBUTION BY STATE, 2001

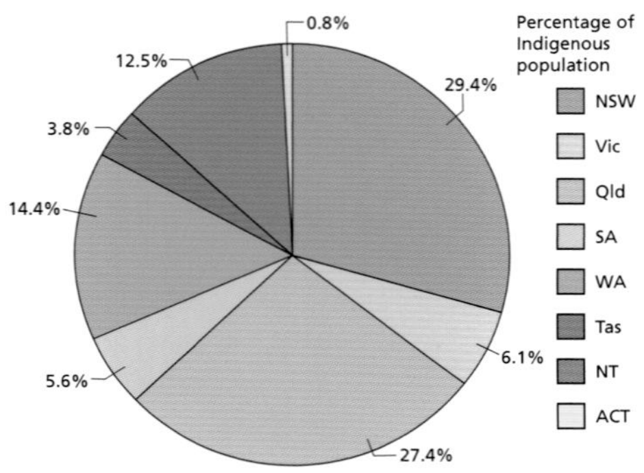

Percentage of Indigenous population
- NSW 29.4%
- Vic
- Qld 27.4%
- SA
- WA 14.4%
- Tas 0.8%
- NT 12.5%
- ACT

3.8%
5.6%
6.1%

F. URBAN/REMOTE POPULATION, 2001

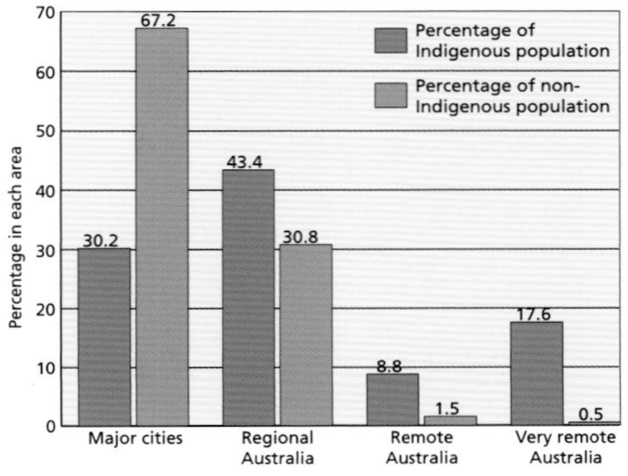

Percentage in each area
■ Percentage of Indigenous population
■ Percentage of non-Indigenous population

	Major cities	Regional Australia	Remote Australia	Very remote Australia
Indigenous	30.2	43.4	8.8	17.6
Non-Indigenous	67.2	30.8	1.5	0.5

Lambert Azimuthal Equal Area projection

1 INDIGENOUS LANDS, 2003

In 2003 approximately 15 per cent of Australia was estimated to be owned or managed by Indigenous people. Indigenous people's understanding of the Australian environment is increasingly being recognised, and their role in conserving the biodiversity of both their own land and national parks and conservation areas is highly valued.

Land tenure
- Reserve
- Freehold
- Leasehold
- Freehold–National Park

Coloured circles represent land less than 100 square kilometres.

SCALE 1:30 000 000

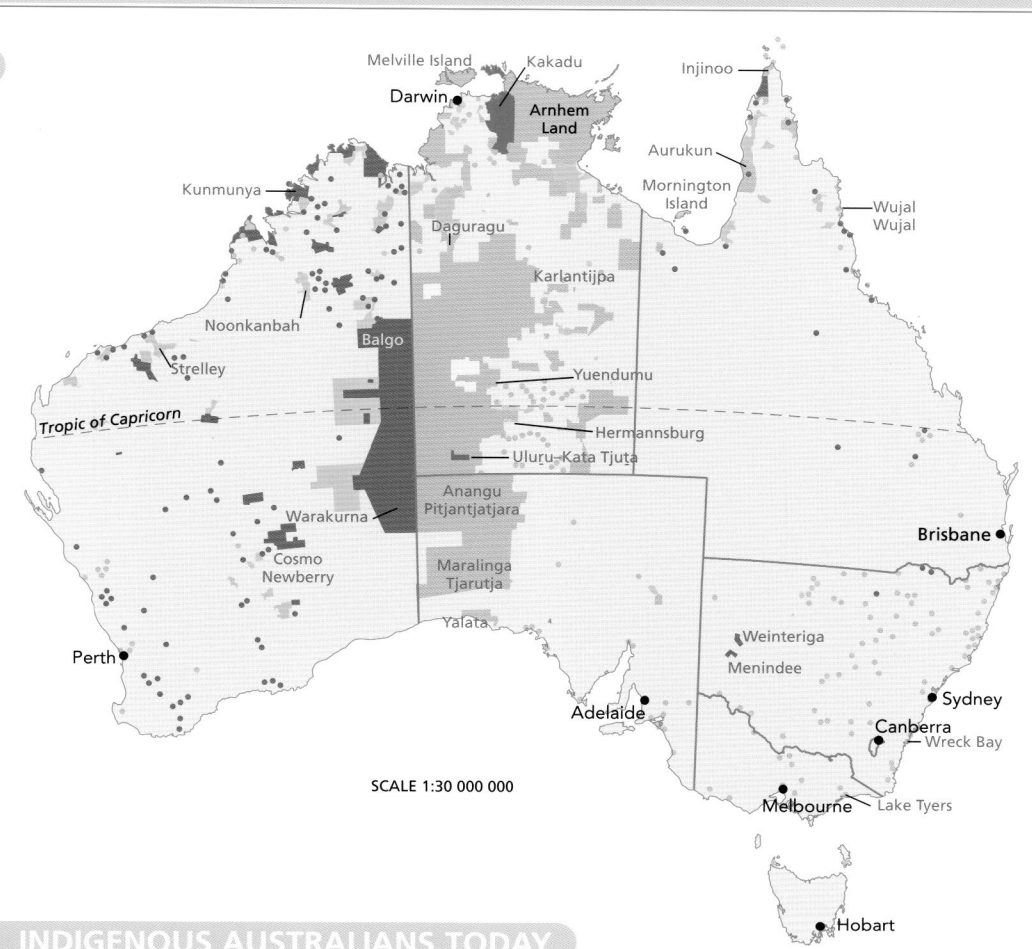

2 INDIGENOUS AUSTRALIANS TODAY

A. LIFE EXPECTANCY AT BIRTH, 1999–2001
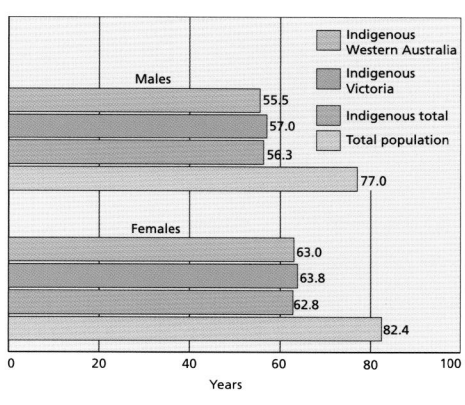

B. INFANT MORTALITY, 1999–2001
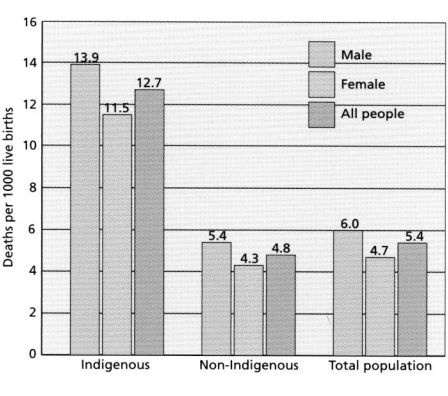

C. INDIGENOUS HEALTH, 2001–02
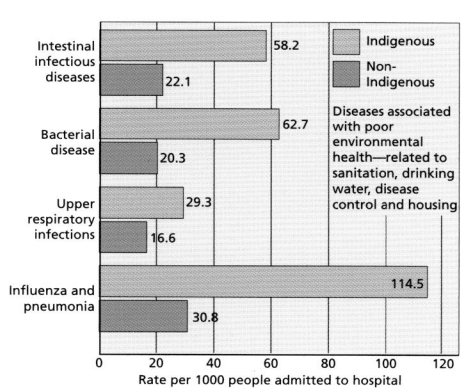

D. YEAR 5 EDUCATIONAL STANDARDS, 2001
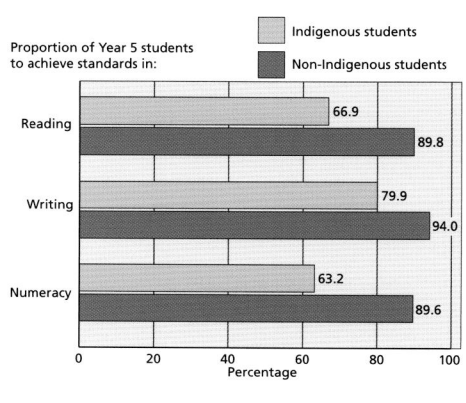

E. LEVEL OF EDUCATION, 2001
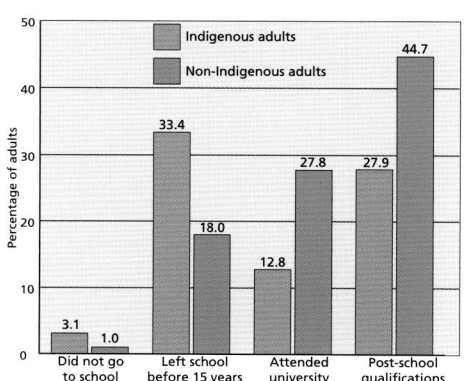

F. DETENTION AND IMPRISONMENT
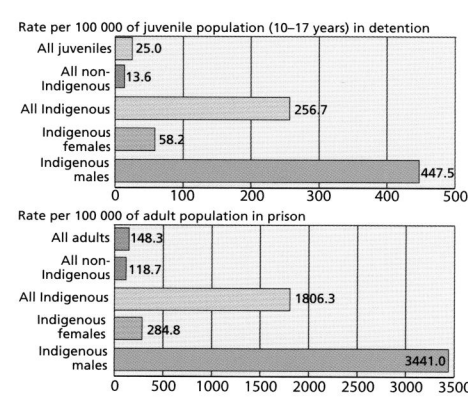

Lambert Azimuthal Equal Area projection

1 MINERALS

Mineral key:

Bx	Bauxite
C	Copper
D	Diamonds
Fe	Iron ore
G	Gold
L	Lead
M	Manganese
MS	Mineral sands
N	Nickel
S	Silver
T	Tin
Z	Zinc

Capel — Operating mine
Jangardup — Possible future development

Map labels (Minerals):

Darwin · Tom's Gully G · Gove Bx · Weipa Bx · Aurukun Bx
Union Reefs · Pine Creek G · Groote Eylandt M
Mitchell Plateau Bx
Cockatoo Island Fe · Argyle G D · McArthur River S L Z
Lady Loretta S L Z · Mt Garnet C S
Cadjebut S L Z · Palm Springs G · Century S L Z · Charters Towers G
Groundrush G · Warrego G · Gecko G · Mammoth C · Ernest Henry G C · Nolans G
Yarrie Fe · The Granites G · George Fisher S L Z · Mount Isa S L Z · Selwyn G C
Marandoo Fe · Telfer G C · Osborne G C · Cannington S L
Robe River Fe · Woodie Woodie M · Miclere G · Byfield MS
Mt Tom Price Fe · Yandi Fe · Tropic of Capricorn
Paraburdoo Fe · Mt Whaleback Fe · Middle Island MS
Channar Fe · West Angelas Fe
Plutonic G · Mt Rawdon G
Honeymoon Well G N · Gympie G
Mt Keith N · Bronzewing G · Brisbane · Stradbroke Island MS
Cosmos N · Leinster N
Mt Magnet G · Granny Smith G · Olympic Dam G C S · Elura C S L
Golden Grove C · Leonora G · Sunrise Dam G · Cobar C S L Z · Girilambone C
Sons of Gwalia G · Murrin Murrin N · Mt Gunson C · Northparkes G C · Peak Hill G
Mt Gibson G · Kalgoorlie G S N · Broken Hill S L Z · Lake Cowal G · Cadia G
Eneabba MS · Koolyanobbing Fe · Kambalda N · Middleback Range Fe · Sydney
Southern Cross G · Norseman G · Adelaide
Perth · Emily Ann N · Canberra
Forestania N · Stawell G · Bendigo G · Benambra C S L Z
Worsley Bx · Huntly Bx · Melbourne · Woods Point G
Capel MS
Jangardup MS
Savage River Fe · Rosebery G C S L Z
Renison · Mt Lyell G C S
Hobart

Australia has the world's largest silver, lead, zinc, uranium, diamond and mineral sands deposits. Its gold, copper, iron ore and nickel resources are in the top six in the world. New discoveries continue to increase Australia's potential as one of the top producers and exporters of minerals in the world.

2 ENERGY

Legend:

- Oil/natural gas producing basin
- Coal producing basin
- Natural gas pipeline (operating)
- Natural gas pipeline (possible future development)
- Oil pipeline
- Basslink undersea power cable

Wanaea — Operating
Kintyre — Possible future development

Major energy fuels
- Oil
- Natural gas
- Black coal
- Brown coal
- Uranium
- Oil shale

Power stations other than coal burning thermal stations
- Hydroelectric
- Wind
- Landfill
- Solar
- Tidal

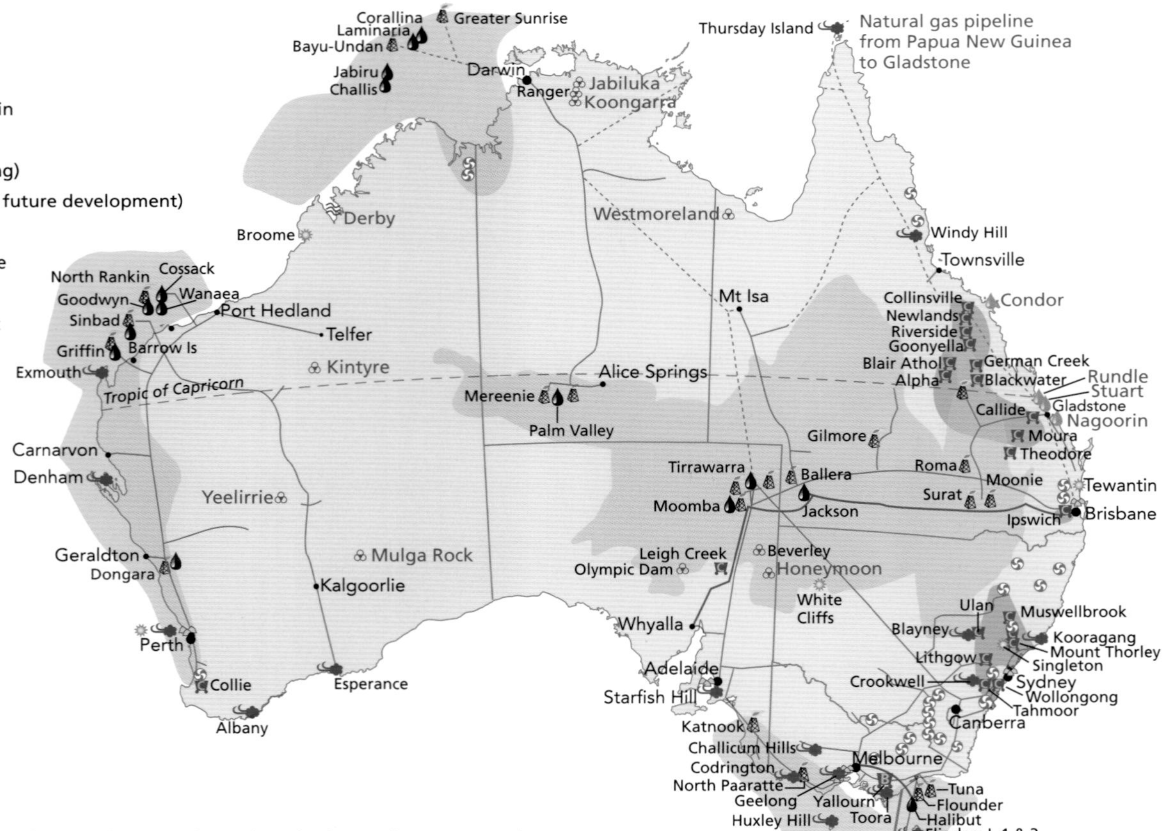

Map labels (Energy):

Corallina · Greater Sunrise
Laminaria · Bayu-Undan · Thursday Island · Natural gas pipeline from Papua New Guinea to Gladstone
Jabiru · Challis · Darwin · Jabiluka · Koongarra · Ranger
Westmoreland · Windy Hill
Broome · Derby · Townsville
North Rankin · Cossack · Collinsville
Goodwyn · Wanaea · Newlands · Condor
Sinbad · Port Hedland · Riverside
Griffin · Telfer · Goonyella
Barrow Is · Blair Athol · German Creek
Exmouth · Kintyre · Alpha · Blackwater · Rundle
Mt Isa · Callide · Stuart
Alice Springs · Gladstone
Mereenie · Nagoorin
Palm Valley · Gilmore · Moura
Carnarvon · Tirrawarra · Ballera · Roma · Theodore
Denham · Moomba · Jackson · Surat · Moonie · Tewantin
Yeelirrie · Ipswich · Brisbane
Geraldton · Leigh Creek · Beverley · Ulan
Dongara · Olympic Dam · Honeymoon · Muswellbrook
Mulga Rock · White Cliffs · Blayney · Kooragang
Kalgoorlie · Whyalla · Lithgow · Mount Thorley · Singleton
Perth · Adelaide · Crookwell · Sydney
Collie · Starfish Hill · Wollongong · Tahmoor
Esperance · Katnook · Canberra
Albany · Challicum Hills · Melbourne
Codrington · Tuna · Flounder
North Paaratte · Yallourn · Halibut
Geelong · Toora · Flinders I. 1 & 2
Huxley Hill · Woolnorth Stage 1 · Musselroe
Heemskirk · Merrywood
Hobart

Australia is fortunate to have abundant coal, natural gas, liquified petroleum gas and uranium to meet its own energy needs and to be a major energy exporter. Reserves of crude oil are, however, limited. There is real potential to develop renewable solar, wind, tidal and geothermal energy resources.

1 TRANSPORT AND MANUFACTURING

Transport and manufacturing make a significant contribution to the Australian economy. Rail transport is essential to the movement of passengers and freight within Australia. Sea transport, mainly by huge bulk carriers, is vital to the export of valuable agricultural, mineral and energy resources. Manufacturing provides about 13 per cent of Australia's gross domestic product (GDP) and employment, while transport provides about 5 per cent of both GDP and employment. Manufacturing is usually located in larger coastal centres.

Manufacturing
- ◻ Major centre
- ● Secondary centre
- ◼ Mineral processing centre
- ◼ Energy processing centre

Ports
- 8 Top 10 ports by weight, 2000–01
- Secondary port

Railways
- Passenger and freight lines
- Freight lines

Airports
- ✈ International airport

SCALE 1:30 000 000

Map labels:
Darwin, Weipa, Wyndham, Yampi Sound, Broome, Cairns, Innisfail, Townsville, Mount Isa, Abbot Point, Mackay, Hay Point, Dampier, Barrow Island, Port Hedland, Port Walcott, Rockhampton, Gladstone, Bundaberg, Cape Cuvier, Carnarvon, Tropic of Capricorn, Alice Springs, Eromanga, Roma, Moomba, Toowoomba, Brisbane, Gold Coast Coolangatta, Geraldton, Dongara, Olympic Dam, Tamworth, Kalgoorlie, Port Bonython, Dubbo, Orange, Kurri, Tomago, Thevenard, Whyalla, Bathurst, Newcastle, Cockle Creek, Perth, Fremantle, Port Pirie, Sydney, Port Kembla, Kwinana, Pinjarra, Wagerup, Berri, Wagga Wagga, Bunbury, Worsley, Port Lincoln, Canberra, Yoganup, Port Adelaide, Adelaide, Esperance, Albury-Wodonga, Albany, Port Stanvac, Bendigo, Shepparton, Mount Gambier, Ballarat, Melbourne, Portland, Longford, Warrnambool, Geelong, Port Westernport, Port Latta, Devonport, Bell Bay, Burnie, Launceston, Risdon, Hobart

2 INTERNATIONAL TRADE

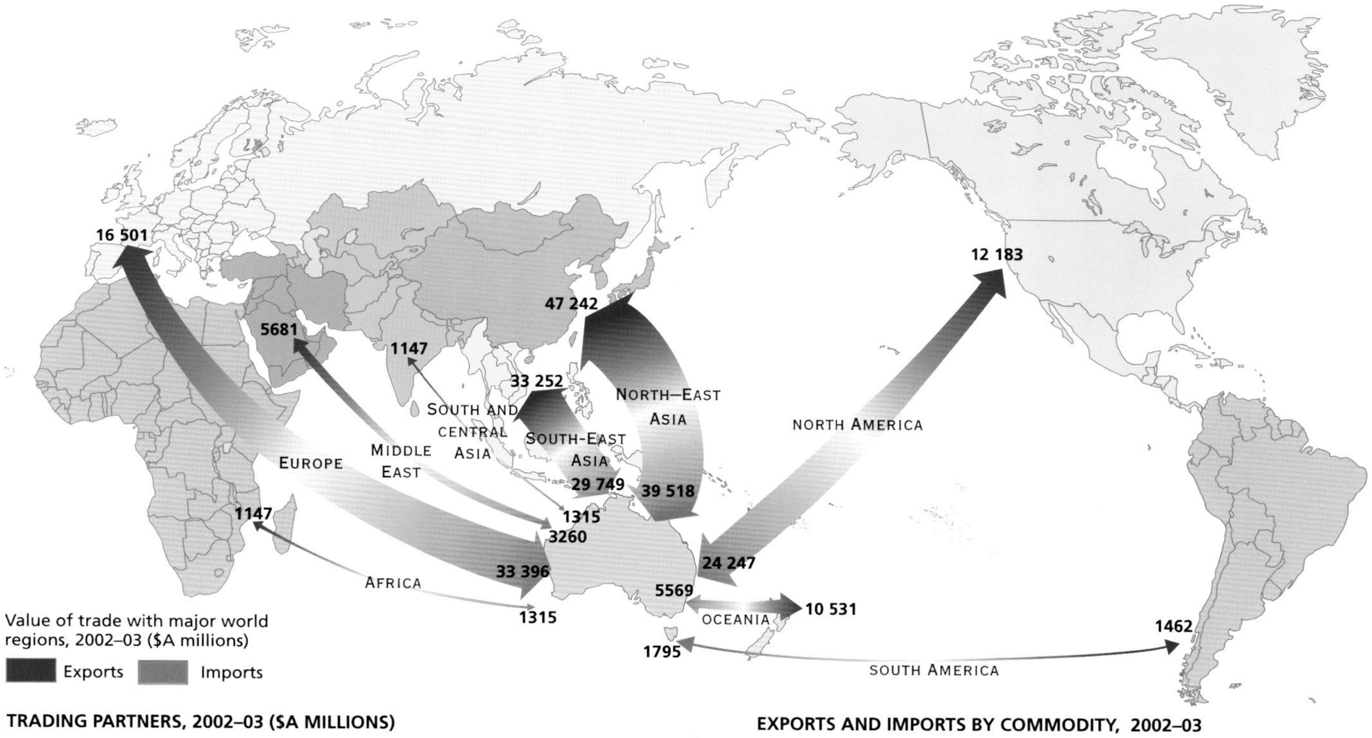

Value of trade with major world regions, 2002–03 ($A millions)
- ◼ Exports ◼ Imports

Region labels and values:
EUROPE 16 501, 5681
MIDDLE EAST 1147
SOUTH AND CENTRAL ASIA 33 252
NORTH-EAST ASIA 47 242
SOUTH-EAST ASIA 29 749, 39 518
NORTH AMERICA 12 183
AFRICA 1147, 1315, 3260, 33 396, 1315
OCEANIA 24 247, 5569, 10 531
SOUTH AMERICA 1795, 1462

TRADING PARTNERS, 2002–03 ($A MILLIONS)

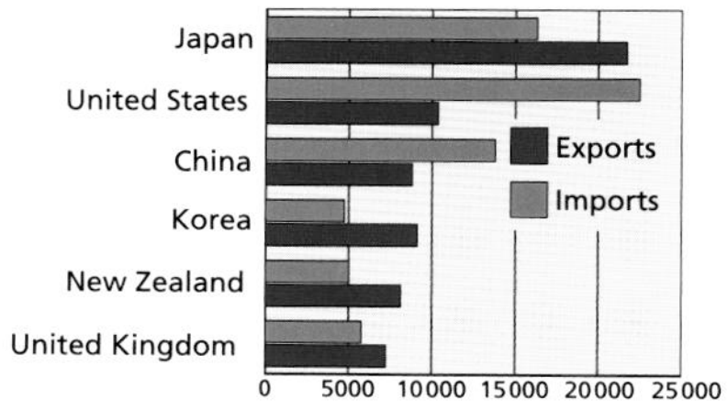

Japan, United States, China, Korea, New Zealand, United Kingdom
- ◼ Exports
- ◼ Imports

0 5000 10000 15000 20000 25000

EXPORTS AND IMPORTS BY COMMODITY, 2002–03

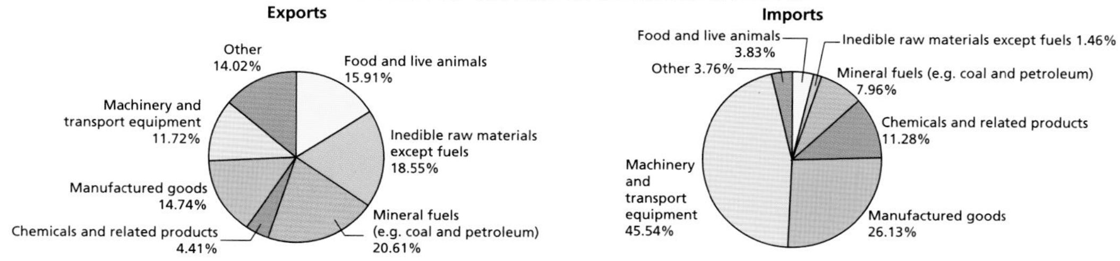

Exports
- Other 14.02%
- Food and live animals 15.91%
- Machinery and transport equipment 11.72%
- Inedible raw materials except fuels 18.55%
- Manufactured goods 14.74%
- Mineral fuels (e.g. coal and petroleum) 20.61%
- Chemicals and related products 4.41%

Imports
- Food and live animals 3.83%
- Other 3.76%
- Inedible raw materials except fuels 1.46%
- Mineral fuels (e.g. coal and petroleum) 7.96%
- Chemicals and related products 11.28%
- Machinery and transport equipment 45.54%
- Manufactured goods 26.13%

Lambert Azimuthal Equal Area projection

1 NATIONAL PARKS

Australia has about 700 national parks and conservation areas, covering over 10 per cent of the land surface area, and a number of very significant marine parks and reserves. Some are very large, but most are relatively small. These areas are protected for a variety of reasons. They may be wilderness areas, contain valuable or rare ecosystems in outstanding natural areas, contain natural monuments of special significance, or they may protect unique habitats for endangered species of flora and fauna.

National parks and conservation areas

Marine parks and reserves

Kakadu World Heritage Area

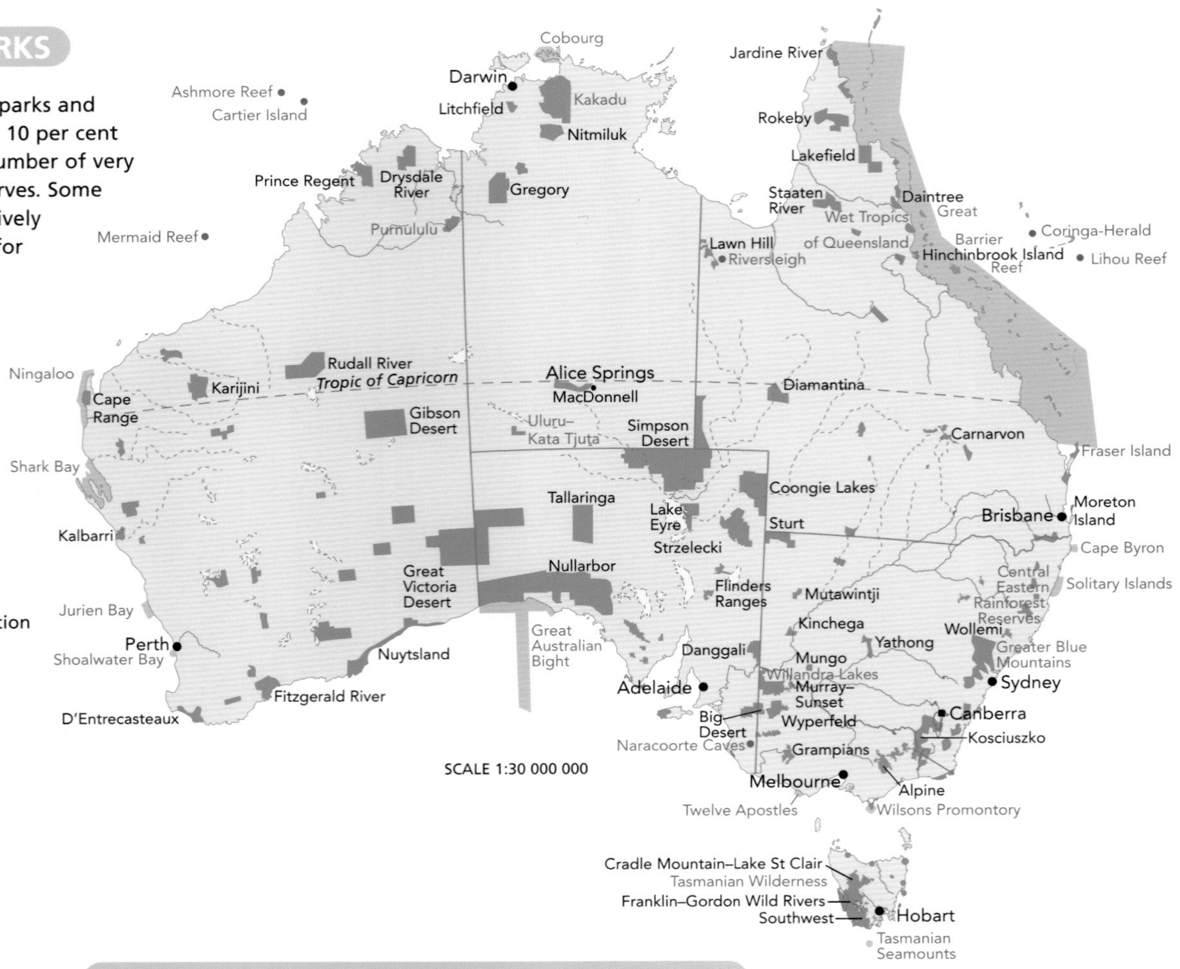

Cobourg
Darwin
Ashmore Reef •
Cartier Island
Litchfield
Kakadu
Nitmiluk
Jardine River
Rokeby
Lakefield
Prince Regent
Drysdale River
Gregory
Staaten River
Daintree
Great Barrier Reef
Purnululu
Wet Tropics of Queensland
Hinchinbrook Island
Coringa-Herald
Mermaid Reef •
Lawn Hill
Riversleigh
Lihou Reef
Ningaloo
Rudall River
Tropic of Capricorn
Alice Springs
MacDonnell
Diamantina
Karijini
Cape Range
Gibson Desert
Uluru–Kata Tjuta
Simpson Desert
Carnarvon
Fraser Island
Shark Bay
Coongie Lakes
Moreton Island
Tallaringa
Lake Eyre
Sturt
Brisbane
Kalbarri
Strzelecki
Cape Byron
Central Eastern Rainforest Reserves
Solitary Islands
Great Victoria Desert
Nullarbor
Flinders Ranges
Mutawintji
Kinchega
Wollemi
Greater Blue Mountains
Jurien Bay
Great Australian Bight
Danggali
Yathong
Perth
Shoalwater Bay
Nuytsland
Mungo
Willandra Lakes
Murray–Sunset
Sydney
Adelaide
Fitzgerald River
Big Desert
Wyperfeld
Canberra
D'Entrecasteaux
Naracoorte Caves
Grampians
Kosciuszko
Melbourne
Alpine
Twelve Apostles
Wilsons Promontory

SCALE 1:30 000 000

Cradle Mountain–Lake St Clair
Tasmanian Wilderness
Franklin–Gordon Wild Rivers
Southwest
Hobart
Tasmanian Seamounts

2 AUSTRALIA'S WORLD HERITAGE AREAS

Australia has 15 World Heritage Sites, identified on the basis of their unique natural heritage (N) and/or their unique cultural heritage (C). Recent additions have been the Greater Blue Mountains Area (N) in 2000 and Purnululu National Park (N) in 2003.

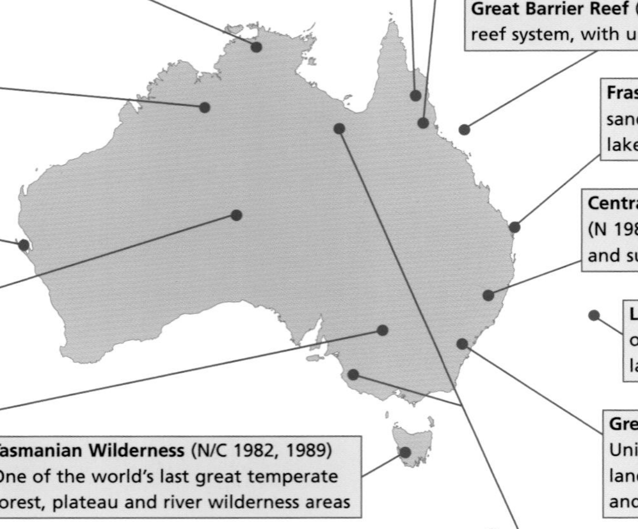

Kakadu National Park (N/C 1981, 1987, 1992) Diverse coastal, floodplain and plateau environments, continuously inhabited by Aboriginal peoples for more than 40 000 years

Purnululu National Park (N 2003) Unique cone-shaped sandstone towers and gorges of the Bungle Bungle Ranges

Shark Bay (N 1991) Coastal peninsulas and marine environments with vast seagrass beds, stromatolites, and habitats of endangered mammals

Uluṟu–Kata Tjuṯa National Park (N/C 1987, 1994) Unique arid landforms of great cultural significance to Aboriginal peoples

Willandra Lakes Region (N/C 1981) Ancient dry lakes with evidence of early Aboriginal occupation and environmental change

Heard and McDonald Islands (N 1997) Sub-Antarctic islands with active volcanoes, glaciers, and rare island ecosystems devoid of human impact

Macquarie Island (N 1997) On the Australian–Pacific plate boundary, with material from the mantle continuously being added to the Earth's crust above sea level

Wet Tropics of Queensland (N 1988) More than 40 tropical rainforest areas with rare and endangered plant and animal species

Great Barrier Reef (N 1981) The world's largest barrier coral reef system, with unique reef habitats and marine life

Fraser Island (N 1992) The world's largest sand island, with perched freshwater dune lakes and unique tropical rainforest habitats

Central Eastern Rainforest Reserves (N 1986, 1994) Outstanding volcanic landforms and subtropical rainforest ecosystems

Lord Howe Island Group (N 1982) Isolated oceanic islands; spectacular volcanic landforms, rare plants and animals

Greater Blue Mountains Area (N 2000) Unique sandstone plateau and canyon landforms, temperate eucalypt forest, and ancient plant species

Tasmanian Wilderness (N/C 1982, 1989) One of the world's last great temperate forest, plateau and river wilderness areas

Australian Fossil Mammal Sites, Riversleigh and Naracoorte (N 1994) Two of the world's greatest fossil sites, showing the evolution of Australia's unique fauna

Lambert Azimuthal Equal Area projection

1 TOURIST ATTRACTIONS

Tourism is important to the Australian economy, contributing about 5 per cent of gross domestic product (GDP) and providing about 6 per cent of all employment. Both figures are higher than the world average, showing Australia's reliance on the travel and tourism industry. Distance from other countries means that domestic tourism is more important than international tourism.

Melville Island
Bathurst Island
Darwin
Litchfield N.P.
Thursday Island
Kakadu
Katherine Gorge (Nitmiluk)
Mataranka Springs
Cape York Peninsula
Lizard Island
Chillagoe Caves
Daintree rainforest
Atherton Tableland
Cairns
Dunk Island
Magnetic Island
Townsville
Kimberley Plateau
Kununurra
Windjana Gorge
Purnululu (Bungle Bungle)
Broome
Geikie Gorge
Karumba
Wet Tropics rainforest
Wolfe Creek Crater
Port Hedland
Roebourne
Tennant Creek
Devils Marbles
Mt Isa
Whitsunday Islands
Mackay
Ningaloo Reef
Wittenoom Gorge
Hamersley Range
Winton
Tropic of Capricorn
Ormiston Gorge
Alice Springs
Kings Canyon
Henbury Craters
Longreach
Great Keppel Island
Heron Island
Carnarvon Gorge
Hervey Bay
Fraser Island
Shark Bay
Monkey Mia
Wiluna
Uluru–Kata Tjuta
Birdsville
Noosa–Sunshine Coast
Murchison River Gorge
Birdsville Track
Brisbane
Coober Pedy
Lake Eyre
Lamington N.P.
Gold Coast
Geraldton
Arkaroola
Lightning Ridge
Byron Bay
Gibralter Range N.P.
The Pinnacles
Kalgoorlie
Nullarbor coastline
Woomera
Flinders Ranges
Mutawintji N.P.
Coffs Harbour
Warrumbungles
Port Macquarie
Perth
York
Wave Rock
Broken Hill
Dubbo
Barrington Tops
Burra
Willandra Lakes
Hill End
Port Stephens
Bunbury
Barossa Valley
Mildura
Hunter Valley
Margaret River
Adelaide
Blue Mountains
Sydney
Karri forests
Stirling Range
Esperance
Port Lincoln
Swan Hill
Jervis Bay
Albany
Kangaroo Island
Canberra
Bendigo
Echuca
NSW snowfields
The Grampians
Ballarat
Vic. snowfields
Mt Gambier
Melbourne
Port Campbell
Gippsland Lakes
Phillip Island
Wilsons Promontory
King Island
Flinders Island
Launceston
Cradle Mountain–Lake St Clair
Freycinet Peninsula
Gordon River–ABT Railway
Hobart
Tasmanian Wilderness
Port Arthur

SCALE 1:25 000 000

Legend:
- ⊙ Capital city with many attractions
- ● Other major tourist centre
- ● Popular tourist holiday centre
- ● Historic settlement
- ■ Mining town
- ■ Spectacular natural scenery
- ◆ World Heritage Area
- ◆ Other place of interest

Marine life:
- Ⓓ Dolphins
- Ⓢ Sea lions
- Ⓦ Whales
- Ⓟ Penguins

2 INTERNATIONAL TOURISM

Australia's 4.5 million international visitors were less than 1 per cent of the world's 703 million international tourist arrivals in 2002, compared with visitors to France (11%), Spain (7.4%) and the United States (6%). International visitors to Australia in 2002 stayed an average of 27 nights. Ten per cent of international visitors in 2002 were backpackers—an increasingly important tourism sector—who on average stayed for 68 nights.

INTERNATIONAL VISITORS BY COUNTRY OF RESIDENCE, 2002

REASONS FOR VISITING AUSTRALIA, 2002

TOP 15 REGIONS VISITED BY INTERNATIONAL VISITORS, 2002

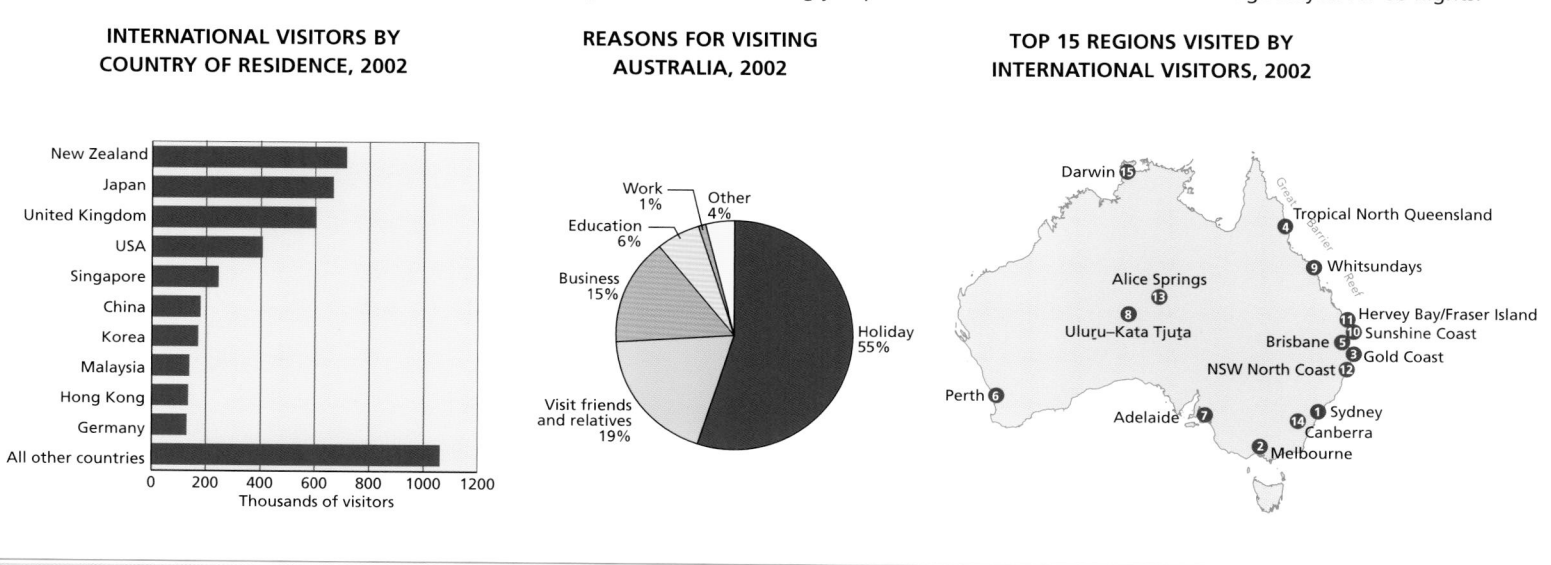

New Zealand, Japan, United Kingdom, USA, Singapore, China, Korea, Malaysia, Hong Kong, Germany, All other countries

0   200   400   600   800   1000   1200
Thousands of visitors

Work 1%
Other 4%
Education 6%
Business 15%
Holiday 55%
Visit friends and relatives 19%

Darwin 15
Tropical North Queensland 4
Whitsundays 9
Alice Springs 13
Hervey Bay/Fraser Island 11
Uluru–Kata Tjuta 8
Sunshine Coast 10
Brisbane 5
Gold Coast 3
NSW North Coast 12
Perth 6
Adelaide 7
Sydney 1
Canberra 14
Melbourne 2

Lambert Azimuthal Equal Area projection

This false colour Landsat TM image shows approximately the same area as the land use map opposite.

0   3   6 km

Approximate scale 1:275 000

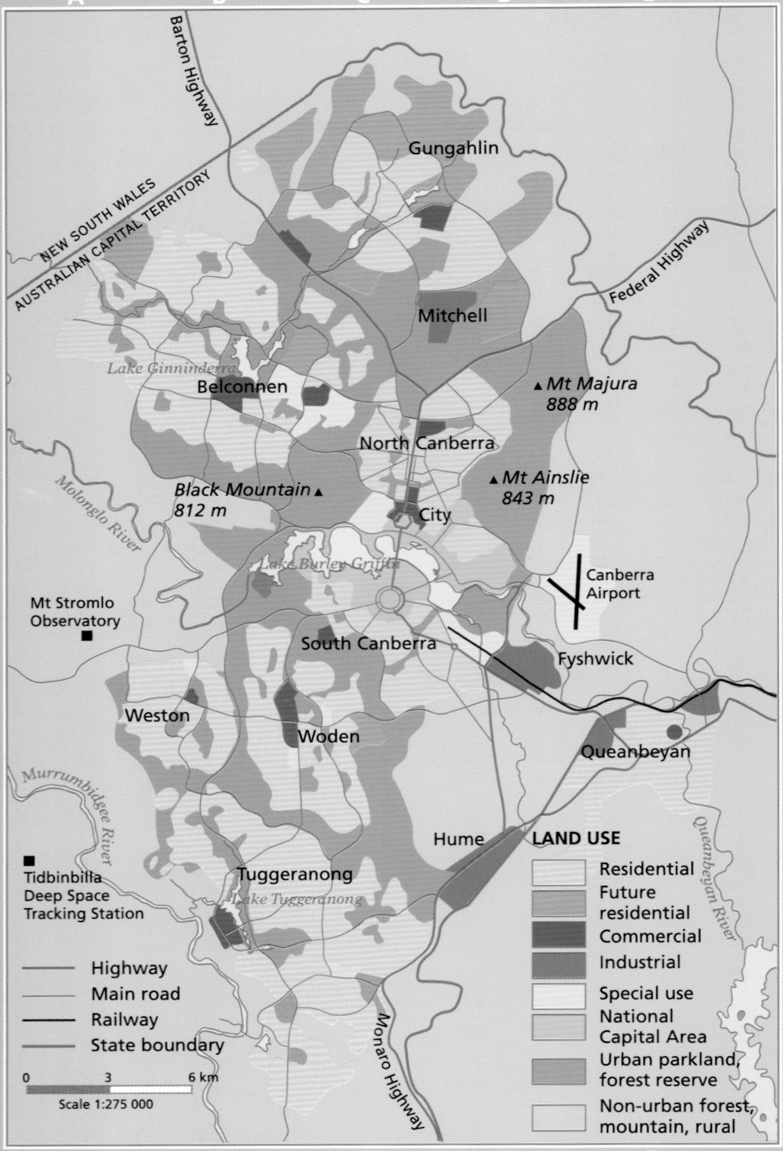

Highway
Main road
Railway
State boundary

0   3   6 km

Scale 1:275 000

NEW SOUTH WALES
AUSTRALIAN CAPITAL TERRITORY

Barton Highway
Federal Highway

Gungahlin

Mitchell

Lake Ginninderra

Belconnen

▲ *Mt Majura*
888 m

North Canberra

Molonglo River

Black Mountain ▲
812 m

City

▲ *Mt Ainslie*
843 m

Lake Burley Griffin

Mt Stromlo
Observatory ■

Canberra
Airport

South Canberra

Fyshwick

Weston

Woden

Queanbeyan

Murrumbidgee River

Queanbeyan River

Hume

LAND USE

Tidbinbilla
Deep Space
Tracking Station ■

Tuggeranong

Lake Tuggeranong

Monaro Highway

Residential
Future residential
Commercial
Industrial
Special use
National Capital Area
Urban parkland, forest reserve
Non-urban forest, mountain, rural

1 POPULATION CHANGE

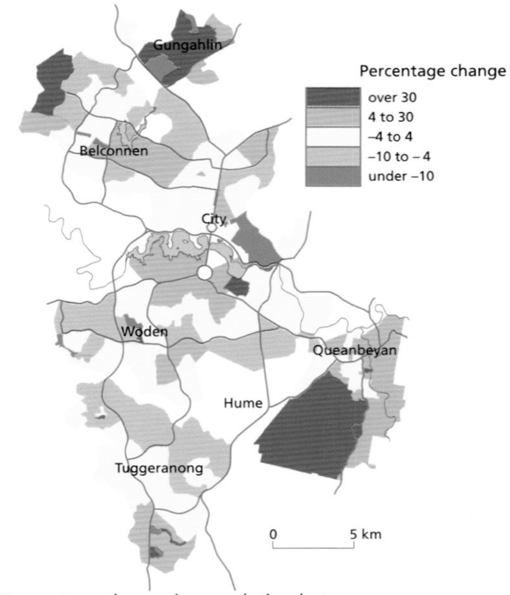

Gungahlin

Belconnen

City

Woden

Queanbeyan

Hume

Tuggeranong

Percentage change
over 30
4 to 30
–4 to 4
–10 to –4
under –10

0   5 km

Percentage change in population between
the 1996 and 2001 censuses

2 PEOPLE BORN OVERSEAS

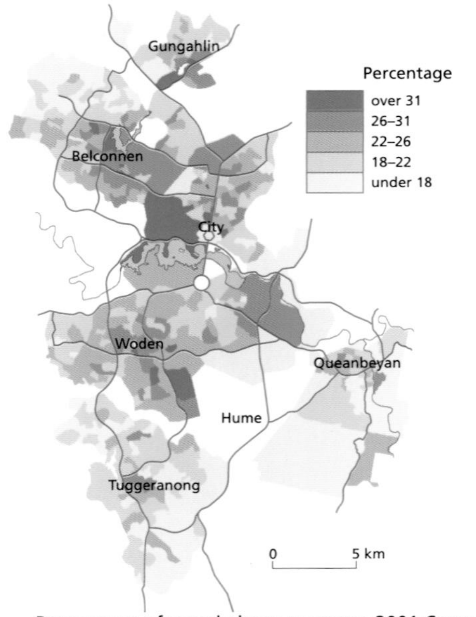

Gungahlin

Belconnen

City

Woden

Queanbeyan

Hume

Tuggeranong

Percentage
over 31
26–31
22–26
18–22
under 18

0   5 km

Percentage of people born overseas, 2001 Census

3 PEOPLE WITH HIGH INCOMES

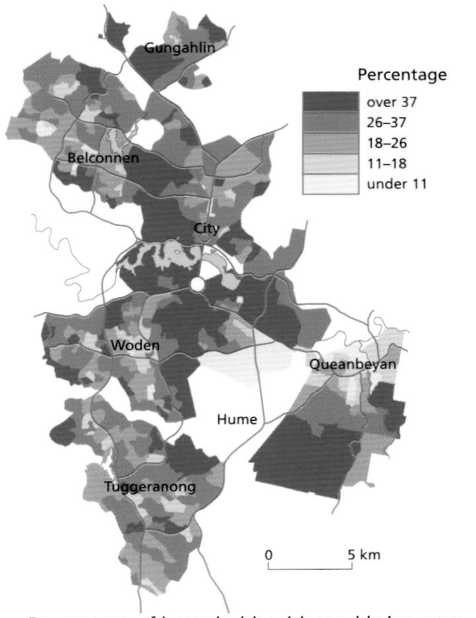

Gungahlin

Belconnen

City

Woden

Queanbeyan

Hume

Tuggeranong

Percentage
over 37
26–37
18–26
11–18
under 11

0   5 km

Percentage of households with weekly incomes
of $1500 or more, 2001 Census

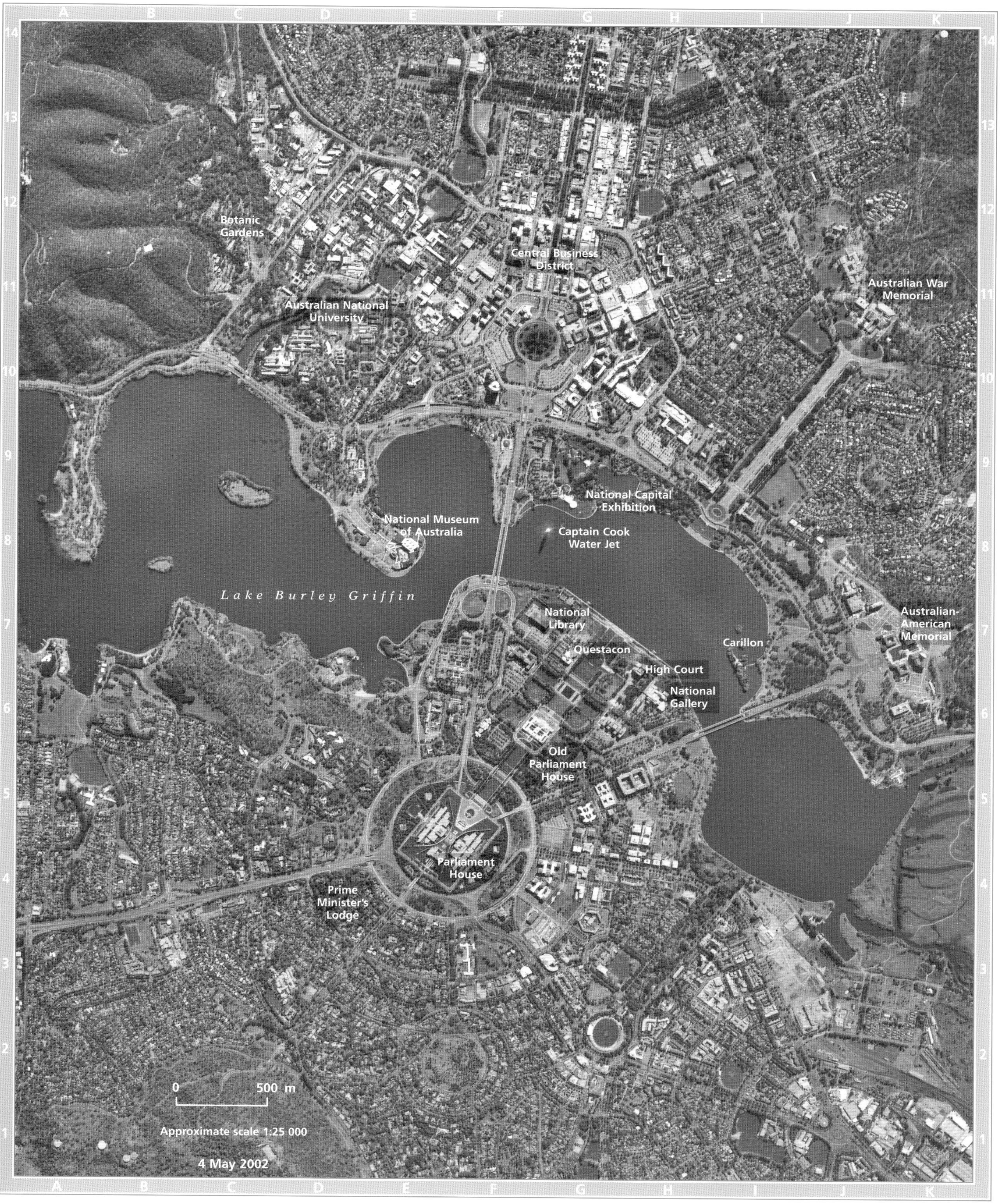

Botanic
Gardens

Central Business
District

Australian War
Memorial

Australian National
University

National Capital
Exhibition

National Museum
of Australia

Captain Cook
Water Jet

Lake Burley Griffin

National
Library

Australian-
American
Memorial

Questacon

Carillon

High Court

National
Gallery

Old
Parliament
House

Parliament
House

Prime
Minister's
Lodge

0   500 m

Approximate scale 1:25 000

4 May 2002

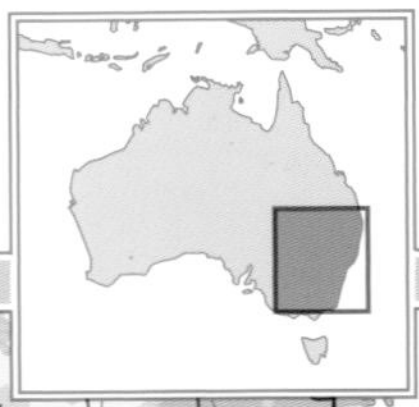

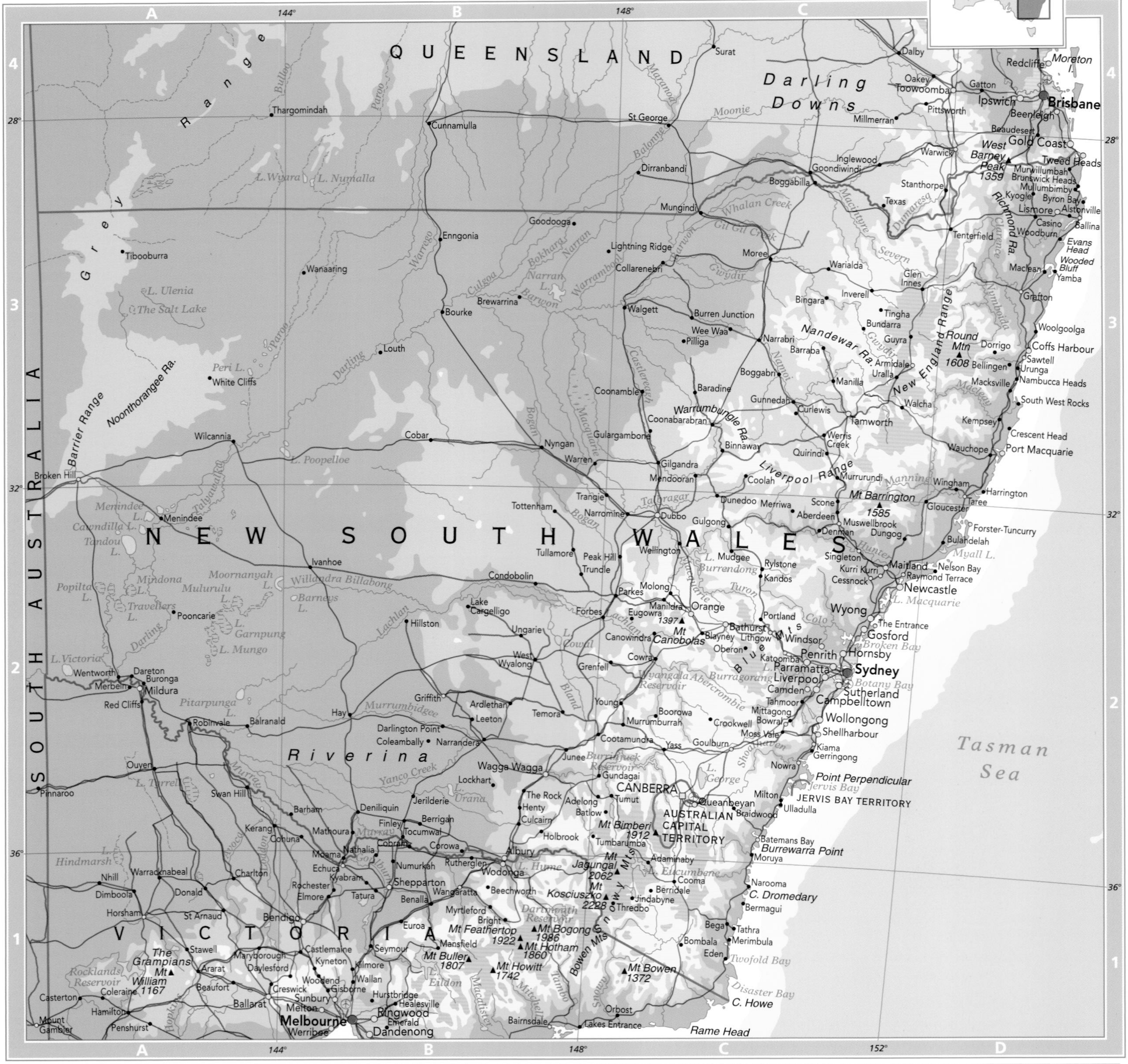

QUEENSLAND

Surat
Redcliffe
Moreton I.
Oakey Toowoomba
Dalby
Gatton
Ipswich
Brisbane
Beaudesert
Beenleigh
Gold Coast
Tweed Heads

Thargomindah
St George
Millmerran
Pittsworth
Warwick
Inglewood
Goondiwindi
West Barney Peak 1359
Murwillumbah
Brunswick Heads
Mullumbimby
Byron Bay

Cunnamulla
Boggabilla
Stanthorpe
Texas
Kyogle
Lismore
Alstonville
Ballina

L. Wyara
L. Numalla
Dirranbandi
Mungindi
Whalan Creek
Tenterfield
Casino
Woodburn
Evans Head
Wooded Bluff
Yamba

Tibooburra
Goodooga
Enngonia
Gil Gil Creek
Glen Innes
Maclean
Grafton

Wanaaring
Lightning Ridge
Moree
Warialda
Inverell
Dorrigo
Woolgoolga
Coffs Harbour

L. Ulenia
The Salt Lake
Bourke
Brewarrina
Collarenebri
Walgett
Burren Junction
Wee Waa
Pilliga
Bingara
Round Mtn 1608
Bellingen
Sawtell
Urunga
Nambucca Heads

Louth
White Cliffs
Peri L.
Narrabri
Barraba
Guyra
Armidale
Uralla
Macksville
South West Rocks

Noonthorangee Ra.
Coonamble
Baradine
Boggabri
Gunnedah
Curlewis
Manilla
Walcha
Kempsey
Crescent Head

Wilcannia
Cobar
Nyngan
Coonabarabran
Warrumbungle Ra.
Tamworth
Wauchope
Port Macquarie

Broken Hill
Warren
Gilgandra
Mendooran
Coolah
Liverpool Range
Mt Barrington 1585
Wingham
Harrington
Taree

Barrier Range
Menindee
Tottenham
Narramine
Dubbo
Dunedoo
Merriwa
Scone
Aberdeen
Gloucester
Forster-Tuncurry

NEW SOUTH WALES
Trangie
Narromine
Gulgong
Wellington
Denman
Muswellbrook
Dungog
Bulahdelah

Menindee
Cawndilla L.
Tandou
Ivanhoe
Tullamore
Peak Hill
Trundle
Mudgee
Rylstone
Kandos
Myall L.

Moornanyah
Mulurulu
Willandra Billabong
Condobolin
Burrendong
Singleton
Kurri Kurri
Nelson Bay

Popilta L.
Mindona
Barnes
Lake Cargelligo
Forbes
Parkes
Molong
Manildra
Orange
Portland
Maitland
Cessnock
Raymond Terrace
Newcastle

Travellers L.
Garnpung L.
Hillston
Eugowra
Mt Canobolas 1397
Bathurst
Lithgow
Wyong
L. Macquarie

L. Victoria
L. Mungo
West Wyalong
Ungarie
Canowindra
Blayney
Oberon
Windsor
Gosford
The Entrance
Broken Bay

Wentworth
Dareton
Buronga
Merbein
Mildura
Pitarpunga L.
Hay
Griffith
Grenfell
Cowra
Young
Katoomba
Penrith
Hornsby
Sydney
Botany Bay

Red Cliffs
Robinvale
Balranald
Darlington Point
Coleambally
Narrandera
Leeton
Ardlethan
Temora
Murrumburrah
Crookwell
Parramatta
Liverpool
Sutherland
Camden
Tahmoor
Campbelltown

Riverina
Ouyen
L. Turrel
Swan Hill
Pinnaroo
Yanco Creek
Urana
Lockhart
Wagga Wagga
Junee
Burrinjuck Reservoir
Gundagai
Goulburn
Yass
Mittagong
Bowral
Moss Vale
Wollongong
Shellharbour
Kiama
Gerringong

Hindmarsh
Barham
Deniliquin
Jerilderie
Berrigan
Tocumwal
The Rock
Henty
Adelong
Tumut
CANBERRA
Queanbeyan
Braidwood
Milton
Ulladulla
Point Perpendicular
JERVIS BAY TERRITORY

Nhill
Warracknabeal
Kerang
Cohuna
Mathoura
Finley
Culcairn
Batlow
Mt Bimberi 1912
AUSTRALIAN CAPITAL TERRITORY
Nowra
Jervis Bay

Dimboola
Charlton
Donald
Rochester
Elmore
Tatura
Numurkah
Shepparton
Corowa
Rutherglen
Albury
Holbrook
Tumbarumba
Adaminaby
Cooma
Batemans Bay
Burrawarra Point
Moruya

Horsham
St Arnaud
Bendigo
Nathalia
Moama
Echuca
Kyabram
Benalla
Wodonga
Mt Jagungal 2062
Berridale
Jindabyne
Narooma
C. Dromedary
Bermagui

Myrtleford
Beechworth
Mt Kosciuszko 2228
Thredbo
Bega
Tathra
Merimbula

VICTORIA
Stawell
Maryborough
Castlemaine
Kyneton
Seymour
Bright
Mt Feathertop 1922
Mt Bogong 1986
Mt Hotham 1860
Bowen Mts
Mt Bowen 1372
Bombala
Eden
Twofold Bay

Rocklands Reservoir
The Grampians
Mt William 1167
Ararat
Daylesford
Woodend
Mansfield
Mt Buller 1807
Mt Howitt 1742
Disaster Bay
C. Howe

Casterton
Coleraine
Beaufort
Ballarat
Creswick
Sunbury
Gisborne
Melton
Healesville
Emerald
Orbost
Rame Head

Mount Gambier
Hamilton
Penshurst
Melbourne
Werribee
Ringwood
Dandenong
Bairnsdale
Lakes Entrance

Tasman Sea

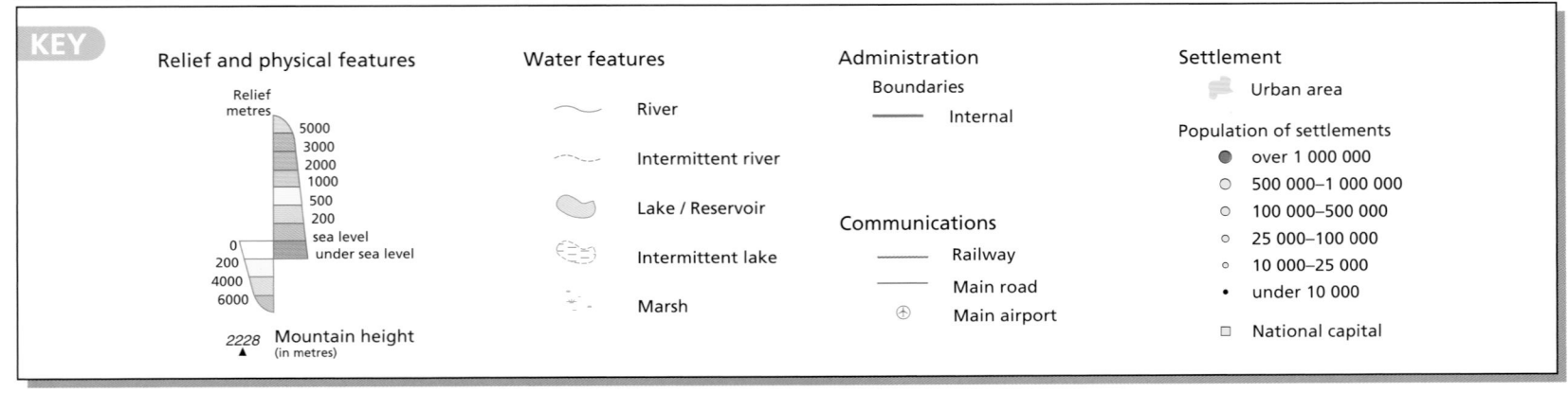

SCALE 1:6 000 000

0   100   200   300 km

Lambert Azimuthal Equal Area projection

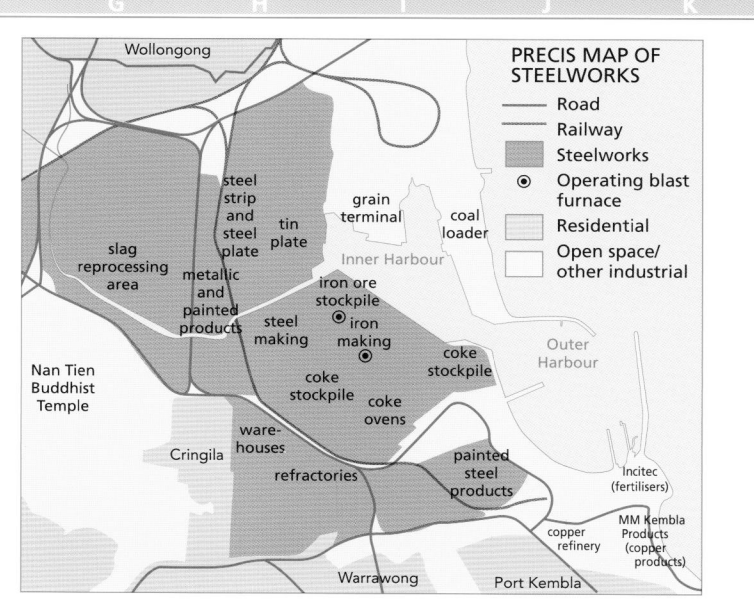

BlueScope (formerly BHP) Steel's Port Kembla steelworks is Australia's largest integrated steel-making centre. The steelworks is a very good example of how various factors can influence the location of an industry over time.

The steelworks was originally located at Port Kembla in 1928 because of its closeness to large quantities of coal and local markets. Other factors taken into consideration at that time included the need for a large area of flat land and a ready labour force, availability of sources of energy and access to transport and other services, and government incentives. Improvements in bulk transporting of materials, and the relatively high cost of handling finished products today, have meant that the deep-water port and its closeness to markets and services are now the two most important factors affecting the steelworks' location.

This July 2002 vertical aerial photograph of the steelworks shows bulk carriers moored in the inner harbour, raw material stockpiles, complex patterns of railways and roads, and steel-making and steel-processing buildings. There are also several other large industries in the same area, some of which have strong links with the steel industry.

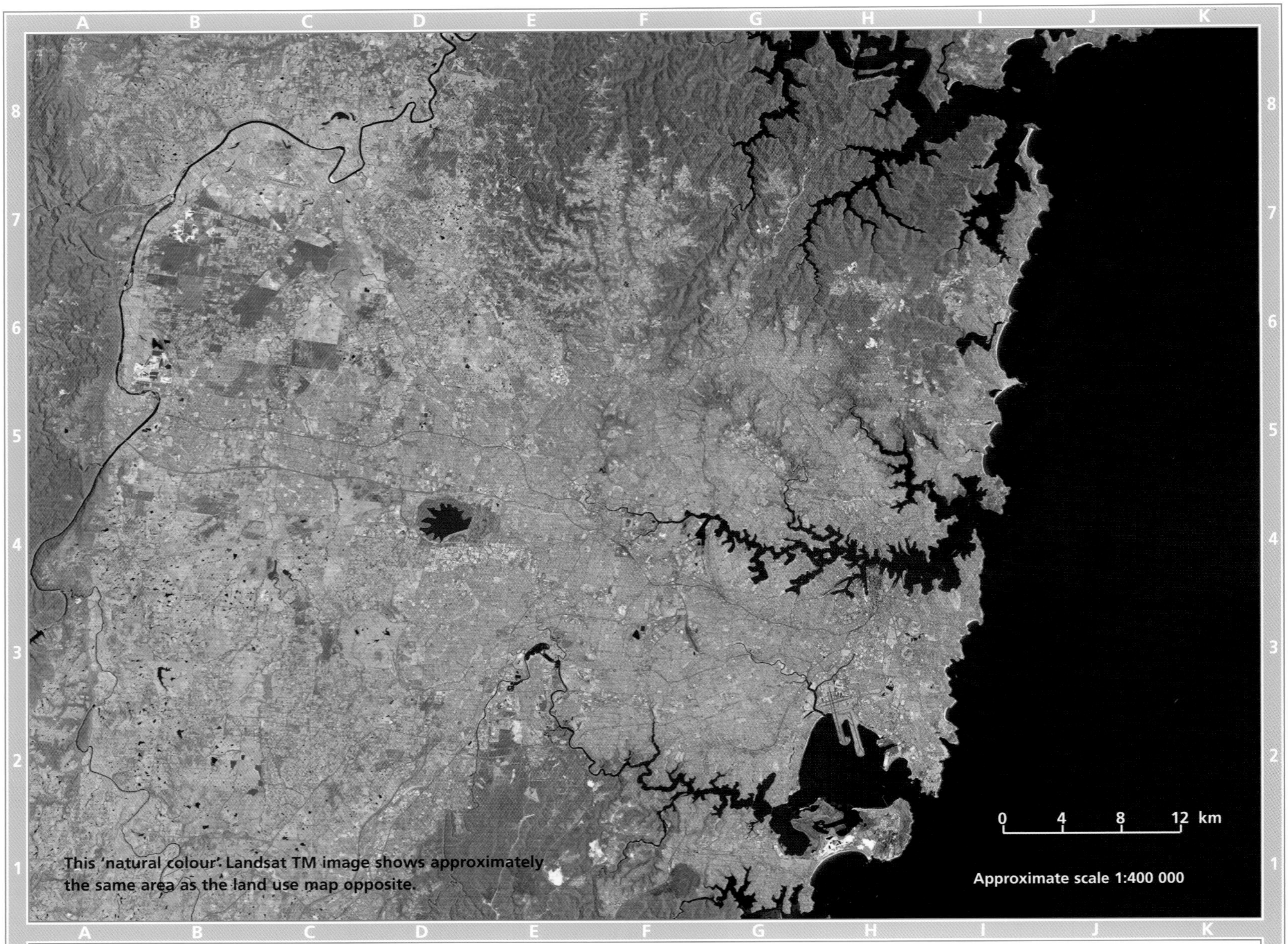

This 'natural colour' Landsat TM image shows approximately the same area as the land use map opposite.

```
0      4      8      12 km
```

Approximate scale 1:400 000

1 POPULATION CHANGE

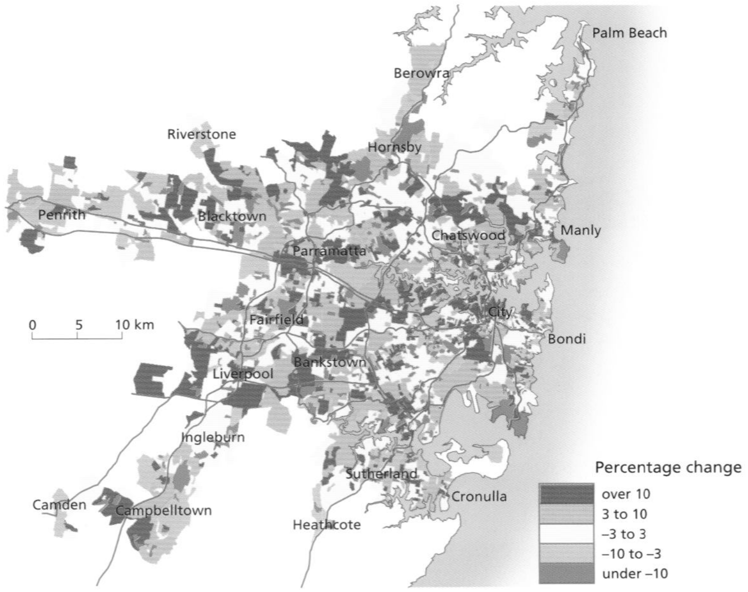

Palm Beach
Berowra
Riverstone
Hornsby
Penrith
Blacktown
Chatswood
Manly
Parramatta
City
Fairfield
Bondi
Bankstown
Liverpool
Ingleburn
Sutherland
Cronulla
Camden Campbelltown
Heathcote

```
0      5      10 km
```

Percentage change

	over 10
	3 to 10
	−3 to 3
	−10 to −3
	under −10

Percentage change in population between the 1996 and 2001 censuses

2 CHILDREN UNDER FIVE

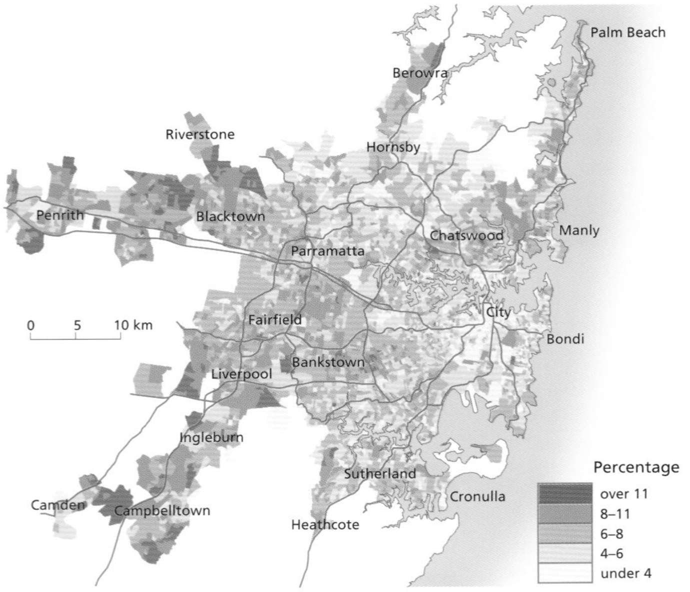

Palm Beach
Berowra
Riverstone
Hornsby
Penrith
Blacktown
Chatswood
Manly
Parramatta
City
Fairfield
Bondi
Bankstown
Liverpool
Ingleburn
Sutherland
Cronulla
Camden Campbelltown
Heathcote

```
0      5      10 km
```

Percentage

	over 11
	8–11
	6–8
	4–6
	under 4

Percentage of total population aged under five years, 2001 Census

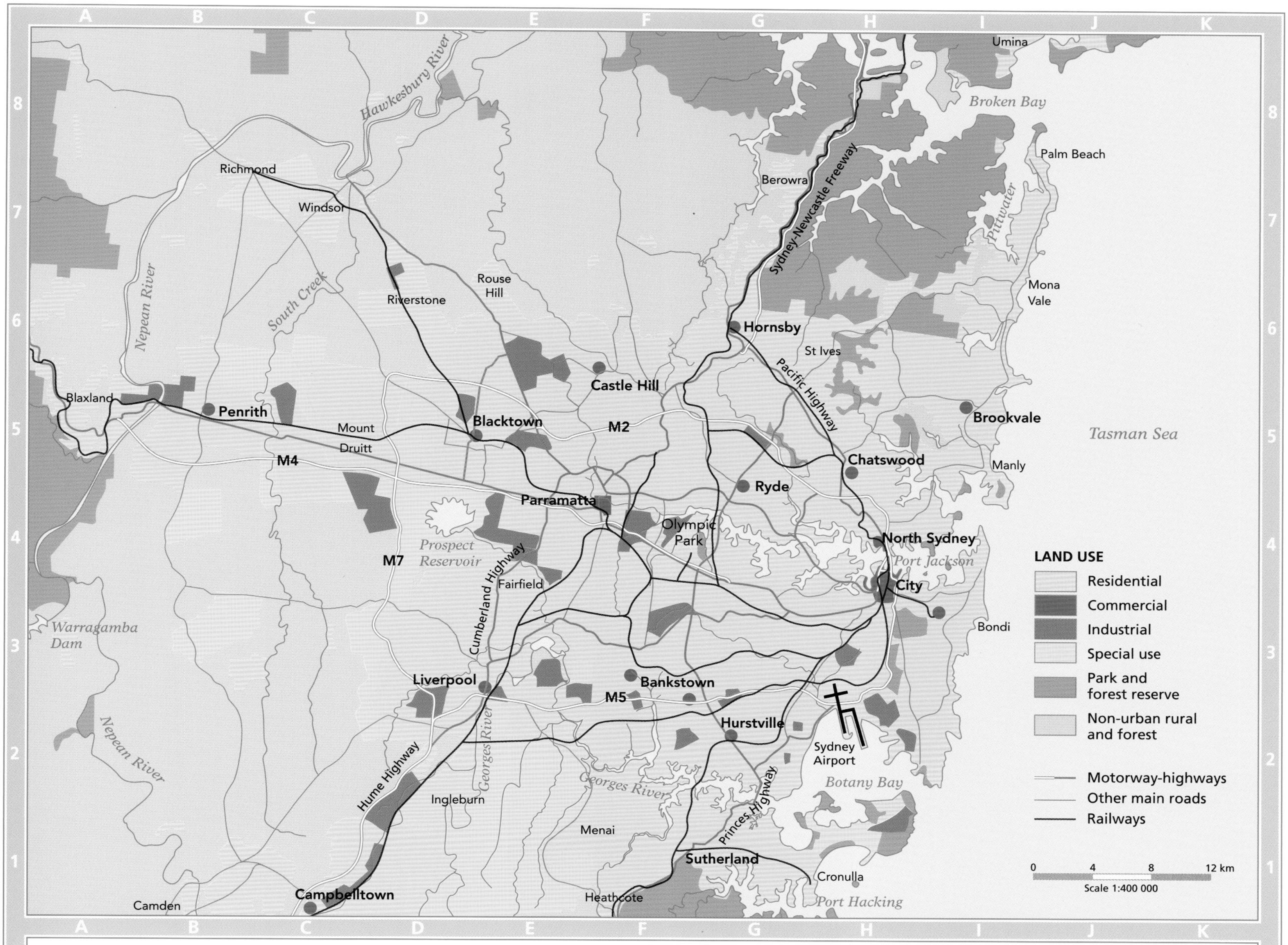

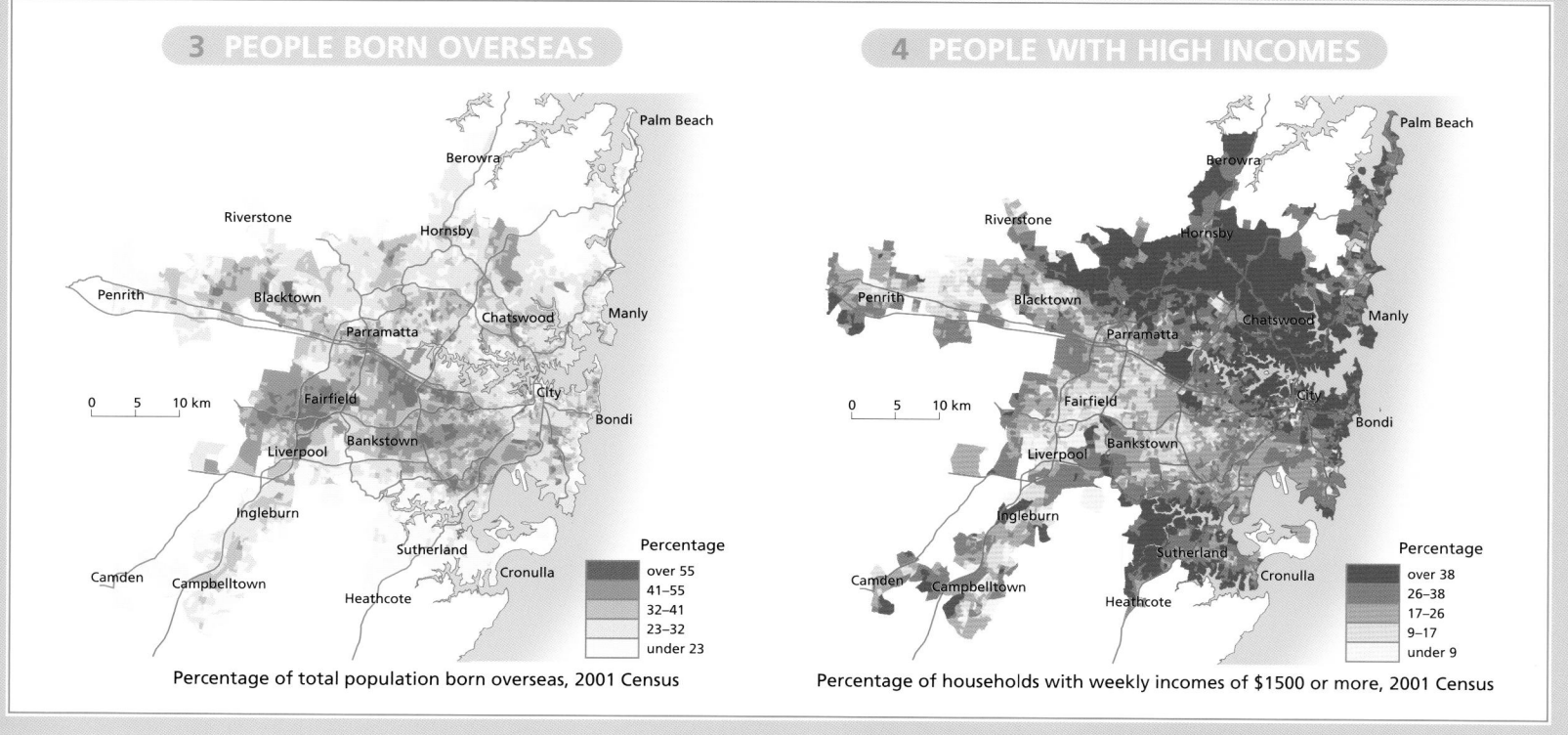

Letter columns										
A	B	C	D	E	F	G	H	I	J	K

Hawkesbury River

Umina

8

Broken Bay

Richmond

Windsor

Berowra

Sydney–Newcastle Freeway

Palm Beach

7

Rouse Hill

Riverstone

Mona Vale

South Creek

Hornsby

St Ives

6

Pittwater

Pacific Highway

Nepean River

Blaxland

Penrith

Castle Hill

Brookvale

5

Tasman Sea

Mount Druitt

Blacktown

M2

Chatswood

Manly

M4

Ryde

Parramatta

Olympic Park

North Sydney

4

Prospect Reservoir

M7

Port Jackson

City

Fairfield

Cumberland Highway

LAND USE

Warragamba Dam

Bondi

3

Liverpool

Bankstown

M5

Residential

Commercial

Industrial

Nepean River

Hurstville

Special use

Sydney Airport

Park and forest reserve

2

Georges River

Georges River

Botany Bay

Non-urban rural and forest

Hume Highway

Ingleburn

Menai

Princes Highway

Motorway-highways

Other main roads

Railways

Sutherland

1

Camden

Campbelltown

Heathcote

Cronulla

Port Hacking

0 4 8 12 km

Scale 1:400 000

3 PEOPLE BORN OVERSEAS

Palm Beach

Berowra

Riverstone

Hornsby

Penrith

Blacktown

Chatswood

Manly

Parramatta

City

Fairfield

Bondi

0 5 10 km

Liverpool

Bankstown

Ingleburn

Sutherland

Camden

Campbelltown

Cronulla

Heathcote

Percentage

over 55

41–55

32–41

23–32

under 23

Percentage of total population born overseas, 2001 Census

4 PEOPLE WITH HIGH INCOMES

Palm Beach

Berowra

Riverstone

Hornsby

Penrith

Blacktown

Chatswood

Manly

Parramatta

City

Fairfield

Bondi

0 5 10 km

Liverpool

Bankstown

Ingleburn

Sutherland

Camden

Campbelltown

Cronulla

Heathcote

Percentage

over 38

26–38

17–26

9–17

under 9

Percentage of households with weekly incomes of $1500 or more, 2001 Census

KEY

Relief and physical features

Relief metres
5000
3000
2000
1000
500
200
0 sea level
under sea level
200
4000
6000

1922 ▲ Mountain height (in metres)

Water features

〜 River

〜 Intermittent river

Lake / Reservoir

Intermittent lake

Communications

—— Railway

—— Main road

⊕ Main airport

Administration

Boundaries

—— Internal

Settlement

Urban area

Population of settlements

● over 1 000 000

○ 500 000–1 000 000

○ 100 000–500 000

○ 25 000–100 000

○ 10 000–25 000

• under 10 000

☐ National capital

YALLOURN AIR PHOTO

SCALE 1:4 000 000

0   50   100   150   200 km

Lambert Azimuthal Equal Area projection

40 41 42 43 44 45

77 .137 SAVIGES ROAD 150 77

MURRAY

SPUR ROAD 150 PURVIS RD

TRACK FERNLEA MILL TRK Tip 155 KELSO Yallourn North

FERNLEA 150 ROAD Water tower ST North

124 PIONEER 150 C BAILLIE

76 TRACK George Bates Reserve C BROWN COAL ROA 76

Fernlea Channel "Woorabinda Camp" BOUNDARY RD C ROAD 100

Boat ramp ROAD 100 C FS Tennis

Thompsons Bay HALL 140 Motor Cycle Club Bowls Oval YALLOURN NORTH OPENCUT

50 Boat ramp 50 129 ANDERSON TRACK THIRD S

75 Boat ramp ROAD RIVER LATROBE 69 SAND WASH RD 75

SULLIVAN TRACK Halls Bay 70 HOWLETT 100 RIVER ROAD 80 RIVER 50

70 TRACK LATROBE Blue Lagoon

100 127 PETTITS Yallourn Power Station Yallourn Power Station Overburden line

SCOUT TRACK DRIVE Car park Conveyor Transmission 63

74 GOLF LINKS Tennis CENTRAL DRIVE line Car park Cooling tower Oval YALLOURN OPENCUT 40 74

Yallourn Heights 120 Yallourn FS Car park Car park

ROAD ROAD SAVIGES Water treatment plant RESERVOIR Pond

170 Tower 130 100 70 73 YALLOURN OPENCUT Pond 41

73 RANGE TRACK DECAMP ROAD Conveyors Conveyors INTERCONNECTING MORWELL 73

TRK 100 YALLOURN OPENCUT
(The detail depicted in the Yallourn Opencut
is subject to continuous change.)

40 41 42 43 44 45

SCALE 1:25 000

0 500 1000 1500 2000 METRES

N

YALLOURN
1:25 000
Contour interval
10 metres

Built-up area	Building, church, police station ▪ • C • PS	Timber, Scattered timber . . . .
Sealed road with bridge, minor road	School, fire station, tank or well ▪ S • FS • Oil	Pine plantation, windbreak . . . .
Vehicular track, foot track	Fence, power transmission line	River, creek, channel or drain . . . . .
Gate, cattlegrid, leveebank	Landmark area, quarry . . . . Tennis	Lake perennial, intermittent . . . .
Embankment, cutting	Spot elevation, landmark object •34 ◦ Silo	Land subject to inundation, Dam or weir
Railway track, siding, bridge	Contours 200	Waterhole, dam, swimming pool . . . . . .

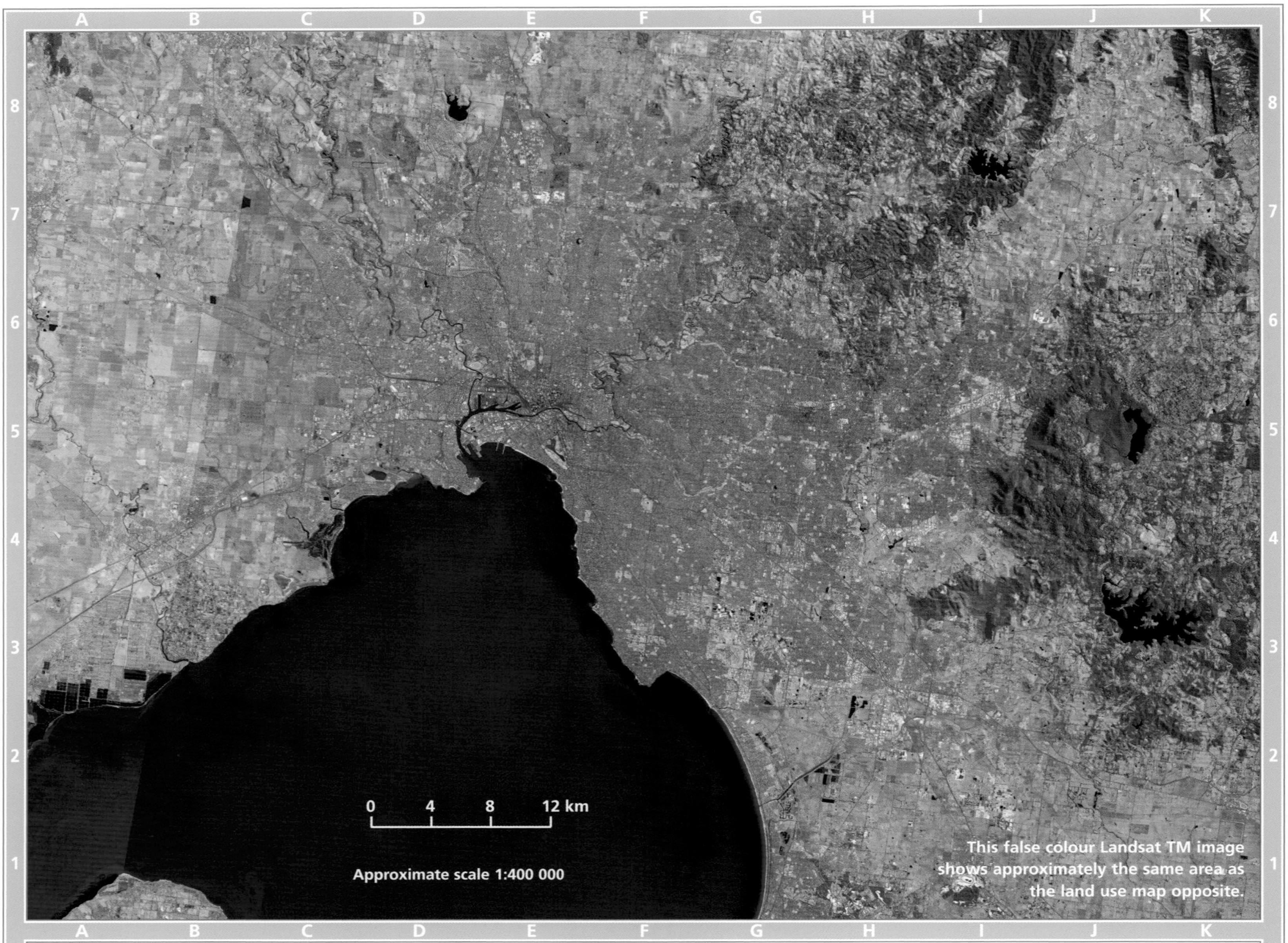

Approximate scale 1:400 000

0   4   8   12 km

This false colour Landsat TM image shows approximately the same area as the land use map opposite.

1 POPULATION CHANGE

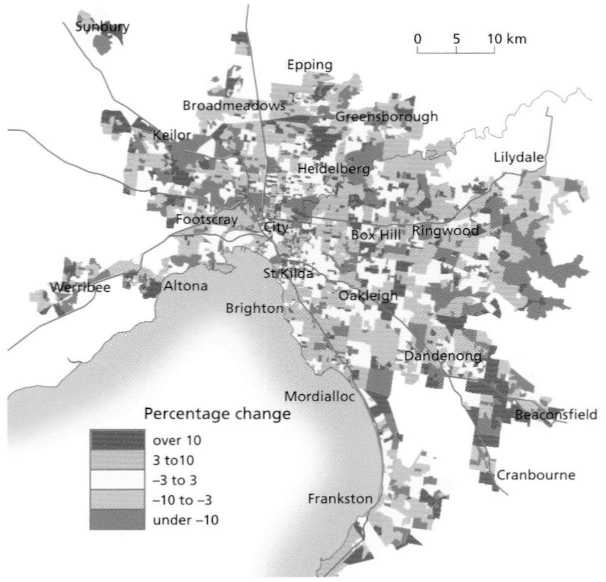

Sunbury

Epping

Broadmeadows

Greensborough

Keilor

Heidelberg

Lilydale

Footscray

City

Box Hill   Ringwood

St Kilda

Werribee   Altona

Oakleigh

Brighton

Dandenong

Mordialloc

Beaconsfield

Cranbourne

Frankston

0   5   10 km

Percentage change

over 10
3 to 10
−3 to 3
−10 to −3
under −10

Percentage change in population between the 1996 and 2001 censuses

2 CHILDREN UNDER FIVE

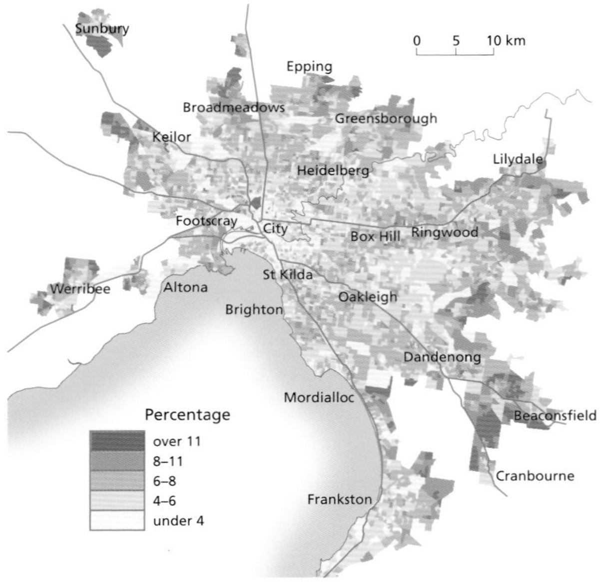

Sunbury

Epping

Broadmeadows

Greensborough

Keilor

Heidelberg

Lilydale

Footscray

City

Box Hill   Ringwood

St Kilda

Werribee   Altona

Oakleigh

Brighton

Dandenong

Mordialloc

Beaconsfield

Cranbourne

Frankston

0   5   10 km

Percentage

over 11
8–11
6–8
4–6
under 4

Percentage of total population aged under five years, 2001 Census

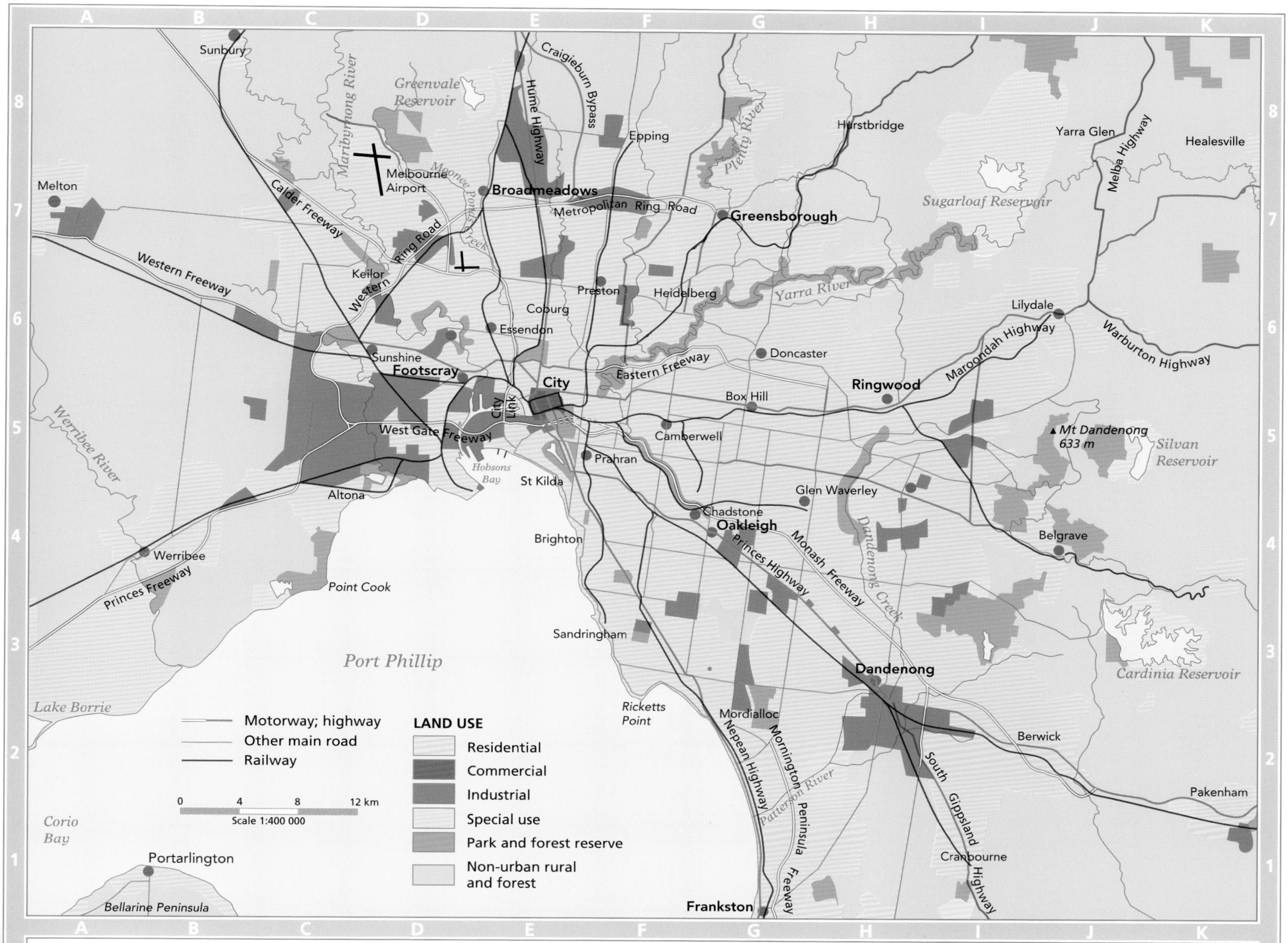

Sunbury

Greenvale
Reservoir

Craigieburn Bypass

Maribyrnong River

Hume Highway

Epping

Plenty River

Hurstbridge

Yarra Glen

Melba Highway

Healesville

Melbourne
Airport

Moonee Ponds Creek

Melton

Calder Freeway

Broadmeadows

Metropolitan Ring Road

Greensborough

Sugarloaf Reservoir

Western Freeway

Keilor

Western Ring Road

Preston

Heidelberg

Yarra River

Lilydale

Warburton Highway

Coburg

Essendon

Maroondah Highway

Sunshine

Footscray

City

Eastern Freeway

Doncaster

Box Hill

Ringwood

Werribee River

West Gate Freeway

City Link

Camberwell

Mt Dandenong
633 m

Silvan
Reservoir

Altona

Hobsons
Bay

St Kilda

Prahran

Glen Waverley

Chadstone

Oakleigh

Princes Highway

Monash Freeway

Dandenong Creek

Belgrave

Brighton

Werribee

Princes Freeway

Point Cook

Sandringham

Dandenong

Cardinia Reservoir

Port Phillip

Ricketts
Point

Lake Borrie

Mordialloc

Nepean Highway

Mornington Peninsula Freeway

Patterson River

South Gippsland Highway

Berwick

Cranbourne Highway

Pakenham

Corio
Bay

Cranbourne

Portarlington

Bellarine Peninsula

Frankston

LAND USE

- Motorway; highway
- Other main road
- Railway

- Residential
- Commercial
- Industrial
- Special use
- Park and forest reserve
- Non-urban rural and forest

0   4   8   12 km
Scale 1:400 000

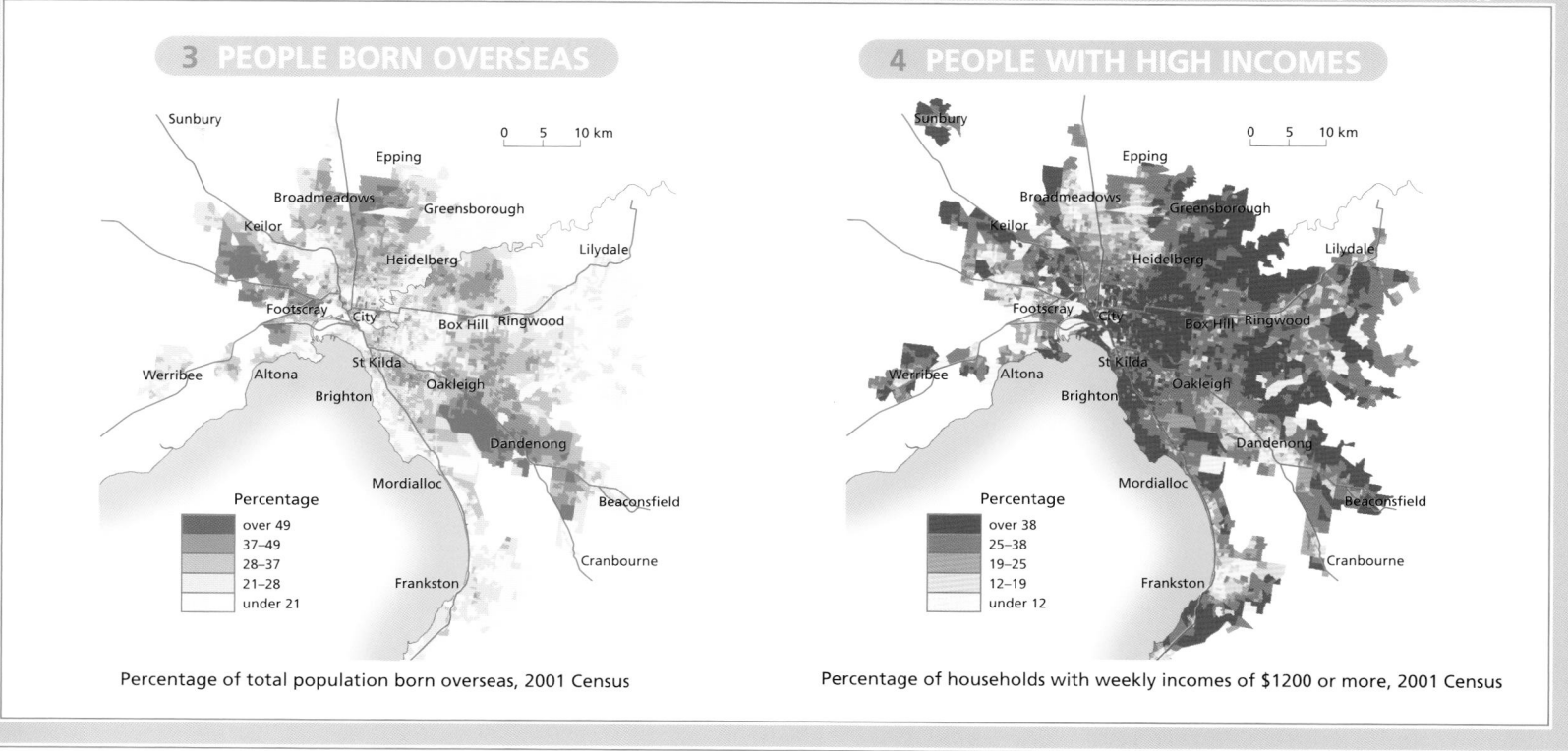

3 PEOPLE BORN OVERSEAS

Sunbury

Epping

Broadmeadows

Greensborough

Keilor

Heidelberg

Lilydale

Footscray

City

Box Hill   Ringwood

Werribee

Altona

St Kilda

Oakleigh

Brighton

Dandenong

Mordialloc

Beaconsfield

Cranbourne

Frankston

0   5   10 km

Percentage
- over 49
- 37–49
- 28–37
- 21–28
- under 21

Percentage of total population born overseas, 2001 Census

4 PEOPLE WITH HIGH INCOMES

Sunbury

Epping

Broadmeadows

Greensborough

Keilor

Heidelberg

Lilydale

Footscray

City

Box Hill   Ringwood

Werribee

Altona

St Kilda

Oakleigh

Brighton

Dandenong

Mordialloc

Beaconsfield

Cranbourne

Frankston

0   5   10 km

Percentage
- over 38
- 25–38
- 19–25
- 12–19
- under 12

Percentage of households with weekly incomes of $1200 or more, 2001 Census

KEY

Relief and physical features

Relief metres

5000
3000
2000
1000
500
200
0 sea level
200 under sea level
4000
6000

1612 ▲ Mountain height (in metres)

Water features

River
Intermittent river
Lake / Reservoir
Intermittent lake
Marsh
Coral reef

Communications

Railway
Main road
⊕ Main airport

Administration

Boundaries

International
Internal

Settlement

Urban area

Population of settlements

● over 1 000 000
◉ 500 000–1 000 000
◎ 100 000–500 000
◦ 25 000–100 000
· 10 000–25 000
· under 10 000

Map labels

Gulf of Papua

PAPUA NEW GUINEA

Daru

Boigu I.
Saibai I.
Torres Strait
Badu I.
Mba I.
Thursday I.
Horn I.
Thursday Island
C. York
Prince of Wales I.
Utingico
Injinoo
Bamaga

Coral Sea

Cape York

Mapoon
C. Grenville

Duifken Pt
Weipa
Napranum
C. Weymouth
Lockhart River
C. Direction

Peninsula
Aurukun

Gulf of Carpentaria

Archer

Coen
Princess Charlotte Bay
C. Melville

Pormpuraaw

Osprey Reef

Lizard I.
C. Flattery

Kowanyama

Holroyd

Hope Vale
Cooktown

Mitchell
Wujal Wujal
C. Tribulation

Mornington I.
C. Van Diemen
Wellesley Is.

Staaten
Mossman
Trinity Bay
Port Douglas

Karumba
Gilbert
Mareeba
Cairns
Gordonvale

Normanton
Atherton
Mt Bartle Frere
Babinda
Herberton
Ravenshoe
1612
Innisfail

Doomadgee
Burketown
Croydon
Georgetown

Tully
Dunk I.

Cardwell
Hinchinbrook I.
Ingham
Great Palm I.
Palm Island
Magnetic I.

Gulf Country

Gregory Range

Seaview Range

Flinders Reefs

Nicholson

Townsville
C. Bowling Green
Ayr

Camooweal
Home Hill

Leichhardt

Norman
Bowen
Hayman I.
Whitsunday Group
Lindeman Group

Julia Creek
Cloncurry
Flinders
Richmond
Charters Towers
Airlie Beach
Proserpine
Collinsville

Mount Isa
Hughenden
Burdekin

Selwyn Range
Mt Dalrymple 1277
Mackay

Dajarra
L. Buchanan
Sarina

Georgina
L. Galilee
Moranbah
Northumberland Isles

Boulia
Winton
QUEENSLAND
Dysart
Clermont
Swain Reefs

Burke

Channel Country
Aramac
Townshend I.
Saumarez Reef

Diamantina
Longreach
Barcaldine
Thomson
Alpha
Emerald
Blackwater
Yeppoon
Great Keppel I.
Rockhampton
Heron I.

Bedourie
L. Machattie
Barcoo
Springsure
Mount Morgan
Curtis I.
Gladstone
Tropic of Capricorn

Eyre
Blackall
Moura
Biloela
Bustard Head

Birdsville
Consuelo Peak 1174
Monto
Miriam Vale

Windorah
Theodore
Bundaberg
Sandy C.
Hervey Bay

Goyder Lagoon
L. Yamma Yamma
Augathella
Taroom
Eidsvold
Howard
Fraser I.

Sturt Stony Desert
Injune
Wandoan
Gayndah
Hervey Bay
Maryborough

Quilpie
Charleville
Mitchell
Roma
Murgon
Gympie

Warburton
Cooper Creek
Wondai
Kingaroy
Noosa

SOUTH AUSTRALIA
Kittakittaooloo
Miles
Chinchilla
Nanango
Nambour
Maroochydore
Caloundra
Caboolture

L. Howitt
Innamincka
Moomba
Surat
Dalby
Kilcoy
Moreton I.

Thargomindah
St George
Oakey
Toowoomba
Gatton
Redcliffe
Brisbane

L. Eyre (South)
L. Gregory
L. Blanche
L. Callabonna
Marree

Tibooburra
Cunnamulla
Dirranbandi
Goondiwindi
Millmerran
Pittsworth
Ipswich
Beenleigh
Gold Coast
Tweed Heads

NEW SOUTH WALES
Enngonia
Goodooga
Mungindi
Inglewood
Warwick
Beaudesert
West Barney Peak 1359
Murwillumbah
Brunswick Heads
Mullumbimby

Moree
Boggabilla
Texas
Stanthorpe
Kyogle
Byron Bay
Ballina

Warialda
Tenterfield
Casino
Lismore
Woodburn

0 100 200 300 400 km

Lambert Azimuthal Equal Area projection

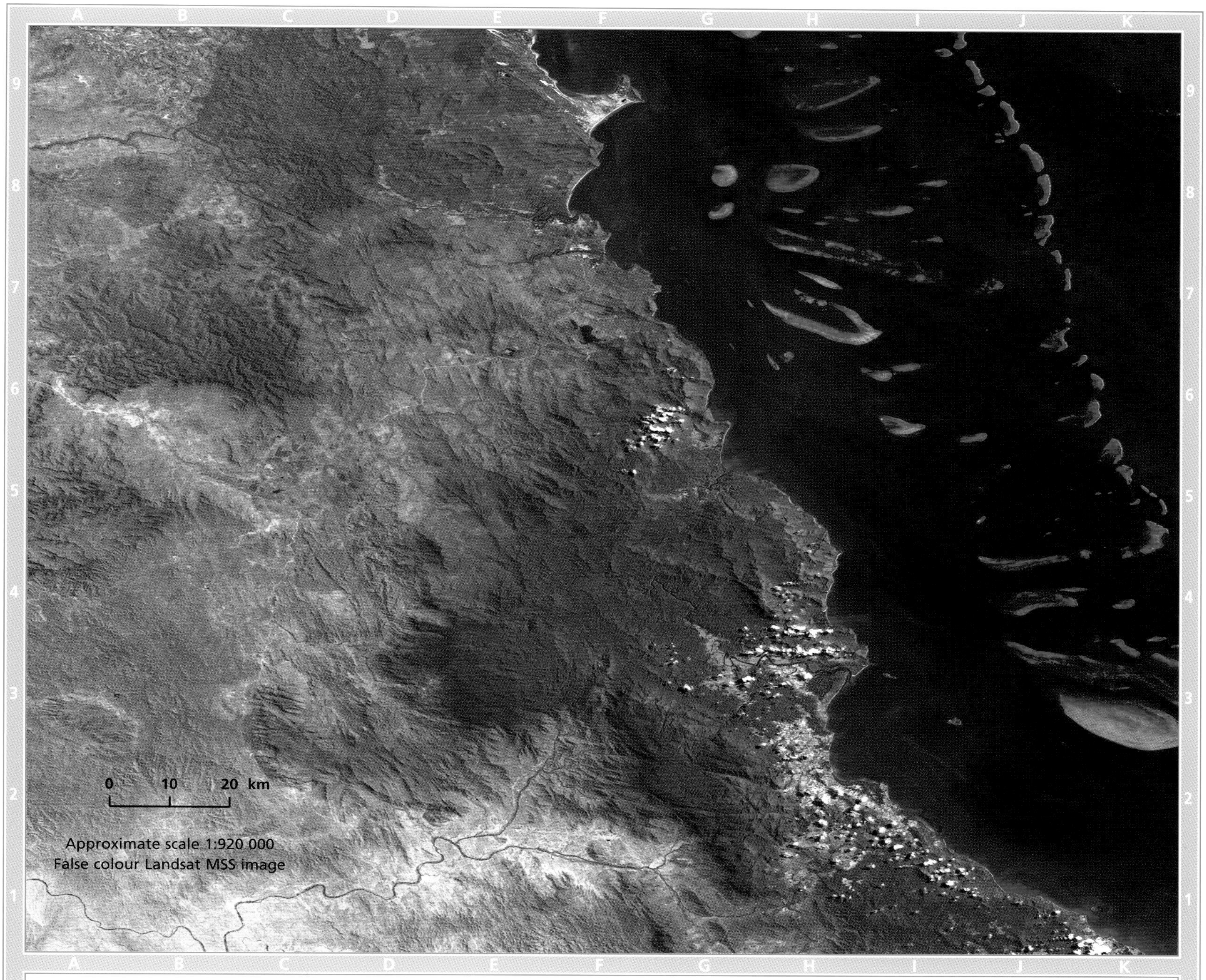

0   10   20 km

Approximate scale 1:920 000
False colour Landsat MSS image

Far northern Queensland is the site of two very important World Heritage Areas:

(a) **The Great Barrier Reef World Heritage Area** covers an area of 34.87 million hectares. There are about 3400 coral reefs, coral cays and islands which stretch more than 2000 kilometres down the north-east coast of Queensland. It is the world's longest coral reef system and probably has the world's most diverse collection of fauna.

(b) **The Wet Tropics World Heritage Area** is a series of national parks and state forests, including the Daintree National Park, which stretch from Cooktown to Townsville. The region has spectacular mountain scenery and lush tropical rainforests which contain many rare species of plants and animals.

This Landsat image clearly shows the Great Barrier Reef with its fine line of ribbon reefs about 50 kilometres off the Queensland coast, from **J9** to **K5**, and the coral cays closer to the coast, e.g. **H7**. In the centre of the image are the World Heritage tropical rainforests which show as bright red, e.g. the Daintree National Park at **G2** and **H4**, while the white spots are clouds. The lighter blue-grey colours to the west of the rainforests are large areas of open eucalypt woodland. These areas have low rainfall and poor soils, and are only suitable for extensive beef cattle grazing. There is a small basin of intensive farming 60 kilometres inland from the coast at **C5**. Because of image distortion, the map and image do not match exactly.

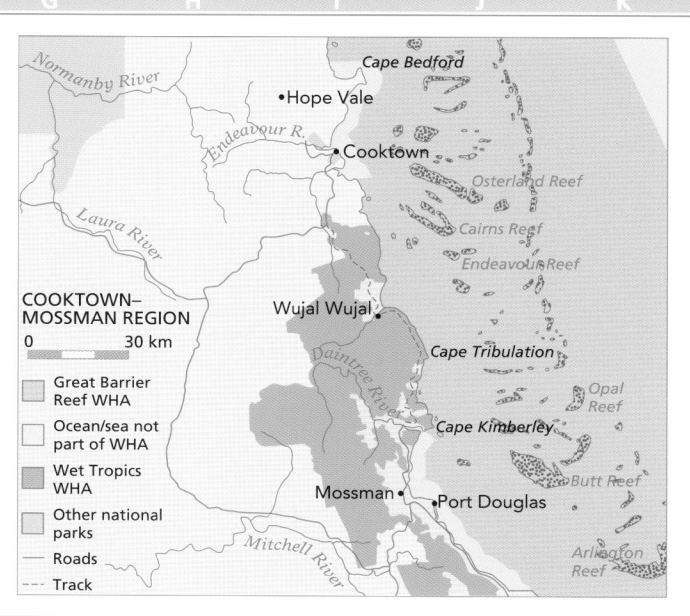

COOKTOWN–
MOSSMAN REGION

0   30 km

- Great Barrier Reef WHA
- Ocean/sea not part of WHA
- Wet Tropics WHA
- Other national parks
- Roads
- Track

0   4   8   12 km

Approximate scale 1:400 000

This 'natural colour' Landsat TM image shows approximately the same area as the land use map opposite.

1 POPULATION CHANGE

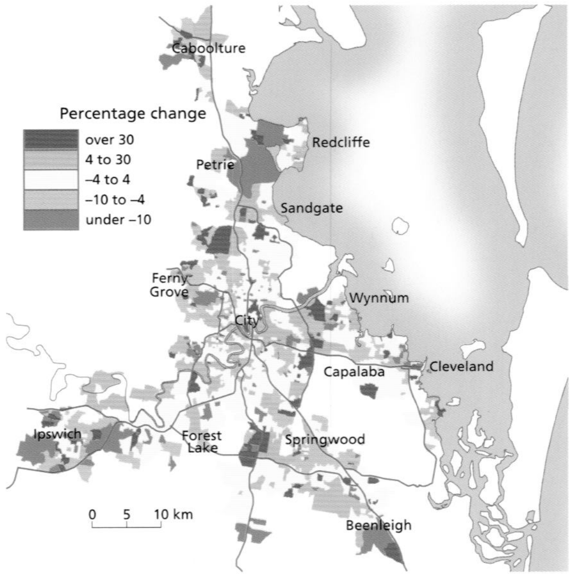

Percentage change

	over 30
	4 to 30
	−4 to 4
	−10 to −4
	under −10

Caboolture
Redcliffe
Petrie
Sandgate
Ferny Grove
City
Wynnum
Capalaba
Cleveland
Ipswich
Forest Lake
Springwood
Beenleigh

0   5   10 km

Percentage change in population between the 1996 and 2001 censuses

2 CHILDREN UNDER FIVE

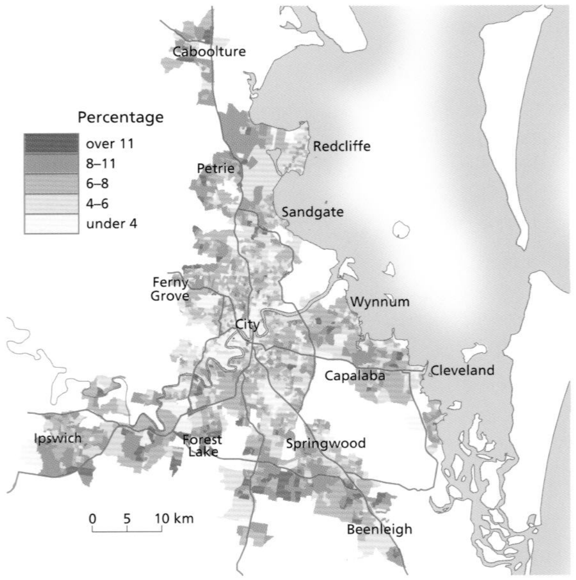

Percentage

	over 11
	8–11
	6–8
	4–6
	under 4

Caboolture
Redcliffe
Petrie
Sandgate
Ferny Grove
City
Wynnum
Capalaba
Cleveland
Ipswich
Forest Lake
Springwood
Beenleigh

0   5   10 km

Percentage of total population aged under five years, 2001 Census

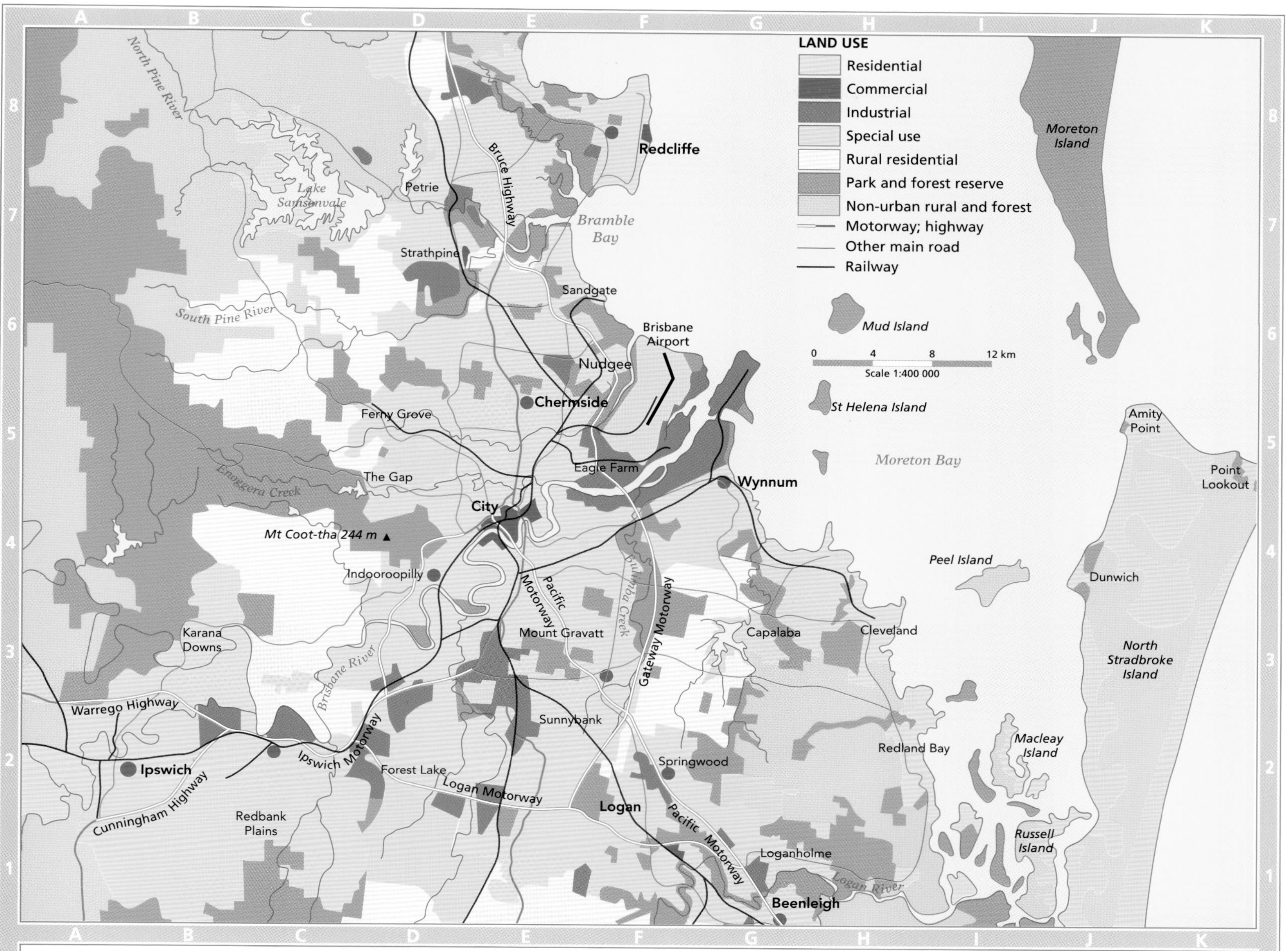

LAND USE

- Residential
- Commercial
- Industrial
- Special use
- Rural residential
- Park and forest reserve
- Non-urban rural and forest
- Motorway; highway
- Other main road
- Railway

North Pine River

Lake Samsonvale

Petrie

Strathpine

South Pine River

Sandgate

Bramble Bay

Redcliffe

Bruce Highway

Brisbane Airport

Nudgee

Chermside

Ferny Grove

Enoggera Creek

The Gap

Eagle Farm

City

Mt Coot-tha 244 m ▲

Indooroopilly

Wynnum

Moreton Island

Mud Island

St Helena Island

Moreton Bay

Amity Point

Point Lookout

0   4   8   12 km

Scale 1:400 000

Peel Island

Dunwich

North Stradbroke Island

Karana Downs

Mount Gravatt

Brisbane River

Pacific Motorway

Bulimba Creek

Gateway Motorway

Capalaba

Cleveland

Warrego Highway

Ipswich Motorway

Sunnybank

Redland Bay

Macleay Island

Cunningham Highway

Forest Lake

Logan Motorway

Springwood

Logan

Pacific Motorway

Russell Island

Redbank Plains

Loganholme

Logan River

Beenleigh

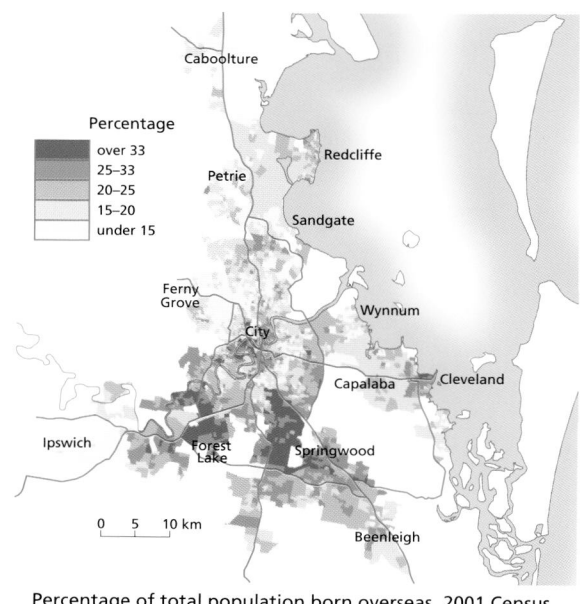

3 PEOPLE BORN OVERSEAS

Caboolture

Percentage
- over 33
- 25–33
- 20–25
- 15–20
- under 15

Petrie

Redcliffe

Sandgate

Ferny Grove

City

Wynnum

Ipswich

Capalaba   Cleveland

Forest Lake   Springwood

0   5   10 km

Beenleigh

Percentage of total population born overseas, 2001 Census

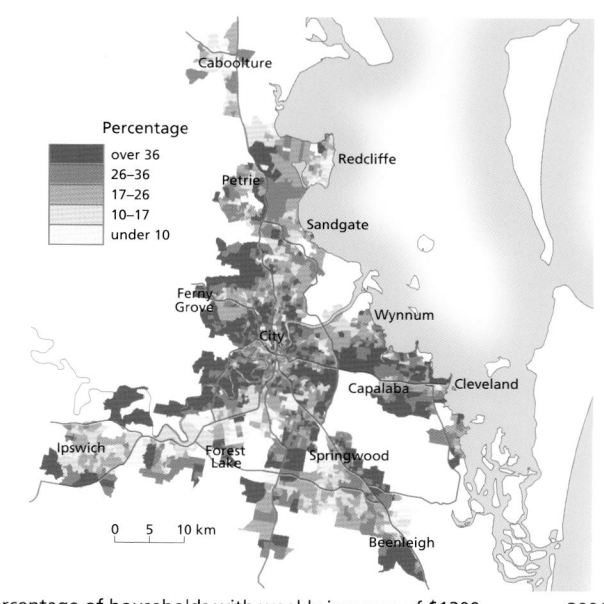

4 PEOPLE WITH HIGH INCOMES

Caboolture

Percentage
- over 36
- 26–36
- 17–26
- 10–17
- under 10

Petrie

Redcliffe

Sandgate

Ferny Grove

City

Wynnum

Ipswich

Capalaba   Cleveland

Forest Lake   Springwood

0   5   10 km

Beenleigh

Percentage of households with weekly incomes of $1200 or more, 2001 Census

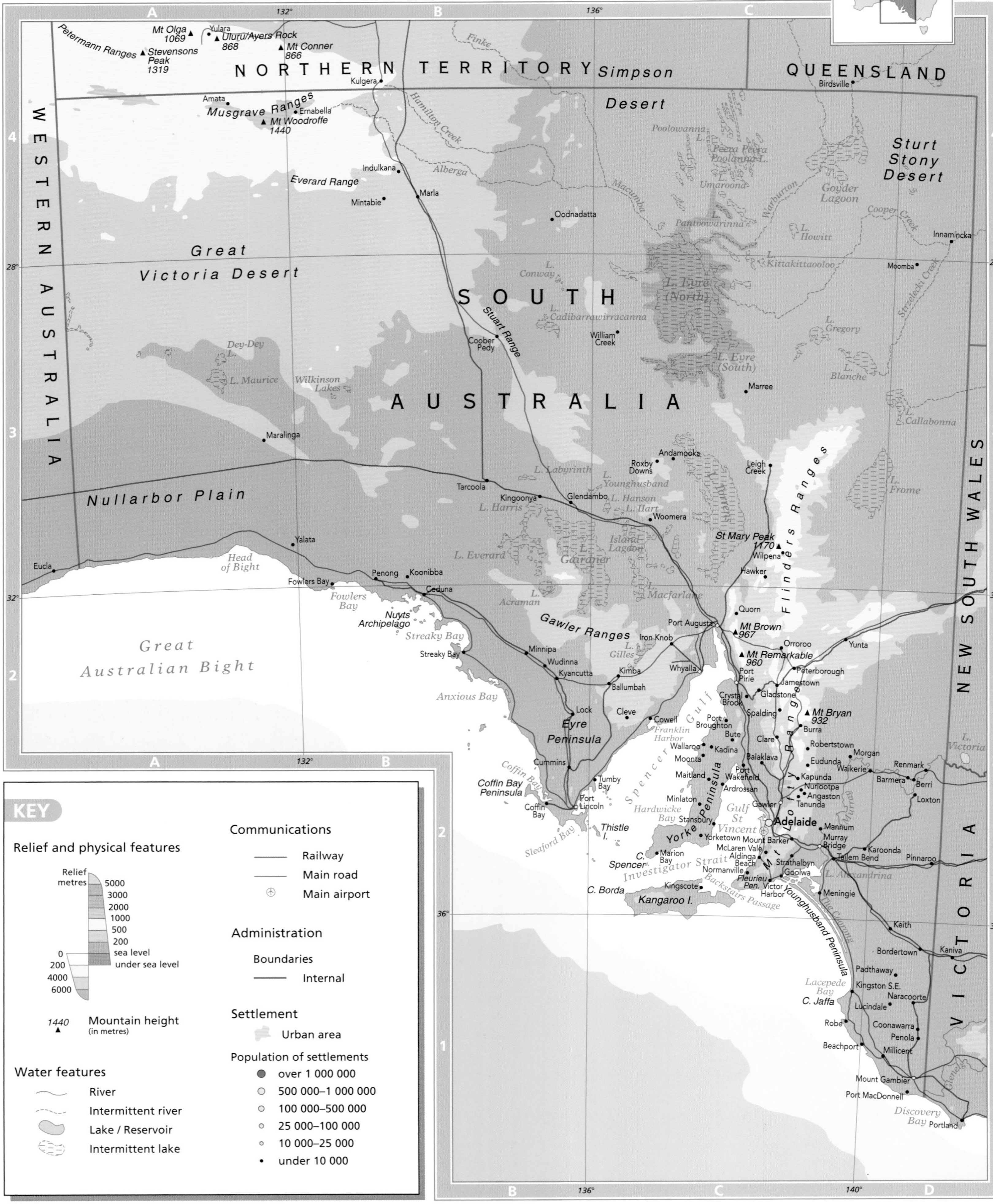

A   132°   B   136°   C

NORTHERN TERRITORY *Simpson* **QUEENSLAND**

Desert

Petermann Ranges
Mt Olga 1069
Yulara
Uluru/Ayers Rock 868
Mt Conner 866
Stevensons Peak 1319
Kulgera
Finke
Birdsville

Amata
Musgrave Ranges
Ernabella
Mt Woodroffe 1440
Hamilton Creek
Poolowanna L.
Peera Peera Poolanna L.

Indulkana
Alberga
Umaroona
Macumba
Cooper Creek

Everard Range
Marla
L.
Oodnadatta
Pantoowarinna
Innamincka

Mintabie
28°

Great
Victoria Desert
L. Conway
L. Cadibarrawirracanna
William Creek
L. Eyre (North)
L. Howitt
Moomba
28°

S O U T H

Stuart Range
Coober Pedy
L. Eyre (South)
L. Gregory

Dey-Dey L.
L. Maurice
Wilkinson Lakes
Marree
L. Blanche

A U S T R A L I A
L. Callabonna

3
Maralinga
L. Labyrinth
Andamooka
Roxby Downs
Leigh Creek
L. Frome
3

Nullarbor Plain
Tarcoola
Kingoonya
Glendambo
L. Younghusband
L. Hanson
L. Hart
Woomera

Yalata
L. Everard
L. Harris
Island Lagoon
Gairdner
St Mary Peak 1170
Wilpena

Head of Bight
Fowlers Bay
Penong
Koonibba
Ceduna
L. Acraman
Gawler Ranges
L. Macfarlane
Hawker

Eucla
Fowlers Bay
Nuyts Archipelago
Streaky Bay
L. Gilles
Quorn
Port Augusta
Mt Brown 967

Great
Australian Bight
Streaky Bay
Minnipa
Wudinna
Iron Knob
Orroroo
Yunta
Mt Remarkable 960

2
Anxious Bay
Kyancutta
Kimba
Whyalla
Port Pirie
Peterborough
2
Ballumbah
Port Jamestown

Lock
Cleve
Cowell
Port Broughton
Crystal Brook
Gladstone
Spalding
Mt Bryan 932
Burra

Eyre Peninsula
Cummins
Bute
Clare
Robertstown
Morgan

Coffin Bay
Tumby Bay
Wallaroo
Kadina
Balaklava
Kapunda
Eudunda
Waikerie
Renmark
Barmera

Coffin Bay Peninsula
Port Lincoln
Maitland
Moonta
Port Wakefield
Nuriootpa
Angaston
Tanunda
Berri
Loxton

Coffin Bay
Minlaton
Ardrossan
Gawler
Yorke Peninsula
Adelaide

Sleaford Bay
Thistle I.
Stansbury
Yorketown
Mount Barker
Mannum

Hardwicke Bay
Gulf St Vincent
Murray Bridge

C. Spencer
Marion Bay
McLaren Vale
Aldinga Beach
Strathalbyn
Karoonda
Pinnaroo

Investigator Strait
Normanville
Fleurieu Pen.
Goolwa
Victor Harbor
L. Alexandrina
Tailem Bend

C. Borda
Kingscote
Backstairs Passage
Meningie

Kangaroo I.
C. Jaffa
Keith

Lacepede Bay
Bordertown
Kaniva

36°
Padthaway
Kingston S.E.
36°

C. Jaffa
Lucindale
Naracoorte

Robe
Coonawarra
Penola

Beachport
Millicent

Mount Gambier

Port MacDonnell

Discovery Bay
Portland

WESTERN AUSTRALIA

NEW SOUTH WALES

VICTORIA

KEY

Relief and physical features

Relief metres
5000
3000
2000
1000
500
200
0 sea level
200 under sea level
4000
6000

1440 ▲ Mountain height (in metres)

Water features

〜 River
‑‑‑ Intermittent river
Lake / Reservoir
Intermittent lake

Communications

—— Railway
—— Main road
⊕ Main airport

Administration

Boundaries
—— Internal

Settlement

Urban area

Population of settlements
● over 1 000 000
◉ 500 000–1 000 000
◯ 100 000–500 000
○ 25 000–100 000
∘ 10 000–25 000
• under 10 000

SCALE 1:6 000 000

0   100   200   300 km

Lambert Azimuthal Equal Area projection

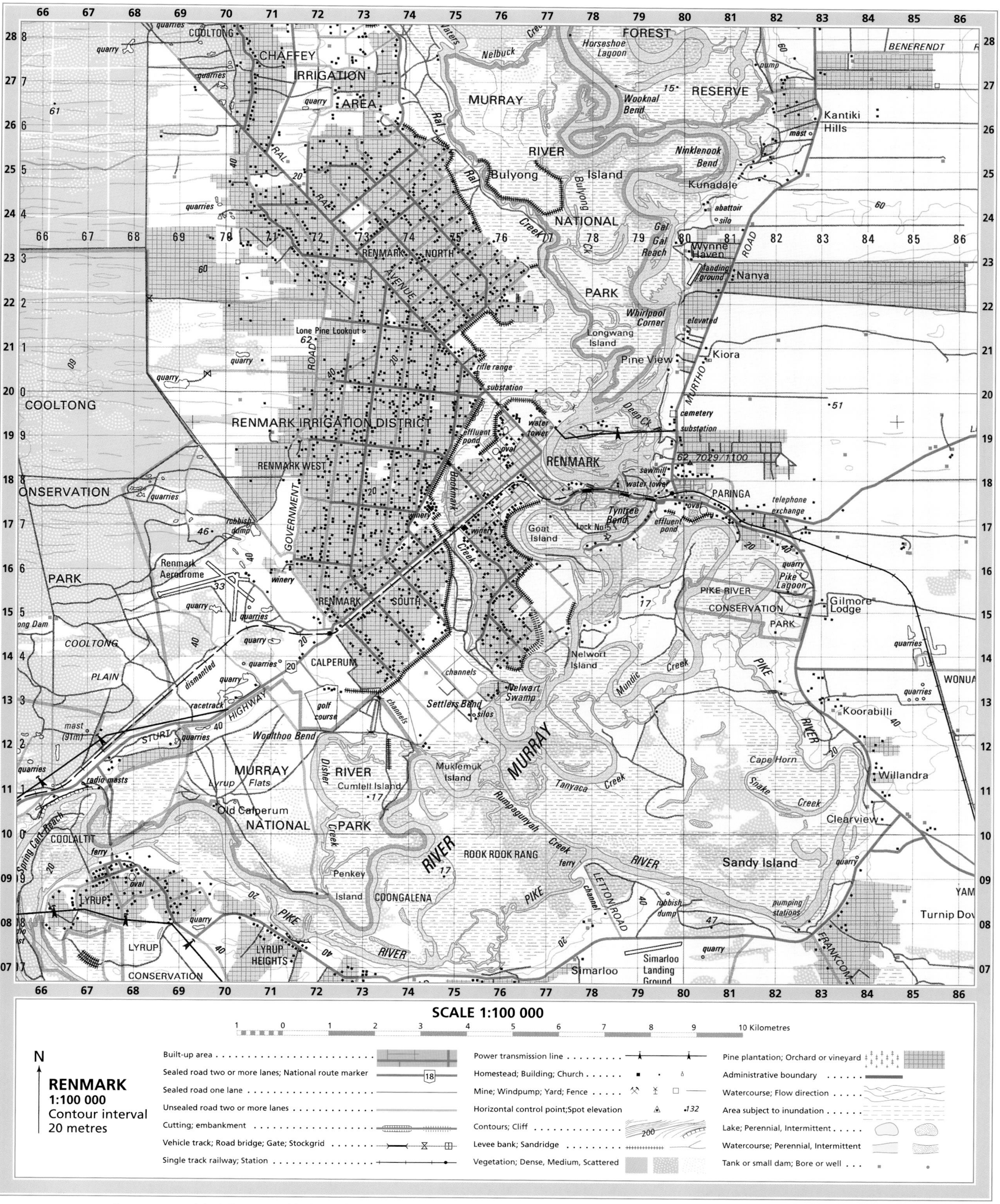

28 8 quarries COOLTONG quarry BENERENDT
CHAFFEY Nelbuck Horseshoe pump
27 7 IRRIGATION quarries Lagoon RESERVE
MURRAY 15 Kantiki
26 6 61 quarry AREA Wooknal FOREST Hills
quarry Bend mast
RAL RIVER Ninklenook
25 5 quarries RAL Bulyong Island Bend Kunadale
RAL Creek NATIONAL abattoir
24 4 66 67 68 69 78 71 72 73 74 75 76 77 78 79 Gal 80 81 82 83 84 85 86
40 60 Gal silo
23 3 60 RENMARK NORTH Reach Wynne landing Nanya
AVENUE PARK Haven ground ROAD
22 2 Whirlpool
Lone Pine Lookout Corner elevated
21 1 62 Longwang ROAD
ROAD Island Pine View Kiora
20 0 COOLTONG quarry 40 rifle range MURTHO 51
substation Dean Ck cemetery substation
19 9 RENMARK IRRIGATION DISTRICT effluent water RENMARK 62 70/29/1100
pond tower oval sawmill
18 8 CONSERVATION quarries RENMARK WEST GOVERNMENT Bookmark 20 winery water tower PARINGA telephone
46 winery Creek Goat Lock No 5 oval exchange
17 7 PARK rubbish 40 winery Island Tyntree effluent
dump Bend pond
16 6 Renmark 40 Goat Island PIKE RIVER Pike quarry
Aerodrome winery Island CONSERVATION Lagoon Gilmore
15 5 ong Dam 33 RENMARK SOUTH 17 PARK Lodge
COOLTONG quarry quarry Nelwort quarries
14 4 PARK 40 quarries 20 Island Mundic WONUA
dismantled 20 CALPERUM channels Creek PIKE Koorabilli
13 3 PLAIN racetrack quarry golf channels Settlers Bend silos RIVER 40 quarries
mast HIGHWAY course Nelwart Swamp Cape Horn
12 2 (91m) quarries STURT 40 Woolthoo Bend Muklemuk MURRAY Snake Willandra
radio masts Disher Island Tanyaca Creek Creek
11 1 quarries RIVER Cumlell Island 17 Clearview
Lyrup Flats RIVER quarry
10 0 ferry Old Calperum MURRAY Sandy Island
COOLALTIT NATIONAL PARK Creek RIVER ferry
09 9 Spring oval 20 Penkey channel LETTON ROAD YAM
Cars Reach Island COONGALENA PIKE 40 rubbish pumping Turnip Dov
08 8 LYRUP quarry ROOK ROOK RANG dump 47 stations
Rumpagumyah Creek
07 7 LYRUP LYRUP PIKE Creek quarry Simarloo
CONSERVATION HEIGHTS 40 RIVER 20 Simarloo Landing

SCALE 1:100 000

1   0   1   2   3   4   5   6   7   8   9   10 Kilometres

N

RENMARK
1:100 000
Contour interval
20 metres

Built-up area . . . .

Sealed road two or more lanes; National route marker

Sealed road one lane . . . .

Unsealed road two or more lanes . . . .

Cutting; embankment . . . .

Vehicle track; Road bridge; Gate; Stockgrid . . . .

Single track railway; Station . . . .

Power transmission line . . . .

Homestead; Building; Church . . . . .

Mine; Windpump; Yard; Fence . . . . .

Horizontal control point; Spot elevation

Contours; Cliff . . . .

Levee bank; Sandridge . . . .

Vegetation; Dense, Medium, Scattered

Pine plantation; Orchard or vineyard

Administrative boundary . . . . . .

Watercourse; Flow direction . . . . .

Area subject to inundation . . . . . .

Lake; Perennial, Intermittent . . . . .

Watercourse; Perennial, Intermittent

Tank or small dam; Bore or well . . .

A B C D E F G H I J K

8 7 6 5 4 3 2 1

0 4 8 12 km

**Approximate scale
1:400 000**

This false colour Landsat TM
image shows approximately
the same area as the land use
map opposite.

A B C D E F G H I J K

1 POPULATION CHANGE

Elizabeth

0 5 10 km

Grange

Rostrevor

City

Glenelg

Stirling

Brighton

Reynella

Christies Beach

Percentage change

	over 15
	5 to 15
	−5 to 5
	−10 to −5
	under −10

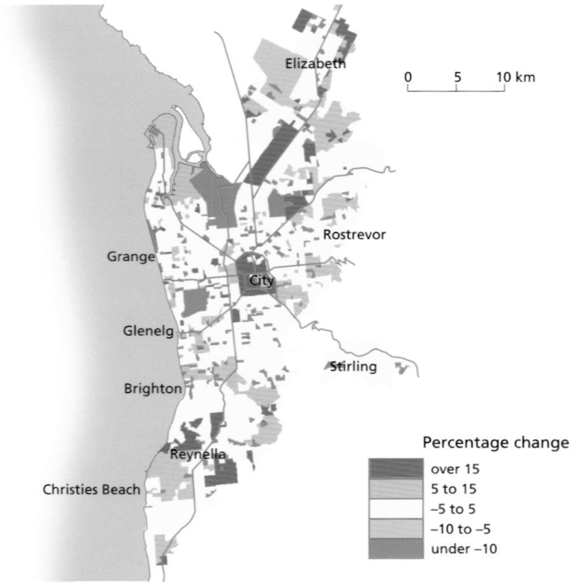

Percentage change in population between the 1996 and 2001 censuses

2 CHILDREN UNDER FIVE

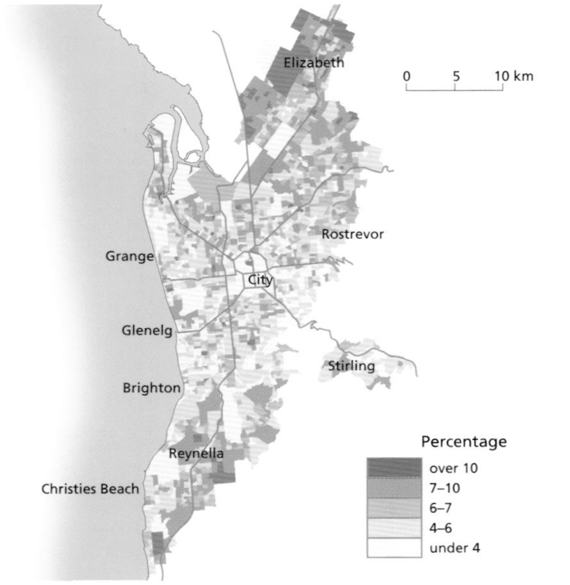

Elizabeth

0 5 10 km

Grange

Rostrevor

City

Glenelg

Stirling

Brighton

Reynella

Christies Beach

Percentage

	over 10
	7–10
	6–7
	4–6
	under 4

Percentage of total population aged under five years, 2001 Census

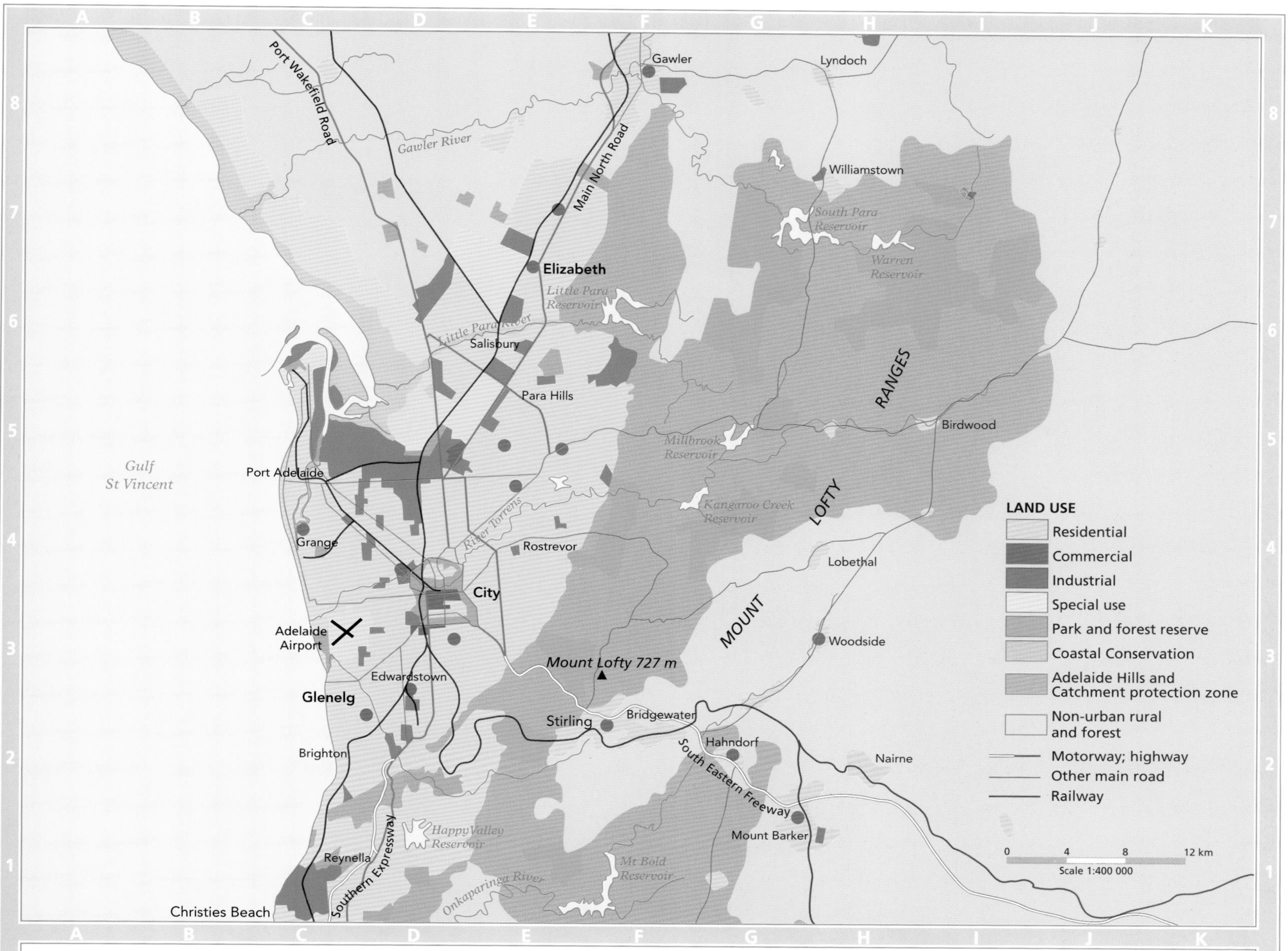

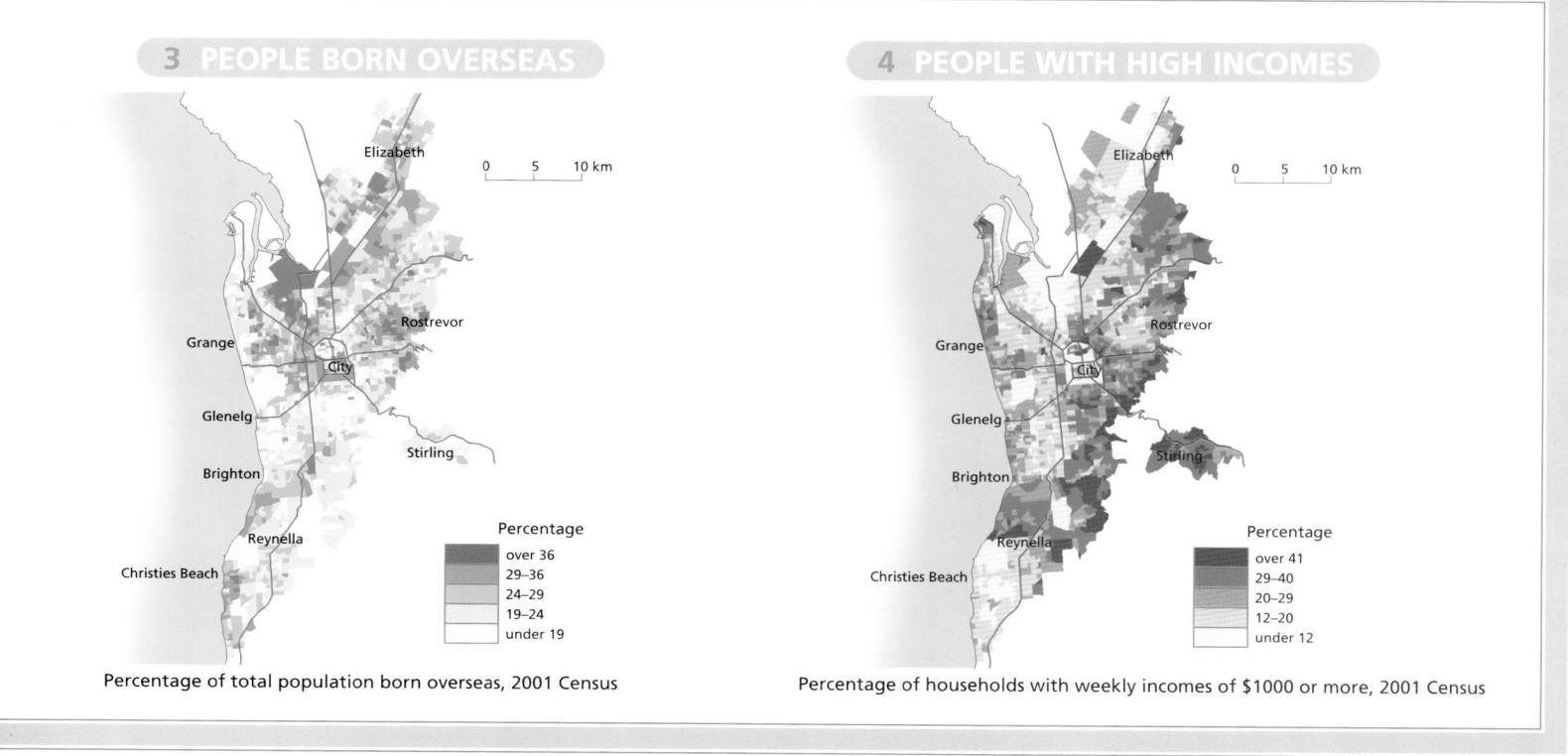

LAND USE

- Residential
- Commercial
- Industrial
- Special use
- Park and forest reserve
- Coastal Conservation
- Adelaide Hills and Catchment protection zone
- Non-urban rural and forest
- Motorway; highway
- Other main road
- Railway

0   4   8   12 km

Scale 1:400 000

3 PEOPLE BORN OVERSEAS

Percentage
- over 36
- 29–36
- 24–29
- 19–24
- under 19

0   5   10 km

Percentage of total population born overseas, 2001 Census

4 PEOPLE WITH HIGH INCOMES

Percentage
- over 41
- 29–40
- 20–29
- 12–20
- under 12

0   5   10 km

Percentage of households with weekly incomes of $1000 or more, 2001 Census

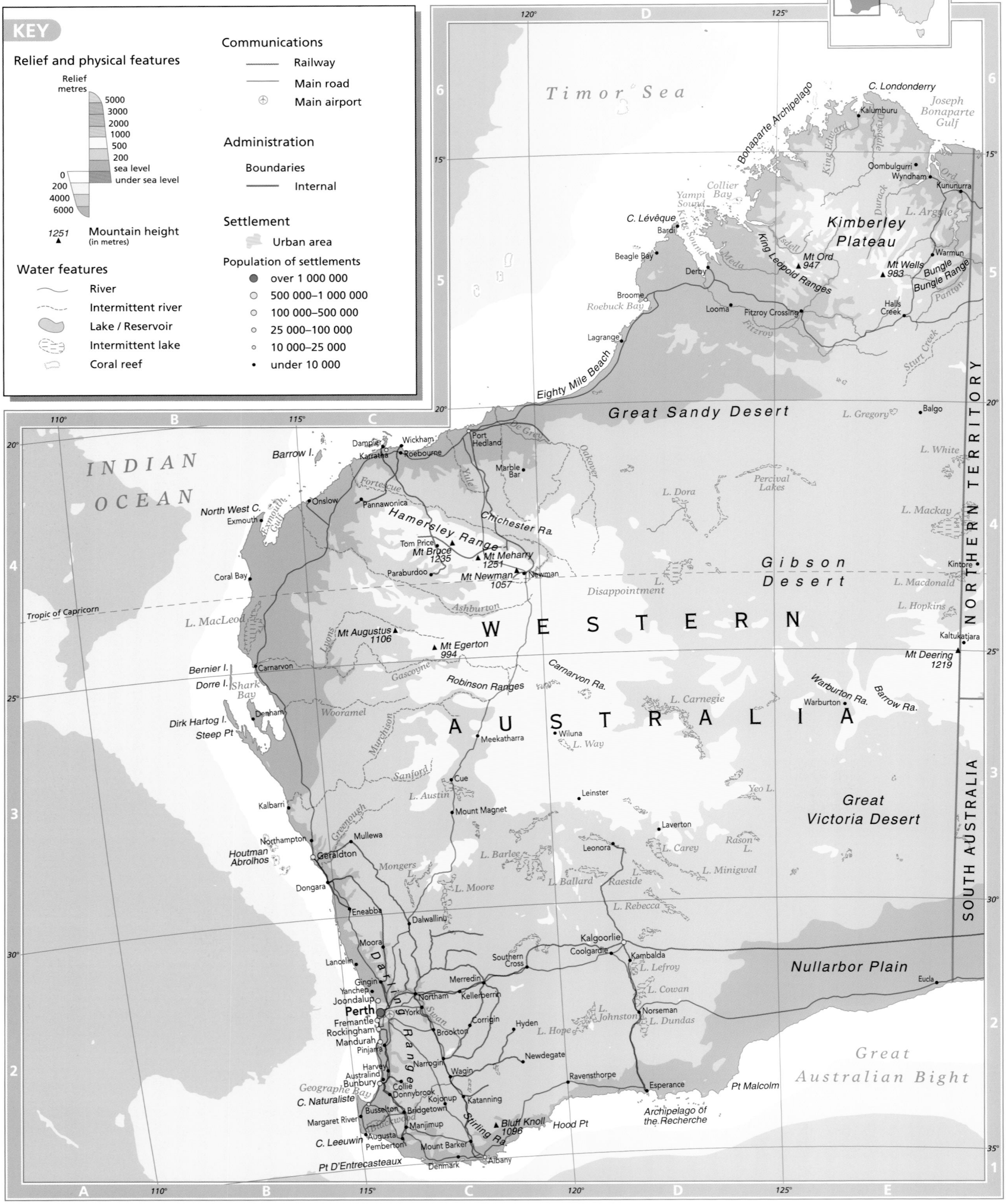

KEY

Relief and physical features

Relief metres

5000
3000
2000
1000
500
200
sea level
0
under sea level
200
4000
6000

▲ 1251 Mountain height (in metres)

Water features

～～～ River

- - - Intermittent river

Lake / Reservoir

Intermittent lake

Coral reef

Communications

——— Railway

——— Main road

⊕ Main airport

Administration

Boundaries

——— Internal

Settlement

Urban area

Population of settlements

● over 1 000 000

◉ 500 000–1 000 000

○ 100 000–500 000

○ 25 000–100 000

○ 10 000–25 000

• under 10 000

Timor Sea

Bonaparte Archipelago
C. Londonderry
Joseph Bonaparte Gulf
Kalumburu
Oombulgurri
Wyndham
Kununurra
Collier Bay
Yampi Sound
C. Lévêque
Bardi
Beagle Bay
Derby
Kimberley Plateau
Mt Ord ▲ 947
King Leopold Ranges
Mt Wells ▲ 983
Bungle Bungle Range
Halls Creek
Broome
Roebuck Bay
Looma
Fitzroy Crossing
Lagrange
Fitzroy
Eighty Mile Beach

Great Sandy Desert
L. Gregory
Balgo

L. White

NORTHERN TERRITORY

INDIAN OCEAN

Barrow I.
Dampier
Wickham
Karratha
Roebourne
Port Hedland
Marble Bar
Fortescue
Yule
Chichester Ra.
North West C.
Onslow
Pannawonica
Exmouth
Hamersley Range
Tom Price
Mt Bruce ▲ 1235
Mt Meharry ▲ 1251
Paraburdoo
Mt Newman ▲ 1057
Newman
Coral Bay
Ashburton
L. Disappointment
Gibson Desert
L. Macdonald
L. Hopkins
Tropic of Capricorn
L. MacLeod
Lyons
Mt Augustus ▲ 1106
Mt Egerton ▲ 994
W E S T E R N
Kintore
Kaltukatjara
Bernier I.
Carnarvon
Gascoyne
Mt Deering ▲ 1219
Dorre I.
Shark Bay
Robinson Ranges
Carnarvon Ra.
Dirk Hartog I.
Denham
Wooramel
L. Carnegie
Warburton
Warburton Ra.
Barrow Ra.
Steep Pt
A U S T R A L I A
Meekatharra
Wiluna
Murchison
L. Way
Kalbarri
Sanford
Cue
Yeo L.
Great Victoria Desert
L. Austin
Mount Magnet
Leinster
Northampton
Mullewa
Leonora
Laverton
Rason L.
Houtman Abrolhos
L. Barlee
L. Carey
L. Minigwal
Geraldton
Mongers
L. Moore
L. Ballard
Raeside
SOUTH AUSTRALIA
Dongara
L. Rebecca
Eneabba
Dalwallinu
Kalgoorlie
Moora
Coolgardie
Kambalda
Southern Cross
L. Lefroy
Nullarbor Plain
Lancelin
Merredin
L. Cowan
Eucla
Gingin
Kellerberrin
Yanchep
Joondalup
Perth
York
Corrigin
Hyden
L. Johnston
Norseman
L. Dundas
Fremantle
Rockingham
Swan
Brookton
Mandurah
L. Hope
Pinjarra
Narrogin
Wagin
Newdegate
Great Australian Bight
Harvey
Australind
Ravensthorpe
Bunbury
Collie
Esperance
Pt Malcolm
Geographe Bay
Donnybrook
Kojonup
C. Naturaliste
Busselton
Bridgetown
Katanning
Archipelago of the Recherche
Margaret River
Manjimup
Bluff Knoll ▲ 1096
Hood Pt
Augusta
C. Leeuwin
Pemberton
Mount Barker
Stirling Ra.
Pt D'Entrecasteaux
Denmark
Albany

Darling Range

Blackwood

Greenough

SCALE 1:10 000 000

0   100   200   300   400 km

Lambert Azimuthal Equal Area projection

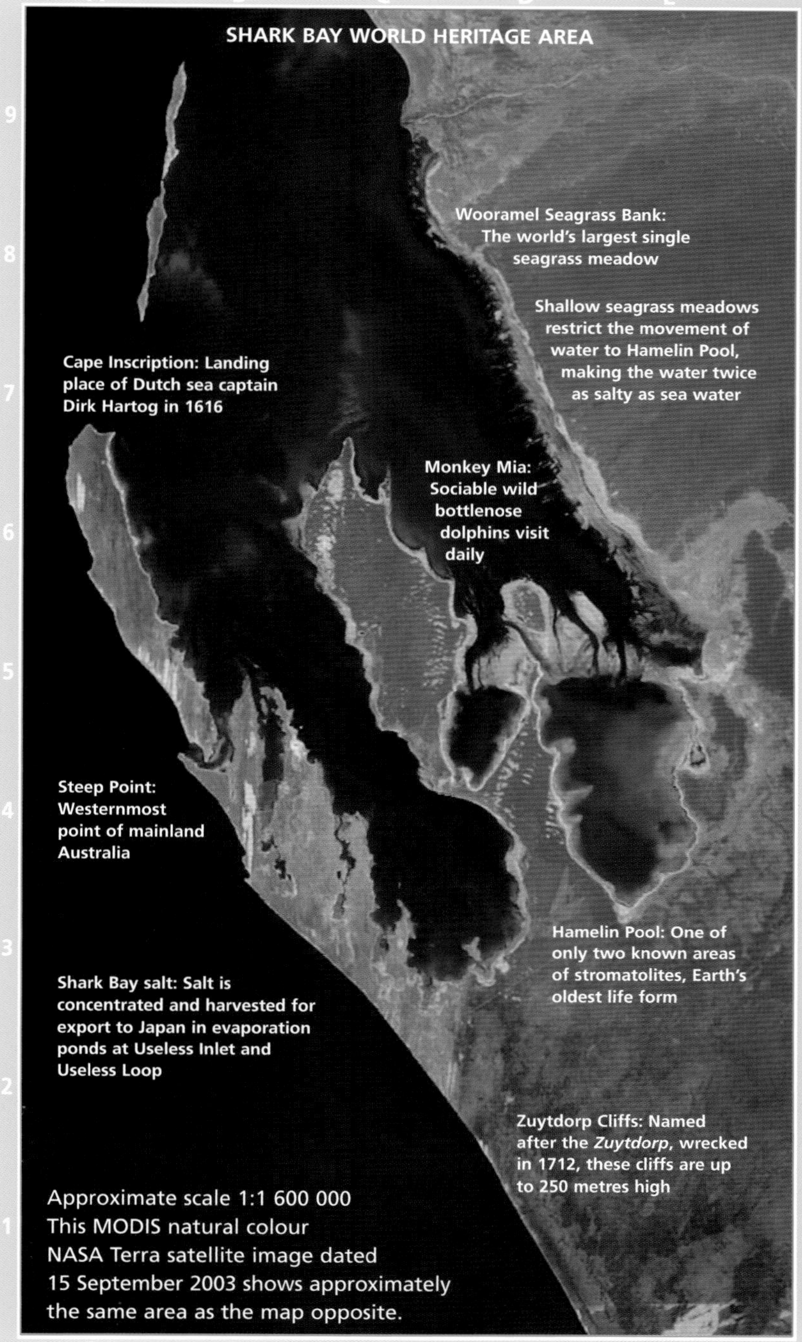

SHARK BAY WORLD HERITAGE AREA

(satellite image)

Wooramel Seagrass Bank: The world's largest single seagrass meadow

Shallow seagrass meadows restrict the movement of water to Hamelin Pool, making the water twice as salty as sea water

Cape Inscription: Landing place of Dutch sea captain Dirk Hartog in 1616

Monkey Mia: Sociable wild bottlenose dolphins visit daily

Steep Point: Westernmost point of mainland Australia

Shark Bay salt: Salt is concentrated and harvested for export to Japan in evaporation ponds at Useless Inlet and Useless Loop

Hamelin Pool: One of only two known areas of stromatolites, Earth's oldest life form

Zuytdorp Cliffs: Named after the *Zuytdorp*, wrecked in 1712, these cliffs are up to 250 metres high

Approximate scale 1:1 600 000
This MODIS natural colour NASA Terra satellite image dated 15 September 2003 shows approximately the same area as the map opposite.

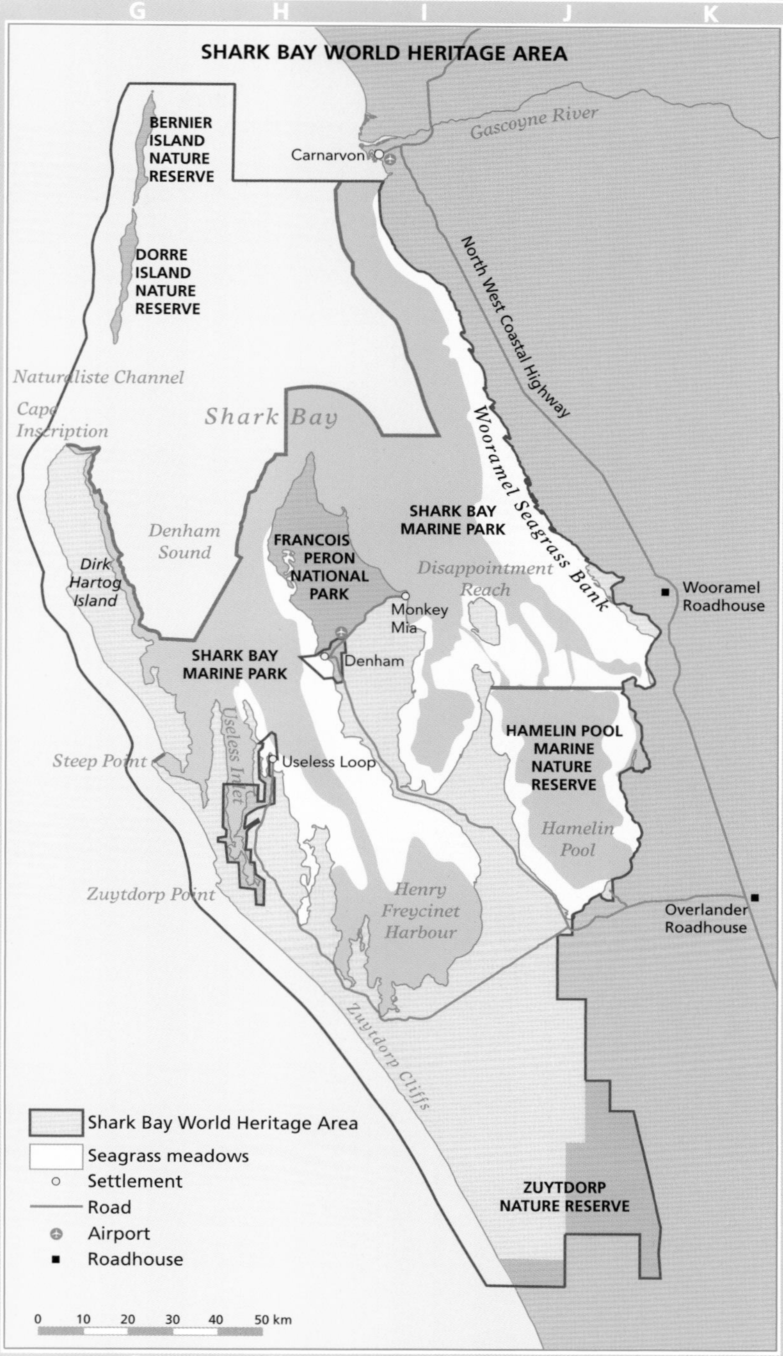

SHARK BAY WORLD HERITAGE AREA

(map)

BERNIER ISLAND NATURE RESERVE

DORRE ISLAND NATURE RESERVE

Gascoyne River

Carnarvon

Naturaliste Channel

Cape Inscription

Shark Bay

North West Coastal Highway

Wooramel Seagrass Bank

Denham Sound

Dirk Hartog Island

FRANCOIS PERON NATIONAL PARK

SHARK BAY MARINE PARK

Disappointment Reach

Wooramel Roadhouse

Monkey Mia

SHARK BAY MARINE PARK

Denham

Useless Inlet

Steep Point

Useless Loop

HAMELIN POOL MARINE NATURE RESERVE

Hamelin Pool

Zuytdorp Point

Henry Freycinet Harbour

Overlander Roadhouse

Zuytdorp Cliffs

ZUYTDORP NATURE RESERVE

Shark Bay World Heritage Area
Seagrass meadows
○ Settlement
— Road
⊕ Airport
■ Roadhouse

0 10 20 30 40 50 km

Shark Bay—800 kilometres north of Perth at Australia's most westerly point—is an arid wilderness where a series of peninsulas and islands jut out into the Indian Ocean, creating Australia's largest coastal bay. Its calm, shallow, warm, clear waters provide unique environments for:
- the world's largest seagrass meadows—covering 4800 square kilometres of the bay—including the 130-kilometre-long Wooramel Seagrass Bank
- stromatolites, prehistoric life forms which survive in the supersaline water of Hamelin Pool
- tropical and temperate marine species including bottlenose dolphins and threatened dugongs and loggerhead turtles.
The surrounding peninsulas, islands and mainland provide valuable habitats for rare and threatened plants, mammals, birds and reptiles.

The region was recognised as a World Heritage Site in 1991, and is one of very few sites to satisfy all four natural selection criteria. The World Heritage Area covers approximately 23 000 sq km—of which 60 per cent is sea, and about half is protected in terrestrial and marine parks and reserves.

The MODIS natural colour NASA Terra satellite image contrasts the red sand and brown shrub/grasslands of the desert with the marine environment. The paler blue-green colour shows shallow water and the extent of the seagrass meadows. These create rich habitats for seaweeds, fish, dugongs, turtles, dolphins and other fauna, and restrict water movement into Hamelin Pool, creating a supersaline environment in which stromatolites thrive.

Aboriginal peoples have occupied the region for over 22 000 years. The first recorded European contact was in 1616 when Dirk Hartog landed at Cape Inscription. Today there is some extensive grazing, and a small area at Useless Inlet and Useless Loop is used to produce salt for export. Increasing numbers of tourists visit Denham and Monkey Mia to enjoy the bottlenose dolphins and marvel at the unique natural scenery.

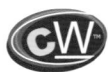

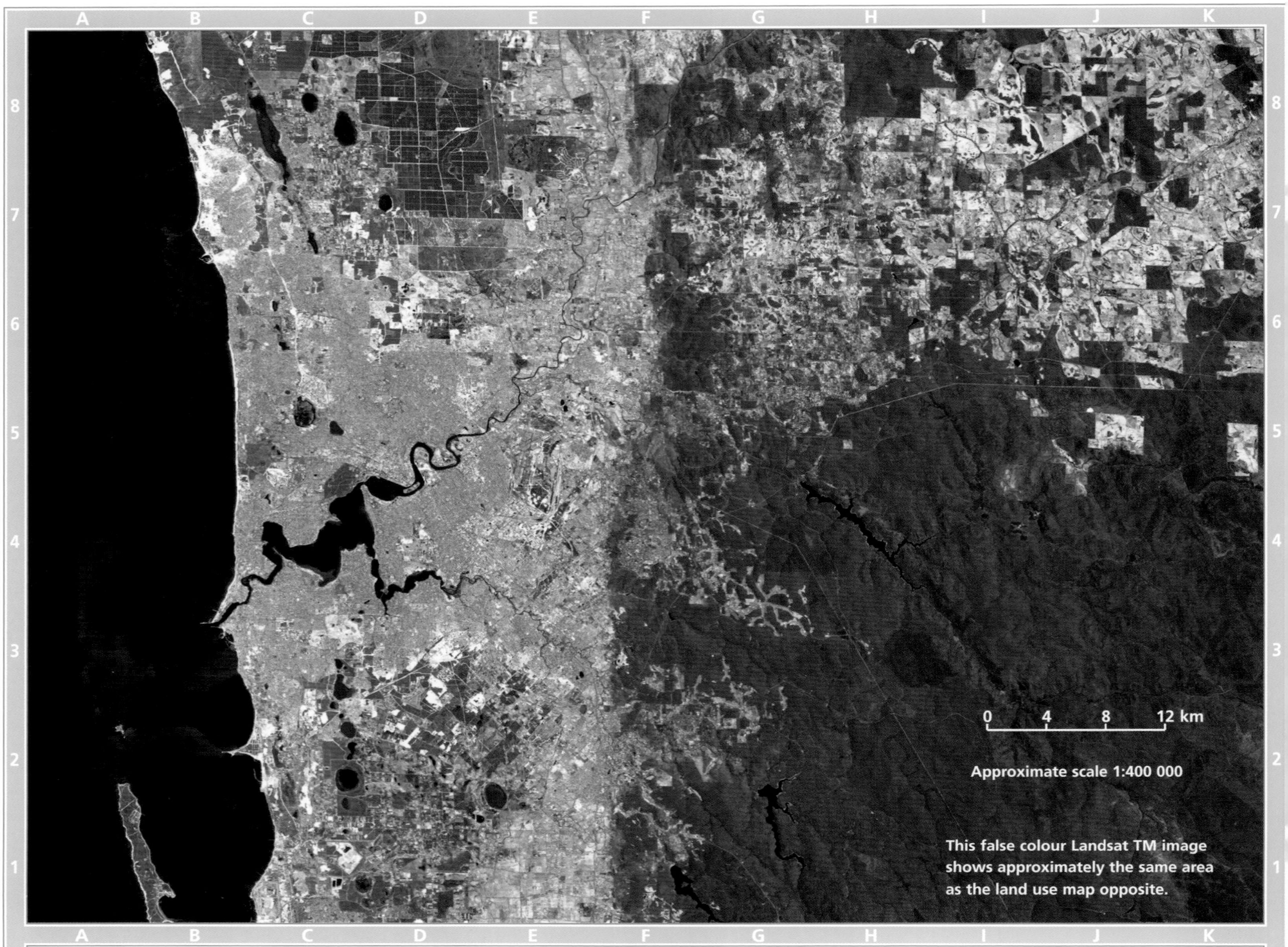

A
B
C
D
E
F
G
H
I
J
K
8
7
6
5
4
3
2
1
0 4 8 12 km
Approximate scale 1:400 000
This false colour Landsat TM image shows approximately the same area as the land use map opposite.

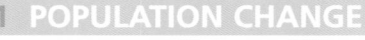

1 POPULATION CHANGE

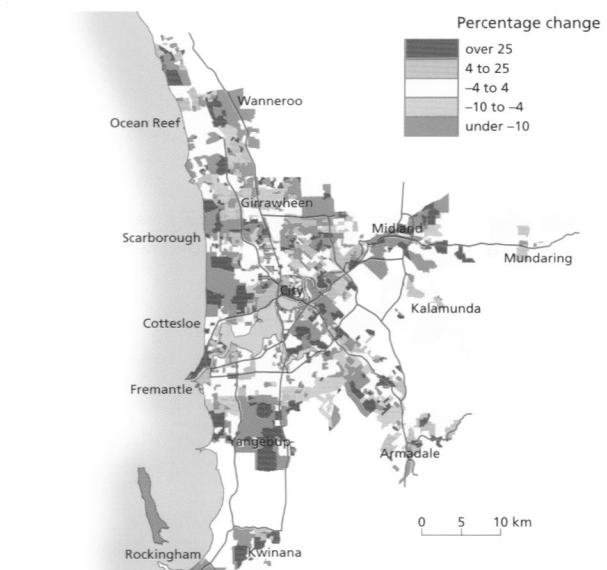

Percentage change
over 25
4 to 25
–4 to 4
–10 to –4
under –10
Wanneroo
Ocean Reef
Girrawheen
Scarborough
Midland
Mundaring
City
Kalamunda
Cottesloe
Fremantle
Yangebup
Armadale
Rockingham
Kwinana
0 5 10 km

Percentage change in population between the 1996 and 2001 censuses

2 CHILDREN UNDER FIVE

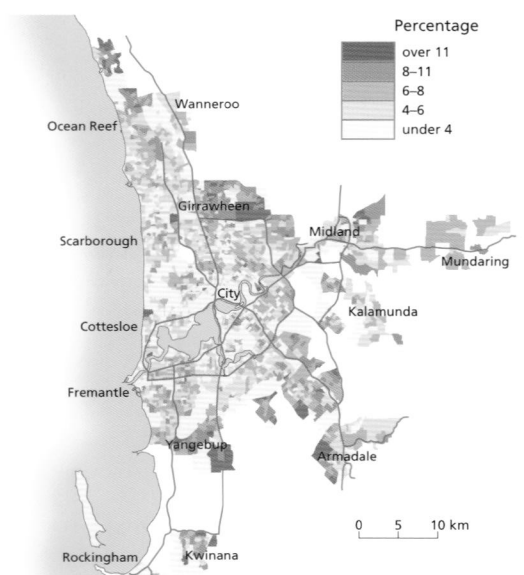

Percentage
over 11
8–11
6–8
4–6
under 4
Wanneroo
Ocean Reef
Girrawheen
Scarborough
Midland
Mundaring
City
Kalamunda
Cottesloe
Fremantle
Yangebup
Armadale
Rockingham
Kwinana
0 5 10 km

Percentage of total population aged under five years, 2001 Census

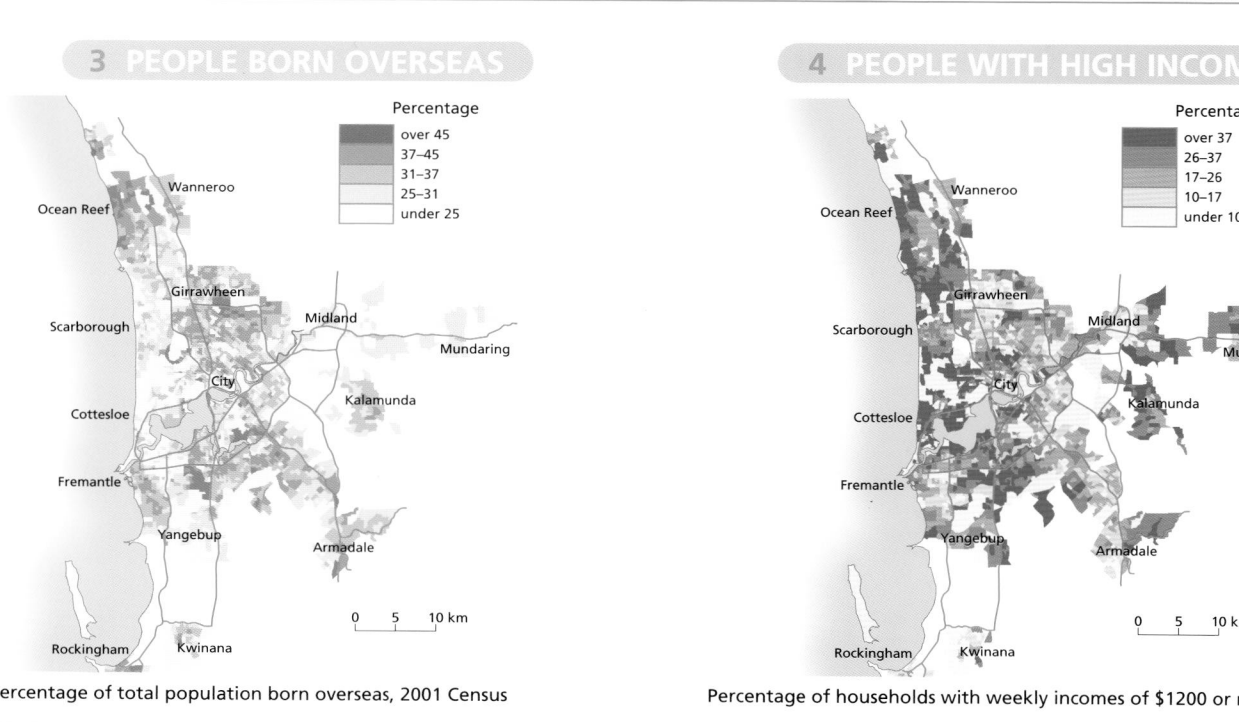

LAND USE

- Residential
- Commercial
- Industrial
- Special use
- Park and forest reserve
- State forest
- Non-urban rural and forest
- Freeway; highway
- Other main road
- Railway

0   4   8   12 km

Scale: 1:400 000

3 PEOPLE BORN OVERSEAS

Percentage
- over 45
- 37–45
- 31–37
- 25–31
- under 25

Percentage of total population born overseas, 2001 Census

4 PEOPLE WITH HIGH INCOMES

Percentage
- over 37
- 26–37
- 17–26
- 10–17
- under 10

Percentage of households with weekly incomes of $1200 or more, 2001 Census

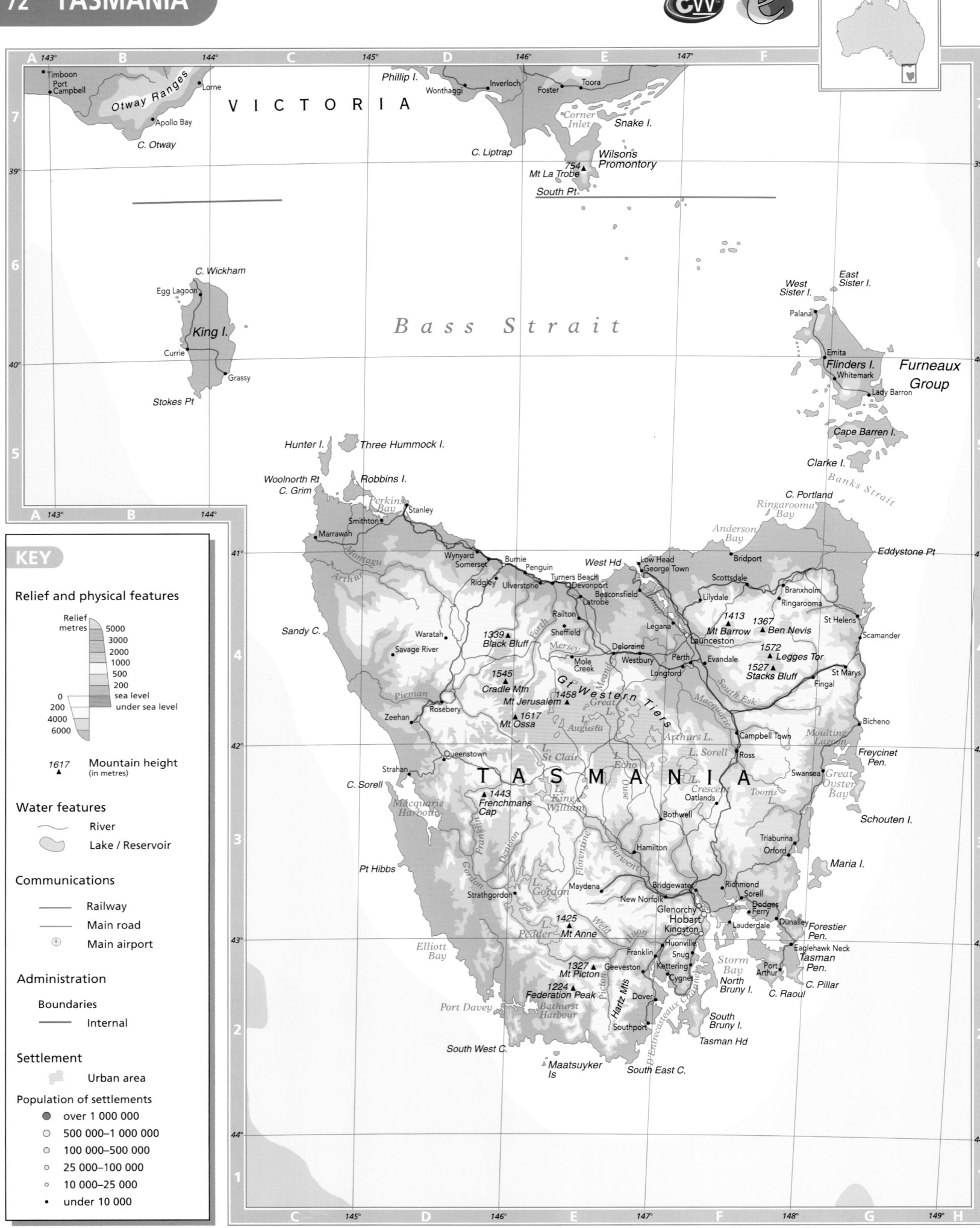

KEY

Relief and physical features

Relief metres	
5000	
3000	
2000	
1000	
500	
200	
0	sea level
200	under sea level
4000	
6000	

1617 ▲ Mountain height (in metres)

Water features

~ River

Lake / Reservoir

Communications

—— Railway

—— Main road

⊕ Main airport

Administration

Boundaries

—— Internal

Settlement

Urban area

Population of settlements

● over 1 000 000
○ 500 000–1 000 000
○ 100 000–500 000
○ 25 000–100 000
○ 10 000–25 000
• under 10 000

SCALE 1:2 500 000

0 20 40 60 80 100 km

Lambert Azimuthal Equal Area projection

This NOAA satellite image uses NDVI (Normalised Difference Vegetation Index) data collected during 1991 and 1992 to give us a long-term, cloud-free view of Tasmania and the estimated percentage cover of trees, tall shrubs, grasses, pastures and crops throughout the year.

The image provides a spectacular impression of the Tasmanian landscape. It clearly shows the very high quality of the wilderness in the west and south-west, reflecting the extent to which this area is remote from and undisturbed by the impacts of post-European settlement. It also vividly shows the extent of land clearing and the intensity of farming in the north and east, including:

(a) **the undulating northern coastal lands**, which have intensive mixed farming of fruit, vegetables, pastures, dairying and fat lambs in the west, and intensive mixed farming of fruit, vegetables and sheep in the east

(b) **the midlands**, with its sheep and cattle grazing which becomes more extensive towards the south

(c) **the south-east**, with its intensive mixed dairying, cattle and lamb fattening, fruit, vegetables and hop-growing in the Derwent and Huon river valleys, and extensive sheep grazing on the hill lands.

This image is an excellent example of the use of satellite computer technology to assist with environmental studies and conservation management. NDVI data collected by satellite was analysed and processed to estimate the percentage of tree and tall shrub cover, and herbaceous cover (i.e. grasses, pastures and crops) in every square kilometre of land. This processing to show the dominant vegetation has resulted in a 'pixel effect' in the image, i.e. the image being fragmented into tiny squares.

The Tasmanian Wilderness World Heritage Area is known for its unique natural and cultural values and its variety of landscape. These include:

(a) Australia's largest glaciated area

(b) spectacular rugged glaciated mountain scenery, treeless plateaus scraped bare by ice, steep gorges, wild rivers and hundreds of lakes

(c) temperate rainforests with Australia's oldest living trees

(d) rare fauna which is extinct or threatened on the mainland

(e) signs of an Aboriginal hunter and gatherer society for at least 30 000 years before European settlement.

The World Heritage Area is made up of five main areas:

1 Cradle Mountain–Lake St Clair National Park

2 Walls of Jerusalem National Park

3 Franklin–Gordon Wild Rivers National Park

4 Southwest National Park

5 Central Plateau Conservation Area.

Estimated grass, pasture and crop cover (%)— only shown where this cover is greater than the tree cover, or where the tree cover is very low

Over 30% cover all year
20–30% cover all year
Over 30% seasonal cover
20–30% seasonal cover
10–20% seasonal cover

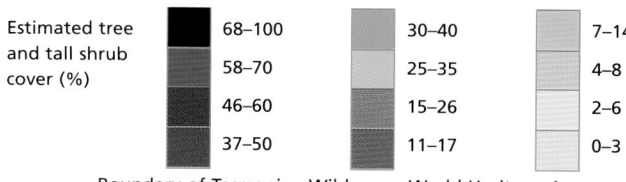

Estimated tree and tall shrub cover (%)

68–100	30–40	7–14
58–70	25–35	4–8
46–60	15–26	2–6
37–50	11–17	0–3

Boundary of Tasmanian Wilderness World Heritage Area

APPROXIMATE SCALE 1:2 500 000

0 20 40 60 80 100 km

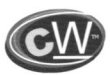

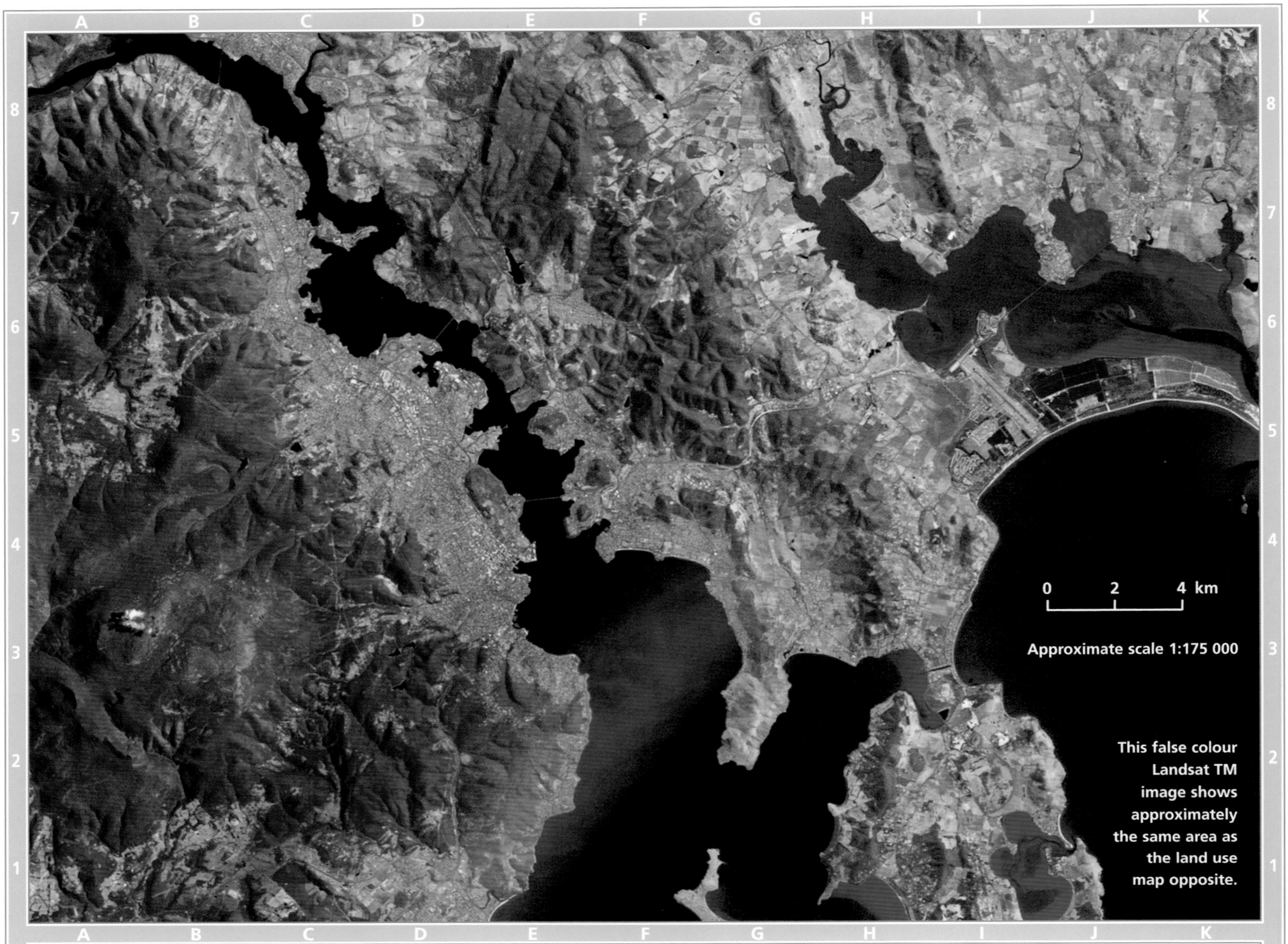
A B C D E F G H I J K
8 7 6 5 4 3 2 1
0 2 4 km
Approximate scale 1:175 000

This false colour Landsat TM image shows approximately the same area as the land use map opposite.

1 POPULATION CHANGE

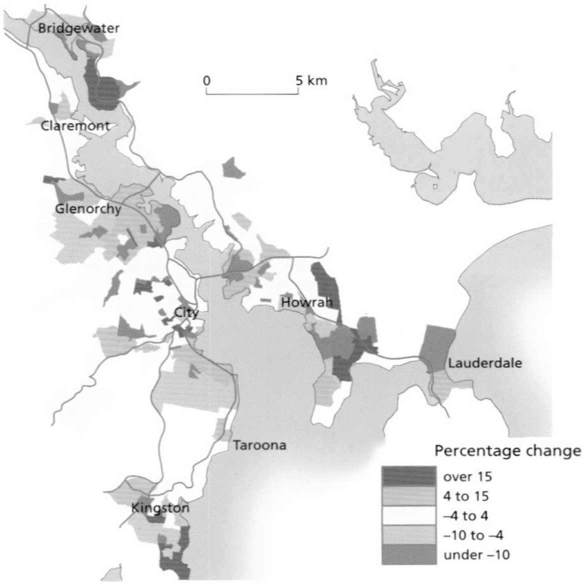
Bridgewater
0 5 km
Claremont
Glenorchy
City
Howrah
Lauderdale
Taroona
Kingston
Percentage change
over 15
4 to 15
–4 to 4
–10 to –4
under –10

Percentage change in population between the 1996 and 2001 censuses

2 CHILDREN UNDER FIVE

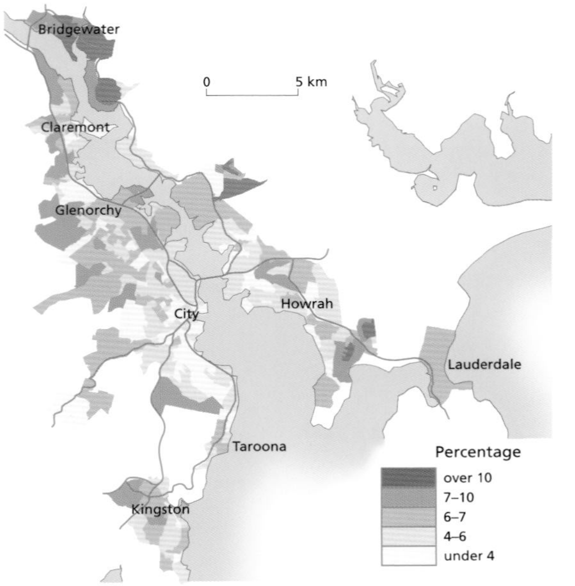
Bridgewater
0 5 km
Claremont
Glenorchy
City
Howrah
Lauderdale
Taroona
Kingston
Percentage
over 10
7–10
6–7
4–6
under 4

Percentage of total population aged under five years, 2001 Census

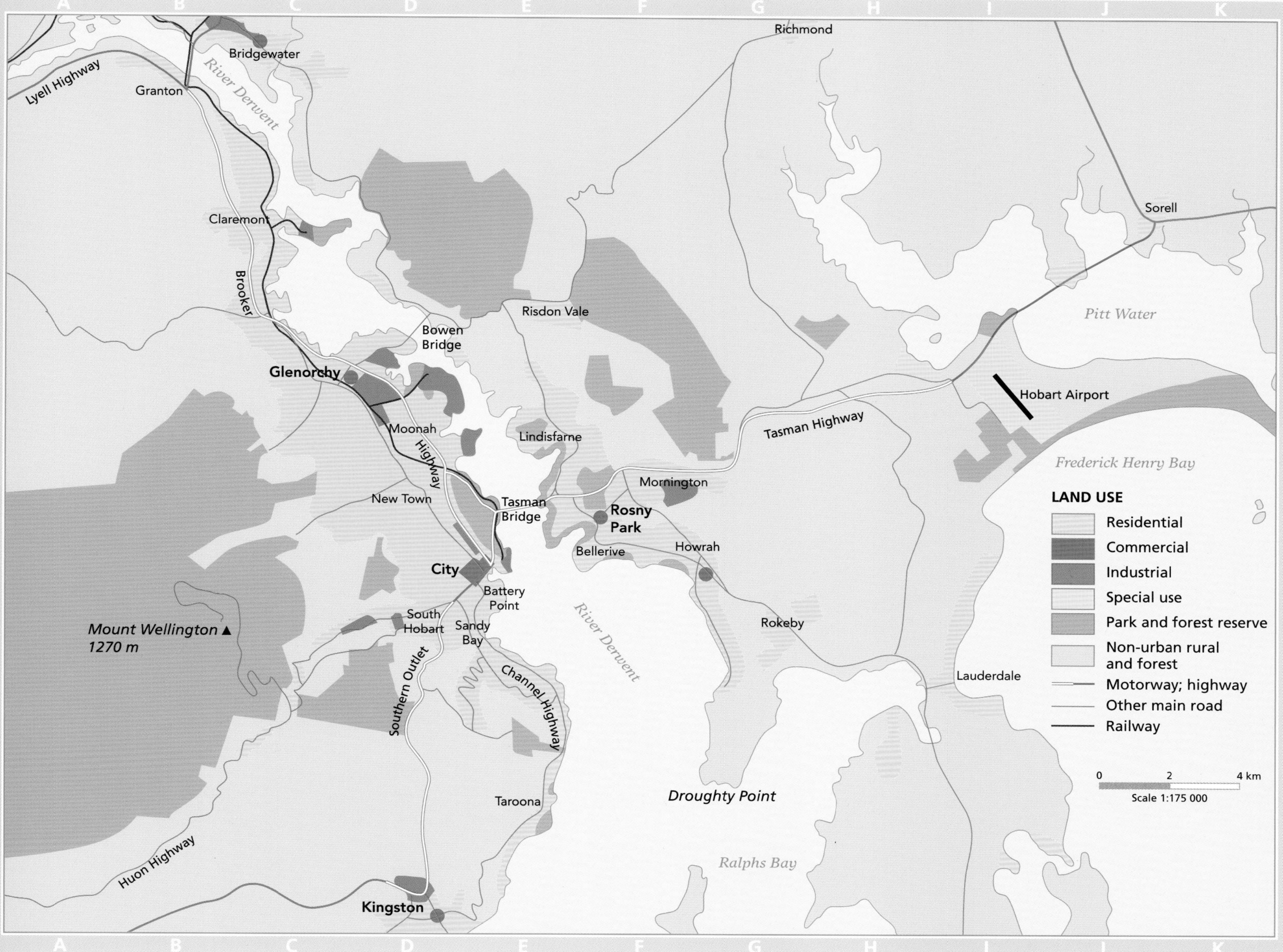

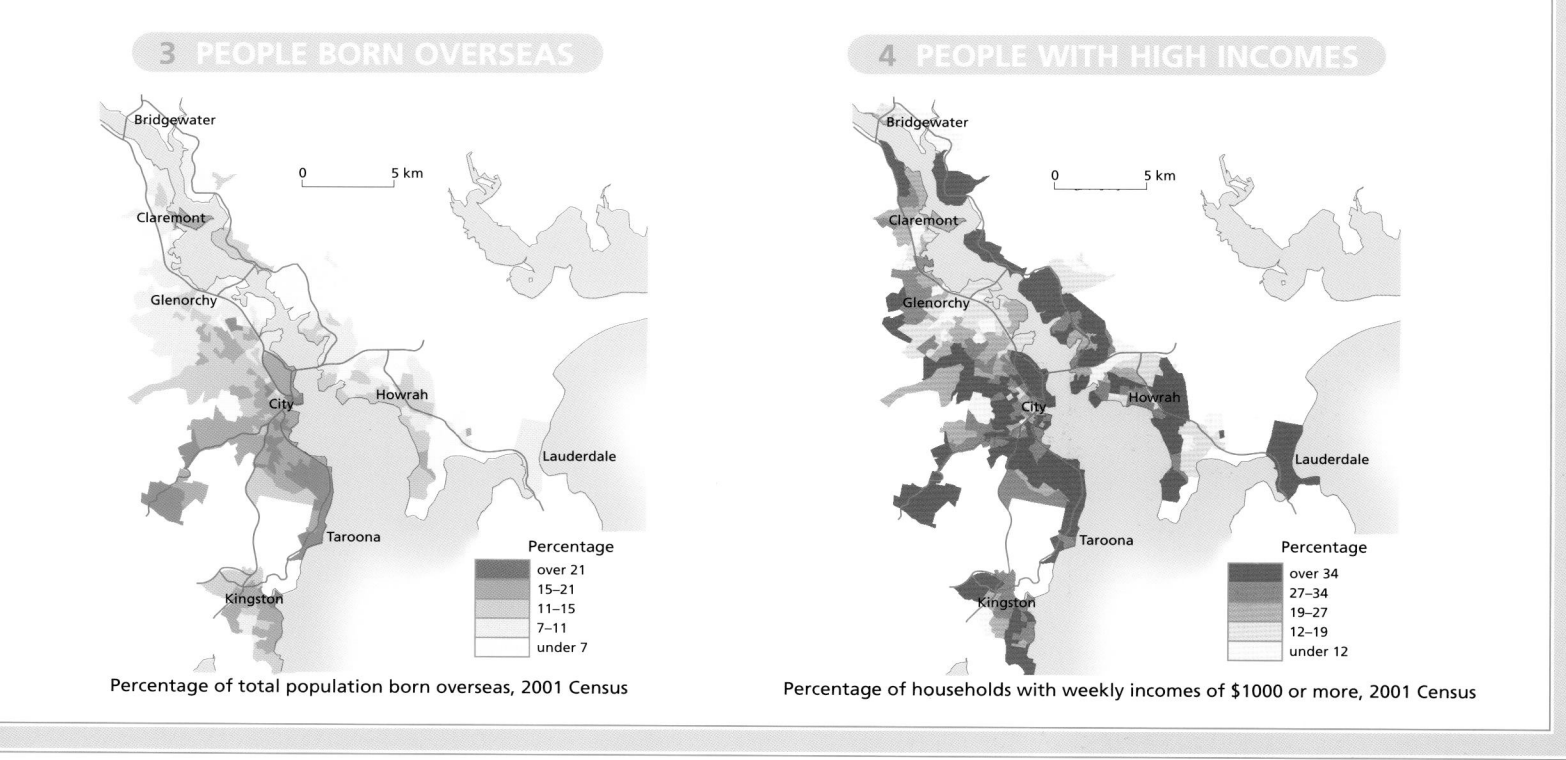

8

7

6

5

4

3

2

1

A B C D E F G H I J K

Richmond

Lyell Highway

Bridgewater

Granton

River Derwent

Claremont

Brooker

Bowen
Bridge

Risdon Vale

Sorell

Pitt Water

Glenorchy

Hobart Airport

Moonah

Highway

Lindisfarne

Tasman Highway

New Town

Tasman
Bridge

Mornington

Rosny
Park

Frederick Henry Bay

City

Battery
Point

Bellerive

Howrah

South
Hobart

Sandy
Bay

River Derwent

Rokeby

Mount Wellington ▲
1270 m

Lauderdale

Southern Outlet

Channel Highway

Droughty Point

Taroona

Huon Highway

Ralphs Bay

Kingston

LAND USE

Residential
Commercial
Industrial
Special use
Park and forest reserve
Non-urban rural
and forest
Motorway; highway
Other main road
Railway

0   2   4 km

Scale 1:175 000

3 PEOPLE BORN OVERSEAS

Bridgewater

Claremont

Glenorchy

City   Howrah

Lauderdale

Taroona

Kingston

0   5 km

Percentage

over 21
15–21
11–15
7–11
under 7

Percentage of total population born overseas, 2001 Census

4 PEOPLE WITH HIGH INCOMES

Bridgewater

Claremont

Glenorchy

City   Howrah

Lauderdale

Taroona

Kingston

0   5 km

Percentage

over 34
27–34
19–27
12–19
under 12

Percentage of households with weekly incomes of $1000 or more, 2001 Census

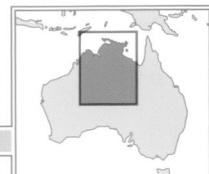

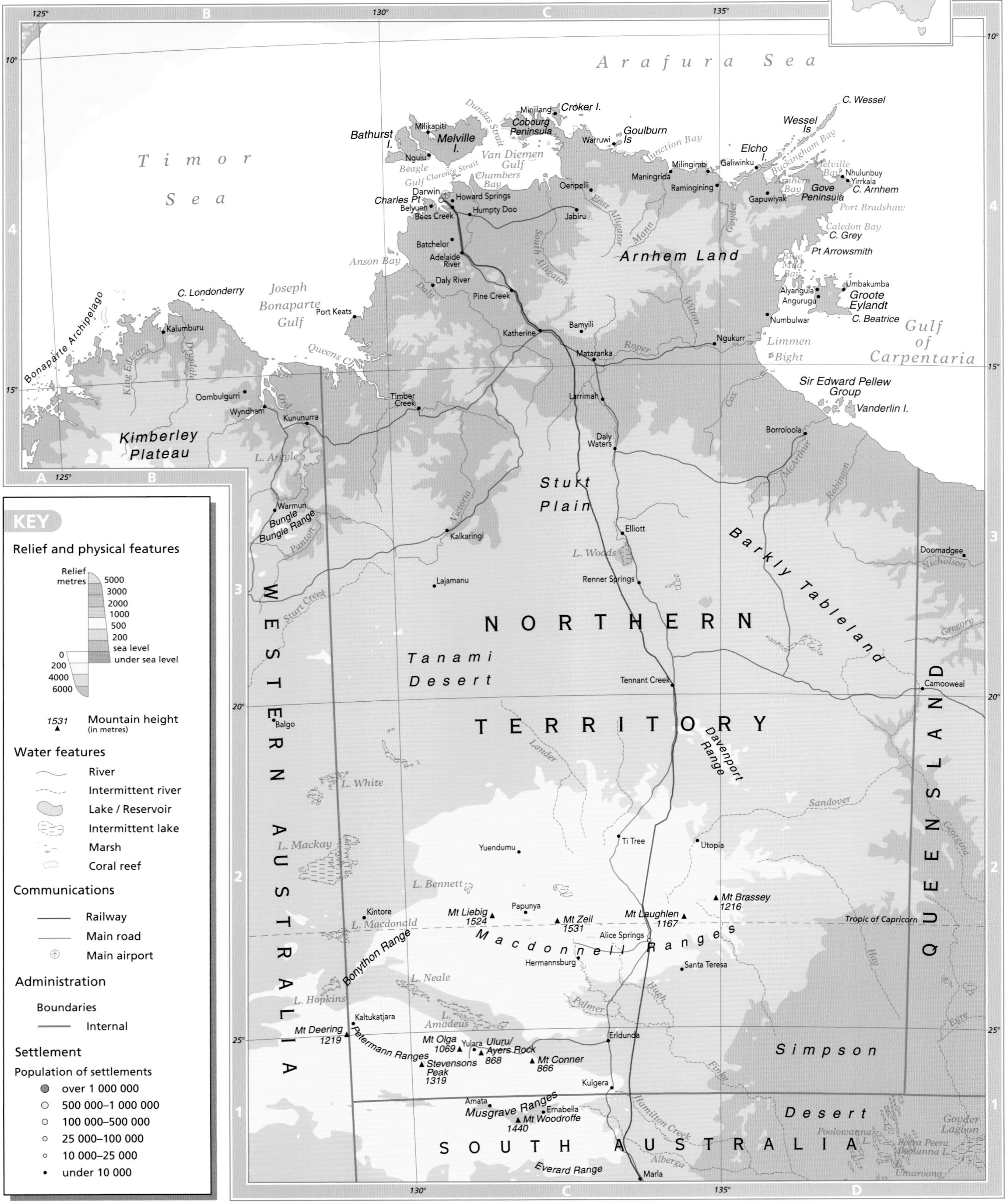

Arafura Sea
Timor Sea
Gulf of Carpentaria
NORTHERN TERRITORY
WESTERN AUSTRALIA
SOUTH AUSTRALIA
QUEENSLAND
Arnhem Land
Sturt Plain
Barkly Tableland
Tanami Desert
Simpson Desert
Kimberley Plateau
Macdonnell Ranges
Davenport Range
Bonython Range
Petermann Ranges
Musgrave Ranges
Everard Range
Bungle Bungle Range
Bonaparte Archipelago
Joseph Bonaparte Gulf
Van Diemen Gulf
Beagle Gulf
Chambers Bay
Anson Bay
Queens Ch.
Dundas Strait
Clarence Strait
Junction Bay
Buckingham Bay
Melville Bay
Arnhem Bay
Port Bradshaw
Caledon Bay
Blue Mud Bay
Limmen Bight
Bathurst I.
Melville I.
Croker I.
Cobourg Peninsula
Goulburn Is
Elcho I.
Wessel Is
C. Wessel
Gove Peninsula
C. Arnhem
C. Grey
Pt Arrowsmith
Groote Eylandt
C. Beatrice
Sir Edward Pellew Group
Vanderlin I.
C. Londonderry
Charles Pt
Darwin
Howard Springs
Humpty Doo
Belyuen
Bees Creek
Batchelor
Adelaide River
Daly River
Pine Creek
Jabiru
Oenpelli
Minjilang
Milikapiti
Nguiu
Warruwi
Maningrida
Milingimbi
Galiwinku
Ramingining
Gapuwiyak
Nhulunbuy
Yirrkala
Umbakumba
Alyangula
Angurugu
Numbulwar
Ngukurr
Bamyili
Katherine
Mataranka
Larrimah
Daly Waters
Borroloola
Port Keats
Kalumburu
Oombulgurri
Wyndham
Kununurra
Timber Creek
Warmun
Kalkaringi
Lajamanu
Elliott
Renner Springs
Tennant Creek
Doomadgee
Camooweal
Balgo
Ti Tree
Utopia
Yuendumu
Papunya
Kintore
Alice Springs
Hermannsburg
Santa Teresa
Kaltukatjara
Yulara
Erldunda
Kulgera
Amata
Ernabella
Marla
Mt Liebig 1524
Mt Zeil 1531
Mt Laughlen 1167
Mt Brassey 1216
Mt Deering 1219
Mt Olga 1069
Uluru/ Ayers Rock 868
Stevensons Peak 1319
Mt Conner 866
Mt Woodroffe 1440
Tropic of Capricorn
King Edward
Drysdale
Ord
L. Argyle
Panton
Victoria
Sturt Creek
Daly
South Alligator
East Alligator
Mann
Goyder
Wilton
Roper
Cox
McArthur
Robinson
Nicholson
Gregory
L. Woods
Lander
L. White
L. Mackay
L. Bennett
L. Macdonald
L. Neale
L. Hopkins
L. Amadeus
Palmer
Hugh
Finke
Sandover
Georgina
Hay
Eyre
Hamilton Creek
Alberga
Poolowanna L.
Peera Peera Poolanna L.
Goyder Lagoon
Umaroona
125°
130°
135°
10°
15°
20°
25°
A
B
C
D
1
2
3
4
KEY
Relief and physical features
Relief metres
5000
3000
2000
1000
500
200
sea level
under sea level
0
200
4000
6000
1531 Mountain height (in metres)
Water features
River
Intermittent river
Lake / Reservoir
Intermittent lake
Marsh
Coral reef
Communications
Railway
Main road
Main airport
Administration
Boundaries
Internal
Settlement
Population of settlements
over 1 000 000
500 000–1 000 000
100 000–500 000
25 000–100 000
10 000–25 000
under 10 000

SCALE 1:7 500 000

0 100 200 300 400 km

Lambert Azimuthal Equal Area projection

1 THE RED CENTRE

Central Australia is often called the 'Red Centre' because, with little vegetation cover in this vast desert area, the bright orange-red of the rocks, sand and soil is the dominant colour. As a result, the MacDonnell Ranges appear as a rugged, bare, orange-red chain of mountains and the surrounding area appears as a red sea of low hills and sand dunes.

The satellite image on the right is a Landsat 7 ETM false colour image of Uluṟu/Ayers Rock. Uluṟu is an excellent example of a monolith, that is, one single solid block of rock, much of which is below ground level. It is approximately 2.5 kilometres long, 1.5 kilometres wide, 9.4 kilometres around its base, and covers 3.33 square kilometres. It is made of orange-red arkose sandstone rock, and rises 348 metres above the surrounding desert.

Uluṟu is part of Uluṟu–Kata Tjuṯa National Park. The park covers an area of 132 556 hectares and is one of Australia's most important World Heritage Areas. It was recognised for its outstanding natural qualities in 1987 and for its outstanding cultural values in 1994.

The park also contains Kata Tjuṯa/The Olgas, a group of 36 very large, steep-sided rounded rock domes about 32 kilometres to the west of Uluṟu. The highest dome in the group is Mt Olga, which rises 546 metres above the desert.

Uluṟu was named 'Ayers Rock' by a European explorer in 1873. Its Aboriginal name, Uluṟu, was first recognised in 1977. In 1985 the Australian government returned Uluṟu to Anangu (Western Desert Aboriginals) with traditional ties to the area, who manage the park jointly with the government.

2 ULURU SATELLITE IMAGE

Landsat 7 ETM false colour satellite image, 16 October 1999

0   1 km

Approximate scale 1:50 000

3 MAJOR TOURIST ATTRACTIONS

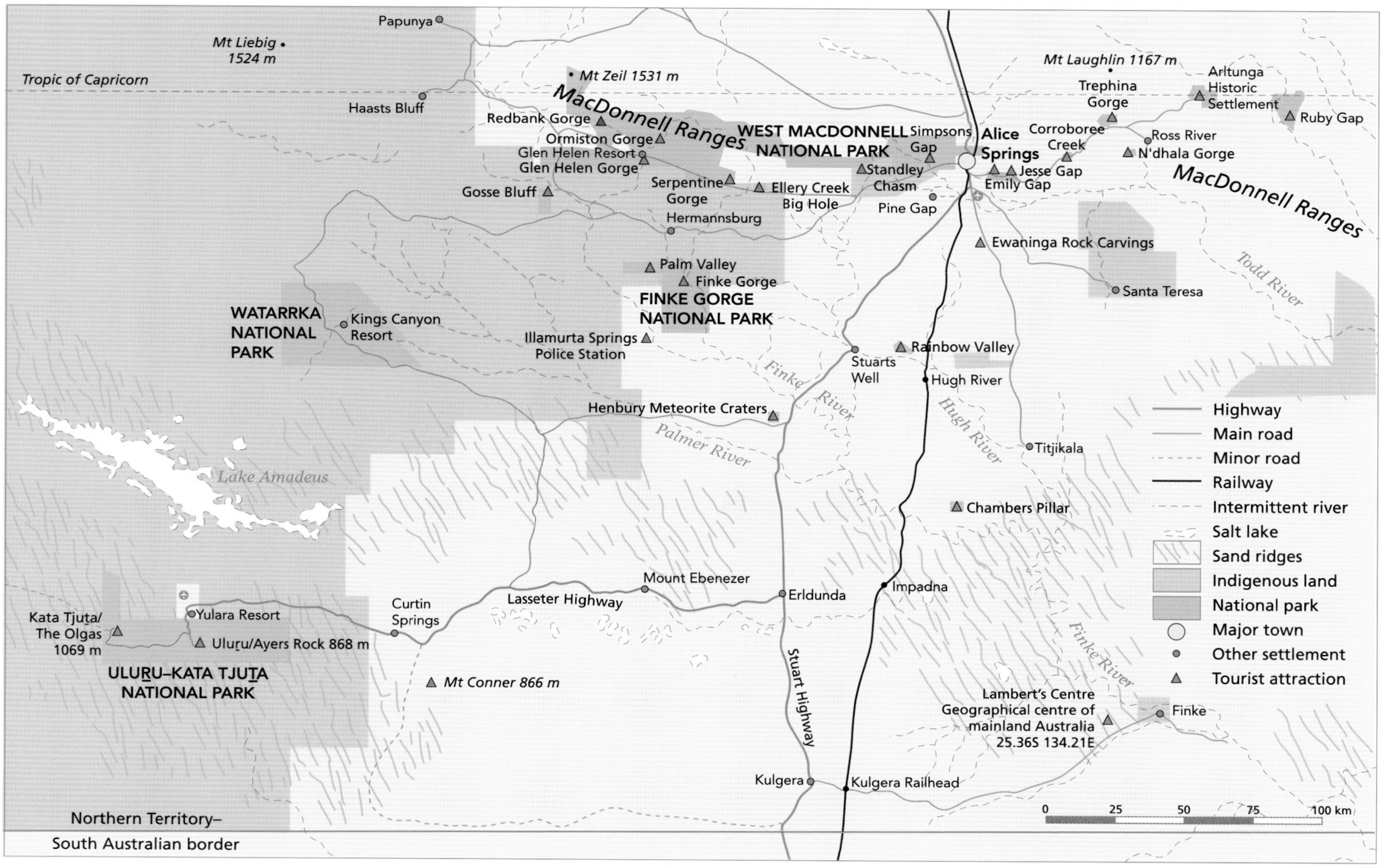

Papunya

Mt Liebig 1524 m

Tropic of Capricorn

Mt Zeil 1531 m

Mt Laughlin 1167 m

Arltunga Historic Settlement

Trephina Gorge

Ruby Gap

Haasts Bluff

MacDonnell Ranges

Redbank Gorge

WEST MACDONNELL NATIONAL PARK

Simpsons Gap

Alice Springs

Corroboree Creek

Ross River

N'dhala Gorge

Ormiston Gorge

Glen Helen Resort

Glen Helen Gorge

Standley Chasm

Jesse Gap

Emily Gap

MacDonnell Ranges

Gosse Bluff

Serpentine Gorge

Ellery Creek Big Hole

Pine Gap

Hermannsburg

Ewaninga Rock Carvings

Todd River

Palm Valley

Finke Gorge

FINKE GORGE NATIONAL PARK

Santa Teresa

WATARRKA NATIONAL PARK

Kings Canyon Resort

Illamurta Springs Police Station

Rainbow Valley

Stuarts Well

Hugh River

Finke River

Henbury Meteorite Craters

Palmer River

Hugh River

Titjikala

Lake Amadeus

Chambers Pillar

Kata Tjuṯa/ The Olgas 1069 m

Yulara Resort

Uluṟu/Ayers Rock 868 m

Curtin Springs

Lasseter Highway

Mount Ebenezer

Erldunda

Impadna

Stuart Highway

Finke River

Mt Conner 866 m

ULURU–KATA TJUṮA NATIONAL PARK

Lambert's Centre Geographical centre of mainland Australia 25.36S 134.21E

Finke

Kulgera

Kulgera Railhead

Northern Territory– South Australian border

——	Highway
——	Main road
- - -	Minor road
——	Railway
- - -	Intermittent river
	Salt lake
	Sand ridges
	Indigenous land
	National park
○	Major town
•	Other settlement
△	Tourist attraction

0   25   50   75   100 km

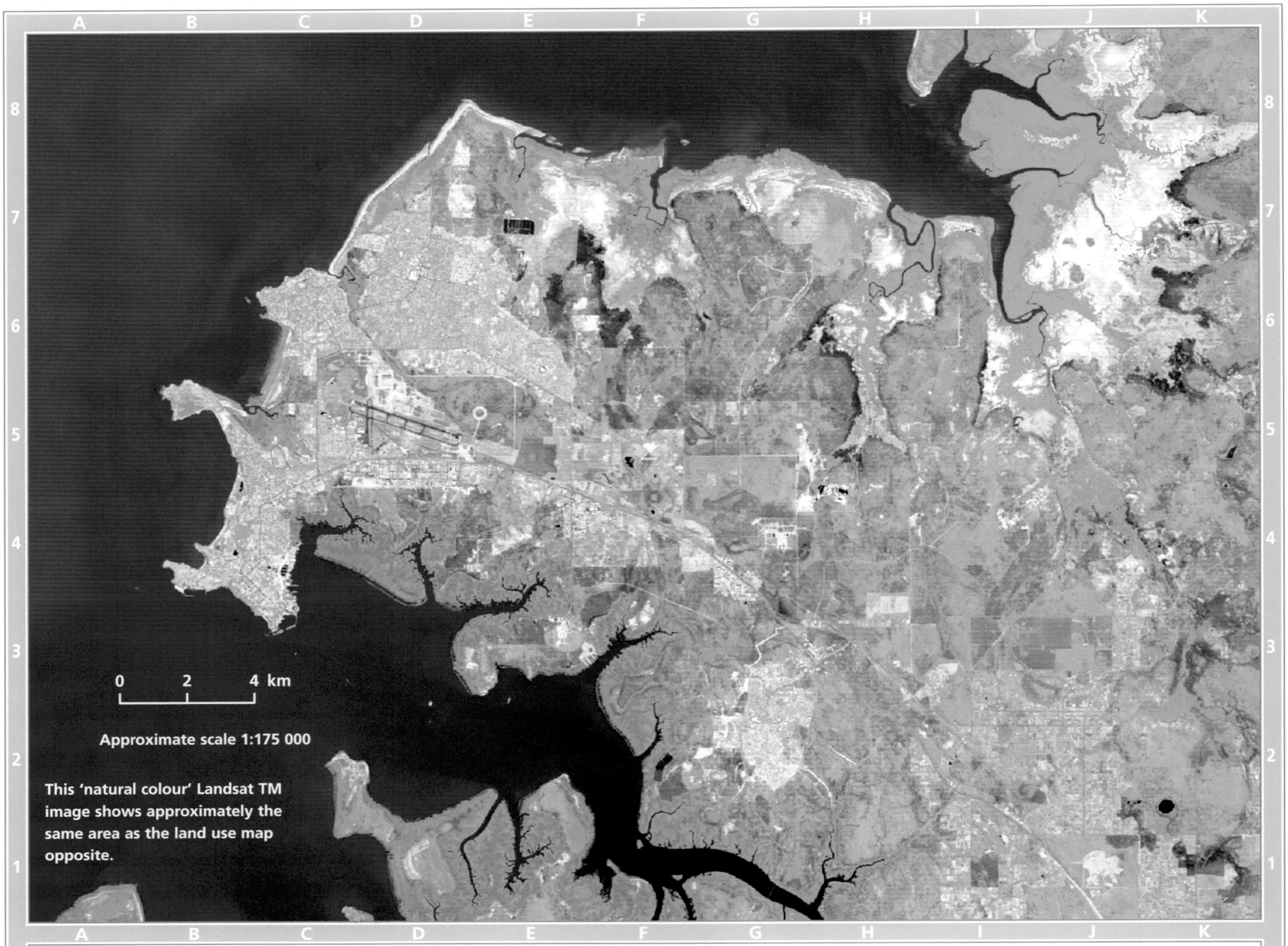

Approximate scale 1:175 000

This 'natural colour' Landsat TM image shows approximately the same area as the land use map opposite.

0   2   4 km

1 POPULATION CHANGE

Casuarina

Nightcliff

Sanderson

Fannie Bay

Winnellie

City

Palmerston

Percentage change
- over 30
- 3 to 30
- −3 to 3
- −8 to −3
- under −8

0   5   10 km

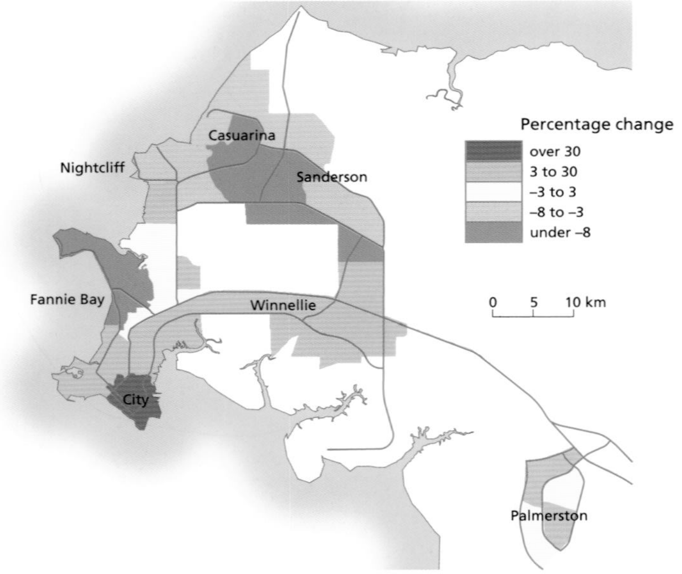

Percentage change in population between the 1996 and 2001 censuses

2 CHILDREN UNDER FIVE

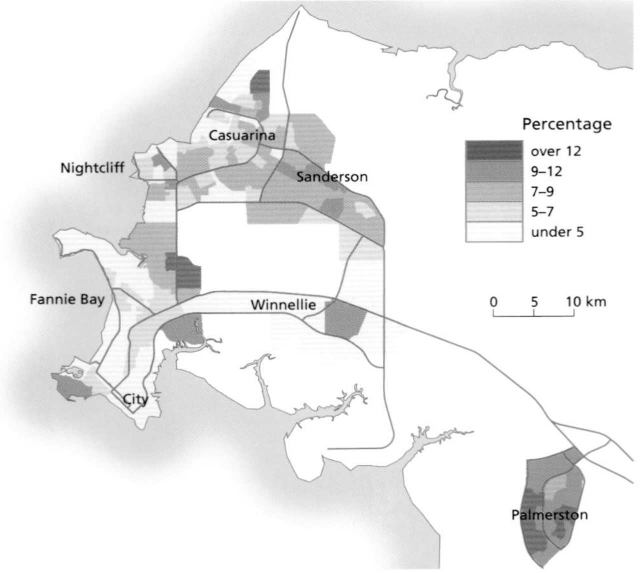

Casuarina

Nightcliff

Sanderson

Fannie Bay

Winnellie

City

Palmerston

Percentage
- over 12
- 9–12
- 7–9
- 5–7
- under 5

0   5   10 km

Percentage of total population aged under five years, 2001 Census

Timor Sea

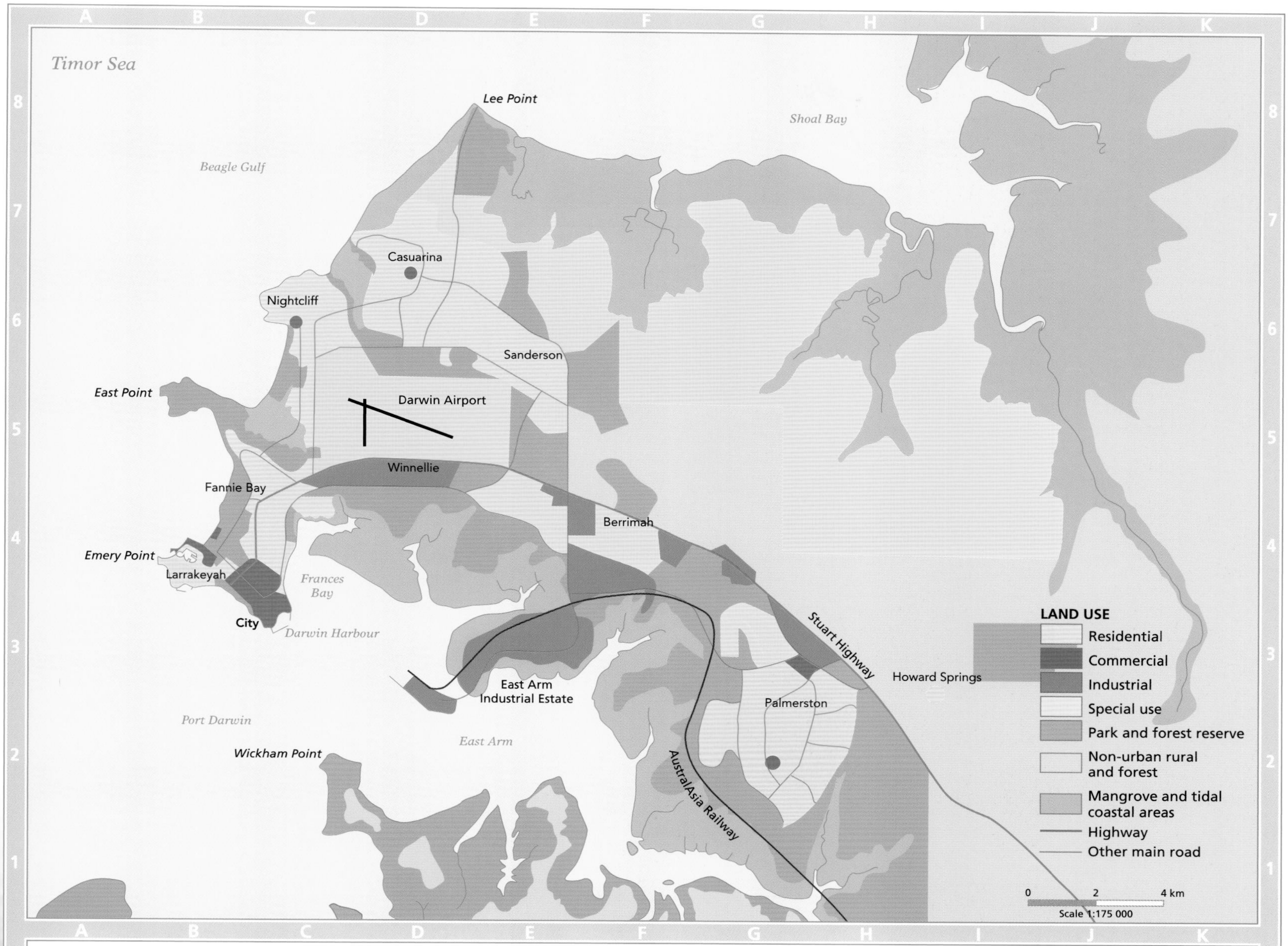

Shoal Bay

Lee Point

Beagle Gulf

Casuarina

Nightcliff

Sanderson

East Point

Darwin Airport

Winnellie

Fannie Bay

Berrimah

Emery Point

Stuart Highway

Larrakeyah

Frances Bay

Howard Springs

City

Darwin Harbour

East Arm
Industrial Estate

Palmerston

Port Darwin

East Arm

AustralAsia Railway

Wickham Point

LAND USE

Residential

Commercial

Industrial

Special use

Park and forest reserve

Non-urban rural
and forest

Mangrove and tidal
coastal areas

Highway

Other main road

0   2   4 km

Scale 1:175 000

3 PEOPLE BORN OVERSEAS

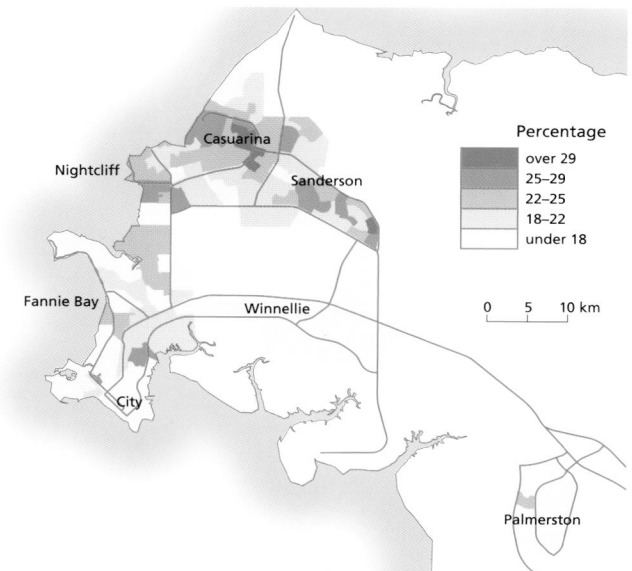

Casuarina

Nightcliff

Sanderson

Percentage

over 29

25–29

22–25

18–22

under 18

Fannie Bay

Winnellie

0   5   10 km

City

Palmerston

Percentage of total population born overseas, 2001 Census

4 PEOPLE WITH HIGH INCOMES

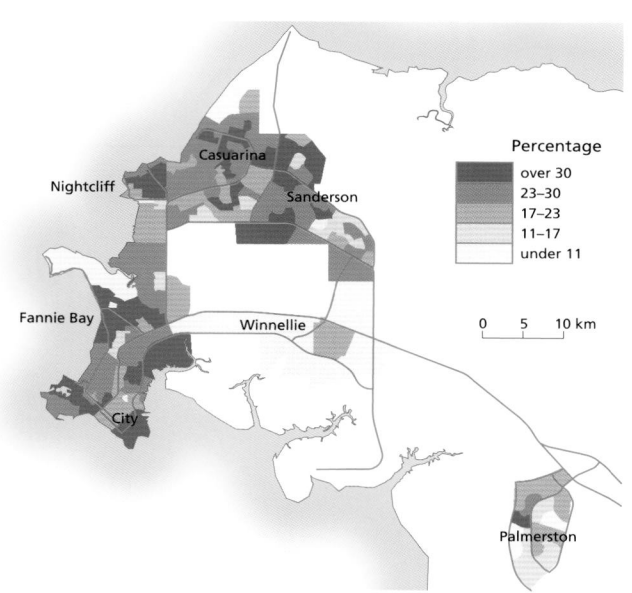

Casuarina

Nightcliff

Sanderson

Percentage

over 30

23–30

17–23

11–17

under 11

Fannie Bay

Winnellie

0   5   10 km

City

Palmerston

Percentage of households with weekly incomes of $1500 or more, 2001 Census

Caspian Sea
Aral Sea
Sor Darya
UZB.
KYRGYZSTAN
Tien Shan
TAJ.
AFG.
Kunlun Shan
Tibetan Plateau
C H I N A
Himalaya
NEPAL
BHUTAN
KATHMANDU
INDIA
BANGLADESH
Tropic of Cancer
DHAKA
Bay of Bengal
MYANMAR
YANGON
VIENTIANE
THAILAND LAOS
BANGKOK VIETNAM
CAMBODIA
PHNOM PENH
Hô Chi Minh City
Gulf of Thailand
Andaman Sea
Medan
KUALA LUMPUR
PUTRAJAYA
M A L A Y S I A
SINGAPORE Singapore
Batu Is
Mentawai Islands
Sumatra
Enggano
JAKARTA
Java
Christmas I. (Aust.)
Cocos Is (Aust.)
I N D I A N   O C E A N

KAZAKHSTAN
Karaganda
ASTANA
Lake Balkhash
Altai Mts
Bosten Hu
MONGOLIA
Gobi
ULAANBAATAR
Hovsgol Nuur
Lake Baikal
RUSSIAN FEDERATION
Stanovoy Range
Dzhugdzhur Range
Amur
Manchuria
Harbin
Sikhote Alin Range
Shenyang
BEIJING
Tianjin
NORTH KOREA
PYONGYANG
SEOUL
SOUTH KOREA
Xi'an
Nanjing
Hangzhou
Shanghai
Wuhan
Chongqing
Nanchang
Fuzhou
Taibei
Guangzhou
Hong Kong
Taiwan
Hainan I.
Huang He
Chang Jiang (Yangtze)
Kobe
Osaka
Honshu
Shikoku
TOKYO
Hachijo-jima
Kyushu
Sakhalin
Sea of Okhotsk
Kamchatka Pen.
Kuril Islands (Rus. Fed.)
Hokkaido
Sea of Japan
Yellow Sea
East China Sea
Okinawa
Ryukyu Islands (Japan)
Tori-shima (Japan)
Ogasawara-shoto (Japan)
Kazan-retto (Japan)
Luzon Strait
South China Sea
Luzon
MANILA
PHILIPPINES
Mindoro
Samar
Panay
Leyte
Palawan
Negros
Mindanao
BRUNEI
BANDAR SERI BEGAWAN
Celebes Sea
Talaud Is
Sulu Sea
Borneo
Sulawesi
Moluccas
Sula Is
Seram
Seram Sea
Banda Sea
Halmahera
Flores Sea
Makassar Strait
Java Sea
Bali Sumbawa
Flores
DILI EAST TIMOR
Sumba
Timor
Roti
Timor Sea
Darwin
Gulf of Carpentaria
I N D O N E S I A
Pk Jaya 5030
New Guinea
PAPUA NEW GUINEA
PORT MORESBY
Torres Strait
Arafura Sea
Admiralty Is
New Ireland
Bismarck Sea
New Britain
Bougainville
SOLOMON ISLANDS
HONIARA
Guadalcanal
Santa Isabel
Malaita
Santa Cruz Is
NORTHERN MARIANA ISLANDS (USA)
Pagan
SAIPAN
Saipan
Tinian
AGANA
GUAM (USA)
PALAU
KOROR
Yap
Gaferut
Hall Is
Chuuk
PALIKIR
Pohnpei
Kosrae
Nomoi Is
FED. STATES OF MICRONESIA
Caroline Islands
Wake I. (USA)
MARSHALL ISLANDS
MAJURO
KIRIBATI
BAIRIKI
Gilbert Islands
NAURU
YAREN
Banaba
Beru
Baker I. (USA)
Howland I. (USA)
KIRIBATI
Phoenix Islands
Kanton I.
Manra
Rawaki
Nikumaroro
Nanumea
TUVALU
Nui
Vaitupu
Funafuti
FUNAFUTI
Nukunonu
Atafu
Tokelau (NZ)
Fakaofo
Swains I. (USA)
AMERICAN SAMOA
Savai'i
SAMOA
APIA
Upolu
Tutuila
PAGO PAGO
AMERICAN SAMOA (USA)
MATA-UTU
WALLIS AND FUTUNA (Fr.)
Espíritu Santo
VANUATU
PORT VILA
Tanna
Vanua Levu
FIJI
Viti Levu
SUVA
Ono-i-Lau
TONGA
Vava'u Group
NUKU'ALOFA
'Niue (NZ)
Tongatapu Group
Palmerston (NZ)
Coral Sea
Iles Loyauté
NEW CALEDONIA (Fr.)
NOUMÉA
Great Barrier Reef
Great Dividing Range
Great Sandy Desert
Simpson Desert
A U S T R A L I A
Brisbane
NORFOLK I. (Aust.)
Raoul
Kermadec Is (NZ)
Lord Howe I. (Aust.)
Tropic of Capricorn
Great Victoria Desert
Great Australian Bight
Perth
Adelaide
Murray
CANBERRA
Sydney
Melbourne
Bass Strait
Tasmania
Hobart
Tasman Sea
Auckland
NEW ZEALAND
North Island
WELLINGTON
Aoraki/Mt Cook 3754
South Island
Chatham Is (NZ)
Stewart I./Rakiura
Bounty Is (NZ)
Snares Is
Antipodes Is (NZ)
Auckland Is (NZ)
Campbell I. (NZ)
Macquarie I. (Aust.)
Kerguelen Is (France)
SOUTHERN OCEAN
NORTH PACIFIC OCEAN
Aleutian Is (USA)
Midway Is (USA)
Kure Atoll
Laysan I.
Hawa
Johnston I. (USA)
Palm
Bering
Palmyra

SCALE 1:50 000 000

0   500   1000   1500   2000 km

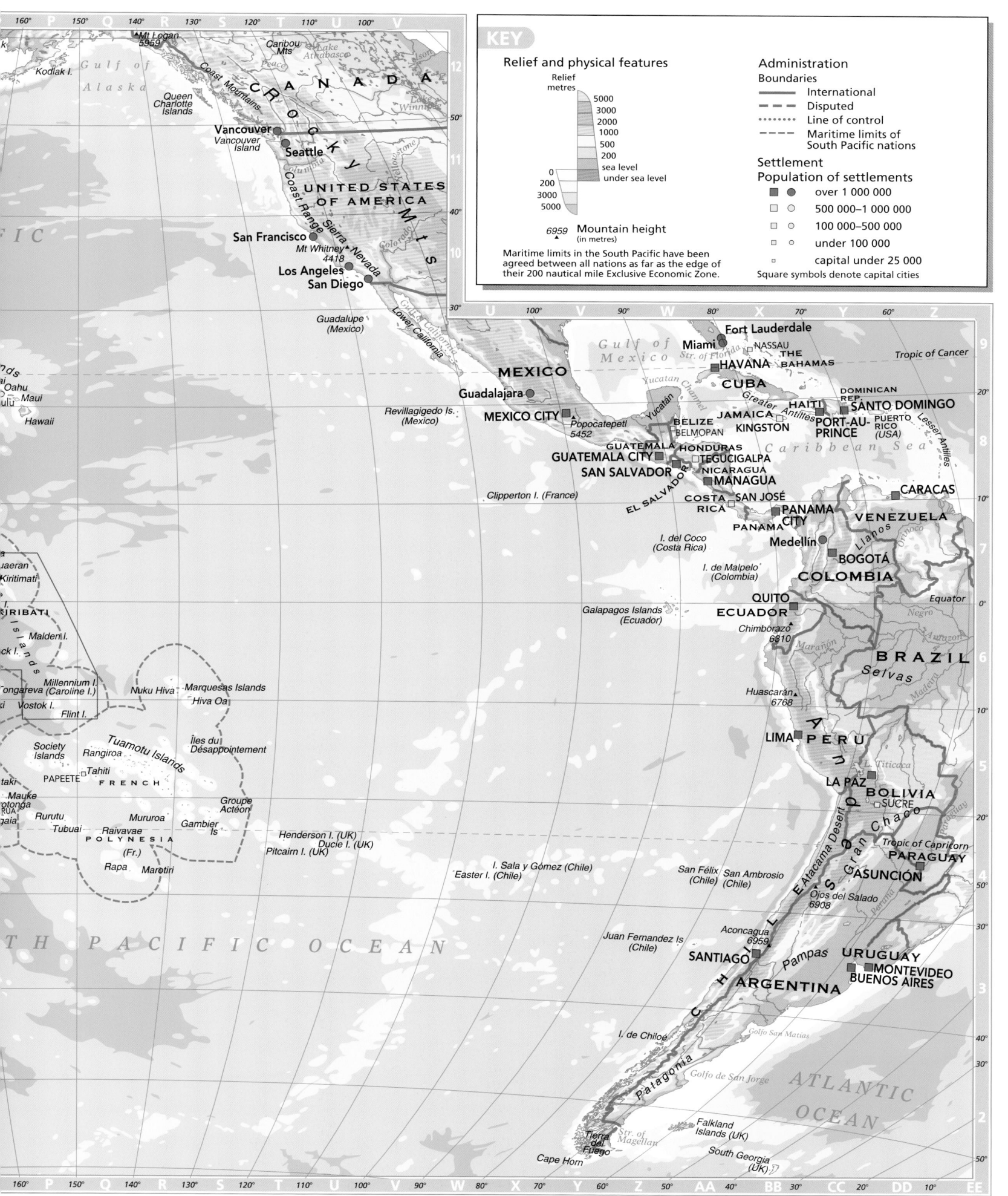

KEY

Relief and physical features

Relief
metres
5000
3000
2000
1000
500
200
0   sea level
200   under sea level
3000
5000

6959 ▲ Mountain height
(in metres)

Administration

Boundaries
— International
— — Disputed
······· Line of control
— — — Maritime limits of
South Pacific nations

Settlement
Population of settlements

■ ● over 1 000 000
□ ○ 500 000–1 000 000
□ ○ 100 000–500 000
□ ○ under 100 000
▫ capital under 25 000
Square symbols denote capital cities

Maritime limits in the South Pacific have been
agreed between all nations as far as the edge of
their 200 nautical mile Exclusive Economic Zone.

Hammer–Aitoff projection

SOLOMON ISLANDS

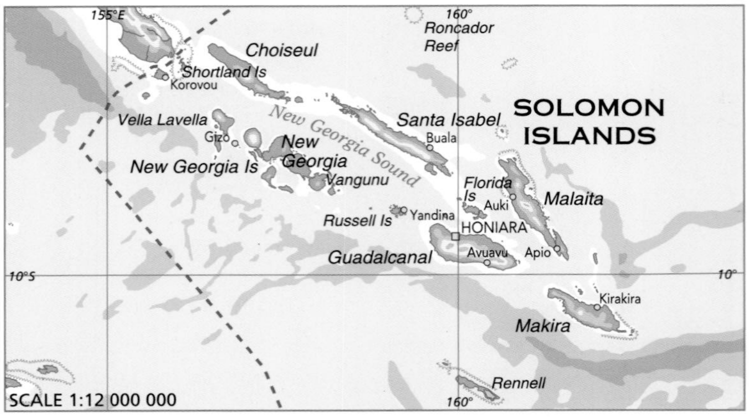

155°E
Choiseul
Roncador
Reef
160°
Shortland Is
Korovou
**SOLOMON
ISLANDS**
Vella Lavella
Gizo
New Georgia Sound
Santa Isabel
New
Georgia
New Georgia Is
Buala
Vangunu
Florida
Is
Auki
Malaita
Russell Is
Yandina
HONIARA
Avuavu
Apio
Guadalcanal
10°S
Kirakira
10°
Makira
Rennell
160°

SCALE 1:12 000 000

HAWAIIAN ISLANDS

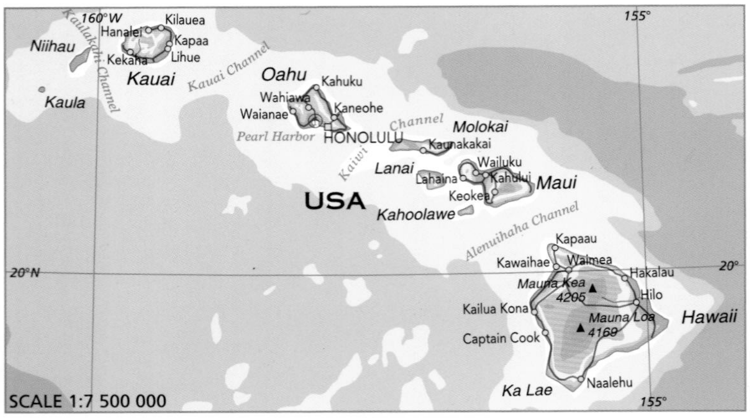

160°W
Kilauea
Niihau
Hanalei
Kapaa
Kekaha
Lihue
155°
Kauai
Kaula
Oahu
Kahuku
Wahiawa
Kaneohe
Waianae
HONOLULU
Molokai
Pearl Harbor
Kamakakai
Lanai
Wailuku
Kahului
Lahaina
Maui
Keokea
USA
Kahoolawe
Alenuihaha Channel
Kapaau
20°N
Kawaihae
Walmea
Hakalau
Mauna Kea
4205
Hilo
Kailua Kona
Mauna Loa
4169
Hawaii
Captain Cook
Ka Lae
Naalehu
155°

SCALE 1:7 500 000

VANUATU AND NEW CALEDONIA

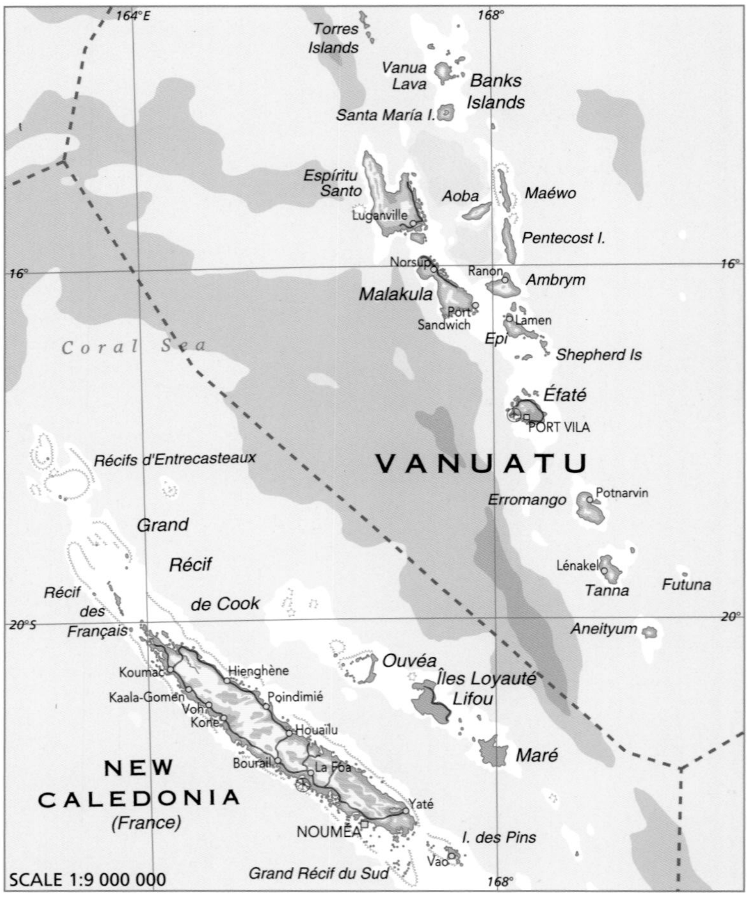

164°E
168°
Torres
Islands
Vanua
Lava
Banks
Islands
Santa María I.
Espíritu
Santo
Aoba
Maéwo
Luganville
16°
Pentecost I.
Norsup
Ranon
Ambrym
Malakula
Port
Lamen
Sandwich
Epi
Shepherd Is
Éfaté
PORT VILA
Récifs d'Entrecasteaux
VANUATU
Erromango
Potnarvin
Grand
Récif
Lénakel
Récif
de Cook
Tanna
Futuna
des
Aneityum
20°S
Français
20°
Koumac
Hienghène
Ouvéa
Kaala-Gomen
Poindimié
Îles Loyauté
Voh
Lifou
Koné
Houaïlou
Bourail
La Foa
Maré
NEW
Yaté
CALEDONIA
(France)
I. des Pins
NOUMÉA
Vao
Grand Récif du Sud
168°

SCALE 1:9 000 000

SAMOA AND AMERICAN SAMOA

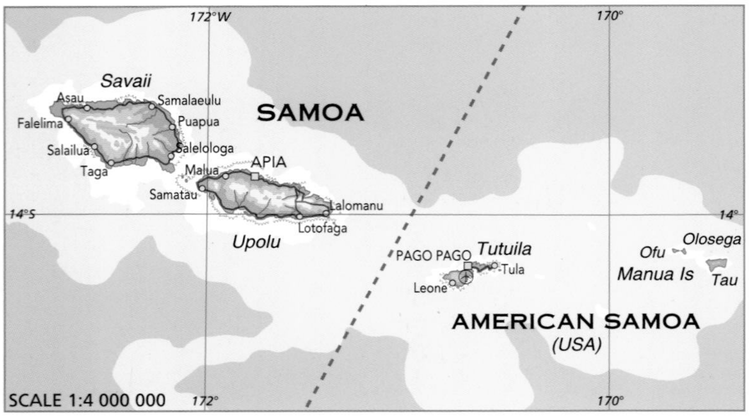

172°W
170°
Savaii
Asau
Samalaeulu
Falelima
Puapua
SAMOA
Salailua
Salelologa
APIA
Taga
Malua
14°S
Samatau
Lalomanu
14°
Upolu
Lotofaga
PAGO PAGO
Tutuila
Ofu
Olosega
Leone
Tula
Manua Is
Tau
AMERICAN SAMOA
(USA)
172°
170°

SCALE 1:4 000 000

TONGA

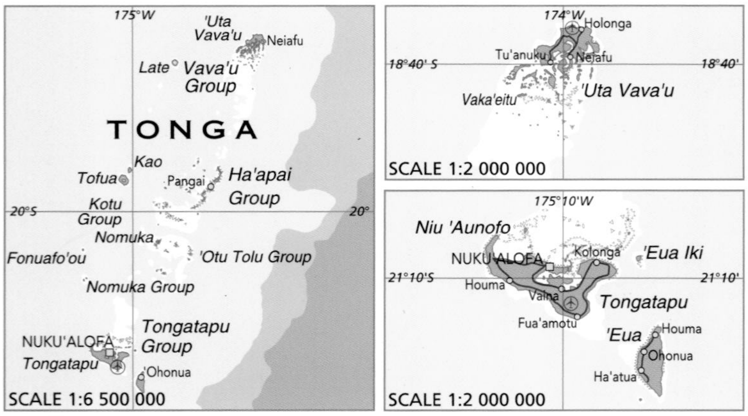

175°W
'Uta
Vava'u
Neiafu
Late
Vava'u
Group
TONGA
Tofua
Kao
Pangai
Ha'apai
Group
20°S
Kotu
Nomuka
20°
Group
'Otu Tolu Group
Fonuafo'ou
Nomuka Group
Tongatapu
NUKU'ALOFA
Group
Tongatapu
'Ohonua

SCALE 1:6 500 000

174°W
Holonga
Tu'anuku
Neiafu
18°40'S
18°40'
Vaka'eitu
'Uta Vava'u

SCALE 1:2 000 000

175°10'W
Niu 'Aunofo
Kolonga
'Eua Iki
NUKU'ALOFA
21°10'S
Houma
Vaini
21°10'
Fua'amotu
Tongatapu
Houma
'Eua
Ohonua
Ha'atua

SCALE 1:2 000 000

LORD HOWE ISLAND

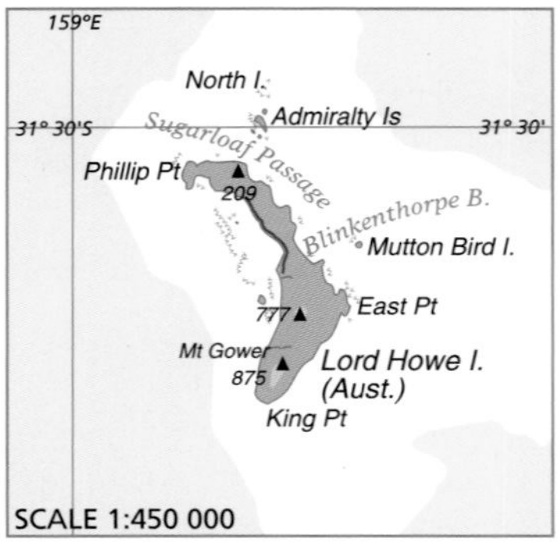

159°E
North I.
Admiralty Is
31°30'S
31°30'
Sugarloaf Passage
Phillip Pt
209
Blinkenthorpe B.
Mutton Bird I.
777
East Pt
Mt Gower
Lord Howe I.
875
(Aust.)
King Pt

SCALE 1:450 000

NORFOLK ISLAND

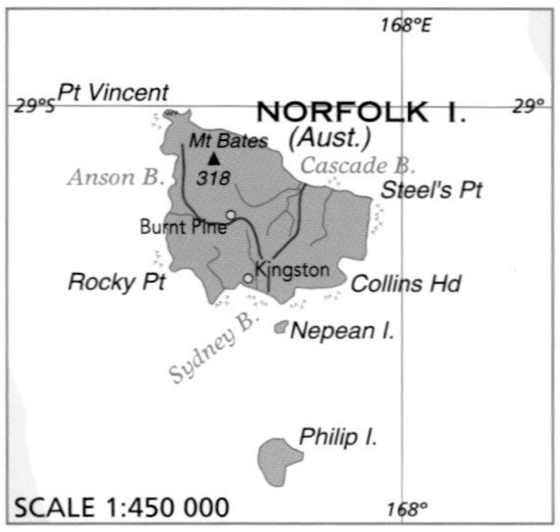

168°E
Pt Vincent
NORFOLK I.
29°S
(Aust.)
29°
Anson B.
Mt Bates
318
Cascade B.
Steel's Pt
Burnt Pine
Rocky Pt
Kingston
Collins Hd
Sydney B.
Nepean I.
Philip I.

SCALE 1:450 000
168°

FIJI

16°
178°E
180°
178°W
16°
Great Sea Reef
Vanua
Labasa
Rabi
Yasawa
Levu
Group
Lau or Eastern Group
Bligh
Nabouwalu
Taveuni
Mamanuca
Water
Koro
Lomaloma
Group
Tavua
Ellington
Koro Sea
Exploring Is
Ovalau
Nadi
Levuka
18°S
Viti Levu
Nausori
Gau
18°
SUVA
Vatulele
FIJI
Lakeba
Great Astrolabe
Reef
Kadavu Passage
Vunisea
178°
Kadavu
180°
178°

SCALE 1:8 000 000

Administration

Boundaries
- International
- Maritime limits of the South Pacific nations

Settlement
Population of settlements
- ◼ ● over 1 000 000
- ◻ ○ 500 000–1 000 000
- ◻ ○ 100 000–500 000
- ◻ ○ under 100 000
- ◻ capital under 25 000

Square symbols denote capital cities
Maritime limits in the South Pacific have been agreed between all nations as far as the edge of their 200 nautical mile Exclusive Economic Zone.

KEY

Relief and physical features

Relief metres
- 6000
- 4000
- 2000
- 1000
- 500
- 200
- 0 sea level
- 200 under sea level
- 4000
- 6000

▲ 5030 Mountain height (in metres)

Water features
- River
- Lake / Reservoir
- Intermittent lake
- Marsh

Communications
- Railway
- Road
- ✈ Main airport

SCALE 1:45 000 000

0   400   800   1200   1600 km

Mercator projection

CW

KEY

Relief and physical features

Relief metres
5000
3000
2000
1000
500
200
sea level
0
under sea level
200
4000
6000

3754 ▲ Mountain height (in metres)

Permanent ice

Water features

River
Lake / Reservoir
Marsh

Communications

Railway
Main road
⊕ Main airport

Settlement

Population of settlements
● over 1 000 000
○ 500 000–1 000 000
○ 100 000–500 000
○ 25 000–100 000
○ 10 000–25 000
• under 10 000
□ National capital

North Island

Three Kings Is
C. Maria van Diemen
North C.
Doubtless Bay
Ninety Mile Beach
Bay of Islands
Kaitaia
Kerikeri
C. Brett
Kaikohe
Paihia
Whangarei
Dargaville
Bream Bay
Great Barrier I.
Warkworth
Hauraki Gulf
Kaipara Harbour
Coromandel Peninsula
Takapuna
Manukau
Auckland
Thames
Manukau Harbour
Pukekohe
Waiuku
Paeroa
Waihi
Mayor I.
Huntly
Te Aroha
Matakana I.
White I.
Ngaruawahia
Tauranga
Te Puke
Bay of Plenty
Hamilton
Cambridge
Whakatane
Hikurangi 1754 ▲
East C.
Te Awamutu
Rotorua
Kawerau
Opotiki
L. Rotorua
Te Kuiti
Tokoroa
Murupara
Huiarau Ra.
Waikato
Taupo
Gisborne
North Taranaki Bight
Taumarunui
L. Taupo
Hawke Bay
Waitara
Turangi
Kaimanawa Mts
Wairoa
New Plymouth
Inglewood
Mt Ngauruhoe 2291 ▲
2797 ▲
Mahia Pen.
Mt Taranaki 2518 ▲
Stratford
Mt Ruapehu
Napier
Hawera
Waiouru
Hastings
South Taranaki Bight
Taihape
Wanganui
Ruahine Ra.
Marton
Feilding
Waipukurau
Palmerston North
Dannevirke
Foxton
Levin
Otaki
Masterton
Upper Hutt
Carterton
Porirua
Featherston
C. Farewell
Golden Bay
D'Urville I.
Kapiti I.
Tasman Motueka Mts
Tasman Bay
Nelson
Picton
WELLINGTON
Lower Hutt
Richmond
Cook Strait
C. Palliser
Karamea Bight
Wairau
Blenheim
Westport
Mt Travers 2338 ▲
C. Campbell
C. Foulwind
Inland Kaikoura Ra.
Greymouth
Lewis Pass
Clarence
Kaikoura
Hokitika
Arthur's Pass
Waipara
Pegasus Bay
Southern Alps / Kā Tiritiri o te Moana
Rangiora
Kaiapoi
Darfield
Christchurch
Aoraki/Mt Cook 3754 ▲
Lincoln
Banks Peninsula
Cascade Pt
L. Tekapo
Ashburton
Mt Aspiring/Tititea 3027 ▲
Geraldine
Canterbury Bight
Milford Sound/ Piopiotahi
L. Pukaki
Twizel
Temuka
Timaru
Milford Sound
L. Hawea
Homer Tunnel
L. Wanaka
Wanaka
L. Benmore
Dunstan Mts
Waimate
Queenstown
L. Wakatipu
Cromwell
Waitaki
L. Anau
Eyre Mts
Garvie Mts
Alexandra
Oamaru
Te Anau
Clutha
L. Manapouri
Port Chalmers
Resolution I.
Mosgiel
Otago Peninsula
Caroline Pk 1722 ▲
Winton
Gore
Dunedin
Puysegur Pt
Riverton/Aparima
Balclutha
Invercargill
Bluff
Ruapuke I.
Foveaux Strait
980 ▲
Stewart I./Rakiura
South West C./ Puhiwaero

South Island

Tasman Sea

South Pacific Ocean

0   100   200   300 km

Conic Equidistant projection

1 AVERAGE ANNUAL TEMPERATURE

The coldest areas in New Zealand are in the mountains which run up the centre of both islands. South Island has a large number of glaciers.

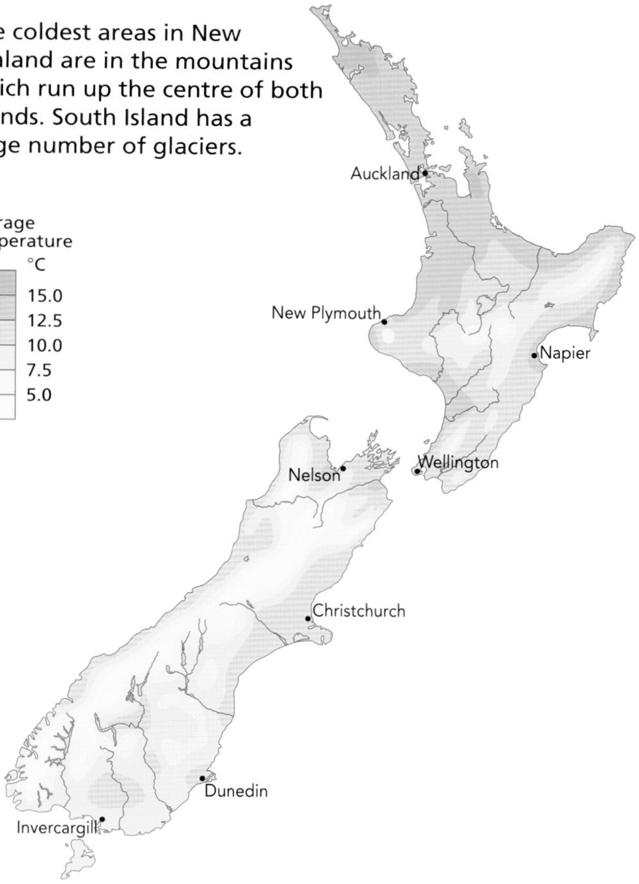

Average temperature
°C
15.0
12.5
10.0
7.5
5.0

Auckland

New Plymouth

Napier

Nelson

Wellington

Christchurch

Dunedin

Invercargill

2 AVERAGE ANNUAL RAINFALL

New Zealand's location between 35° and 47° south means that it is in the path of westerly winds which bring heavy rain to the west coast of South Island.

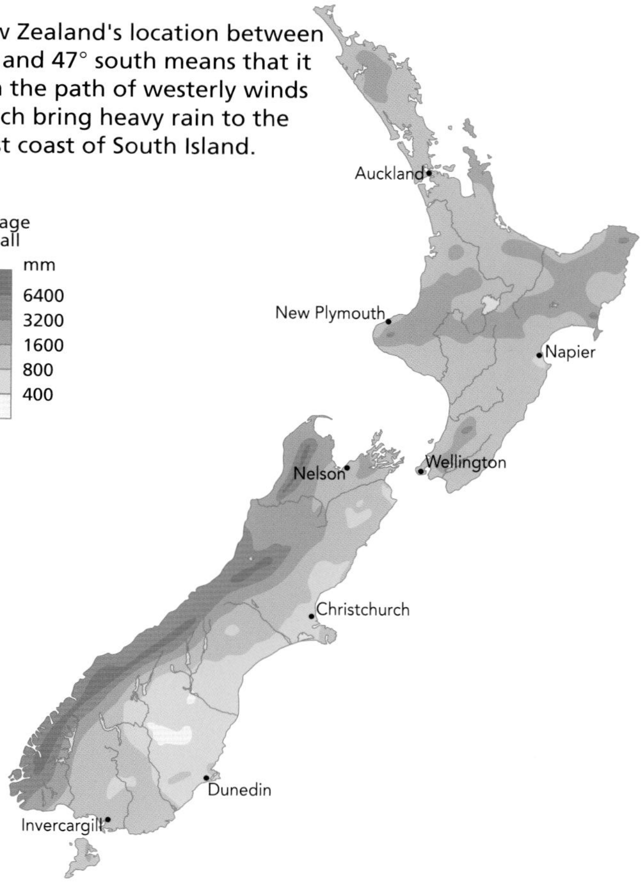

Average rainfall
mm
6400
3200
1600
800
400

Auckland

New Plymouth

Napier

Nelson

Wellington

Christchurch

Dunedin

Invercargill

3 POPULATION

Auckland is New Zealand's largest urban area with just over one million people. More than three-quarters of the people live in North Island.

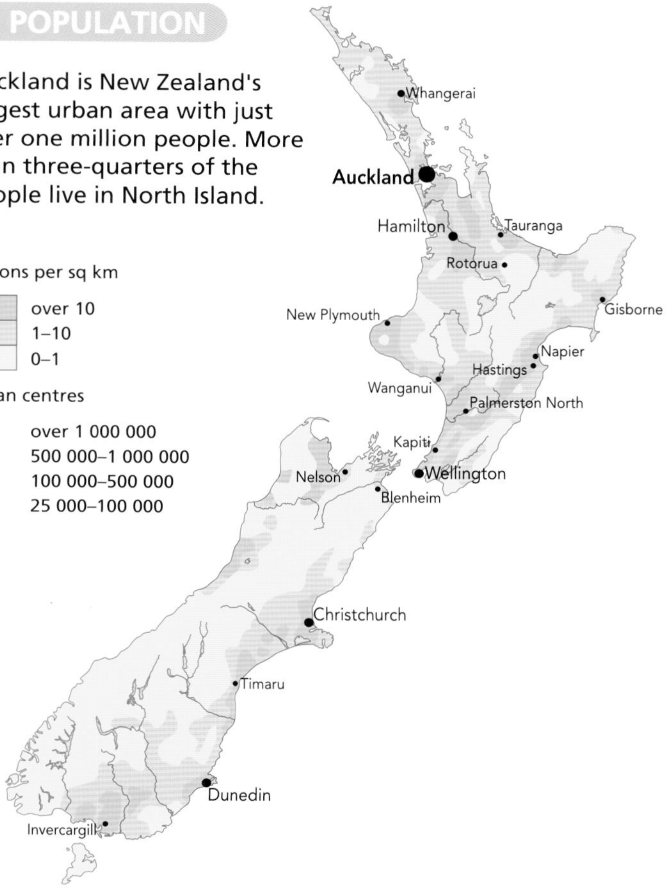

Persons per sq km

over 10
1–10
0–1

Urban centres

● over 1 000 000
● 500 000–1 000 000
● 100 000–500 000
· 25 000–100 000

Whangerai

Auckland

Hamilton
Tauranga
Rotorua

New Plymouth
Gisborne

Napier
Wanganui
Hastings
Palmerston North

Kapiti
Nelson
Wellington
Blenheim

Christchurch

Timaru

Dunedin

Invercargill

4 LAND USE

Half the farms in New Zealand are sheep farms, with beef cattle and dairy cattle next most important. Only 15% of people live in rural areas.

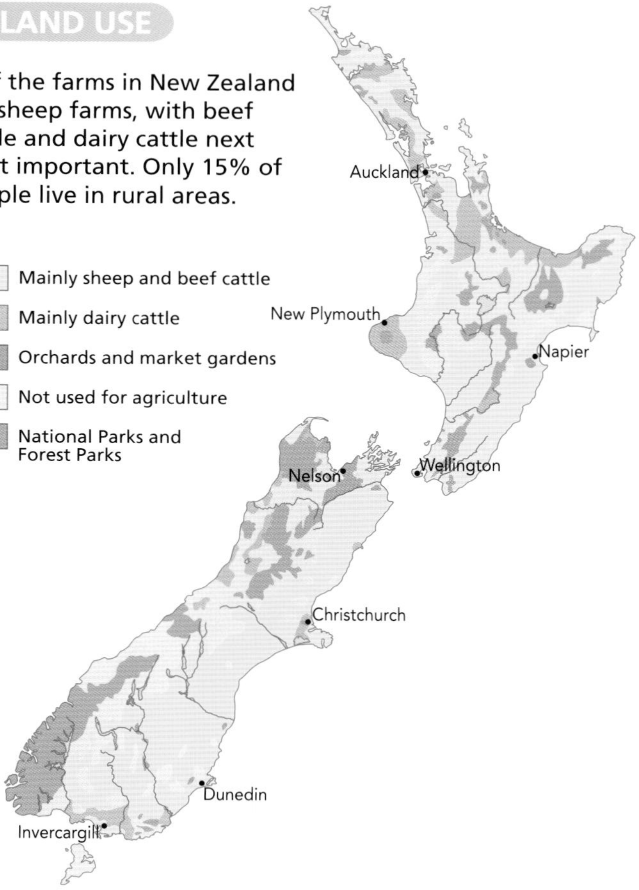

Mainly sheep and beef cattle

Mainly dairy cattle

Orchards and market gardens

Not used for agriculture

National Parks and Forest Parks

Auckland

New Plymouth

Napier

Nelson
Wellington

Christchurch

Dunedin

Invercargill

SCALE 1:12 000 000

0   100   200   300   400 km

Conic projection

This natural colour Landsat 7 ETM image of Aoraki/Mt Cook, New Zealand, dated 31 March 2001, shows approximately the same area as the topographic map opposite, at approximate scale 1:110 000. See the line scale on page 87 opposite.

The permanently snow-capped peaks and deep valleys of the Aoraki/Mt Cook region are the most striking alpine environment of the Southern Alps/Kā Tiritiri o te Moana. Both satellite image and map extract include Aoraki/Mt Cook (3754 metres), many other peaks above 3000 metres, and the Tasman Glacier, New Zealand's largest glacier.

The Southern Alps are still being formed today—firstly, by the collision of the Pacific Plate with the Indo-Australian Plate, forcing the edge of the Pacific Plate to fold and rise about 10 millimetres per year over the subducting Indo-Australian Plate, and secondly, by glacial erosion.

The Southern Alps are an orographic barrier to the winds of the Southern Ocean, causing heavy falls of rain and snow which collects as ice to feed the glaciers. Though the glaciers are now only a fraction of their former size, their enormous power to erode is shown by the dark lines of lateral and medial moraine and the moraine which covers the valley floors.

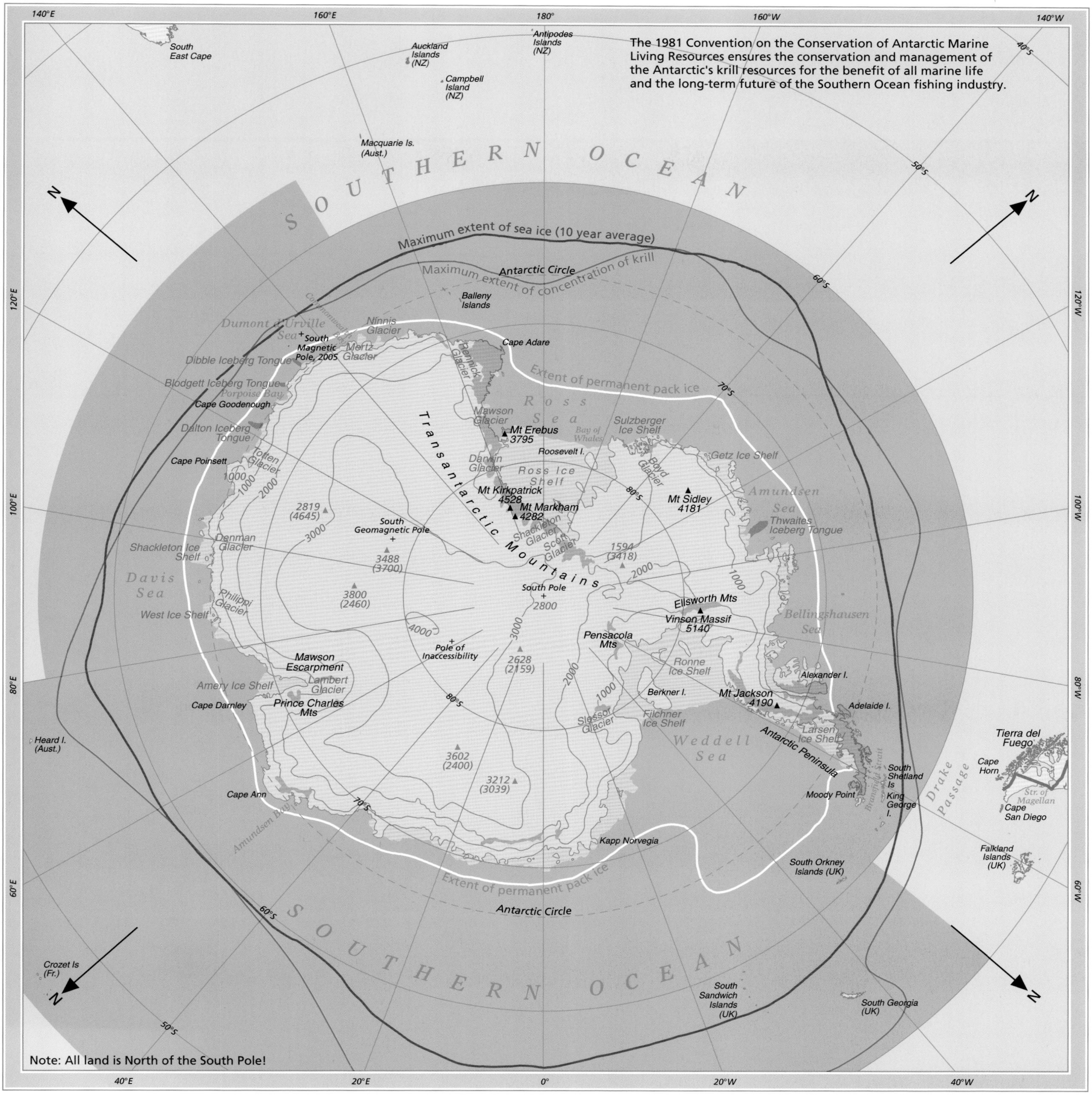

The 1981 Convention on the Conservation of Antarctic Marine Living Resources ensures the conservation and management of the Antarctic's krill resources for the benefit of all marine life and the long-term future of the Southern Ocean fishing industry.

SOUTHERN OCEAN

140°E 160°E 180° 160°W 140°W
40°S 50°S 60°S 70°S 80°S

South East Cape
Auckland Islands (NZ)
Antipodes Islands (NZ)
Campbell Island (NZ)
Macquarie Is. (Aust.)
Balleny Islands
Cape Adare

Maximum extent of sea ice (10 year average)
Maximum extent of concentration of krill
Antarctic Circle
Extent of permanent pack ice

Dumont d'Urville Sea
Ninnis Glacier
South Magnetic Pole, 2005
Mertz Glacier
Dibble Iceberg Tongue
Porpoise Bay
Blodgett Iceberg Tongue
Cape Goodenough
Dalton Iceberg Tongue
Cape Poinsett
Totten Glacier
1000 2000

Ross Sea
Mawson Glacier
Mt Erebus 3795
Bay of Whales
Sulzberger Ice Shelf
Roosevelt I.
Getz Ice Shelf
Darwin Glacier
Ross Ice Shelf
Mt Kirkpatrick 4528
Mt Markham 4282
Shackleton Glacier
Scott Glacier
Amundsen Sea
Mt Sidley 4181
Thwaites Iceberg Tongue

Transantarctic Mountains

2819 (4645)
3000
South Geomagnetic Pole
3488 (3700)
3800 (2460)
4000
Pole of Inaccessibility
South Pole 2800
2628 (2159)
1594 (3418)
2000
1000
Ellsworth Mts
Vinson Massif 5140
Pensacola Mts
Ronne Ice Shelf
Berkner I.
Mt Jackson 4190
Bellingshausen Sea
Alexander I.
Adelaide I.

Denman Glacier
Shackleton Ice Shelf
Davis Sea
Philippi Glacier
West Ice Shelf
Mawson Escarpment
Lambert Glacier
Amery Ice Shelf
Cape Darnley
Prince Charles Mts
Cape Ann
Heard I. (Aust.)

3602 (2400)
3212 (3039)
Slessor Glacier
Filchner Ice Shelf
Kapp Norvegia
Weddell Sea
Larsen Ice Shelf
Antarctic Peninsula
Moody Point
South Shetland Is
King George I.
South Orkney Islands (UK)

Tierra del Fuego
Cape Horn
Str. of Magellan
Cape San Diego
Drake Passage
Falkland Islands (UK)

Extent of permanent pack ice
Antarctic Circle

SOUTHERN OCEAN

Heard I. (Aust.)
Crozet Is (Fr.)
South Sandwich Islands (UK)
South Georgia (UK)

40°E 20°E 0° 20°W 40°W
60°E 80°E 100°E 120°E
60°W 80°W 100°W 120°W
50°S 60°S 70°S 80°S

Note: All land is North of the South Pole!

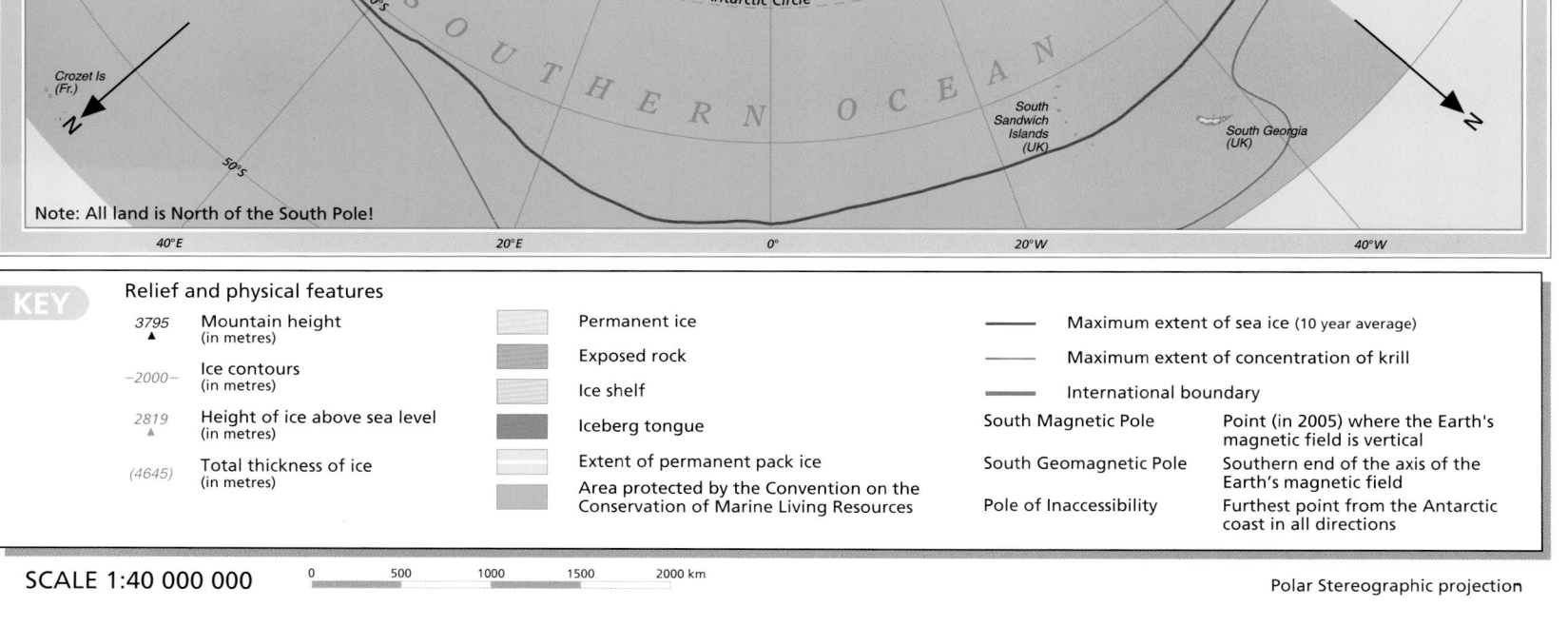

KEY

Relief and physical features

- 3795 ▲ Mountain height (in metres)
- –2000– Ice contours (in metres)
- 2819 ▲ Height of ice above sea level (in metres)
- (4645) Total thickness of ice (in metres)

- Permanent ice
- Exposed rock
- Ice shelf
- Iceberg tongue
- Extent of permanent pack ice
- Area protected by the Convention on the Conservation of Marine Living Resources

- Maximum extent of sea ice (10 year average)
- Maximum extent of concentration of krill
- International boundary

- South Magnetic Pole — Point (in 2005) where the Earth's magnetic field is vertical
- South Geomagnetic Pole — Southern end of the axis of the Earth's magnetic field
- Pole of Inaccessibility — Furthest point from the Antarctic coast in all directions

SCALE 1:40 000 000

0 500 1000 1500 2000 km

Polar Stereographic projection

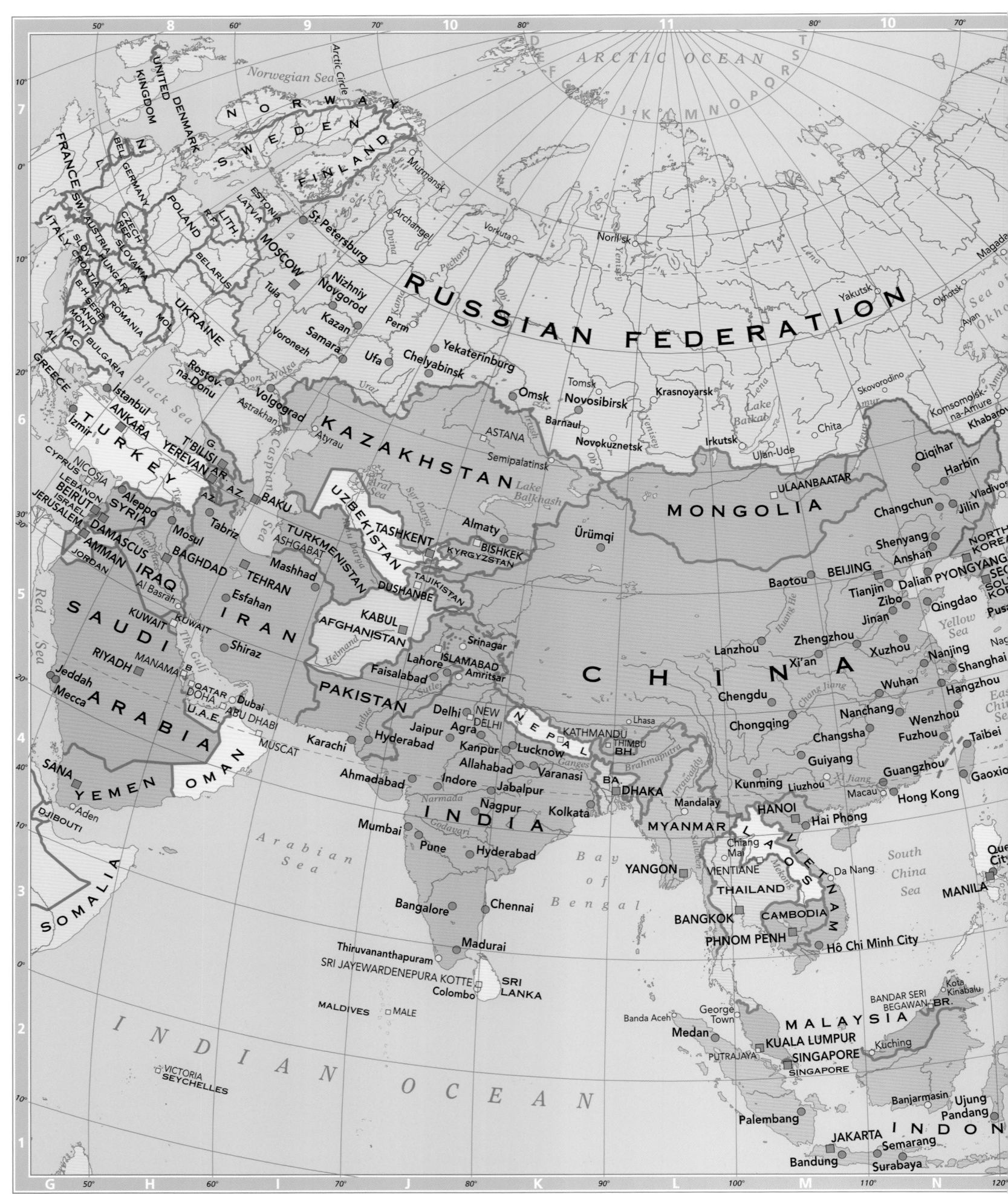

SCALE 1:40 000 000

0   400   800   1200   1600 km

Lambert Azimuthal Equal Area projection

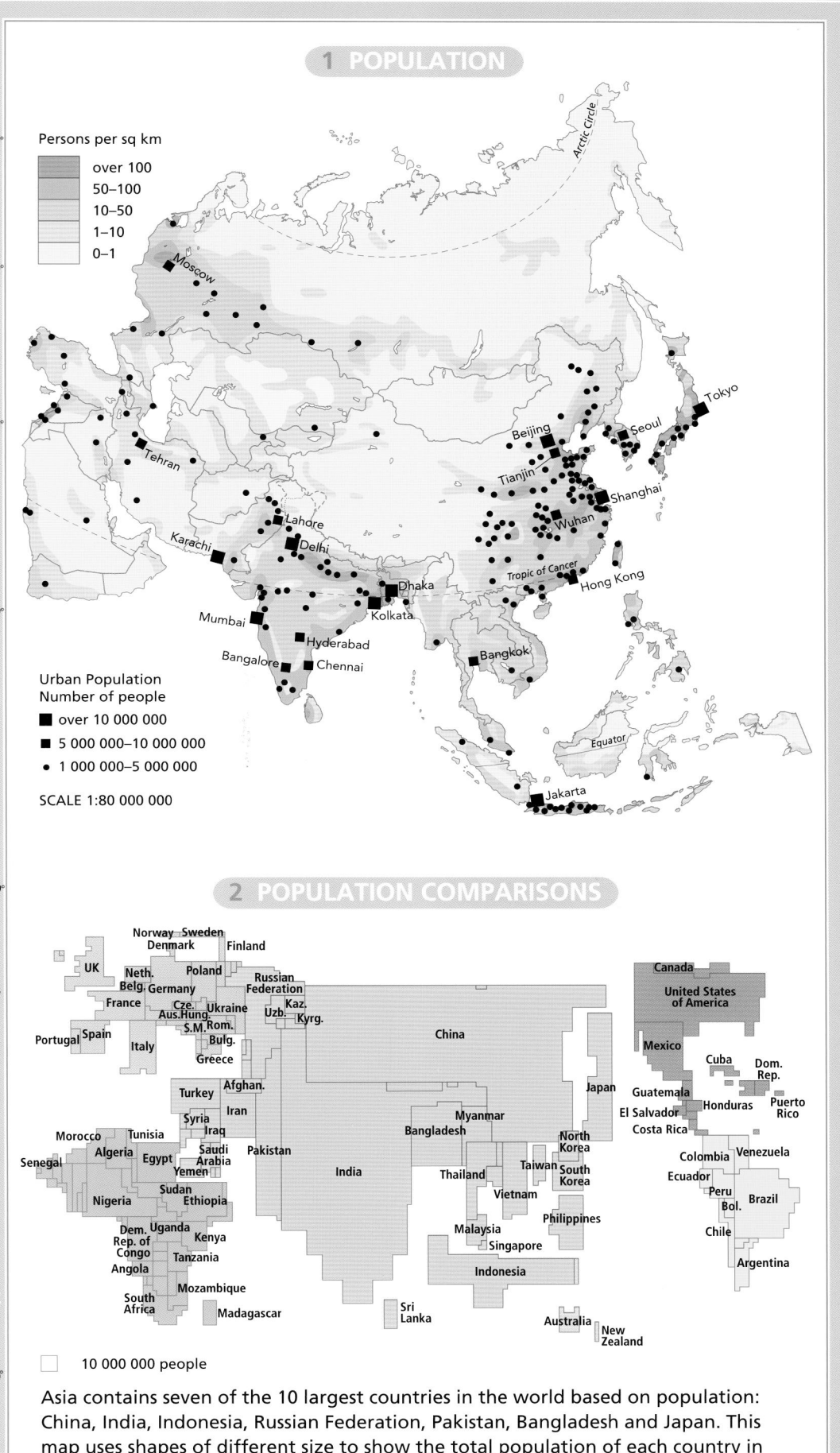

Boundaries

——————	International
— — —	Disputed
··········	Ceasefire line
– – – –	Maritime Limits of South Pacific nations

Population of settlements

■	●	over 1 000 000
☐	○	500 000–1 000 000
☐	○	100 000–500 000
□	○	under 100 000

Square symbols denote capital cities

Maritime limits in the South Pacific have been agreed between all nations as far as the edge of their 200 nautical mile Exclusive Economic Zone.

AR. ARMENIA
AZ. AZERBAIJAN
B. BAHRAIN
BA. BANGLADESH
BH. BHUTAN
BR. BRUNEI
G. GEORGIA
U.A.E. UNITED ARAB EMIRATES

1 POPULATION

Persons per sq km

	over 100
	50–100
	10–50
	1–10
	0–1

Urban Population
Number of people

■	over 10 000 000
■	5 000 000–10 000 000
●	1 000 000–5 000 000

SCALE 1:80 000 000

2 POPULATION COMPARISONS

☐ 10 000 000 people

Asia contains seven of the 10 largest countries in the world based on population: China, India, Indonesia, Russian Federation, Pakistan, Bangladesh and Japan. This map uses shapes of different size to show the total population of each country in the world and how it compares to the others.

Countries with population of less than 1 000 000 are not shown.

ARCTIC OCEAN

Norwegian Sea

North Sea

Baltic Sea

Bay of Biscay

Apennines

Carpathian Mts

North European Plain

Central Russian Uplands

Spitsbergen

Franz Josef Land

Severnaya Zemlya

New Siberian Islands

Wrangel I.

Kolyma Range

North Cape

Arctic Circle

Kola Peninsula

Novaya Zemlya

C. Chelyuskin

Laptev Sea

Taymyr Peninsula

Verkhoyansk Range

Dzhugdzhur Range

Sea of Okho

West Siberian Plain

Central Siberian Plateau

S I B E R I A

Narodnaya 1894

Lower Tunguska

Ural Mountains

Black Sea

Caucasus

Kirghiz Steppe

Caspian Sea

Lake Baikal

Yablonovyy Range

Stanovoy Range

Amur

Sikh

Taurus Mts

Mt Ararat 5165

Cyprus

Mediterranean Sea

Elburz Mts

Aral Sea

Lake Balkhash

Lake Zaysan

Altai Mts

Gobi

Da Hinggan Ling

Manchuria

Zagros Mts

Dasht-e Kavir

Iranian Plateau

Tien Shan

Turpan Pendi

Lop Nur

Taklimakan Shamo

Kunlun Shan

Tibetan Plateau

North China Plain

Bo Hai

Yellow Sea

An Nafud

The Gulf

Hindu Kush

K2 8611

Karakoram Ra.

Sulaiman Range

Sutlej

Himalaya

Chang Jiang

East China Sea

Hijaz

Red Sea

Arabian Peninsula

Asir

Rub' al Khali

Makran

Gulf of Oman

Thar Desert

Indus

Dhaulagiri 8167

Annapurna 8091

Mt Everest 8848

Gongga Shan 7514

Nan Ling

Taiwan

Masirah

Narmada

Yamuna

Ganges

Brahmaputra

Ganges Delta

Arakan

Hainan

Luzon Strait

Gulf of Aden

Socotra

Arabian Sea

Deccan

Western Ghats

Eastern Ghats

Godavari

Bay of Bengal

Andaman

South China Sea

Luzon

Philippin

Laccadive Is

2633

Andaman Islands

Andaman Sea

Gulf of Thailand

Palawan

Sulu Sea

C. Comorin

Sri Lanka

Nicobar Islands

Mekong

Cele

Maldives

Strait of Malacca

Malay Peninsula

Borneo

Sulawe

Equator

Seychelles

INDIAN OCEAN

Mentawai Islands

Sumatra

Aldabra Is

Chagos Archipelago

Java Sea

J a v a

Lombok

Bali

Flore

North European Plain

Rhine

Danube

Dnieper

Don

Volga

Dvina

Lake Ladoga

Lake Onega

White Sea

Barents Sea

Pechora

Ob

Yenisey

Lena

Ob'

Irtysh

Syr Darya

Amu Darya

Helmand

Euphrates

Tigris

Xi Jiang

Salween

Irrawaddy

Huang He

0   400   800   1200   1600 km

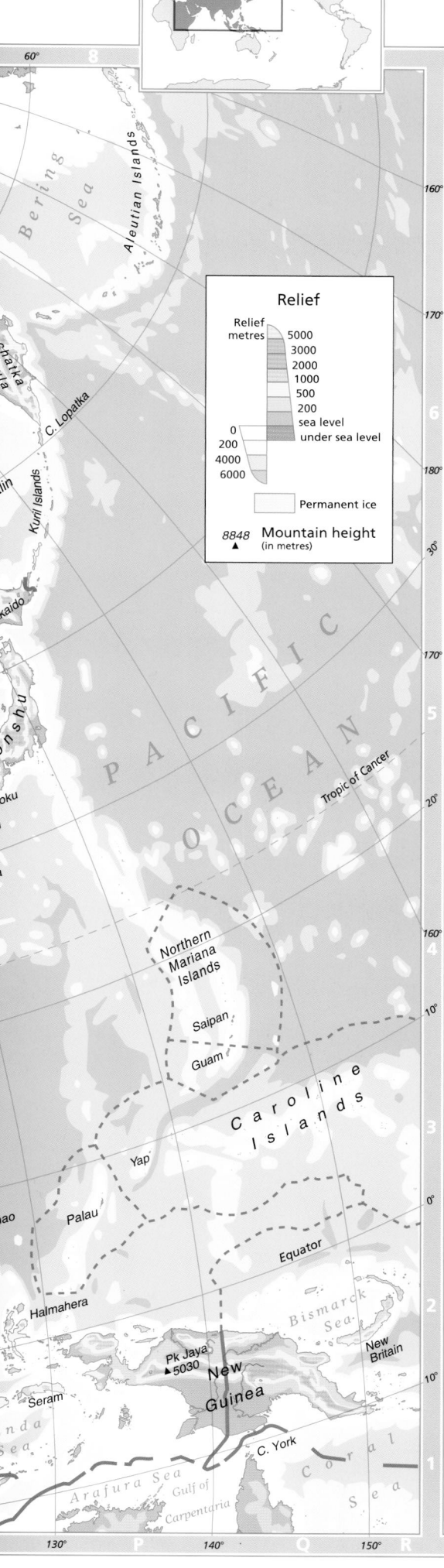

Relief

Relief metres
5000
3000
2000
1000
500
200
0 sea level
200 under sea level
4000
6000

Permanent ice

8848 ▲ Mountain height (in metres)

1 LAND REGIONS

In most continents of the world, landforms are used to divide the continent into land regions. Asia's landforms, however, are very complex. As a result, Asia is usually divided into land regions based on *location* or *direction*, rather than landforms. In northern Asia the Ural Mountains are regarded as the dividing line between Asia and Europe. As a result, the Russian Federation is in both Asia and Europe.

SCALE 1:120 000 000

2 GANGES SATELLITE IMAGE

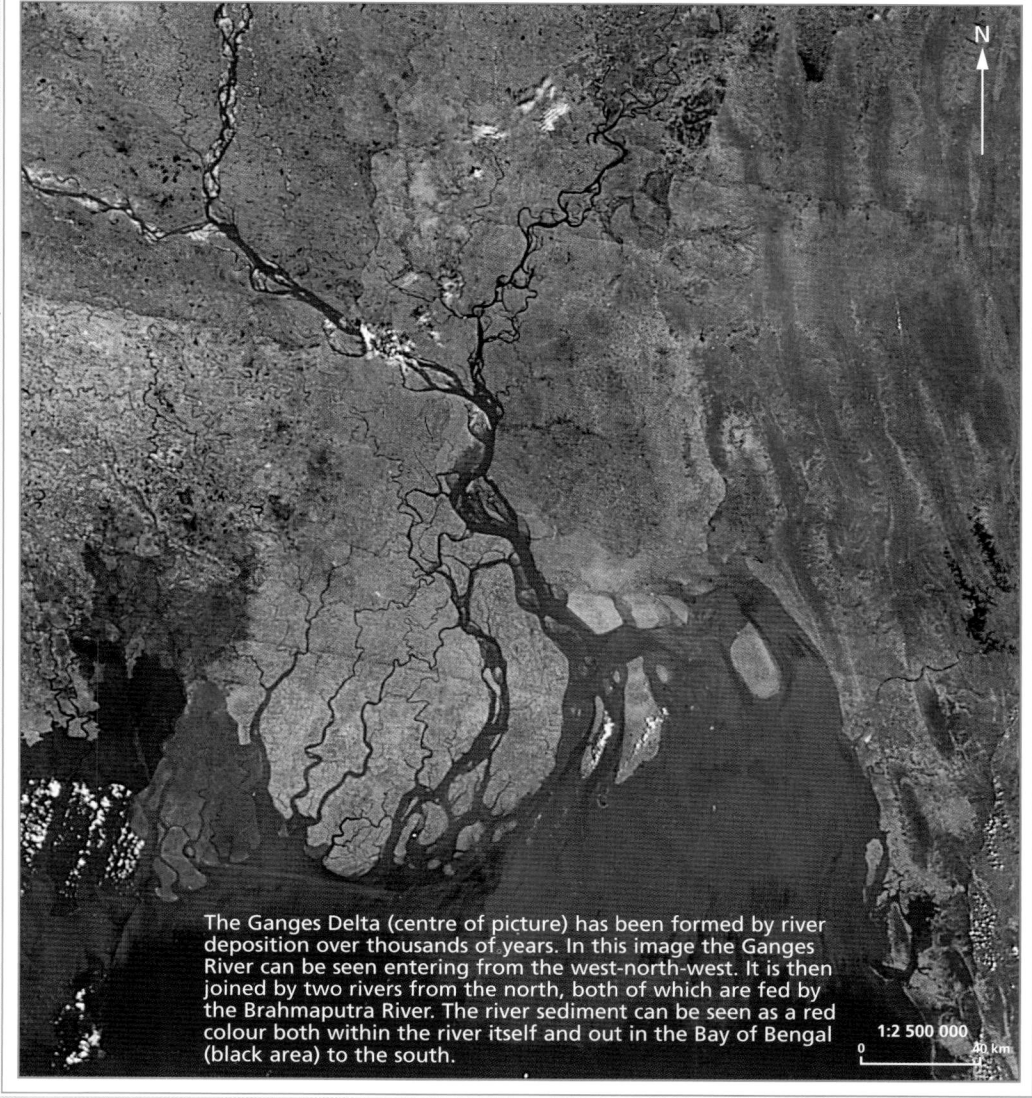

The Ganges Delta (centre of picture) has been formed by river deposition over thousands of years. In this image the Ganges River can be seen entering from the west-north-west. It is then joined by two rivers from the north, both of which are fed by the Brahmaputra River. The river sediment can be seen as a red colour both within the river itself and out in the Bay of Bengal (black area) to the south.

1:2 500 000

Lambert Azimuthal Equal Area projection

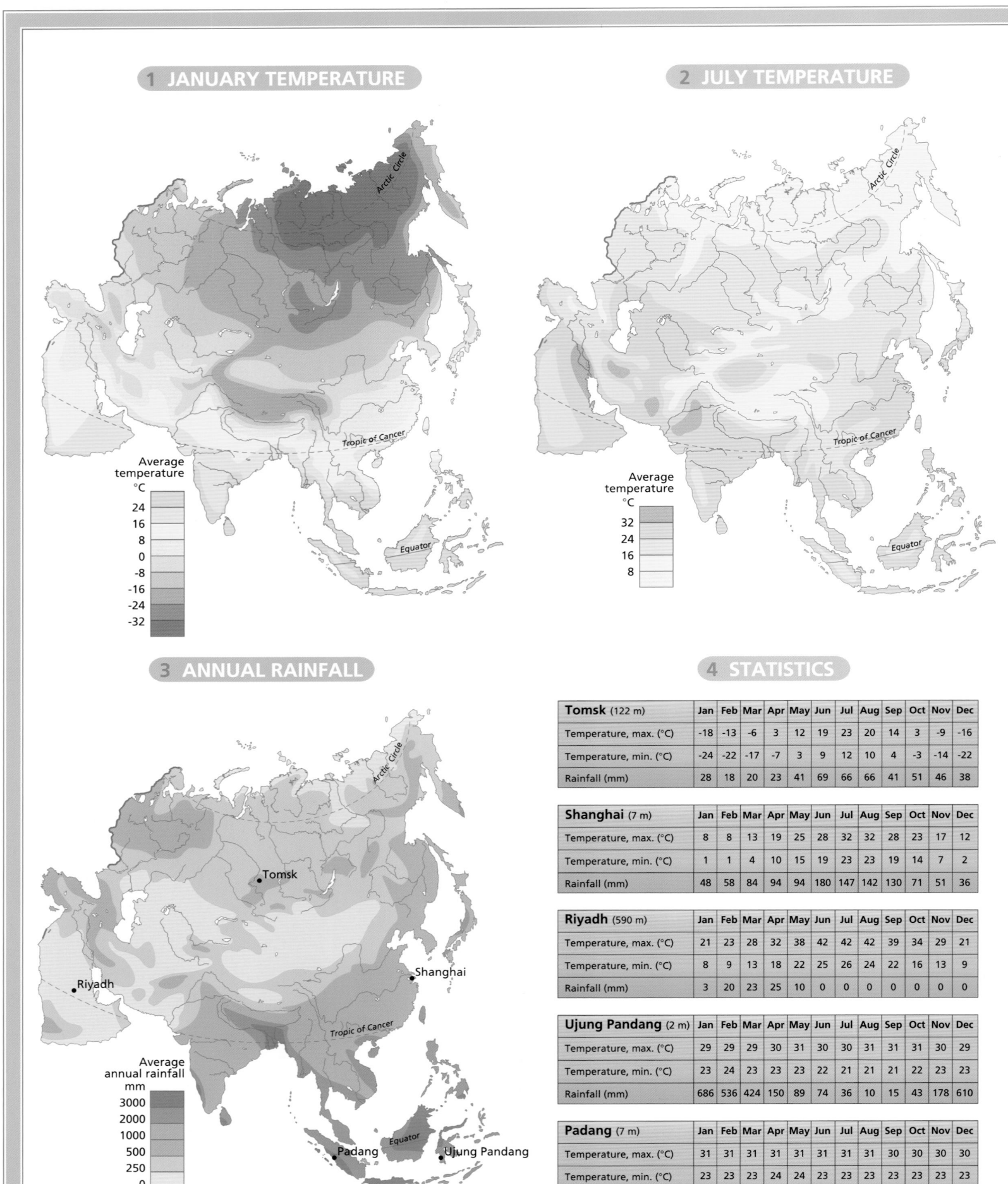

1 JANUARY TEMPERATURE

Average temperature °C

| 24 |
| 16 |
| 8 |
| 0 |
| -8 |
| -16 |
| -24 |
| -32 |

2 JULY TEMPERATURE

Average temperature °C

| 32 |
| 24 |
| 16 |
| 8 |

3 ANNUAL RAINFALL

Average annual rainfall mm

| 3000 |
| 2000 |
| 1000 |
| 500 |
| 250 |
| 0 |

4 STATISTICS

Tomsk (122 m)	Jan	Feb	Mar	Apr	May	Jun	Jul	Aug	Sep	Oct	Nov	Dec
Temperature, max. (°C)	-18	-13	-6	3	12	19	23	20	14	3	-9	-16
Temperature, min. (°C)	-24	-22	-17	-7	3	9	12	10	4	-3	-14	-22
Rainfall (mm)	28	18	20	23	41	69	66	66	41	51	46	38

Shanghai (7 m)	Jan	Feb	Mar	Apr	May	Jun	Jul	Aug	Sep	Oct	Nov	Dec
Temperature, max. (°C)	8	8	13	19	25	28	32	32	28	23	17	12
Temperature, min. (°C)	1	1	4	10	15	19	23	23	19	14	7	2
Rainfall (mm)	48	58	84	94	94	180	147	142	130	71	51	36

Riyadh (590 m)	Jan	Feb	Mar	Apr	May	Jun	Jul	Aug	Sep	Oct	Nov	Dec
Temperature, max. (°C)	21	23	28	32	38	42	42	42	39	34	29	21
Temperature, min. (°C)	8	9	13	18	22	25	26	24	22	16	13	9
Rainfall (mm)	3	20	23	25	10	0	0	0	0	0	0	0

Ujung Pandang (2 m)	Jan	Feb	Mar	Apr	May	Jun	Jul	Aug	Sep	Oct	Nov	Dec
Temperature, max. (°C)	29	29	29	30	31	30	30	31	31	31	30	29
Temperature, min. (°C)	23	24	23	23	23	22	21	21	21	22	23	23
Rainfall (mm)	686	536	424	150	89	74	36	10	15	43	178	610

Padang (7 m)	Jan	Feb	Mar	Apr	May	Jun	Jul	Aug	Sep	Oct	Nov	Dec
Temperature, max. (°C)	31	31	31	31	31	31	31	31	30	30	30	30
Temperature, min. (°C)	23	23	23	24	24	23	23	23	23	23	23	23
Rainfall (mm)	351	259	307	363	315	307	277	348	152	495	518	480

SCALE 1:100 000 000

0 1000 2000 3000 4000 km

Lambert Azimuthal Equal Area projection

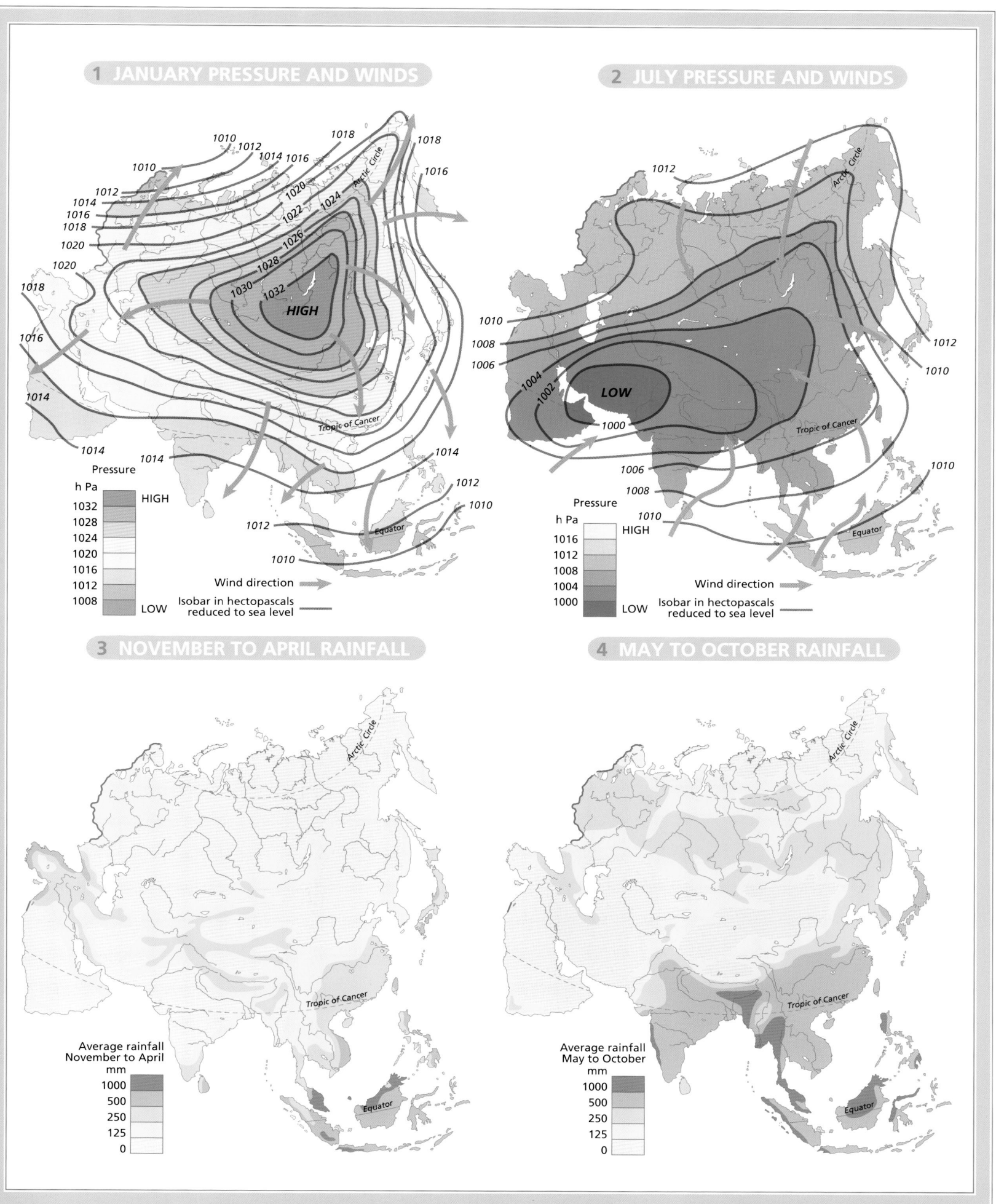

1 JANUARY PRESSURE AND WINDS

1010 1012 1014 1016 1018
1010
1012
1014
1016
1018
1020
1020
1018
1016
1014
1014
1020 1022 1024 1026 1028 1030 1032
Arctic Circle
1018
1016
HIGH
Tropic of Cancer
1014
1012
1010
1012
1010
Equator

Pressure
h Pa
1032 HIGH
1028
1024
1020
1016
1012
1008 LOW

→ Wind direction
— Isobar in hectopascals
reduced to sea level

2 JULY PRESSURE AND WINDS

1012
Arctic Circle
1010
1008
1006
1004 1002
LOW
1000
1006
1008
1010
1012
1010
1010
Tropic of Cancer
Equator

Pressure
h Pa
1016 HIGH
1012
1008
1004
1000 LOW

→ Wind direction
— Isobar in hectopascals
reduced to sea level

3 NOVEMBER TO APRIL RAINFALL

Arctic Circle
Tropic of Cancer
Equator

Average rainfall
November to April
mm
1000
500
250
125
0

4 MAY TO OCTOBER RAINFALL

Arctic Circle
Tropic of Cancer
Equator

Average rainfall
May to October
mm
1000
500
250
125
0

SCALE 1:100 000 000

0   1000   2000   3000   4000 km

Lambert Azimuthal Equal Area projection

CHINA

INDIA
Chittagong
BANGLA-DESH
Monywa
Shwebo
Mt Victoria
3053
Pakokku
Mandalay
Myingyan
Meiktila
Magwe
Taung-gyi
Kengtung
Louang Namtha
Phôngsali
Lao Cai
Cao Bang
Yunjinghong
Pingxiang
Nanning
Yulin
GUANGDONG
CHINA
Macau
Hong Kong
Gaoxi
TAIWAN
MYANMAR
Sittwe
Arakan Yoma
Sandoway
Pyinmana
Pye
Henzada
Regu
Chiang Rai
Phayao
Chiang Mai
Nan
Lampang
Phrae
Louangphrabang
Xiangkhoang
Thanh Hoa
Vinh
Ha Tinh
Qinzhou
Beihai
Zhanjiang
Leizhou Peninsula
HAINAN
Haikou
Hainan
Qionghai
Dongfang
Thai Nguyên
HANOI
Nam Dinh
Hai Phong
Thai Binh
Gulf of Tongking
Son La

Bay of Bengal

Bassein
Pyapon
YANGON
Thaton
Martaban
Moulmein
Mouths of the Irrawaddy
Gulf of Martaban
Shwegyin
Uttaradit
VIENTIANE
Udon Thani
Khon Kaen
Savannakhét
Quang Tri
Huê
Da Nang
Quang Ngai

Preparis I.
Tavoy
Nakhon Pathom
Phitsanulok
Tak
Nakhon Sawan
Sara Buri
Ayutthaya
Nonthaburi
BANGKOK
THAILAND
Nakhon Ratchasima
Surin
Ubon Ratchathani
Pakxé
Qui Nhon
LAOS
VIETNAM
SOUTH

Andaman Islands (India)
Mergui
Mergui
Tenasserim
Rat Buri
Phet Buri
Chon Buri
Sisophon
Batdâmbâng
Chanthaburi
Pouthisat
Tônlé Sap
Krâcheh
Kâmpóng Cham
Buôn Mê Thuôt
Nha Trang
Cam Ranh
Da Lat
CHINA

Port Blair
Little Andaman
Archipelago
Prachuap Khiri Khan
CAMBODIA
PHNOM PENH
Tây Ninh
Phan Thiêt
SEA

Ten Degree Channel
Car Nicobar
Andaman Sea
Chumphon
Ranong
Gulf of Thailand
Sihanoukville
Kâmpôt
Long Xuyên
Rach Gia
My Tho
Hô Chi Minh City
Vung Tau
Paracel Is
Spratly Is
Palawan
Puerto Princ

Nicobar Islands (India)
Great Nicobar
Nakhon Si Thammarat
Krabi
Phuket
Phatthalung
Songkhla
Bac Lieu
Cân Tho
Mui Ca Mau
Mouths of the Mekong
Con Son
Brooke's Point

Ban Hat Yai
Yala
Kota Bharu
Alor Setar
George Town
Butterworth
Pinang
Banda Aceh
Lhokseumawe
Langsa
Taiping
Ipoh
Kuala Terengganu
Dungun
MALAYSIA
BRUNEI
BANDAR SERI BEGAWAN
Miri
Seria
G. Kinabalu 4094
Kota Kinabalu
SABAH
Sandakan
Lahad Datu
Tawau
Tawit

G. Leuser 3145
Medan
Tebingtinggi
Prapat
Balige
Sibolga
MALAYA
Kuantan
Kuala Lumpur
PUTRAJAYA
Seremban
Melaka
Muar
Keluang
Natuna Besar
Anambas Is
Natuna Is
Igan
Sibu
Bintulu
SARAWAK
Iran Ra. 2988
Tarakan
Simeuluë
Lake Toba
Rantauprapat
Johor Bahru
SINGAPORE
SINGAPORE
Sambas
Kuching
Debak
Simanggang
Singkawang
Tanjungredeb

Nias
Pakanbaru
SUMATRA
Riau Is
Strait of Malacca
Tambelan Is
Pontianak
BORNEO
Kalimantan
Samarinda
Balikpapan
Palu
Sulaw

Batu Is
Bukittinggi
Padangpanjang
Muarabungo
Jambi
Bangka
Mentok
Pangkalpinang
Ketapang
Sukadana
Schwaner Mts
Palangkaraya
Sampit
Amuntai
Mamuju
3074
Bt Gandadiwata
Majene
Parepare

Padang
Siberut
Sipura
Utara I.
Barisan Range
G. Kerinci 3805
Sungaipenuh
Palembang
Belitung
Tanjungpandan
Toboali
Karimata Strait
Tg Puting
Kendawangan
Pangkalanbuun
Banjarmasin
Tg Selatan
Watampone
Makassar Strait

Mentawai Is
Selatan I.
Lubuklinggau
Prabumulih
Lahat
Dempo 3159
Bengkulu
Martapura
Kotabumi
INDIAN
OCEAN
Java Sea
Laut

Enggano
Tanjungkarang Telukbetung
Bawean
Ujung Pandang 2871
Bontosunggu
Bulu

Sunda Str.
JAKARTA
Serang
Bogor
Sukabumi
Bandung
Cirebon
Pekalongan
Tuban
Madura
Kangean Is
INDONE

Tasikmalaya
Cilacap
Slamet 3428
Semarang
Surakarta
Surabaya
Probolinggo
Bali Sea
Flor

JAVA
Yogyakarta
Malang 3676
Jember
Bali
Singaraja
Denpasar
Mataram 3726
Lombok
Raba
Ruteng
Sumbawa

Christmas I. (Aust.)
Sumba
Waingapi

0   200   400   600   800 km

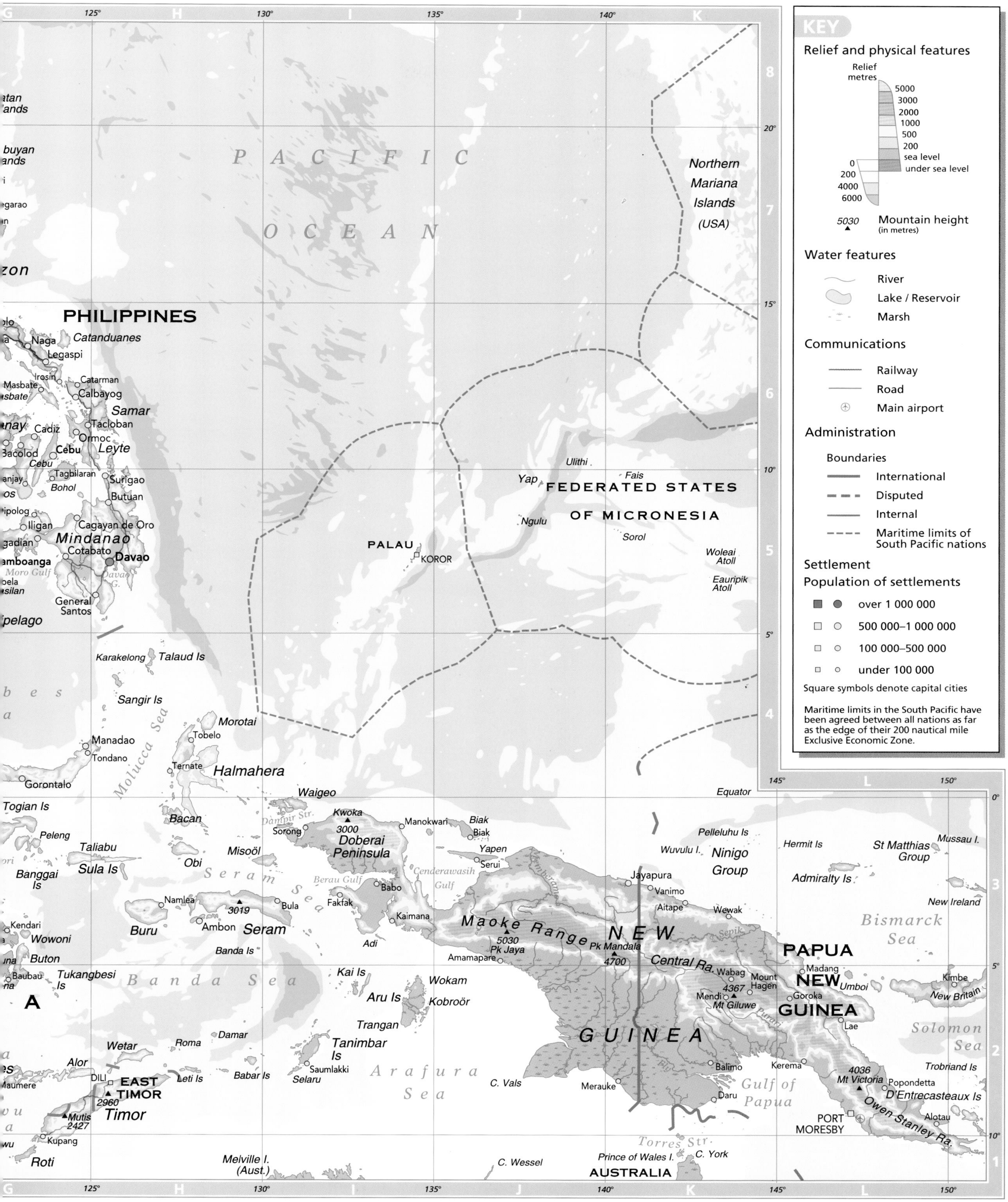

KEY

Relief and physical features

Relief metres

5000
3000
2000
1000
500
200
0 sea level
200 under sea level
4000
6000

5030 ▲ Mountain height (in metres)

Water features

River

Lake / Reservoir

Marsh

Communications

Railway

Road

⊕ Main airport

Administration

Boundaries

International

Disputed

Internal

Maritime limits of South Pacific nations

Settlement

Population of settlements

■ ● over 1 000 000

□ ○ 500 000–1 000 000

□ ○ 100 000–500 000

□ ○ under 100 000

Square symbols denote capital cities

Maritime limits in the South Pacific have been agreed between all nations as far as the edge of their 200 nautical mile Exclusive Economic Zone.

PACIFIC OCEAN

PHILIPPINES

atan ands
buyan ands
i
garao
zon
olo
Naga *Catanduanes*
Legaspi
Irosin Catarman
Masbate Calbayog
sbate
Samar
nay Cadiz *Tacloban*
Ormoc *Leyte*
3acolod **Cebu**
Cebu
anjay Tagbilaran Surigao
os *Bohol* Butuan
ipolog Iligan
gadian Cagayan de Oro
Mindanao Cotabato
amboanga Davao
bela *Davao G.*
asilan *Moro Gulf*
General Santos
pelago

Northern Mariana Islands (USA)

Ulithi *Fais*

Yap **FEDERATED STATES**

OF MICRONESIA

Ngulu

Sorol

PALAU

☐ KOROR

Woleai Atoll

Eauripik Atoll

Karakelong *Talaud Is*

Sangir Is

Morotai

Manadao Tobelo
Tondano Ternate *Halmahera*

Gorontalo

Togian Is

Molucca Sea

Waigeo

Equator

Dampir Str. Kwoka ▲ 3000 Manokwari *Biak*
Sorong *Doberai Peninsula* *Biak*
Yapen
Misoöl Serui

Peleng
Taliabu
Banggai Is *Sula Is* Obi
Seram Sea Babo
Namlea Fakfak
3019 ▲ Bula
Ambon *Seram* Kaimana
Buru
Banda Is
Kendari *Adi*
Wowoni
na *Buton*
Baubau *Tukangbesi Is*
ria

Berau Gulf *Cenderawasih Gulf*

Jayapura
Vanimo
Aitape
Wewak

Pelleluhu Is
Wuvulu I. *Ninigo Group*

Hermit Is *St Matthias Group* *Mussau I.*

Admiralty Is *New Ireland*

Bismarck Sea

A

Banda Sea

Maoke Range **N E W**
5030 ▲ Pk Mandala ▲
Pk Jaya 4700 *Central Ra.*
Amamapare

PAPUA
Madang **NEW**
Wabag Umboi Kimbe
Mount Hagen *New Britain*
4367 ▲ Goroka
Mendi *Mt Giluwe* Lae **GUINEA**

Kai Is Wokam
Aru Is Kobroör

Trangan

Tanimbar Is

Saumlakki
Selaru

Arafura Sea

C. Vals Merauke

G U I N E A

Balimo

Kerema

Solomon Sea

4036 ▲ Mt Victoria *Trobriand Is*
Popondetta
D'Entrecasteaux Is

PORT MORESBY ☐
Alotau

Gulf of Papua

Owen Stanley Ra.

Wetar Roma *Damar*
Alor
DILI **EAST** Leti Is *Babar Is*
2960 ▲ **TIMOR**
Mutis ▲ *Timor*
2427
wu Kupang
Roti

Melville I. (Aust.)

Torres Str.
C. Wessel Prince of Wales I. C. York

AUSTRALIA

Mercator projection

1 THE INDONESIAN WILDFIRES 1997–98

Wildfires have been a major problem in Indonesia for many years. Almost without exception these fires are deliberately lit by farmers, plantation companies and timber companies wanting to clear the land in the cheapest possible way. During late 1997 and early 1998, the fires were so numerous and widespread that their smoke created a thick pollution haze over much of South-East Asia. The map below shows the locations of some of the major fires between 23 September and 2 October 1997. It was during these 10 days that nearby Malaysia declared a 'State of Emergency' because of the severe smoke pollution and the problems which it caused.

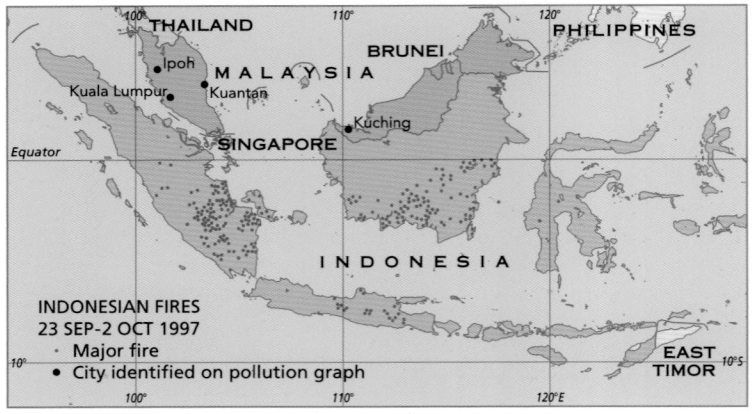

The fires and their smoke haze lasted in the area for many months. The haze created severe health problems, disrupted air and sea transport and caused a plane crash which killed 234 people. The fires destroyed millions of hectares of natural forest and plantation timber, set alight a million hectares of peat swamp, polluted rivers and coral reefs and threatened many animals and birds including the endangered orangutan, Sumatran tiger and Asian elephant.

2 AIR POLLUTION LEVELS

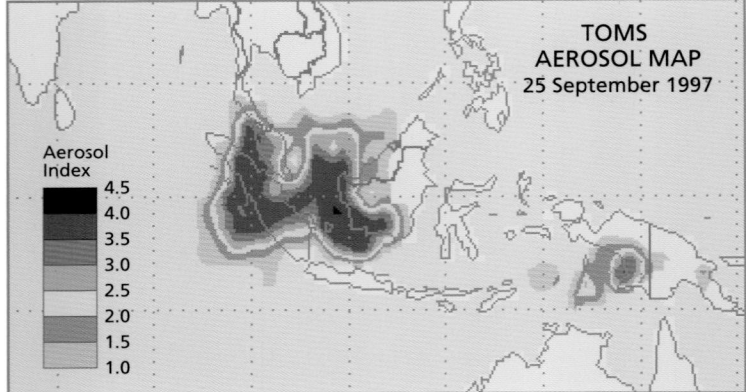

NASA's Total Ozone Mapping Spectrometer, mounted in a satellite, measures ozone and sulphur dioxide in the atmosphere. Data from the TOMS has been used to draw this aerosol map. It shows the very heavy pollution over South-East Asia on 25 September 1997.

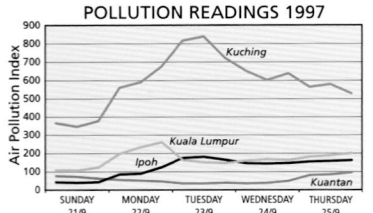

Air Pollution Index	Pollution Level	Air Quality
0–50	Low	Good
51–100	Standard	Moderate
101–200	Alert	Unhealthy
201–300	Warning	Very Unhealthy
301–400	Emergency	Hazardous
401–500	Critical	Very Hazardous

Readings above 500 are extremely rare.
See map on left for location of cities

The dense haze over South-East Asia has had very serious health effects on people. These have included eye, skin and respiratory problems. It is believed that the worst air pollution ever recorded anywhere in the world occurred in Kuching on 23 September 1997.

3 NOAA SATELLITE IMAGES OF THE FIRES

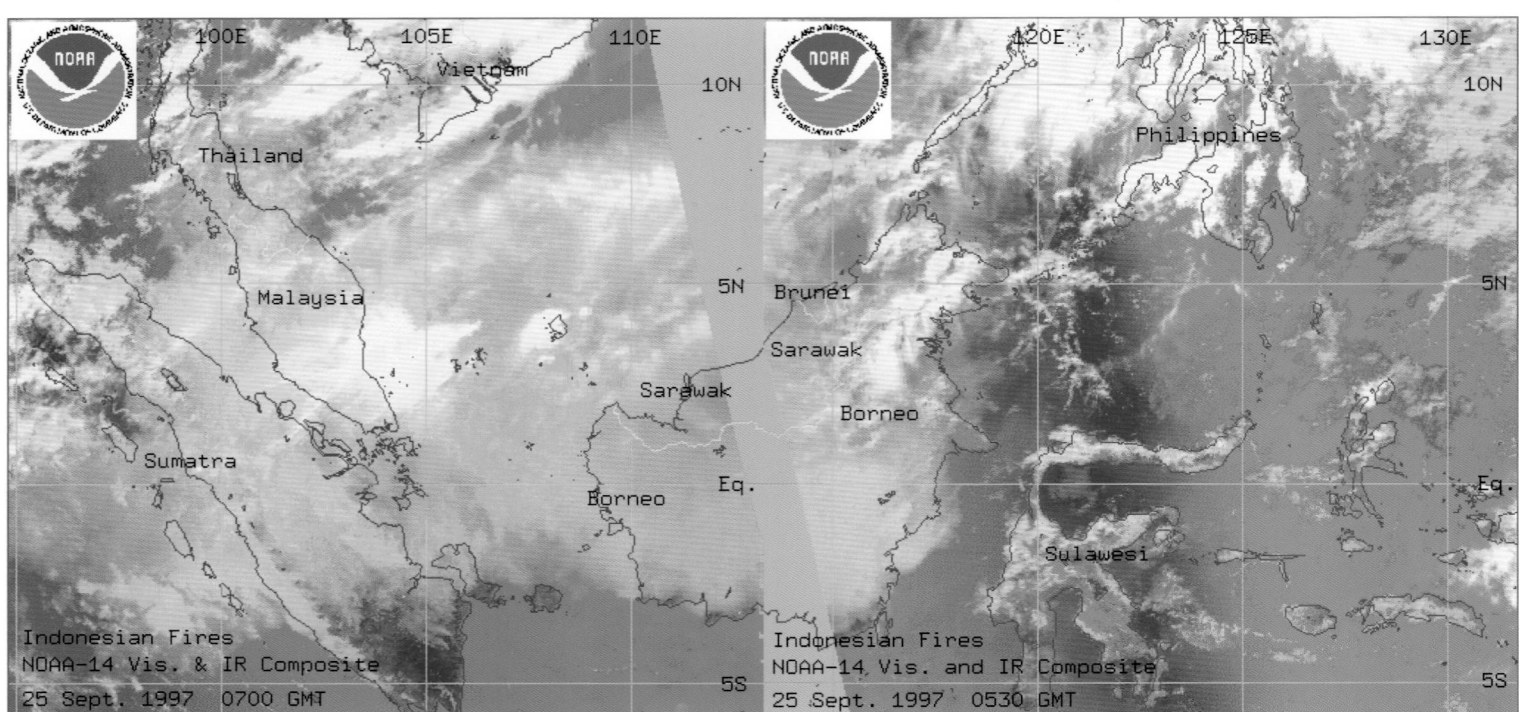

These two NOAA-14 satellite images show South-East Asia on 25 September 1997, one of the worst days for smoke pollution. The smoke shows up as a pink haze on these images. The bright blue gap between the two images is due to the path taken by the satellite.

1 THE 1991 ERUPTION

Mt Pinatubo is one of 22 active volcanoes in the Philippines. After lying dormant for more than 600 years it erupted unexpectedly in April, May and June 1991. This eruption became the most violent and destructive volcanic eruption of the 20th century.

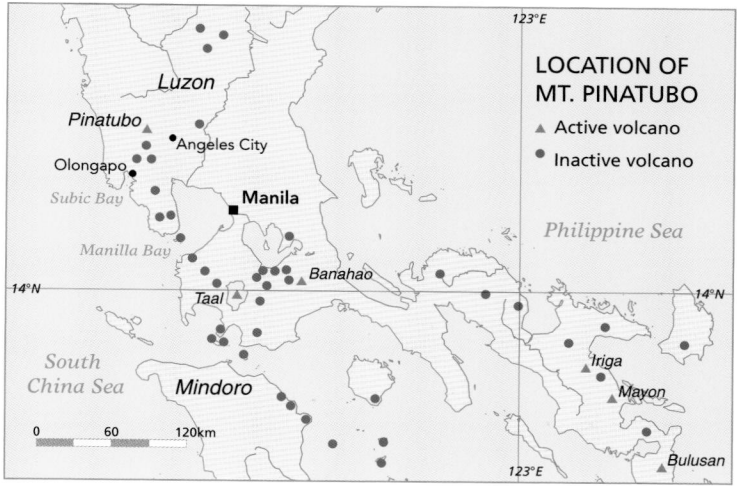

LOCATION OF MT. PINATUBO
▲ Active volcano
● Inactive volcano

2 AFTER THE ERUPTION

By the time the volcanic eruption was over, the top 260 metres of the mountain had been blasted away to leave a 2 km wide *caldera*, more than 20 000 sq km of land around Pinatubo was covered in volcanic ash, and ash had even fallen in mainland South-East Asia, 1200 km away. More than 300 people died during the eruption and about 500 have died since then, mainly as a result of mud flows.

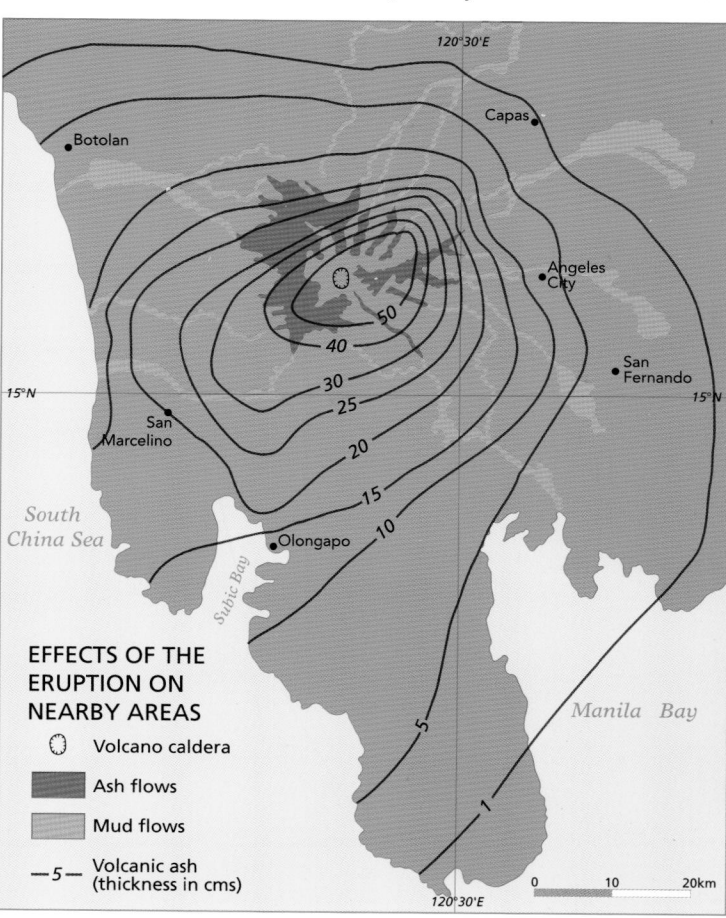

EFFECTS OF THE ERUPTION ON NEARBY AREAS
○ Volcano caldera
Ash flows
Mud flows
—5— Volcanic ash (thickness in cms)

3 EFFECTS ON CLIMATE

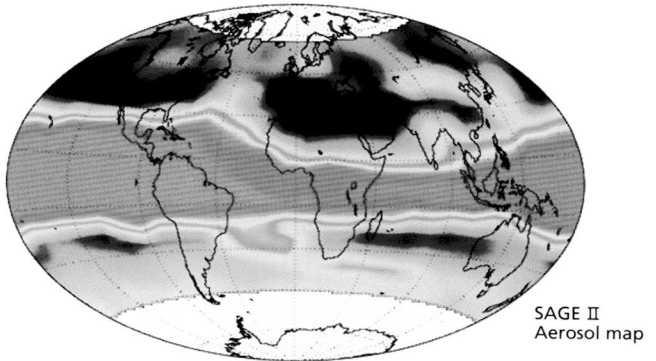

SAGE II Aerosol map

The Mt Pinatubo eruption had a significant impact on world climate. It injected huge amounts of ash, dust and sulphur dioxide gas into the atmosphere. The satellite image above shows the very highly concentrated gas and dust cloud soon after the eruption as a broad band of purple and red along the Equator. This cloud then spread out right across the whole stratosphere, showing up in a satellite image 18 months later as the whole world in purple and red.

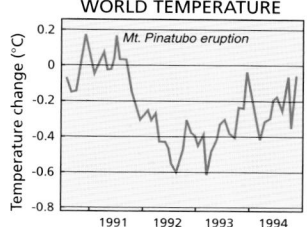

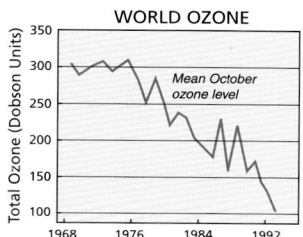

The huge ash and gas cloud created an atmospheric haze across the earth which lowered world temperatures by more than 0.5°C and increased world ozone depletion faster than ever before recorded.

4 SATELLITE IMAGE, DECEMBER 1991

MOS-1 satellite image

This satellite image shows in shades of pink the large mud flows (lahars), ash flows and ash deposits six months after the eruption. Further mud flows will remain a danger for the next 10 to 15 years.

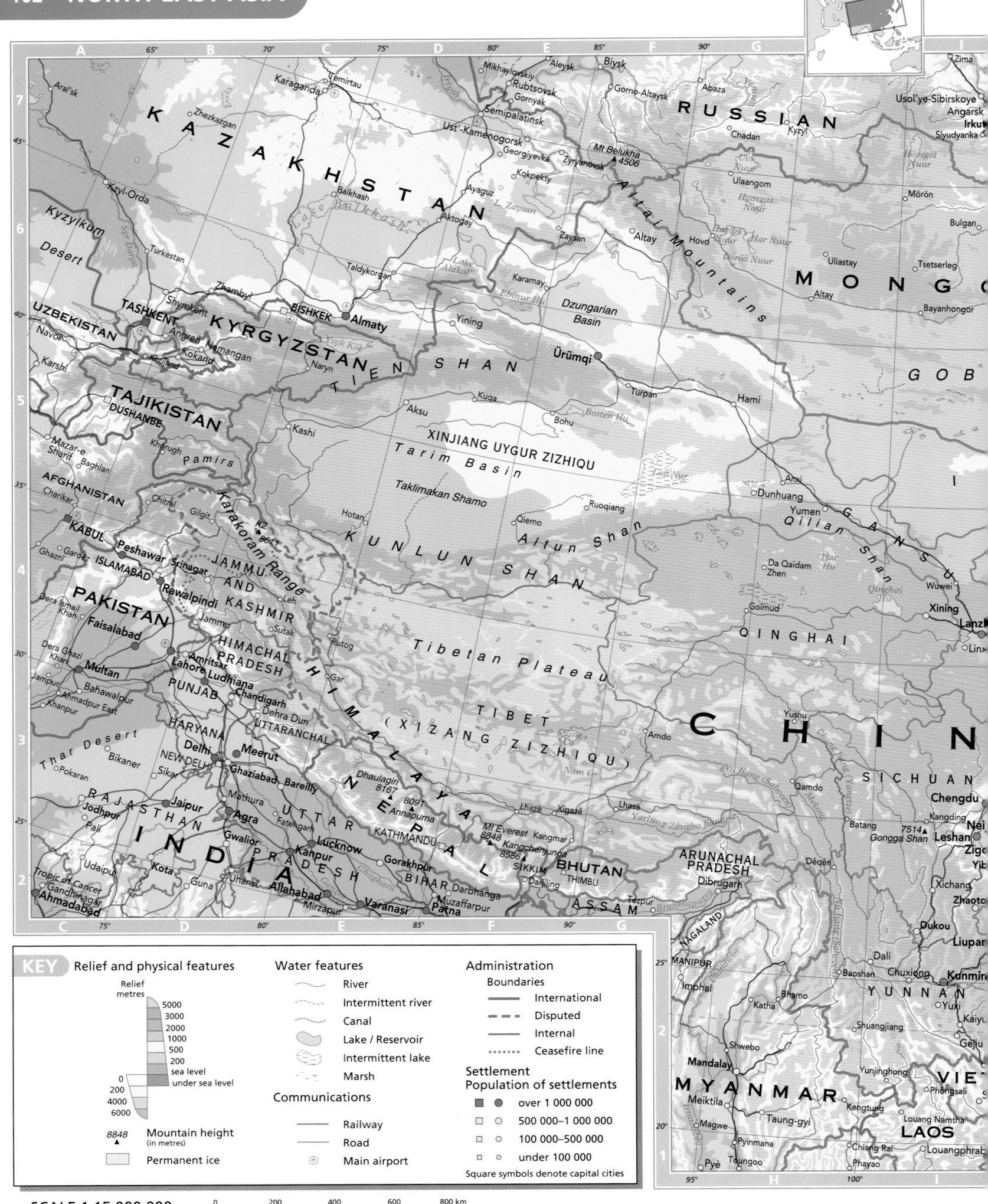

KEY

Relief and physical features

Relief metres
5000
3000
2000
1000
500
200
sea level
under sea level
0
200
4000
6000

8848 ▲ Mountain height (in metres)

Permanent ice

Water features

~ River

~ Intermittent river

~ Canal

Lake / Reservoir

Intermittent lake

Marsh

Communications

— Railway

— Road

⊕ Main airport

Administration

Boundaries

— International

--- Disputed

— Internal

····· Ceasefire line

Settlement

Population of settlements

■ ● over 1 000 000

□ ○ 500 000–1 000 000

□ ○ 100 000–500 000

□ ○ under 100 000

Square symbols denote capital cities

SCALE 1:15 000 000

0   200   400   600   800 km

Conic projection

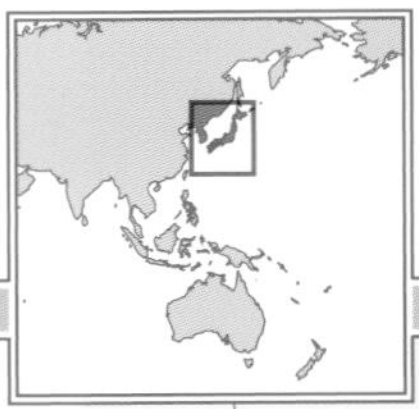

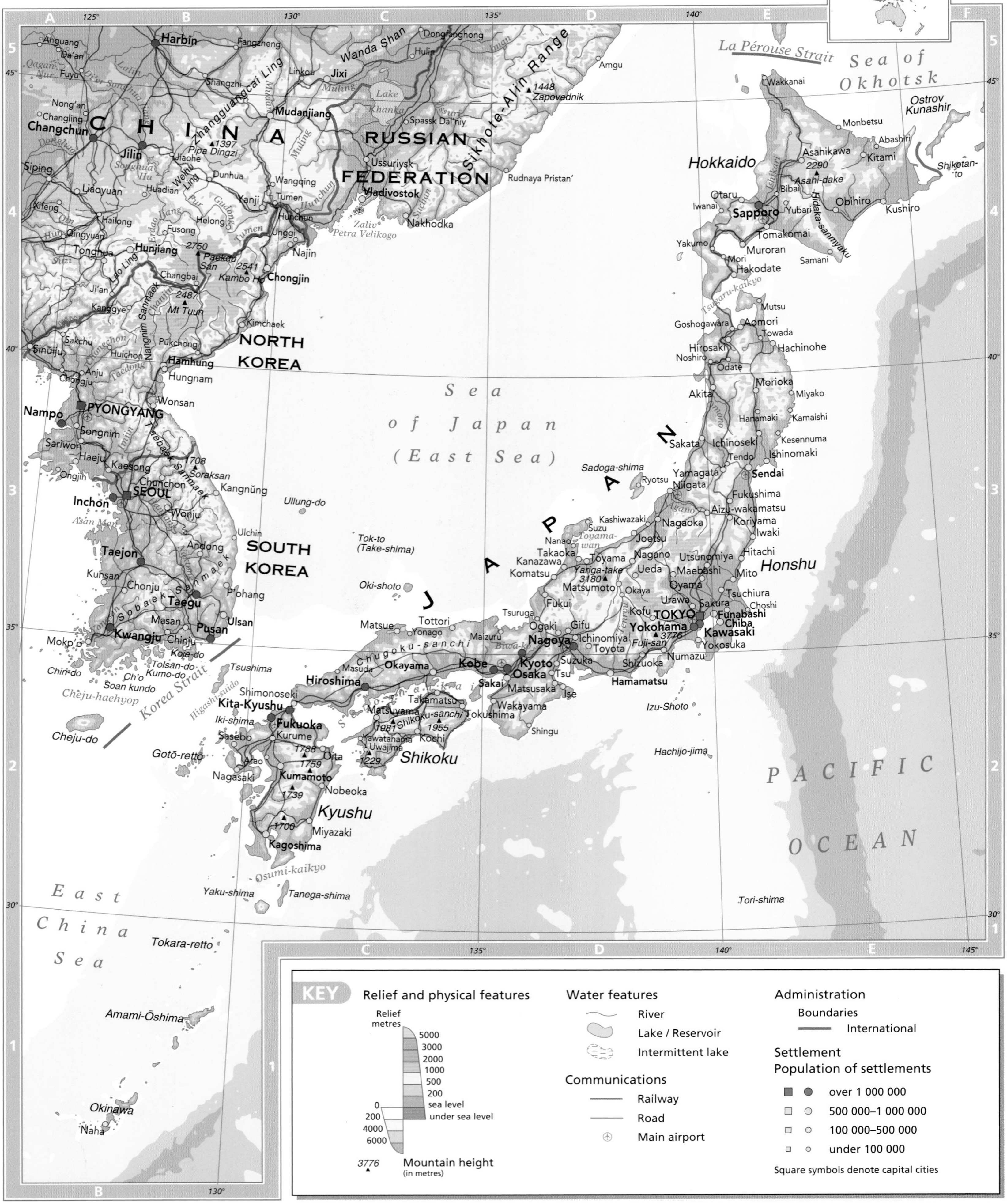

KEY

Relief and physical features

Relief metres
5000
3000
2000
1000
500
200
0 sea level
200 under sea level
4000
6000

3776 ▲ Mountain height (in metres)

Water features

River
Lake / Reservoir
Intermittent lake

Communications

Railway
Road
⊕ Main airport

Administration

Boundaries
International

Settlement
Population of settlements

■ ● over 1 000 000
□ ○ 500 000–1 000 000
□ ○ 100 000–500 000
□ ○ under 100 000

Square symbols denote capital cities

SCALE 1:9 000 000

0   100   200   300   400 km

Albers Equal Area Conic projection

A B C D E F G H I J K

Approximate scale 1:420 000

False colour Landsat 7 ETM image
of Tokyo, Japan

Tokyo Metropolitan Area—the world's largest city with 35.3 million people in 2005—is expected to grow to 36.2 million by 2015. The continuous built-up area—usually referred to as Tokyo—spreads around Tokyo Bay to include the coastal cities of Tokyo, Yokohama, Kawasaki and Chiba, and extends some 45 kilometres west across the Kanto Plain.

The image is dominated by the urban area and by Tokyo Bay with its almost continuous development of port facilities from Yokohama and Tokyo to south of Chiba, making Tokyo Bay one of the world's major ports. So much of the bay has been reclaimed for port facilities that less than 5 per cent of its shoreline is natural.

Many of the characteristics of megacities are evident, such as the continuous urban sprawl, high density of land use—an average population density of 3313 persons per square kilometre—and intensive development of transport infrastructure. Haneda Airport, for example, is built on land reclaimed from Tokyo Bay, and the Trans Tokyo Bay Highway, with its 4.4 kilometre bridge and 9.5 kilometre tunnel linking Kisarazu to Kawasaki, cuts 70 kilometres from the trip around the bay.

Tokyo's great size has created massive problems, including atmospheric pollution from vehicle exhausts, road and rail traffic congestion, and waste disposal. Pressure on the environment of Tokyo Bay is extreme. The demands of Tokyo are so great that its urban footprint—the amount of land needed to sustain the city, provide the materials it needs and process all its wastes—is more than 3.5 times the total productive land area of Japan.

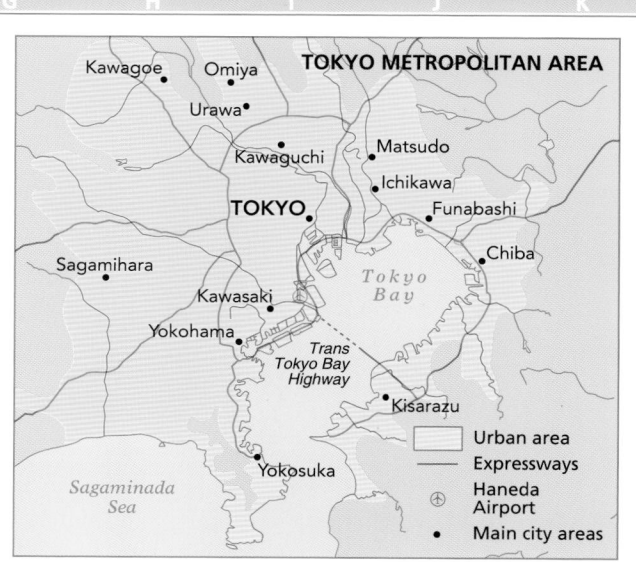

TOKYO METROPOLITAN AREA

Kawagoe
Omiya
Urawa
Kawaguchi
Matsudo
Ichikawa
TOKYO
Funabashi
Sagamihara
Chiba
Kawasaki
Tokyo Bay
Yokohama
Trans Tokyo Bay Highway
Kisarazu
Yokosuka
Sagaminada Sea

Urban area
Expressways
Haneda Airport
Main city areas

KEY

Relief and physical features

Relief metres

5000
3000
2000
1000
500
200
0 sea level
200 under sea level
4000
6000

8848 ▲ Mountain height (in metres)

Permanent ice

Water features

River
Intermittent river
Canal
Lake / Reservoir
Intermittent lake
Marsh

Communications

Railway
Road
⊕ Main airport

Administration

Boundaries

International
Disputed
Internal
Ceasefire line

Settlement

Population of settlements

■ ● over 1 000 000
□ ○ 500 000–1 000 000
□ ○ 100 000–500 000
□ ○ under 100 000

Square symbols denote capital cities

POLITICAL

B. BAHRAIN
U.A.E. UNITED ARAB EMIRATES
UZB. UZBEKISTAN
SCALE 1:40 000 000

SCALE 1:15 000 00●

Conic projection

200 400 600 800 km

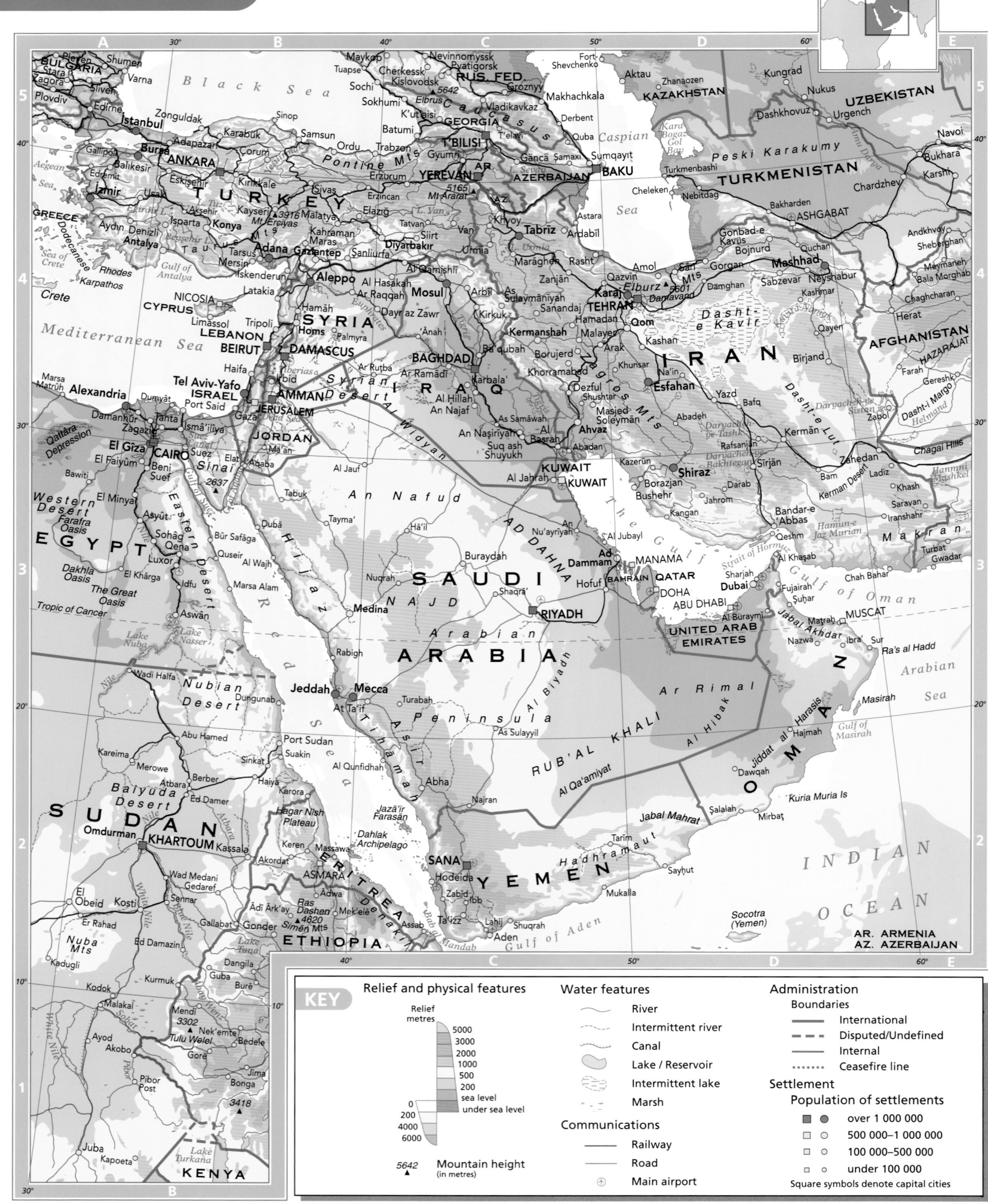

KEY

Relief and physical features

Relief metres
5000
3000
2000
1000
500
200
sea level
under sea level
0
200
4000
6000

▲ 5642 Mountain height (in metres)

Water features

~ River
~ Intermittent river
~ Canal
Lake / Reservoir
Intermittent lake
Marsh

Communications

Railway
Road
⊕ Main airport

Administration

Boundaries

International
Disputed/Undefined
Internal
Ceasefire line

Settlement

Population of settlements

■ ●	over 1 000 000	
□ ○	500 000–1 000 000	
□ ○	100 000–500 000	
□ ○	under 100 000	

Square symbols denote capital cities

SCALE 1:17 500 000

0 150 300 450 600 750 km

Albers Equal Area Conic projection

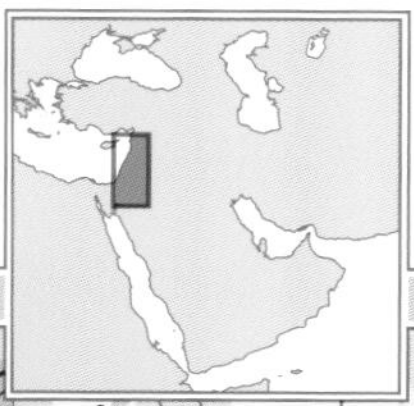

1 ISRAEL AND LEBANON

CYPRUS

Refer to the Key on p108 for explanation of symbols used on this map.

Mediterranean Sea

Latakia
Al Huwayz
Khān Shaykhūn
Jablah
Shūrān
Bāniyās
Ḥamāh
Al Qadmūs
Maṣyāf
Jabal an Nuṣayriyah
1385
SYRIA
Ṭarṭūs
Ṣāfītā
Tall Kalakh
Homs
Halba
2216
Tripoli
Hermel
Hisyah
Batroûn
3087 Qornet es Saouda
El Beqa'a
Tal 'at Mūsá 2659
Ba'albek
An Nabk
Yabrūd
BEIRUT
Zaḥlé
Jayrūd
Ṭaalabaya
LEBANON
1910
Az Zabadānī
Dūmā
Dumayr
Sidon
Jezzine
2814
DAMASCUS
Marjayoûn
Tyre
Bāniyās
Buḥayrat al Ḥijānah
SYRIA
Nawá
Har Meron 1208
Golan Heights
Acre
Rama
Zefat
Nazareth
As Suwaydā'
1735 Jabal ad Durūz
Tiberias
B. of Haifa
L. Tiberias (Sea of Galilee)
Haifa
'Afula
Dar'ā
Zikhron Ya'aqov
Irbid
Aṛ Ramthā
Ṣalkhad
Ḥadera
Jenīn
1247
Al Mafraq
Netanya
Nāblus
Zarqā'
ISRAEL
Plain of Sharon
WEST BANK
As Salṭ
Tel Aviv-Yafo
Petaḥ Tiqwa
Qā' Khannā
Ḥolon
AMMAN
Rishon le Ziyyon
Ramla
Zarqā'
Lod
Ramallah
Jericho
Ashdod
Reḥovot
JERUSALEM
Ashqelon
Bethlehem
963
Gaza
Qiryat Gat
Hebron
GAZA
Dhībān
Rafah
J. Abu Hallūfah 979
Khān Yūnis
Beersheba
'Arad
JORDAN
Dimona
Al Qaṭrānah
Sedom
Kārak
Aṣ Ṣāfi
Al Ghawr
W. al Ḥasāh
Al Hasā
Negev
Jurf ad Darāwīsh
J. al Hādī
Edom
Beer Menuha
J. Mubrak 1727
Ma'ān
Ḥiyon
Gharandal
EGYPT
1555
Sinai
J. Ramm 1754
Elat
Aqaba
Gulf of Aqaba

Conic Equidistant projection

SCALE 1:2 750 000

0 30 60 90 120 km

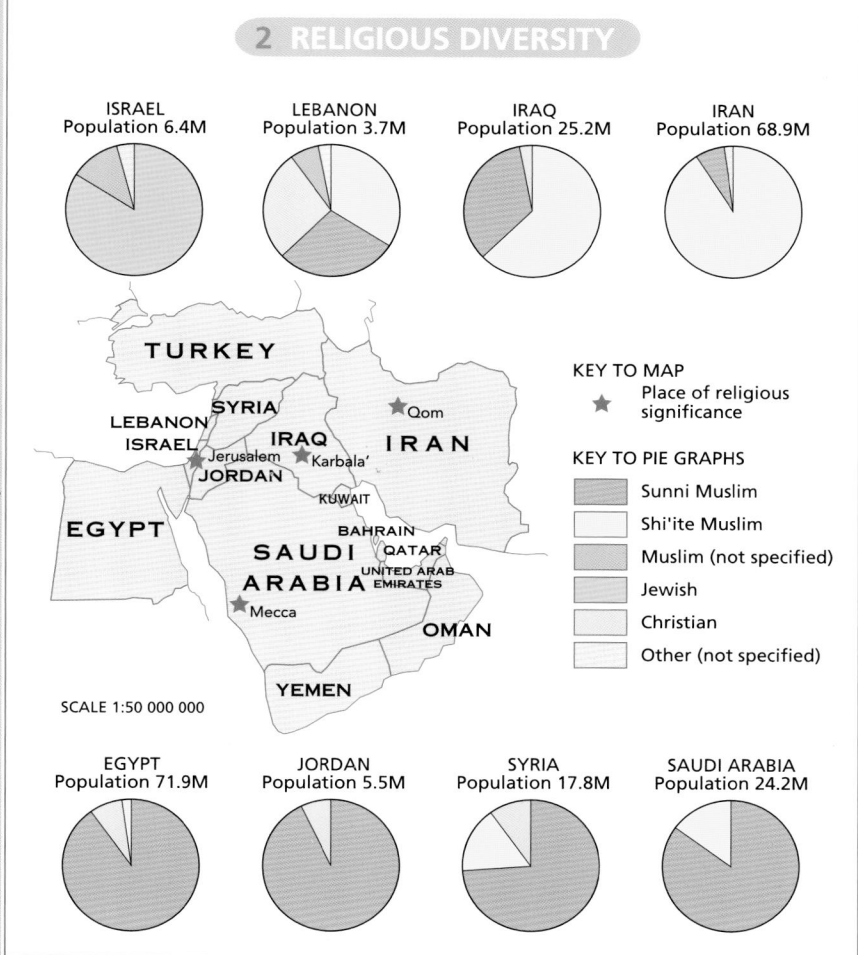

2 RELIGIOUS DIVERSITY

ISRAEL Population 6.4M
LEBANON Population 3.7M
IRAQ Population 25.2M
IRAN Population 68.9M

TURKEY
LEBANON
SYRIA
Qom
ISRAEL
IRAQ
IRAN
Jerusalem
JORDAN
Karbala'
EGYPT
KUWAIT
BAHRAIN
SAUDI ARABIA
QATAR
UNITED ARAB EMIRATES
Mecca
OMAN
YEMEN

SCALE 1:50 000 000

KEY TO MAP
★ Place of religious significance

KEY TO PIE GRAPHS
Sunni Muslim
Shi'ite Muslim
Muslim (not specified)
Jewish
Christian
Other (not specified)

EGYPT Population 71.9M
JORDAN Population 5.5M
SYRIA Population 17.8M
SAUDI ARABIA Population 24.2M

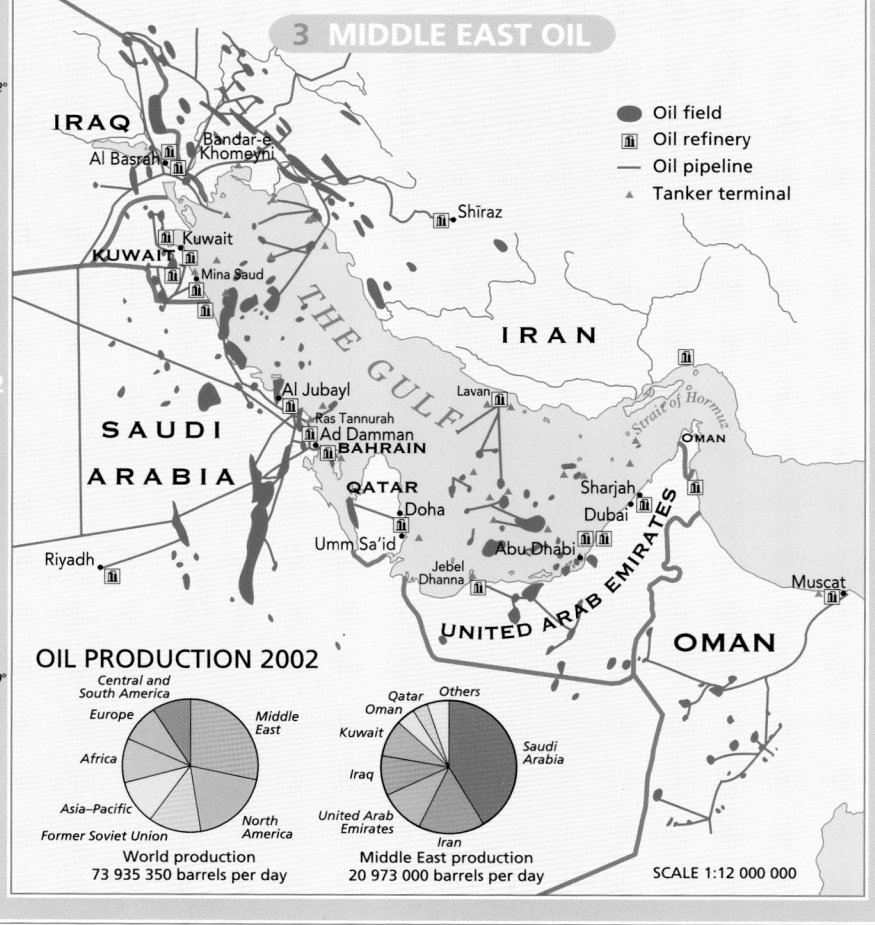

3 MIDDLE EAST OIL

IRAQ
Al Başrah
Bandar-e Khomeyni
Shīrāz
Kuwait
KUWAIT
Mina Saud
IRAN
Al Jubayl
Lavan
Ras Tannurah
Ad Damman
OMAN
SAUDI ARABIA
BAHRAIN
Sharjah
QATAR
Dubai
Doha
Abu Dhabi
Riyadh
Umm Sa'id
Jebel Dhanna
UNITED ARAB EMIRATES
Muscat
OMAN
THE GULF
Strait of Hormuz

⬤ Oil field
🏭 Oil refinery
— Oil pipeline
▲ Tanker terminal

OIL PRODUCTION 2002

Central and South America
Europe
Middle East
Africa
Asia-Pacific
Former Soviet Union
North America

World production
73 935 350 barrels per day

Qatar Others
Oman
Kuwait
Saudi Arabia
Iraq
United Arab Emirates
Iran

Middle East production
20 973 000 barrels per day

SCALE 1:12 000 000

A 30° B 20° C 10° D 0° E 10° F 20° G 30° H 40° I 50° J 60° K 70°

Arctic Circle

ATLANTIC OCEAN

Barents Sea

North Cape
Kolguyev
Cape Kanin
Kanin Pen.
Cheshskaya Bay
Pechora

Ísafjörður
Iceland
1833 Snæfell
Vatnajökull
Vestmannaeyjar

Norwegian Sea

Vesterålen
Lofoten
Lappland
Inarijärvi
Lake Imandra
Kola Peninsula
White Sea
Mezen

Scandinavia
Lule
Ume
Indals
Gulf of Bothnia
Lake Onega
Dvina
Rybinsk Reservoir
Nycbegda

Faeroes

Shetland

North Sea

Åland
Mälaren
Vänern
Vättern
Hiiumaa
Saaremaa
Gulf of Finland
Lake Ladoga
Lake Peipus
Volga
Klyubushev Reservoir

Orkney
Outer Hebrides
Ben Nevis 1344
British Isles
Malin Head

Skagerrak
Kattegat
Sjælland
Fyn
Gotland
Öland
Bornholm
Baltic Sea

North European Plain
Volga Uplands
Central Russian Uplands

Ural Mountains

Ireland
Cape Clear
The Pennines
Great Britain
Land's End
English Channel
St George's Channel
Irish Sea

Frisian Is
Ijsselmeer
Weser
Elbe
Oder
Warta
Vistula
Bug
Pripet Marshes
Kiev Reservoir
Don
Kirghiz Steppe

Strait of Dover

Bay of Biscay

Brittany
Seine
Marne
Rhine
Loire
Jura
Vosges
Taunus
Bodeltsee
Dniester
Carpathian Mountains
Dnieper
Tsimlyansk Reservoir
Volga
Ural

Cape Finisterre

Rhône
Garonne
Lake Geneva
Mont Blanc 4808
ALPS
Matterhorn 4478
3798 Gross Glockner
Balaton
Hungarian Plain
Mureş
Sava
Transylvanian Alps
Crimea
Sea of Azov
Elbrus 5642
Caucasus
Caspian Sea

Cantabrian Mountains
Massif Central
Pyrenees 3404 Pico de Aneto
Gulf of Lions
Apennines
Dinaric Alps
Danube
Balkan Mts
Rhodope Mts
Black Sea
Mt Ararat 5165

Douro
Duero
Ebro
Tagus
Sierra Morena
Guadalquivir
Sierra Nevada
Corsica
Balearic Islands
Menorca
Mallorca
Ibiza
Sardinia
Ligurian Sea
Adriatic Sea
Tyrrhenian Sea
Vesuvius 1281
Corfu
Pindus Mts
Mt Olympus 2911
Evvoia
Aegean Sea
Sea of Marmara
Kelkit
Lake Van
Zagros Mts

Cape St Vincent
Strait of Gibraltar
Mediterranean Sea
Sicily
Mt Etna 3323
Ionian Sea
Zakynthos
Naxos
Rhodes
Crete
Mt Olympus 1952
Cyprus
Taurus Mts
Lake Tuz
Tigris
Euphrates

Hauts Plateaux
Saharan Atlas

Suez Canal
Qattâra Depression
Sinai
An Nafud
Red Sea

Libyan Desert
Nile
Tropic of Cancer
Sahara
Lake Nasser
Darfur

LAND REGIONS

North-West Highlands
Scandinavian Highlands
Arctic Circle
North-West Highlands
Coastal Lowlands and Great European Plain
Central Uplands and Plateaux
Alpine Mountain System

SCALE 1:45 000 000

Relief

Relief metres	
5000	
3000	
2000	
1000	
500	
200	
sea level	
0	under sea level
200	
4000	
6000	

Permanent ice

5642 ▲ Mountain height (in metres)

SCALE 1:25 000 000

0 300 600 900 km

Conic Equidistant projection

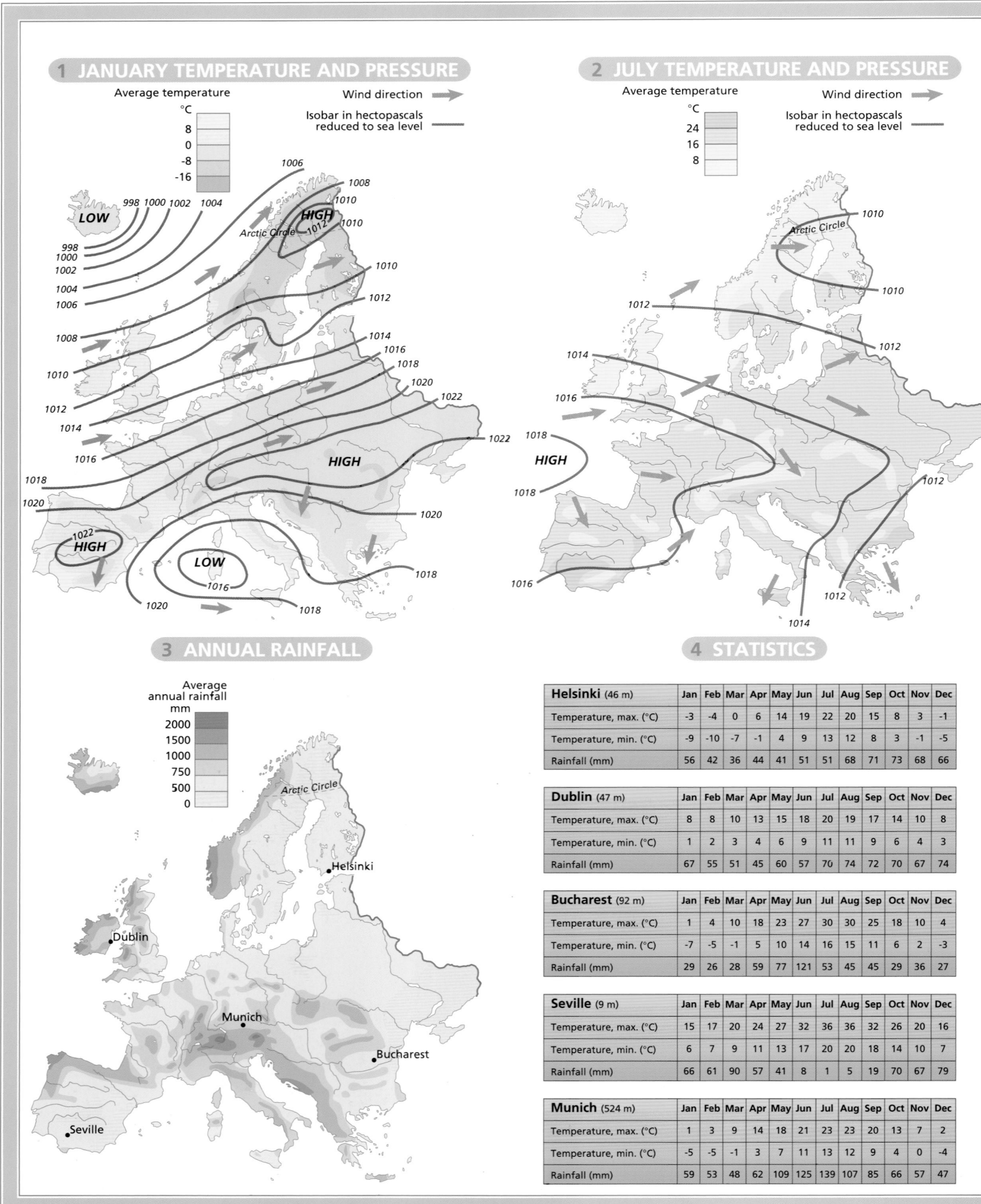

1 JANUARY TEMPERATURE AND PRESSURE

Average temperature

°C
8
0
-8
-16

Wind direction →

Isobar in hectopascals reduced to sea level ——

2 JULY TEMPERATURE AND PRESSURE

Average temperature

°C
24
16
8

Wind direction →

Isobar in hectopascals reduced to sea level ——

3 ANNUAL RAINFALL

Average annual rainfall
mm
2000
1500
1000
750
500
0

4 STATISTICS

Helsinki (46 m)	Jan	Feb	Mar	Apr	May	Jun	Jul	Aug	Sep	Oct	Nov	Dec
Temperature, max. (°C)	-3	-4	0	6	14	19	22	20	15	8	3	-1
Temperature, min. (°C)	-9	-10	-7	-1	4	9	13	12	8	3	-1	-5
Rainfall (mm)	56	42	36	44	41	51	51	68	71	73	68	66

Dublin (47 m)	Jan	Feb	Mar	Apr	May	Jun	Jul	Aug	Sep	Oct	Nov	Dec
Temperature, max. (°C)	8	8	10	13	15	18	20	19	17	14	10	8
Temperature, min. (°C)	1	2	3	4	6	9	11	11	9	6	4	3
Rainfall (mm)	67	55	51	45	60	57	70	74	72	70	67	74

Bucharest (92 m)	Jan	Feb	Mar	Apr	May	Jun	Jul	Aug	Sep	Oct	Nov	Dec
Temperature, max. (°C)	1	4	10	18	23	27	30	30	25	18	10	4
Temperature, min. (°C)	-7	-5	-1	5	10	14	16	15	11	6	2	-3
Rainfall (mm)	29	26	28	59	77	121	53	45	45	29	36	27

Seville (9 m)	Jan	Feb	Mar	Apr	May	Jun	Jul	Aug	Sep	Oct	Nov	Dec
Temperature, max. (°C)	15	17	20	24	27	32	36	36	32	26	20	16
Temperature, min. (°C)	6	7	9	11	13	17	20	20	18	14	10	7
Rainfall (mm)	66	61	90	57	41	8	1	5	19	70	67	79

Munich (524 m)	Jan	Feb	Mar	Apr	May	Jun	Jul	Aug	Sep	Oct	Nov	Dec
Temperature, max. (°C)	1	3	9	14	18	21	23	23	20	13	7	2
Temperature, min. (°C)	-5	-5	-1	3	7	11	13	12	9	4	0	-4
Rainfall (mm)	59	53	48	62	109	125	139	107	85	66	57	47

SCALE 1:40 000 000

0 400 800 1200 1600 km

Conic projection

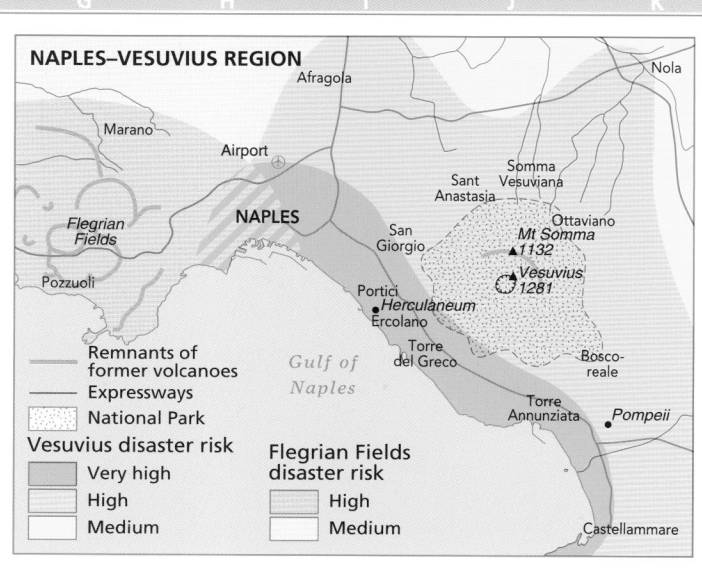

A B C D E F G H I J K

9 8 7 6 5 4 3 2 1

```
0      2      4 km
```

Approximate scale 1:160 000

**False colour Advanced Spaceborne Thermal Emission
and Reflection Radiometer (ASTER) image of Vesuvius,
Italy, dated 26 September 2000**

**Built-up urban
area of the
Naples region**

**Areas of intensive
agriculture on rich
volcanic soils**

**Woodland and
scrub on slopes
and rugged areas**

**The bare ash and
lava-covered cone
of Vesuvius**

Naples, Italy's third-largest city, is dominated by Vesuvius, the world's most famous and most hazardous active volcano. More people live close to Vesuvius than any other volcano. People have always farmed the rich volcanic soils on its lower slopes, but rapid urbanisation since its last eruption in 1944 has consumed most of the farming land and spread up the lower slopes of Vesuvius.

Naples is located between Vesuvius and the Flegrian Fields, a remnant of an earlier volcano which contains 40 small cinder cones, explosion craters and thermal pools. With one million people in towns and villages around Vesuvius and 3.4 million in the Naples region, it is one of the world's highest risk areas.

Vesuvius is most famous for its devastating 79 AD eruption, which buried the surrounding area in up to 30 metres of ash and left only a remnant of the original volcano. An estimated 3500 people were suffocated, buried or burned alive in Pompeii and Herculaneum.

With so many more people in the region, the new Vesuvius which has grown in the remnant of the former volcano is considered even more dangerous and is constantly monitored for activity that could signal a new eruption. Italian authorities are now paying families most at risk to move to safe areas and hoping that Vesuvius gives sufficient warning to evacuate the remaining residents.

NAPLES–VESUVIUS REGION

Nola, Afragola, Marano, Airport, Somma Vesuviana, Sant Anastasia, Flegrian Fields, NAPLES, San Giorgio, Ottaviano, Mt Somma ▲1132, Vesuvius 1281, Pozzuoli, Portici, Herculaneum Ercolano, Torre del Greco, Bosco-reale, *Gulf of Naples*, Torre Annunziata, *Pompeii*, Castellammare

— Remnants of former volcanoes
— Expressways
National Park

Vesuvius disaster risk
Very high
High
Medium

Flegrian Fields disaster risk
High
Medium

Norwegian Sea

ATLANTIC OCEAN

North Sea

Faeroes (Denmark)
Tórshavn

Shetland

Orkney
Thurso
Lewis
Outer Hebrides
The Minch
Skye
Inverness
Moray Firth
Ben Nevis 1344
Mull
Grampian Mountains
Aberdeen
Perth
Dundee
Stirling
Kirkcaldy
Firth of Forth
Glasgow
Edinburgh
Southern Uplands
Dumfries

UNITED KINGDOM

Malin Head
Londonderry
Donegal Bay
Achill Island
Belfast
Isle of Man
Bangor
Solway Firth
Carlisle
Newcastle upon Tyne
Sunderland
Middlesbrough
Darlington

REPUBLIC OF IRELAND

Galway
Galway Bay
Dublin
Wicklow Mts
Limerick
Shannon
Dingle B.
Cape Clear
Cork
Waterford
St George's Channel
Fishguard
Cardigan Bay
Cambrian Mts
Snowdon 1085
Anglesey
Irish Sea
Liverpool
Manchester
Sheffield
Leeds
Huddersfield
York
Kingston upon Hull
Humber
Blackpool
Preston
Lancaster
Bradford
Pennines
Derby
Nottingham
The Wash
Stoke-on-Trent
Shrewsbury
Birmingham
Leicester
Peterborough
Norwich
Cambridge
Ipswich
Milton Keynes
Oxford
Luton
Swansea
Newport
Gloucester
Cardiff
Bristol
Swindon
Watford
Southend-on-Sea
Bristol Channel
Taunton
Reading
LONDON
Brighton
Hastings
Barnstaple
Southampton
Bournemouth
Portsmouth
Isle of Wight
Dover
Plymouth
Torquay
Penzance
Land's End
Isles of Scilly

English Channel
Strait of Dover

Guernsey
Channel Islands
Jersey
Cherbourg
Dieppe
Le Havre
Golfe de St-Malo
St-Malo
Caen
Rouen
Brest
Quimper
Lorient
Vannes
Belle Île
Rennes
Laval
Le Mans
Alençon
Chartres
St-Nazaire
Nantes
Angers
Tours
Cholet
Île d'Oléron
La Rochelle
Rochefort
Poitiers
Angoulême
Limoges

FRANCE
PARIS
Marne-la-Vallée
Beauvais
Amiens
Arras
Boulogne
Calais
Dunkerque
Lille
Charleroi
Reims
Châlons-en-Champagne
Troyes
Auxerre
Orléans
Vierzon
Châteauroux
Moulins
Vichy
Roanne
Mâcon
Dijon
Chalon-sur-Saône
Nancy
Metz
Thionville
Strasbourg
Mulhouse
Belfort
Besançon

Bay of Biscay

NORWAY
Vikna
Namsos
Verdalsøra
Frøya
Hitra
Smøla
Stjørdalshalsen
Trondheim
Kristiansund
Molde
Ålesund
Storskrymten 1985
Galdhøpiggen 2470
Gudbrandsdalen
Lillehammer
Østerdalen
Elverum
Hamar
Gjøvik
Bergen
Voss
Hardangervidda 1690
Harteigan
Haugesund
Drammen
Kongsberg
OSLO
Stavanger
Horten
Moss
Sandnes
Skien
Porsgrunn
Sarpsborg
Arendal
Lindesnes
Kristiansand

Storsjön
Östersund
Sylarna 1761
SWEDEN
Borlänge
Mora
Arvika
Karlstad
Vänern
Uddevalla
Vänersborg
Trollhättan
Borås
Göteborg
Frederikshavn
Varberg
Falkenberg
Skagerrak
Kattegat

DENMARK
Ålborg
Viborg
Randers
Holstebro
Århus
Vejle
Esbjerg
Fredericia
Odense
Fyn
COPENHAGEN
Malmö
Helsingborg
Helsingør
Lund
Landskrona
Trelleborg
Næstved
Lolland
Bornholm (Denmark)
Flensburg
Schleswig
Kiel
North Frisian Islands
Neumünster
Cuxhaven

NETHERLANDS
AMSTERDAM
THE HAGUE
Haarlem
Rotterdam
Utrecht
Apeldoorn
Arnhem
Nijmegen
Eindhoven
Tilburg
Gent
Antwerpen
Brugge
Oostende
Leeuwarden
West Frisian Islands
Den Helder
Groningen
Assen
Wilhelmshaven

BELGIUM
BRUSSELS
Lille
Charleroi
Namur
Liège
Aachen
LUXEMBOURG
LUX
Ardennes
Charleville-Mézières

GERMANY
Hamburg
Bremerhaven
Bremen
Lübeck
Schwerin
Rostock
Neustrelitz
Uelzen
Salzgitter
Hannover
Wolfsburg
Brandenburg
BERLIN
Osnabrück
Münster
Duisburg
Essen
Dortmund
Düsseldorf
Cologne
Bonn
Siegen
Kassel
Göttingen
Nordhausen
Halle
Leipzig
Magdeburg
Potsdam
Wittenberg
Frankfurt an der Oder
Zielona Góra
Dresden
Chemnitz
Erfurt
Jena
Zwickau
Thuringian Forest
Frankfurt am Main
Offenbach am Main
Mainz
Darmstadt
Würzburg
Mannheim
Heidelberg
Bayreuth
Erlangen
Nürnberg
Regensburg
Saarbrücken
Karlsruhe
Pforzheim
Stuttgart
Reutlingen
Ingolstadt
Augsburg
Munich
Landshut
Passau
Ulm
Freiburg im Breisgau
Konstanz
Black Forest
Swabian Alps
Danube
Straubing
Deggendorf
Linz

CZECH REPUBLIC
PRAGUE
Plzeň
Tábor
České Budějovice
Bohemian Forest
Ústí nad Labem

SWITZERLAND
BERN
Zürich
Luzern
Basel
Neuchâtel
Lausanne
Jungfrau 4158
LIECH.
VADUZ
Innsbruck
ALPS
AUSTRIA
Gross Glockner 3798
Salzburg

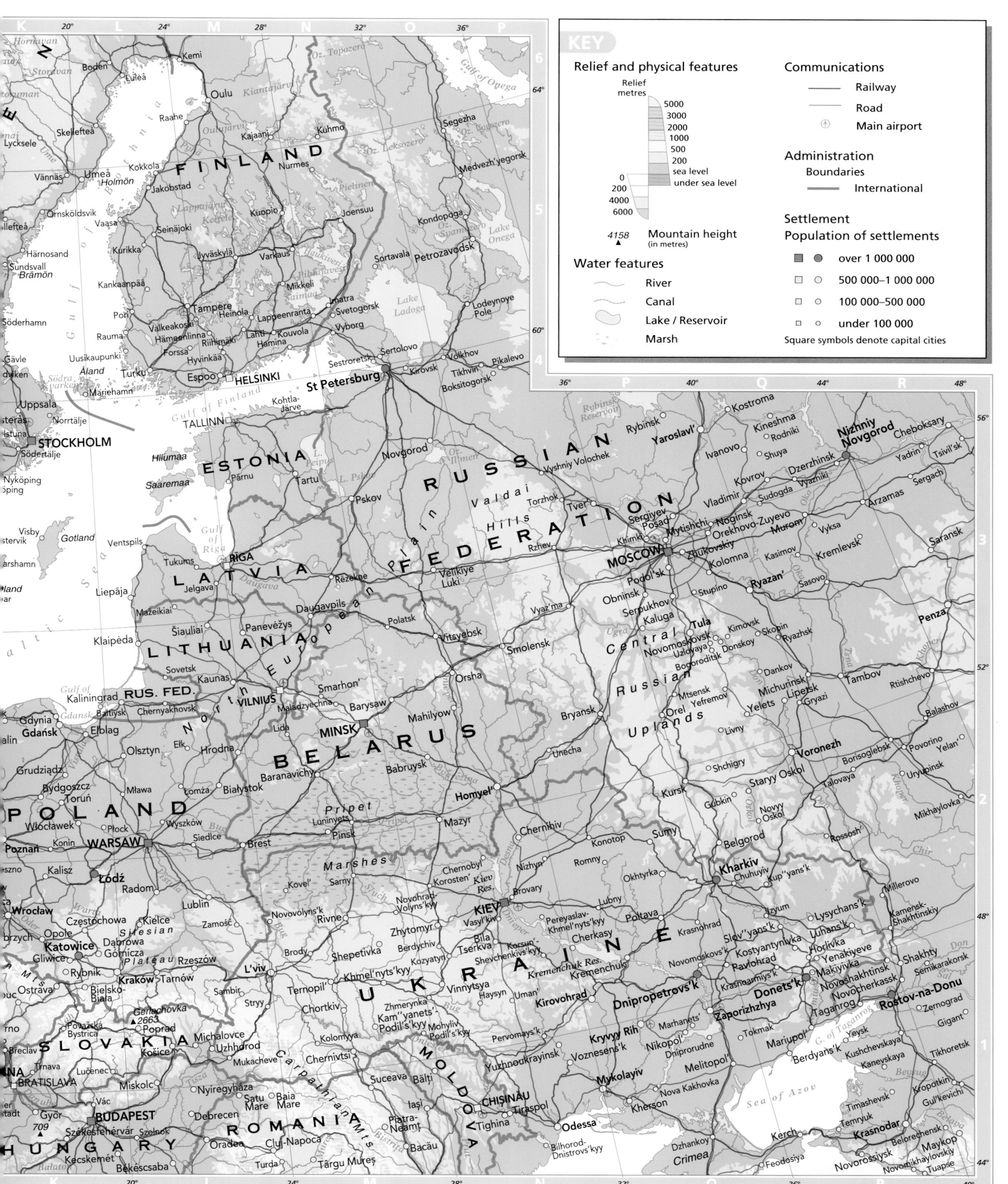

KEY

Relief and physical features

Relief metres
5000
3000
2000
1000
500
200
sea level
0
under sea level
200
4000
6000

4158 ▲ Mountain height (in metres)

Water features

River
Canal
Lake / Reservoir
Marsh

Communications

——— Railway
——— Road
⊕ Main airport

Administration

Boundaries
——— International

Settlement
Population of settlements

■ ● over 1 000 000
□ ○ 500 000–1 000 000
□ ○ 100 000–500 000
□ ○ under 100 000

Square symbols denote capital cities

FINLAND
SWEDEN
ESTONIA
LATVIA
LITHUANIA
RUSSIAN FEDERATION
BELARUS
POLAND
UKRAINE
SLOVAKIA
HUNGARY
ROMANIA
MOLDOVA

STOCKHOLM
HELSINKI
TALLINN
St Petersburg
RIGA
VILNIUS
MINSK
WARSAW
MOSCOW
KIEV
CHIŞINĂU
BUDAPEST
BRATISLAVA

Conic Equidistant projection

Map labels

Bay of Biscay
Gulf of Gascony
Gulf of Lions
Gulf of Valencia
Ligurian Sea
Tyrrhenian Sea
Mediterranean
Strait of Gibraltar
Strait of Bonifacio
Gulf of Genoa
Gulf of Hammamet
Gulf of Gabes

GERMANY
Nürnberg, Regensburg, Augsburg, Munich, Stuttgart, Ulm, Karlsruhe, Strasbourg, Mannheim, Freiburg im Breisgau, Salzburg, Innsbruck, Rosenheim

FRANCE
Brest, St-Malo, St-Brieuc, Quimper, Lorient, St-Nazaire, Nantes, Rennes, Vannes, Alençon, Versailles, Dreux, Chartres, Le Mans, Angers, Orléans, PARIS, Reims, Châlons-en-Champagne, LUXEMBOURG, Metz, Nancy, Fontainebleau, St Dizier, Chaumont, Épinal, Lunéville, Troyes, Blois, Tours, Gien, Vierzon, Bourges, Poitiers, Châtellerault, La Rochelle, Saintes, Angoulême, Limoges, Montluçon, Moulins, Vichy, Clermont-Ferrand, Dijon, Besançon, Dole, Mulhouse, Mâcon, Lyon, St-Étienne, Chambéry, Annecy, Mont Blanc 4808, Grenoble, Gap, Bordeaux, Bergerac, Périgueux, Brive-la-Gaillarde 1885, Rodez, Cahors, Montauban, Albi, Mende, Montélimar, Valence, Digne-les-Bains, Bayonne, Pau, Tarbes, Toulouse, Montpellier, Nîmes, Alès, Avignon, Aix-en-Provence, Nice, Cannes, Monte-Carlo, Narbonne, Béziers, Marseille, Toulon, Perpignan
Massif Central
Pyrenees 3404
Corsica (France), Bastia, Ajaccio, Bonifacio

SWITZERLAND
BERN, Lausanne, Geneva, Zürich, Luzern, Basel

LIECH, VADUZ

ALPS
Bernina Pass, Bellinzona, Dolomites, Bolzano, Trento

ITALY / ITAL
Milan, Monza, Novara, Pavia, Turin, Cuneo, Savona, Genoa, La Spezia, Bergamo, Verona, Vicenza, Padua, Parma, Modena, Bologna, Forlì, Ferrara, Ravenna, Livorno, Pisa, Florence, Viterbo, Civitavecchia, Perugia, ROME, Latina, SAN MAR, Capraia, Elba
Sardinia (Italy), Sassari, Olbia, Oristano, Nuoro, Cagliari, C. Carbonara, C. Spartivento
Palermo, Trapani, Marsala, Pantelleria (Italy), Agrig

SPAIN
A Coruña, Cape Finisterre, Santiago, Lugo, Oviedo, Gijón, Pontevedra, Vigo, Tui, Ourense, Ponferrada, León, Santander, Donostia/San Sebastián, Bilbao, Vitoria-Gasteiz, Miranda de Ebro, Burgos, Palencia, Valladolid, Zamora, Salamanca, Segovia, Ávila, MADRID, Alcalá de Henares, Guadalajara, Soria, Logroño, Pamplona, Zaragoza, Calatayud, ANDORRA, ANDORRA LA VELLA, Lleida, Sabadell, Barcelona, Tarragona, Figueres, Girona, Tortosa, Castelló de la Plana, Valencia, Gandía, Alicante, Elche, Murcia, Cartagena, Almería, Lorca, Jaén, Mulhacén 3482, Sa Nevada, Granada, Linares, Andújar, Ciudad Real, Valdepeñas, Albacete, Villarrobledo, Alcázar, Talavera de la Reina, Toledo, Aranjuez, Puertollano, Córdoba, Sierra Morena, Mérida, Badajoz, Zafra, Seville, Huelva, Cádiz, Jerez de la Frontera, Algeciras, Gibraltar (UK), Málaga
Cantabrian Mountains
Balearic Islands, Menorca, Mahón, Alcúdia, Manacor, Palma de Mallorca, Mallorca, Ibiza, Eivissa, Formentera

PORTUGAL
Oporto, Braga, Bragança, Viseu, Guarda, Coimbra, Covilhã, Portalegre, LISBON, Setúbal, Évora, Beja, Sines, Lagos, Faro, Cape St Vincent

MOROCCO
Tangier, Larache, Ksar el Kebir, Kénitra, RABAT, Casablanca, El Jadida, Settat, Khouribga, Safi, Beni Mellal, Marrakesh, Jbel Toubkal 4167, Taroudannt, Ouarzazate, Er Rachidia, Meknès, Fez, Azrou, Khenifra, Moyen Atlas, High Atlas, Ceuta (Sp.), Tétouan, Chaouen, Al Hoceima, Melilla (Sp.), Nador, Ouezzane, Sidi Kacem, Taza, Oujda, Taourirt

ALGERIA
Oran, Mostaganem, Relizane, Mascara, Beni-Saf, Ghazaouet, Tlemcen, Sidi Bel Abbès, Tiaret, Ech Chélif, Blida, ALGIERS, Tizi Ouzou, Bejaïa, Skikda, Annaba, Constantine, Guelma, Sétif, Bou Saâda, Souk Ahras, Aïn Beïda, El Eulma, Ksar El Boukhari, Djelfa, Laghouat, Batna, Biskra, Khenchela, Tébessa, El Meghaïer, Touggourt, El Oued, Ghardaïa, Béchar, Figuig, Aïn Sefra, Bouârfa, Mecheria, El Bayadh, Hauts Plateaux, Saharan Atlas, Chott ech Chergui, Chott el Hodna, Chott Melrhir, Abadla
Mts des Nementcha

TUNISIA
TUNIS, Bizerte, Menzel Bourguiba, C. Bon, Nabeul, Sousse, M'Saken, Kairouan, Kasserine, Sfax, Gafsa, Tozeur, Gabès, Chott el Jerid, Zarzis, Medenine, Jendouba, Zuwārah, TRI

Bordj Messaouda, Ghadames, Nalut, Al Jawsh, Gharyan, TRIPOLI
Al Hamadah al Ham
Idhan Awbari
Illizi

KEY

Relief and physical features
Relief metres
5000, 3000, 2000, 1000, 500, 200, sea level, under sea level, 0, 200, 4000, 6000

4808 ▲ Mountain height (in metres)

Water features
~ River
⋯ Intermittent river
~ Canal
▢ Lake / Reservoir
Intermittent lake
Marsh

Communications
— Railway
— Road
⊕ Main airport

Administration
Boundaries
—— International
－－ Disputed
⋯⋯ Ceasefire line

Settlement
Population of settlements
■ ● over 1 000 000
□ ○ 500 000–1 000 000
□ ○ 100 000–500 000
□ ○ under 100 000
Square symbols denote capital cities

SCALE 1:10 000 000
0   100   200   300   400 km

Conic projection

KEY

Relief and physical features

Relief metres
5000
3000
2000
1000
500
200
sea level
0
200 under sea level
4000
6000

▲ 4750 Mountain height (in metres)

Permanent ice

Water features

River

Intermittent river

Lake / Reservoir

Intermittent lake

Marsh

Communications

Railway

Road

⊕ Main airport

Administration

Boundaries

International

Internal

Settlement

Population of settlements

■ ● over 1 000 000

□ ○ 500 000–1 000 000

□ ○ 100 000–500 000

□ ○ under 100 000

Square symbols denote capital cities

ICELAND

Faeroes (Den.)
Torshavn

Jan Mayen (Nor.)

Arctic Circle

Norwegian Sea

NORWAY
Bergen
Oslo
Trondheim
Narvik
Tromso
North Cape

SWEDEN
STOCKHOLM
Norrkoping
Uppsala

Baltic Sea
Gulf of Bothnia
Tampere
Turku

FINLAND
HELSINKI

Svalbard (Norway)
Longyearbyen
Spitsbergen
Nordaustlandet
Bear Island

Barents Sea

Franz Josef Land

Novaya Zemlya

Kara Sea

Murmansk
C. Kanin
Kola Pen.
Kem'
White Sea
Archangel
Kanin Pen.
Kolguyev
Vaygach
Yamal Pen.
Gydanskiy
Peninsula

LIEPĀJA
RIGA
LATVIA
ESTONIA
TALLINN
Tartu
Pskov
Narva

St Petersburg
Lake Ladoga
Petrozavodsk
Novgorod
Cherepovets

LITHUANIA
VILNIUS
Kaunas
Šiauliai

BELARUS
MINSK
Homyel
Mahilyow
Vitsyebsk

Velikiye Luki
Tver
Rybinsk
Yaroslavl
MOSCOW
Smolensk
Bryansk
Kaluga
Tula
Serpukhov
Ryazan'
Murom
Vladimir
Ivanovo
Kostroma

Vologda
Kotlas
Syktyvkar
Ukhta
Troitsko-Pechorsk
Narodnaya ▲1894

R U S S I A N

U R A L S

Pechora G.
Naryan Mar
Mezen
Pinega
Novodvinsk
Vel'sk

Vorkuta
Salekhard
Novyy Port
Vorkuta

UKRAINE
Chernihiv
Sumy
Kharkiv
Kirovohrad
Kursk
Belgorod
Staryy Oskol
Lipetsk
Voronezh
Tambov
Penza
Saransk
Nizhniy Novgorod
Dzerzhinsk
Novomoskovsk
Michurinsk
Cheboksary
Kazan

Izhevsk
Perm
Solikamsk
Berezniki
Kirov
Vyatka
Serov
Khanty-Mansiysk
Nizhniy Tagil

West Siberian Plain

Nadym
Noyabr'sk
Urengoy
Pangody

MOLD
CHIŞINĂU
ROMANIA
BUCHAREST
Galaţi
Ploieşti
Ruse
BULGARIA
Varna
Burgas
Constanţa

Odessa
Mykolayiv
Kherson
Crimea
Simferopol
Sevastopol
Kerch
Dnipropetrovs'k
Zaporizhzhya
Donets'k
Luhans'k
Mariupol'

Black Sea
Sea of Azov
Rostov-na-Donu
Krasnodar
Novorossiysk
Sochi

Saratov
Engels
Kamyshin
Volgograd
Volzhskiy
Don

Tol'yatti
Samara
Syzran'
Kuznetsk
Ul'yanovsk
Naberezhnyye Chelny

Ufa ▲1639
Sterlitamak
Salavat
Zlatoust
Miass
Yaman-Tau
Magnitogorsk

Yekaterinburg
Kamensk-Ural'skiy
Chelyabinsk
Kurgan
Tyumen
Tobol'sk

Siberian Plain
Surgut
Nizhnevartovsk
Kolpashevo
Ob'

Tomsk
Kuybyshev
Anzhero-Sudzhensk
Kemero
Leni Kuznets
Novokuzne

İstanbul
Adapazari
TURKEY
ANKARA
Karabük
Samsun
Ordu
Kayseri
Malatya
Diyarbakir
Van
SYRIA
Aleppo
Ar Raqqah
Ar Rutba
IRAQ
Mosul

Caucasus
Elbrus ▲5642
Stavropol Highlands
GEORGIA
T'BILISI
Sokhumi
Batumi
Groznyy
ARM.
YEREVAN
Mt Ararat ▲5165
AZER.
Ganca
Sumqayit
BAKU
Tabriz
Lake Urmia
IRAN

Caspian Depression
Astrakhan'
Neftekumsk
Makhachkala
Ust Urt Plateau
Aktau

Caspian Sea
Fort Shevchenko
Atyrau
Ural'sk
Orenburg
Orsk
Aktyubinsk
Rudnyy
Kostanay
Petropavlovsk
Omsk
Tatarsk
Novosibirsk

KAZAKHSTAN
ASTANA
Kokshetau
Pavlodar
Temirtau
Karaganda
Zhezkazgan
Aralsk
Aral Sea
Lake Tengiz
Karasuk
Rubtsovsk
Biy
Semipalatinsk

UZBEKISTAN
Kungrad
Nukus
Kzyl-Orda
Syr Darya

TURKMENISTAN
Turkmenbashi
Kara-Bogaz-Gol Bay

CHINA
Mt Be
Ust-Kamenogorsk
Ayaguz
L. Zaysan
Balkhash
Aktogay
Zaysan

0   200   400   600   800 km

Conic Equidistant projection

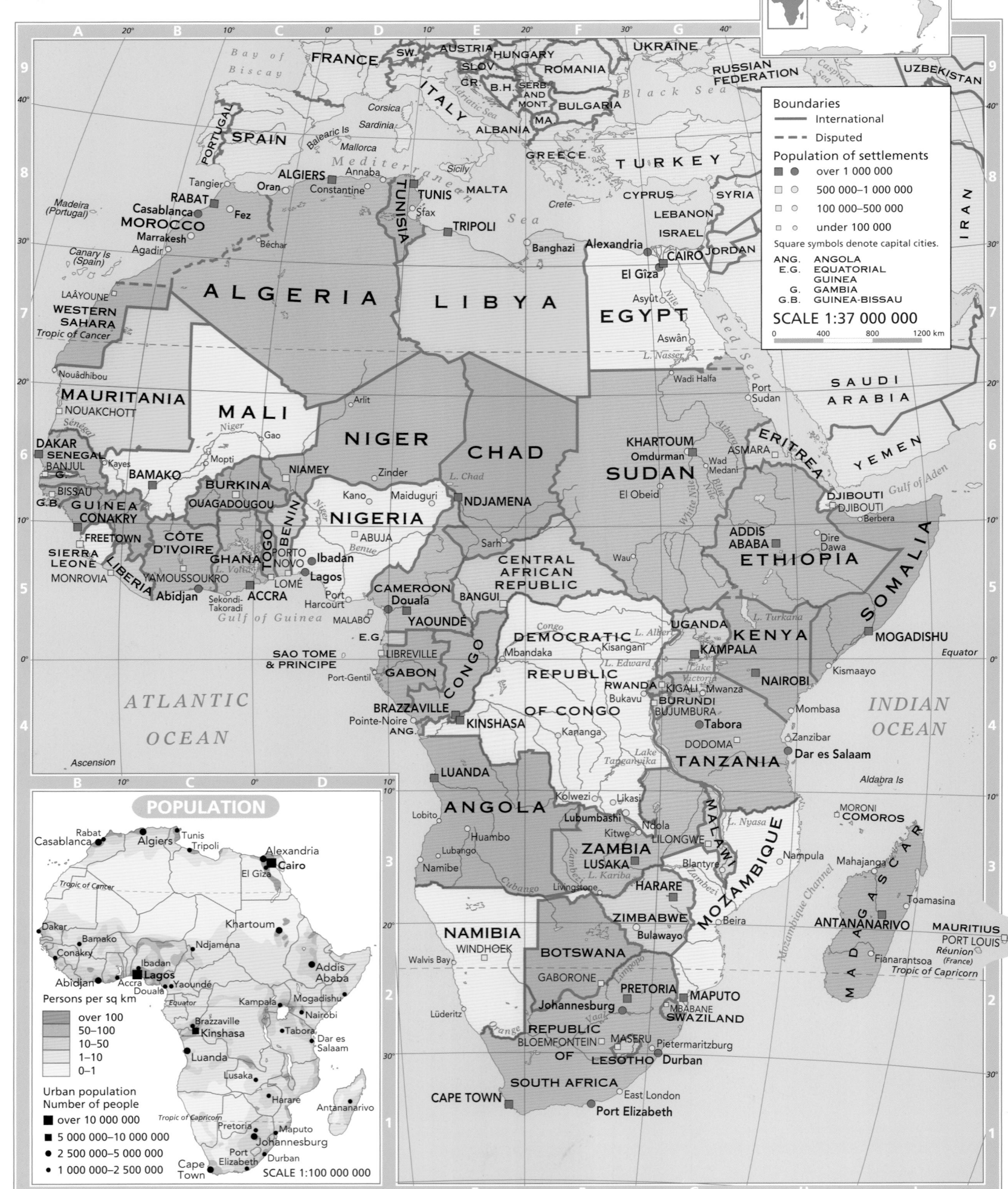

CW

Boundaries
— International
-- Disputed

Population of settlements
■ ● over 1 000 000
□ ○ 500 000–1 000 000
□ ○ 100 000–500 000
□ ○ under 100 000

Square symbols denote capital cities.
ANG.   ANGOLA
E.G.   EQUATORIAL
        GUINEA
G.   GAMBIA
G.B.   GUINEA-BISSAU

SCALE 1:37 000 000
0   400   800   1200 km

POPULATION

Persons per sq km
over 100
50–100
10–50
1–10
0–1

Urban population
Number of people
■ over 10 000 000
■ 5 000 000–10 000 000
● 2 500 000–5 000 000
● 1 000 000–2 500 000

SCALE 1:100 000 000

Lambert Azimuthal Equal Area projection

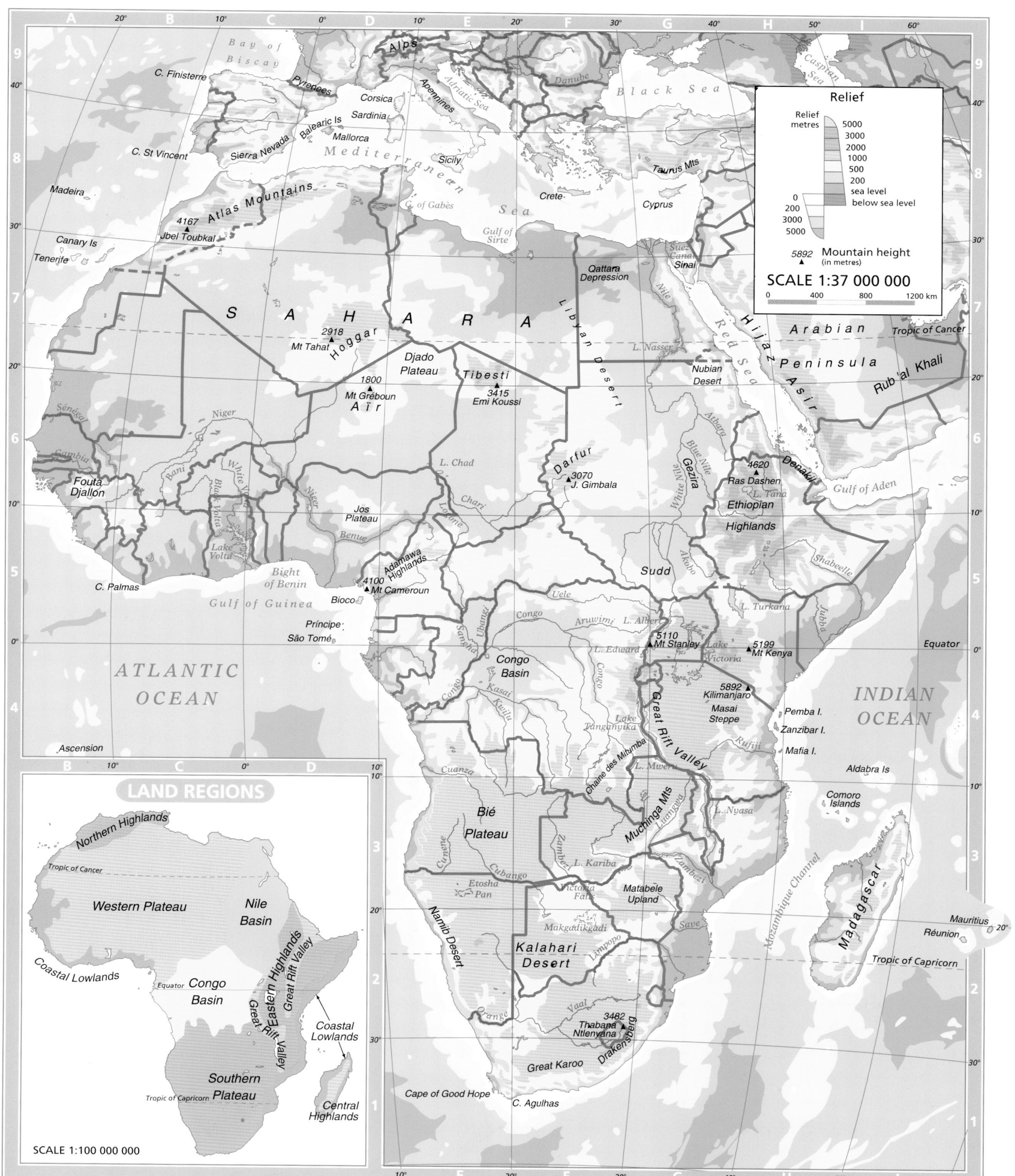

Relief

Relief metres
5000
3000
2000
1000
500
200
sea level
below sea level
0
200
3000
5000

5892 ▲ Mountain height (in metres)

SCALE 1:37 000 000

0   400   800   1200 km

LAND REGIONS

Northern Highlands

Tropic of Cancer

Western Plateau

Nile Basin

Coastal Lowlands

Equator   Congo Basin

Eastern Highlands

Great Rift Valley

Coastal Lowlands

Southern Plateau

Tropic of Capricorn

Central Highlands

SCALE 1:100 000 000

Lambert Azimuthal Equal Area projection

1 JANUARY TEMPERATURE AND PRESSURE

1020
1018
1016
Tropic of Cancer
1014
1020
1018
1016
1014
1012

Average temperature °C
32
24
16
8

LOW

Equator
1010

1012
1014

Wind direction
Isobar in hectopascals reduced to sea level

Tropic of Capricorn
1012
1010
1014

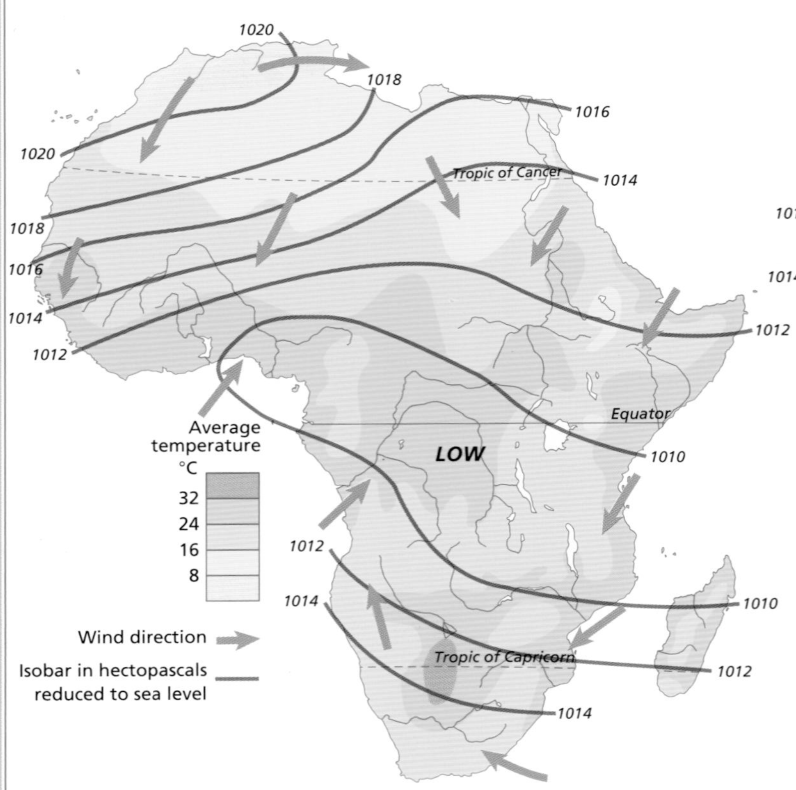

2 JULY TEMPERATURE AND PRESSURE

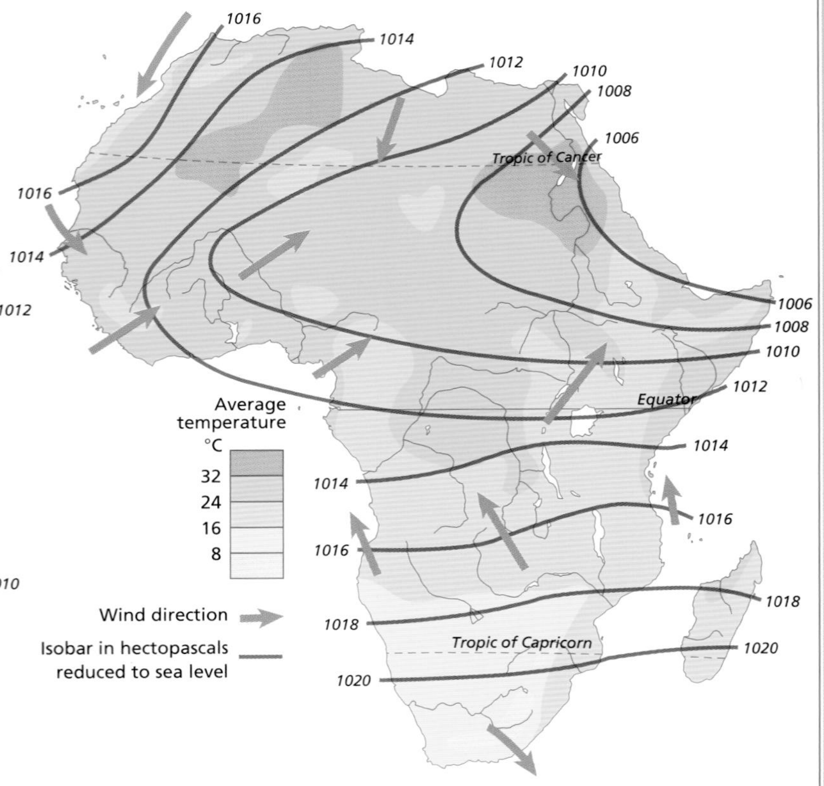

1016
1014
1012
1010
1008
Tropic of Cancer
1006
1016
1014
1006
1008
1010
1012

Average temperature °C
32
24
16
8

1014
1016

Equator
1014
1016
1018

Wind direction
Isobar in hectopascals reduced to sea level

1018
Tropic of Capricorn
1020
1020

3 ANNUAL RAINFALL

Algiers

Tropic of Cancer

Conakry

Equator
Nairobi

Average annual rainfall mm
3000
2000
1000
500
250
0

Walvis Bay
Beira
Tropic of Capricorn

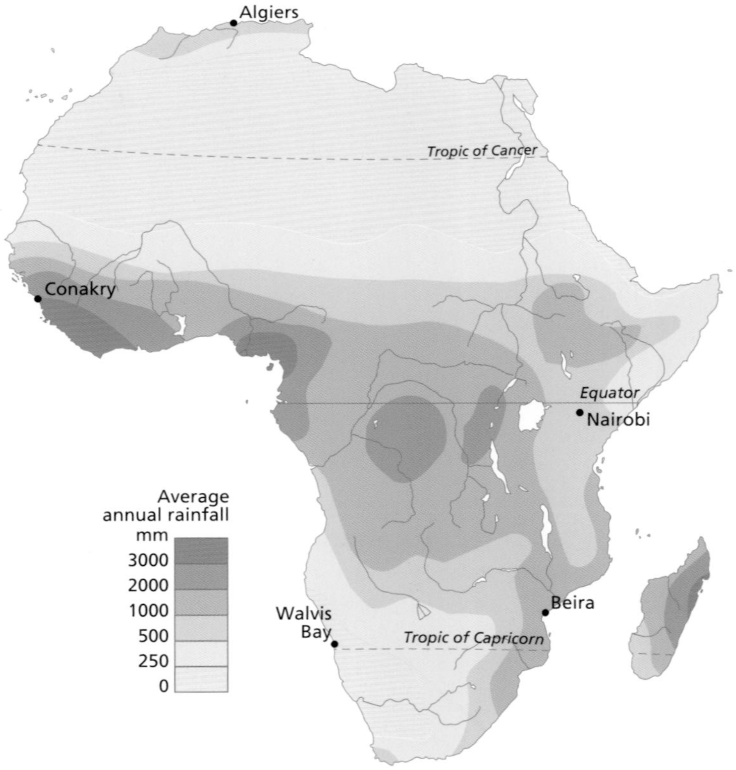

4 STATISTICS

Algiers (59 m)	Jan	Feb	Mar	Apr	May	Jun	Jul	Aug	Sep	Oct	Nov	Dec
Temperature, max. (°C)	15	16	17	20	23	26	28	29	27	23	19	16
Temperature, min. (°C)	9	9	11	13	15	18	21	22	21	17	13	11
Rainfall (mm)	112	84	74	41	46	15	0	5	41	79	130	137

Conakry (7 m)	Jan	Feb	Mar	Apr	May	Jun	Jul	Aug	Sep	Oct	Nov	Dec
Temperature, max. (°C)	31	31	32	32	32	30	28	28	29	31	31	31
Temperature, min. (°C)	22	23	23	23	24	23	22	22	23	23	24	23
Rainfall (mm)	3	3	10	23	158	559	1298	1054	683	371	122	10

Nairobi (1820 m)	Jan	Feb	Mar	Apr	May	Jun	Jul	Aug	Sep	Oct	Nov	Dec
Temperature, max. (°C)	25	26	25	24	22	21	21	21	24	24	23	23
Temperature, min. (°C)	12	13	14	14	13	12	11	11	11	13	13	13
Rainfall (mm)	38	64	125	211	158	46	15	23	31	53	109	86

Walvis Bay (7 m)	Jan	Feb	Mar	Apr	May	Jun	Jul	Aug	Sep	Oct	Nov	Dec
Temperature, max. (°C)	23	23	23	24	23	23	21	20	19	19	22	22
Temperature, min. (°C)	15	16	15	13	11	9	8	8	9	11	12	14
Rainfall (mm)	0	5	8	3	3	0	0	3	0	0	0	0

Beira (9 m)	Jan	Feb	Mar	Apr	May	Jun	Jul	Aug	Sep	Oct	Nov	Dec
Temperature, max. (°C)	32	32	31	30	28	26	25	26	28	31	31	31
Temperature, min. (°C)	24	24	23	22	18	16	16	17	18	22	22	23
Rainfall (mm)	277	213	257	107	56	33	31	28	20	132	135	234

SCALE 1:77 000 000

0   1000   2000   3000 km

Lambert Azimuthal Equal Area projection

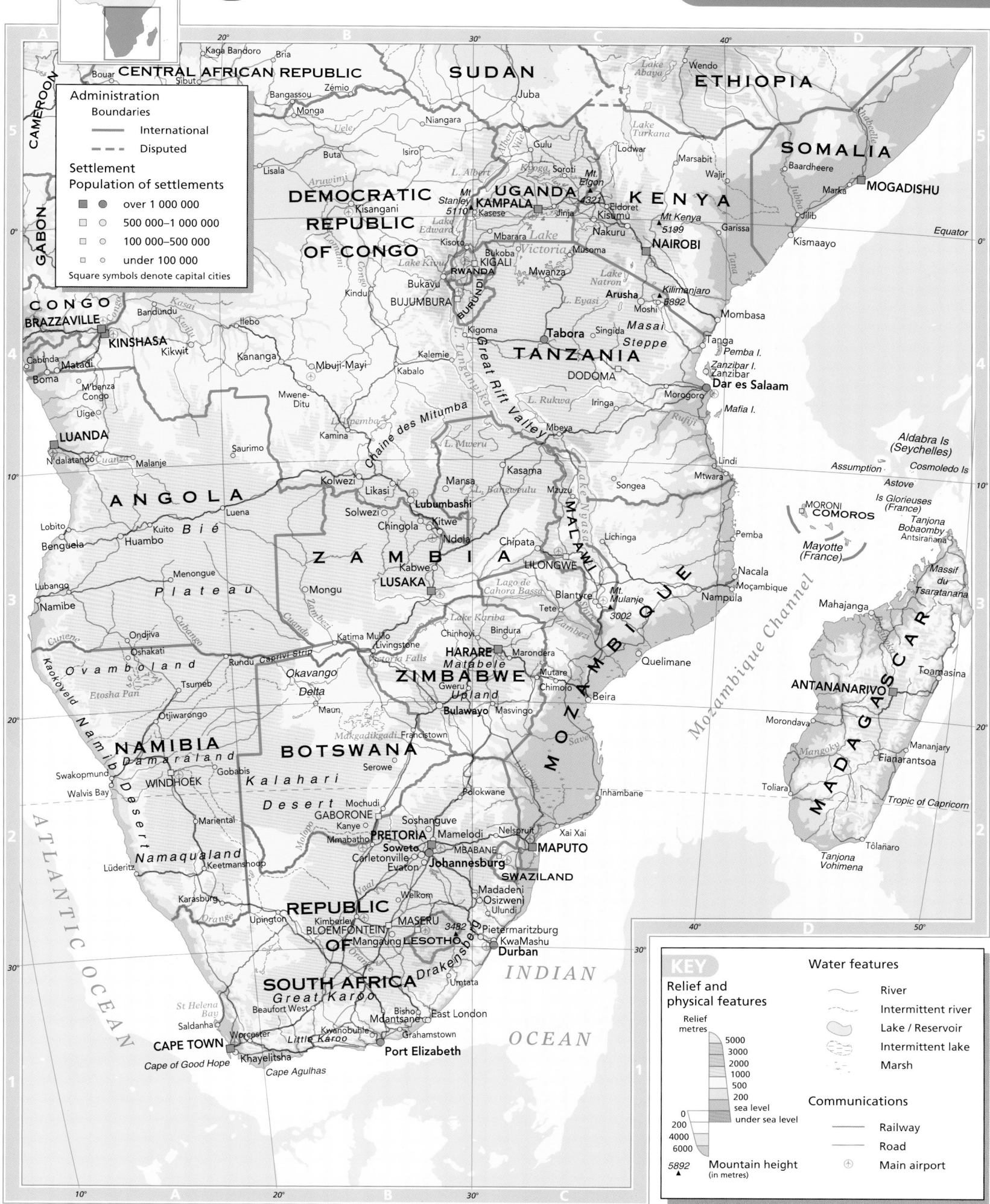

CW

Administration
Boundaries
——— International
----- Disputed

Settlement
Population of settlements
▪ ● over 1 000 000
▫ ○ 500 000–1 000 000
▫ ○ 100 000–500 000
▫ ○ under 100 000
Square symbols denote capital cities

CAMEROON

CENTRAL AFRICAN REPUBLIC

Bouar
Kaga Bandoro
Bria
Sibut
Bangassou
Zémio
Monga
Niangara
Buta
Lisala
Isiro
Gulu

SUDAN
Juba

ETHIOPIA

Lake Abaya
Wendo

SOMALIA

Baardheere
Marka
MOGADISHU
Jilib

GABON
CONGO
BRAZZAVILLE
Bandundu
KINSHASA
Kikwit
Cabinda
Matadi
Boma
M'banza Congo
Uige
LUANDA
N'dalatando
Cuanza
Malanje

DEMOCRATIC REPUBLIC OF CONGO

Kisangani
Ilebo
Kananga
Mbuji-Mayi
Mwene-Ditu
Kabalo
Kamina
Kalemie

L. Albert
Aruwimi
L. Edward
Kivu
Kisoto
Mbarara
Bukoba
RWANDA
KIGALI
Bukavu
BUJUMBURA
BURUNDI
Kindu
Kigoma
Kisangani

Mt Stanley 5110
Kasese
UGANDA
KAMPALA
Jinja

L. Albert
Kyoga
Soroti
Mt. Elgon 4321
Eldoret
Kisumu

KENYA

Lodwar
Lake Turkana
Marsabit
Wajir
Garissa

Nakuru
NAIROBI
Mt Kenya 5199

Equator

Kismaayo

Lake Victoria
Musoma
Mwanza
Singida
Mombasa
Tanga
Pemba I.
Zanzibar I.
Zanzibar

Arusha
Kilimanjaro 5892
Moshi
Masai Steppe

TANZANIA
Tabora
DODOMA
Iringa
Morogoro
Dar es Salaam

L. Rukwa
Mbeya
L. Eyasi
L. Natron

ANGOLA

Lobito
Benguela
Kuito
Huambo
Menongue
Lubango
Namibe

Bié
Plateau

Saurimo
Luena

Kolwezi
Likasi
Lubumbashi
Solwezi
Chingola
Kitwe
Ndola

Mansa
L. Bangweulu
Kasama
Mzuzu
Songea
Lichinga

ZAMBIA

Kabwe
LUSAKA
Chipata
LILONGWE

MALAWI

Mtwara
Lindi
Assumption
Astove
Is Glorieuses (France)
Cosmoledo Is
Aldabra Is (Seychelles)

MORONI
COMOROS
Mayotte (France)

Tanjona Bobaomby
Antsiranana

MADAGASCAR

Massif du Tsaratanana
Mahajanga

ANTANANARIVO
Toamasina

Curoca
Ondjiva
Oshakati
Kaokoveld

Ovamboland
Etosha Pan
Rundu
Caprivi Strip
Katima Mulilo
Livingstone
Victoria Falls

NAMIBIA
Damaraland
Tsumeb
Otjiwarongo
Swakopmund
WINDHOEK
Walvis Bay

Zambezi
Cuando
Okavango Delta
Maun
Makgadikgadi
Francistown

BOTSWANA

Kalahari Desert

Gobabis
Serowe
Mochudi
GABORONE
Kanye

Namib Desert

Mariental
Namaqualand

Lüderitz
Karasburg
Keetmanshoop

Lake Kariba
Chinhoyi
Bindura
HARARE
Marondera
Mutare

ZIMBABWE
Matabele Upland
Gweru
Bulawayo
Masvingo
Chimoio

Lago de Cahora Bassa
Blantyre
Tete
Mt Mulanje 3002
Nampula
Nacala
Moçambique
Quelimane
Beira

MOZAMBIQUE

Mozambique Channel

Save
Inhambane
Xai Xai

Morondava
Mananjary
Fianarantsoa
Toliara
Tanjona Vohimena
Tôlañaro

Polokwane
Soshanguve
PRETORIA
Mamelodi
Nelspruit
MBABANE
MAPUTO
SWAZILAND

Mmabatho
Soweto
Johannesburg
Carletonville
Evaton
Welkom
Madadeni
Osizweni
Ulundi

ATLANTIC OCEAN

Upington
Kimberley
BLOEMFONTEIN
Mangaung
MASERU
LESOTHO
3482
Pietermaritzburg
KwaMashu
Durban

REPUBLIC OF SOUTH AFRICA

Great Karoo
Beaufort West
Bisho
Mdantsane
East London
Grahamstown

INDIAN OCEAN

St Helena Bay
Saldanha
Worcester
Little Karoo
Kwanobuhle
Khayelitsha
CAPE TOWN
Cape of Good Hope
Cape Agulhas
Port Elizabeth

Umtata

Orange
Drakensberg
Vaal

KEY
Relief and physical features
Relief metres
5000
3000
2000
1000
500
200
sea level
under sea level
0
200
4000
6000
5892 ▲ Mountain height (in metres)

Water features
〰 River
Intermittent river
Lake / Reservoir
Intermittent lake
Marsh

Communications
——— Railway
——— Road
⊕ Main airport

SCALE 1:20 000 000

0   200   400   600   800 km

Bonne projection

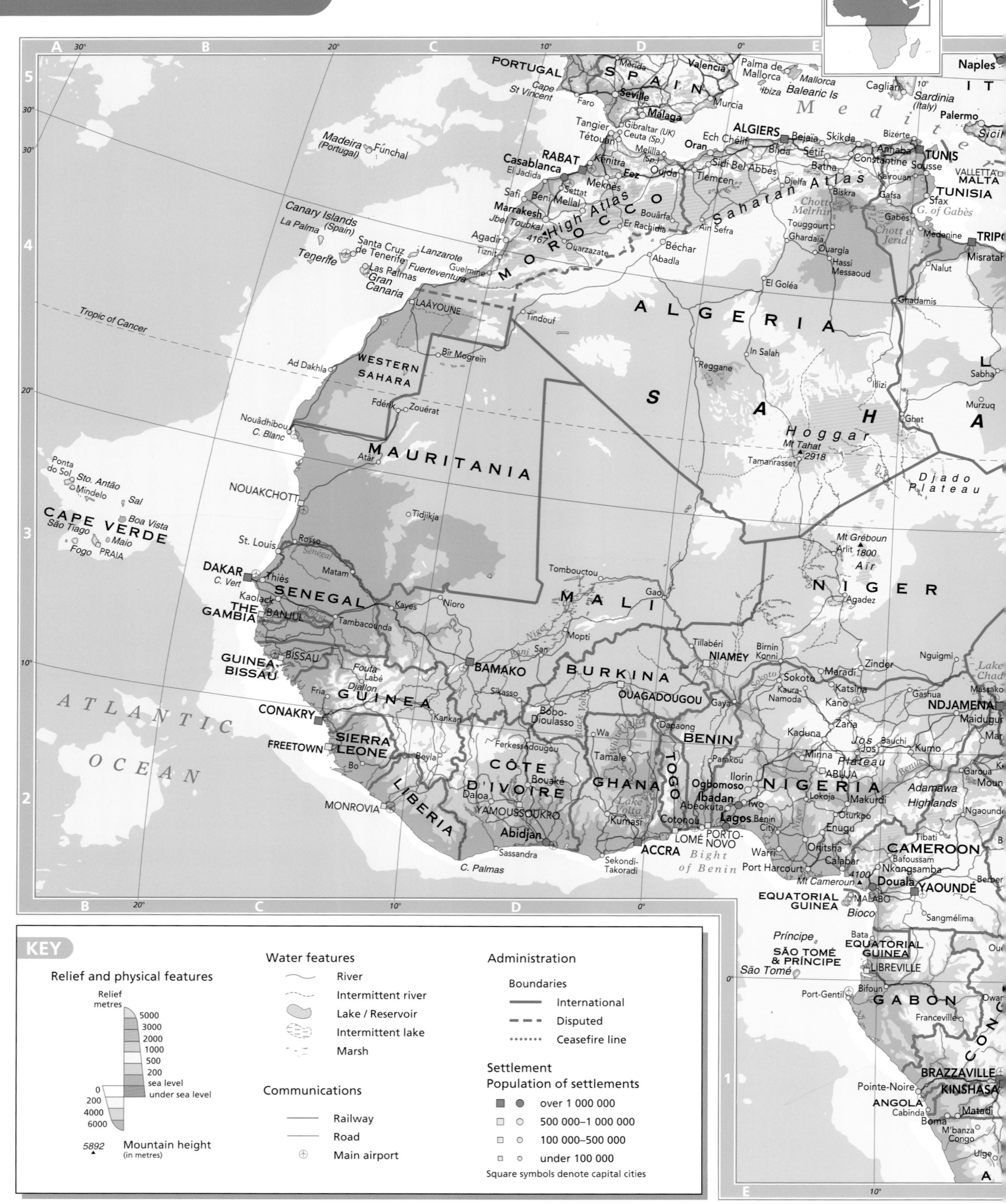

KEY

Relief and physical features

Relief
metres
5000
3000
2000
1000
500
200
0 sea level
under sea level
200
4000
6000

5892 Mountain height
(in metres)

Water features

River
Intermittent river
Lake / Reservoir
Intermittent lake
Marsh

Communications

Railway
Road
Main airport

Administration

Boundaries

International
Disputed
Ceasefire line

Settlement
Population of settlements

over 1 000 000
500 000–1 000 000
100 000–500 000
under 100 000

Square symbols denote capital cities

SCALE 1:20 000 000

0   200   400   600   800 km

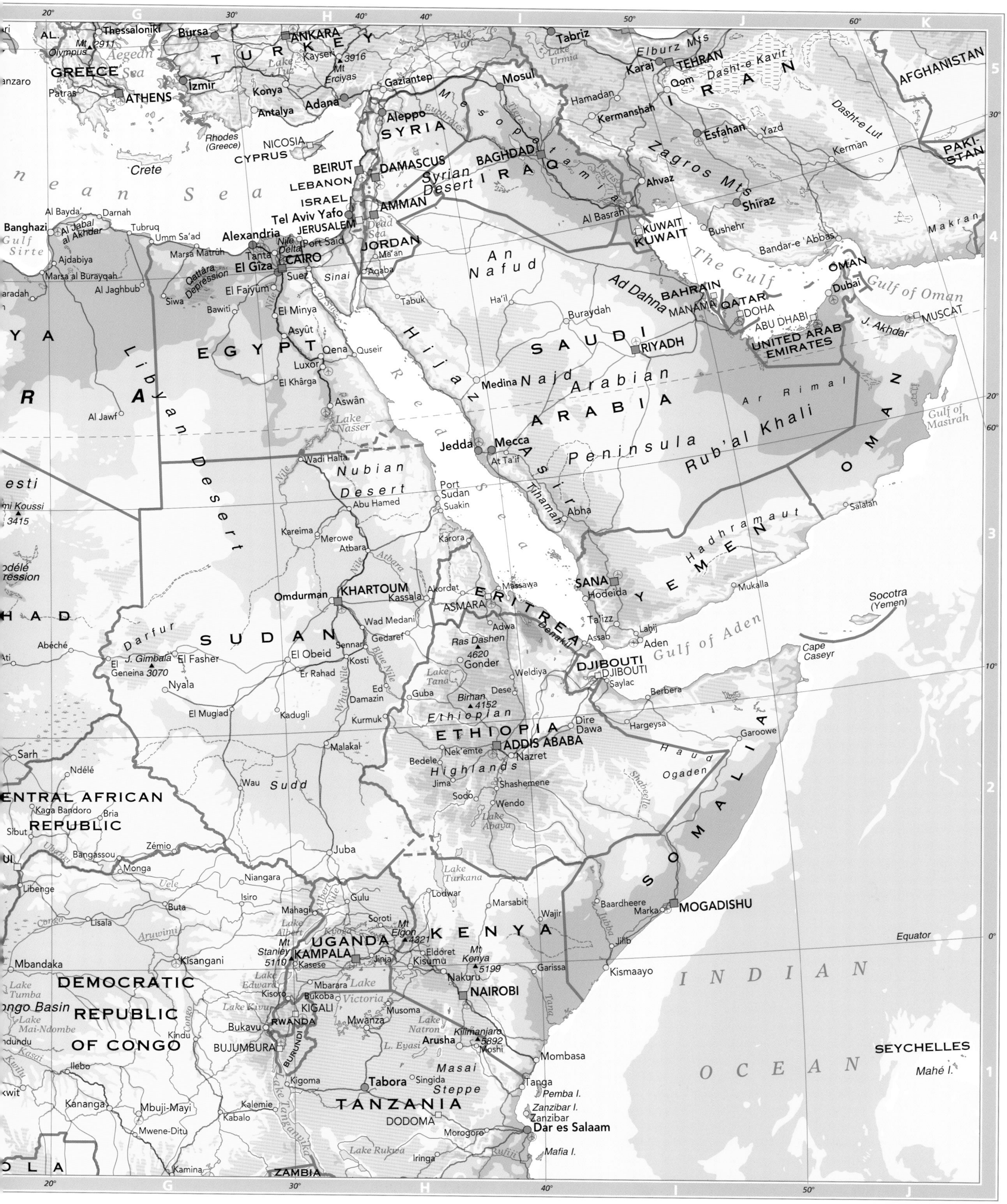

Millers Stereographic projection

CW

Boundaries
—— International

Population of settlements
- ■ ● over 1 000 000
- □ ○ 500 000–1 000 000
- □ ○ 100 000–500 000
- □ ○ under 100 000

Square symbols denote capital cities.

- **D.R.** DOMINICAN REPUBLIC
- **E.S.** EL SALVADOR
- **H.** HAITI
- **P.R.** PUERTO RICO

SCALE 1:40 000 000
0   400   800   1200 km

ARCTIC OCEAN

PACIFIC OCEAN

RUSSIAN FEDERATION

U.S.A. ALASKA
Fairbanks
Anchorage
Inuvik
Whitehorse
Yellowknife

GREENLAND (KALAALLIT NUNAAT) (Denmark)
NUUK

Arctic Circle
ICELAND

CANADA
Edmonton
Saskatoon
Calgary
Regina
Winnipeg
Churchill
Hudson Bay
Iqaluit
St John's
Charlottetown
Saint John
Halifax

Vancouver
Victoria
Seattle
Portland
Spokane
Boise
Billings

Québec
Montréal
OTTAWA
Toronto
Thunder Bay
Duluth
Sudbury
Hamilton
Detroit
Buffalo
Cleveland
Boston
Providence
New York
Philadelphia
Baltimore
WASHINGTON D.C.

Minneapolis-St Paul
Milwaukee
Chicago
Omaha
Indianapolis
Pittsburgh
Cincinnati
Norfolk
Greensboro

UNITED STATES OF AMERICA

San Francisco
Sacramento
Reno
Fresno
Salt Lake City
Denver
Kansas City
St Louis

Las Vegas
Los Angeles
San Diego
Tijuana
Phoenix
Tucson
El Paso
Albuquerque
Oklahoma City
Tulsa
Little Rock
Memphis
Greenville
Atlanta
Birmingham
Jackson
Savannah
Mobile
Jacksonville

ATLANTIC OCEAN
BERMUDA (UK)

Tropic of Cancer

Fort Worth
Dallas
Austin
Houston
San Antonio
Monterrey
Mazatlán

New Orleans
Tampa-St Petersburg
Fort Lauderdale
Miami
NASSAU
THE BAHAMAS

HAVANA
CUBA

Gulf of Mexico

MEXICO
Guadalajara
León
Cancún
MEXICO CITY
Puebla
Acapulco

JAMAICA
Kingston
H.
PORT-AU PRINCE
D.R.
SANTO DOMINGO
P.R. (USA)
SAN JUAN

Caribbean Sea

GUATEMALA
GUATEMALA CITY
SAN SALVADOR
BELMOPAN
BELIZE
HONDURAS
TEGUCIGALPA
E.S.
MANAGUA
NICARAGUA

VENEZUELA

SAN JOSÉ
COSTA RICA
PANAMA
PANAMA CITY

PACIFIC OCEAN

COLOMBIA
Equator
ECUADOR

PERU   BRAZIL

POPULATION

Persons per sq km
- over 100
- 50–100
- 10–50
- 1–10
- 0–1

Arctic Circle

Toronto
Detroit
Montréal
Boston
Chicago
New York
Philadelphia
Washington D.C.
San Francisco
Los Angeles
Phoenix
San Diego
Dallas
Atlanta
Monterrey
Houston
Miami
Tropic of Cancer
Guadalajara
Mexico City
Santo Domingo
Guatemala City

Urban population
Number of people
- ■ over 10 000 000
- ■ 5 000 000–10 000 000
- ● 2 500 000–5 000 000
- ● 1 000 000–2 500 000

SCALE 1:100 000 000

Chamberlin Trimetric projection

ARCTIC OCEAN

Bering Sea

Wrangel I.

Greenland

Iceland

Faeroes

Arctic Circle

St Lawrence I.

Nunivak I.

Bristol Bay

Pt Barrow

Brooks Range

Yukon

Beaufort Sea

Queen Elizabeth Islands

Parry Islands

Banks Island

Ellesmere Island

Baffin Bay

Denmark Strait

Cape Farewell

Alaska Range
▲Mt McKinley 6194

Aleutian Range

Kodiak I.

Gulf of Alaska

Mackenzie Mts

Victoria Island

Baffin Island

Davis Strait

Labrador Sea

▲Mt Logan 5959

Alexander Archipelago

Coast Mountains

Great Bear L.

Foxe Basin

Southampton I.

Hudson Strait

Péninsule d'Ungava

Queen Charlotte Islands

Mt Waddington 4042▲

Peace

Great Slave L.

Lake Athabasca

Churchill

Nelson

Hudson Bay

Belcher Is

Churchill

PACIFIC OCEAN

Vancouver Island

Fraser

Saskatchewan

Severn

Albany

CANADIAN SHIELD

L. St Lawrence

Gulf of St Lawrence

Cape Breton I.

Newfoundland

Mt Rainier 4392▲

Columbia

Cascade Ra

Snake

Lake Winnipeg

ROCKY MOUNTAINS

GREAT PLAINS

Yellowstone

Gannett Pk 4202▲

Missouri

Lake Superior

Lake Huron

Lake Michigan

L. Ontario

Lake Erie

Long I.

C. Cod

C. Sable

ATLANTIC OCEAN

Bermuda

Sierra Nevada

Great Salt L.

Great Basin

Platte

Appalachian Mts

Chesapeake B.

C. Hatteras

Mt Whitney 4418▲

Colorado

Grand Canyon

Colorado Plateau

Arkansas

Ohio

Tennessee

Ozark Plateau

Mississippi

Alabama

C. Fear

Red

C. Canaveral

Tropic of Cancer

Guadalupe

Lower California

Rio Grande

Edwards Plateau

Brazos

Gulf of California

Bahamas

Gulf of Mexico

C. San Lucas

Sierra Madre Occidental

Altiplano Mexicano

Sierra Madre Oriental

Yucatán Channel

Cuba

Hispaniola

Jamaica

Puerto Rico

Greater Antilles

Lesser Antilles

Curaçao

Campeche Bay

Yucatán

Caribbean Sea

Popocatépetl 5452▲

Sierra Madre del Sur

Sierra Madre

G. of Honduras

L. Nicaragua

Isthmus of Panama

G. of Darién

G. of Panama

Orinoco

PACIFIC OCEAN

I. de Coco

I. de Malpelo

Galapagos Islands

G. of Guayaquil

Cordillera Occidental

Cordillera Central

Colopaxi 5896▲

Chimborazo 6310▲

Equator

Relief

Relief metres
5000
3000
2000
1000
500
200
0 sea level
below sea level
200
4000
6000

Permanent ice

6194 ▲ Mountain height (in metres)

SCALE 1:40 000 000

0   400   800   1200 km

LAND REGIONS

Arctic Circle

Pacific Ranges

Canadian Shield

Rocky Mountains

Interior Plains and Lowlands

Appalachian Highlands

Western Plateaus, Ranges and Basins

Coastal Lowlands

Tropic of Cancer

Caribbean Islands

Central American Highlands

SCALE 1:100 000 000

Chamberlin Trimetric projection

1 JANUARY TEMPERATURE AND PRESSURE

HIGH
Arctic Circle
Tropic of Cancer
1020
1018
1016
1014
1012
1010
1008
1006
Average temperature °C
24
16
8
0
-8
-16
-24
-32
Wind direction
Isobar in hectopascals reduced to sea level

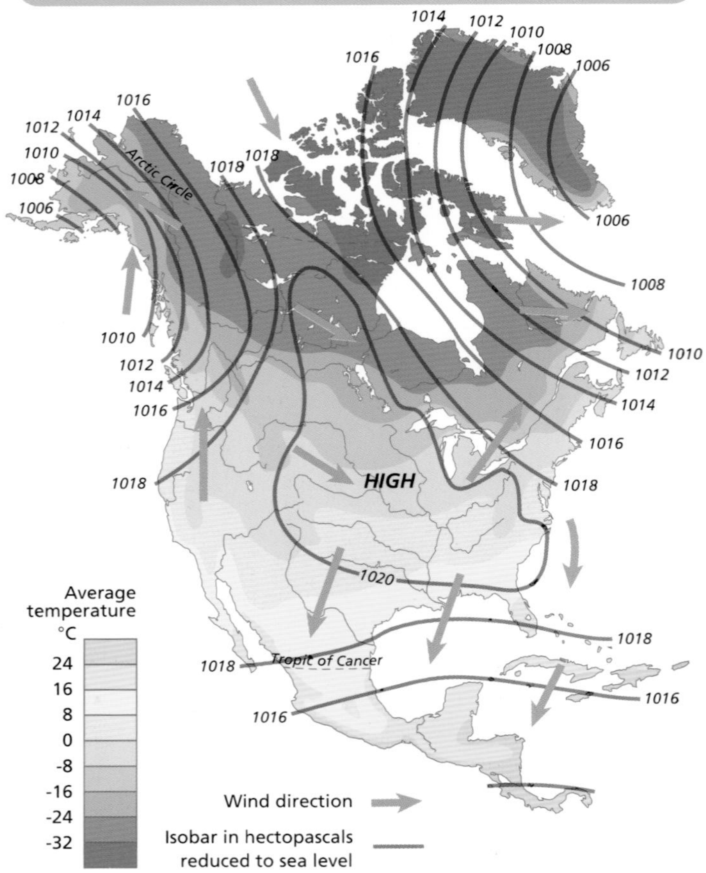

2 JULY TEMPERATURE AND PRESSURE

LOW
LOW
HIGH
LOW
Arctic Circle
Tropic of Cancer
1016
1014
1012
1010
1008
1006
Average temperature °C
32
24
16
8
0
-8
Wind direction
Isobar in hectopascals reduced to sea level

3 ANNUAL RAINFALL

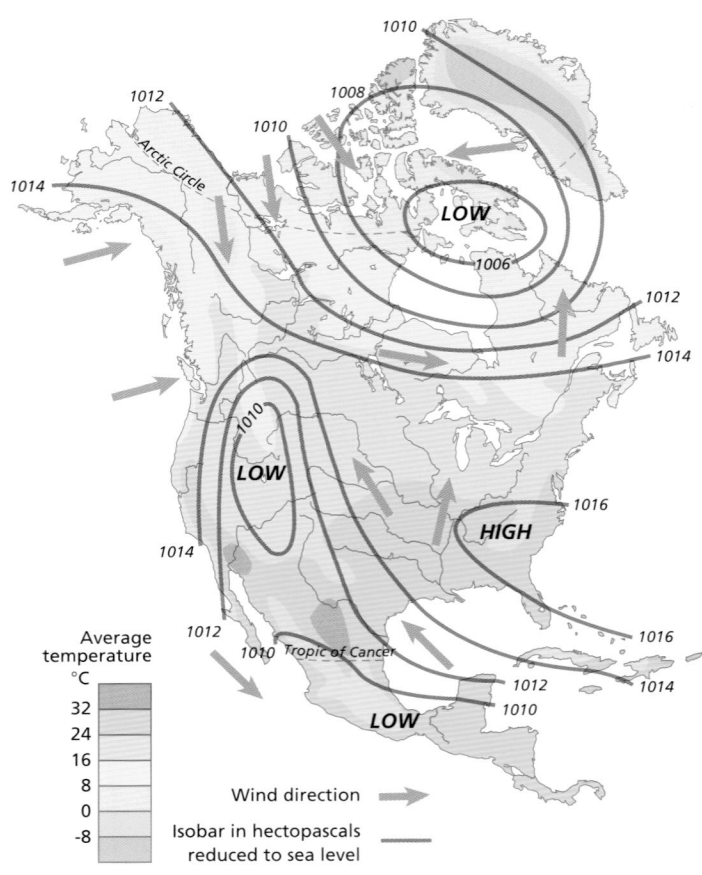

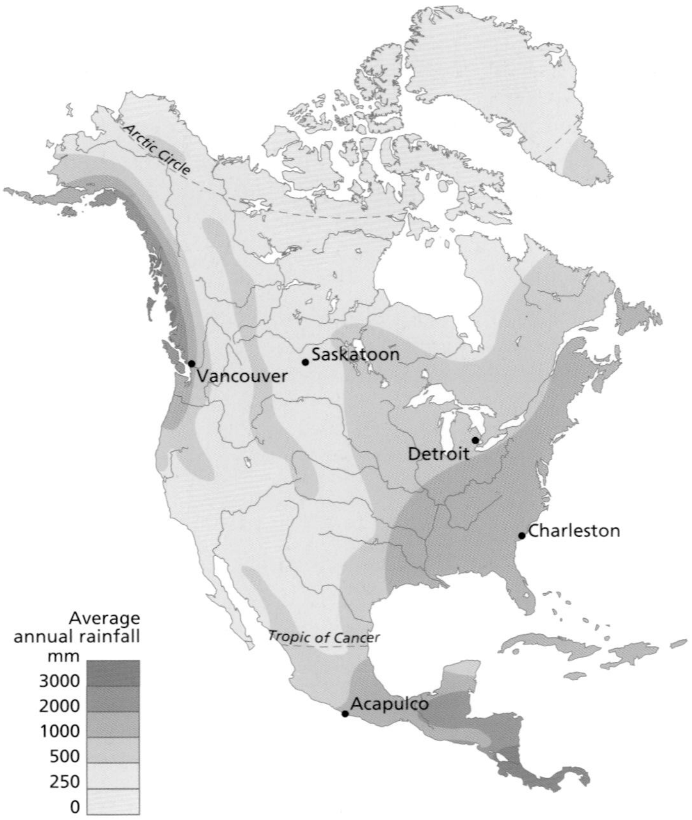

Arctic Circle
Vancouver
Saskatoon
Detroit
Charleston
Tropic of Cancer
Acapulco
Average annual rainfall mm
3000
2000
1000
500
250
0

4 STATISTICS

Saskatoon (515 m)	Jan	Feb	Mar	Apr	May	Jun	Jul	Aug	Sep	Oct	Nov	Dec
Temperature, max. (°C)	-13	-11	-3	9	18	22	25	24	17	11	-1	-9
Temperature, min. (°C)	-24	-22	-14	-3	3	9	11	9	3	-3	-11	-19
Rainfall (mm)	23	13	18	18	36	66	61	48	38	23	13	15

Vancouver (14 m)	Jan	Feb	Mar	Apr	May	Jun	Jul	Aug	Sep	Oct	Nov	Dec
Temperature, max. (°C)	5	7	10	14	18	21	23	23	18	14	9	6
Temperature, min. (°C)	0	1	3	4	8	11	12	12	9	7	4	2
Rainfall (mm)	218	147	127	84	71	64	31	43	91	147	211	224

Charleston (3 m)	Jan	Feb	Mar	Apr	May	Jun	Jul	Aug	Sep	Oct	Nov	Dec
Temperature, max. (°C)	14	15	19	23	27	30	31	31	28	24	19	15
Temperature, min. (°C)	6	7	10	14	19	23	24	24	22	16	11	7
Rainfall (mm)	74	84	86	71	81	119	185	168	130	81	58	71

Acapulco (3 m)	Jan	Feb	Mar	Apr	May	Jun	Jul	Aug	Sep	Oct	Nov	Dec
Temperature, max. (°C)	31	31	31	32	32	33	32	33	32	32	32	31
Temperature, min. (°C)	22	22	22	23	25	25	25	25	24	24	23	22
Rainfall (mm)	6	1	0	1	36	281	256	252	349	159	28	8

Detroit (189 m)	Jan	Feb	Mar	Apr	May	Jun	Jul	Aug	Sep	Oct	Nov	Dec
Temperature, max. (°C)	-1	0	6	13	19	25	28	27	23	16	8	2
Temperature, min. (°C)	-7	-8	-3	3	9	14	17	17	13	7	1	-4
Rainfall (mm)	53	53	64	64	84	91	84	69	71	61	61	58

SCALE 1:80 000 000 — 0 800 1600 2400 3200 km

Bonne projection

The image and map show that San Francisco is a city built between the rugged San Andreas, Hayward and Calaveras Faults. Not surprisingly, earthquakes are common. Recent US Geological Survey research indicates that there is a 62 per cent probability of one or more magnitude 6.7 earthquakes in the San Francisco Bay region before 2032.

 The heavily built-up urban area around San Francisco Bay shows up in this image as a fine pattern of light blue. Four bridges cross the bay. San Francisco City is in the top left corner of the image, **B8.**

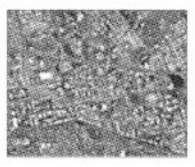

 Areas of dense woodland to the south-west and north-east of the built-up area show as bright red on this image. Much of this woodland has been left uncleared because the land is very rugged.

 Areas of lighter blue/green in the bay represent shallower waters. Areas of blue/black and the dark blue/green patterns along the edge of the bay are salt marshes and other marshlands.

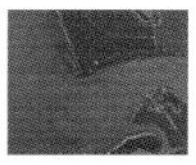

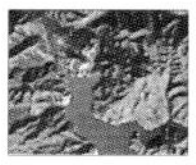

 Lakes and reservoirs stand out from the surrounding countryside as mid-blue shapes within the rugged red woodland. The effects of the shadows are to highlight the ruggedness of the mountain areas.

Approximate scale 1:375 000

0   5   10 km

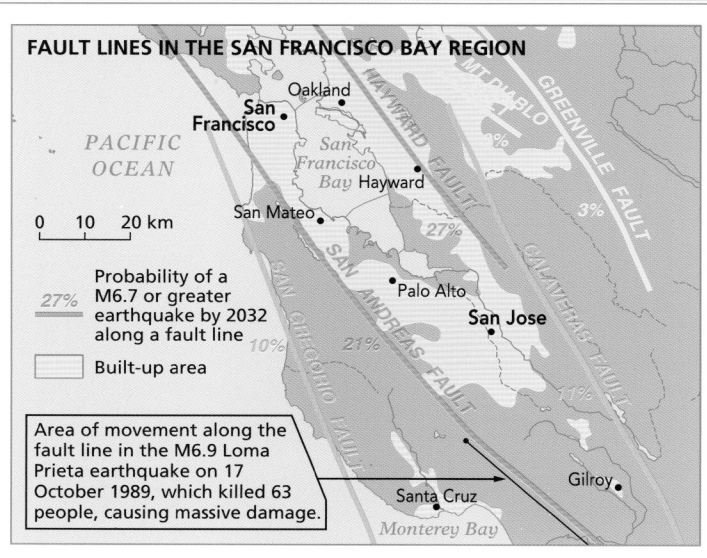

FAULT LINES IN THE SAN FRANCISCO BAY REGION

PACIFIC OCEAN

0   10   20 km

Oakland
San Francisco
San Francisco Bay   Hayward
San Mateo
Palo Alto
San Jose
Santa Cruz
Gilroy
Monterey Bay

HAYWARD FAULT
GREENVILLE FAULT
CALAVERAS FAULT
SAN ANDREAS FAULT
SAN GREGORIO FAULT

27% Probability of a M6.7 or greater earthquake by 2032 along a fault line

Built-up area

Area of movement along the fault line in the M6.9 Loma Prieta earthquake on 17 October 1989, which killed 63 people, causing massive damage.

KEY

Relief and physical features

Relief metres
5000
3000
2000
1000
500
200
0 sea level
200
4000 under sea level
6000

▲ 6194 Mountain height (in metres)

Permanent ice

Water features

~ River

Lake / Reservoir

Intermittent lake

Marsh

Communications

— Railway

Road

⊕ Main airport

Administration

Boundaries

International

Internal

Settlement
Population of settlements

■ ● over 1 000 000

□ ○ 500 000–1 000 000

□ ○ 100 000–500 000

□ ○ under 100 000

Square symbols denote capital cities

SCALE 1:17 000 000

0   200   400   600   800 km

GREENLAND (KALAALLIT NUNAAT) (Denmark)

ICELAND

Kong Christian IX Land
Gunnbjørn Field 3700
Kong Frederik VI Kyst
Arctic Circle
Siglufjördhur
Akureyri
1763 Hvannadalshnúkur
Höfn
Seydhisfjördhur
Ísafjördhur
Faxaflói
REYKJAVÍK
Keflavík
Hotsjökull

Denmark Strait

Axel Heiberg Island
Ellesmere Island
Cape Parry
Qaanaaq (Thule)
Cape York
Melville Bay
Upernavik
Disko
Saqqaq
Qasigianguit
Ilulissat
Maniitsoq
Sisimiut
NUUK (Godthåb)
Paamiut
Ivittuut
Nanortalik
Cape Farewell

Nares Strait
Jones Sound
Devon Island
Lancaster Sound
Baffin Bay
Somerset Island
Resolute Bay
Brodeur Peninsula
Arctic Bay
Borden Peninsula
Bylot Island
Mittimatalik (Pond Inlet)
Prince Charles I.
Clyde River
Home Bay
Penny Icecap
Pangnirtung
C. Dyer
Davis Strait
Cumberland Sound

Gulf of Boothia
Taloyoak
Melville Peninsula
Hall Beach
Repulse Bay
Foxe Basin
Nettilling Lake
Amadjuak Lake
Foxe Peninsula
Iqaluit
Frobisher Bay
NUNAVUT

Labrador Sea

Southampton Island
Coral Harbour
Foxe Channel
Fisher Str.
Coats I.
Mansel I.
Resolution Island
Akpatok I.
C. Chidley

ATLANTIC OCEAN

CANADA

Salluit
Kangiqsujuaq
Ungava Bay
Kangiqsualujjuaq
NEWFOUNDLAND AND LABRADOR
Puvurnituq
Ottawa Is
Inukjuak
Kuujjuaq
Nain
Hopedale
Cape Harrison

Cape Churchill
Churchill
Hudson Bay
Belcher Islands
Cape Henrietta Maria
Labrador
Smallwood Reservoir
Schefferville
Happy Valley–Goose Bay
Port Hope Simpson
St Anthony

MANITOBA
Fort Severn
Fort Albany
Big Trout Lake
Sandy Lake
James Bay
Akimiski Island
Eastmain
Waskaganish (Fort Rupert)
Moosonee
Chisasibi (Fort George)
Réservoir La Grande 2
Réservoir La Grande 3
QUÉBEC
Gagnon
Labrador City
Wabush
Sept-Îles
Havre-St-Pierre
Strait of Belle Isle
Grand Falls
Gander
Bonavista
Corner Brook
Newfoundland
St John's
Channel-Port aux Basques

Red Lake
Sioux Lookout
ONTARIO
Lac St Joseph
Mistissini (Baie-du-Poste)
Île d'Anticosti
Gulf of St Lawrence
Cabot Strait
St Pierre & Miquelon (Fr.)

Longlac
Kapuskasing
Nipigon
Thunder Bay
Lake Nipigon
Timmins
Chibougamau
Baie Comeau
Péninsule de Gaspé
Gaspé
Rimouski
Bathurst
PRINCE EDWARD ISLAND
Charlottetown
Sydney
Glace Bay
Cape Breton Island

Kirkland Lake
Val d'Or
Amos
Roberval
Chicoutimi
Jonquière
Rivière-du-Loup
Edmundston
NEW BRUNSWICK
Moncton
Fredericton
NOVA SCOTIA
Truro
Sable I.

MINNESOTA
Duluth
Chapleau
Sudbury
North Bay
Montmagny
Québec
Trois Rivières
Sherbrooke
MAINE
St John
Bangor
Bay of Fundy
Halifax
Cape Sable

WISCONSIN
Minneapolis
Green Bay
Ashland
Escanaba
Marquette
MICHIGAN
Sault Ste Marie
OTTAWA
Montréal
VER. 1917
Mt Washington
N.H.
Manchester
Augusta
Portland
Yarmouth

Albert Lea
Cedar Rapids
Milwaukee
Rockford
Chicago
Cadillac
Bay City
Flint
Grand Rapids
Detroit
Toledo
Owen Sound
Oshawa
Toronto
London
Rochester
Buffalo
Erie
Cleveland
PENNSYLVANIA
Williamsport
Binghamton
Scranton
NEW YORK
Syracuse
Albany
Worcester
Hartford
CONN.
New Haven
MASS.
Lowell
Boston
Providence
R.I.
Cape Cod
Long Island
N.J.
New York

CONN. CONNECTICUT
MASS. MASSACHUSETTS
N.H. NEW HAMPSHIRE
N.J. NEW JERSEY
R.I. RHODE ISLAND
VER. VERMONT

Chamberlin Trimetric projection

The states of Hawaii and Alaska are not shown on this map. You can find a map of Hawaii on page 82 and a map of Alaska on page 130.

SCALE 1:12 000 000

0   150   300   450   600 km

KEY

Relief and physical features

Relief metres

5000
3000
2000
1000
500
200
0
sea level
under sea level
200
4000
6000

▲ 4418 Mountain height (in metres)

Water features

~ River

- - - Intermittent river

Lake / Reservoir

Intermittent lake

Marsh

Communications

——— Railway

——— Road

✈ Main airport

Administration

Boundaries

——— International

——— Internal

Settlement
Population of settlements

■ ● over 1 000 000

□ ○ 500 000–1 000 000

□ ○ 100 000–500 000

□ ○ under 100 000

Square symbols denote capital cities

Lambert Conformal Conic projection

CONN. CONNECTICUT
MARYL. MARYLAND
MASS. MASSACHUSETTS
NEW. HAMP. NEW HAMPSHIRE
R.I. RHODE ISLAND
VER. VERMONT

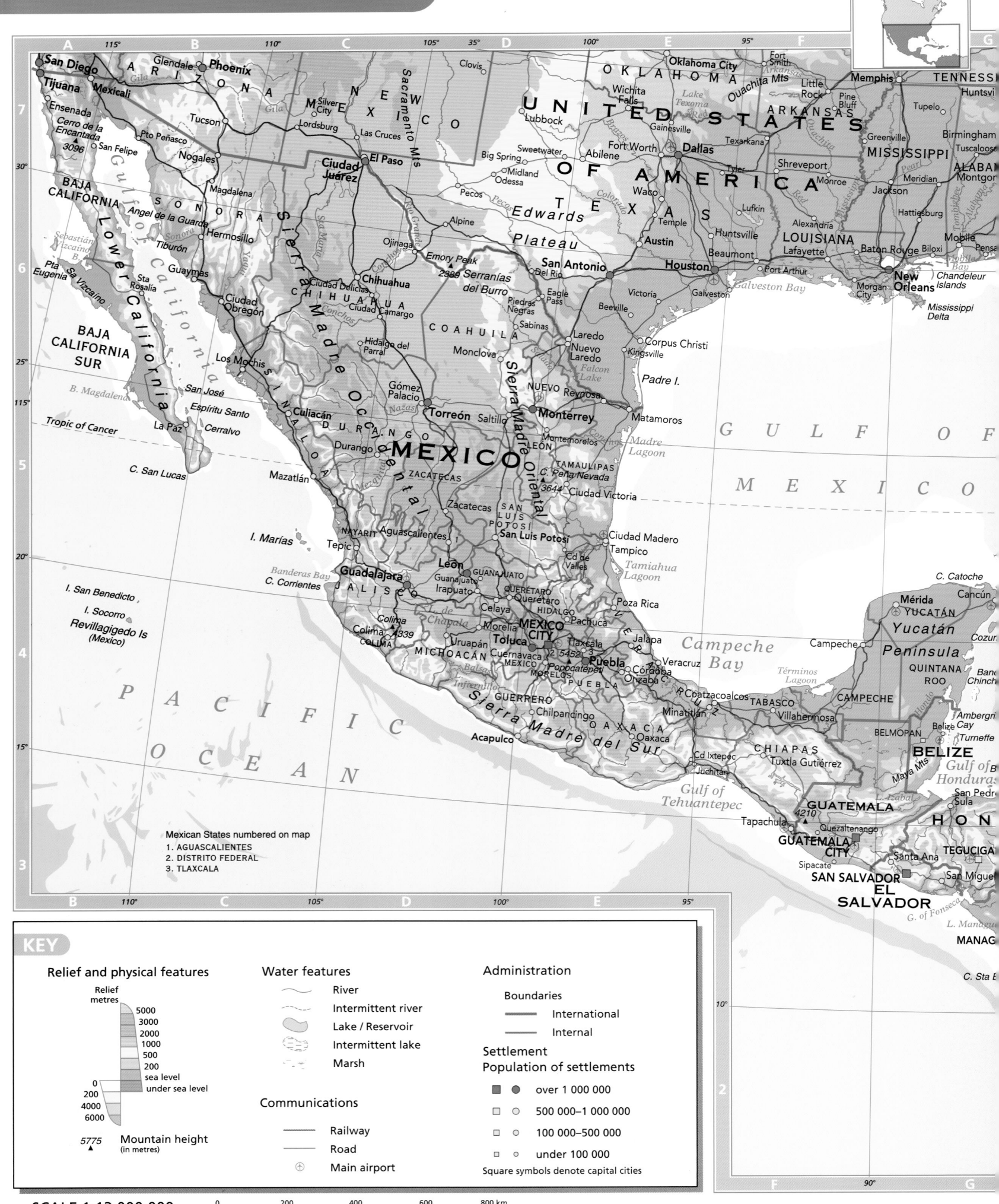

KEY

Relief and physical features

Relief metres

| 5000 |
| 3000 |
| 2000 |
| 1000 |
| 500 |
| 200 |
| sea level |
| under sea level |
| 200 |
| 4000 |
| 6000 |

5775 ▲ Mountain height (in metres)

Water features

～ River
⋯ Intermittent river
◗ Lake / Reservoir
⋯ Intermittent lake
⋯ Marsh

Communications

━━ Railway
── Road
⊕ Main airport

Administration

Boundaries
━━ International
── Internal

Settlement
Population of settlements

■ ●	over 1 000 000
□ ○	500 000–1 000 000
▫ ○	100 000–500 000
▫ ○	under 100 000

Square symbols denote capital cities

SCALE 1:13 000 000

0   200   400   600   800 km

CW

MEXICO
BELIZE
GUATEMALA
HONDURAS
EL SALVADOR
NICARAGUA
COSTA RICA
PANAMA

CUBA
THE BAHAMAS
JAMAICA
HAITI
DOMINICAN REP.
PUERTO RICO (USA)

G. of Honduras
CARIBBEAN SEA

ATLANTIC OCEAN

Barranquilla
Cartagena
Maracaibo
Valencia
Cabimas
CARACAS
Maracay
TRINIDAD AND TOBAGO

Cúcuta
San Cristóbal
Ciudad Bolívar
Ciudad Guayana
GEORGETOWN
PARAMARIBO
CAYENNE

Medellín
Manizales
Bucaramanga
VENEZUELA
GUYANA
SURINAME
FRENCH GUIANA

BOGOTÁ
COLOMBIA
Buenaventura
I. de Coco (Costa Rica)
I. de Malpelo (Colombia)
Cali

Orinoco
Meta
Esequibo

QUITO
ECUADOR
Guayaquil
Galapagos Islands (Ecuador)
G. of Guayaquil

Japurá
Amazon
Negro
Manaus
Santarém
Belém
São Luís
Fernando de Noronha (Brazil)

Equator

Iquitos
Marañón
Juruá
Purús
Madeira

Chiclayo
Trujillo
Porto Velho
Rio Branco

P E R U
Tapajós
Xingu
Araguaia
Tocantins
Parnaíba

B R A Z I L

Fortaleza
Teresina
Natal
João Pessoa
Campina Grande
Recife
Maceió
Aracaju
Salvador

LIMA
Callao
Huancayo
Cuzco

L. Titicaca
BOLIVIA
LA PAZ
Cochabamba
L. Poopó
SUCRE
Santa Cruz
Corumbá
Cuiabá

São Francisco

BRASÍLIA
Goiânia
Belo Horizonte
Vitória

Arequipa
Arica
Iquique
Antofagasta

PACIFIC OCEAN

Salta
San Miguel de Tucumán

PARAGUAY
ASUNCIÓN
Corrientes

Paraná

Ribeirão Prêto
Campinas
Nova Iguaçu
Campos
São Paulo
Santos
Rio de Janeiro
Curitiba
Florianopolis

Trindade (Brazil)
Martin Vaz Is

Tropic of Capricorn

Córdoba
Santa Fé
Rosario
Paraná
Mendoza
URUGUAY
MONTEVIDEO
Porto Alegre
Pelotas

Valparaíso
SANTIAGO
Talcahuano
Concepción
BUENOS AIRES
La Plata
Mar del Plata
Bahía Blanca

C H I L E
A R G E N T I N A
Uruguay

ATLANTIC OCEAN

Puerto Montt
Golfo San Matías

Comodoro Rivadavia

Bahía Grande
Str. of Magellan
Punta Arenas

Stanley
Falkland Islands (UK)

South Georgia (UK)

South Sandwich Is (UK)

POPULATION

Persons per sq km
over 100
50–100
10–50
1–10
0–1

Caracas
Medellín
Bogotá
Equator
Fortaleza
Recife
Salvador
Lima
Belo Horizonte
Rio de Janeiro
São Paulo
Curitiba
Tropic of Capricorn
Porto Alegre
Santiago
Buenos Aires

Urban Population
Number of people
■ over 10 000 000
■ 5 000 000–10 000 000
● 2 500 000–5 000 000
• 1 000 000–2 500 000

SCALE 1:80 000 000

Boundaries
——— International

Population of settlements
■ ● over 1 000 000
□ ○ 500 000–1 000 000
□ ○ 100 000–500 000
□ ○ under 100 000

Square symbols denote capital cities

SCALE 1:35 000 000
0   400   800   1200 km

Lambert Azimuthal Equal Area projection

ATLANTIC OCEAN

CARIBBEAN SEA

Yucatan Channel
Cuba
Bahamas
Yucatán Peninsula
Greater Antilles
Hispaniola
Puerto Rico
Jamaica
Leeward Is
Sierra Madre
G. of Honduras
Lesser Antilles
L. Nicaragua
Gallinas Pt
Curaçao
Windward Is

G. of Darien
Trinidad
Orinoco Delta
L. Maracaibo
Llanos
Orinoco
Meta
2810 Mt Roraima
Guiana Highlands
Essequibo

I. de Coco
Cordillera Central

I. de Malpelo

Amazon Delta

5896
Cotopaxi
6310 Chimborazo
Equator
Japurá
Amazon
Negro
Amazon

Galapagos Islands

G. of Guayaquil
Marañón
Juruá
Purús
Madeira
Tapajós
Xingu
Tocantins
Araguaia
Parnaíba

Pta Negra
Selvas

Fernando de Noronha
C. de São Roque

6768
Huascarán

Mato Grosso Plateau

Brazilian

A N D E S

L. Titicaca
Altiplano
L. Poopó

São Francisco

Highlands

PACIFIC OCEAN

Atacama Desert
Gran Chaco
Paraguay
Paraná

2797
Agulhas Negras

Trindade
Martin Vaz Is

Tropic of Capricorn

6908
Ojos del Salado

Paraná
Uruguay

6959
Aconcagua

Pampas

Rio de la Plata

ATLANTIC OCEAN

Golfo San Matías

Patagonia

Isla de Chiloé

Bahía Grande
Str. of Magellan

Falkland Islands

Tierra del Fuego

Cape Horn

South Georgia

South Sandwich Is

LAND REGIONS

Guiana Highlands
Equator
Central Plains and Lowlands
Brazilian Plateau
Andes Mountains
Tropic of Capricorn

SCALE 1:80 000 000

Relief

Relief metres	
	5000
	3000
	2000
	1000
	500
	200
	sea level
0	below sea level
200	
3000	
5000	

▲ 6959   Mountain height (in metres)

SCALE 1:35 000 000

0   400   800   1200 km

Lambert Azimuthal Equal Area projection

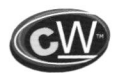

1 JANUARY TEMPERATURE AND PRESSURE

1014
1014
Equator
1012
1012
1012
LOW
1010
1014
1014
Tropic of Capricorn
1012
1012
1014
1012
1012
Average temperature °C
24
16
8
Wind direction
Isobar in hectopascals reduced to sea level
1010
1010
1008
1008
1006
1006
1004
1004

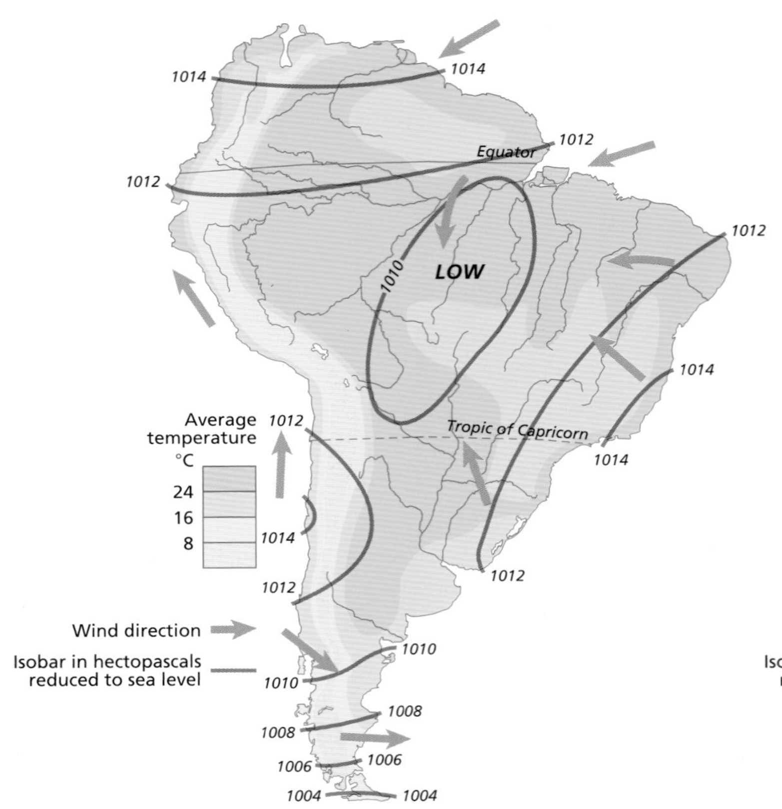

2 JULY TEMPERATURE AND PRESSURE

1010
LOW
1010
Equator
1012
1012
1014
1014
1016
1016
1018
1020
Tropic of Capricorn
1018
1018
1020
1018
Average temperature °C
24
16
8
0
Wind direction
Isobar in hectopascals reduced to sea level
1016
1016
1014
1014
1012
1012
1010
1010

3 ANNUAL RAINFALL

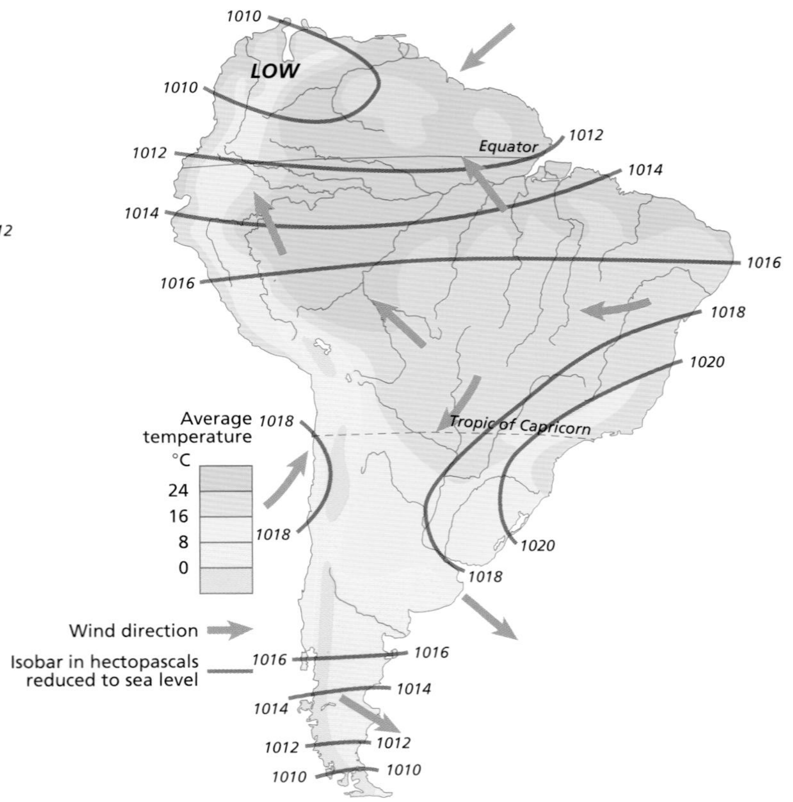

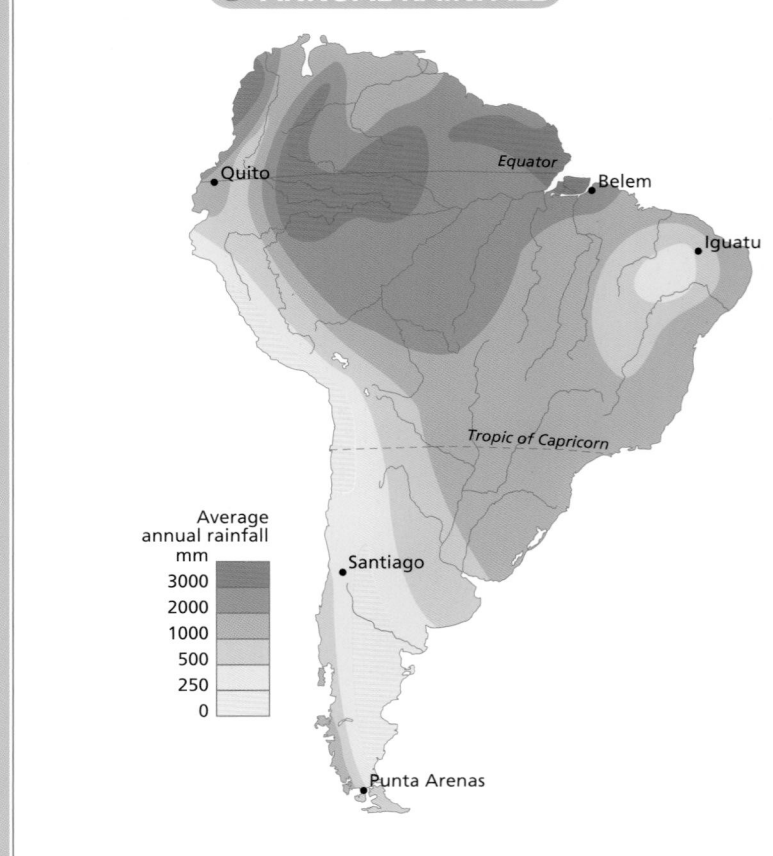

Equator
Quito
Belem
Iguatu
Tropic of Capricorn
Santiago
Punta Arenas
Average annual rainfall mm
3000
2000
1000
500
250
0

4 STATISTICS

Quito (2879 m)	Jan	Feb	Mar	Apr	May	Jun	Jul	Aug	Sep	Oct	Nov	Dec
Temperature, max. (°C)	22	22	22	21	21	22	22	23	23	22	22	22
Temperature, min. (°C)	8	8	8	8	8	7	7	7	7	8	7	8
Rainfall (mm)	99	112	142	175	137	43	20	31	69	112	97	79

Belem (13 m)	Jan	Feb	Mar	Apr	May	Jun	Jul	Aug	Sep	Oct	Nov	Dec
Temperature, max. (°C)	31	30	31	31	31	31	31	31	32	32	32	32
Temperature, min. (°C)	22	22	23	23	23	22	22	22	22	22	22	22
Rainfall (mm)	318	358	358	320	259	170	150	112	89	84	66	155

Iguatu (209 m)	Jan	Feb	Mar	Apr	May	Jun	Jul	Aug	Sep	Oct	Nov	Dec
Temperature, max. (°C)	34	33	32	31	31	31	32	32	35	36	36	36
Temperature, min. (°C)	23	23	23	23	22	22	21	21	22	23	23	23
Rainfall (mm)	89	173	185	160	61	61	36	5	18	18	10	33

Santiago (520 m)	Jan	Feb	Mar	Apr	May	Jun	Jul	Aug	Sep	Oct	Nov	Dec
Temperature, max. (°C)	29	29	27	23	18	14	15	17	19	22	26	28
Temperature, min. (°C)	12	11	9	7	5	3	3	4	6	7	9	11
Rainfall (mm)	3	3	5	13	64	84	76	56	31	15	8	5

Punta Arenas (8 m)	Jan	Feb	Mar	Apr	May	Jun	Jul	Aug	Sep	Oct	Nov	Dec
Temperature, max. (°C)	14	14	12	10	7	5	4	6	8	11	12	14
Temperature, min. (°C)	7	7	5	4	2	1	-1	1	2	3	4	6
Rainfall (mm)	38	23	33	36	33	41	28	31	23	28	18	36

SCALE 1:70 000 000

0 1000 2000 3000 km

Lambert Azimuthal Equal Area projection

Severe tropical forest destruction has been widespread in Rondonia, Brazil. More than half its tropical forests have been destroyed or degraded either by timber logging or land clearing for small agricultural plots, plantations or pasture land. This satellite image shows several of these situations.

 Area **E4** represents an early 'slash and burn' farming area. The forest has been cleared along tracks which follow the higher ground. The tracks are probably the result of early logging company activities.

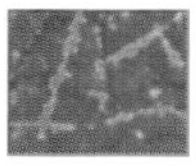

 Area **G3** represents extensive 'slash and burn' farming. The roads have been cut through the forest in a rectangular pattern, possibly the result of a government colonisation or development scheme.

 Area **F7** represents large-scale forest clearance, probably by large companies. These companies usually establish large cattle ranches or large plantations to grow crops on a commercial scale.

 Area **I8** represents large-scale forest clearance for timber. The logging companies are gradually working their way along the top of each of the mountain ridges, leaving bare ground behind them.

The blue areas from **A3** to **F1** are extensive grasslands on the river floodplains.

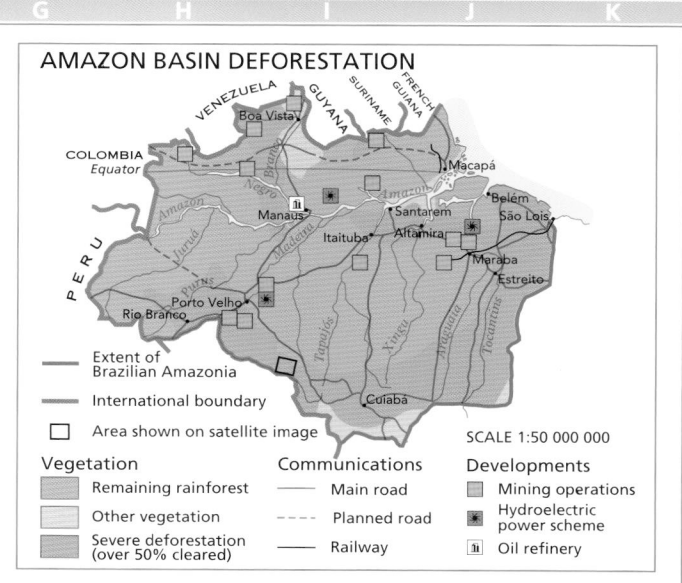

AMAZON BASIN DEFORESTATION

SCALE 1:50 000 000

Vegetation
- Remaining rainforest
- Other vegetation
- Severe deforestation (over 50% cleared)

Communications
- —— Main road
- ---- Planned road
- —— Railway

Developments
- Mining operations
- Hydroelectric power scheme
- Oil refinery

—— Extent of Brazilian Amazonia
—— International boundary
□ Area shown on satellite image

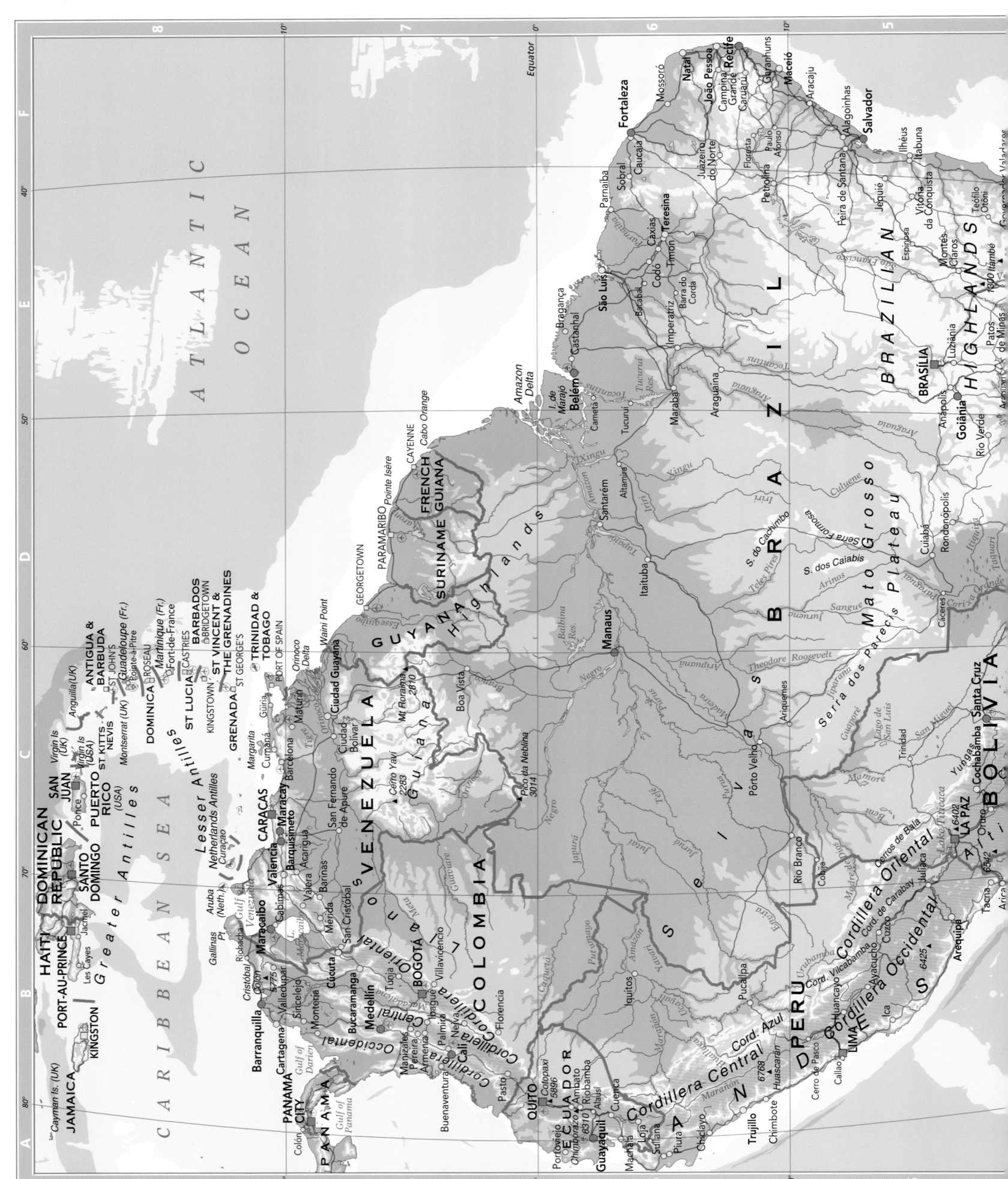

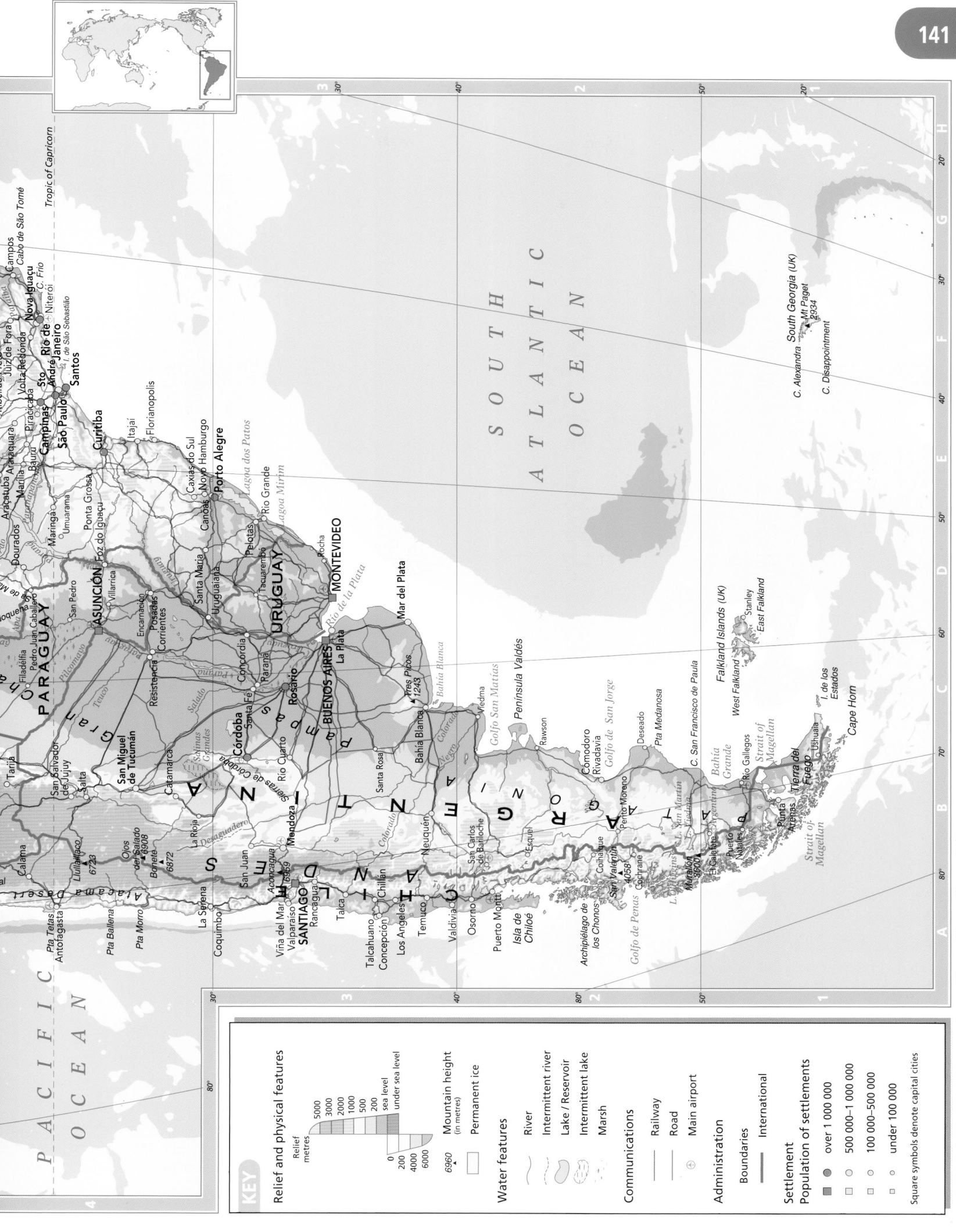

KEY

Relief and physical features

Relief
metres

5000
3000
2000
1000
500
200
sea level
under sea level

Mountain height
(in metres)

6960 ▲

Permanent ice

0
200
4000
6000

Water features

River

Intermittent river

Lake / Reservoir

Intermittent lake

Marsh

Communications

Railway

Road

⊕ Main airport

Administration

Boundaries

International

Settlement

Population of settlements

● over 1 000 000

◐ 500 000–1 000 000

○ 100 000–500 000

○ under 100 000

Square symbols denote capital cities

SCALE 1:20 000 000

0   200   400   600   800 km

Sinusoidal projection

PACIFIC
OCEAN

Tropic of Capricorn

Campos
Cabo de São Tomé
C. Frio
Nova Iguaçu
Niterói
Rio de Janeiro
I. de São Sebastião
Sto. André
Santos
São Paulo
Campinas
Piracicaba
Bauru
Curitiba
Araçatuba Araraquara
Matão
Maringá
Dourados
Ponta Grossa
Umuarama
Itajaí
Florianópolis

Juiz de Fora
Volta Redonda

Laguna dos Patos
Caxias do Sul
Novo Hamburgo
Porto Alegre
Canoas
Rio Grande
Lagoa Mirim
Pelotas
Santa Maria
Uruguaiana
Tacuarembó

Pedro Juan Caballero
Filadélfia
San Pedro
Villarrica
ASUNCIÓN
Encarnación
Posadas
Corrientes
Resistencia

PARAGUAY

Gran

Pilcomayo
Bermejo

Tarija
Calama
Antofagasta
Pta Tetas
Pta Ballena
Pta Morro
La Serena
Coquimbo

San Salvador
de Jujuy
Salta
Llullaillaco
6723
Ojos del Salado
6908
Bonete
6872

San Miguel
de Tucumán
Catamarca
La Rioja
San Juan

Atacama Desert

Salinas Grandes

ARGENTINA

Córdoba
Sierras de Córdoba
Río Cuarto
Desaguadero

URUGUAY
Rocha
MONTEVIDEO
Mar del Plata

Santa Fé
Paraná
Rosario
BUENOS AIRES
La Plata
Río de la Plata

Santa Rosa

Colorado
Bahía Blanca
Tres Picos
1243
Bahía Blanca

Aconcagua
6959
Mendoza
ANDES
SANTIAGO
Viña del Mar
Valparaíso
Rancagua
Chillán
Talca
Concepción
Talcahuano
Los Ángeles
Temuco
Valdivia
Osorno
Puerto Montt
Isla de Chiloé

Neuquén

San Carlos
de Bariloche

Negro
Viedma
Golfo San Matías
Península Valdés
Rawson

Colorado

CHILE

PATAGONIA

Golfo de Penas
Archipiélago de los Chonos

Coihaique
Esquel

L. Buenos Aires
L. San Martín
Perito Moreno
Murallón
3600
San Valentín
4058
Cochrane

Comodoro
Rivadavia
Golfo de San Jorge
Deseado
Pta Medanosa

C. San Francisco de Paula

Bahía Grande
L. Argentino
El Calafate
Puerto
Natales
Puerto Moreno
Punta
Arenas
Río Gallegos
Strait of Magellan

Strait of Magellan

Falkland Islands (UK)
Stanley
West Falkland
East Falkland

Tierra del Fuego
Ushuaia
I. de los Estados
Cape Horn

SOUTH
ATLANTIC
OCEAN

C. Alexandra *South Georgia (UK)*
Mt Paget
2934
C. Disappointment

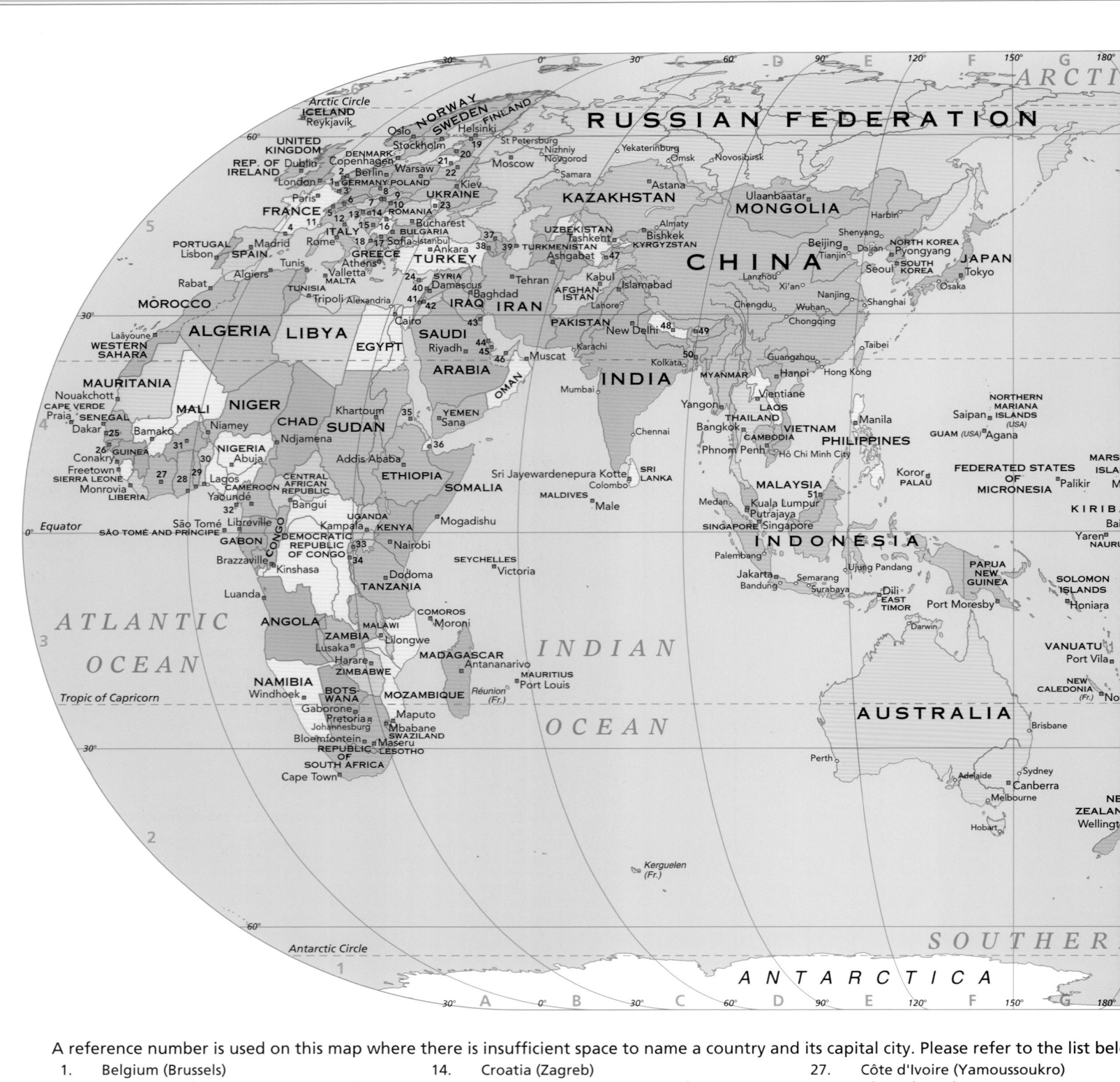

A reference number is used on this map where there is insufficient space to name a country and its capital city. Please refer to the list bel◀

1.	Belgium (Brussels)	14.	Croatia (Zagreb)	27.	Côte d'Ivoire (Yamoussoukro)	
2.	Netherlands (The Hague, Amsterdam)	15.	Bosnia-Herzegovina (Sarajevo)	28.	Ghana (Accra)	
3.	Luxembourg (Luxembourg)	16.	Serbia and Montenegro (Belgrade)	29.	Togo (Lomé)	
4.	Andorra (Andorra la Vella)	17.	Macedonia (Skopje)	30.	Benin (Porto-Novo)	
5.	Switzerland (Bern)	18.	Albania (Tiranë)	31.	Burkina (Ouagadougou)	
6.	Liechtenstein (Vaduz)	19.	Estonia (Tallinn)	32.	Equatorial Guinea (Malabo)	
7.	Austria (Vienna)	20.	Latvia (Riga)	33.	Rwanda (Kigali)	
8.	Czech Republic (Prague)	21.	Lithuania (Vilnius)	34.	Burundi (Bujumbura)	
9.	Slovakia (Bratislava)	22.	Belarus (Minsk)	35.	Eritrea (Asmara)	
10.	Hungary (Budapest)	23.	Moldova (Chișinău)	36.	Djibouti (Djibouti)	
11.	Monaco (Monaco)	24.	Cyprus (Nicosia)	37.	Georgia (T'bilisi)	
12.	San Marino (San Marino)	25.	The Gambia (Banjul)	38.	Armenia (Yerevan)	
13.	Slovenia (Ljubljana)	26.	Guinea-Bissau (Bissau)			

SCALE 1:90 000 000

0   900   1800   2700   3600 km

LARGEST LAND AREAS	sq km
Russian Federation	17 075 400
Canada	9 984 670
USA	9 826 635
China	9 562 000
Brazil	8 514 819
Australia	7 692 024
India	3 064 898
Argentina	2 766 889
Kazakhstan	2 717 300
Sudan	2 505 813

LARGEST POPULATIONS	'000
China	1 289 161
India	1 065 462
USA	294 043
Indonesia	219 883
Brazil	178 470
Pakistan	153 578
Bangladesh	146 736
Russian Federation	143 246
Japan	127 654
Nigeria	124 009

HIGHEST DENSITIES	persons per sq km
Monaco	17 000
Singapore	6 554
Malta	1 244
Maldives	1 037
Bangladesh	996
Bahrain	959
Barbados	626
Nauru	619
Mauritius	578
South Korea	477

LOWEST DENSITIES	persons per sq km
Guyana	3.6
Canada	3.1
Libya	3.1
Iceland	2.8
Mauritania	2.8
Botswana	2.7
Suriname	2.6
Australia	2.5
Namibia	2.2
Mongolia	1.7

e capital city is named in brackets after the name of the country.

39. Azerbaijan (Baku)
40. Lebanon (Beirut)
41. Israel (Jerusalem)
42. Jordan (Amman)
43. Kuwait (Kuwait)
44. Bahrain (Manama)
45. Qatar (Doha)
46. United Arab Emirates (Abu Dhabi)
47. Tajikistan (Dushanbe)
48. Nepal (Kathmandu)
49. Bhutan (Thimbu)
50. Bangladesh (Dhaka)

51. Brunei (Bandar Seri Begawan)
52. Belize (Belmopan)
53. El Salvador (San Salvador)
54. St Kitts-Nevis (Basseterre)
55. Antigua and Barbuda (St John's)
56. Dominica (Roseau)
57. St Lucia (Castries)
58. Barbados (Bridgetown)
59. St Vincent and the Grenadines (Kingstown)
60. Grenada (St George's)
61. Trinidad and Tobago (Port of Spain)
62. French Guiana (Cayenne)

LIFE EXPECTANCY	years
Highest	
Japan	81
Iceland, Sweden, Switzerland	80
Australia, Austria, Belgium, Canada, France, Israel, Norway	79
Lowest	
Sierra Leone, Zambia	37
Botswana, Malawi	38
Zimbabwe	39
Rwanda	40
Mali, Mozambique	41

Eckert IV projection

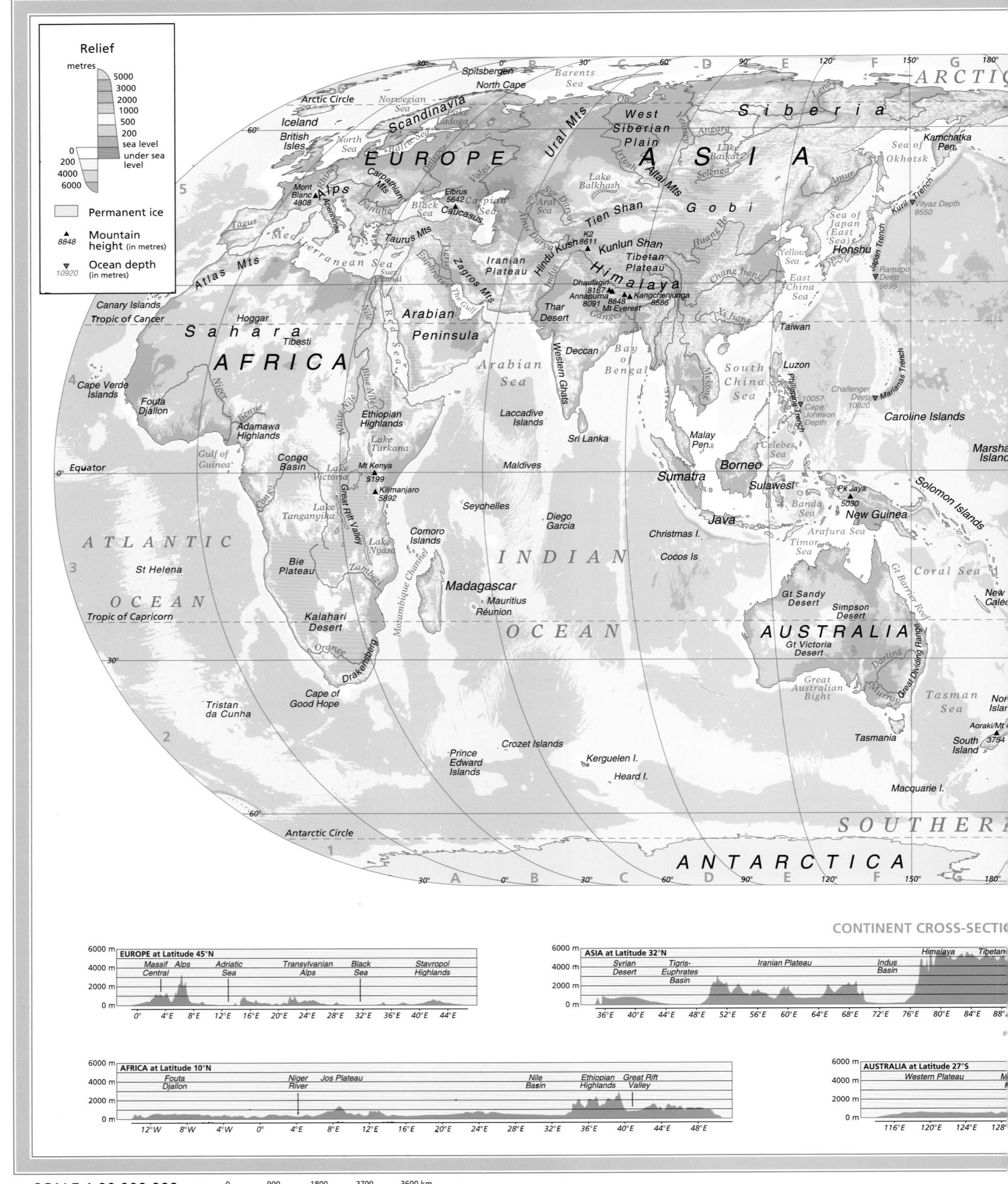

Relief

metres
5000
3000
2000
1000
500
200
sea level
0
under sea
200 level
4000
6000

Permanent ice

▲ Mountain
8848 height (in metres)

▽ Ocean depth
10920 (in metres)

CONTINENT CROSS-SECTION

EUROPE at Latitude 45°N

6000 m
4000 m   Massif   Alps   Adriatic   Transylvanian   Black   Stavropol
2000 m   Central   Sea   Alps   Sea   Highlands
0 m
0° 4°E 8°E 12°E 16°E 20°E 24°E 28°E 32°E 36°E 40°E 44°E

ASIA at Latitude 32°N

6000 m
4000 m   Syrian   Tigris-   Iranian Plateau   Indus   Himalaya   Tibetan
2000 m   Desert   Euphrates   Basin
         Basin
0 m
36°E 40°E 44°E 48°E 52°E 56°E 60°E 64°E 68°E 72°E 76°E 80°E 84°E 88°

AFRICA at Latitude 10°N

6000 m
4000 m   Fouta   Niger Jos Plateau   Nile   Ethiopian Great Rift
2000 m   Djallon   River   Basin   Highlands Valley
0 m
12°W 8°W 4°W 0° 4°E 8°E 12°E 16°E 20°E 24°E 28°E 32°E 36°E 40°E 44°E 48°E

AUSTRALIA at Latitude 27°S

6000 m
4000 m   Western Plateau
2000 m
0 m
116°E 120°E 124°E 128°

SCALE 1:90 000 000

0   900   1800   2700   3600 km

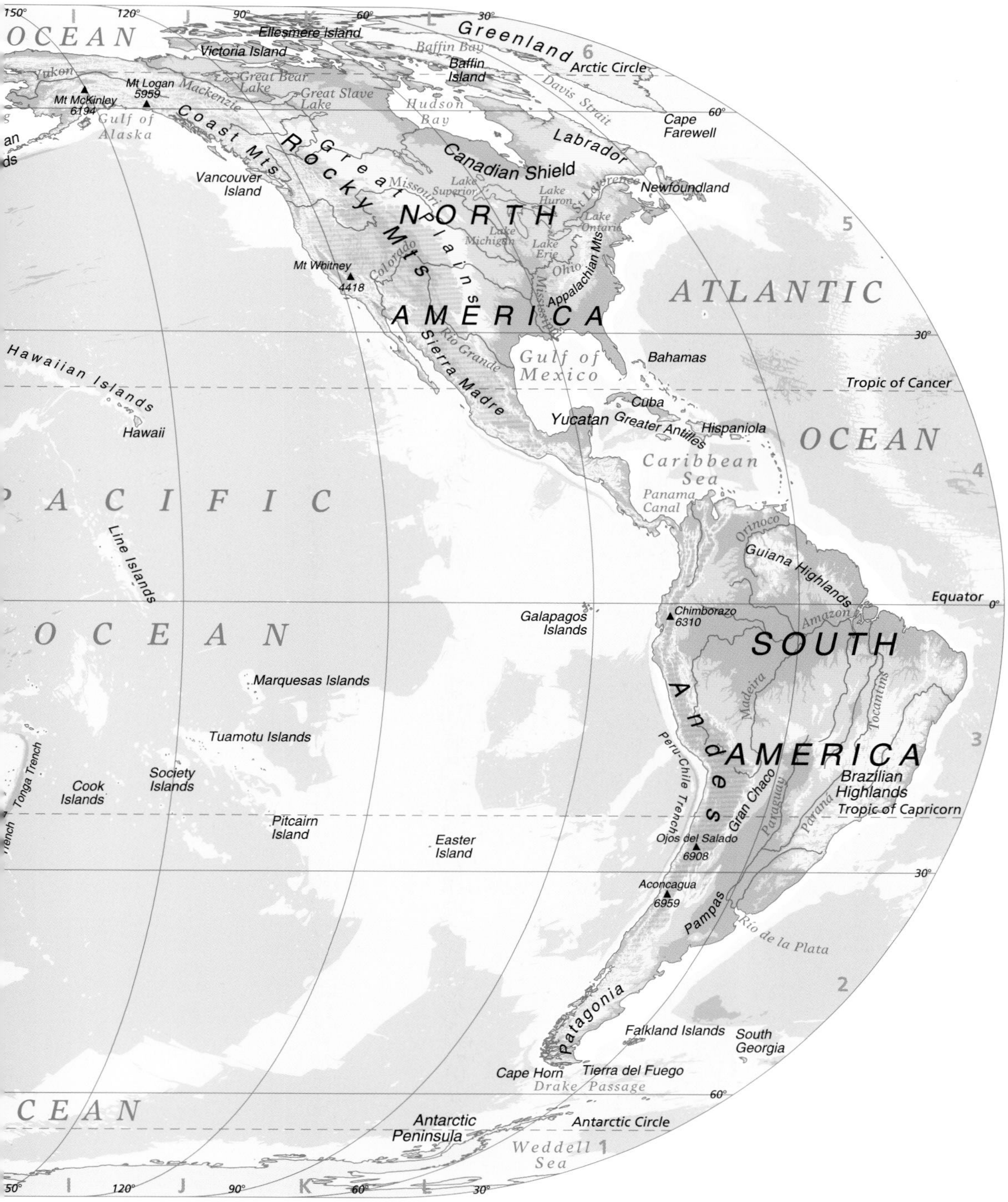

OCEAN
Ellesmere Island
Victoria Island
Greenland
Baffin Bay
Baffin Island
Arctic Circle
Davis Strait
Yukon
Mt McKinley 6194
Mt Logan 5959
Mackenzie
Great Bear Lake
Great Slave Lake
Hudson Bay
Gulf of Alaska
Coast Mts
Great Plains
Rocky Mts
Cape Farewell
Labrador
Canadian Shield
Vancouver Island
Missouri
Lake Superior
Lake Huron
St Lawrence
Newfoundland
NORTH AMERICA
Lake Michigan
Lake Ontario
Lake Erie
Ohio
Appalachian Mts
Mt Whitney 4418
Colorado
Mississippi
ATLANTIC OCEAN
Rio Grande
Sierra Madre
Gulf of Mexico
Bahamas
Tropic of Cancer
Hawaiian Islands
Hawaii
Cuba
Yucatan
Greater Antilles
Hispaniola
Caribbean Sea
Panama Canal
PACIFIC OCEAN
Line Islands
Orinoco
Guiana Highlands
Equator
Chimborazo 6310
Galapagos Islands
Amazon
SOUTH AMERICA
Marquesas Islands
Madeira
Tocantins
Andes
Tuamotu Islands
Peru-Chile Trench
Tonga Trench
Cook Islands
Society Islands
Gran Chaco
Brazilian Highlands
Paraguay
Paraná
Tropic of Capricorn
Pitcairn Island
Easter Island
Ojos del Salado 6908
Aconcagua 6959
Pampas
Río de la Plata
Patagonia
Falkland Islands
South Georgia
Cape Horn
Tierra del Fuego
Drake Passage
Antarctic Peninsula
Antarctic Circle
Weddell Sea
150°
120°
90°
60°
30°
0°
I
J
K
L
1
2
3
4
5
6

…zontal scale 1 cm to 500 km, Vertical scale in metres, Vertical exaggeration = 105)

hang Jiang
North China Plain
100°E
104°E
108°E
112°E
116°E
120°E

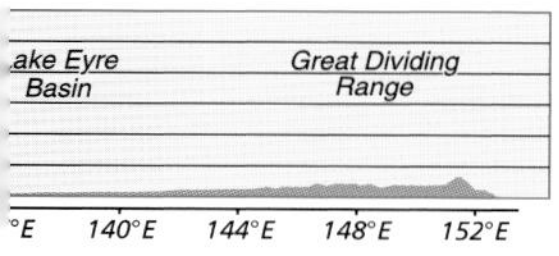

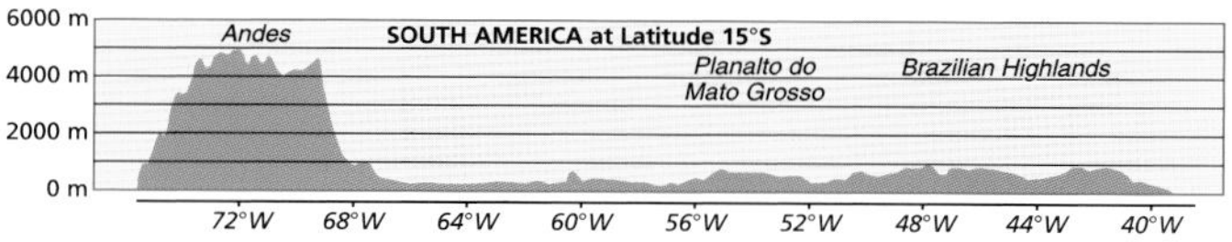

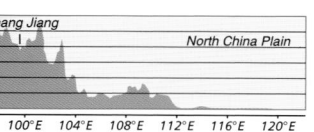

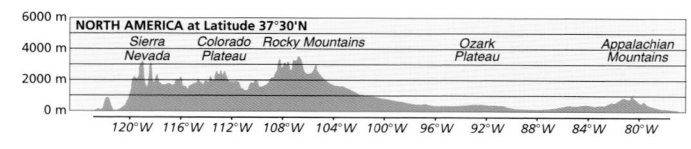

NORTH AMERICA at Latitude 37°30'N
6000 m
4000 m
2000 m
0 m
Sierra Nevada
Colorado Plateau
Rocky Mountains
Ozark Plateau
Appalachian Mountains
120°W
116°W
112°W
108°W
104°W
100°W
96°W
92°W
88°W
84°W
80°W

ake Eyre Basin
Great Dividing Range
°E
140°E
144°E
148°E
152°E

SOUTH AMERICA at Latitude 15°S
6000 m
4000 m
2000 m
0 m
Andes
Planalto do Mato Grosso
Brazilian Highlands
72°W
68°W
64°W
60°W
56°W
52°W
48°W
44°W
40°W

CONTINENTS	sq km
Asia	45 036 492
Africa	30 343 578
North America	24 680 331
South America	17 815 420
Antarctica	12 093 000
Europe	9 908 599
Australia	7 682 300

OCEANS	sq km
Pacific Ocean	166 241 000
Atlantic Ocean	86 557 000
Indian Ocean	73 427 000
Arctic Ocean	9 485 000

ISLANDS	sq km
Greenland	2 175 600
New Guinea	808 510
Borneo	745 561
Madagascar	587 040
Baffin Island	507 451
Sumatra	473 606
Honshu	227 414
Great Britain	218 476
Victoria Island	217 291
Ellesmere Island	196 236

MOUNTAINS	metres
Mt Everest *(Nepal/China)*	8848
K2 *(Jammu & Kashmir/China)*	8611
Kangchenjunga *(Nepal/India)*	8586
Dhaulagiri *(Nepal)*	8167
Annapurna *(Nepal)*	8091
Aconcagua *(Argentina)*	6959
Ojos del Salado *(Argentina/Chile)*	6908
Chimborazo *(Ecuador)*	6310
Mt McKinley *(USA)*	6194
Mt Logan *(Canada)*	5959

RIVERS	km
Nile *(Africa)*	6695
Amazon *(S. America)*	6516
Chang Jiang *(Asia)*	6380
Mississippi-Missouri *(N. America)*	5969
Ob-Irtysh *(Asia)*	5568
Yenisey-Angara-Selenga *(Asia)*	5500
Huang-He *(Asia)*	5464
Congo *(Africa)*	4667
Río de la Plata-Paraná *(S. America)*	4500
Mekong *(Asia)*	4425

LAKES	sq km
Caspian Sea *(Europe/Asia)*	371 000
Lake Superior *(N. America)*	82 100
Lake Victoria *(Africa)*	68 800
Lake Huron *(N. America)*	59 600
Lake Michigan *(N. America)*	57 800
Lake Tanganyika *(Africa)*	32 900
Great Bear Lake *(N. America)*	31 328
Lake Baikal *(Asia)*	30 500
Lake Nyasa *(Africa)*	30 044

Eckert IV projection

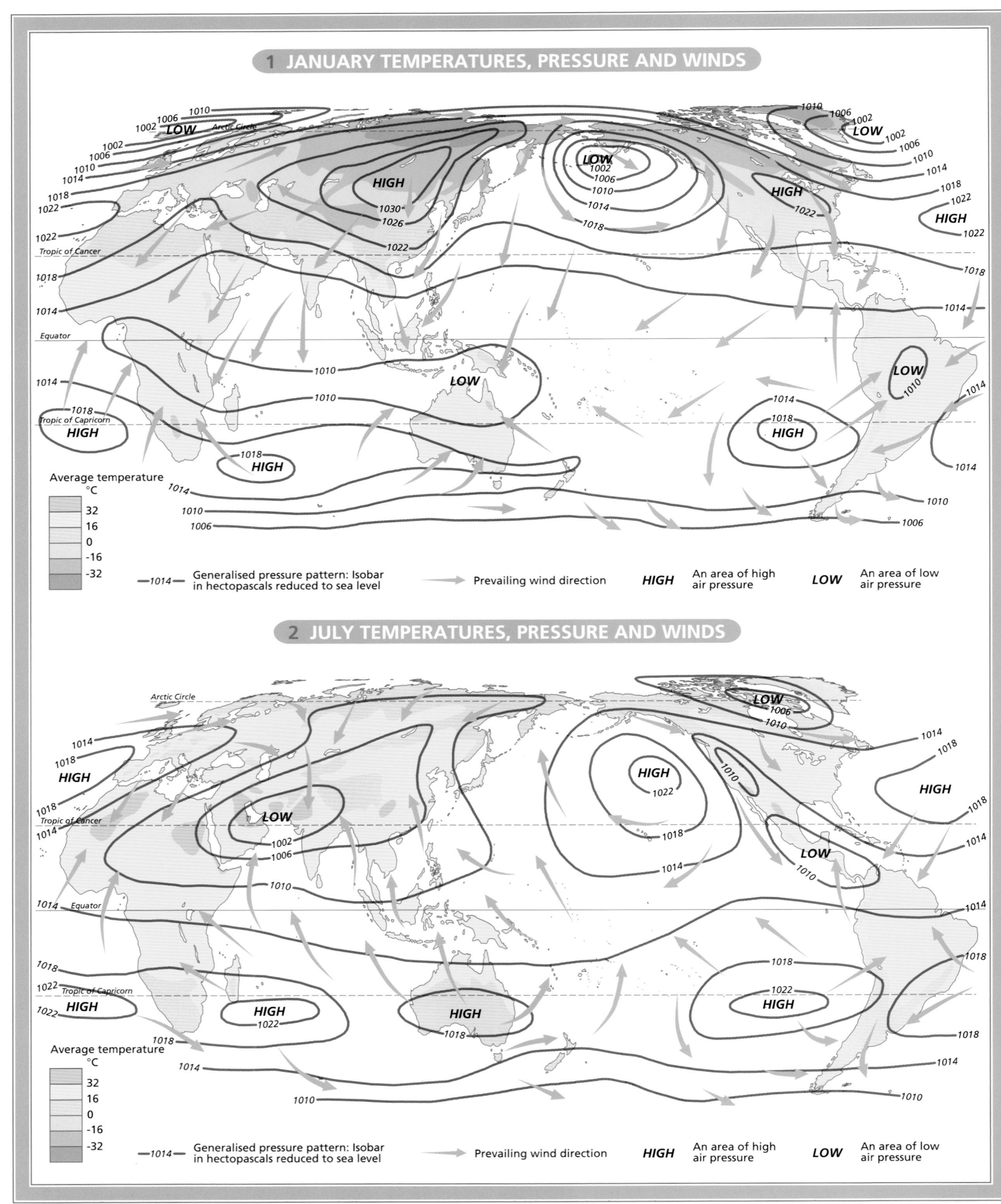

1 JANUARY TEMPERATURES, PRESSURE AND WINDS

Average temperature
°C

| 32 |
| 16 |
| 0 |
| -16 |
| -32 |

——1014— Generalised pressure pattern: Isobar in hectopascals reduced to sea level

→ Prevailing wind direction

HIGH An area of high air pressure

LOW An area of low air pressure

2 JULY TEMPERATURES, PRESSURE AND WINDS

Average temperature
°C

| 32 |
| 16 |
| 0 |
| -16 |
| -32 |

——1014— Generalised pressure pattern: Isobar in hectopascals reduced to sea level

→ Prevailing wind direction

HIGH An area of high air pressure

LOW An area of low air pressure

SCALE 1:160 000 000

0   2000   4000   6000   8000 km

Eckert IV projection

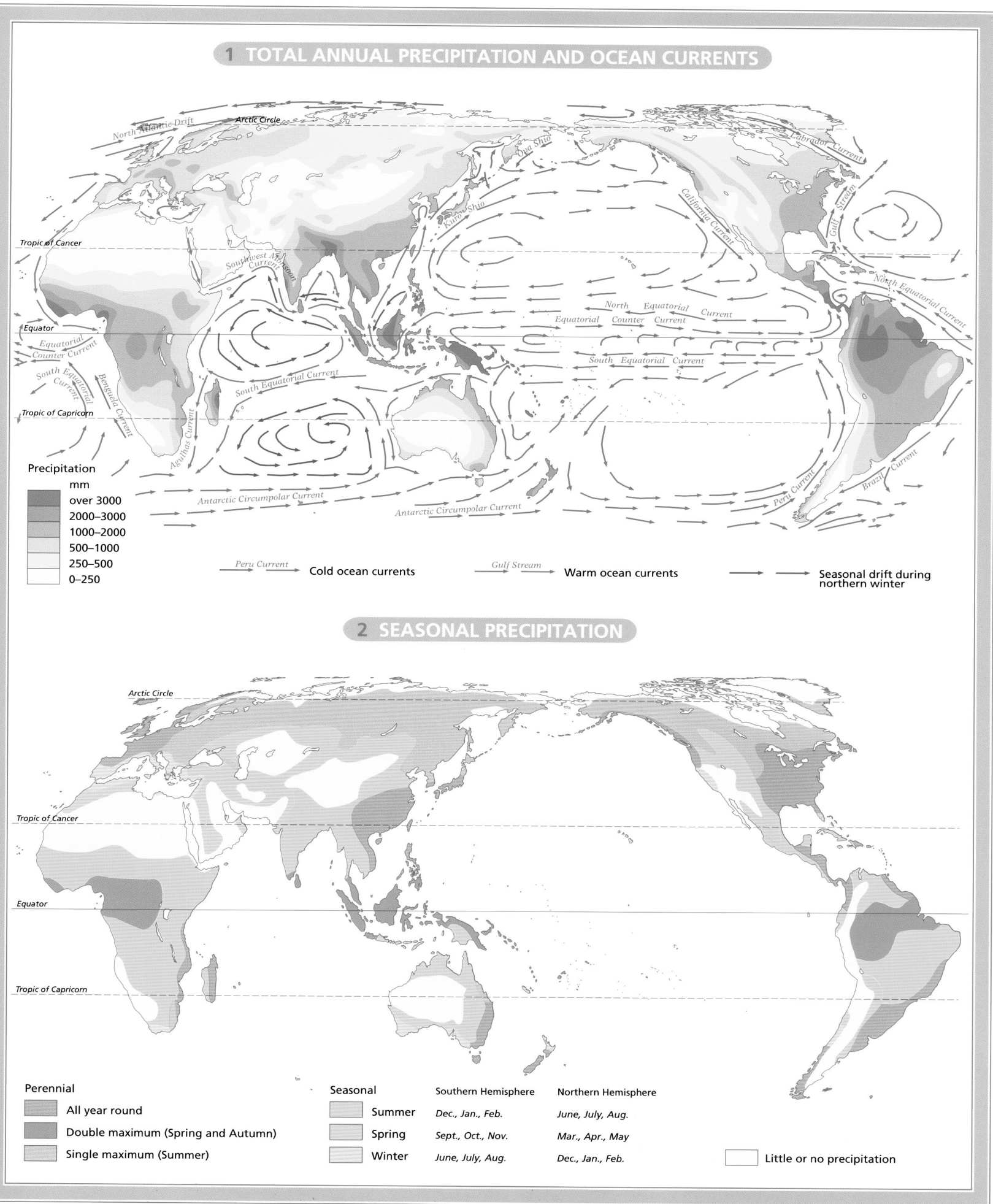

1 TOTAL ANNUAL PRECIPITATION AND OCEAN CURRENTS

Arctic Circle

North Atlantic Drift

Oya Shio

Kuro Shio

Labrador Current

California Current

Gulf Stream

Tropic of Cancer

Southwest Monsoon Current

North Equatorial Current

Equator

Equatorial Counter Current

North Equatorial Current

Equatorial Counter Current

South Equatorial Current

South Equatorial Current

South Equatorial Current

Benguela Current

Agulhas Current

Tropic of Capricorn

Peru Current

Brazil Current

Antarctic Circumpolar Current

Antarctic Circumpolar Current

Precipitation
mm
- over 3000
- 2000–3000
- 1000–2000
- 500–1000
- 250–500
- 0–250

Peru Current → Cold ocean currents

Gulf Stream → Warm ocean currents

→ Seasonal drift during northern winter

2 SEASONAL PRECIPITATION

Arctic Circle

Tropic of Cancer

Equator

Tropic of Capricorn

Perennial
- All year round
- Double maximum (Spring and Autumn)
- Single maximum (Summer)

Seasonal	Southern Hemisphere	Northern Hemisphere
Summer	Dec., Jan., Feb.	June, July, Aug.
Spring	Sept., Oct., Nov.	Mar., Apr., May
Winter	June, July, Aug.	Dec., Jan., Feb.

Little or no precipitation

SCALE 1:160 000 000

0   2000   4000   6000   8000 km

Eckert IV projection

1 CLIMATE

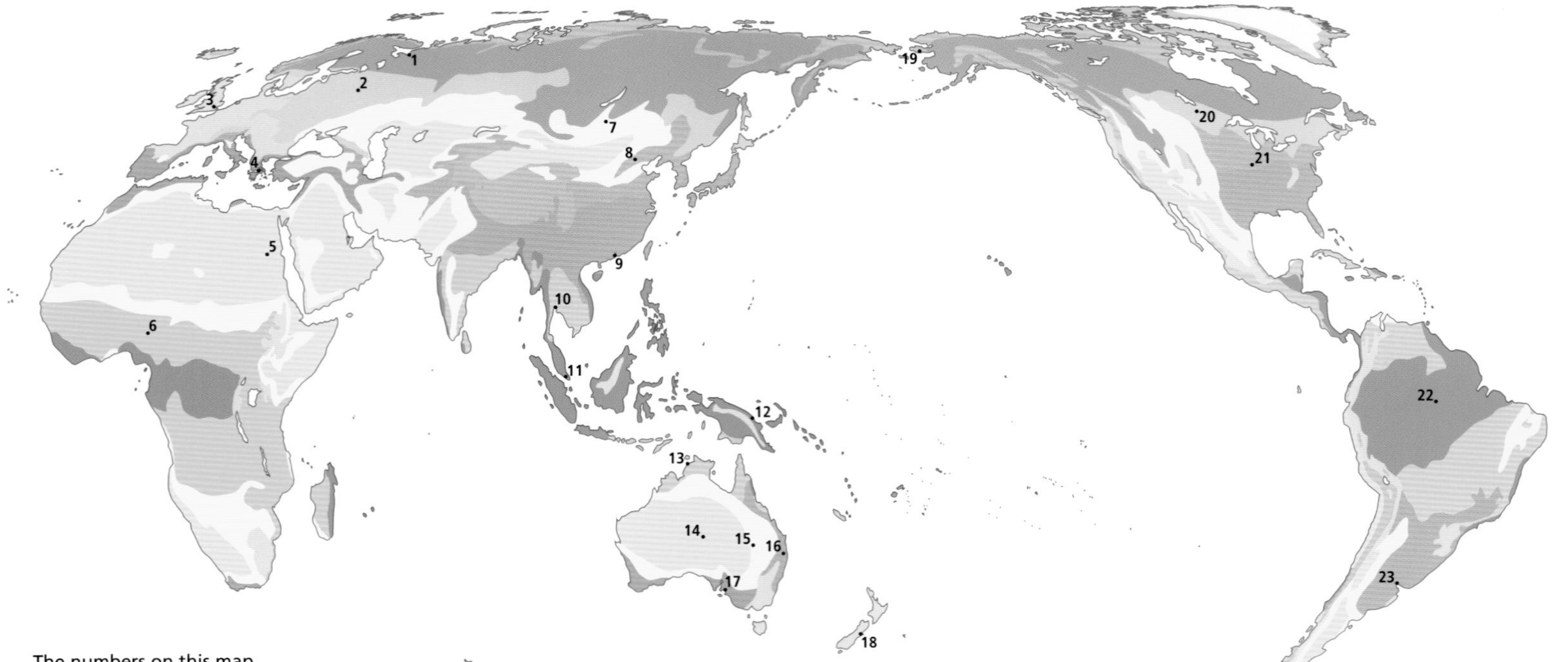

The numbers on this map refer to the climatic graphs below and on page 149.

	Ice cap Ice and snow all year		**Continental** Rainy; warm summer, cold winter		**Semi-arid** Cool and dry or hot and dry
	Tundra Cool short summer, very severe winter		**Temperate** Rainy; mild winter, warm summer		**Desert** Very dry all year
	Sub-arctic Rainy; cool short summer, severe winter		**Wet subtropical** Rainy; mild winter, warm to hot summer		**Tropical wet and dry** Warm to hot, with a distinct wet and dry season
	Continental Rainy; cool summer, cold winter		**Mediterranean** Mild wet winter, dry warm to hot summer		**Rainy tropical** Hot and wet all year

2 CLIMATIC GRAPHS

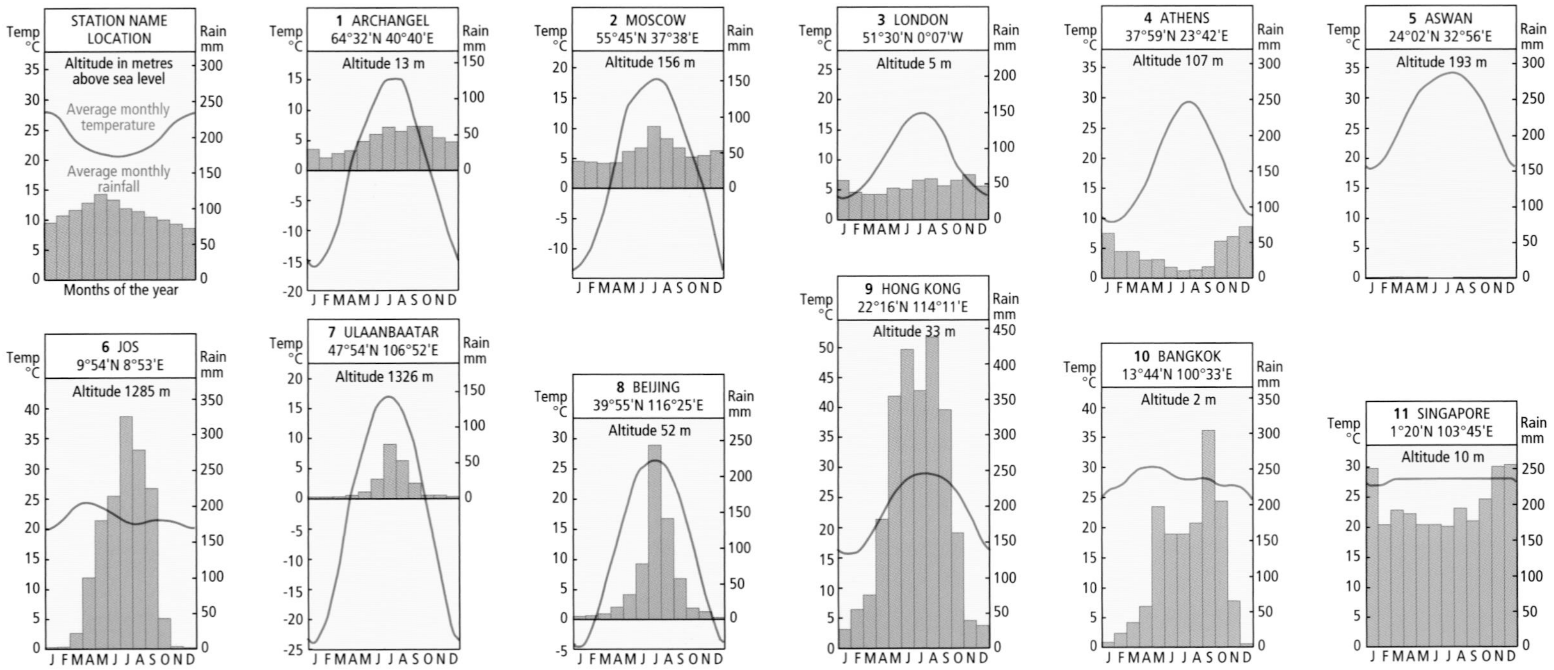

STATION NAME LOCATION
Temp °C — Rain mm
Altitude in metres above sea level
Average monthly temperature
Average monthly rainfall
Months of the year

1 ARCHANGEL 64°32'N 40°40'E — Altitude 13 m

2 MOSCOW 55°45'N 37°38'E — Altitude 156 m

3 LONDON 51°30'N 0°07'W — Altitude 5 m

4 ATHENS 37°59'N 23°42'E — Altitude 107 m

5 ASWAN 24°02'N 32°56'E — Altitude 193 m

6 JOS 9°54'N 8°53'E — Altitude 1285 m

7 ULAANBAATAR 47°54'N 106°52'E — Altitude 1326 m

8 BEIJING 39°55'N 116°25'E — Altitude 52 m

9 HONG KONG 22°16'N 114°11'E — Altitude 33 m

10 BANGKOK 13°44'N 100°33'E — Altitude 2 m

11 SINGAPORE 1°20'N 103°45'E — Altitude 10 m

SCALE 1:160 000 000

0   2000   4000   6000   8000 km

Eckert IV projection

1 VEGETATION

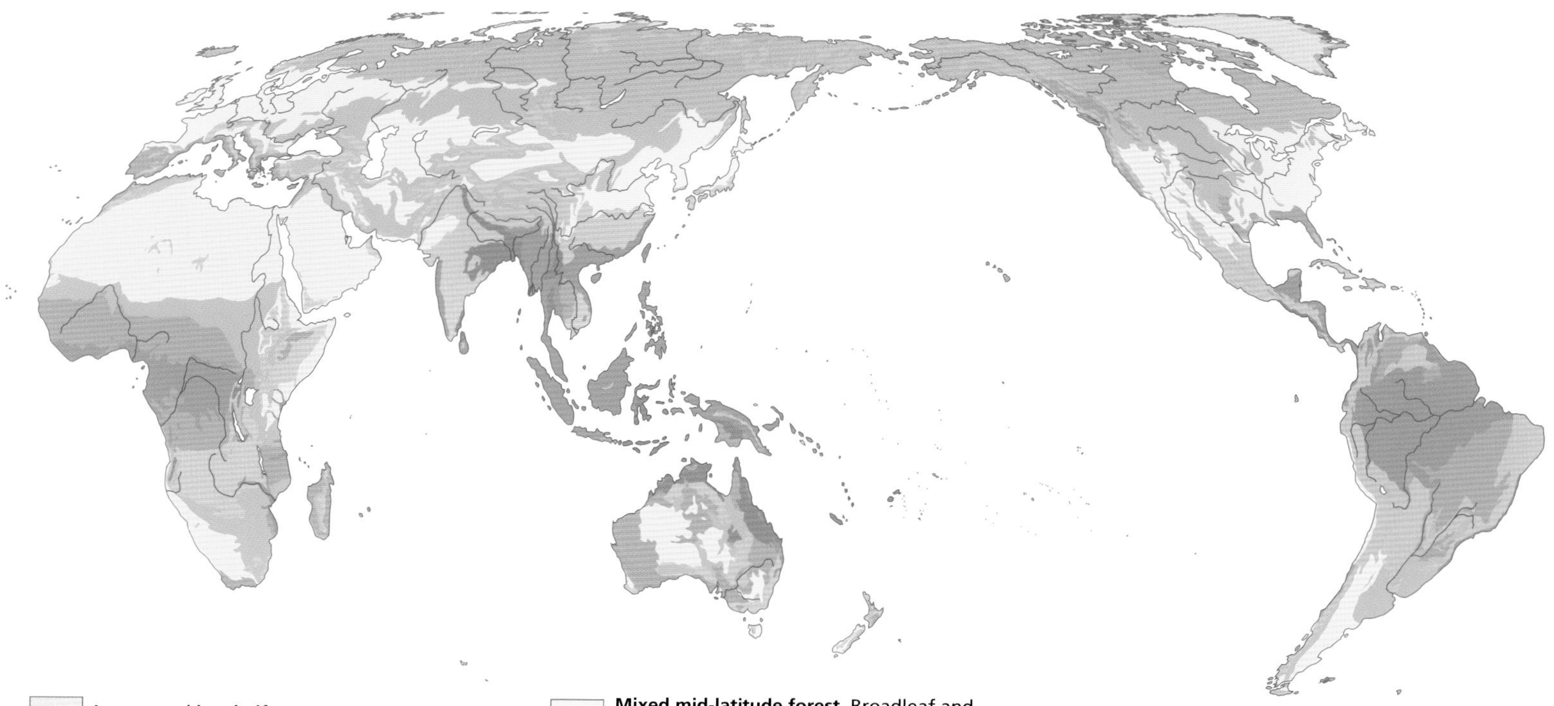

Ice cap and ice shelf

Mountain vegetation Mosses, lichens with few trees

Tundra Mosses, lichens, rushes, grasses

Boreal forest (Taiga) High-latitude coniferous forests

Coniferous forest Mid-latitude coniferous forests

Mixed mid-latitude forest Broadleaf and coniferous forests

Mediterranean scrub Drought-hardy shrubs and trees

Temperate grasslands Broad grasslands with few trees

Savanna Tropical grasslands with few trees

Tropical rainforest Tall dense multi-layered forests

Monsoon forest Tropical wet and dry deciduous forest

Dry tropical forest and scrub Semi-deciduous forest and shrubs

Sub-tropical forest Hard leaf evergreen forests

Desert vegetation Drought-tolerant trees, shrubs and grasses

2 CLIMATIC GRAPHS

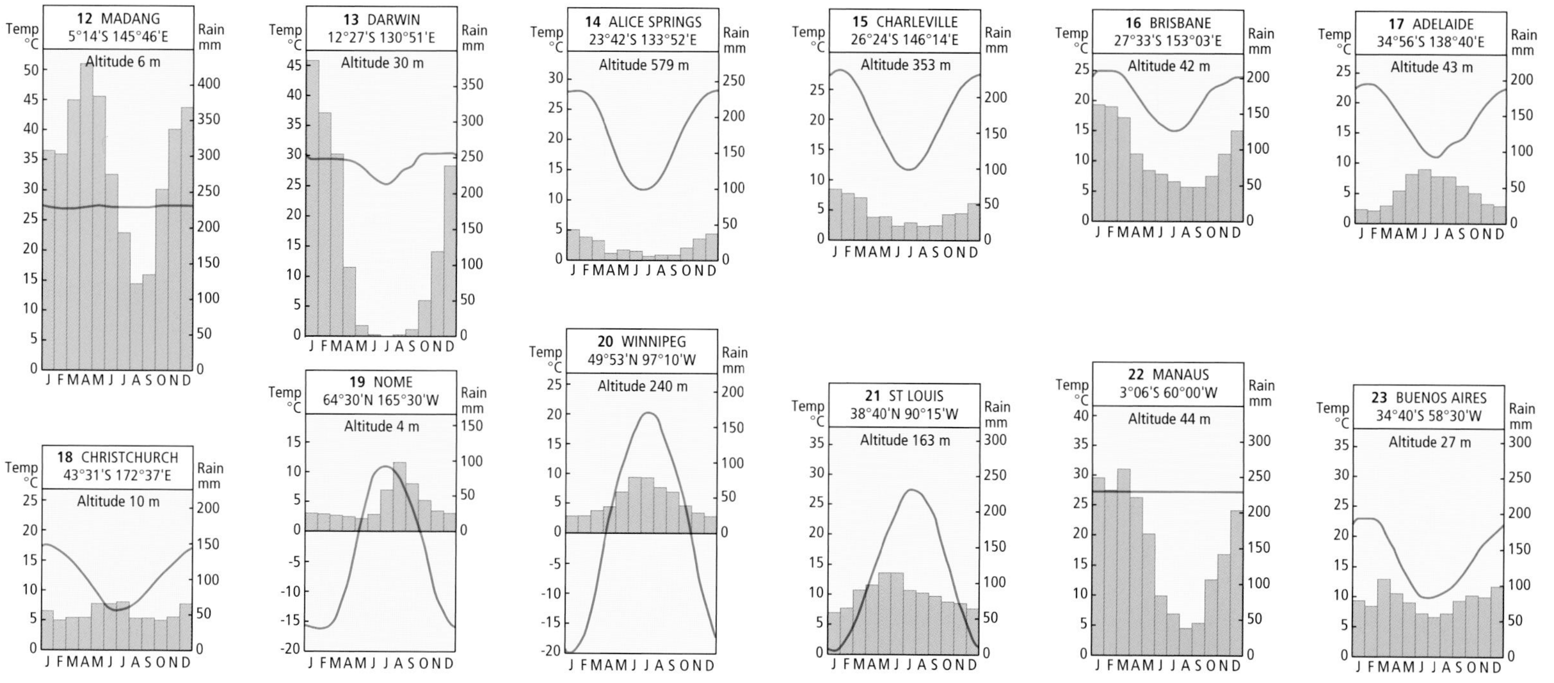

12 MADANG 5°14'S 145°46'E
Altitude 6 m

13 DARWIN 12°27'S 130°51'E
Altitude 30 m

14 ALICE SPRINGS 23°42'S 133°52'E
Altitude 579 m

15 CHARLEVILLE 26°24'S 146°14'E
Altitude 353 m

16 BRISBANE 27°33'S 153°03'E
Altitude 42 m

17 ADELAIDE 34°56'S 138°40'E
Altitude 43 m

18 CHRISTCHURCH 43°31'S 172°37'E
Altitude 10 m

19 NOME 64°30'N 165°30'W
Altitude 4 m

20 WINNIPEG 49°53'N 97°10'W
Altitude 240 m

21 ST LOUIS 38°40'N 90°15'W
Altitude 163 m

22 MANAUS 3°06'S 60°00'W
Altitude 44 m

23 BUENOS AIRES 34°40'S 58°30'W
Altitude 27 m

SCALE 1:160 000 000

0   2000   4000   6000   8000 km

Eckert IV projection

1 PLATE TECTONICS

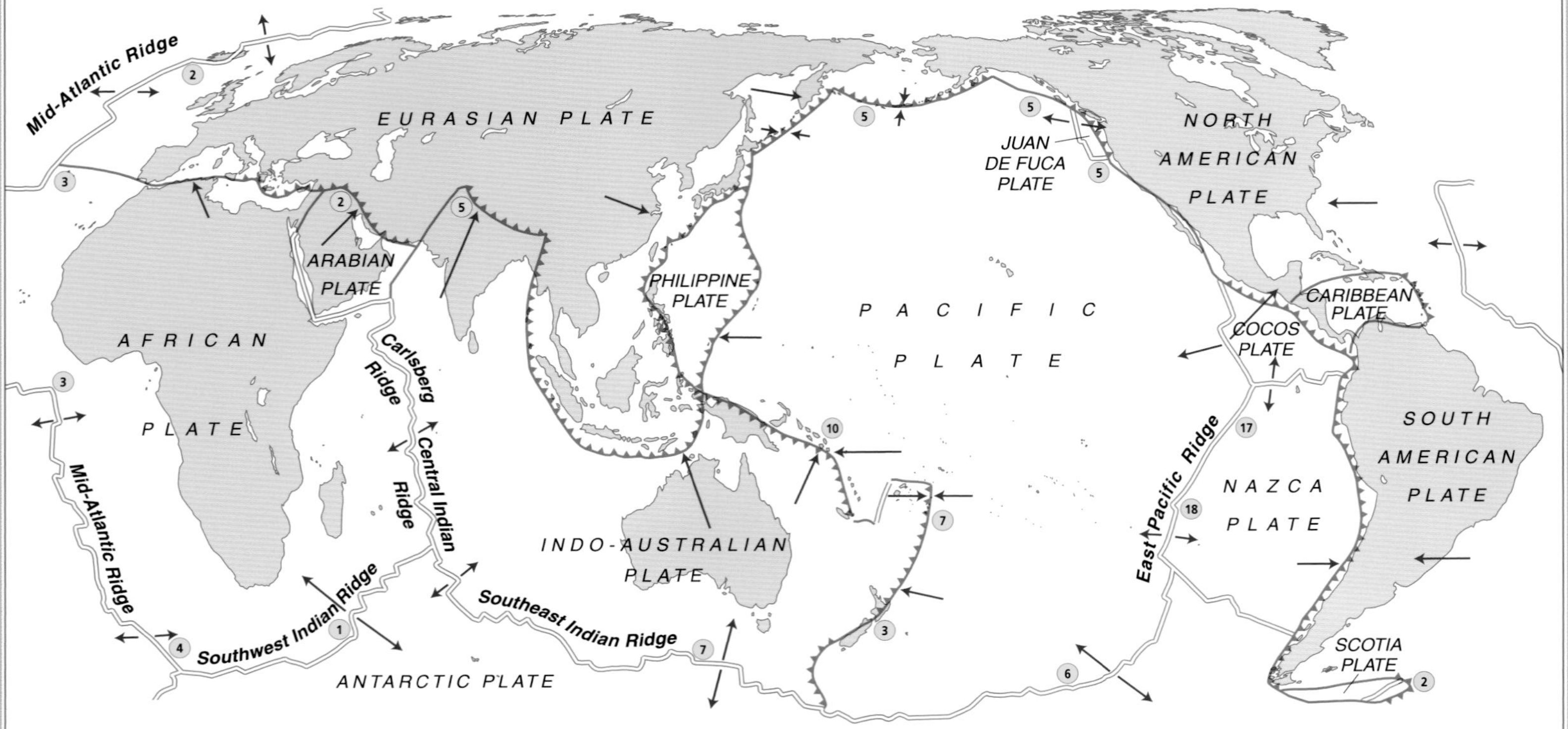

EURASIAN PLATE

Mid-Atlantic Ridge

NORTH AMERICAN PLATE

JUAN DE FUCA PLATE

ARABIAN PLATE

PHILIPPINE PLATE

CARIBBEAN PLATE

AFRICAN PLATE

P A C I F I C   P L A T E

COCOS PLATE

Carlsberg Ridge

Central Indian Ridge

SOUTH AMERICAN PLATE

East Pacific Ridge

NAZCA PLATE

Mid-Atlantic Ridge

INDO-AUSTRALIAN PLATE

Southeast Indian Ridge

Southwest Indian Ridge

ANTARCTIC PLATE

SCOTIA PLATE

Constructive or divergent boundaries	Destructive or convergent boundaries	Conservative or transform boundaries	⑥ Rate of plate movement (cm per year)
Where two plates move apart or diverge, new crust is created where magma reaches the surface, forming a mid-ocean ridge.	Where two plates collide or converge, one plate is pulled down into the mantle forming a subduction zone, where crust is destroyed.	Where two plates moves horizontally past each other, crust is conserved, that is, neither created nor destroyed.	← Direction of plate movement

2 EARTHQUAKES AND VOLCANOES

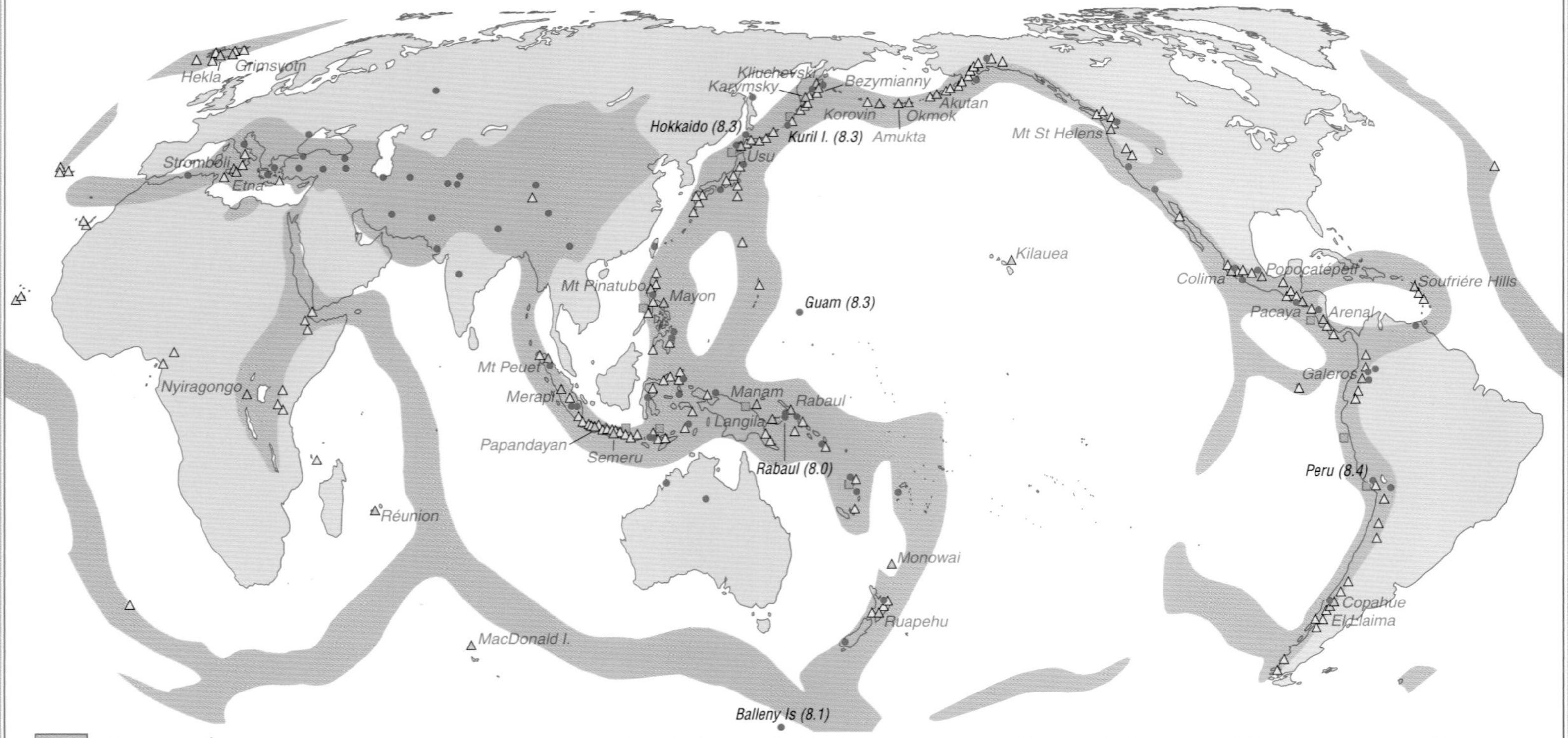

Hekla Grímsvötn

Kliuchevsk
Karymsky Bezymianny
Korovin Okmok Akutan

Hokkaido (8.3)

Kuril I. (8.3) Amukta

Mt St Helens

Usu

Stromboli
Etna

Kilauea

Colima Popocatepetl Soufrière Hills

Mt Pinatubo Mayon

Guam (8.3)

Pacaya Arenal

Nyiragongo

Mt Peuet

Manam Rabaul

Galeros

Merapi Langila

Papandayan Semeru

Rabaul (8.0)

Peru (8.4)

Réunion

Monowai

Copahue
El Daima

Ruapehu

MacDonald I.

Balleny Is (8.1)

	Earthquake* and volcano zone	• Major earthquake since 1990 (6.0 to 7.9*)	△ Active volcano	■ Major tsunami since 1990
	*Earthquake force is measured on the Richter scale	*Guam (8.3)* • Great earthquake since 1990 (8.0 and over*)	*Rabaul* △ Active volcano with eruption since 1990	See the case studies of Mt Pinatubo (p. 101), Vesuvius (p. 113) and San Francisco (p. 129)

SCALE 1:160 000 000

0   2000   4000   6000   8000 km

Eckert IV projection

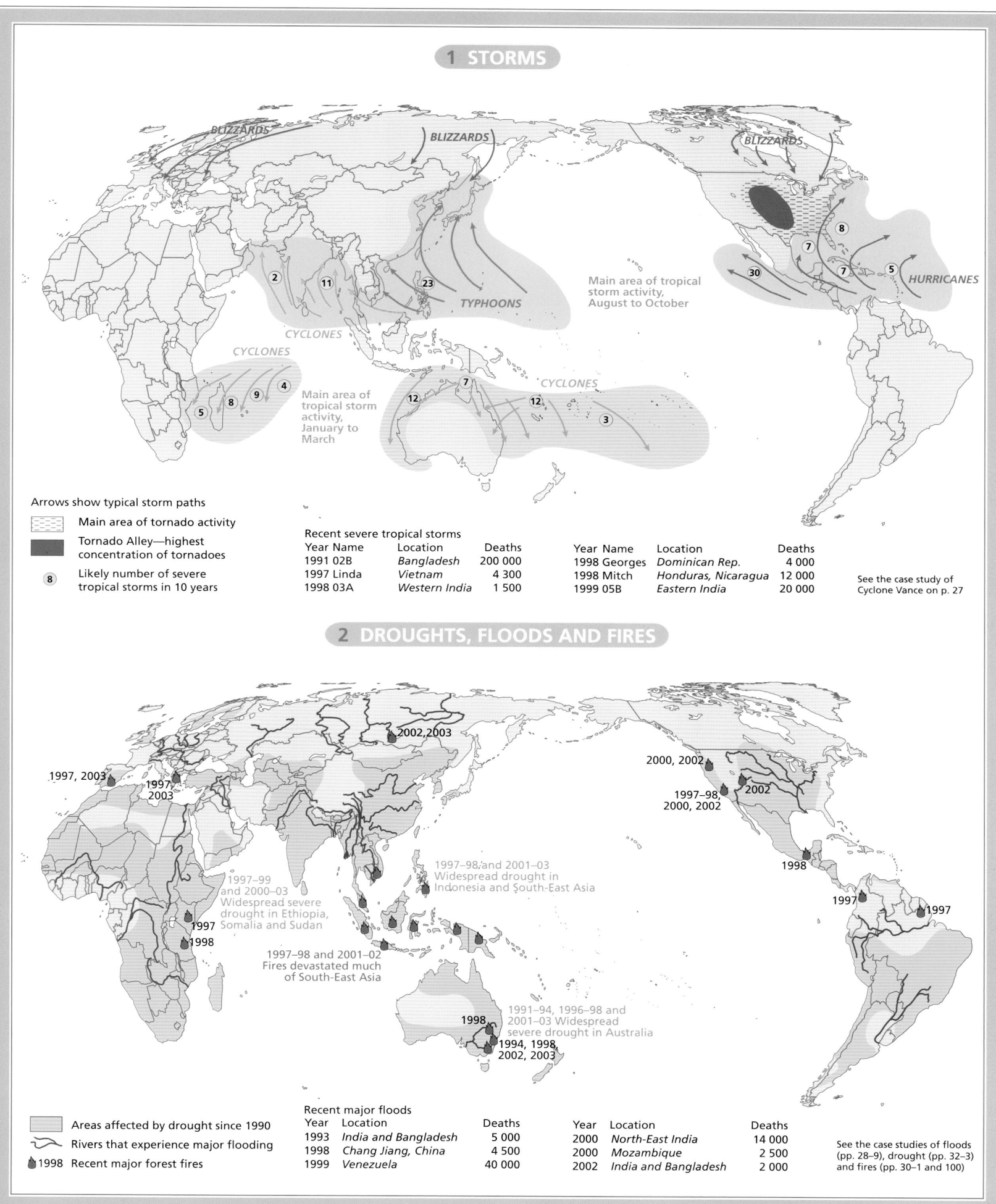

1 STORMS

BLIZZARDS

BLIZZARDS

BLIZZARDS

HURRICANES

Main area of tropical
storm activity,
August to October

TYPHOONS

CYCLONES

CYCLONES

CYCLONES

Main area of
tropical storm
activity,
January to
March

Arrows show typical storm paths

Main area of tornado activity

Tornado Alley—highest
concentration of tornadoes

8 Likely number of severe
tropical storms in 10 years

Recent severe tropical storms

Year	Name	Location	Deaths
1991	02B	Bangladesh	200 000
1997	Linda	Vietnam	4 300
1998	03A	Western India	1 500

Year	Name	Location	Deaths
1998	Georges	Dominican Rep.	4 000
1998	Mitch	Honduras, Nicaragua	12 000
1999	05B	Eastern India	20 000

See the case study of
Cyclone Vance on p. 27

2 DROUGHTS, FLOODS AND FIRES

1997, 2003

1997, 2003

2002, 2003

2000, 2002

1997–98,
2000, 2002

2002

1998

1997–99
and 2000–03
Widespread severe
drought in Ethiopia,
Somalia and Sudan

1997

1998

1997–98, and 2001–03
Widespread drought in
Indonesia and South-East Asia

1997

1997

1997–98 and 2001–02
Fires devastated much
of South-East Asia

1998

1991–94, 1996–98 and
2001–03 Widespread
severe drought in Australia

1994, 1998,
2002, 2003

Areas affected by drought since 1990

Rivers that experience major flooding

1998 Recent major forest fires

Recent major floods

Year	Location	Deaths
1993	India and Bangladesh	5 000
1998	Chang Jiang, China	4 500
1999	Venezuela	40 000

Year	Location	Deaths
2000	North-East India	14 000
2000	Mozambique	2 500
2002	India and Bangladesh	2 000

See the case studies of floods
(pp. 28–9), drought (pp. 32–3)
and fires (pp. 30–1 and 100)

SCALE 1:160 000 000

0   2000   4000   6000   8000 km

Eckert IV projection

1 LOSING THE FORESTS

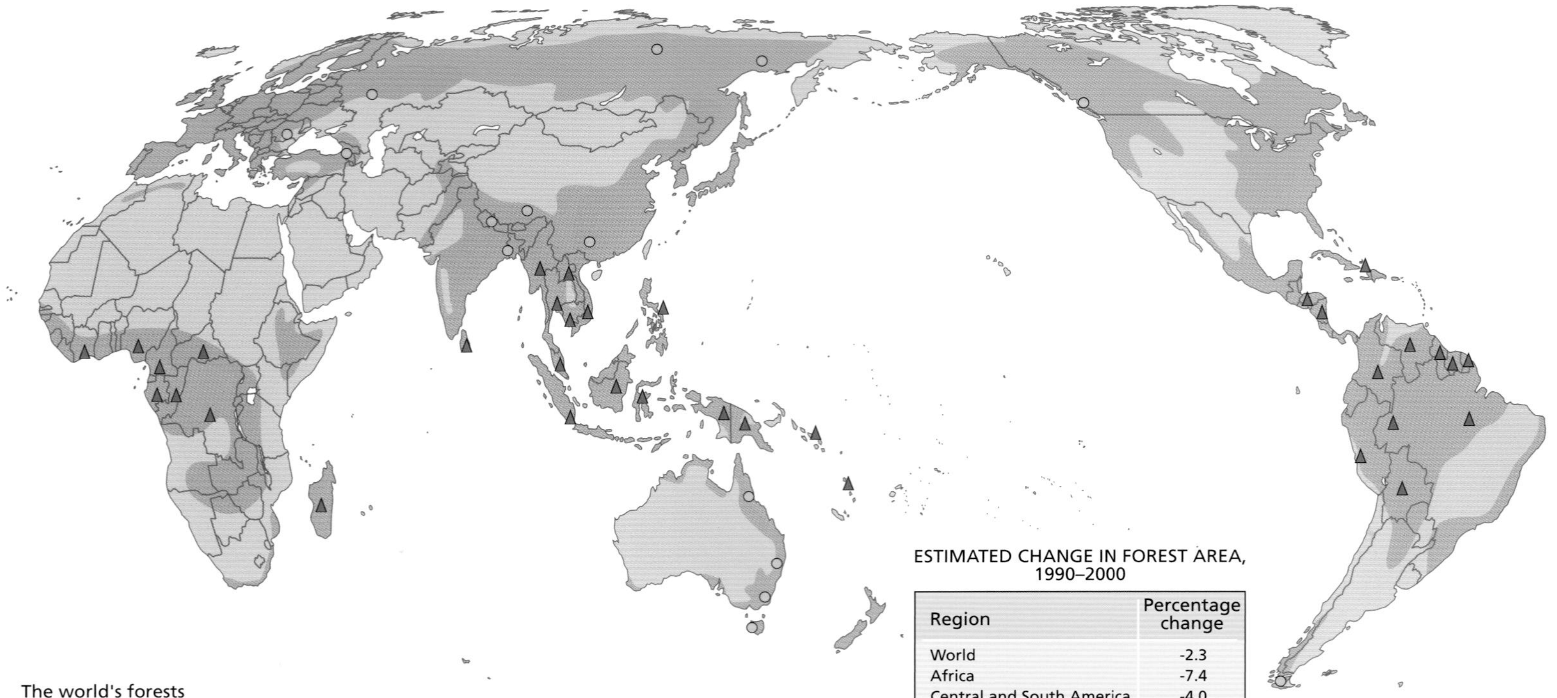

The world's forests

- No major forest areas originally
- Original forests now mostly cleared
- Original forests still remaining

See the case study of Amazon Deforestation on p. 139

▲ Areas of tropical forest with a very high rate of deforestation

⦿ Other forest areas where deforestation is a major issue

ESTIMATED CHANGE IN FOREST AREA, 1990–2000

Region	Percentage change
World	-2.3
Africa	-7.4
Central and South America	-4.0
Australia	-1.8
Asia	-0.6
Europe	+0.8
North America	+1.0

2 DEGRADING THE LAND AND SEA

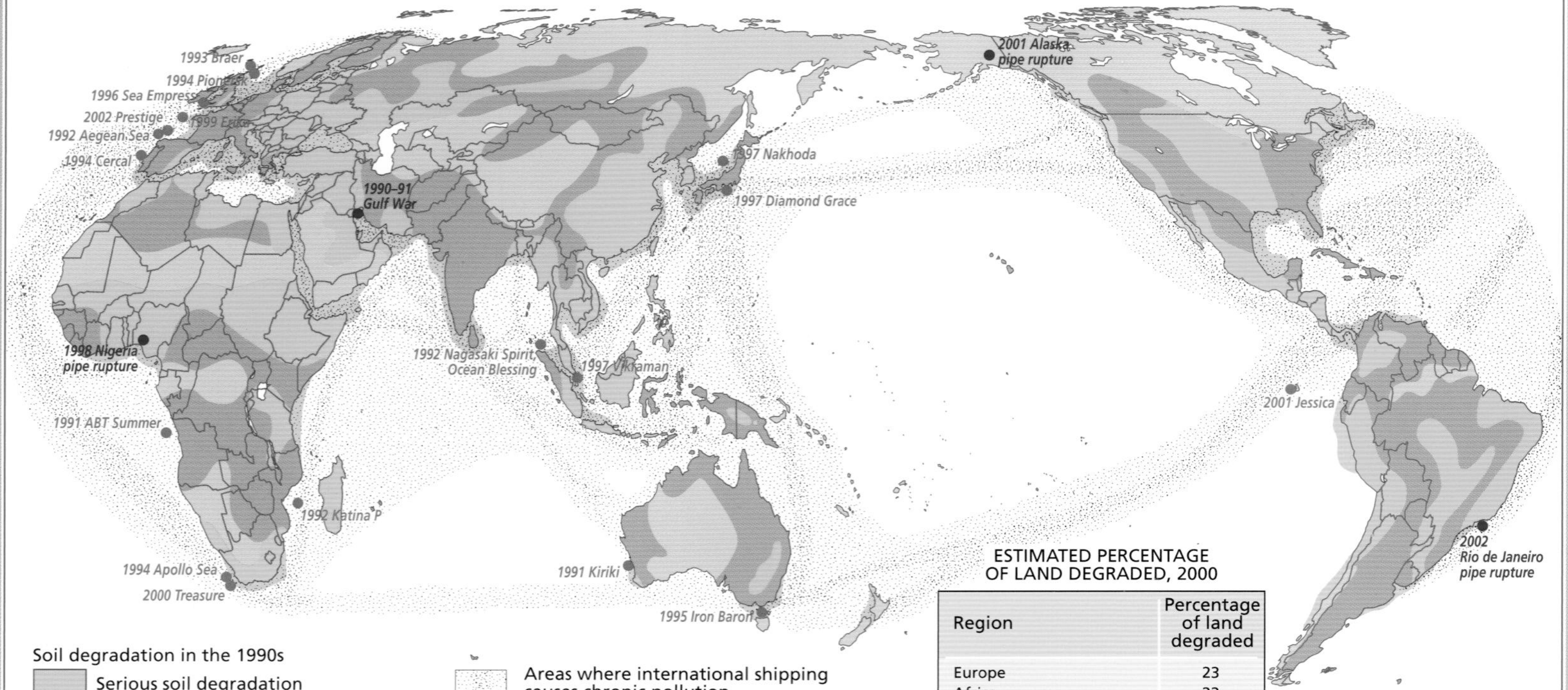

1993 Braer
1994 Pioneer
1996 Sea Empress
2002 Prestige
1992 Aegean Sea
1999 Erika
1994 Cercal
1990–91 Gulf War
1997 Nakhoda
1997 Diamond Grace
2001 Alaska pipe rupture
1998 Nigeria pipe rupture
1991 ABT Summer
1992 Nagasaki Spirit, Ocean Blessing
1997 Katman
2001 Jessica
1992 Katina P
1994 Apollo Sea
2000 Treasure
1991 Kiriki
1995 Iron Baron
2002 Rio de Janeiro pipe rupture

Soil degradation in the 1990s

- Serious soil degradation
- Some soil degradation
- Relatively stable land
- Areas of severe coastal pollution

Areas where international shipping causes chronic pollution

● 1993 Braer — Shipping accidents causing major oil spills since 1990

● 1990–91 Gulf War — Other major oil pollution since 1990

ESTIMATED PERCENTAGE OF LAND DEGRADED, 2000

Region	Percentage of land degraded
Europe	23
Africa	22
Asia	20
Central and South America	20
Australia	13
North America	10

SCALE 1:160 000 000

0 2000 4000 6000 8000 km

Eckert IV projection

1 NUCLEAR ENERGY

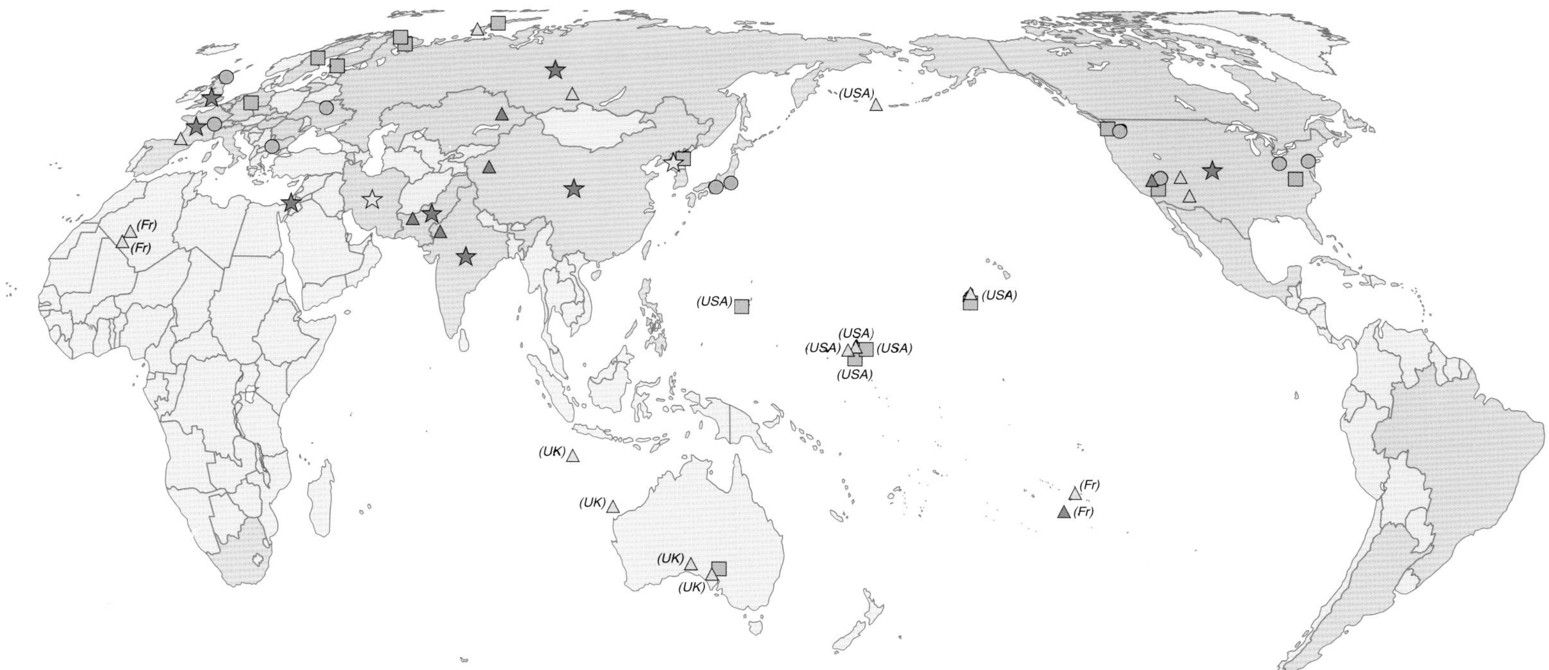

Countries using nuclear energy to generate electricity, 2004

▪ Storage site for nuclear material

● Nuclear reactors considered dangerous since 1990

Nuclear test sites

▲ used since 1990

△ used before 1990

(USA) Country which has conducted nuclear tests beyond its borders at this site

★ Countries known to have nuclear weapons, 2004

☆ Countries likely to have nuclear weapons, 2004

2 GLOBAL WARMING

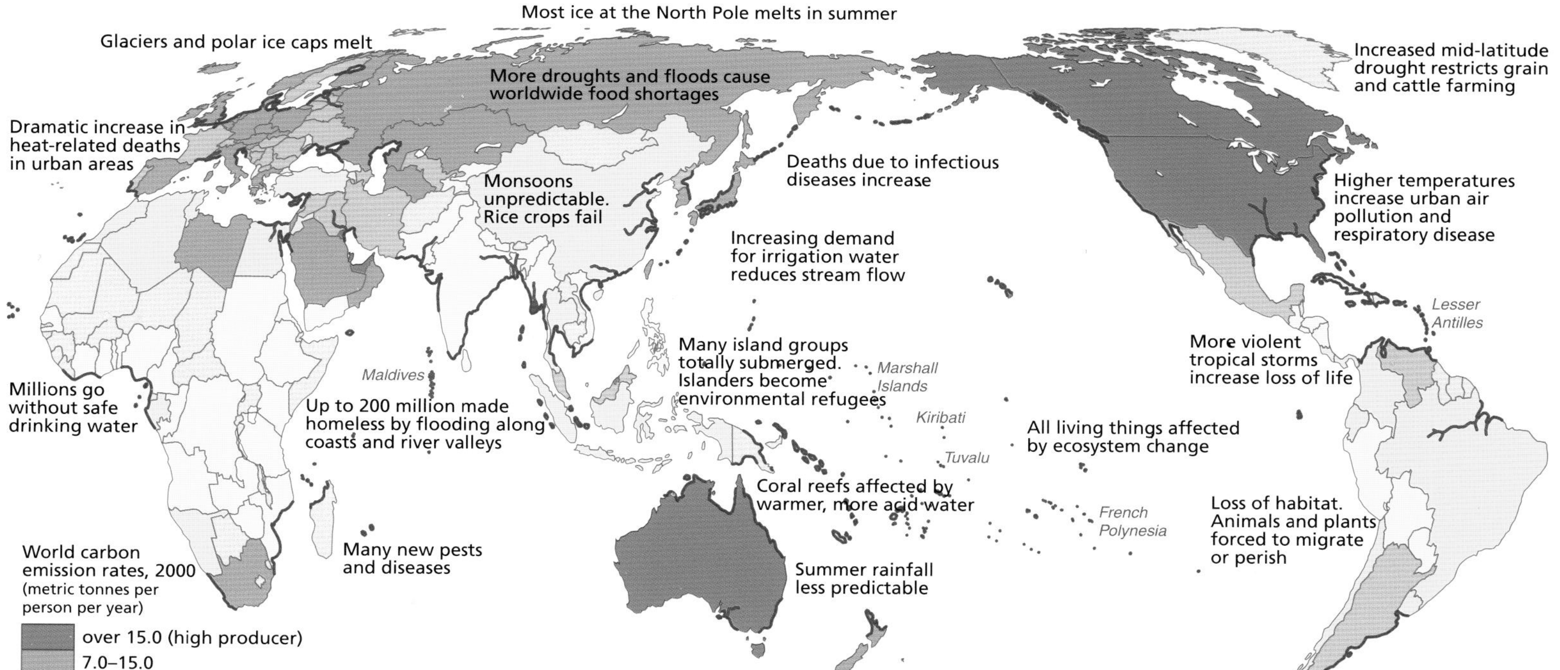

Most ice at the North Pole melts in summer

Glaciers and polar ice caps melt

Increased mid-latitude drought restricts grain and cattle farming

More droughts and floods cause worldwide food shortages

Dramatic increase in heat-related deaths in urban areas

Deaths due to infectious diseases increase

Higher temperatures increase urban air pollution and respiratory disease

Monsoons unpredictable. Rice crops fail

Increasing demand for irrigation water reduces stream flow

Lesser Antilles

Maldives

Many island groups totally submerged. Islanders become environmental refugees

Marshall Islands

More violent tropical storms increase loss of life

Millions go without safe drinking water

Up to 200 million made homeless by flooding along coasts and river valleys

Kiribati

All living things affected by ecosystem change

Tuvalu

Coral reefs affected by warmer, more acid water

French Polynesia

Loss of habitat. Animals and plants forced to migrate or perish

Many new pests and diseases

Summer rainfall less predictable

World carbon emission rates, 2000 (metric tonnes per person per year)

over 15.0 (high producer)

7.0–15.0

3.0–6.9

1.0–2.9 (low producer)

less than 1.0 (low producer)

no data

Area likely to be flooded with ice melt and sea-level rise

Predicted global warming by 2100 may cause:
- world mean temperature to increase by between 1.4 and 5.8°C compared with 1990 temperatures
- greatest warming in northern high latitudes, particularly in winter
- rainfall to increase in northern high latitudes, and increase and decrease in low latitudes
- more unpredictable weather, with more severe storms, droughts, floods and cyclones
- average sea level to increase by between 9 and 88 cm by 2100

SCALE 1:160 000 000

0   2000   4000   6000   8000 km

Eckert IV projection

1 POPULATION DISTRIBUTION

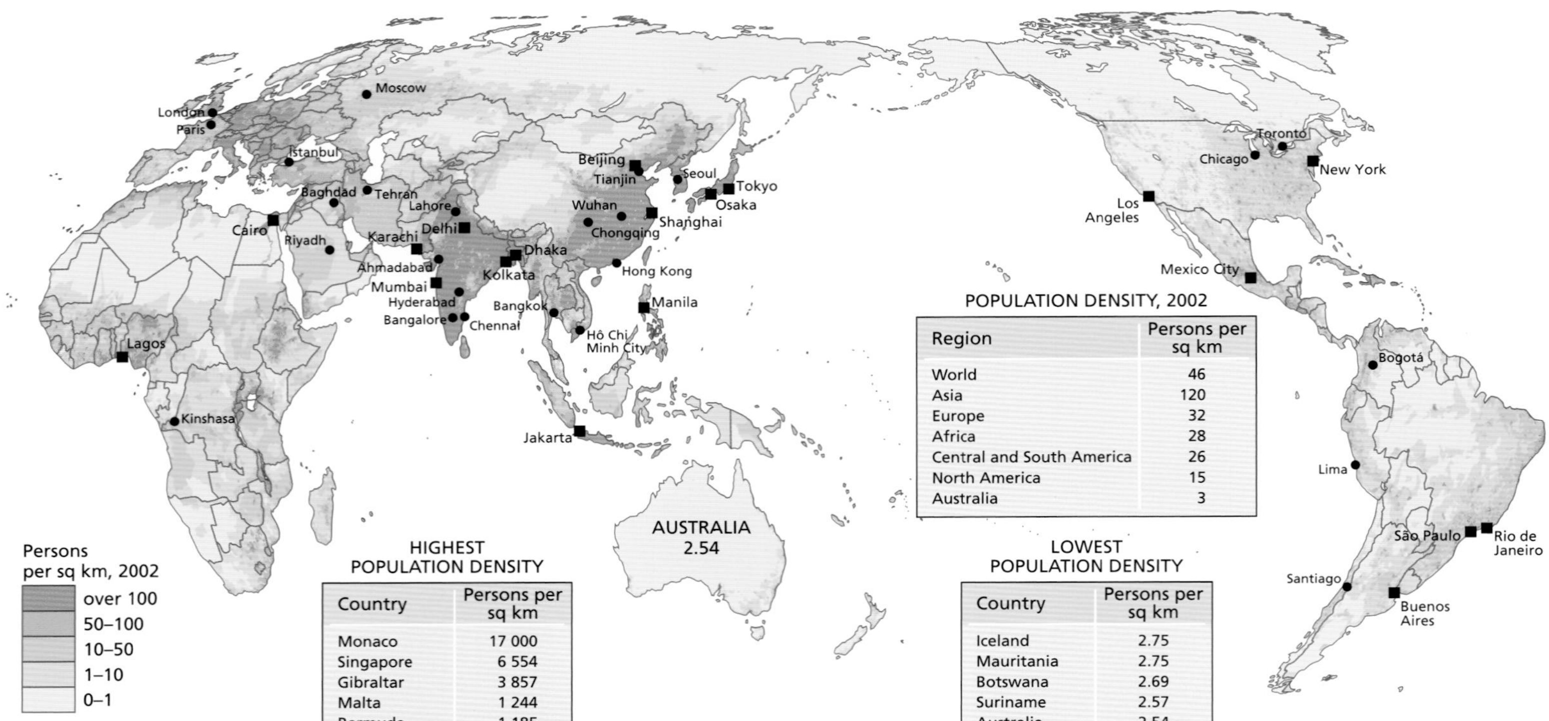

London
Paris
Moscow
Istanbul
Baghdad Tehran
Cairo Riyadh
Lahore
Karachi Delhi
Ahmadabad
Mumbai
Hyderabad
Bangalore Chennai
Lagos
Kinshasa
Beijing
Tianjin Seoul
Wuhan Tokyo
Chongqing Osaka
Shanghai
Dhaka
Kolkata
Hong Kong
Bangkok Manila
Hô Chi
Minh City
Jakarta
Toronto
Chicago New York
Los
Angeles
Mexico City
Bogotá
Lima
São Paulo
Santiago Rio de Janeiro
Buenos
Aires

AUSTRALIA
2.54

POPULATION DENSITY, 2002

Region	Persons per sq km
World	46
Asia	120
Europe	32
Africa	28
Central and South America	26
North America	15
Australia	3

Persons per sq km, 2002
- over 100
- 50–100
- 10–50
- 1–10
- 0–1

Cities
- ■ over 10 million people
- ● 5–10 million people

HIGHEST POPULATION DENSITY

Country	Persons per sq km
Monaco	17 000
Singapore	6 554
Gibraltar	3 857
Malta	1 244
Bermuda	1 185
Maldives	1 037
Bangladesh	996
Bahrain	959

LOWEST POPULATION DENSITY

Country	Persons per sq km
Iceland	2.75
Mauritania	2.75
Botswana	2.69
Suriname	2.57
Australia	2.54
Namibia	2.21
French Guiana	1.96
Mongolia	1.65

2 POPULATION CHANGE

POPULATION CHANGE
Population change is the average annual percentage increase or decrease in the population.

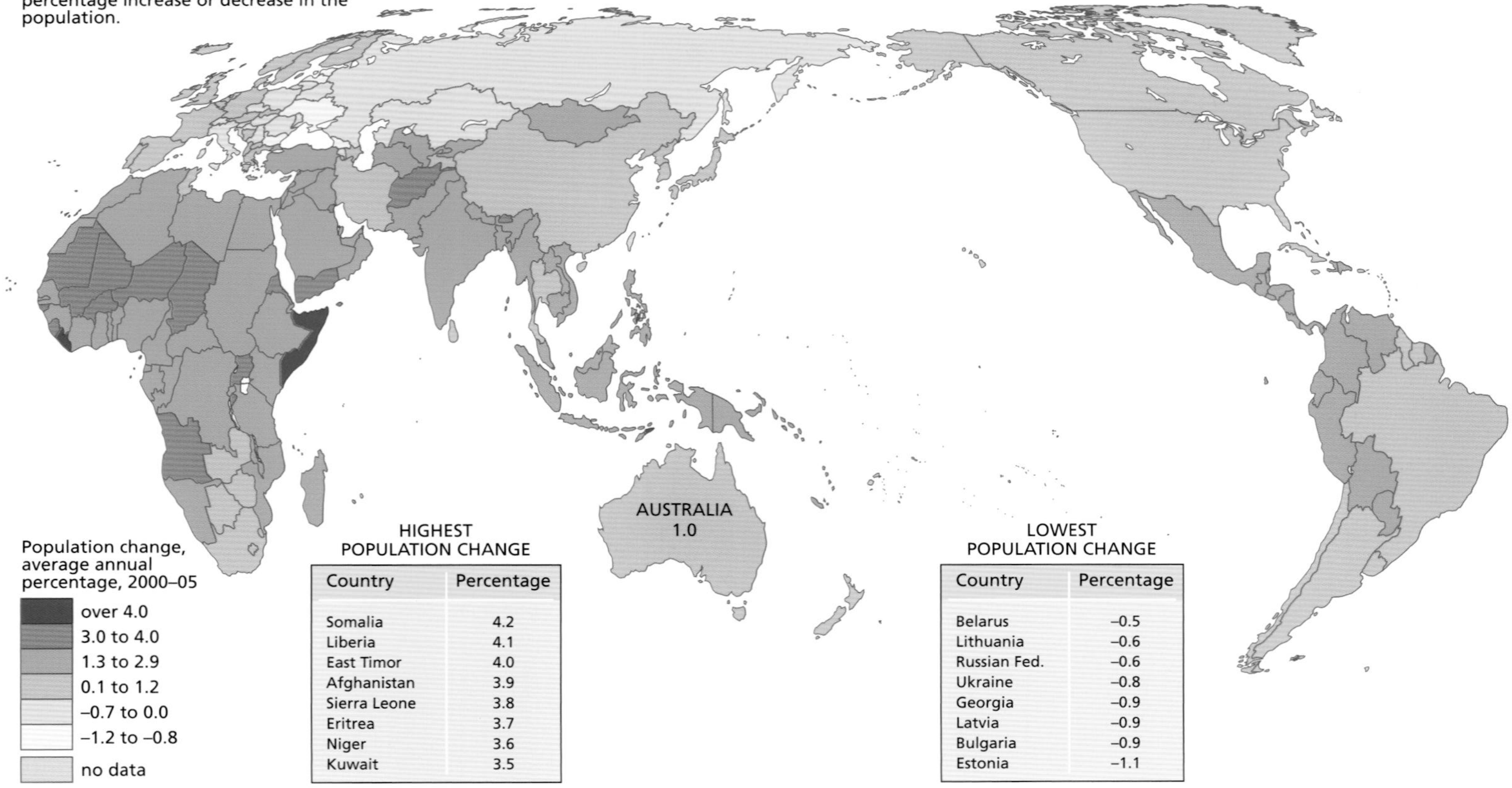

AUSTRALIA
1.0

Population change, average annual percentage, 2000–05
- over 4.0
- 3.0 to 4.0
- 1.3 to 2.9
- 0.1 to 1.2
- –0.7 to 0.0
- –1.2 to –0.8
- no data

HIGHEST POPULATION CHANGE

Country	Percentage
Somalia	4.2
Liberia	4.1
East Timor	4.0
Afghanistan	3.9
Sierra Leone	3.8
Eritrea	3.7
Niger	3.6
Kuwait	3.5

LOWEST POPULATION CHANGE

Country	Percentage
Belarus	–0.5
Lithuania	–0.6
Russian Fed.	–0.6
Ukraine	–0.8
Georgia	–0.9
Latvia	–0.9
Bulgaria	–0.9
Estonia	–1.1

SCALE 1:160 000 000

0   2000   4000   6000   8000 km

Eckert IV projection

1 BIRTH RATES

BIRTH RATE

Birth rate is the number of births per
thousand of the population in one year.

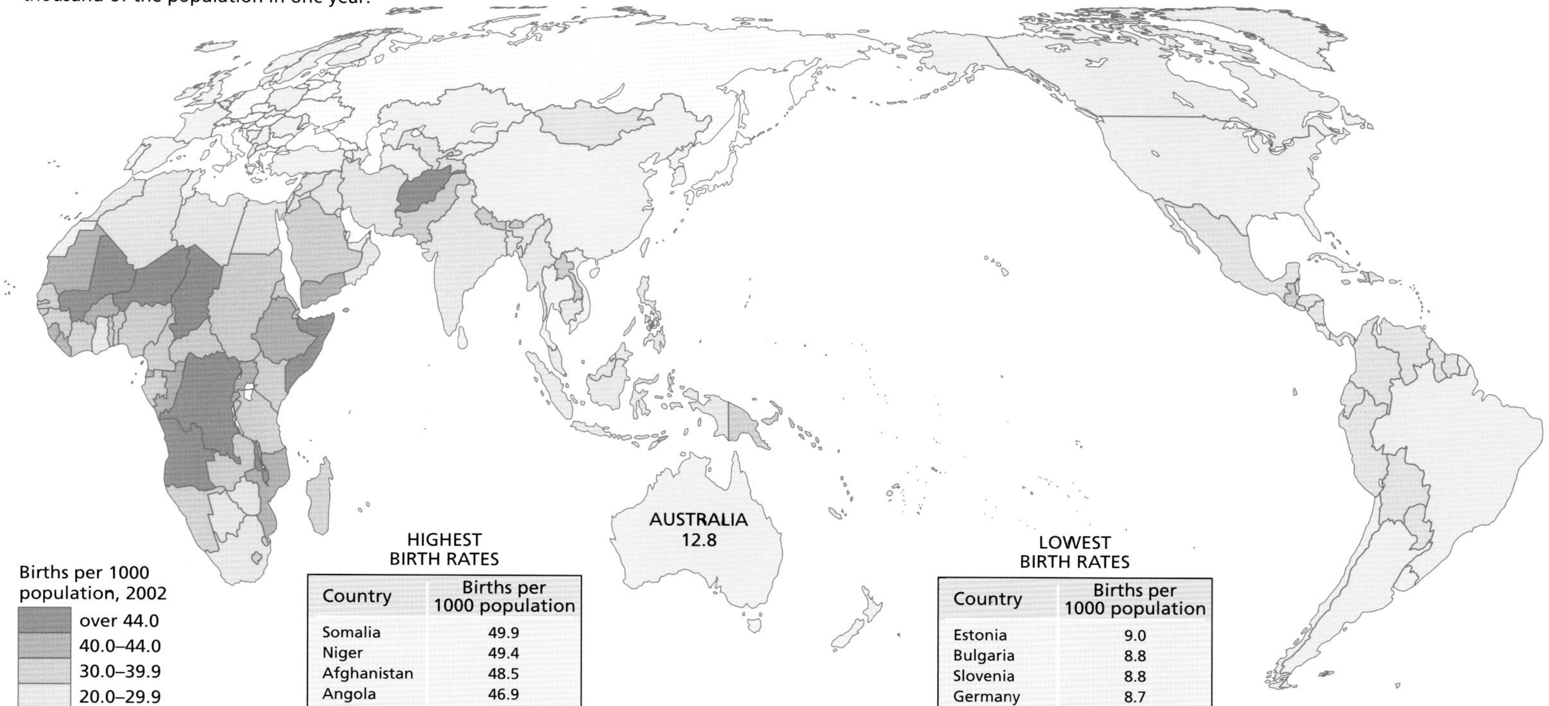

AUSTRALIA
12.8

Births per 1000
population, 2002

	over 44.0
	40.0–44.0
	30.0–39.9
	20.0–29.9
	10.0–19.9
	0.0–9.9
	no data

HIGHEST BIRTH RATES

Country	Births per 1000 population
Somalia	49.9
Niger	49.4
Afghanistan	48.5
Angola	46.9
Mali	45.5
D. R. Congo	45.1
Malawi	44.9
Chad	44.8

LOWEST BIRTH RATES

Country	Births per 1000 population
Estonia	9.0
Bulgaria	8.8
Slovenia	8.8
Germany	8.7
Ukraine	8.7
Italy	8.6
Georgia	8.2
Latvia	8.2

2 DEATH RATES

DEATH RATE

Death rate is the number of deaths per
thousand of the population in one year.

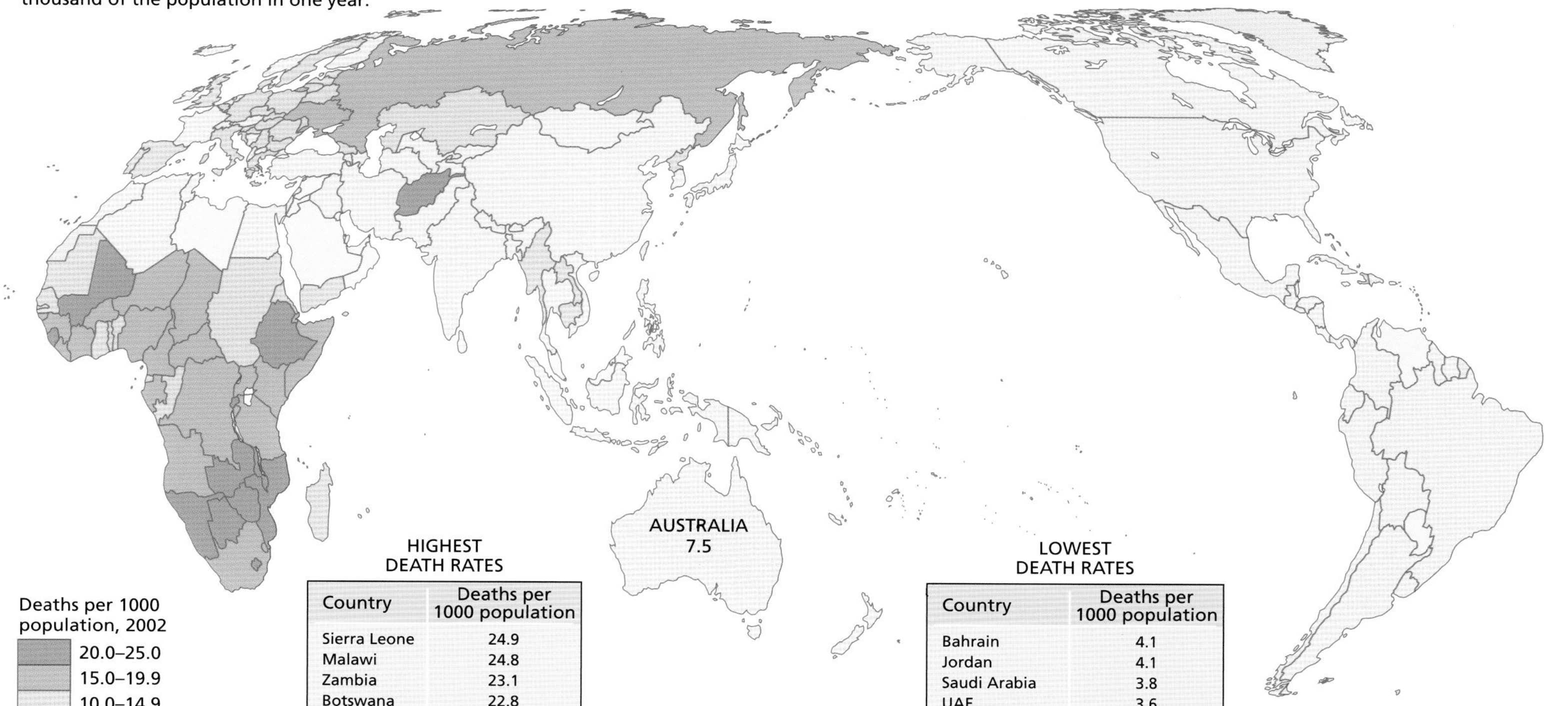

AUSTRALIA
7.5

Deaths per 1000
population, 2002

	20.0–25.0
	15.0–19.9
	10.0–14.9
	5.0–9.9
	0.0–4.9
	no data

HIGHEST DEATH RATES

Country	Deaths per 1000 population
Sierra Leone	24.9
Malawi	24.8
Zambia	23.1
Botswana	22.8
Rwanda	21.6
Mali	21.4
Zimbabwe	21.3
Afghanistan	21.2

LOWEST DEATH RATES

Country	Deaths per 1000 population
Bahrain	4.1
Jordan	4.1
Saudi Arabia	3.8
UAE	3.6
Qatar	3.5
Oman	3.0
Brunei	2.8
Kuwait	2.7

SCALE 1:160 000 000

0   2000   4000   6000   8000 km

Eckert IV projection

1 URBAN POPULATION

URBAN POPULATION

This map shows the percentage of people living in towns and cities. The definition of 'urban' may vary greatly.

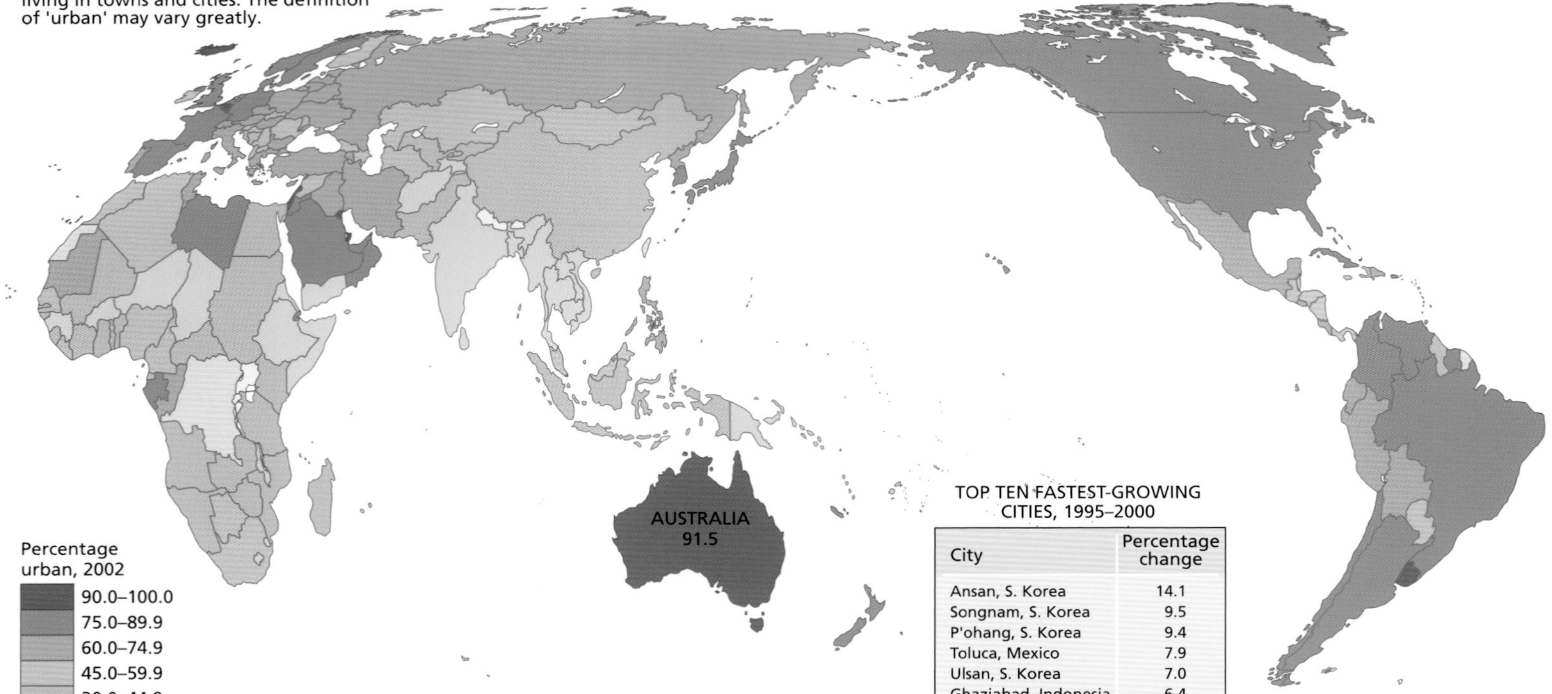

AUSTRALIA
91.5

Percentage urban, 2002

- 90.0–100.0
- 75.0–89.9
- 60.0–74.9
- 45.0–59.9
- 30.0–44.9
- 15.0–29.9
- 0.0–14.9
- no data

TOP TEN FASTEST-GROWING CITIES, 1995–2000

City	Percentage change
Ansan, S. Korea	14.1
Songnam, S. Korea	9.5
P'ohang, S. Korea	9.4
Toluca, Mexico	7.9
Ulsan, S. Korea	7.0
Ghaziabad, Indonesia	6.4
Sana, Yemen	6.4
Rajshahi, Bangladesh	6.3
Dubai, UAE	6.2
Surat, India	6.2

2 URBAN GROWTH

URBAN GROWTH

Urban growth is the average annual percentage increase or decrease in the urban population.

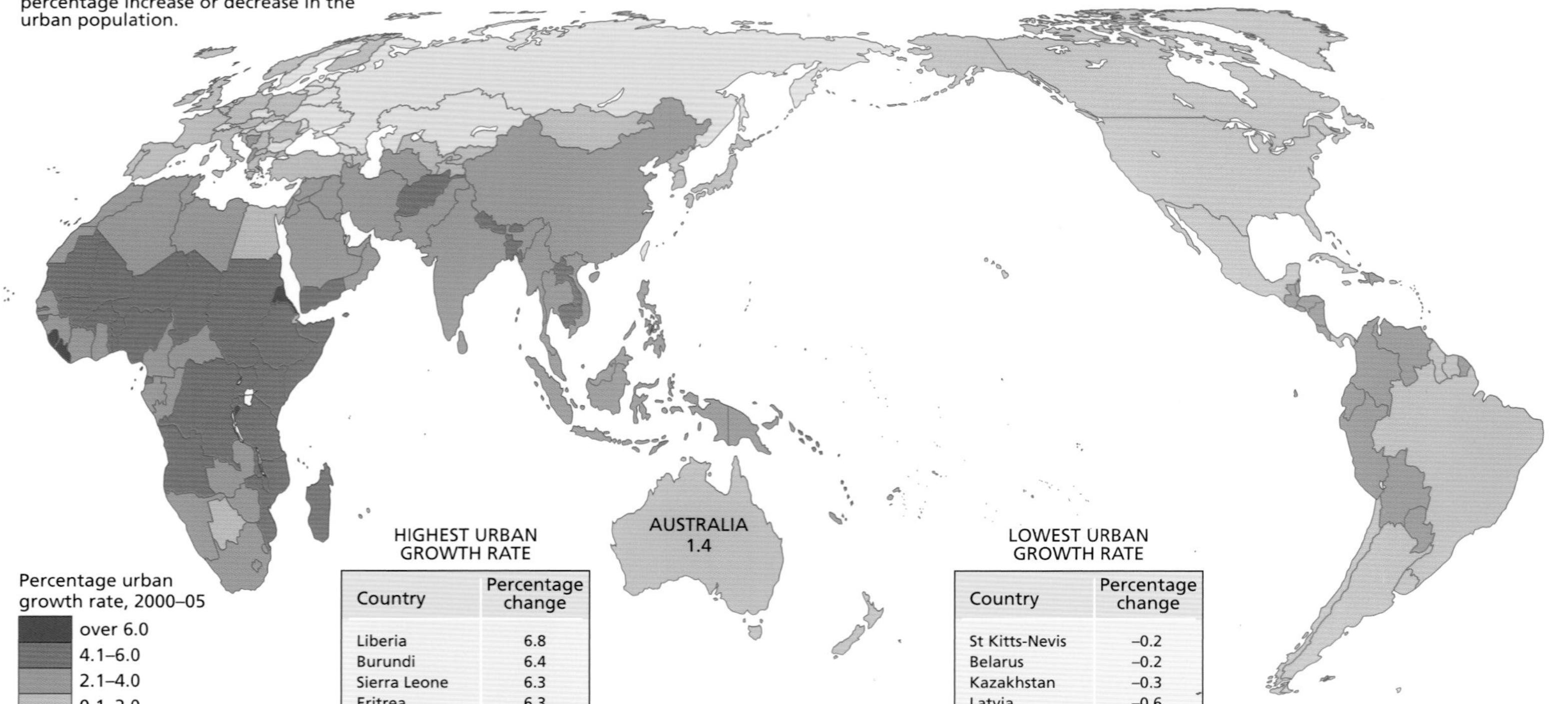

AUSTRALIA
1.4

Percentage urban growth rate, 2000–05

- over 6.0
- 4.1–6.0
- 2.1–4.0
- 0.1–2.0
- –1.0–0.0
- under –1.0
- no data

HIGHEST URBAN GROWTH RATE

Country	Percentage change
Liberia	6.8
Burundi	6.4
Sierra Leone	6.3
Eritrea	6.3
Niger	6.0
Solomon Islands	6.0
Bhutan	5.9
Somalia	5.8

LOWEST URBAN GROWTH RATE

Country	Percentage change
St Kitts-Nevis	–0.2
Belarus	–0.2
Kazakhstan	–0.3
Latvia	–0.6
Russian Fed.	–0.6
Ukraine	–0.8
Bulgaria	–0.9
Estonia	–1.1

SCALE 1:160 000 000

0   2000   4000   6000   8000 km

Eckert IV projection

1 MILLION CITIES

MILLION CITIES

Cities shown on the map are urban agglomerations that have over 1 000 000 people living in the city and adjacent areas.

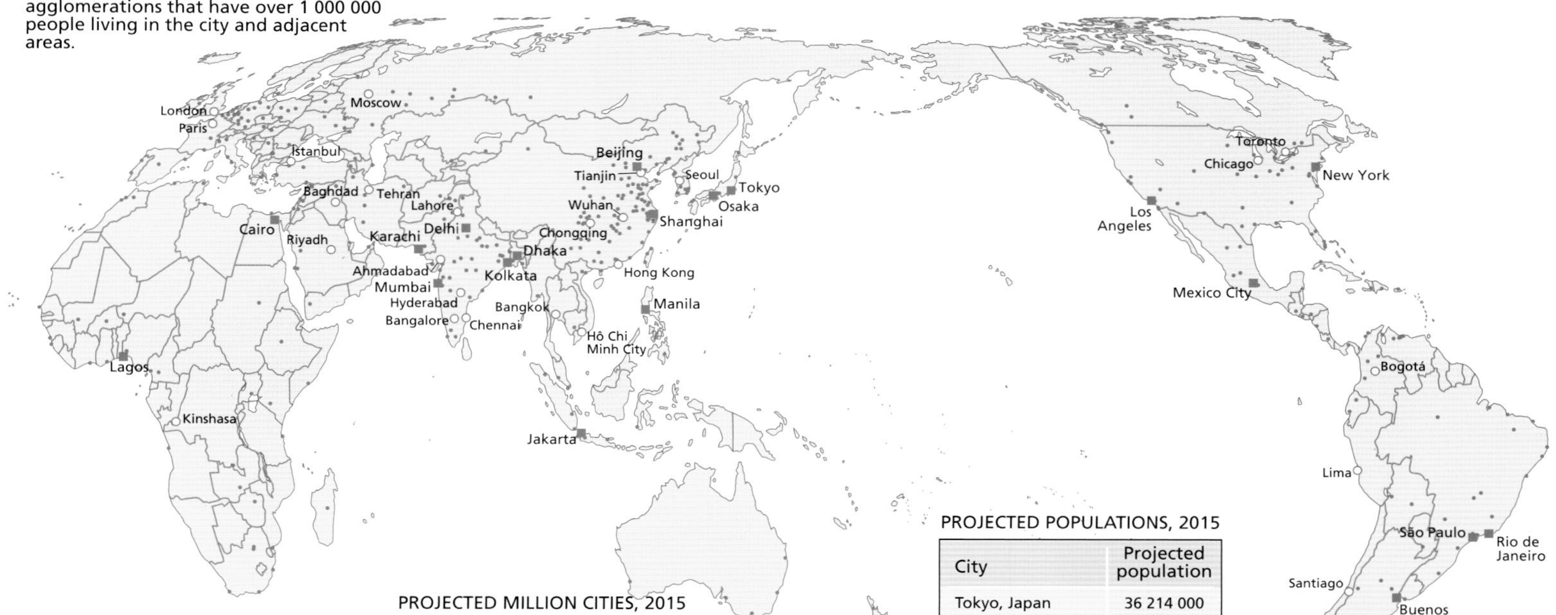

Million Cities, 2002

- ■ over 10 000 000 people
- ○ 5 000 000–10 000 000 people
- · 1 000 000–5 000 000 people

PROJECTED MILLION CITIES, 2015

Region	Number of cities
Asia	288
Central and South America	73
Europe	63
Africa	60
North America	51
Australia and Oceania	6

PROJECTED POPULATIONS, 2015

City	Projected population
Tokyo, Japan	36 214 000
Mumbai, India	22 645 000
Delhi, India	20 946 000
Mexico City, Mexico	20 647 000
São Paulo, Brazil	19 963 000
New York, USA	19 717 000
Dhaka, Bangladesh	17 907 000
Jakarta, Indonesia	17 498 000
Lagos, Nigeria	17 036 000
Kolkata, India	16 798 000

2 EMPLOYMENT BY SECTOR

EMPLOYMENT BY SECTOR

Employment by sector is measured as the percentage of the economically active population employed in agriculture, industry and services.

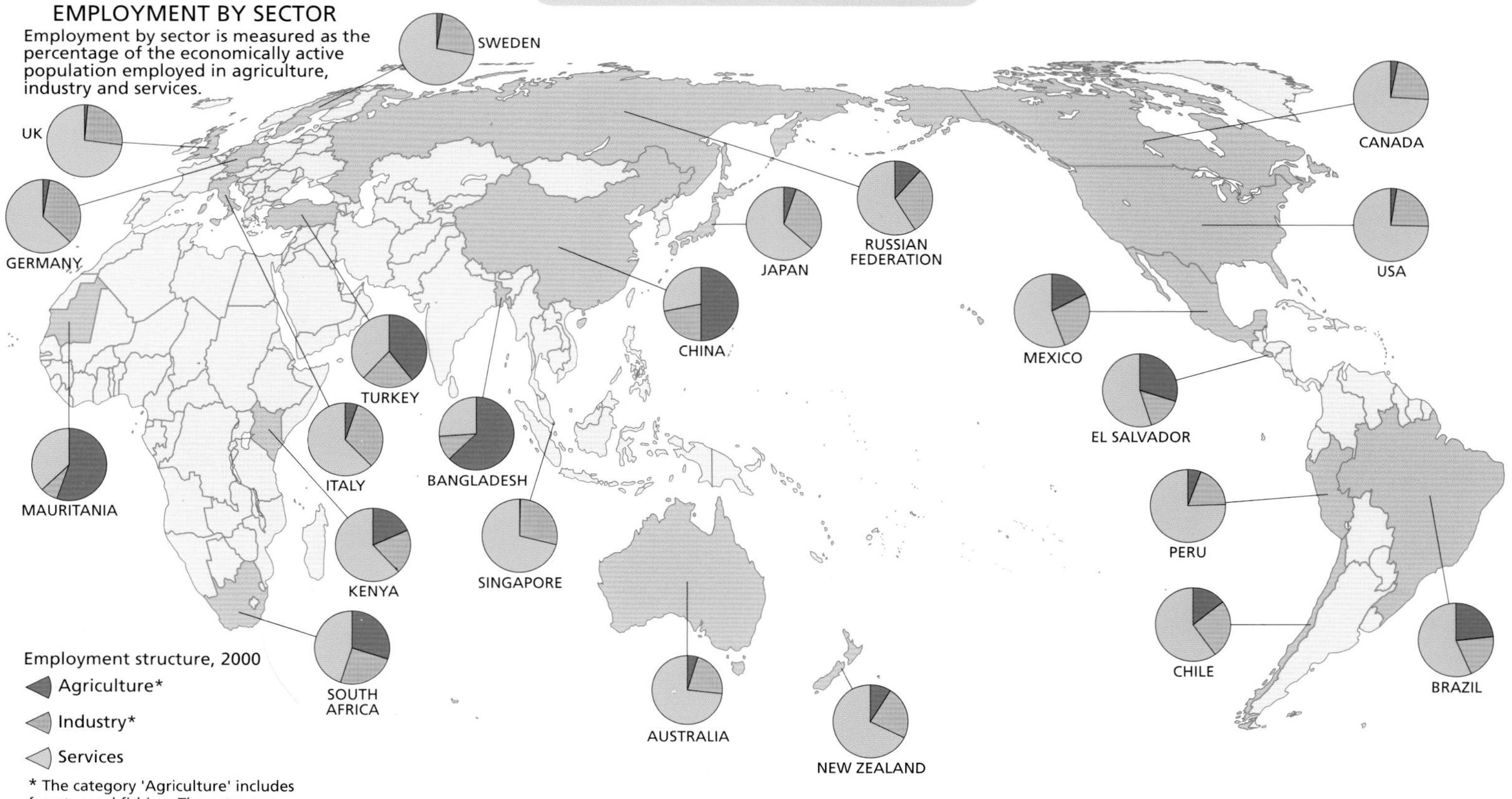

Employment structure, 2000

- ◣ Agriculture*
- ◤ Industry*
- ◁ Services

* The category 'Agriculture' includes forestry and fishing. The category 'Industry' includes mining.

SCALE 1:160 000 000

0   2000   4000   6000   8000 km

Eckert IV projection

1 QUALITY OF LIFE

QUALITY OF LIFE

The Human Development Index is used to measure the quality of life in a country. This index is a measure of life expectancy, educational attainment and adjusted income.

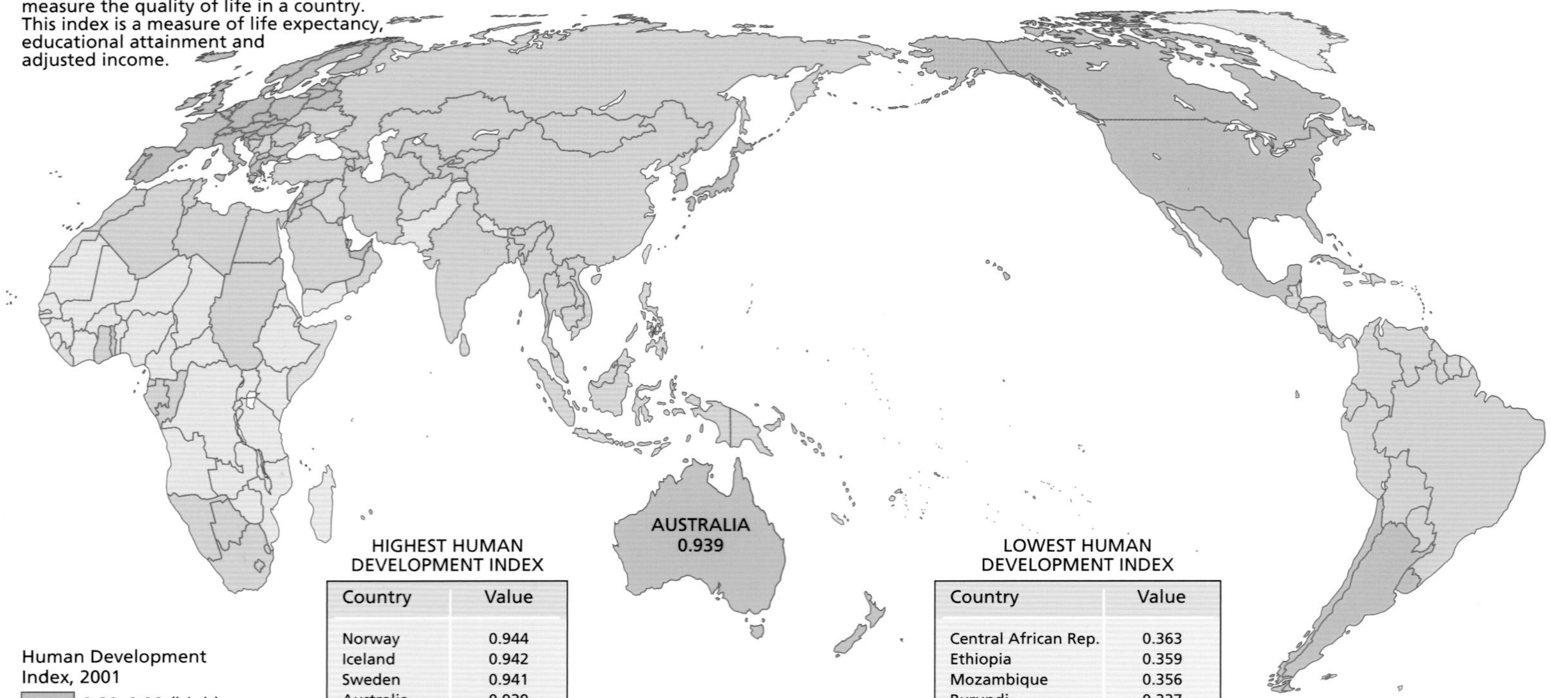

AUSTRALIA
0.939

Human Development Index, 2001

- 0.80–0.99 (high)
- 0.50–0.79 (medium)
- 0.00–0.49 (low)
- no data

HIGHEST HUMAN DEVELOPMENT INDEX

Country	Value
Norway	0.944
Iceland	0.942
Sweden	0.941
Australia	0.939
Netherlands	0.938
Belgium	0.937
USA	0.937
Canada	0.937

LOWEST HUMAN DEVELOPMENT INDEX

Country	Value
Central African Rep.	0.363
Ethiopia	0.359
Mozambique	0.356
Burundi	0.337
Mali	0.337
Burkina	0.330
Niger	0.292
Sierra Leone	0.275

2 LIFE EXPECTANCY

LIFE EXPECTANCY

Life expectancy is the average age a newborn infant would live to if patterns of mortality prevailing for all people at the time of its birth were to stay the same throughout its life.

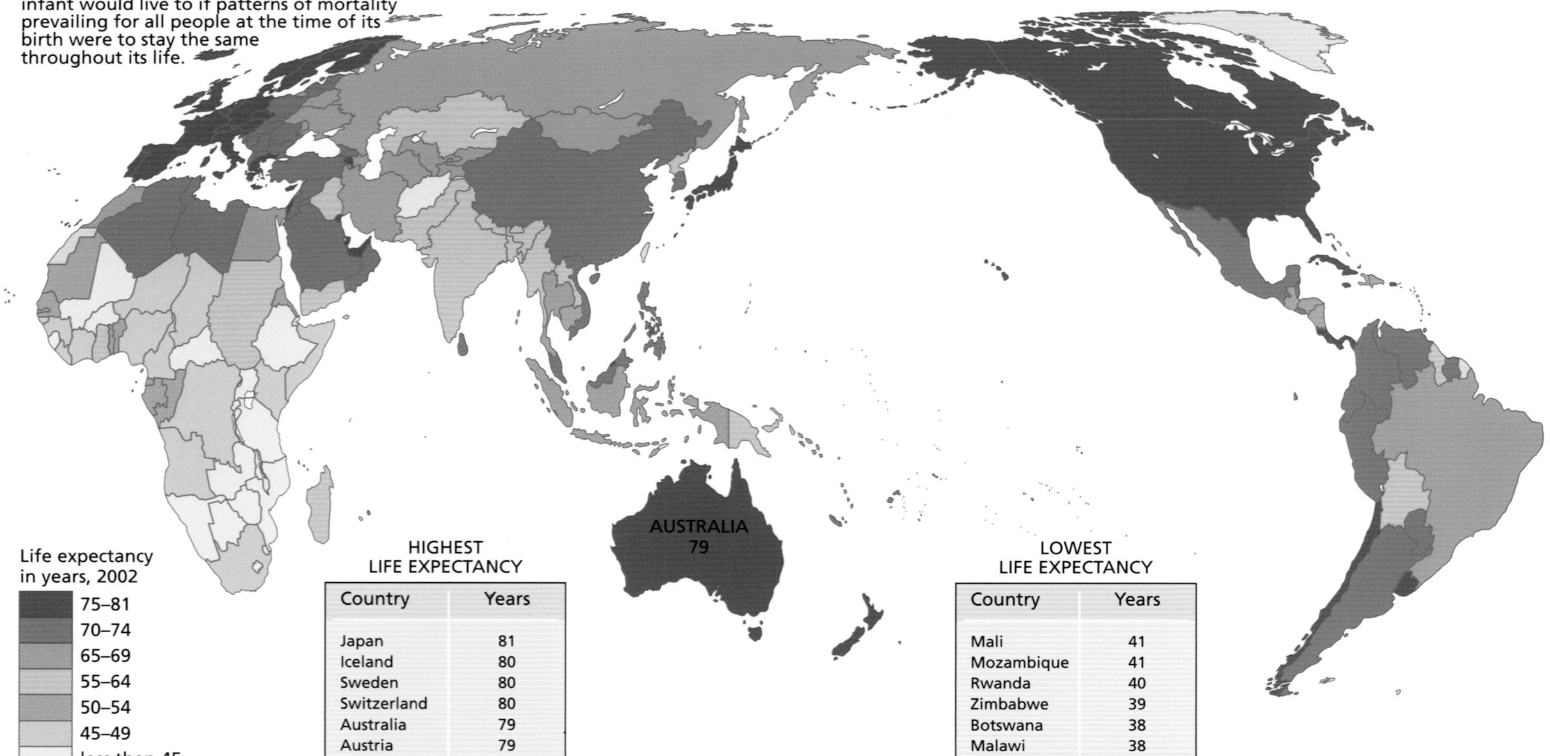

AUSTRALIA
79

Life expectancy in years, 2002

- 75–81
- 70–74
- 65–69
- 55–64
- 50–54
- 45–49
- less than 45
- no data

HIGHEST LIFE EXPECTANCY

Country	Years
Japan	81
Iceland	80
Sweden	80
Switzerland	80
Australia	79
Austria	79
Belgium	79
Canada	79

LOWEST LIFE EXPECTANCY

Country	Years
Mali	41
Mozambique	41
Rwanda	40
Zimbabwe	39
Botswana	38
Malawi	38
Sierra Leone	37
Zambia	37

SCALE 1:160 000 000

0   2000   4000   6000   8000 km

Eckert IV projection

1 ACCESS TO DOCTORS

ACCESS TO DOCTORS

The map shows the number of doctors per 100 000 people in each country.

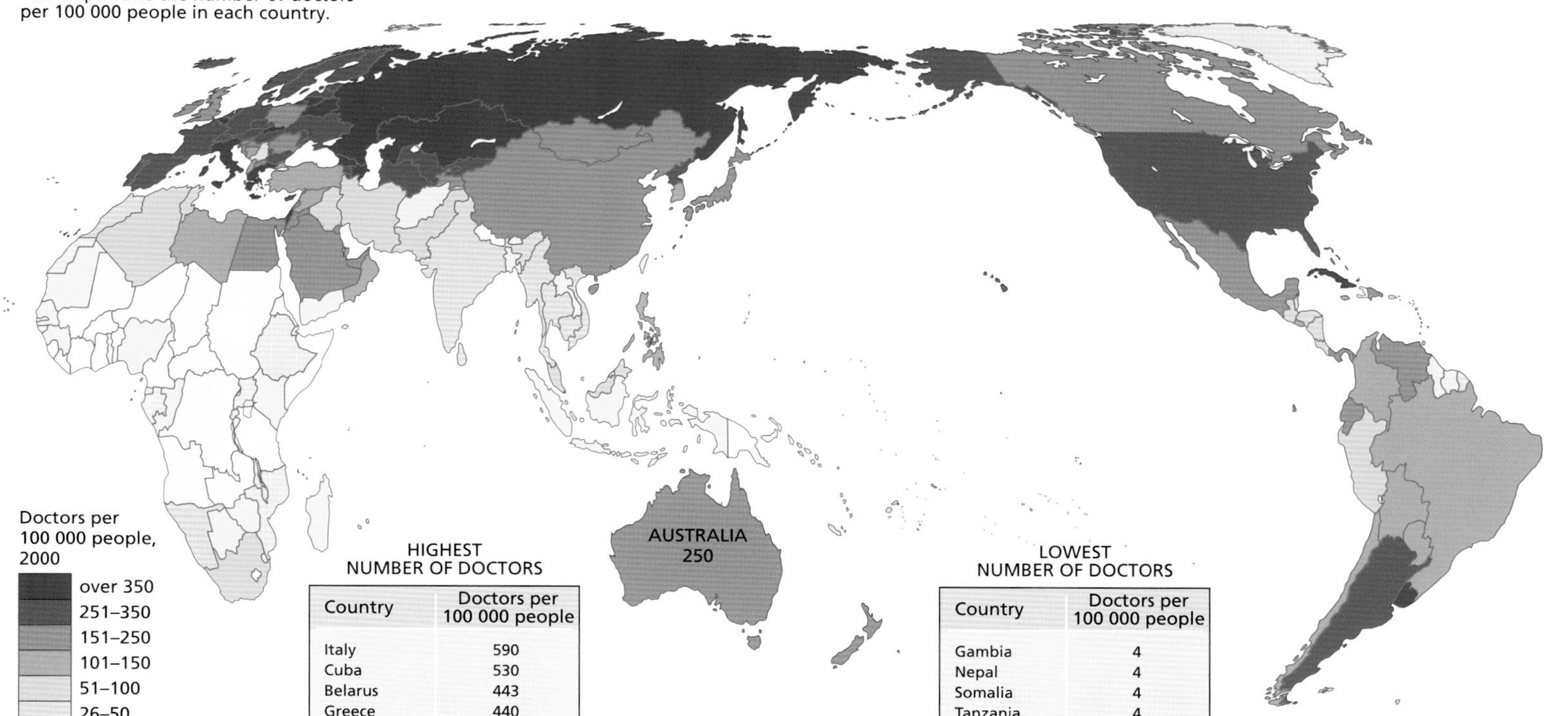

Doctors per 100 000 people, 2000

- over 350
- 251–350
- 151–250
- 101–150
- 51–100
- 26–50
- 10–25
- under 10
- no data

AUSTRALIA
250

HIGHEST NUMBER OF DOCTORS

Country	Doctors per 100 000 people
Italy	590
Cuba	530
Belarus	443
Greece	440
Georgia	436
Russian Fed.	421
Lithuania	400
Belgium	390

LOWEST NUMBER OF DOCTORS

Country	Doctors per 100 000 people
Gambia	4
Nepal	4
Somalia	4
Tanzania	4
Chad	3
Eritrea	3
Niger	3
Liberia	2

2 INFANT MORTALITY

INFANT MORTALITY

Infant mortality is the probability of dying between birth and one year of age, expressed as deaths per 1000 live births.

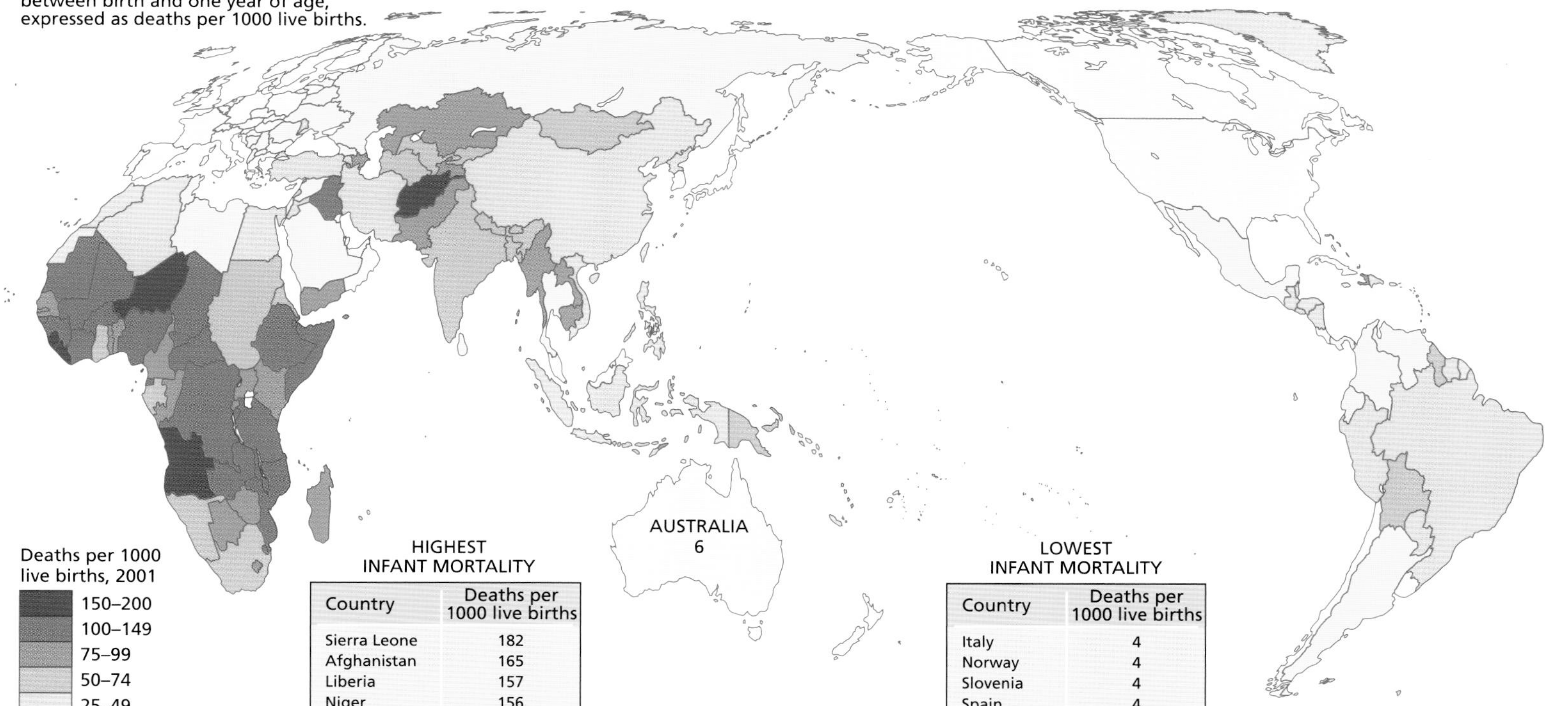

Deaths per 1000 live births, 2001

- 150–200
- 100–149
- 75–99
- 50–74
- 25–49
- 15–24
- 0–14
- no data

AUSTRALIA
6

HIGHEST INFANT MORTALITY

Country	Deaths per 1000 live births
Sierra Leone	182
Afghanistan	165
Liberia	157
Niger	156
Angola	154
Mali	141
Somalia	133
Guinea-Bissau	130

LOWEST INFANT MORTALITY

Country	Deaths per 1000 live births
Italy	4
Norway	4
Slovenia	4
Spain	4
Iceland	3
Japan	3
Singapore	3
Sweden	3

SCALE 1:160 000 000

0   2000   4000   6000   8000 km

Eckert IV projection

1 ACCESS TO SAFE DRINKING WATER

ACCESS TO SAFE DRINKING WATER
The map shows the percentage of the total population with access to safe drinking water.

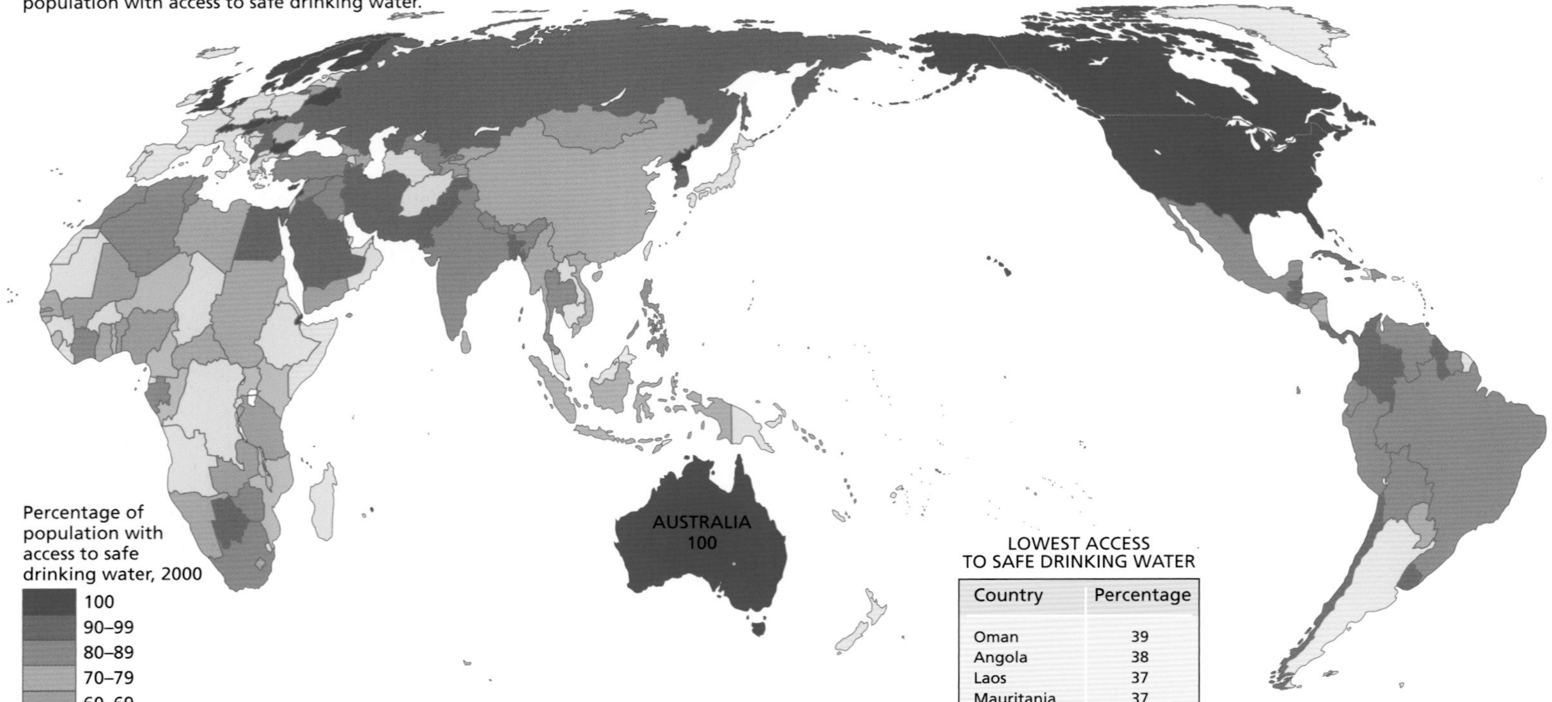

AUSTRALIA
100

Percentage of population with access to safe drinking water, 2000

- 100
- 90–99
- 80–89
- 70–79
- 60–69
- 50–59
- 12–49
- no data

LOWEST ACCESS TO SAFE DRINKING WATER

Country	Percentage
Oman	39
Angola	38
Laos	37
Mauritania	37
Cambodia	30
Chad	27
Ethiopia	24
Afghanistan	13

2 FOOD SUPPLY

FOOD SUPPLY
The map shows the percentage of the total population who are undernourished, that is, they consume too little food to maintain normal levels of activity.

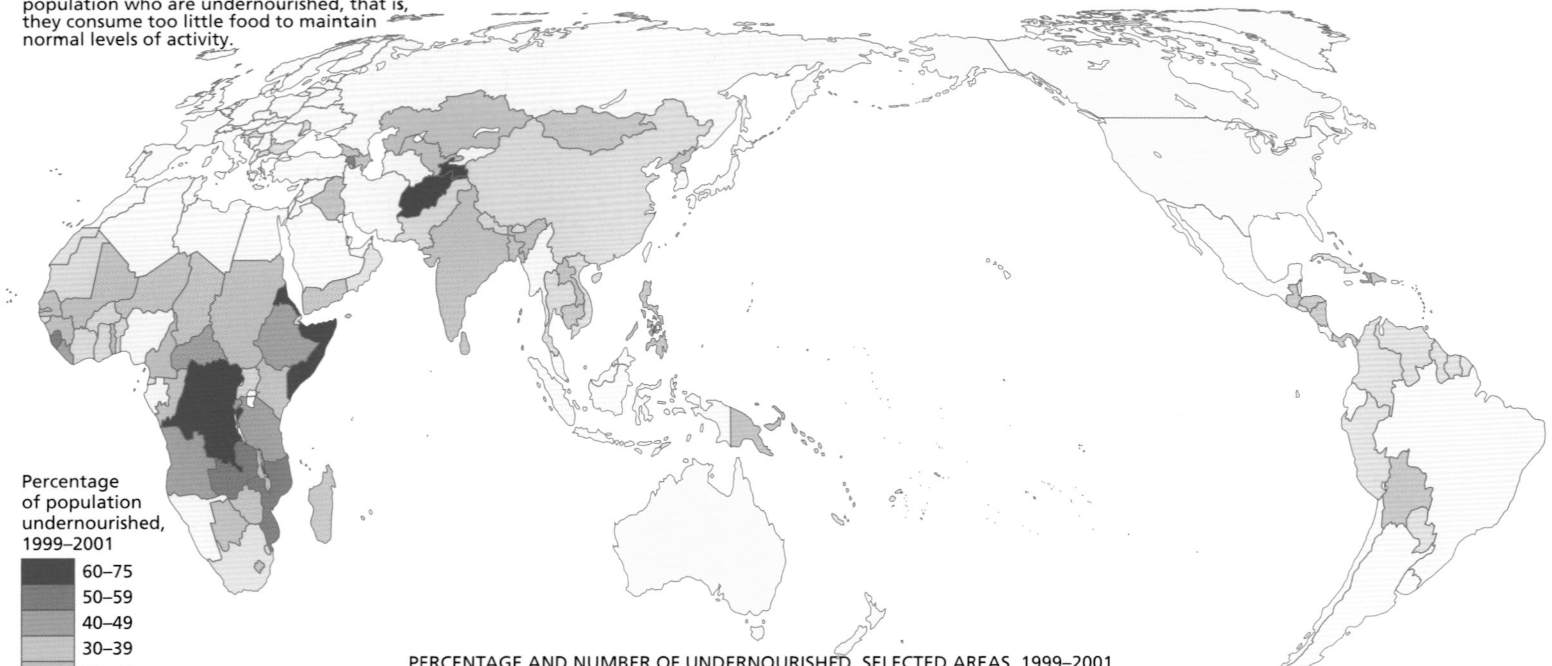

Percentage of population undernourished, 1999–2001

- 60–75
- 50–59
- 40–49
- 30–39
- 20–29
- 10–19
- under 10
- developed country
- no data

PERCENTAGE AND NUMBER OF UNDERNOURISHED, SELECTED AREAS, 1999–2001

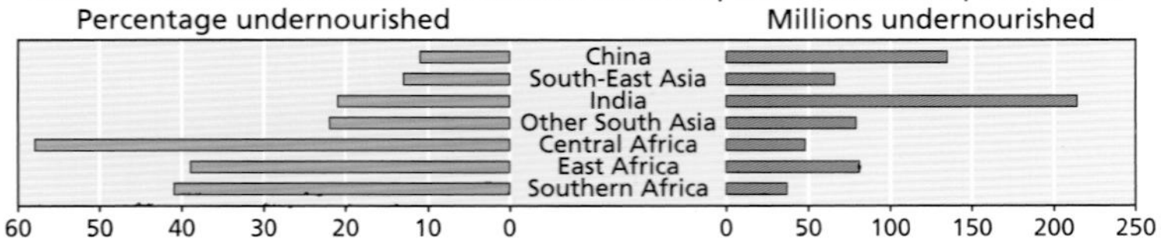

Percentage undernourished   Millions undernourished

China
South-East Asia
India
Other South Asia
Central Africa
East Africa
Southern Africa

60 50 40 30 20 10   0   0 50 100 150 200 250

SCALE 1:160 000 000

0   2000   4000   6000   8000 km

Eckert IV projection

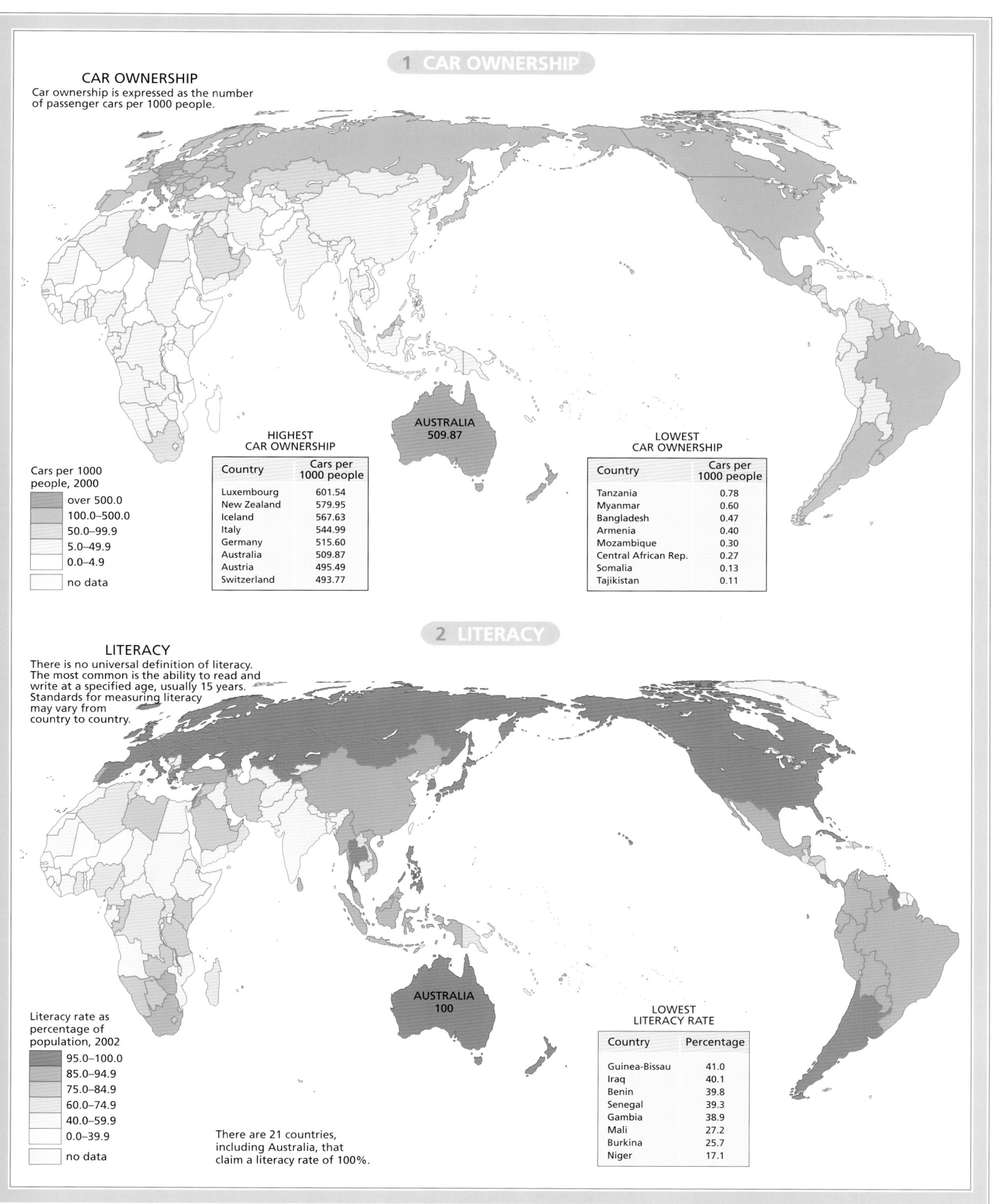

CAR OWNERSHIP

Car ownership is expressed as the number of passenger cars per 1000 people.

AUSTRALIA
509.87

HIGHEST CAR OWNERSHIP

Country	Cars per 1000 people
Luxembourg	601.54
New Zealand	579.95
Iceland	567.63
Italy	544.99
Germany	515.60
Australia	509.87
Austria	495.49
Switzerland	493.77

LOWEST CAR OWNERSHIP

Country	Cars per 1000 people
Tanzania	0.78
Myanmar	0.60
Bangladesh	0.47
Armenia	0.40
Mozambique	0.30
Central African Rep.	0.27
Somalia	0.13
Tajikistan	0.11

Cars per 1000 people, 2000

- over 500.0
- 100.0–500.0
- 50.0–99.9
- 5.0–49.9
- 0.0–4.9
- no data

LITERACY

There is no universal definition of literacy. The most common is the ability to read and write at a specified age, usually 15 years. Standards for measuring literacy may vary from country to country.

AUSTRALIA
100

LOWEST LITERACY RATE

Country	Percentage
Guinea-Bissau	41.0
Iraq	40.1
Benin	39.8
Senegal	39.3
Gambia	38.9
Mali	27.2
Burkina	25.7
Niger	17.1

Literacy rate as percentage of population, 2002

- 95.0–100.0
- 85.0–94.9
- 75.0–84.9
- 60.0–74.9
- 40.0–59.9
- 0.0–39.9
- no data

There are 21 countries, including Australia, that claim a literacy rate of 100%.

SCALE 1:160 000 000

0   2000   4000   6000   8000 km

Eckert IV projection

1 GROSS DOMESTIC PRODUCT

GDP

Gross domestic product (GDP) is the value
of a country's annual domestic production
of goods and services, measured in US$.

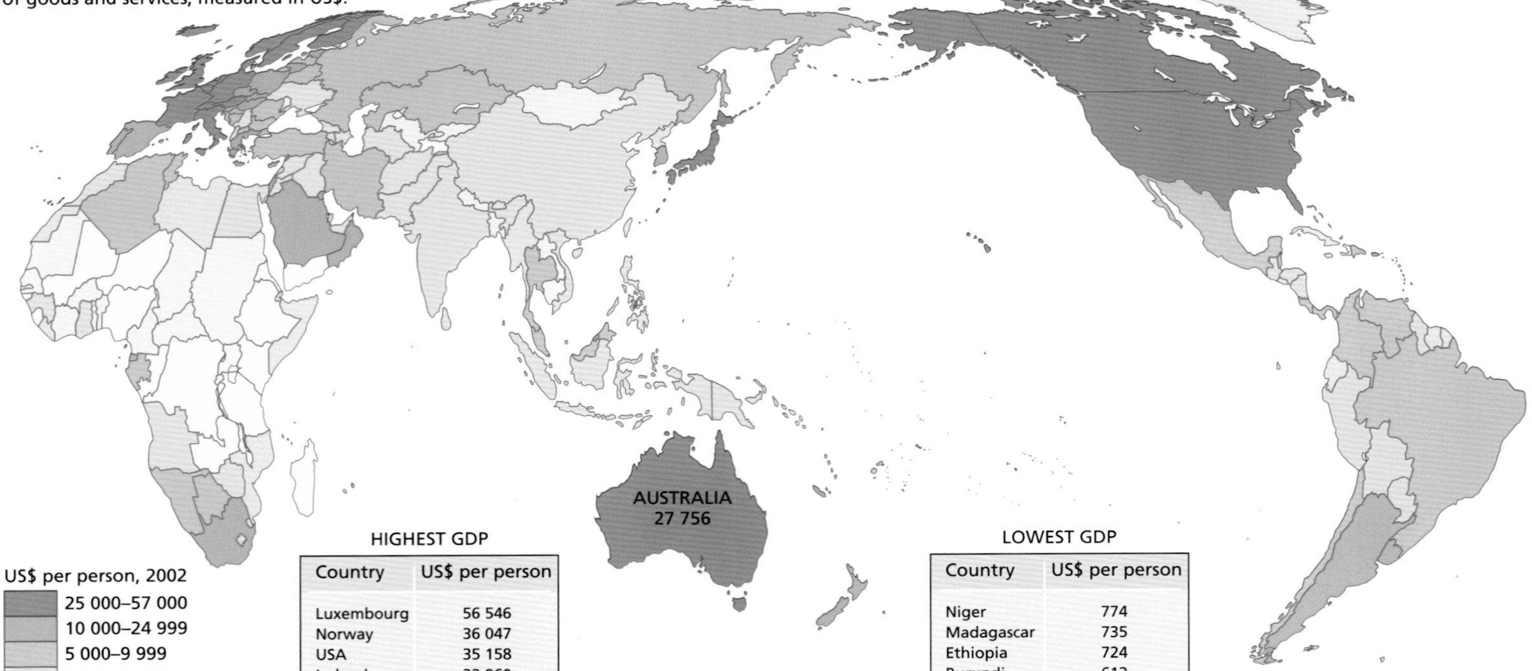

AUSTRALIA
27 756

US$ per person, 2002

- 25 000–57 000
- 10 000–24 999
- 5 000–9 999
- 2 000–4 999
- 1 000–1 999
- 0–999
- no data

HIGHEST GDP

Country	US$ per person
Luxembourg	56 546
Norway	36 047
USA	35 158
Ireland	32 960
Denmark	29 975
Iceland	29 614
Canada	28 699
Austria	28 611

LOWEST GDP

Country	US$ per person
Niger	774
Madagascar	735
Ethiopia	724
Burundi	613
D. R. Congo	606
Malawi	586
Tanzania	557
Sierra Leone	509

2 AGRICULTURE, FORESTRY AND FISHING

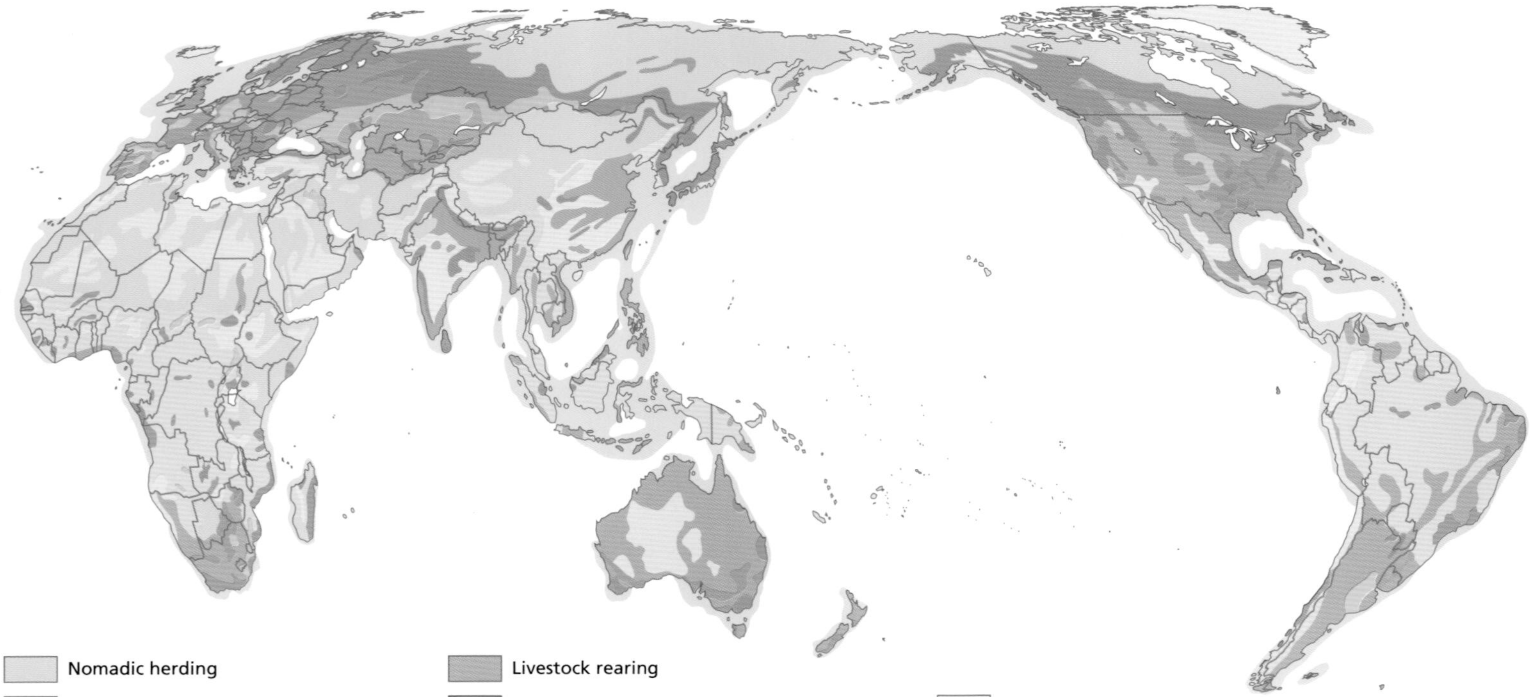

- Nomadic herding
- Shifting and marginal cultivation
- Subsistence farming—crops dominant
- Subsistence farming—crops and livestock
- Livestock rearing
- Commercial farming—grain dominant
- Commercial farming—mixed crops, dairying and livestock
- Specialised crops
- Limited agricultural use
- Forestry
- Fishing

SCALE 1:160 000 000

0   2000   4000   6000   8000 km

Eckert IV projection

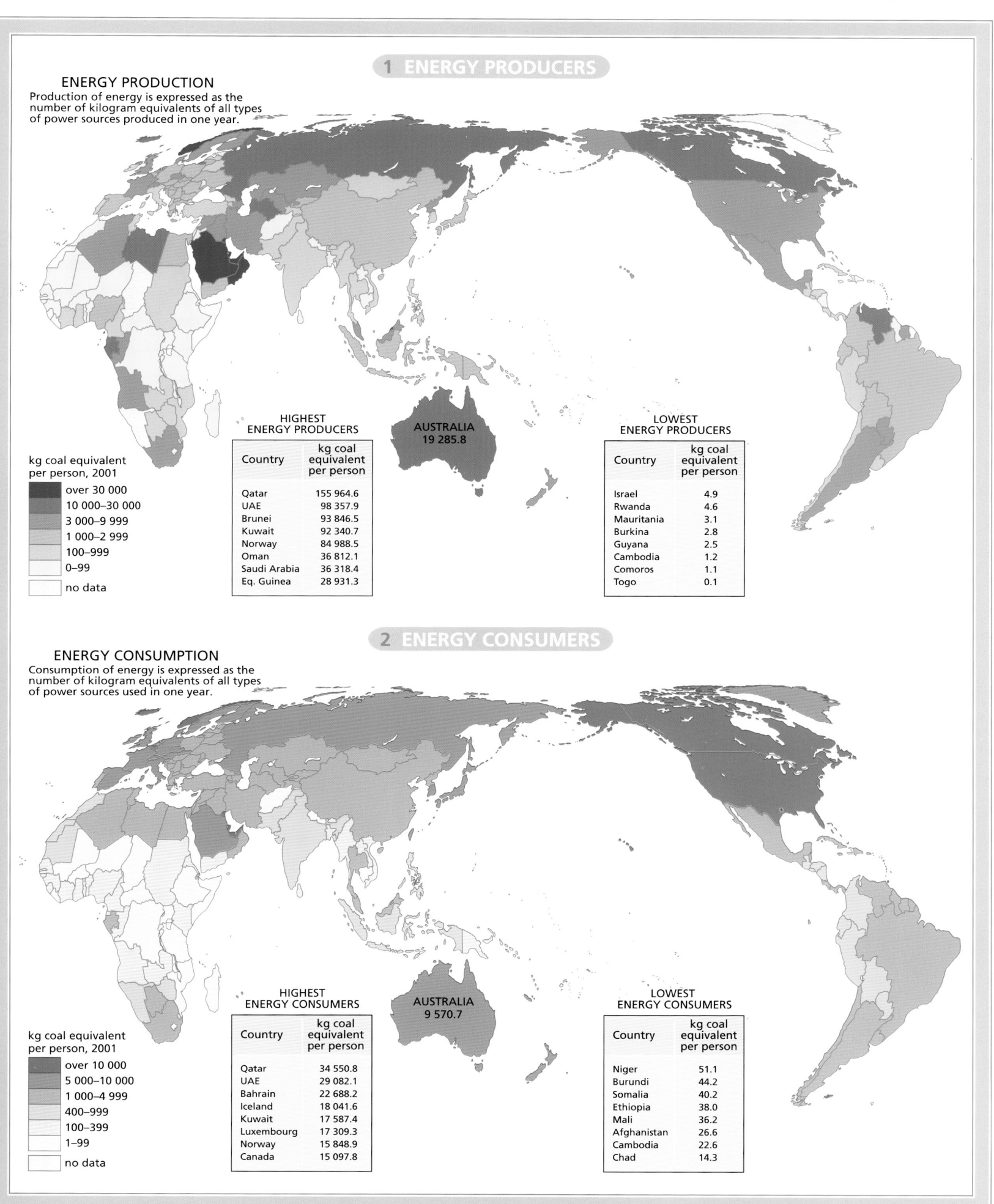

1 ENERGY PRODUCERS

ENERGY PRODUCTION

Production of energy is expressed as the
number of kilogram equivalents of all types
of power sources produced in one year.

kg coal equivalent
per person, 2001

- over 30 000
- 10 000–30 000
- 3 000–9 999
- 1 000–2 999
- 100–999
- 0–99
- no data

AUSTRALIA
19 285.8

HIGHEST ENERGY PRODUCERS

Country	kg coal equivalent per person
Qatar	155 964.6
UAE	98 357.9
Brunei	93 846.5
Kuwait	92 340.7
Norway	84 988.5
Oman	36 812.1
Saudi Arabia	36 318.4
Eq. Guinea	28 931.3

LOWEST ENERGY PRODUCERS

Country	kg coal equivalent per person
Israel	4.9
Rwanda	4.6
Mauritania	3.1
Burkina	2.8
Guyana	2.5
Cambodia	1.2
Comoros	1.1
Togo	0.1

2 ENERGY CONSUMERS

ENERGY CONSUMPTION

Consumption of energy is expressed as the
number of kilogram equivalents of all types
of power sources used in one year.

kg coal equivalent
per person, 2001

- over 10 000
- 5 000–10 000
- 1 000–4 999
- 400–999
- 100–399
- 1–99
- no data

AUSTRALIA
9 570.7

HIGHEST ENERGY CONSUMERS

Country	kg coal equivalent per person
Qatar	34 550.8
UAE	29 082.1
Bahrain	22 688.2
Iceland	18 041.6
Kuwait	17 587.4
Luxembourg	17 309.3
Norway	15 848.9
Canada	15 097.8

LOWEST ENERGY CONSUMERS

Country	kg coal equivalent per person
Niger	51.1
Burundi	44.2
Somalia	40.2
Ethiopia	38.0
Mali	36.2
Afghanistan	26.6
Cambodia	22.6
Chad	14.3

SCALE 1:160 000 000

0   2000   4000   6000   8000 km

Eckert IV projection

1 LANGUAGES

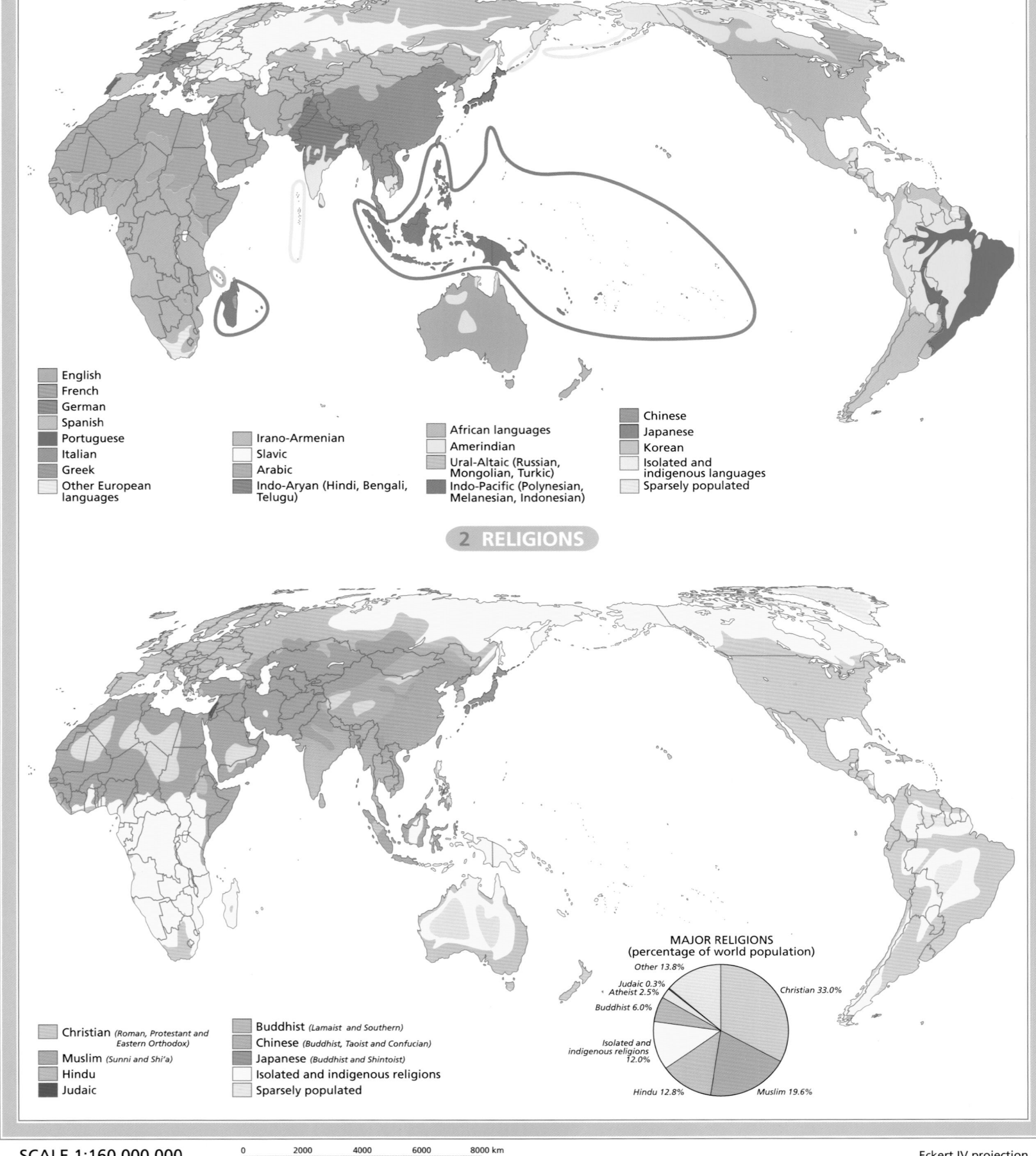

English
French
German
Spanish
Portuguese
Italian
Greek
Other European languages

Irano-Armenian
Slavic
Arabic
Indo-Aryan (Hindi, Bengali, Telugu)

African languages
Amerindian
Ural-Altaic (Russian, Mongolian, Turkic)
Indo-Pacific (Polynesian, Melanesian, Indonesian)

Chinese
Japanese
Korean
Isolated and indigenous languages
Sparsely populated

2 RELIGIONS

Christian (Roman, Protestant and Eastern Orthodox)
Muslim (Sunni and Shi'a)
Hindu
Judaic

Buddhist (Lamaist and Southern)
Chinese (Buddhist, Taoist and Confucian)
Japanese (Buddhist and Shintoist)
Isolated and indigenous religions
Sparsely populated

MAJOR RELIGIONS
(percentage of world population)

Other 13.8%
Judaic 0.3%
Atheist 2.5%
Buddhist 6.0%
Christian 33.0%
Isolated and indigenous religions 12.0%
Hindu 12.8%
Muslim 19.6%

SCALE 1:160 000 000

0   2000   4000   6000   8000 km

Eckert IV projection

1 REFUGEES

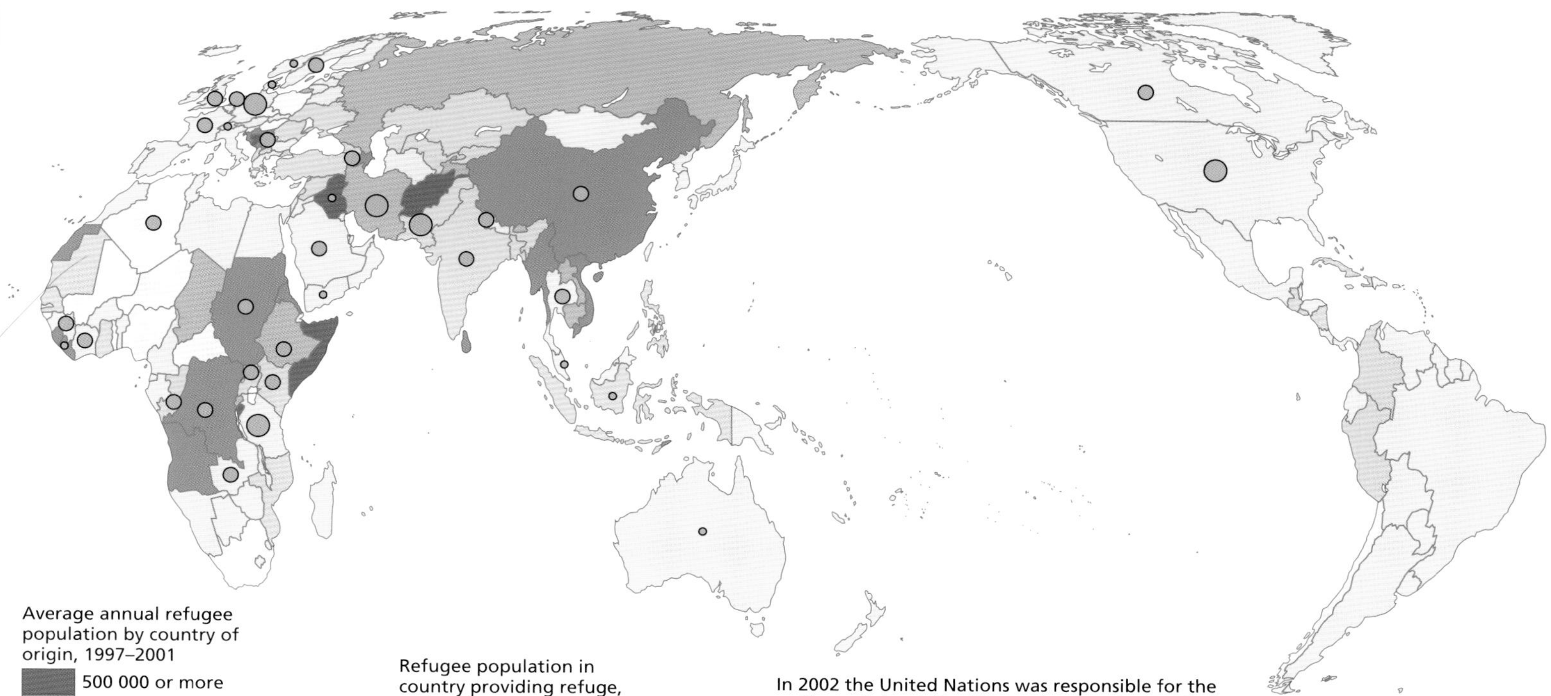

Average annual refugee population by country of origin, 1997–2001

- 500 000 or more
- 100 000–499 999
- 50 000–99 999
- 5 000–49 999
- less than 5 000

Refugee population in country providing refuge, end 2001

- 500 000 or more
- 100 000–499 999
- 50 000–99 999

In 2002 the United Nations was responsible for the welfare of about 12 million refugees who had fled from their homeland in fear for their safety. Many refugees return home when the conflict in their homeland is resolved. There are an additional 4 million people in refugee camps in the Palestinian territory.

2 INDIGENOUS PEOPLES

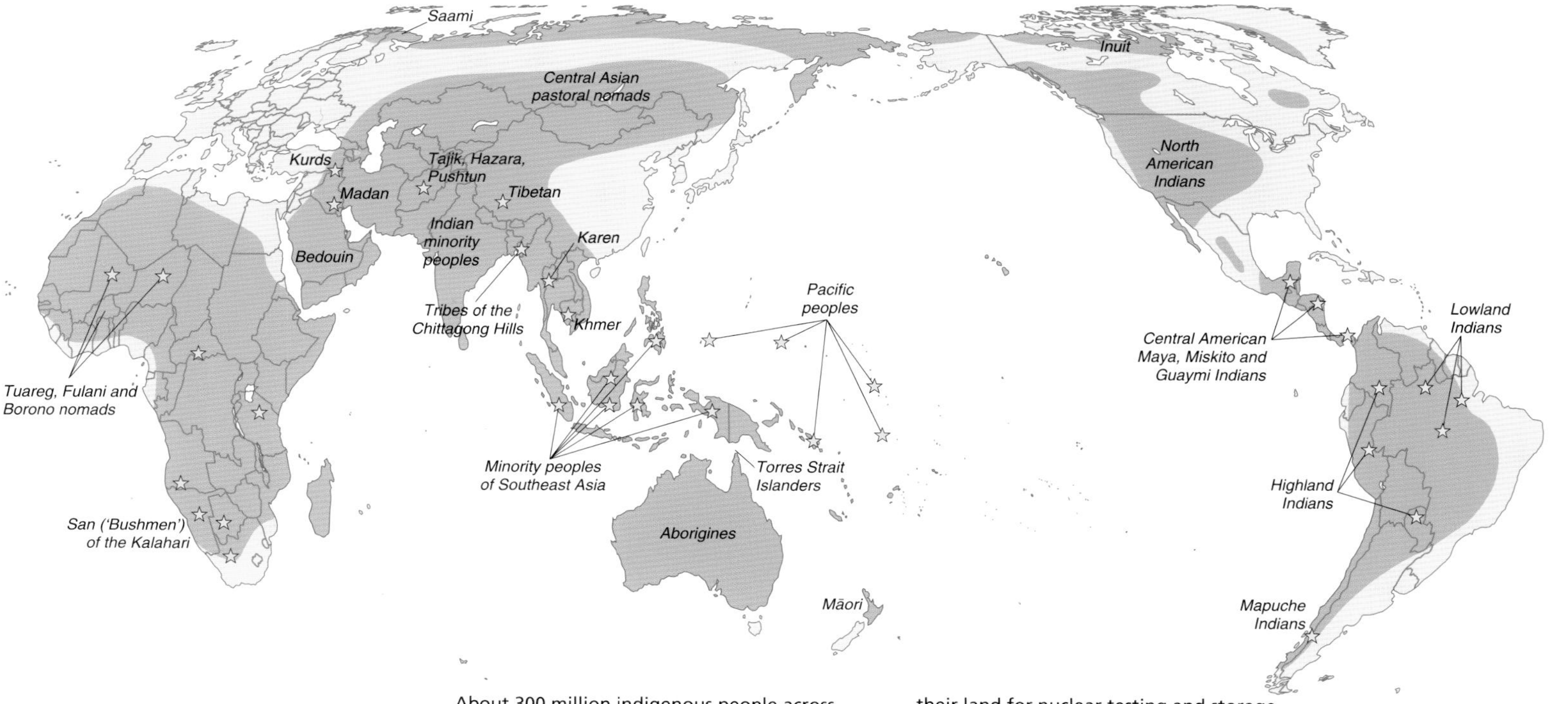

Saami

Inuit

Central Asian pastoral nomads

Kurds

Tajik, Hazara, Pushtun

Madan

Tibetan

North American Indians

Bedouin

Indian minority peoples

Karen

Pacific peoples

Tribes of the Chittagong Hills

Khmer

Central American Maya, Miskito and Guaymi Indians

Lowland Indians

Tuareg, Fulani and Borono nomads

Minority peoples of Southeast Asia

Torres Strait Islanders

Highland Indians

San ('Bushmen') of the Kalahari

Aborigines

Māori

Mapuche Indians

- Areas with significant numbers of indigenous people
- ☆ Indigenous peoples under threat

About 300 million indigenous people across the world are the descendants of the original population of their area. They have suffered natural and human disasters, invasion by others, forced removal from their land, use of their land for nuclear testing and storage, exploitation of the natural resources of their land without approval, and even official government policies of 'cleansing'. Today many groups remain deprived of their rights.

0   2000   4000   6000   8000 km

Eckert IV projection

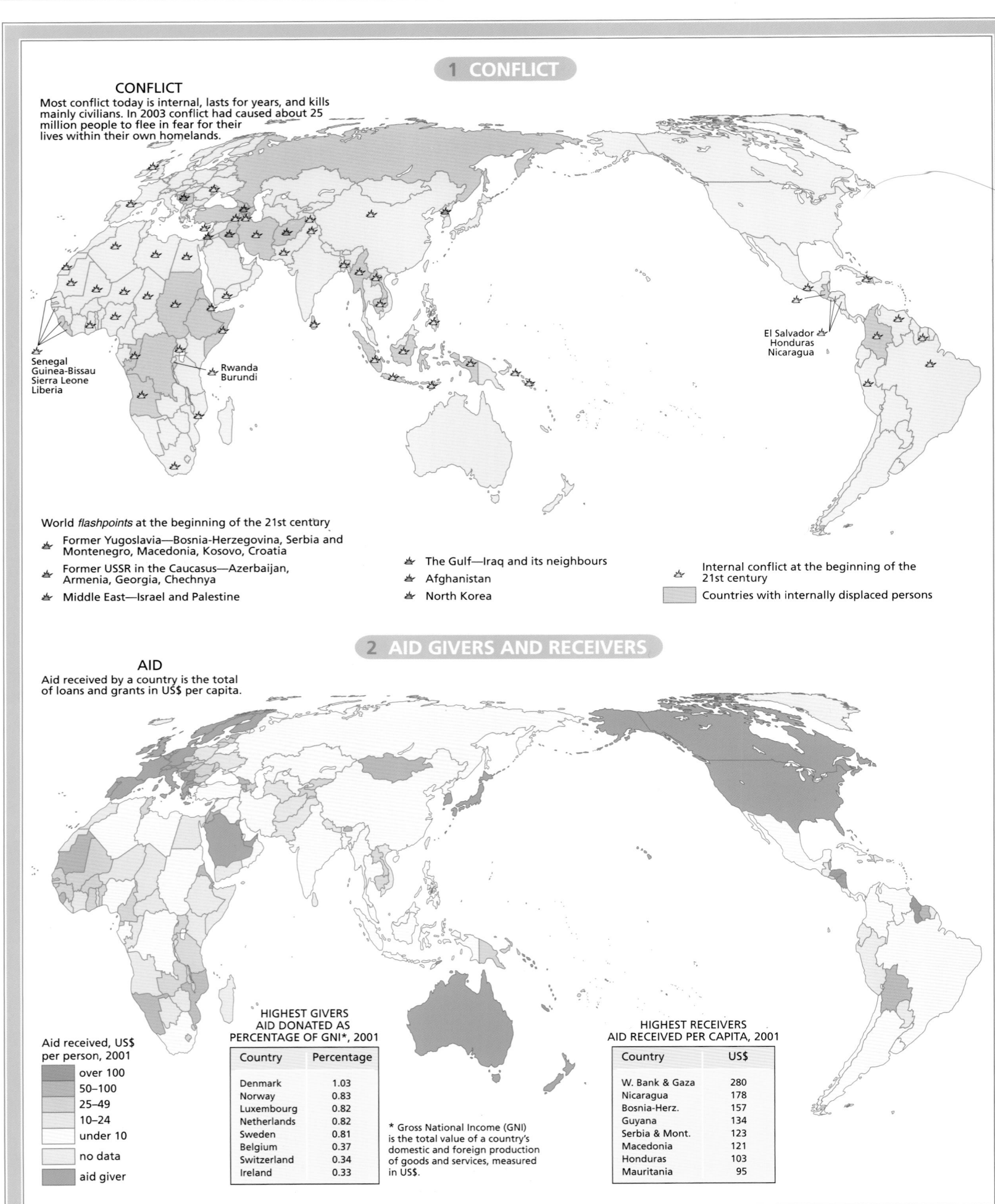

1 CONFLICT

CONFLICT

Most conflict today is internal, lasts for years, and kills mainly civilians. In 2003 conflict had caused about 25 million people to flee in fear for their lives within their own homelands.

Senegal
Guinea-Bissau
Sierra Leone
Liberia

Rwanda
Burundi

El Salvador
Honduras
Nicaragua

World *flashpoints* at the beginning of the 21st century

⚔ Former Yugoslavia—Bosnia-Herzegovina, Serbia and Montenegro, Macedonia, Kosovo, Croatia

⚔ Former USSR in the Caucasus—Azerbaijan, Armenia, Georgia, Chechnya

⚔ Middle East—Israel and Palestine

⚔ The Gulf—Iraq and its neighbours

⚔ Afghanistan

⚔ North Korea

⚔ Internal conflict at the beginning of the 21st century

Countries with internally displaced persons

2 AID GIVERS AND RECEIVERS

AID

Aid received by a country is the total of loans and grants in US$ per capita.

Aid received, US$ per person, 2001

- over 100
- 50–100
- 25–49
- 10–24
- under 10
- no data
- aid giver

HIGHEST GIVERS AID DONATED AS PERCENTAGE OF GNI*, 2001	
Country	Percentage
Denmark	1.03
Norway	0.83
Luxembourg	0.82
Netherlands	0.82
Sweden	0.81
Belgium	0.37
Switzerland	0.34
Ireland	0.33

* Gross National Income (GNI) is the total value of a country's domestic and foreign production of goods and services, measured in US$.

HIGHEST RECEIVERS AID RECEIVED PER CAPITA, 2001	
Country	US$
W. Bank & Gaza	280
Nicaragua	178
Bosnia-Herz.	157
Guyana	134
Serbia & Mont.	123
Macedonia	121
Honduras	103
Mauritania	95

SCALE 1:160 000 000

0   2000   4000   6000   8000 km

Eckert IV projection

1 INTERNATIONAL ORGANISATIONS

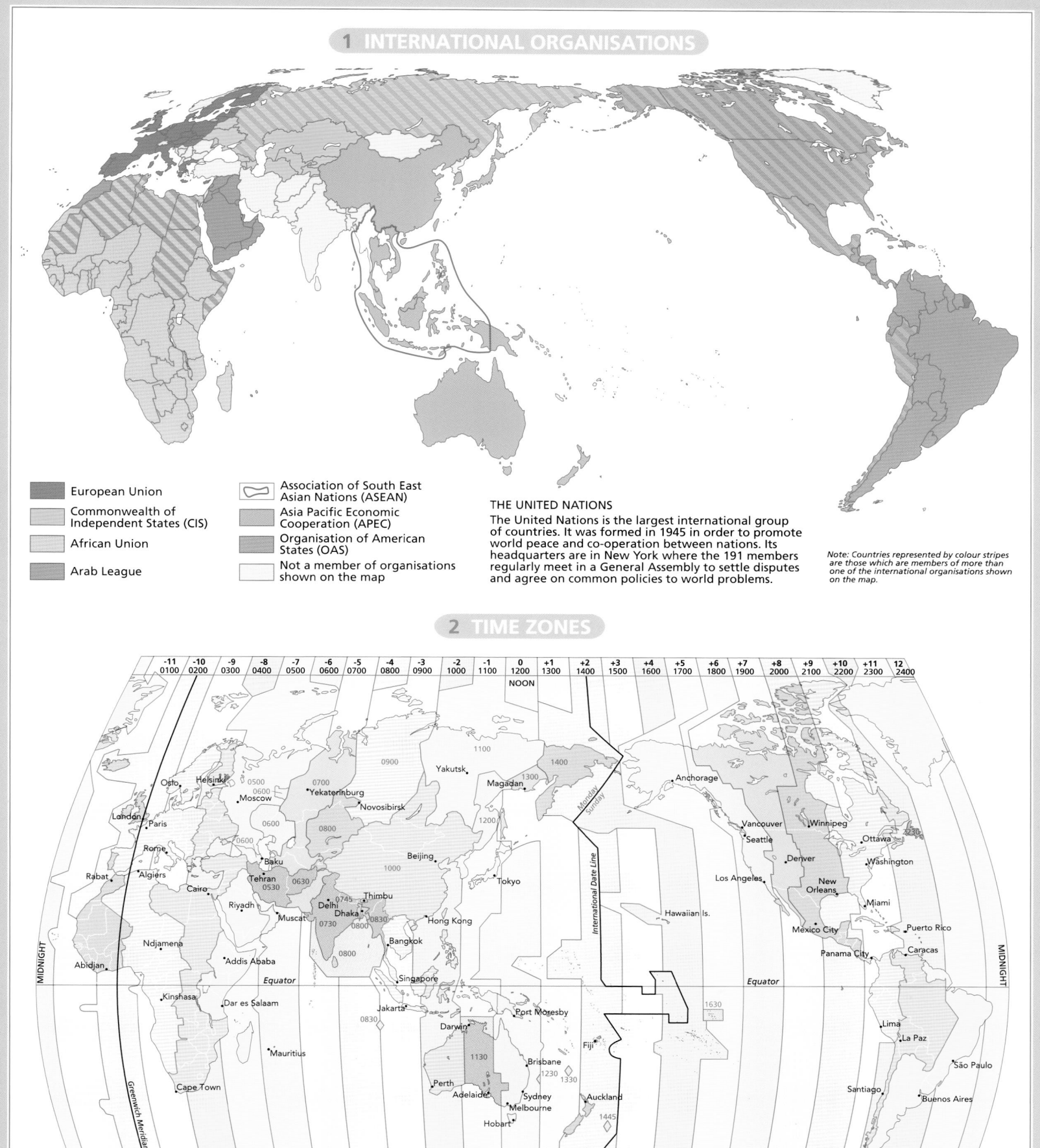

European Union

Commonwealth of Independent States (CIS)

African Union

Arab League

Association of South East Asian Nations (ASEAN)

Asia Pacific Economic Cooperation (APEC)

Organisation of American States (OAS)

Not a member of organisations shown on the map

THE UNITED NATIONS

The United Nations is the largest international group of countries. It was formed in 1945 in order to promote world peace and co-operation between nations. Its headquarters are in New York where the 191 members regularly meet in a General Assembly to settle disputes and agree on common policies to world problems.

Note: Countries represented by colour stripes are those which are members of more than one of the international organisations shown on the map.

2 TIME ZONES

| -11 0100 | -10 0200 | -9 0300 | -8 0400 | -7 0500 | -6 0600 | -5 0700 | -4 0800 | -3 0900 | -2 1000 | -1 1100 | 0 1200 NOON | +1 1300 | +2 1400 | +3 1500 | +4 1600 | +5 1700 | +6 1800 | +7 1900 | +8 2000 | +9 2100 | +10 2200 | +11 2300 | 12 2400 |

This map shows the world's official ("standard") time zones. The first line of numbers across the top shows how many hours ahead (+) or behind (-) each time zone is when compared to Australian Eastern Standard Time. The second line of numbers shows what time it would be in each zone if it was 1200 hours (noon) in Sydney, Melbourne or Brisbane. The red times printed on the map show those time zones which differ from the normal pattern. This map does not identify which places use Daylight Saving Time in summer. Daylight Saving Time is usually one hour ahead of the standard time.

KEY INFORMATION

FLAG	COUNTRY	CAPITAL CITY	LAND AREA sq km	TOTAL POP. 2003	MAIN LANGUAGES	MAIN RELIGIONS	CURRENCY
	AFGHANISTAN	Kabul	652 225	23 897 000	Dari, Pushtu, Uzbek, Turkmen	Sunni Muslim, Shi'a Muslim	Afghani
	ALBANIA	Tiranë	28 748	3 166 000	Albanian, Greek	Sunni Muslim, Albanian Orthodox, Roman Catholic	Lek
	ALGERIA	Algiers	2 381 741	31 800 000	Arabic, French, Berber	Sunni Muslim	Dinar
	ANGOLA	Luanda	1 246 700	13 625 000	Portuguese, Bantu, local languages	Roman Catholic, Protestant, trad. beliefs	Kwanza
	ARGENTINA	Buenos Aires	2 766 889	38 428 000	Spanish, Italian, Amerindian languages	Roman Catholic, Protestant	Peso
	ARMENIA	Yerevan	29 800	3 061 000	Armenian, Azeri	Armenian Orthodox	Dram
	AUSTRALIA	Canberra	7 682 395	19 731 000	English, Italian, Greek	Protestant, Roman Catholic, Orthodox	Dollar
	AUSTRIA	Vienna	83 855	8 116 000	German, Croatian, Turkish	Roman Catholic, Protestant	Euro
	AZERBAIJAN	Baku	86 600	8 370 000	Azeri, Armenian, Russian, Lezgian	Shi'a Muslim, Sunni Muslim, Russian and Armenian Orthodox	Manat
	BAHAMAS, THE	Nassau	13 939	314 000	English, Creole	Protestant, Roman Catholic	Dollar
	BAHRAIN	Manama	691	724 000	Arabic, English	Shi'a Muslim, Sunni Muslim, Christian	Dinar
	BANGLADESH	Dhaka	143 998	146 736 000	Bengali, English,	Sunni Muslim, Hindu	Taka
	BARBADOS	Bridgetown	430	270 000	English, Creole	Protestant, Roman Catholic	Dollar
	BELARUS	Minsk	207 600	9 895 000	Belorussian, Russian	Belorussian Orthodox, Roman Catholic	Rouble
	BELGIUM	Brussels	30 520	10 318 000	Dutch (Flemish), French (Walloon), German	Roman Catholic, Protestant	Euro
	BELIZE	Belmopan	22 965	256 000	English, Spanish, Mayan, Creole	Roman Catholic, Protestant	Dollar
	BENIN	Porto-Novo	112 620	6 736 000	French, Fon, Yoruba, Adja, local languages	Trad. beliefs, Roman Catholic, Sunni Muslim	CFA franc
	BHUTAN	Thimbu	46 620	2 257 000	Dzongkha, Nepali, Assamese	Buddhist, Hindu	Ngultrum, Indian rupee
	BOLIVIA	La Paz/Sucre	1 098 581	8 808 000	Spanish, Quechua, Aymara	Roman Catholic, Protestant, Baha'i	Boliviano
	BOSNIA-HERZEGOVINA	Sarajevo	51 130	4 161 000	Bosnian, Serbian, Croatian	Sunni Muslim, Serbian Orthodox, Roman Catholic, Protestant	Marka
	BOTSWANA	Gaborone	581 370	1 785 000	English, Setswana, Shona, local languages	Trad. beliefs, Protestant, Roman Catholic	Pula
	BRAZIL	Brasília	8 547 379	178 470 000	Portuguese	Roman Catholic, Protestant	Real
	BRUNEI	Bandar Seri Begawan	5 765	358 000	Malay, English, Chinese	Sunni Muslim, Buddhist, Christian	Dollar
	BULGARIA	Sofia	110 994	7 897 000	Bulgarian, Turkish, Romany, Macedonian	Bulgarian Orthodox, Sunni Muslim	Lev
	BURKINA	Ouagadougou	274 200	13 002 000	French, Moore (Mossi), Fulani, local languages	Sunni Muslim, trad. beliefs, Roman Catholic	CFA franc
	BURUNDI	Bujumbura	27 835	6 825 000	Kirundi (Hutu, Tutsi), French	Roman Catholic, trad. beliefs, Protestant	Franc
	CAMBODIA	Phnom Penh	181 035	14 144 000	Khmer, Vietnamese	Buddhist, Roman Catholic, Sunni Muslim	Riel
	CAMEROON	Yaoundé	475 442	16 018 000	French, English, Fang, Bamileke, local languages	Roman Catholic, trad. beliefs, Sunni Muslim, Protestant	CFA franc
	CANADA	Ottawa	9 970 610	31 510 000	English, French	Roman Catholic, Protestant, Eastern Orthodox, Jewish	Dollar
	CENTRAL AFRICAN REPUBLIC	Bangui	622 436	3 865 000	French, Sango, Banda, Baya, local languages	Protestant, Roman Catholic, trad. beliefs, Sunni Muslim	CFA franc
	CHAD	Ndjamena	1 284 000	8 598 000	Arabic, French, Sara, local languages	Sunni Muslim, Roman Catholic, Protestant, trad. beliefs	CFA franc
	CHILE	Santiago	756 945	15 805 000	Spanish, Amerindian languages	Roman Catholic, Protestant	Peso
	CHINA	Beijing	9 584 492	1 289 161 000	Mandarin, Wu, Cantonese, Hsiang, regional languages	Confucian, Taoist, Buddhist, Christian, Sunni Muslim	Yuan, HK dollar, Macau pataca
	COLOMBIA	Bogotá	1 141 748	44 222 000	Spanish, Amerindian languages	Roman Catholic, Protestant	Peso
	COMOROS	Moroni	1 862	768 000	Comorian, French, Arabic	Sunni Muslim, Roman Catholic	Franc
	CONGO	Brazzaville	342 000	3 724 000	French, Kongo, Monokutuba, local languages	Roman Catholic, Protestant, trad. beliefs, Sunni Muslim	CFA franc
	CONGO, DEM. REP. OF	Kinshasa	2 345 410	52 771 000	French, Lingala, Swahili, Kongo, local languages	Christian, Sunni Muslim	Franc
	COSTA RICA	San José	51 100	4 173 000	Spanish	Roman Catholic, Protestant	Colón
	CÔTE D'IVOIRE	Yamoussoukro	322 463	16 631 000	French, Creole, Akan, local languages	Sunni Muslim, Roman Catholic, trad. beliefs, Protestant	CFA franc
	CROATIA	Zagreb	56 538	4 428 000	Croatian, Serbian	Roman Catholic, Serbian Orthodox, Sunni Muslim	Kuna
	CUBA	Havana	110 860	11 300 000	Spanish	Roman Catholic, Protestant	Peso
	CYPRUS	Nicosia	9 251	802 000	Greek, Turkish, English	Greek Orthodox, Sunni Muslim	Pound
	CZECH REPUBLIC	Prague	78 864	10 236 000	Czech, Moravian, Slovak	Roman Catholic, Protestant	Koruna
	DENMARK	Copenhagen	43 075	5 364 000	Danish	Protestant	Krone
	DJIBOUTI	Djibouti	23 200	703 000	Somali, Afar, French, Arabic	Sunni Muslim, Christian	Franc

POPULATION

HEALTH AND EDUCATION

DEVELOPMENT

DENSITY persons per sq km 2003	BIRTH RATE per 1000 population 2002	DEATH RATE per 1000 population 2002	LIFE EXPECT-ANCY in years 2002	POP. CHANGE % 2000–05	URBAN POP. % 2002	INFANT MORTALITY deaths under one year per 1000 live births 2000–05	DOCTORS PER 100 000 PEOPLE 2000	FOOD INTAKE % population under-nourished 1999–2001	ADULT LITERACY % 2002	SCHOOL ENROLMENT Secondary, gross % 2000	ENERGY CONSUM-PTION kg per capita, coal eq. 2001	GNI PER CAPITA US $ 2002
37	49	21	43	3.9	22.8	162	11	70	...	...	27	...
110	17	6	74	0.7	43.6	25	129	4	86	78	1 336	1 380
13	22	5	71	1.7	58.3	44	100	6	69	71	1 545	1 720
11	47	19	47	3.2	35.5	140	7.7	49	...	15	259	660
14	19	8	74	1.2	88.5	20	268	<2.5	97	97	2 664	4 060
103	12	7	75	-0.5	67.4	17	316	51	99	73	1 114	790
3	13	8	79	1.0	91.5	6	250	dev.	100	161	9 571	19 740
97	9	10	79	0.1	67.6	5	310	dev.	100	99	6 588	23 390
97	16	7	65	0.9	51.9	29	360	21	100	80	2 613	710
23	18	8	70	1.1	89.1	18	152	dev.	96	84	5 946	...
1 048	21	4	73	2.2	92.8	14	100	dev.	89	101	22 688	11 130
1 019	28	8	62	2.0	26.1	64	20	32	41	46	137	360
628	14	8	75	0.4	51.1	11	125	dev.	100	102	3 325	9 750
48	9	14	68	-0.5	69.7	11	443	3	100	84	4 540	1 360
338	10	10	79	0.2	97.5	4	390	dev.	100	...	10 137	23 250
11	25	4	74	2.1	48.2	31	55	...	94	74	1 760	2 960
60	38	13	53	2.7	43.7	93	57	16	40	22	173	380
48	37	9	63	3.0	7.6	54	16	...	...	...	141	590
8	29	8	64	1.9	63.4	56	130	22	87	80	716	900
81	12	8	74	1.1	43.9	14	143	8	...	...	2 041	1 270
3	30	23	38	0.9	49.9	57	24	24	79	93	1 676	2 980
21	19	7	69	1.2	82.2	38	127	9	88	108	1 910	2 850
62	19	3	77	2.3	73.2	6	85	dev.	92	113	8 696	...
71	9	14	72	-0.9	67.5	15	345	16	99	94	4 422	1 790
47	43	19	43	3.0	17.2	93	4	17	26	10	56	220
245	39	20	42	3.1	9.6	107	...	70	50	10	44	100
78	27	12	54	2.4	18.0	73	30	38	69	19	23	280
34	36	16	48	1.8	50.4	88	7	27	74	...	201	560
3	11	8	79	0.8	79.1	5	210	dev.	100	103	15 098	22 300
6	36	20	42	1.3	42.2	100	4	44	50	...	58	260
7	45	16	48	3.0	24.5	115	3	34	46	11	14	220
21	16	6	76	1.2	86.3	12	110	4	96	75	2 582	4 260
135	15	8	71	0.7	37.6	37	168	11	86	63	1 158	940
39	21	6	72	1.6	76.0	26	116	13	92	70	993	1 830
412	32	8	61	2.8	34.4	67	7	...	56	21	76	390
11	41	14	52	2.6	66.6	84	25	30	83	42	208	700
22	45	18	45	2.9	...	120	7	75	64	...	56	90
82	20	4	78	1.9	60.0	11	90	6	96	60	1 493	4 100
52	37	17	45	1.6	44.5	101	...	15	51	23	265	610
78	10	12	45	-0.2	58.6	8	229	12	99	...	3 454	4 640
102	12	8	74	0.3	75.7	7	530	11	97	85	1 304	...
87	13	8	77	0.8	70.5	8	255	dev.	98	93	5 049	12 320
130	9	11	78	-0.1	74.6	6	310	<2.5	100	95	5 578	5 560
125	12	12	75	0.2	85.1	5	340	dev.	100	128	6 299	30 290
30	36	20	77	1.6	84.4	102	14	...	67	15	1 457	900

... no data available

dev. developed country

KEY INFORMATION

FLAG	COUNTRY	CAPITAL CITY	LAND AREA sq km	TOTAL POP. 2003	MAIN LANGUAGES	MAIN RELIGIONS	CURRENCY
	DOMINICA	Roseau	750	70 000	English, Creole	Roman Catholic, Protestant	E. Carib. dollar
	DOMINICAN REPUBLIC	Santo Domingo	48 442	8 745 000	Spanish, Creole	Roman Catholic, Protestant	Peso
	EAST TIMOR	Dili	14 874	778 000	Portuguese, Tetun, English	Roman Catholic	US dollar
	ECUADOR	Quito	272 045	13 003 000	Spanish, Quechua and other Amerindian languages	Roman Catholic	US dollar
	EGYPT	Cairo	1 000 250	71 931 000	Arabic	Sunni Muslim, Coptic Christian	Pound
	EL SALVADOR	San Salvador	21 041	6 515 000	Spanish	Roman Catholic, Protestant	Colón, US dollar
	EQUATORIAL GUINEA	Malabo	28 051	494 000	Spanish, French, Fang	Roman Catholic, trad. beliefs	CFA franc
	ERITREA	Asmara	117 400	4 141 000	Tigrinya, Tigre	Sunni Muslim, Coptic Christian	Nakfa
	ESTONIA	Tallinn	45 200	1 323 000	Estonian, Russian	Protestant, Estonian and Russian Orthodox	Kroon
	ETHIOPIA	Addis Ababa	1 133 880	70 678 000	Oromo, Amharic, Tigrinya, local languages	Ethiopian Orthodox, Sunni Muslim, trad. beliefs	Birr
	FIJI	Suva	18 330	839 000	English, Fijian, Hindi	Christian, Hindu, Sunni Muslim	Dollar
	FINLAND	Helsinki	338 145	5 207 000	Finnish, Swedish	Protestant, Finnish Orthodox	Euro
	FRANCE	Paris	543 965	60 144 000	French, Arabic	Roman Catholic, Protestant, Sunni Muslim	Euro
	GABON	Libreville	267 667	1 329 000	French, Fang, local languages	Roman Catholic, Protestant, trad. beliefs	CFA franc
	GAMBIA, THE	Banjul	11 295	1 426 000	English, Malinke, Fulani, Wolof	Sunni Muslim, Protestant	Dalasi
	GEORGIA	T'bilisi	69 700	5 126 000	Georgian, Russian, Armenian, Azeri, Ossetian, Abkhaz	Georgian Orthodox, Russian Orthodox, Sunni Muslim	Lari
	GERMANY	Berlin	357 028	82 476 000	German, Turkish	Protestant, Roman Catholic	Euro
	GHANA	Accra	238 537	20 922 000	English, Hausa, Akan, local languages	Christian, Sunni Muslim, trad. beliefs	Cedi
	GREECE	Athens	131 957	10 976 000	Greek	Greek Orthodox, Sunni Muslim	Euro
	GUATEMALA	Guatemala City	108 890	12 347 000	Spanish, Mayan languages	Roman Catholic, Protestant	Quetzal, US dollar
	GUINEA	Conakry	245 857	8 480 000	French, Fulani, Malinke, local languages	Sunni Muslim, trad. beliefs, Christian	Franc
	GUINEA-BISSAU	Bissau	36 125	1 493 000	Portuguese, Crioulo, local languages	Trad. beliefs, Sunni Muslim, Christian	CFA franc
	GUYANA	Georgetown	214 969	765 000	English, Creole, Amerindian languages	Protestant, Hindu, Roman Catholic, Sunni Muslim	Dollar
	HAITI	Port-au-Prince	27 750	8 326 000	French, Creole	Roman Catholic, Protestant, Voodoo	Gourde
	HONDURAS	Tegucigalpa	112 088	6 941 000	Spanish, Amerindian languages	Roman Catholic, Protestant	Lempira
	HUNGARY	Budapest	93 030	9 877 000	Hungarian	Roman Catholic, Protestant	Forint
	ICELAND	Reykjavík	102 820	290 000	Icelandic	Protestant	Króna
	INDIA	New Delhi	3 065 027	1 065 462 000	Hindi, English, many regional languages	Hindu, Sunni Muslim, Shi'a Muslim, Sikh, Christian	Rupee
	INDONESIA	Jakarta	1 919 445	219 883 000	Indonesian, local languages	Sunni Muslim, Protestant, Roman Catholic, Hindu, Buddhist	Rupiah
	IRAN	Tehran	1 648 000	68 920 000	Farsi, Azeri, Kurdish, regional languages	Sunni Muslim, Shi'a Muslim	Rial
	IRAQ	Baghdad	438 317	25 175 000	Arabic, Kurdish, Turkmen	Sunni Muslim, Shi'a Muslim, Christian	Dinar
	IRELAND, REPUBLIC OF	Dublin	70 282	3 956 000	English, Irish	Roman Catholic, Protestant	Euro
	ISRAEL	*Jerusalem	20 770	6 433 000	Hebrew, Arabic	Jewish, Sunni Muslim, Christian, Druze	Shekel
	ITALY	Rome	301 245	57 423 000	Italian	Roman Catholic	Euro
	JAMAICA	Kingston	10 991	2 651 000	English, Creole	Protestant, Roman Catholic	Dollar
	JAPAN	Tokyo	377 727	127 654 000	Japanese	Shintoist, Buddhist, Christian	Yen
	JORDAN	Amman	89 206	5 473 000	Arabic	Sunni Muslim, Christian	Dinar
	KAZAKHSTAN	Astana	2 717 300	15 433 000	Kazak, Russian, Ukrainian, German, Uzbek, Tatar	Sunni Muslim, Russian Orthodox, Protestant	Tenge
	KENYA	Nairobi	582 646	31 987 000	Swahili, English, local languages	Christian, trad. beliefs	Shilling
	KIRIBATI	Tarawa	717	86 000	Gilbertese, English	Roman Catholic, Protestant	Australian dollar
	KUWAIT	Kuwait	17 818	2 521 000	Arabic	Sunni Muslim, Shi'a Muslim, Christian, Hindu	Dinar
	KYRGYZSTAN	Bishkek	198 500	5 138 000	Kirghiz, Russian, Uzbek	Sunni Muslim, Russian Orthodox	Som
	LAOS	Vientiane	236 800	5 657 000	Lao, local languages	Buddhist, trad. beliefs	Kip
	LATVIA	Riga	63 700	2 307 000	Latvian, Russian	Protestant, Roman Catholic, Russian Orthodox	Lat
	LEBANON	Beirut	10 452	3 653 000	Arabic, Armenian, French	Shi'a Muslim, Sunni Muslim, Christian	Pound

* not internationally recognised

POPULATION						HEALTH AND EDUCATION					DEVELOPMENT	
DENSITY persons per sq km 2003	BIRTH RATE per 1000 population 2002	DEATH RATE per 1000 population 2002	LIFE EXPECT-ANCY in years 2002	POP. CHANGE % 2000–05	URBAN POP. % 2002	INFANT MORTALITY deaths under one year per 1000 live births 2000–05	DOCTORS PER 100 000 PEOPLE 2000	FOOD INTAKE % population under-nourished 1999–2001	ADULT LITERACY % 2002	SCHOOL ENROLMENT Secondary, gross % 2000	ENERGY CONSUM-PTION kg per capita, coal eq. 2001	GNI PER CAPITA US $ 2002
93	18	6	44	0.3	71.7	...	49	...	...	...	820	3 180
181	23	7	77	1.5	66.5	36	216	25	84	59	1 201	2 320
52	43	...	67	4.0	7.6	124	...	...	...	...	...	520
48	24	6	70	1.5	63.9	42	170	4	92	57	985	1 450
72	24	6	69	2.0	42.8	41	160	3	57	86	1 178	1 470
310	26	6	70	1.6	62.4	26	107	14	80	54	672	2 080
18	41	15	52	2.7	50.3	101	25	...	98	31	393	700
35	38	13	51	3.7	19.5	73	3	61	58	28	105	160
29	9	14	71	-1.1	69.5	9	297	4	100	92	2 600	4 130
62	42	20	42	2.5	16.2	100	...	42	42	18	38	100
46	22	6	70	1.0	50.9	18	48	...	94	...	732	2 160
15	11	10	78	0.2	59.0	4	310	dev.	100	126	9 581	23 510
111	13	10	79	0.5	75.7	5	300	dev.	100	108	6 666	22 010
5	35	15	53	1.8	82.9	57	...	7	...	60	1 086	3 120
126	37	14	53	2.7	31.9	81	4	27	39	36	102	280
74	8	10	73	-0.9	56.8	18	436	26	100	73	1 259	650
231	9	11	78	0.1	87.9	5	350	dev.	100	99	6 535	22 670
88	29	13	55	2.2	36.7	58	6	12	74	36	326	270
83	9	11	78	0.1	60.6	6	440	dev.	97	98	4 929	11 660
113	33	7	65	2.6	40.3	41	93	25	70	37	510	1 750
34	38	17	46	1.6	28.4	102	13	28	...	...	104	410
41	39	20	45	3.0	33.1	120	17	...	41	20	161	150
4	22	10	62	0.2	37.1	51	18	14	99	...	1 152	840
300	32	14	52	1.3	37.0	63	8	49	52	...	115	440
62	30	6	66	2.3	54.5	32	83	20	76	...	493	920
106	10	14	72	-0.5	65.1	9	320	<2.5	99	99	4 133	5 280
3	13	7	80	0.8	92.8	3	340	dev.	100	109	18 042	27 970
348	24	9	63	1.5	28.1	65	48	21	59	49	472	480
115	20	7	67	1.3	43.0	42	16	6	88	57	808	710
42	22	6	69	1.2	65.4	33	85	5	78	78	3 012	1 710
57	29	8	63	2.7	67.5	83	55	27	40	38	1 710	...
56	14	8	77	1.1	59.6	6	230	dev.	100	...	5 950	23 870
310	20	6	79	2.0	91.9	6	385	dev.	95	93	4 605	...
191	9	11	78	-0.1	67.3	5	590	dev.	99	96	5 249	18 960
241	20	6	76	0.9	57.1	20	140	9	88	83	2 121	2 820
338	9	9	81	0.1	79.1	3	190	dev.	100	102	6 456	33 550
61	28	4	72	2.7	79.0	24	166	6	91	88	1 264	1 760
6	15	12	62	-0.4	55.9	52	353	22	99	88	4 386	1 510
55	35	16	46	1.5	35.2	69	13	37	84	31	168	360
120	28	7	63	1.4	39.1	...	30	...	...	...	166	810
141	20	3	77	3.5	96.2	11	189	4	83	56	17 587	18 270
26	19	8	65	1.4	34.4	37	301	7	...	86	1 864	290
24	36	12	55	2.3	20.2	88	24	22	66	38	103	310
36	8	14	70	-0.9	60.4	14	282	6	100	91	3 271	3 480
350	19	6	71	1.6	90.3	17	210	3	87	76	2 553	3 990

... no data available   *dev.* developed country

KEY INFORMATION

FLAG	COUNTRY	CAPITAL CITY	LAND AREA sq km	TOTAL POP. 2003	MAIN LANGUAGES	MAIN RELIGIONS	CURRENCY
	LESOTHO	Maseru	30 355	1 802 000	Sesotho, English, Zulu	Christian, trad. beliefs	Loti, S. African rand
	LIBERIA	Monrovia	111 369	3 367 000	English, Creole, local languages	Trad. beliefs, Christian, Sunni Muslim	Dollar
	LIBYA	Tripoli	1 759 540	5 551 000	Arabic, Berber	Sunni Muslim	Dinar
	LITHUANIA	Vilnius	65 200	3 444 000	Lithuanian, Russian, Polish	Roman Catholic, Protestant, Russian Orthodox	Litas
	LUXEMBOURG	Luxembourg	2 586	453 000	Luxembourgian, German, French	Roman Catholic	Euro
	MACEDONIA	Skopje	25 713	2 056 000	Macedonian, Albanian, Turkish	Macedonian Orthodox, Sunni Muslim	Denar
	MADAGASCAR	Antananarivo	587 041	17 404 000	Malagasy, French	Trad. beliefs, Christian, Sunni Muslim	Franc
	MALAWI	Lilongwe	118 484	12 105 000	Chichewa, English, local languages	Christian, trad. beliefs, Sunni Muslim	Kwacha
	MALAYSIA	Kuala Lumpur/Putrajaya	332 965	24 425 000	Malay, English, Chinese, Tamil, local languages	Sunni Muslim, Buddhist, Hindu, Christian, trad. beliefs	Ringgit
	MALDIVES	Male	298	318 000	Divehi (Maldivian)	Sunni Muslim	Rufiyaa
	MALI	Bamako	1 240 140	13 007 000	French, Bambara, local languages	Sunni Muslim, trad. beliefs, Christian	CFA franc
	MALTA	Valletta	316	394 000	Maltese, English	Roman Catholic	Lira
	MAURITANIA	Nouakchott	1 030 700	2 893 000	Arabic, French, local languages	Sunni Muslim	Ouguiya
	MAURITIUS	Port Louis	2 040	1 221 000	English, Creole, Hindi, Bhojpurī, French	Hindu, Roman Catholic, Sunni Muslim	Rupee
	MEXICO	Mexico City	1 972 545	103 457 000	Spanish, Amerindian languages	Roman Catholic, Protestant	Peso
	MICRONESIA, FEDERATED STATES OF	Palikir	701	109 000	English, Trukese, Pohnpeian, local languages	Roman Catholic, Protestant	US dollar
	MOLDOVA	Chişinău	33 700	4 267 000	Romanian, Ukrainian, Gagauz, Russian	Romanian Orthodox, Russian Orthodox	Leu
	MONGOLIA	Ulaanbaatar	1 565 000	2 594 000	Khalka (Mongolian), Kazakh, local languages	Buddhist, Sunni Muslim	Tugrik
	MOROCCO	Rabat	446 550	30 566 000	Arabic, Berber, French	Sunni Muslim	Dirham
	MOZAMBIQUE	Maputo	799 380	18 863 000	Portuguese, Makua, Tsonga, local languages,	Trad. beliefs, Roman Catholic, Sunni Muslim	Metical
	MYANMAR	Yangon	676 577	49 485 000	Burmese, Shan, Karen, local languages	Buddhist, Christian, Sunni Muslim	Kyat
	NAMIBIA	Windhoek	824 292	1 987 000	English, Afrikaans, German, Ovambo, local languages	Protestant, Roman Catholic	Dollar
	NAURU	Yaren	21	13 000	Nauruan, English	Protestant, Roman Catholic	Australian dollar
	NEPAL	Kathmandu	147 181	25 164 000	Nepali, Maithili, Bhojpuri, English, local languages	Hindu, Buddhist, Sunni Muslim	Rupee
	NETHERLANDS	Amsterdam/The Hague	41 526	16 149 000	Dutch, Frisian	Roman Catholic, Protestant, Sunni Muslim	Euro
	NEW ZEALAND	Wellington	270 534	3 875 000	English, Māori	Protestant, Roman Catholic	Dollar
	NICARAGUA	Managua	130 000	5 466 000	Spanish, Amerindian languages	Roman Catholic, Protestant	Córdoba
	NIGER	Niamey	1 267 000	11 972 000	French, Hausa, Fulani, local languages	Sunni Muslim, trad. beliefs	CFA franc
	NIGERIA	Abuja	923 768	124 009 000	English, Hausa, Yoruba, Ibo, Fulani, local languages	Sunni Muslim, Christian, trad. beliefs	Naira
	NORTH KOREA	Pyongyang	120 538	22 664 000	Korean	Trad. beliefs, Chondoist, Buddhist	Won
	NORWAY	Oslo	323 878	4 533 000	Norwegian	Protestant, Roman Catholic	Krone
	OMAN	Muscat	309 500	2 851 000	Arabic, Baluchi, Indian languages	Ibadhi Muslim, Sunni Muslim	Riyal
	PAKISTAN	Islamabad	803 940	153 578 000	Urdu, Punjabi, Sindhi, Pushtu, English	Sunni Muslim, Shi'a Muslim, Christian, Hindu	Rupee
	PALAU	Koror	497	20 000	Palauan, English	Roman Catholic, Protestant, trad. beliefs	US dollar
	PANAMA	Panama City	77 082	3 120 000	Spanish, English, Amerindian languages	Roman Catholic, Protestant, Sunni Muslim	Balboa
	PAPUA NEW GUINEA	Port Moresby	462 840	5 711 000	English, Tok Pisin (Creole), local languages	Protestant, Roman Catholic, trad. beliefs	Kina
	PARAGUAY	Asunción	406 752	5 878 000	Spanish, Guaraní	Roman Catholic, Protestant	Guaraní
	PERU	Lima	1 285 216	27 167 000	Spanish, Quechua, Aymara	Roman Catholic, Protestant	Sol
	PHILIPPINES	Manila	300 000	79 999 000	English, Pilipino, Cebuano, local languages	Roman Catholic, Protestant, Sunni Muslim, Aglipayan	Peso
	POLAND	Warsaw	312 683	38 587 000	Polish, German	Roman Catholic, Polish Orthodox	Złoty
	PORTUGAL	Lisbon	88 940	10 062 000	Portuguese	Roman Catholic, Protestant	Euro
	QATAR	Doha	11 437	610 000	Arabic	Sunni Muslim	Riyal
	ROMANIA	Bucharest	237 500	22 334 000	Romanian, Hungarian	Romanian Orthodox, Protestant, Roman Catholic	Leu
	RUSSIAN FEDERATION	Moscow	17 075 400	143 246 000	Russian, Tatar, Ukrainian, local languages	Russian Orthodox, Sunni Muslim, Protestant	Rouble
	RWANDA	Kigali	26 338	8 387 000	Kinyarwanda, French, English	Roman Catholic, trad. beliefs, Protestant	Franc

POPULATION						HEALTH AND EDUCATION					DEVELOPMENT	
DENSITY persons per sq km 2003	BIRTH RATE per 1000 population 2002	DEATH RATE per 1000 population 2002	LIFE EXPECT-ANCY in years 2002	POP. CHANGE % 2000–05	URBAN POP. % 2002	INFANT MORTALITY deaths under one year per 1000 live births 2000–05	DOCTORS PER 100 000 PEOPLE 2000	FOOD INTAKE % population under-nourished 1999–2001	ADULT LITERACY % 2002	SCHOOL ENROLMENT Secondary, gross % 2000	ENERGY CONSUM-PTION kg per capita, coal eq. 2001	GNI PER CAPITA US $ 2002
59	31	20	43	0.1	29.5	92	5	25	84	33	60	470
30	43	20	47	4.1	46.1	147	2	41	56	38	79	150
3	27	4	72	1.9	88.2	21	128	<2.5	82	90	4 503	...
53	10	12	73	-0.6	68.8	9	400	<2.5	100	95	3 537	3 660
175	12	10	77	1.3	92.2	5	310	dev.	100	94	17 309	38 830
80	13	9	73	0.5	59.5	16	225	...	...	84	2 350	1 700
30	39	12	55	2.8	30.7	92	11	36	68	...	75	240
102	45	25	38	2.0	15.5	115	...	33	62	36	63	160
73	22	4	73	1.9	58.7	10	66	<2.5	88	70	3 610	3 540
1 067	29	6	69	3.0	28.5	38	40	...	97	55	906	2 090
10	46	21	41	3.0	31.5	119	6	21	27	...	36	240
1 247	12	8	78	0.4	91.4	7	261	...	97	89	4 944	...
3	40	15	51	3.0	60.3	97	14	10	41	21	686	410
599	17	7	73	1.0	41.9	16	85	5	85	77	1 464	3 850
52	22	5	74	1.5	74.8	28	180	5	92	75	2 213	5 910
155	25	6	69	0.8	29.0	34	57	...	...	132	...	1 980
127	11	13	67	-0.1	41.8	...	350	12	99	71	1 178	460
2	23	6	65	1.3	56.7	58	243	38	99	61	1 036	440
68	21	6	68	1.6	56.7	42	46	7	51	39	614	1 190
24	40	21	41	1.8	34.3	122	...	53	47	12	79	210
73	23	12	57	1.3	28.7	84	30	7	85	39	159	...
2	35	21	42	1.4	31.9	60	30	7	83	62	681	1 780
619	28	7	61	2.3	100.0	25	140	...	95	...	8 290	...
171	32	10	60	2.2	12.5	71	4	17	44	51	98	230
389	12	9	78	0.5	89.7	5	320	dev.	100	124	9 892	23 960
14	14	8	78	0.8	86.0	6	220	dev.	100	112	8 222	13 710
42	29	5	69	2.4	56.9	36	86	29	67	54	418	...
9	49	20	46	3.6	21.6	126	3	34	17	6	51	170
134	39	17	45	2.5	45.7	79	19	8	67	...	294	290
188	18	11	62	0.5	60.8	45	297	34	...	...	4 780	...
14	13	10	79	0.4	75.3	5	290	dev.	100	115	15 849	37 850
9	26	3	74	2.9	77.0	20	133	...	74	68	4 930	7 720
191	33	8	64	2.4	33.8	87	57	19	45	24	484	410
40	...	...	...	2.1	69.5	...	...	...	...	84	...	7 140
40	20	5	75	1.8	56.9	21	167	26	92	69	1 815	4 020
12	32	10	57	2.2	17.9	62	7	27	65	21	331	530
14	30	5	71	2.4	57.3	37	110	13	94	60	738	1 170
21	22	6	70	1.5	73.5	33	93	11	91	...	783	2 050
267	26	6	70	1.8	60.1	29	123	22	95	77	610	1 020
123	10	10	74	-0.1	62.8	9	220	<2.5	100	101	3 432	4 570
113	11	11	76	0.1	66.8	6	320	dev.	93	114	4 073	10 840
53	14	4	75	1.5	93.1	12	126	dev.	82	89	34 551	...
94	10	13	70	-0.2	55.5	20	184	<2.5	98	82	2 740	1 850
8	10	15	66	-0.6	72.9	16	421	4	100	83	7 323	2 140
318	44	22	40	2.2	6.4	112	...	41	69	12	60	230

... no data available   dev. developed country

KEY INFORMATION

FLAG	COUNTRY	CAPITAL CITY	LAND AREA sq km	TOTAL POP. 2003	MAIN LANGUAGES	MAIN RELIGIONS	CURRENCY
	SAMOA	Apia	2 831	178 000	Samoan, English	Protestant, Roman Catholic	Tala
	SAUDI ARABIA	Riyadh	2 200 000	24 217 000	Arabic	Sunni Muslim, Shi'a Muslim	Riyal
	SENEGAL	Dakar	196 720	10 095 000	French, Wolof, Fulani, local languages	Sunni Muslim, Roman Catholic, trad. beliefs	CFA franc
	SERBIA AND MONTENEGRO	Belgrade	102 173	10 527 000	Serbian, Albanian, Hungarian	Serbian Orthodox, Montenegrin Orthodox, Sunni Muslim	Dinar, Euro
	SEYCHELLES	Victoria	455	84 000	English, French, Creole	Roman Catholic, Protestant	Rupee
	SIERRA LEONE	Freetown	71 740	4 971 000	English, Creole, Mende, Temne, local languages	Sunni Muslim, trad. beliefs	Leone
	SINGAPORE	Singapore	639	4 253 000	Chinese, English, Malay, Tamil	Buddhist, Taoist, Sunni Muslim, Christian, Hindu	Dollar
	SLOVAKIA	Bratislava	49 035	5 402 000	Slovak, Hungarian, Czech	Roman Catholic, Protestant, Orthodox	Koruna
	SLOVENIA	Ljubljana	20 251	1 984 000	Slovene, Croatian, Serbian	Roman Catholic, Protestant	Tólar
	SOLOMON ISLANDS	Honiara	28 370	477 000	English, Creole, local languages	Protestant, Roman Catholic	Dollar
	SOMALIA	Mogadishu	637 657	9 890 000	Somali, Arabic	Sunni Muslim	Shilling
	SOUTH AFRICA, REPUBLIC OF	Pretoria/Cape Town/ Bloemfontein	1 219 090	45 026 000	Afrikaans, English, nine official local languages	Protestant, Roman Catholic, Sunni Muslim, Hindu	Rand
	SOUTH KOREA	Seoul	99 274	47 700 000	Korean	Buddhist, Protestant, Roman Catholic	Won
	SPAIN	Madrid	504 782	41 060 000	Castilian, Catalan, Galician, Basque	Roman Catholic	Euro
	SRI LANKA	Sri Jayewardenepura Kotte	65 610	19 065 000	Sinhalese, Tamil, English	Buddhist, Hindu, Sunni Muslim, Roman Catholic	Rupee
	SUDAN	Khartoum	2 505 813	33 610 000	Arabic, Dinka, Nubian, Beja, Nuer, local languages	Sunni Muslim, trad. beliefs, Christian	Dinar
	SURINAME	Paramaribo	163 820	436 000	Dutch, Surinamese, English, Hindi	Hindu, Roman Catholic, Protestant, Sunni Muslim	Guilder
	SWAZILAND	Mbabane	17 364	1 077 000	Swazi, English	Christian, trad. beliefs	Emalangeni, S. African rand
	SWEDEN	Stockholm	449 964	8 876 000	Swedish	Protestant, Roman Catholic	Krona
	SWITZERLAND	Bern	41 293	7 169 000	German, French, Italian, Romansch	Roman Catholic, Protestant	Franc
	SYRIA	Damascus	185 180	17 800 000	Arabic, Kurdish, Armenian	Sunni Muslim, Shi'a Muslim, Christian	Pound
	*TAIWAN	Taibei	36 179	22 548 000	Mandarin, Min, Hakka, local languages	Buddhist, Taoist, Confucian, Christian	Dollar
	TAJIKISTAN	Dushanbe	143 100	6 245 000	Tajik, Uzbek, Russian	Sunni Muslim	Somoni
	TANZANIA	Dodoma	945 087	36 977 000	Swahili, English, Nyamwezi, local languages	Shi'a Muslim, Sunni Muslim, trad. beliefs, Christian	Shilling
	THAILAND	Bangkok	513 115	62 833 000	Thai, Lao, Chinese, Malay, Mon-Khmer languages	Buddhist, Sunni Muslim	Baht
	TOGO	Lomé	56 785	4 909 000	French, Ewe, Kabre, local languages	Trad. beliefs, Christian, Sunni Muslim	CFA franc
	TONGA	Nuku'alofa	748	104 000	Tongan, English	Protestant, Roman Catholic	Pa'anga
	TRINIDAD AND TOBAGO	Port of Spain	5 130	1 303 000	English, Creole, Hindi	Roman Catholic, Hindu, Protestant, Sunni Muslim	Dollar
	TUNISIA	Tunis	164 150	9 832 000	Arabic, French	Sunni Muslim	Dinar
	TURKEY	Ankara	779 452	71 325 000	Turkish, Kurdish	Sunni Muslim, Shi'a Muslim	Lira
	TURKMENISTAN	Ashgabat	488 100	4 867 000	Turkmen, Uzbek, Russian	Sunni Muslim, Russian Orthodox	Manat
	TUVALU	Funafuti	25	11 000	Tuvaluan, English	Protestant	Australian dollar
	UGANDA	Kampala	241 038	25 827 000	English, Swahili, Luganda, local languages	Roman Catholic, Protestant, Sunni Muslim, trad. beliefs	Shilling
	UKRAINE	Kiev	603 700	48 523 000	Ukrainian, Russian	Ukrainian Orthodox, Ukrainian Catholic, Roman Catholic	Hryvnia
	UNITED ARAB EMIRATES	Abu Dhabi	83 600	2 995 453	Arabic, English	Sunni Muslim, Shi'a Muslim	Dirham
	UNITED KINGDOM	London	244 082	59 251 000	English, Welsh, Gaelic	Protestant, Roman Catholic, Muslim	Pound
	UNITED STATES OF AMERICA	Washington D.C.	9 809 378	294 043 000	English, Spanish	Protestant, Roman Catholic, Sunni Muslim, Jewish	Dollar
	URUGUAY	Montevideo	176 215	3 415 000	Spanish	Roman Catholic, Protestant, Jewish	Peso
	UZBEKISTAN	Tashkent	447 400	26 093 000	Uzbek, Russian, Tajik, Kazakh	Sunni Muslim, Russian Orthodox	Som
	VANUATU	Port Vila	12 190	212 000	English, Bislama (Creole), French	Protestant, Roman Catholic, trad. beliefs	Vatu
	VENEZUELA	Caracas	912 050	25 699 000	Spanish, Amerindian languages	Roman Catholic, Protestant	Bolívar
	VIETNAM	Hanoi	329 565	81 377 000	Vietnamese, Thai, Khmer, Chinese, local languages	Buddhist, Taoist, Roman Catholic, Cao Dai, Hoa Hao	Dong
	YEMEN	Sana	527 968	20 010 000	Arabic	Sunni Muslim, Shi'a Muslim	Riyal
	ZAMBIA	Lusaka	752 614	10 812 000	English, Bemba, Nyanja, Tonga, local languages	Christian, trad. beliefs	Kwacha
	ZIMBABWE	Harare	390 759	12 891 000	English, Shona, Ndebele	Christian, trad. beliefs	Dollar

* not internationally recognised; widely regarded as a province of China

POPULATION

HEALTH AND EDUCATION

DEVELOPMENT

DENSITY persons per sq km 2003	BIRTH RATE per 1000 population 2002	DEATH RATE per 1000 population 2002	LIFE EXPECT-ANCY in years 2002	POP. CHANGE % 2000–05	URBAN POP. % 2002	INFANT MORTALITY deaths under one year per 1000 live births 2000–05	DOCTORS PER 100 000 PEOPLE 2000	FOOD INTAKE % population under-nourished 1999–2001	ADULT LITERACY % 2002	SCHOOL ENROLMENT Secondary, gross % 2000	ENERGY CONSUM-PTION kg per capita, coal eq. 2001	GNI PER CAPITA US $ 2002
63	29	6	69	1.0	22.5	26	34	...	99	75	1 339	1 420
11	32	4	73	2.9	87.1	21	166	3	78	68	8 764	8 460
51	35	13	52	2.4	48.8	61	10	24	39	18	257	470
103	12	12	73	-0.1	51.9	13	...	9	...	...	2 211	1 400
185	19	7	73	0.9	65.3	177	132	...	...	...	3 961	6 530
69	44	25	37	3.8	38.0	...	7	50	...	26	114	140
6 656	12	5	...	1.7	100.0	3	163	dev.	...	...	14 961	20 690
110	11	10	73	0.1	57.8	8	353	...	100	87	5 778	3 950
98	9	10	76	-0.1	49.2	6	228	<2.5	100	...	5 758	9 810
17	39	5	69	2.9	20.8	21	14	...	...	...	212	570
16	50	17	47	4.2	28.4	118	4	71	...	...	40	...
37	25	20	46	0.6	58.4	48	56	...	86	87	3 892	2 600
480	12	7	74	0.6	83.0	5	130	<2.5	98	94	6 383	9 930
81	10	10	78	0.2	78.1	5	330	dev.	98	116	5 307	14 430
291	18	6	74	0.8	23.4	20	37	25	92	...	365	840
13	33	10	58	2.2	37.9	77	9	25	60	29	138	350
3	21	6	70	0.8	75.3	26	25	11	...	87	3 265	1 960
62	35	18	44	0.8	27.0	78	15	12	81	60	815	1 180
20	11	11	80	0.1	83.3	3	290	dev.	100	149	9 433	24 820
174	9	9	80	-0.1	67.5	5	350	dev.	100	100	6 767	37 930
96	29	4	70	2.4	52.1	22	130	4	76	43	1 936	1 130
623	...	...	...	...	...	...	...	...	...	...	6 807	...
44	23	7	67	0.9	27.6	50	201	71	99	79	1 423	180
39	38	18	43	1.9	34.2	100	4	43	77	6	64	280
122	15	8	69	1.0	20.2	20	37	19	96	82	1 731	1 980
86	34	15	50	2.3	34.5	82	8	25	57	39	209	270
139	23	8	71	1.0	33.2	34	44	...	...	100	848	1 410
254	16	7	72	0.3	74.9	14	82	12	99	81	13 696	6 490
60	18	6	73	1.1	66.8	23	70	<2.5	63	78	1 303	2 000
92	20	7	70	1.4	66.6	40	121	3	86	58	1 581	2 500
10	20	7	65	1.5	45.2	49	300	7	...	...	3 668	1 200
440	...	...	...	1.2	...	...	...	...	...	...	...	...
107	44	18	43	3.2	14.9	86	...	19	69	19	59	250
80	9	15	68	-0.8	68.1	14	299	4	100	...	4 640	770
36	17	4	75	1.9	87.6	14	181	<2.5	77	75	29 082	...
243	11	11	77	0.3	89.6	5	180	dev.	100	156	6 179	25 250
30	14	9	78	1.9	77.7	7	280	dev.	100	95	12 816	35 060
19	16	10	75	0.3	92.3	13	370	3	98	98	1 756	4 370
58	20	6	67	1.5	36.7	37	309	26	99	...	3 044	450
17	32	5	69	2.4	22.5	29	12	...	...	28	235	1 080
28	23	5	74	1.9	87.4	19	236	18	93	59	4 497	4 090
247	19	6	70	1.4	24.9	34	48	19	93	67	360	430
38	41	10	57	3.5	25.3	71	20	33	49	...	286	490
14	39	23	37	1.2	40.1	105	7	50	80	24	315	330
33	29	21	39	0.5	36.7	58	14	39	90	44	651	...

... no data available

dev. developed country

How to use the Index

All the names on the maps in this atlas, except some of those on the special topic maps, are included in the index.

The names are arranged in **alphabetical order.** Where the name has more than one word the separate words are considered as one to decide the position of the name in the index:

White Cliffs
Whitecourt
Whitehorse
White I.
Whiteman Range

Where there is more than one place with the same name, the country name is used to decide the order:

Los Angeles Chile
Los Angeles USA

If both places are in the same country, the county or state name is also used:

Fuzhou Fujian China
Fuzhou Jiangxi China

Each entry in the index starts with the name of the place or feature, followed by the name of the country, state or territory in which it is located. This is followed by the number of the most appropriate page on which the name appears, usually the largest scale map. Next comes the alphanumeric reference followed by the latitude and longitude.

Names of physical features such as rivers, capes and mountains are listed with the part that refers to the type of feature in second place:

Newman, Mt

If the name does not include a reference to the type of feature, it is followed by a description, which is usually shortened to one, two or three letters. These abbreviations are keyed below.

Legges Tor *mtn*

Town names are followed by a description only when the name may be confused with that of a physical feature:

Mount Barker *town*

To help to distinguish the different parts of each entry, different styles of type are used:

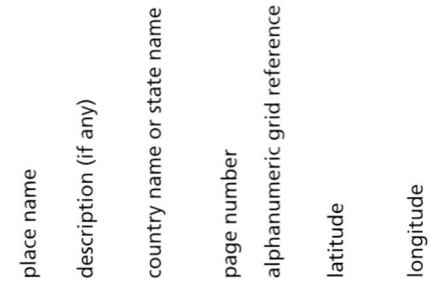

Mitchell *r.* Victoria 56 D2 37.50S 147.36E

To use the **alphanumeric grid reference** to find a feature on the map, first find the correct page and then look at the white letters printed in the blue frame along the top and bottom of the map and the white numbers printed in the blue frame at the sides of the map. When you have found the correct letter and number, follow the grid boxes up or down, and along, until you find the grid box specified by the alphanumeric grid reference. You must then search the grid box until you find the name of the feature.

The **latitude and longitude reference** gives a more exact description of the position of the feature.

Page 6 of the atlas describes lines of latitude and lines of longitude, and explains how they are numbered and divided into degrees and minutes. Each name in the index has a different latitude and longitude reference, so the feature can be located accurately. The lines of latitude and lines of longitude shown on each map are numbered in degrees. These numbers are printed black along the top, bottom and sides of the map.

The drawing above shows part of the map on page 72 and the lines of latitude and lines of longitude.

The index entry for Savage River is given as follows:

Savage River Tasmania 72 D4 41.30S 145.21E

To locate Savage River, first find latitude 41S and estimate 30 minutes south from 41 degrees to find 41.30S, then find longitude 145E and estimate 21 minutes east from 145 degrees to find 145.21E. The symbol for the town of Savage River is where latitude 41.30S and longitude 145.21E meet.

On maps at a smaller scale than this one, it is not possible to show every line of latitude and longitude. Only every 5 or 10 degrees of latitude and longitude may be shown, and you must estimate the degrees and minutes to find the exact location of a feature.

Abbreviations

Afghan.	Afghanistan	*i.*, **I.**, *is*, **Is**	island, Island, islands, Islands	PNG	Papua New Guinea
Ala.	Alabama	Ill.	Illinois	**Pt**	Point
b., **B.**	bay, Bay	*l.*, **L.**	lake, Lake	*r.*, **R.**	river, River
Bangla.	Bangladesh	La	Louisiana	Rep. of Ire.	Republic of Ireland
Bosnia-Herz.	Bosnia-Herzegovina	Liech.	Liechtenstein	*res. stn*	research station
BVIs	British Virgin Islands	Lux.	Luxembourg	**Resr**	Reservoir
c., **C.**	cape, Cape	Man.	Manitoba	RSA	Republic of South Africa
CAR	Central African Republic	Med. Sea	Mediterranean Sea	Russian Fed.	Russian Federation
Carib. Sea	Caribbean Sea	Miss.	Mississippi	Serb. & Mont.	Serbia and Montenegro
Colo.	Colorado	**Mt**	Mount	**Sd**	Sound
Czech Rep.	Czech Republic	*mtn*, **Mtn**	mountain, Mountain	SC	South Carolina
d.	internal division, e.g. county, state	*mts*, **Mts**	mountains, Mountains	S. Korea	South Korea
		NC	North Carolina	*str.*, **Str.**	strait, Strait
Del.	Delaware	N. Cal.	New Caledonia	Switz.	Switzerland
Dem. Rep. of Congo	Democratic Republic of Congo	Neth.	Netherlands	Tex.	Texas
		Neth. Ant.	Netherlands Antilles	UAE	United Arab Emirates
des.	desert	Nev.	Nevada	UK	United Kingdom
Dom. Rep.	Dominican Republic	Nfld	Newfoundland	USA	United States of America
Equat. Guinea	Equatorial Guinea	N. Korea	North Korea	USVIs	United States Virgin Islands
est.	estuary	N. Mex.	New Mexico	Va	Virginia
f.	physical feature, e.g. valley, plain, geographic district	NY	New York	W. Sahara	Western Sahara
		Oc.	Ocean	W. Va	West Virginia
Fla	Florida	Oreg.	Oregon	Wyo.	Wyoming
g., **G.**	Gulf	*pen.*, **Pen.**	peninsula, Peninsula		
Ga	Georgia	Phil.	Philippines		

A

D

Mazar-e Sharif Afghan. **106 D8** 36.43N 67.07E
Mazatlán Mexico **134 C5** 23.11N 106.25W
Mažeikiai Lithuania **115 L4** 56.18N 22.22E
Mazyr Belarus **115 N3** 52.03N 29.15E
Mbabane Swaziland **123 C2** 26.20S 31.08E
Mbandaka Dem. Rep. of Congo **125 F2** 0.03N 18.28E
M'banza Congo Angola **123 A4** 6.18S 14.16E
Mbarara Uganda **123 C4** 0.36S 30.40E
Mbeya Tanzania **123 C4** 8.54S 33.29E
Mbuji-Mayi Dem. Rep. of Congo **123 B4** 6.10S 23.39E
McKinley, Mt USA **130 C4** 63.00N 151.00W
McMurdo *res. stn* Antarctica **90** 77.51S 166.37E
Mdantsane RSA **123 B1** 32.54S 27.54E
Mead, L. USA **132 D4** 36.10N 114.25W
Meander *r.* Tasmania **72 F4** 41.31S 147.03E
Mecca Saudi Arabia **108 B3** 21.25N 39.47E
Mecheria Algeria **116 C3** 33.33N 0.17W
Meda *r.* Western Australia **68 D5** 17.04S 123.54E
Medan Indonesia **98 B4** 3.35N 98.39E
Medanosa, Punta *c.* Argentina **141 C2** 48.08S 65.55W
Medellín Colombia **135 I2** 6.15N 75.36W
Medenine Tunisia **124 F5** 33.24N 10.25E
Medicine Hat Canada **130 G3** 50.03N 110.41W
Medina Saudi Arabia **108 B3** 24.31N 39.32E
Medvezh'yegorsk Russian Fed. **115 O5** 62.55N 34.29E
Meekatharra Western Australia **68 C3** 26.35S 118.29E
Meerut India **107 F6** 29.00N 77.42E
Meghalaya *d.* India **107 I6** 25.30N 91.00E
Meharry, Mt Western Australia **68 C4** 23.01S 118.42E
Meiktila Myanmar **107 J5** 20.53N 95.54E
Meizhou China **103 L2** 24.20N 116.15E
Mek'elē Ethiopia **108 B2** 13.31N 39.28E
Meknès Morocco **124 D5** 33.53N 5.37W
Mekong *r.* Asia **98 D6** 10.00N 106.20E
Mekong, Mouths of the Vietnam **98 D6** 10.00N 106.20E
Melaka Malaysia **98 C4** 2.11N 102.16E
Melbourne Victoria **56 C2** 37.49S 144.58E
Melilla Spain **124 D5** 35.17N 2.57W
Melitopol' Ukraine **115 O1** 46.51N 35.22E
Melton Victoria **56 C2** 37.43S 144.34E
Melville Canada **130 H3** 50.57N 102.49W
Melville, C. Queensland **60 B4** 14.09S 144.31E
Melville B. Greenland **131 L5** 75.00N 63.00W
Melville B. Northern Territory **76 D4** 12.05S 136.38E
Melville I. Canada **130 G5** 75.30N 110.00W
Melville I. Northern Territory **76 C4** 11.37S 130.55E
Melville Pen. Canada **131 J4** 68.00N 84.00W
Memberamo *r.* Indonesia **99 J3** 1.45S 137.25E
Memphis USA **133 I4** 35.05N 90.00W
Mendawai *r.* Indonesia **98 E3** 3.17S 113.20E
Mende France **116 D5** 44.32N 3.30E
Mendī Ethiopia **108 B1** 9.49N 35.03E
Mendi PNG **88 A2** 6.09S 143.40E
Mendooran New South Wales **52 C3** 31.49S 149.05E
Mendoza Argentina **141 C3** 33.00S 68.52W
Menindee New South Wales **52 A2** 32.22S 142.28E
Menindee L. New South Wales **52 A2** 32.18S 142.20E
Meningie South Australia **64 C2** 35.41S 139.19E
Menongue Angola **123 A3** 14.40S 17.41E
Menorca *i.* Spain **116 D4** 40.00N 4.00E
Mentawai Is Indonesia **98 B3** 2.50S 99.00E
Mentok Indonesia **98 D3** 2.04S 105.12E
Menzel Bourguiba Tunisia **116 E4** 37.10N 9.48E
Merano Italy **116 F6** 46.41N 11.10E
Merauke Indonesia **99 K2** 8.30S 140.22E
Merbein Victoria **56 B3** 34.12S 142.03E
Merced USA **132 B4** 37.17N 120.29W
Mergui Myanmar **107 J3** 12.26N 98.34E
Mergui Archipelago *is* Myanmar **107 J3** 11.30N 98.30E
Mérida Mexico **134 G5** 20.59N 89.39W
Mérida Spain **116 B4** 38.55N 6.20W
Mérida Venezuela **135 J2** 8.24N 71.08W
Mérida, Cordillera de *mts* Venezuela **135 J2** 8.00N 71.30W
Meridian USA **133 I3** 32.21N 88.42W
Merimbula New South Wales **52 C1** 36.51S 149.55E
Meron, Har *mtn* Israel **109 A3** 32.59N 35.25E
Merowe Sudan **108 B2** 18.27N 31.51E
Merredin Western Australia **68 C2** 31.29S 118.14E
Merriwa New South Wales **52 C2** 32.10S 150.19E
Mersey *r.* Tasmania **72 E4** 41.14S 146.25E
Mersey *r.* UK **114 F3** 53.21N 2.56W
Mersin Turkey **117 J4** 36.47N 34.37E
Mertz Glacier Antarctica **91** 67.38S 144.30E
Merzifon Turkey **117 K5** 40.52N 35.28E
Mesolóngion Greece **117 H4** 38.23N 21.23E
Mesopotamia *f.* Iraq **125 I5** 33.30N 44.30E
Messina Italy **117 G4** 38.13N 15.34E
Metkovic Croatia **117 G5** 43.03N 17.38E
Metz France **114 H2** 49.07N 6.11E
Mexicali Mexico **134 A7** 32.26N 115.30W
Mexico C. America **134 D5** 20.00N 100.00W
México *d.* Mexico **134 E4** 19.45N 99.30W
Mexico, G. of N. America **134 F5** 25.00N 90.00W
Mexico City Mexico **134 E4** 19.25N 99.10W
Meymaneh Afghan. **106 C8** 35.56N 64.45E
Mezen Russian Fed. **118 G4** 65.50N 44.20E
Mezen *r.* Russian Fed. **111 H6** 65.50N 44.18E
Mezquital *r.* Mexico **134 C5** 21.58N 105.30W
Miami USA **133 J2** 25.42N 80.18W
Miass Russian Fed. **118 I3** 55.00N 60.00E
Michalovce Slovakia **115 L2** 48.45N 21.55E
Michigan *d.* USA **133 I5** 45.00N 85.00W
Michigan, L. USA **133 I5** 44.00N 87.00W
Michipicoten I. Canada **133 I6** 47.40N 85.50W
Michoacán *d.* Mexico **134 D4** 19.20N 101.00W
Michurinsk Russian Fed. **115 Q3** 52.55N 40.30E
Middlesbrough UK **114 F3** 54.35N 1.14W
Midland USA **132 F3** 32.00N 102.05W
Midway Is Hawaiian Is **80 N9** 28.15N 177.25W
Mikhaylovka Russian Fed. **115 Q2** 50.04N 43.15E
Mikhaylovskiy Russian Fed. **102 D8** 51.41N 79.47E
Mikkeli Finland **115 M5** 61.41N 27.17E
Milan Italy **116 E6** 45.28N 9.16E
Mildura Victoria **56 B3** 34.12S 142.11E
Miles Queensland **60 D1** 26.40S 150.11E
Miles City USA **132 E6** 46.24N 105.48W
Milford Sd/Piopiotahi New Zealand **84 B2** 44.20S 167.40E
Milford Sound *town* New Zealand **84 B2** 44.34S 167.48E
Milikapiti Northern Territory **76 C4** 11.24S 130.41E
Milingimbi Northern Territory **76 C4** 12.05S 134.50E
Milk *r.* USA **132 E6** 47.55N 106.15W
Mille Lacs *l.* USA **133 H6** 46.15N 93.40W
Millennium I. Kiribati **81 Q6** 10.00S 150.30W
Millerovo Russian Fed. **115 Q2** 48.56N 40.23E
Millicent South Australia **64 D1** 37.37S 140.21E
Millmerran Queensland **60 D1** 27.53S 151.18E
Milos *i.* Greece **117 H4** 36.40N 24.26E
Milton New South Wales **52 C2** 35.18S 150.25E
Milton Keynes UK **114 F3** 52.01N 0.44W
Milwaukee USA **133 I5** 43.03N 87.56W
Minatitlán Mexico **134 F4** 17.59N 94.32W
Mindanao *i.* Phil. **99 H5** 7.30N 125.00E
Mindelo Cape Verde **124 B3** 16.54N 25.00W
Mindona L. New South Wales **52 A2** 33.06S 142.02E
Mindoro *i.* Phil. **98 G6** 13.00N 121.00E
Mindoro Str. Pacific Oc. **98 G6** 12.30N 120.10E
Minigwal, L. Western Australia **68 D3** 29.36S 123.13E
Minjilang Northern Territory **76 C4** 11.11S 132.36E
Minlaton South Australia **64 C2** 34.39S 137.34E
Minna Nigeria **124 E2** 9.39N 6.32E
Minneapolis-St Paul USA **133 H5** 45.00N 93.15W
Minnesota *d.* USA **133 H5** 46.00N 95.00W
Minnipa South Australia **64 B2** 32.47S 135.08E
Minot USA **132 F6** 48.16N 101.19W
Minsk Belarus **115 M3** 53.53N 27.34E
Mintabie South Australia **64 B4** 27.19S 133.15E
Miranda de Ebro Spain **116 C5** 42.41N 2.57W
Mirbāţ Oman **108 D2** 17.02N 54.43E
Mirboo North Victoria **56 D1** 38.23S 146.11E
Miri Malaysia **98 E4** 4.28N 114.00E
Miriam Vale Queensland **60 D2** 24.20S 151.35E
Mirim, Lagoa *l.* Brazil **141 D3** 33.10S 53.30W
Mirny *res. stn* Antarctica **90** 66.33S 93.01E
Mirpur Khas Pakistan **106 D6** 25.33N 69.05E
Mirzapur India **107 G6** 25.09N 82.34E
Miskolc Hungary **115 L2** 48.06N 20.48E
Misoöl *i.* Indonesia **99 I3** 1.50S 130.10E
Misratah Libya **124 F5** 32.24N 15.04E
Missinaibi *r.* Canada **131 J3** 50.44N 81.29W
Mississippi *d.* USA **133 I3** 33.00N 90.00W
Mississippi *r.* USA **133 I2** 28.55N 89.05W
Mississippi Delta *f.* USA **133 I2** 29.00N 89.10W
Missoula USA **132 D6** 46.52N 114.00W
Missouri *d.* USA **133 H4** 39.00N 93.00W
Missouri *r.* USA **133 H4** 38.40N 90.20W
Mistassini, L. Canada **131 K3** 50.45N 73.40W
Mistissini Canada **131 K3** 50.13N 73.48W
Mitchell Queensland **60 C1** 26.29S 147.57E
Mitchell *r.* Queensland **60 B3** 15.14S 141.37E
Mitchell USA **132 G5** 43.40N 98.01W
Mitchell *r.* Victoria **56 D2** 37.50S 147.36E
Mitchell, Mt USA **133 J4** 35.57N 82.16W
Mito Japan **104 E3** 36.30N 140.29E
Mittagong New South Wales **52 C2** 34.25S 150.27E
Mittimatalik *see* **Pond Inlet** Canada **131**
Mitumba, Chaine des *mts* Dem. Rep. of Congo **123 B4** 8.00S 28.00E
Miyako Japan **104 E3** 39.40N 141.59E
Miyazaki Japan **104 C2** 31.58N 131.50E
Mizdah Libya **116 F3** 31.26N 12.59E
Mizoram *d.* India **107 I5** 23.40N 92.40E
Mława Poland **115 L3** 53.07N 20.23E
Mmabatho RSA **123 B2** 25.46S 25.37E
Moa I. Queensland **60 B4** 10.10S 142.18E
Moama New South Wales **52 B1** 36.07S 144.44E
Mobile USA **133 I3** 30.40N 88.05W
Mobile B. USA **133 I3** 30.30N 87.50W
Mobridge USA **132 F6** 45.31N 100.25W
Moçambique *town* Mozambique **123 D3** 15.00S 40.55E
Mochudi Botswana **123 B2** 24.26S 26.07E
Modena Italy **116 F5** 44.39N 10.55E
Moe Victoria **56 D1** 38.12S 146.20E
Mogadishu Somalia **125 I2** 2.02N 45.21E
Mohyliv Podil's'kyy Ukraine **115 M2** 48.27N 27.48E
Mokp'o S. Korea **104 B2** 34.50N 126.25E
Molde Norway **114 H5** 62.44N 7.10E
Moldova Europe **115 N1** 46.59N 28.55E
Mole Creek *town* Tasmania **72 E4** 41.33S 146.25E
Molodezhnaya *res. stn* Antarctica **90** 67.40S 45.51E
Molokai *i.* Hawaiian Is **82 I12** 21.09N 157.00W
Molong New South Wales **52 C2** 33.07S 148.51E
Molopo *r.* RSA **123 B2** 28.30S 20.07E
Moluccas *is* Indonesia **83 C4** 2.00S 128.00E
Molucca Sea Pacific Oc. **99 H4** 2.00N 126.30E
Mombasa Kenya **123 C4** 4.04S 39.40E
Monaco Europe **116 E5** 43.40N 7.25E
Mona I. Puerto Rico **135 K4** 18.06N 67.54W
Mona Passage Dom. Rep. **135 K4** 18.10N 68.00W
Monbetsu Japan **104 E4** 44.21N 143.18E
Monclova Mexico **134 D6** 26.55N 101.20W
Moncton Canada **131 L2** 46.06N 64.50W
Monga Dem. Rep. of Congo **125 G2** 4.05N 22.50E
Mongers L. Western Australia **68 C3** 29.27S 116.47E
Mongolia Asia **102 I7** 46.30N 104.00E
Mongu Zambia **123 B3** 15.10S 23.09E
Monroe USA **133 H3** 32.31N 92.06W
Monrovia Liberia **124 C2** 6.20N 10.46W
Montagu *r.* Tasmania **72 C5** 40.46S 144.55E
Montana *d.* USA **132 D6** 47.00N 110.00W
Montauban France **116 D5** 44.01N 1.20E
Monte-Carlo Monaco **116 E5** 43.44N 7.25E
Montego Bay *town* Jamaica **135 I4** 18.27N 77.56W
Montélimar France **116 D5** 44.33N 4.45E
Montemorelos Mexico **134 E6** 25.12N 99.50W
Montenegro *d.* Serb. & Mont. **117 G5** 42.49N 19.24E
Montería Colombia **135 I2** 8.45N 75.54W
Monterrey Mexico **134 D6** 25.40N 100.20W
Montes Claros Brazil **140 E5** 16.45S 43.52W
Montevideo Uruguay **141 D3** 34.55S 56.10W
Montgomery USA **133 I3** 32.22N 86.20W
Montmagny Canada **131 L2** 46.59N 70.33W
Monto Queensland **60 D2** 24.51S 151.10E
Montpelier USA **133 L5** 44.16N 72.34W
Montpellier France **116 D5** 43.36N 3.53E
Montréal Canada **131 K2** 45.30N 73.36W
Montrose USA **132 E4** 38.29N 107.53W
Montserrat *i.* Leeward Is **135 L4** 16.45N 62.14W
Monywa Myanmar **107 I5** 22.07N 95.11E
Monza Italy **116 E6** 45.35N 9.16E
Moomba South Australia **64 D3** 28.02S 140.17E
Moonie *r.* New South Wales/Queensland **60 C1** 29.21S 148.42E
Moonta South Australia **64 C2** 34.04S 137.36E
Moora Western Australia **68 C2** 30.39S 116.00E
Moore, L. Western Australia **68 C3** 29.49S 117.28E
Moorhead USA **132 G6** 46.51N 96.44W
Moornanyah L. New South Wales **52 A2** 33.03S 143.58E
Moose Jaw Canada **130 H3** 50.23N 105.35W
Moosonee Canada **131 J3** 51.18N 80.40W
Mopti Mali **124 D3** 14.29N 4.10W
Mora Sweden **114 J5** 11.04N 14.10E
Moranbah Queensland **60 C2** 21.58S 148.03E
Moray Firth *est.* UK **114 E4** 57.31N 4.11W
Morden Canada **130 I2** 49.15N 98.10W
Moree New South Wales **52 C3** 29.28S 149.52E
Morehead PNG **88 A2** 8.44S 141.39E
Morelia Mexico **134 D4** 19.40N 101.11W
Morelos *d.* Mexico **134 E4** 18.40N 99.00W
Morena, Sierra *mts* Spain **116 C4** 38.10N 5.00W
Moreton I. Queensland **60 D1** 27.10S 153.23E
Morgan South Australia **64 C2** 34.02S 139.39E
Morgan City USA **133 H2** 29.41N 91.13W
Mori Japan **104 E4** 42.07N 140.30E
Morioka Japan **104 E3** 39.43N 141.10E
Mornington I. Queensland **60 A3** 16.34S 139.25E
Morobe PNG **88 B2** 7.46S 147.34E
Morocco Africa **124 D5** 31.00N 5.00W
Moro G. Phil. **99 G5** 6.30N 123.20E
Morogoro Tanzania **123 C4** 6.49S 37.40E
Mörön Mongolia **102 I7** 49.36N 100.08E
Morondava Madagascar **123 D2** 20.17S 44.17E
Moroni Comoros **123 D3** 11.40S 43.19E
Morotai *i.* Indonesia **99 H4** 2.10N 128.30E
Morro, Punta *c.* Chile **141 B4** 27.06S 71.00W
Morrosquillo, G. of Colombia **135 I2** 9.30N 75.50W
Mortlake Victoria **56 B1** 38.05S 142.50E
Moruya New South Wales **52 C2** 35.55S 150.06E
Morwell Victoria **56 D1** 38.14S 146.26E
Moscow Russian Fed. **115 P3** 55.45N 37.38E
Moselle *r.* Germany **114 H2** 50.23N 7.37E
Mosgiel New Zealand **84 D2** 45.52S 170.21E
Moshi Tanzania **123 C4** 3.20S 37.21E
Mosquitos, G. of Panama **135 H2** 9.00N 81.00W
Mosquito Coast *f.* Nicaragua **135 H3** 13.00N 84.00W
Moss Norway **114 I4** 59.26N 10.39E
Mossman Queensland **60 C3** 16.29S 145.26E
Mossoró Brazil **140 F6** 5.10S 37.20W
Moss Vale New South Wales **52 C2** 34.34S 150.23E
Mostaganem Algeria **116 D4** 35.56N 0.05E
Mostar Bosnia-Herz. **117 G5** 43.20N 17.50E
Mosul Iraq **108 C4** 36.18N 43.05E
Motueka New Zealand **84 E4** 41.07S 173.01E
Moulins France **114 G1** 46.34N 3.20E
Moulmein Myanmar **107 J4** 16.20N 97.50E
Moulting Lagoon Tasmania **72 G3** 42.02S 148.11E
Moundou Chad **124 F2** 8.36N 16.02E
Mount Barker *town* South Australia **64 C2** 35.05S 138.53E
Mount Barker *town* Western Australia **68 C2** 34.38S 117.36E
Mount Beauty *town* Victoria **56 D2** 36.41S 147.09E
Mount Gambier *town* South Australia **64 D1** 37.52S 140.48E
Mount Hagen *town* PNG **88 A2** 5.51S 144.14E
Mount Isa *town* Queensland **60 A2** 20.45S 139.29E
Mount Lofty Range *mts* South Australia **64 C2** 35.29S 138.41E
Mount Magnet *town* Western Australia **68 C3** 28.05S 117.48E
Mount Morgan *town* Queensland **60 D2** 23.39S 150.27E
Moura Queensland **60 C2** 24.35S 149.59E
Moyen Atlas *mts* Morocco **116 B3** 33.30N 5.00W
Mozambique Africa **123 C3** 18.00S 35.00E
Mozambique Channel Indian Oc. **123 D3** 16.00S 42.30E
M'Saken Tunisia **116 F4** 35.42N 10.33E
Mtsensk Russian Fed. **115 P3** 53.17N 36.36E
Mtwara Tanzania **123 D3** 10.17S 40.11E
Muar Malaysia **98 C4** 2.01N 102.35E
Muarabungo Indonesia **98 C3** 1.29S 102.06E
Mubrak, Jabal *mtn* Jordan **109 A2** 30.12N 35.28E
Muchinga Mts Zambia **121 G3** 12.00S 31.00E
Mudan *r.* China **104 B5** 45.54N 129.49E
Mudanjiang China **103 N6** 44.36N 129.42E
Mudgee New South Wales **52 C2** 32.37S 149.35E
Mui Ca Mau *c.* Vietnam **98 C5** 8.30N 104.35E
Mukacheve Ukraine **115 L2** 48.27N 22.43E
Mukalla Yemen **108 C2** 14.34N 49.06E
Mulanje, Mt Malawi **123 C3** 15.57S 35.33E
Mulhacén *mtn* Spain **116 C4** 37.04N 3.22W
Mulhouse France **114 H1** 47.45N 7.20E
Muling *r.* China **104 C5** 45.45N 132.13E
Mull *i.* UK **114 E4** 56.27N 5.58W
Mullewa Western Australia **68 C3** 28.31S 115.30E
Mullumbimby New South Wales **52 D3** 28.33S 153.30E
Multan Pakistan **106 E7** 30.10N 71.36E
Mulurulu L. New South Wales **52 A2** 33.16S 143.25E
Mumbai India **106 E4** 18.56N 72.51E
Mumeng PNG **88 B2** 6.59S 146.36E
Muna *i.* Indonesia **99 G2** 5.00S 122.30E
Munger India **107 H6** 25.24N 86.29E
Mungindi New South Wales **52 C3** 28.59S 149.00E
Mungo, L. New South Wales **52 A2** 33.46S 143.11E
Munich Germany **114 I2** 48.08N 11.35E
Münster Germany **114 H2** 51.57N 7.38E
Murallón *mtn* Argentina/Chile **141 B2** 49.48S 73.26W
Murchison Victoria **56 C2** 36.39S 145.15E
Murchison *r.* Western Australia **68 B3** 27.39S 114.09E
Murcia Spain **116 C4** 37.59N 1.08W
Mureş *r.* Romania **115 M1** 46.18N 20.49E
Murgon Queensland **60 D1** 26.15S 151.58E
Murmansk Russian Fed. **118 F4** 68.59N 33.08E
Murom Russian Fed. **115 Q3** 55.34N 42.04E
Muroran Japan **104 E4** 42.21N 140.59E
Murray *r.* South Australia **64 C2** 34.36S 139.55E
Murray, L. PNG **88 A2** 7.03S 141.32E
Murray Bridge *town* South Australia **64 C2** 35.07S 139.17E
Murrumbidgee *r.* New South Wales **52 A2** 34.42S 143.13E
Murrumburrah New South Wales **52 C2** 34.34S 148.25E
Murrurundi New South Wales **52 C3** 31.47S 150.51E
Murtoa Victoria **56 B2** 36.39S 142.30E
Murupara New Zealand **84 G5** 38.28S 176.42E
Mururoa *i.* French Polynesia **81 Q4** 22.00S 140.00W
Murwara India **107 G5** 23.49N 80.28E
Murwillumbah New South Wales **52 D3** 28.20S 153.25E
Murzuq Libya **124 F4** 25.56N 13.57E
Muscat Oman **108 D3** 23.36N 58.35E
Musgrave Ranges *mts* South Australia **64 A4** 26.17S 131.43E
Muskegon USA **133 I5** 43.13N 86.10W
Muskogee USA **133 G4** 35.45N 95.21W
Musoma Tanzania **123 C4** 1.29S 33.48E
Muswellbrook New South Wales **52 C2** 32.17S 150.55E
Mutare Zimbabwe **123 C3** 18.58S 32.38E
Mutis *mtn* Indonesia **99 G2** 9.35S 124.15E
Mutsu Japan **104 E4** 41.16N 141.12E
Mutton Bird I. Lord Howe I. **82 B2** 31.33S 159.08E
Muzaffarpur India **107 H6** 26.07N 85.23E
Mwanza Tanzania **123 C4** 2.30S 32.54E
Mwene-Ditu Dem. Rep. of Congo **123 B4** 7.01S 23.27E
Mweru, L. Zambia/Dem. Rep. of Congo **123 B4** 9.00S 28.40E
Myall L. New South Wales **52 D2** 32.25S 152.20E
Myanmar Asia **107 J5** 21.00N 95.00E
Myingyan Myanmar **107 J5** 21.25N 95.20E
Mykolayiv Ukraine **115 O1** 46.57N 32.02E
Myrtleford Victoria **56 D2** 36.35S 146.44E
Mysore India **106 F3** 12.18N 76.37E
My Tho Vietnam **98 D6** 10.21N 106.21E
Mytishchi Russian Fed. **115 P3** 55.55N 37.46E
Mzuzu Malawi **123 C3** 11.26S 34.02E

N

Naalehu Hawaiian Is **82 J10** 19.04N 155.36W

O

Oakover *r.* Western Australia **68 D4** 20.48S 120.40E
Oamaru New Zealand **84 D2** 45.06S 170.58E
Oates Land *f.* Antarctica **90** 70.13S 157.04E
Oatlands Tasmania **72 F3** 42.18S 147.22E
Oaxaca Mexico **134 E4** 17.05N 96.41W
Oaxaca *d.* Mexico **134 E4** 17.30N 97.00W
Ob *r.* Russian Fed. **118 I4** 66.50N 69.00E
Ob, G. of Russian Fed. **118 J4** 68.30N 74.00E
Oberon New South Wales **52 C2** 33.40S 149.51E
Obi *i.* Indonesia **99 H3** 1.45S 127.30E
Obihiro Japan **104 E4** 42.55N 143.00E
Obninsk Russian Fed. **115 P3** 55.04N 36.38E
Occidental, Cordillera *mts* Chile **140 C5** 20.00S 69.00W
Occidental, Cordillera *mts* Colombia **140 B7** 5.00N 76.15W
Occidental, Cordillera *mts* Peru **140 B5** 14.00S 74.00W
Ocean Falls *town* Canada **130 F3** 52.24N 127.42W
Ocean Grove Victoria **56 C1** 38.17S 144.28E
October Revolution *i.* Russian Fed. **119 L5** 79.30N 96.00E
Odate Japan **104 E4** 40.16N 140.34E
Odense Denmark **114 I3** 55.24N 10.23E
Oder *r.* Germany/Poland **114 K2** 49.54N 18.19E
Odessa Ukraine **115 N1** 46.28N 30.39E
Odessa USA **132 F3** 31.50N 102.23W
Oenpelli Northern Territory **76 C4** 12.20S 133.05E
Offenbach am Main Germany **114 I2** 50.06N 8.46E
Ofu *i.* Amer. Samoa **82 J8** 14.12S 169.47W
Ogaden *f.* Ethiopia **125 I2** 7.50N 45.40E
Ogaki Japan **104 D3** 35.25N 136.36E
Ogasawara-shoto *is* Japan **83 D6** 27.00N 142.10E
Ogbomoso Nigeria **124 E2** 8.05N 4.11E
Ogden USA **132 D5** 41.14N 111.59W
Ogilvie *r.* Canada **130 E4** 66.10N 134.10W
Ogoki *r.* Canada **133 I7** 51.35N 86.00W
O'Higgins, L. Chile **141 B2** 48.53S 73.10W
Ohio USA **133 J5** 40.00N 83.00W
Ohio *r.* USA **133 I4** 37.07N 89.10W
'Ohonua Tonga **82 J4** 21.22S 174.58W
Oil City USA **133 K5** 41.26N 79.30W
Oita Japan **104 C2** 33.15N 131.40E
Ojinaga Mexico **134 D6** 29.35N 104.26W
Ojos del Salado *mtn* Chile/Argentina **141 C4** 27.05S 68.05W
Oka *r.* Russian Fed. **115 Q4** 56.20N 43.59E
Okanogan *r.* USA **132 B6** 47.45N 120.05W
Okavango Delta *f.* Botswana **123 B3** 19.30S 23.00E
Okaya Japan **104 D3** 36.03N 138.00E
Okayama Japan **104 C2** 34.40N 133.54E
Okeechobee, L. USA **133 J2** 27.00N 80.45W
Okefenokee Swamp *f.* USA **133 J3** 30.40N 82.40W
Okha India **106 D5** 22.25N 69.00E
Okha Russian Fed. **119 Q3** 53.35N 142.50E
Okhotsk Russian Fed. **119 Q3** 59.20N 143.15E
Okhotsk, Sea of Russian Fed. **119 Q3** 55.00N 150.00E
Okhtyrka Ukraine **115 O2** 50.19N 34.54E
Okinawa *i.* Japan **103 N3** 26.30N 128.00E
Oki-shoto *is* Japan **104 C3** 36.10N 133.10E
Oklahoma *d.* USA **132 G4** 35.00N 97.00W
Oklahoma City USA **132 G4** 35.28N 97.33W
Oksskolten *mtn* Norway **114 J6** 66.00N 14.24E
Öland *i.* Sweden **115 K4** 56.50N 16.50E
Olbia Italy **116 E5** 40.55N 9.29E
Old Crow Canada **130 E4** 67.34N 139.43W
Olean USA **133 K5** 42.05N 78.26W
Olekminsk Russian Fed. **119 O4** 60.25N 120.00E
Olenek Russian Fed. **119 N4** 68.38N 112.15E
Olenek *r.* Russian Fed. **119 O5** 73.00N 120.00E
Oléron, Île d' *i.* France **114 F1** 45.55N 1.16W
Olga, Mt Northern Territory **76 C1** 25.17S 130.47E
Olomouc Czech Rep. **115 K2** 49.35N 17.16E
Olongapo Phil. **98 G7** 14.52N 120.16E
Olosega *i.* Amer. Samoa **82 J8** 14.12S 169.45W
Olsztyn Poland **115 L3** 53.47N 20.29E
Olympus *mtn* Greece **117 H5** 40.04N 22.20E
Omaha USA **132 G5** 41.15N 96.00W
Oman Asia **108 D2** 20.00N 556.00E
Oman, G. of Asia **108 D3** 25.00N 58.00E
Omdurman Sudan **108 B2** 15.38N 32.28E
Omeo Victoria **56 D2** 37.07S 147.37E
Omolon *r.* Russian Fed. **119 R4** 68.50N 158.30E
Omono *r.* Japan **104 E3** 39.44N 140.05E
Omsk Russian Fed. **118 J3** 55.00N 73.22E
Ondjiva Angola **123 A3** 17.03S 15.41E
Onega, G. of Russian Fed. **115 P6** 64.30N 36.30E
Onega, L. Russian Fed. **115 O5** 61.38N 35.32E
Ongjin N. Korea **104 B3** 37.56N 125.21E
Ongole India **107 G4** 15.31N 80.04E
Onitsha Nigeria **124 E2** 6.10N 6.47E
Ono-i-Lau *i.* Fiji **80 N4** 19.00S 178.30W
Onslow Western Australia **68 C4** 21.39S 115.11E
Ontario *d.* Canada **131 J3** 52.00N 86.00W
Ontario, L. N. America **133 K5** 43.40N 78.00W
Oodnadatta South Australia **64 B4** 27.35S 135.27E
Oombulgurri Western Australia **68 E5** 15.15S 127.49E
Oostende Belgium **114 G2** 51.13N 2.55E
Opole Poland **115 K2** 50.40N 17.56E
Oporto Portugal **116 B5** 41.09N 8.37W
Opotiki New Zealand **84 G5** 38.01S 177.17E
Oradea Romania **115 L1** 47.04N 21.57E
Oran Algeria **124 D5** 35.45N 0.38W
Orange New South Wales **52 C2** 33.19S 149.07E
Orange *r.* RSA **123 A2** 28.43S 16.30E
Orange, Cabo *c.* Brazil **140 D7** 4.25N 51.32W
Orangeburg USA **133 J3** 33.28N 80.53W
Orbost Victoria **56 E2** 37.42S 148.30E
Orchila *i.* Venezuela **135 K3** 11.52N 66.10W
Ord *r.* Western Australia **68 E5** 15.24S 128.18E
Ord, Mt Western Australia **68 E5** 17.19S 125.29E
Ordu Turkey **117 K5** 41.00N 37.52E
Örebro Sweden **114 J4** 59.16N 15.14E
Oregon *d.* USA **132 B5** 44.00N 120.00W
Orekhovo-Zuyevo Russian Fed. **115 P3** 55.48N 38.58E
Orel Russian Fed. **115 P3** 52.58N 36.05E
Ore Mts Czech Rep./Germany **114 J2** 50.33N 13.07E
Orenburg Russian Fed. **118 H3** 51.50N 55.00E
Orford Tasmania **72 F3** 42.34S 147.52E
Oriental, Cordillera *mts* Colombia **140 B7** 5.00N 74.30W
Oriental, Cordillera *mts* Peru/Bolivia **140 B5** 14.00S 70.00W
Orissa *d.* India **107 G5** 20.15N 84.00E
Oristano Italy **116 E4** 39.53N 6.36E
Orizaba Mexico **134 E4** 18.51N 97.08W
Orkney *is* UK **114 F4** 59.06N 3.20W
Orlando USA **133 J2** 28.33N 81.21W
Orléans France **114 G1** 47.55N 1.54E
Ormoc Phil. **99 G6** 11.01N 124.36E
Örnsköldsvik Sweden **115 K5** 63.18N 18.43E
Orroroo South Australia **64 C2** 32.44S 138.38E
Orsha Belarus **115 N3** 54.30N 30.26E
Orsk Russian Fed. **118 H3** 51.13N 58.35E
Oruro Bolivia **140 C5** 18.05S 67.00W
Osaka Japan **104 D2** 34.40N 135.30E
Osa Pen. Costa Rica **135 H2** 8.20N 83.30W
Oshakati Namibia **123 A3** 17.47S 15.30E
Oshawa Canada **131 K2** 43.53N 78.51W
Osijek Croatia **117 G6** 45.33N 18.41E
Osizweni RSA **123 C2** 27.45S 30.11E
Ösjön *l.* Sweden **114 J5** 63.51N 15.40E
Oskarshamn Sweden **115 K4** 57.16N 16.26E
Oskol *r.* Russian Fed. **115 P2** 49.59N 37.57E
Oslo Norway **114 I4** 59.55N 10.46E
Oslofjorden *est.* Norway **114 I4** 59.12N 10.39E
Osnabrück Germany **114 I3** 52.17N 8.04E
Osorno Chile **141 B2** 40.35S 73.14W
Osprey Reef Queensland **60 C4** 13.57S 146.39E
Ossa, Mt Tasmania **72 E4** 41.52S 146.01E
Österdal *r.* Sweden **114 J5** 61.40N 13.15E
Østerdalen *f.* Norway **114 I5** 62.05N 11.00E
Östersund Sweden **114 J5** 63.11N 14.39E
Ostrava Czech Rep. **115 K2** 49.51N 18.17E
Osumi-kaikyo *str.* Japan **104 C2** 31.30N 131.00E
Otago Pen. New Zealand **84 D2** 45.49S 170.44E
Otaki New Zealand **84 F4** 40.46S 175.08E
Otaru Japan **104 E4** 43.14N 140.59E
Otjiwarongo Namibia **123 A2** 20.30S 16.39E
Ottawa Canada **131 K2** 45.25N 75.43W
Ottawa *r.* Canada **131 K2** 45.23N 73.55W
Ottawa Is Canada **131 J3** 59.50N 80.00W
Oturkpo Nigeria **124 E2** 7.16N 8.16E
Otu Tolu Group *is* Tonga **82 G5** 20.20S 174.30W
Otway, C. Victoria **56 B1** 38.51S 143.33E
Otway Ranges *mts* Victoria **56 B1** 38.40S 143.32E
Ouachita *r.* USA **133 H3** 31.52N 91.48W
Ouachita Mts USA **133 H3** 34.40N 94.30W
Ouagadougou Burkina **124 D3** 12.20N 1.40W
Ouargla Algeria **124 E5** 32.00N 5.16E
Ouarzazate Morocco **124 D5** 30.57N 6.50W
Ouésso Congo **124 F2** 1.38N 16.03E
Ouezzane Morocco **116 B3** 34.52N 5.35W
Oujda Morocco **124 D5** 34.41N 1.45W
Oulu Finland **115 M6** 65.01N 25.30E
Oulujärvi *l.* Finland **115 M6** 64.17N 27.15E
Ourense Spain **116 B5** 42.20N 7.52W
Ouse *r.* Tasmania **72 E3** 42.31S 146.43E
Outer Hebrides *is* UK **114 E4** 57.53N 7.21W
Ouvéa *i.* N. Cal. **82 C5** 20.30S 166.34E
Ouyen Victoria **56 B3** 35.06S 142.22E
Ovalau *i.* Fiji **82 G2** 17.42S 178.50E
Ovamboland *f.* Namibia **123 A3** 17.45S 17.00E
Oviedo Spain **116 B5** 43.21N 5.50W
Owando Congo **124 F1** 0.30S 15.48E
Owensboro USA **133 I4** 37.46N 87.07W
Owen Sound *town* Canada **131 J2** 44.34N 80.56W
Owen Stanley Range *mts* PNG **88 B2** 8.59S 147.57E
Oxford UK **114 F2** 51.45N 1.15W
Oxnard USA **132 C3** 34.12N 119.11W
Oyama Japan **104 D3** 36.18N 139.48E
Ozark Plateau USA **133 H4** 36.00N 93.35W

P

Paamiut Greenland **131 N4** 62.05N 49.30W
Pachuca Mexico **134 E5** 20.10N 98.44W
Pacific Oc. **80-1**
Padang Indonesia **98 C3** 0.55S 100.21E
Padangpanjang Indonesia **98 C3** 0.30S 100.26E
Padre I. USA **132 G2** 27.00N 97.20W
Padthaway South Australia **64 D1** 36.38S 140.27E
Padua Italy **116 F6** 45.27N 11.52E
Paekdu San N. Korea **104 B4** 42.03N 128.13E
Paeroa New Zealand **84 F6** 37.23S 175.40E
Pagadian Phil. **99 G5** 7.50N 123.30E
Pagan *i.* N. Mariana Is **83 E6** 18.08N 145.46E
Paget, Mt South Georgia **141 F1** 54.23S 36.45W
Pago Pago Amer. Samoa **82 I8** 14.16S 170.43W
Paihai New Zealand **84 F7** 35.16S 174.05E
Pakanbaru Indonesia **98 C4** 0.34N 101.30E
Pakenham Victoria **56 C1** 38.04S 145.31E
Pakistan Asia **106 D6** 30.00N 70.00E
Pakokku Myanmar **107 J5** 21.20N 95.10E
Pakxé Laos **98 D7** 15.05N 105.50E
Palana Russian Fed. **119 R3** 59.05N 159.59E
Palana Tasmania **72 F6** 39.45S 147.54E
Palangkaraya Indonesia **98 E3** 2.18S 113.55E
Palau Pacific Oc. **99 I5** 7.00N 134.25E
Palawan *i.* Phil. **98 F5** 9.30N 118.30E
Palembang Indonesia **98 C3** 2.59S 104.50E
Palencia Spain **116 C5** 42.01N 4.34W
Palermo Italy **116 F4** 38.09N 13.22E
Palestine *f.* Asia **109 A2** 31.40N 35.10E
Pali India **106 E6** 25.46N 73.20E
Palikir Fed. States of Micronesia **83 E5** 6.56N 158.10E
Palk Str. India/Sri Lanka **107 F2** 10.00N 79.40E
Palliser, C. New Zealand **84 F4** 41.37S 175.16E
Palma de Mallorca Spain **116 D4** 39.36N 2.39E
Palmas, C. Liberia **124 D2** 4.30N 7.55W
Palmer *r.* Northern Territory **76 C2** 24.46S 133.22E
Palmer *res. stn* Antarctica **90** 64.46S 64.05W
Palmer Land *f.* Antarctica **90** 69.37S 66.18W
Palmerston I. Cook Is **80 O5** 18.04S 163.10W
Palmerston North New Zealand **84 F4** 40.22S 175.37E
Palmira Colombia **140 B7** 3.33N 76.17W
Palm Island *town* Queensland **60 C3** 18.42S 146.33E
Palmyra Syria **108 B4** 34.34N 38.17E
Palmyra I. Pacific Oc. **80 O7** 5.52N 162.05W
Palopo Indonesia **98 G3** 3.01S 120.12E
Palu Indonesia **98 F3** 0.54S 119.52E
Pamirs *mts* Tajikistan **102 C5** 37.50N 73.30E
Pampa USA **132 F4** 35.32N 100.58W
Pampas *f.* Argentina **141 C3** 35.00S 63.00W
Pamplona Spain **116 C5** 42.29N 1.39W
Panaji India **106 E4** 15.29N 73.50E
Panama C. America **135 H2** 9.00N 80.00W
Panamá, G. of Panama **135 I2** 8.30N 79.00W
Panama Canal Panama **135 I2** 9.21N 79.54W
Panama City Panama **135 I2** 8.57N 79.30W
Panama City USA **133 I3** 30.10N 85.41W
Panay *i.* Phil. **99 G6** 11.10N 122.30E
Panevėžys Lithuania **115 M3** 55.44N 24.23E
Pangai Tonga **82 G5** 19.50S 174.23W
Pangkalanbuun Indonesia **98 E3** 2.43S 111.38E
Pangkalpinang Indonesia **98 D3** 2.05S 106.09E
Pangnirtung Canada **131 L4** 66.05N 65.45W
Pannawonica Western Australia **68 C4** 21.42S 116.17E
Pantelleria *i.* Italy **116 F4** 36.48N 12.00E
Panton *r.* Western Australia **68 E5** 17.52S 128.12E
Pantoowarinna, L. South Australia **64 C4** 27.23S 137.37E
Papua, G. of PNG **88 A2** 8.30S 145.00E
Papua New Guinea Pacific Oc. **88 B2** 6.05S 146.34E
Papunya Northern Territory **76 C2** 23.16S 131.54E
Paraburdoo Western Australia **68 C4** 23.18S 117.40E
Paracel Is S. China Sea **98 E7** 16.20N 112.00E
Paraguay *r.* Argentina **141 D4** 27.30S 58.50W
Paraguay S. America **141 D4** 23.00S 58.00W
Paraíba *r.* Brazil **141 E4** 21.45S 41.10W
Parakow Benin **124 E2** 9.23N 2.40E
Paramaribo Suriname **140 D7** 5.52N 55.14W
Paraná Argentina **141 C3** 31.45S 60.30W
Paraná *r.* Argentina **141 D3** 34.00S 58.30W
Paraná *r.* Brazil **141 D4** 12.30S 48.10W
Paranaíba *r.* Brazil **140 D5** 20.00S 51.00W
Paranapanema *r.* Brazil **141 D4** 22.30S 53.03W
Pardo *r.* Brazil **141 D4** 21.56S 52.07W
Pardubice Czech Rep. **114 J2** 50.03N 15.47E
Parecis, Serra dos *mts* Brazil **140 C5** 13.30S 60.00W
Parepare Indonesia **98 F3** 4.03S 119.40E
Paria Pen. Venezuela **135 L3** 10.45N 62.30W
Paris France **114 G2** 48.52N 2.21E
Parkes New South Wales **52 C2** 33.09S 148.10E
Parma Italy **116 F5** 44.48N 10.18E
Parnaíba Brazil **140 E6** 2.58S 41.46W
Parnaíba *r.* Brazil **140 E6** 3.00S 42.00W
Pärnu Estonia **115 M4** 58.23N 24.30E
Paroo *r.* New South Wales **52 A3** 30.27S 143.59E
Paros *i.* Greece **117 I4** 34.04N 25.11E
Parramatta New South Wales **52 C2** 33.49S 150.58E
Parry, C. Canada **130 F5** 70.10N 124.33W
Parry, C. Greenland **131 K5** 76.50N 71.00W
Parry Is Canada **130 H5** 76.00N 106.00W
Pasadena USA **132 C3** 34.10N 118.09W
Pasig Phil. **98 G6** 14.30N 120.54E
Passau Germany **114 J2** 48.34N 13.25E
Pasto Colombia **140 B7** 1.12N 77.17W
Patagonia *f.* Argentina **141 C2** 45.00S 68.00W
Paterson USA **133 L5** 40.55N 74.10W
Pathfinder Resr USA **132 E5** 42.25N 106.55W
Patna India **107 H6** 25.37N 85.12E
Patos, Lagoa dos *l.* Brazil **141 D3** 31.00S 51.10W
Patos de Minas Brazil **140 E5** 18.35S 46.32W
Patras Greece **117 H4** 38.15N 21.45E
Pau France **116 C5** 43.18N 0.22W
Paulo Afonso Brazil **140 F6** 9.25S 38.15W
Pavia Italy **116 E6** 45.10N 9.10E
Pavlodar Kazakhstan **118 J3** 52.21N 76.59E
Pavlohrad Ukraine **115 O2** 48.31N 35.53E
Pavlovskaya Russian Fed. **117 K6** 46.18N 39.48E
Peace *r.* Canada **130 G3** 59.00N 111.26W
Peace River *town* Canada **130 G3** 56.15N 117.18W
Peak Hill *town* New South Wales **52 C2** 32.47S 148.11E
Peale, Mt USA **132 E4** 38.26N 109.14W
Pearl *r.* USA **133 I3** 30.15N 89.25W
Pearl Harbor Hawaiian Is **82 H12** 21.22N 158.00W
Peć Serb. & Mont. **117 H5** 42.40N 20.17E
Pechora *r.* Russian Fed. **118 H4** 68.10N 54.00E
Pechora G. Russian Fed. **118 H4** 69.00N 56.00E
Pecos USA **132 F3** 31.25N 103.30W
Pecos *r.* USA **132 F2** 29.45N 101.25W
Pécs Hungary **117 G6** 46.05N 18.14E
Pedder, L. Tasmania **72 E3** 42.55S 146.08E
Pedro Juan Caballero Paraguay **141 D4** 22.30S 55.44W
Peel *r.* Canada **130 E4** 68.13N 135.00W
Peera Peera Poolanna L. South Australia **64 C4** 26.50S 138.07E
Pegasus B. New Zealand **84 E3** 43.20S 172.49E
Pegu Myanmar **107 J4** 17.18N 96.31E
Peipus, L. Estonia/Russian Fed. **115 M4** 58.38N 27.28E
Pekalongan Indonesia **98 D2** 6.54S 109.37E
Peleng *i.* Indonesia **99 G3** 1.30S 123.10E
Pelleluhu Is PNG **99 K3** 1.09S 144.23E
Pelotas Brazil **141 D3** 31.45S 52.20W
Pemba Mozambique **123 D3** 13.02S 40.30E
Pemba I. Tanzania **123 C4** 5.10S 39.45E
Pemberton Western Australia **68 C2** 34.28S 115.59E
Peña Nevada, Cerro *mtn* Mexico **134 E5** 23.49N 99.51W
Penas, Golfo de *g.* Chile **141 B2** 47.20S 75.00W
Penguin Tasmania **72 E4** 41.06S 146.04E
Pennsylvania *d.* USA **133 K5** 41.00N 78.00W
Penny Icecap *f.* Canada **131 L4** 67.10N 66.50W
Penola South Australia **64 D1** 37.23S 140.50E
Penong South Australia **64 B3** 31.55S 133.03E
Penrith New South Wales **52 C2** 33.47S 150.51E
Pensacola USA **133 I3** 30.30N 87.12W
Pensacola Mts Antarctica **91** 85.24S 73.42W
Penshurst Victoria **56 B2** 37.52S 142.19E
Pentecost I. Vanuatu **82 D8** 15.48S 168.10E
Penza Russian Fed. **115 R3** 53.12N 45.01E
Penzance UK **114 E2** 50.07N 5.33W
Penzhina, G. of Russian Fed. **119 S4** 61.00N 163.00E
Peoria USA **133 I5** 40.43N 89.38W
Percival Lakes Western Australia **68 D4** 21.19S 124.55E
Pereira Colombia **140 B7** 4.47N 75.46W
Pereyaslav-Khmel'nyts'kyy Ukraine **115 N2** 50.04N 31.28E
Pérgueux France **116 D6** 45.12N 0.44E
Perija, Sierra de *mts* Venezuela **135 J2** 9.00N 73.00W
Peri L. New South Wales **52 A3** 30.45S 143.36E
Perito Moreno Argentina **141 B2** 46.35S 71.00W
Perkins B. Tasmania **72 D5** 40.45S 145.10E
Perlas Pt Nicaragua **135 H3** 12.23N 83.30W
Perm Russian Fed. **118 H3** 58.01N 56.10E
Pernik Bulgaria **117 H5** 42.35N 23.03E
Perpendicular, Pt New South Wales **52 C2** 35.03S 150.51E
Perpignan France **116 D5** 42.42N 2.54E
Perth Tasmania **72 F4** 41.34S 147.11E
Perth UK **114 F4** 56.24N 3.26W
Perth Western Australia **68 C2** 31.56S 115.47E
Peru S. America **140 B5** 10.00S 75.00W
Perugia Italy **116 F5** 43.06N 12.24E
Pervomays'k Ukraine **115 N2** 48.03N 30.51E
Pescara Italy **117 F5** 42.27N 14.13E
Peshawar Pakistan **106 E7** 34.01N 71.40E
Petah Tiqwa Israel **109 A3** 32.05N 34.53E
Peterborough Canada **131 K2** 44.18N 78.19W
Peterborough South Australia **64 C2** 32.59S 138.50E
Peterborough UK **114 F3** 52.34N 0.14W
Petermann Ranges *mts* Northern Territory **76 B1** 25.18S 129.44E
Petersville USA **130 C4** 62.30N 150.48W
Petrolina Brazil **140 E6** 9.22S 40.30W
Petropavlovsk Kazakhstan **118 I3** 54.53N 69.13E
Petropavlovsk-Kamchatskiy Russian Fed. **119 R3** 53.03N 158.43E
Petrozavodsk Russian Fed. **115 O5** 61.48N 34.19E
Pforzheim Germany **114 I2** 48.53N 8.42E
Phan Thiêt Vietnam **98 D6** 10.56N 108.06E
Phatthalung Thailand **98 C5** 7.38N 100.05E
Phayao Thailand **98 B7** 19.10N 99.55E
Phet Buri Thailand **98 B6** 13.01N 99.55E
Philadelphia USA **133 K5** 39.55N 75.10W
Philip I. Pacific Oc. **82 D1** 29.13S 167.58E
Philippines Asia **99 G6** 13.00N 123.00E
Philippine Trench *f.* Pacific Oc. **144 F4**
Phillip I. Victoria **56 C1** 38.30S 145.14E
Phillip Pt Lord Howe I. **82 A2** 31.32S 159.03E

Q

R

Temuka New Zealand 84 D2 44.15S 171.17E
Tenasserim Myanmar 107 J3 12.05N 99.00E
Ten Degree Channel Indian Oc. 107 I2 10.00N 92.30E
Tendo Japan 104 E3 38.22N 140.22E
Tengiz, L. Kazakhstan 118 I3 50.30N 69.00E
Tennant Creek *town* Northern Territory 76 C3 19.32S 134.16E
Tennessee *d.* USA 133 I4 36.00N 86.00W
Tennessee *r.* USA 133 I4 37.10N 88.25W
Tenryu *r.* Japan 104 D2 34.42N 137.44E
Tenterfield New South Wales 52 D3 29.03S 152.02E
Teófilo Otôni Brazil 140 E5 17.52S 41.31W
Tepic Mexico 134 D5 21.30N 104.51W
Te Puke New Zealand 84 G6 37.47S 176.19E
Teraina *i.* Kiribati 81 O7 4.30N 160.02W
Terang Victoria 56 B1 38.16S 142.57E
Teresina Brazil 140 E6 4.50S 42.50W
Términos Lagoon Mexico 134 F4 18.30N 91.30W
Ternate Indonesia 99 H4 0.48N 127.23E
Terni Italy 116 F5 42.34N 12.44E
Ternopil' Ukraine 115 M2 49.33N 25.36E
Terrace Canada 130 F3 54.31N 128.32W
Terre Adélie *f.* Antarctica 90 69.21S 139.02E
Terre Haute USA 133 I4 39.27N 87.24W
Teslin Canada 130 E4 60.10N 132.42W
Tetas, Punta *c.* Chile 141 B4 23.32S 70.39W
Tete Mozambique 123 C3 16.10S 33.30E
Tétouan Morocco 124 D5 35.34N 5.22W
Texarkana USA 133 H3 33.28N 94.02W
Texas Queensland 60 D1 28.50S 151.12E
Texas *d.* USA 132 G3 32.00N 100.00W
Texoma, L. USA 132 G3 34.00N 96.40W
Tezpur India 107 I6 26.38N 92.49E
Thai Binh Vietnam 98 D8 20.27N 106.20E
Thailand Asia 98 C7 16.00N 101.00E
Thailand, G. of Asia 98 C6 11.00N 101.00E
Thai Nguyên Vietnam 98 D8 21.31N 105.55E
Thames New Zealand 84 F6 37.09S 175.33E
Thames *r.* UK 114 G2 51.27N 0.21E
Thanh Hoa Vietnam 98 D7 19.50N 105.48E
Thar Desert India 106 E6 28.00N 72.00E
Thargomindah Queensland 60 B1 27.59S 143.49E
Thasos *i.* Greece 117 H5 40.40N 24.39E
Thaton Myanmar 107 J4 16.56N 97.20E
The Coorong *inlet* South Australia 64 C2 35.52S 139.24E
The Entrance New South Wales 52 C2 33.21S 151.28E
The Everglades *f.* USA 133 J2 26.00N 80.30W
The Great Oasis Egypt 108 B3 24.30N 30.40E
The Grenadines *is* Windward Is 135 L3 12.35N 61.20W
The Gulf Asia 108 D3 27.00N 50.00E
The Hague Neth. 114 H3 52.04N 4.18E
Thelon *r.* Canada 130 I4 64.23N 96.15W
The Minch *str.* UK 114 E4 58.02N 5.50W
Theodore Queensland 60 D2 24.59S 150.08E
Theodore Roosevelt *r.* Brazil 140 C6 7.33S 60.24W
The Pas Canada 130 H3 53.50N 101.15W
The Pennines *hills* UK 114 F3 54.23N 2.18W
The Rock New South Wales 52 B2 35.18S 147.07E
The Salt L. New South Wales 52 A3 30.05S 142.08E
The Snares *is* New Zealand 80 L2 48.00S 166.30E
Thessaloniki Greece 117 H5 40.38N 22.56E
The Wash *b.* UK 114 G3 52.55N 0.11E
Thiès Senegal 124 C3 14.48N 16.56W
Thimbu Bhutan 107 H6 27.29N 89.40E
Thionville France 114 H2 49.22N 6.10E
Thira *i.* Greece 117 I4 36.24N 25.27E
Thiruvananthapuram India 106 F2 8.41N 76.57E
Thistle I. South Australia 64 C2 34.59S 136.07E
Thompson Canada 130 I3 55.45N 97.54W
Thomson *r.* Queensland 60 B1 25.11S 142.54E
Thredbo New South Wales 52 C1 36.30S 148.21E
Three Hummock I. Tasmania 72 C5 40.28S 144.55E
Three Kings Is New Zealand 84 E7 34.11S 172.05E
Thule *see* Qaanaaq Greenland 131
Thunder Bay *town* Canada 131 J2 48.25N 89.14W
Thuringian Forest *mts* Germany 114 I2 50.52N 10.50E
Thursday Island *town* Queensland 60 B4 10.33S 142.14E
Thursday I. Queensland 60 B4 10.34S 142.13E
Thurso UK 114 F4 58.36N 3.31W
Thwaites Iceberg Tongue Antarctica 91 75.11S 106.38W
Tianjin China 103 L5 39.08N 117.12E
Tianshui China 103 J4 34.25N 105.58E
Tiaret Algeria 116 D4 35.28N 1.21E
Tibati Cameroon 124 F2 6.25N 12.33E
Tiberias Israel 109 A3 32.46N 35.33E
Tiberias, L. Israel 109 A3 32.49N 35.37E
Tibesti *mts* Chad 125 F4 21.00N 17.30E
Tibet *d.* China 102 F4 31.26N 88.11E
Tibetan Plateau *f.* China 102 F4 34.00N 86.15E
Tibooburra New South Wales 52 A3 29.27S 142.02E
Tiburón *i.* Mexico 134 B6 29.00N 112.25W
Tidjikja Mauritania 124 C3 18.29N 11.31W
Tien Shan *mts* Asia 102 D6 42.00N 80.30E
Tierra del Fuego *i.* S. America 141 C1 54.00S 68.30W
Tighina Moldova 115 N1 46.49N 29.29E
Tigre *r.* Venezuela 135 L2 9.20N 62.30W
Tigris *r.* Iraq/Syria 108 C4 30.59N 47.25E
Tihāmah *f.* Saudi Arabia 108 C2 19.18N 42.30E
Tijuana Mexico 134 A7 32.29N 117.10W
Tikhoretsk Russian Fed. 115 Q1 45.52N 40.06E
Tikhvin Russian Fed. 115 O4 59.39N 33.32E
Tiksi Russian Fed. 119 O5 71.40N 128.45E
Tilburg Neth. 114 H2 51.33N 5.05E
Tillabéri Niger 124 E3 14.28N 1.27E
Timaru New Zealand 84 D2 44.24S 171.14E
Timashevsk Russian Fed. 115 P1 45.37N 38.56E
Timber Creek *town* Northern Territory 76 C3 15.35S 130.27E
Timboon Victoria 56 B1 38.31S 142.59E
Timişoara Romania 117 H6 45.47N 21.15E
Timmins Canada 131 J2 48.30N 81.20W
Timon Brazil 140 E6 5.08S 42.52W
Timor *i.* East Timor/Indonesia 99 H2 9.30S 125.00E
Timor Sea Australia/Indonesia 11 B4 13.00S 122.00E
Tindouf Algeria 124 D4 27.42N 8.10W
Tingha New South Wales 52 C3 29.57S 151.15E
Tinian *i.* N. Mariana Is 83 E5 14.58N 145.38E
Tinos *i.* Greece 117 H4 37.36N 25.08E
Tiranë Albania 117 G5 41.20N 19.48E
Tiraspol Moldova 115 N1 46.51N 29.37E
Tiruchchirappalli India 107 F3 10.50N 78.43E
Tiruppur India 106 F3 11.05N 77.20E
Tisza *r.* Hungary 115 L1 46.09N 20.04E
Titicaca, L. Bolivia/Peru 140 C5 16.00S 69.00W
Titiea *see* Aspiring, Mt/Titiea New Zealand 84
Titovo Užice Serb. & Mont. 117 G5 43.52N 19.51E
Ti Tree *town* Northern Territory 76 C2 22.08S 133.24E
Tizi Ouzou Algeria 116 D4 36.44N 4.05E
Tiznit Morocco 124 D4 29.43N 9.44W
Tlaxcala Mexico 134 E4 19.20N 98.12W
Tlaxcala *d.* Mexico 134 E4 19.45N 98.20W
Tlemcen Algeria 124 D5 34.53N 1.21W
Toamasina Madagascar 123 D3 18.10S 49.23E
Toba, L. Indonesia 98 B4 2.45N 98.50E
Tobago *i.* S. America 135 L3 11.15N 60.40W
Tobelo Indonesia 99 H4 1.45N 127.59E
Toboali Indonesia 98 D3 3.00S 106.30E
Tobol *r.* Russian Fed. 118 I3 58.15N 68.12E
Tobol'sk Russian Fed. 118 I3 58.15N 68.12E
Tocantins *r.* Brazil 140 E6 2.40S 49.20W
Tocumwal New South Wales 52 B2 35.51S 145.35E
Tofua *i.* Tonga 82 G5 19.45S 175.05W
Togian Is Indonesia 99 G3 0.20S 122.00E
Togo Africa 124 E2 8.30N 1.00E
Tok USA 130 D4 63.20N 143.10W
Tokara-retto *is* Japan 104 B1 29.30N 129.00E
Tokelau *i.* Pacific Oc. 80 N6 9.00S 171.45W
Tokmak Ukraine 115 O1 47.15N 35.44E
Tokoroa New Zealand 84 F5 38.14S 175.52E
Tok-to *i.* Sea of Japan 104 C3 37.13N 131.54E
Tokushima Japan 104 C2 34.03N 134.34E
Tokyo Japan 104 D3 35.40N 139.45E
Tôlañaro Madagascar 123 D2 25.01S 47.00E
Toledo Spain 116 C4 39.52N 4.02W
Toledo USA 133 J5 41.40N 83.35W
Toliara Madagascar 123 D2 23.20S 43.41E
Tolitoli Indonesia 98 G4 1.05N 120.50E
Tolsan-do *i.* S. Korea 104 B2 34.35N 127.48E
Toluca Mexico 134 E4 19.20N 99.40W
Tol'yatti Russian Fed. 118 G3 53.32N 49.24E
Tomakomai Japan 104 E4 42.39N 141.33E
Tombigbee *r.* USA 133 I3 31.05N 87.55W
Tombouctou Mali 124 D3 16.49N 2.59W
Tomini G. Indonesia 98 G3 0.30S 120.45E
Tom Price Western Australia 68 C4 22.43S 117.50E
Tomsk Russian Fed. 118 K3 56.30N 85.05E
Tona, G. of Russian Fed. 119 P5 72.00N 136.10E
Tondano Indonesia 99 G4 1.19N 124.56E
Tonga Pacific Oc. 82 G5 20.00S 174.30W
Tongala Victoria 56 C2 36.15S 144.58E
Tongareva Cook Is 81 P6 9.00S 158.00W
Tongatapu *i.* Tonga 82 J4 21.10S 175.10W
Tongatapu Group *is* Tonga 82 F4 21.10S 175.10W
Tonghua China 103 N6 41.40N 126.52E
Tongking, G. of Asia 98 D8 20.00N 107.50E
Tongliao China 103 M6 43.37N 122.15E
Tongling China 103 L4 30.57N 117.40E
Tônlé Sab *l.* Cambodia 98 C6 12.50N 104.00E
Tooms L. Tasmania 72 F3 42.13S 147.48E
Toora Victoria 56 D1 38.40S 146.21E
Toowoomba Queensland 60 D1 27.33S 151.58E
Topeka USA 133 G4 39.03N 95.41W
Topozero, Ozero *l.* Russian Fed. 115 O6 65.42N 32.00E
Tori-shima *i.* Japan 83 D6 30.28N 140.18E
Toronto Canada 131 K2 43.42N 79.25W
Torquay UK 114 F2 50.28N 3.31W
Torquay Victoria 56 C1 38.22S 144.17E
Torrens, L. South Australia 64 C3 30.58S 137.52E
Torrens Creek *r.* Queensland 60 C2 22.22S 145.10E
Torreón Mexico 134 D6 25.34N 103.25W
Torres Is Vanuatu 82 C9 13.40S 166.33E
Torres Str. Queensland 60 B5 9.50S 142.11E
Tórshavn Faeroes 114 E5 62.02N 6.47W
Tortosa Spain 116 D5 40.49N 0.31E
Torzhok Russian Fed. 115 O4 57.02N 34.57E
Tottenham New South Wales 52 B2 32.15S 147.22E
Tottori Japan 104 C3 35.32N 134.12E
Toubkal, Jbel *mtn* Morocco 124 D5 31.03N 7.57W
Touggourt Algeria 124 E5 33.08N 6.04E
Toulon France 116 E5 43.07N 5.53E
Toulouse France 116 D5 43.33N 1.24E
Toungoo Myanmar 107 J4 19.00N 96.30E
Tours France 114 G1 47.23N 0.42E
Towada Japan 104 E4 40.36N 140.47E
Townshend I. Queensland 60 D2 22.17S 150.34E
Townsville Queensland 60 C3 19.15S 146.49E
Towori G. Indonesia 99 G3 2.00S 122.30E
Toyama Japan 104 D3 36.42N 137.14E
Toyama-wan *b.* Japan 104 D3 37.00N 137.20E
Toyota Japan 104 D3 35.05N 137.09E
Tozeur Tunisia 116 E3 33.55N 8.08E
Trabzon Turkey 117 K5 41.00N 39.43E
Trafalgar Victoria 56 D1 38.13S 146.09E
Trangan *i.* Indonesia 99 I2 6.30S 134.15E
Trangie New South Wales 52 B2 32.04S 147.59E
Transantarctic Mts Antarctica 91 73.59S 156.44E
Transylvanian Alps *mts* Romania 117 H6 45.35N 24.40E
Trapani Italy 116 F4 38.02N 12.30E
Traralgon Victoria 56 D1 38.12S 146.34E
Travellers L. New South Wales 52 A2 33.18S 142.00E
Travers, Mt New Zealand 84 E3 42.01S 172.44E
Traverse City USA 133 I5 44.46N 85.38W
Trelleborg Sweden 114 J3 55.22N 13.10E
Trento Italy 116 F6 46.04N 11.06E
Trenton USA 133 L5 40.15N 74.43W
Tres Picos *mtn* Argentina 141 C3 38.13S 61.50W
Triabunna Tasmania 72 F3 42.30S 147.54E
Tribulation, C. Queensland 60 C3 16.01S 145.26E
Trieste Italy 117 F6 45.40N 13.47E
Trikala Greece 117 H4 39.34N 21.46E
Trincomalee Sri Lanka 107 G2 8.34N 81.13E
Trindade *i.* Atlantic Oc. 137 H4 20.30S 29.15W
Trinidad Bolivia 140 C5 15.00S 64.50W
Trinidad *i.* S. America 135 L3 10.20N 61.10W
Trinidad USA 132 F4 37.11N 104.31W
Trinidad & Tobago S. America 135 L3 10.30N 61.20W
Trinity B. Queensland 60 C3 16.37S 145.26E
Tripoli Greece 117 H4 37.31N 22.21E
Tripoli Lebanon 109 A4 34.26N 35.52E
Tripoli Libya 124 F5 32.58N 13.12E
Tripolitania *f.* Libya 116 F3 31.00N 12.00E
Tripura *d.* India 107 I5 23.45N 91.45E
Tristan da Cunha *i.* Atlantic Oc. 144 A2 38.00S 12.00W
Trnava Slovakia 115 K2 48.22N 17.36E
Trobriand Is PNG 88 C2 8.33S 151.09E
Trois Rivières *town* Canada 131 K2 46.21N 72.34W
Troitsko-Pechorsk Russian Fed. 118 H4 62.40N 56.08E
Trollhättan Sweden 114 J4 58.16N 12.18E
Tromsø Norway 118 D4 69.39N 18.57E
Trondheim Norway 114 I5 63.25N 10.22E
Trout L. Canada 133 H7 51.13N 93.20W
Troyes France 114 H2 48.18N 4.05E
Trujillo Peru 140 B6 8.06S 79.00W
Trundle New South Wales 52 B2 32.56S 147.43E
Truro Canada 131 L2 45.24N 63.18W
Tsaratanana, Massif du *mts* Madagascar 123 D3 14.00S 49.00E
Tsetserleg Mongolia 102 I7 47.26N 101.22E
Tsimlyansk Resr Russian Fed. 111 H4 48.00N 43.00E
Tsivil'sk Russian Fed. 115 R3 55.52N 47.29E
Tsna *r.* Russian Fed. 115 Q3 54.28N 42.02E
Tsu Japan 104 D2 34.43N 136.35E
Tsuchiura Japan 104 E3 36.05N 140.12E
Tsugaru-kaikyo *str.* Japan 104 E4 41.30N 140.50E
Tsumeb Namibia 123 A3 19.13S 17.42E
Tsuruga Japan 104 D3 35.40N 136.05E
Tsushima *i.* Japan 104 B2 34.30N 129.20E
Tuamotu Is Pacific Oc. 81 Q5 17.00S 142.00W
Tu'anuku Tonga 82 I6 18.40S 174.02W
Tuapse Russian Fed. 115 P1 44.06N 39.04E
Tuban Indonesia 98 E2 6.55S 112.01E
Tubruq Libya 117 H3 32.04N 23.57E
Tubuai *i.* Pacific Oc. 81 Q4 23.23S 149.27W
Tucson USA 132 D3 32.15N 110.57W
Tucumcari USA 132 F4 35.11N 103.44W
Tucuruí Brazil 140 E6 3.42S 49.44W
Tucuruí Resr Brazil 140 E6 4.35S 49.33W
Tufi PNG 88 B2 9.06S 149.19E
Tuguegarao Phil. 99 G7 17.36N 121.44E
Tui Spain 116 B5 42.03N 8.38W
Tukangbesi Is Indonesia 99 G2 5.30S 124.00E
Tukums Latvia 115 L4 56.58N 23.10E
Tula Amer. Samoa 82 I8 14.15S 170.35W
Tula Russian Fed. 115 P3 54.12N 37.37E
Tulít'a Canada 130 F4 64.55N 125.31W
Tullamore New South Wales 52 B2 32.40S 147.35E
Tully Queensland 60 C3 17.56S 146.00E
Tulsa USA 132 G4 36.07N 95.58W
Tulu Welel *mtn* Ethiopia 108 B1 8.53N 34.49E
Tumba, L. Dem. Rep. of Congo 125 F1 0.45S 18.00E
Tumbarumba New South Wales 52 C2 35.48S 148.03E
Tumby Bay *town* South Australia 64 C2 34.23S 136.06E
Tumen China 104 B4 42.56N 129.47E
Tumen *r.* China/N. Korea 104 C4 42.19N 130.40E
Tumkur India 106 F3 13.20N 77.06E
Tumut New South Wales 52 C2 35.20S 148.15E
Tunis Tunisia 124 F5 36.47N 10.10E
Tunisia Africa 124 E5 34.00N 9.00E
Tunja Colombia 135 J2 5.33N 73.23W
Tunnsjøen *l.* Norway 114 J6 64.42N 13.24E
Tupelo USA 133 I3 34.15N 88.43W
Tura Russian Fed. 119 M4 64.05N 100.00E
Turabah Saudi Arabia 108 C3 21.14N 41.37E
Turangi New Zealand 84 F5 38.59S 175.49E
Turbat Pakistan 106 C6 25.59N 63.04E
Turda Romania 115 L1 46.34N 23.47E
Turhal Turkey 117 K5 40.23N 36.05E
Turin Italy 116 E6 45.04N 7.40E
Turkana, L. Kenya 123 C5 4.00N 36.00E
Turkestan Kazakhstan 102 B6 43.17N 68.16E
Turkey Asia 108 B4 39.19N 34.21E
Turkmenistan Asia 108 D5 40.50N 58.26E
Turks and Caicos Is C. America 135 J5 21.30N 71.50W
Turks Is Turks & Caicos Is 135 J5 21.30N 71.10W
Turku Finland 115 L5 60.27N 22.15E
Turneffe Is Belize 134 G4 17.30N 87.45W
Turners Beach *town* Tasmania 72 E4 41.09S 146.13E
Turon *r.* New South Wales 52 C2 33.06S 149.23E
Turpan China 102 F6 42.55N 89.06E
Turquino *mtn* Cuba 135 I5 20.05N 76.50W
Tuscaloosa USA 133 I3 33.12N 87.33W
Tuticorin India 107 F2 8.48N 78.10E
Tutuila *i.* Amer. Samoa 82 I8 14.18S 170.42W
Tuun, Mt N. Korea 104 B4 41.06N 127.55E
Tuvalu Pacific Oc. 80 M6 7.24S 178.20E
Tuxtla Gutiérrez Mexico 134 F4 16.45N 93.09W
Tuz, L. Turkey 117 J4 38.45N 33.24E
Tuzla Bosnia-Herz. 117 G5 44.33N 18.41E
Tver' Russian Fed. 115 O4 56.50N 35.54E
Tweed Heads *town* New South Wales 52 D3 28.10S 153.35E
Twin Falls *town* USA 132 D5 42.34N 114.30W
Twizel New Zealand 84 D2 44.16S 170.07E
Twofold B. New South Wales 52 C1 37.04S 149.57E
Tyler USA 133 G3 32.22N 95.18W
Tynda Russian Fed. 119 O3 55.11N 124.34E
Tyre Lebanon 109 A3 33.15N 35.14E
Tyrrell, L. Victoria 56 B3 35.20S 142.52E
Tyrrhenian Sea Med. Sea 116 F5 40.00N 12.00E
Tyumen Russian Fed. 118 I3 57.11N 65.29E

U

Ubangi *r.* Congo/Dem. Rep. of Congo 125 F1 0.25S 17.50E
Uberaba Brazil 141 E5 19.47S 47.57W
Uberlândia Brazil 140 E5 18.57S 48.17W
Ubon Ratchathani Thailand 98 C7 15.15N 104.50E
Ucayali *r.* Peru 140 B6 4.00S 73.30W
Udaipur India 106 E5 24.36N 73.47E
Uddevalla Sweden 114 I4 58.21N 11.57E
Uddjaure *l.* Sweden 115 K6 65.56N 17.52E
Udine Italy 116 F6 46.03N 13.15E
Udon Thani Thailand 98 C7 17.29N 102.45E
Udupi India 106 E3 13.21N 74.45E
Ueda Japan 104 D3 36.27N 138.13E
Uele *r.* Dem. Rep. of Congo 123 B5 4.08N 22.25E
Uelzen Germany 114 I3 52.58N 10.34E
Ufa Russian Fed. 118 H3 54.45N 55.58E
Uganda Africa 123 C5 1.00N 33.00E
Uglegorsk Russian Fed. 119 Q2 49.01N 142.04E
Ugra *r.* Russian Fed. 115 P3 54.30N 36.10E
Uíge Angola 123 A4 7.40S 15.09E
Uinta Mts USA 132 D5 40.45N 110.30W
Ujung Pandang Indonesia 98 F2 5.09S 119.28E
Ukhta Russian Fed. 118 H4 63.33N 53.44E
Ukiah USA 132 B4 39.09N 123.12W
Ukraine Europe 115 N2 49.23N 31.18E
Ulaanbaatar Mongolia 103 J7 47.54N 106.52E
Ulaangom Mongolia 102 G7 49.59N 92.00E
Ulan-Ude Russian Fed. 119 M3 51.55N 107.40E
Ulchin S. Korea 104 B3 37.00N 129.26E
Ulenia, L. New South Wales 52 A3 29.57S 142.19E
Uliastay Mongolia 102 H7 47.42N 96.52E
Ulithi *i.* Fed. States of Micronesia 99 J6 10.00N 139.40E
Ulladulla New South Wales 52 C2 35.21S 150.26E
Ullung do *i.* S. Korea 104 C3 37.30N 130.55E
Ulm Germany 114 I2 48.25N 9.59E
Ulsan S. Korea 104 B3 35.32N 129.21E
Ulundi RSA 123 C2 28.17S 31.28E
Uluru/Ayers Rock *f.* Northern Territory 76 C1 25.20S 131.05E
Ulverstone Tasmania 72 E4 41.09S 146.13E
Umagico Queensland 60 B4 10.53S 142.21E
Uman' Ukraine 115 N2 48.45N 30.14E
Umaroona, L. South Australia 64 C4 26.59S 138.04E
Umbakumba Northern Territory 76 D4 13.52S 136.51E
Umboi *i.* PNG 88 B2 5.42S 147.50E
Ume *r.* Sweden 115 L5 63.46N 20.19E
Umeå Sweden 115 L5 63.50N 20.17E
Umingmaktok *see* Bathurst Inlet Canada 130
Umm Sa'ad Libya 117 I3 31.33N 25.03E
Umtata RSA 123 B1 31.35S 28.47E
Umuarama Brazil 141 D4 24.00S 53.20W
Unecha Russian Fed. 115 O3 52.51N 32.41E

Malcolm and Brian wish to thank their wives and families for their support and encouragement, and staff at Pearson Education Australia for their professionalism and enthusiasm. They would also like to thank the following people for their assistance: Mike Archer and Bev Walsh, Bluescope Steel Limited, Port Kembla; Jeff Bailey and Terry Boyd, Resource Industry Associates, Melbourne; Kim Badcock, CSIRO Marine Research Remote Sensing Facility, Hobart; Peter Blackshaw, Yallourn Energy, Yallourn; Edward Codsi, Sydney; Stuart Cohen, NSW National Parks and Wildlife Service, Queanbeyan; George Cresswell, CSIRO Division of Marine Research, Hobart; Peter Dunda, Bureau of Meteorology, Sydney; Neil Freeman, Environmental Resources Information Network, Canberra; Cindy Hahn, Geoscience Australia, Canberra; Robert Hill, Charles Sturt University, Bathurst; Anne Mahon, Neal Jordan-Caws and Mark Steward, Collins Bartholomew, Glasgow; Terry Malone, Bureau of Meteorology, Brisbane; Paul Nanninga, Murray–Darling Basin Commission, Canberra; James Risbey, School of Mathematical Sciences, Monash University, Melbourne; Ray Stacey, Hobart; Andrew Watkins, Bureau of Meteorology, Melbourne; Melissa Webb, National Education Services Unit, Australian Bureau of Statistics, Melbourne.

The authors and publisher are grateful to the following for permission to reproduce original source material in this atlas:

ACT Land Information Centre, ACT Planning and Land Authority: p. 51;
AIATSIS/Aboriginal Studies Press: p. 39 reproduced with permission from *The Encyclopaedia of Aboriginal Australia* by David Horton;
Australian Government Department of the Environment and Heritage © Commonwealth of Australia: pp. 20 (2), 73 (plant cover data);
BlueScope Steel Limited: p. 53;
Bureau of Meteorology © Commonwealth of Australia: pp. 16 (3 & 4) satellite images processed by the Bureau of Meteorology, originally obtained from the Geostationary Meteorological Satellite (GMS-5) of the Japan Meteorological Agency; 27 (2–4), 35 (4—radar images);
CSIRO Marine Research: p. 24;
Department of Lands: pp. 22, 23;
Descloitres, Jacques, MODIS Rapid Response Team, NASA/GSFC: p. 69 (left);
Geoscience Australia Copyright © Commonwealth of Australia 2000 Landsat ETM satellite image acquired by ACRES, Geoscience Australia: pp. 28 (3), 30 (3), 77;
Land Victoria, Department of Sustainability and Environment: p. 57;
Murray–Darling Basin Commission: p. 18;
NASA: pp. 100 (2), 101 (3);
NASA/GSFC Landsat Project Science Office and USGS EROS Data Center: p. 105;
NASA/GSFC/MITI/ERSDAC/JAROS and US/Japan ASTER Science Team: p. 113;
NASA's Earth Observatory: p. 86;
NOAA: pp. 24 (2), 100 (3);
NOAA/NESDIS: pp. 26 (2), 32 (3);
Photolibrary.com: pp. 95 (2), 129 (1), 139;
Resource Industry Associates: pp. 9, 50, 54, 58, 61, 62, 66, 70, 74, 78;
Terralink International Limited, Cartography by, © 2004 Terralink International Limited: p. 87;
Tokai University Research & Information Center: p. 101 (4);
USGS/Earthquake Hazards Program: p. 129 (map);
Yallourn Energy Pty Ltd: p. 56;

The authors and publisher are grateful to the following who supplied data to develop material in this atlas:

ACT Government: p. 50;
AIATSIS: pp. 44–5;
Australian Antarctic Division: pp. 90–1;
Australian Bureau of Statistics: pp. 10, 17, 42–4, 45 (2), 47 (2), 50, 54–5, 58–9, 62–3, 66–7, 70–1, 74–5, 78–9;
Australian Gas Association: p. 45 (2);
Australian Geographic: p. 69 (right);
Australian Institute for Health and Welfare: p. 45;
Australian Institute of Petroleum: p. 46;
Australian Nuclear Science and Technology Organisation/International Nuclear Safety Center at Argonne National Laboratory: p. 153 (1);
Australian Railway Association: p. 47 (1);
Bureau of Meteorology: pp. 12–14, 15, 16, 25 (3), 26 (1), 27 (1), 29, 30 (2), 31 (1), 32, 33, 35 (1);
Bureau of Resource Sciences: p. 46;
Bureau of Tourism Research: p. 49;
Bureau of Transport and Communications Economics: p. 47;
CSIRO Atmospheric Research: p. 15;
Center for World Indigenous Studies: p. 165;
Center for World Indigenous Studies: p. 165;
Centre for Aboriginal Economic Policy Research, Australian National University: p. 45 (2 e) source data from *Monitoring Practical Reconciliation: Evidence from the Reconciliation Decade* by J.C. Altman and B. H. Hunter;
Convention on the Conservation of Antarctic Marine Living Resources: pp. 90–1;
Department of Environment and Conservation NSW (National Parks and Wildlife Service): p. 31 (2);
Department of Industry and Resources, Western Australia: p. 46;
Department of Natural Resources, Mines and Energy, Queensland: p. 46;
Department of Primary Industries, Victoria: p. 46;
Department of the Chief Minister: p. 45 (1);
Department of the Environment and Heritage: p. 48 (1);
Disaster Mitigation Unit, Queensland: p. 29;
Emergency Management Australia: pp. 28 (1 & 2), 30 (1);
Food and Agriculture Organization of the United Nations: p. 152 (1);
Forum Fisheries Agency: p. 80–1;
Goddard Institute for Space Studies: p. 100;
Greenpeace: p. 152 (2);
International Energy Agency: p. 153 (2);
Land and Water Australia: pp. 36 (1), 36 (4) adapted with permission from *Australian Agriculture Assessment 2001 Vol. 1*, Land and Water Australia © Commonwealth of Australia; 37 (3 & 4) reproduced with permission from *Landscape Health in Australia*, Land and Water Australia, 2001 © Commonwealth of Australia;
Land Victoria, Department of Sustainability and Environment: p. 59;
Metcalf, Thomas R., University of Hawaii: p. 26 (3);
Murray–Darling Basin Commission: p. 19 (1);
NOAA: p. 25 (1 & 2);
NSW Department of Mineral Resources: p. 46;
NSW Department of Infrastructure, Planning and Natural Resources: p. 55;
National Land and Water Resources Audit, Commonwealth of Australia: p. 17 (3) reproduced with permission from *Australian Water Resources Assessment 2000*;
National Statistical Office of Papua New Guinea: pp. 88–9;
Northern Territory Department of Infrastructure, Planning & Environment: p. 79;
Planning SA, the Department for Transport and Urban Planning: p. 67;
Primary Industries and Resources South Australia: p. 46
Productivity Commission, Canberra: p. 45 (2) source data from *Overcoming Indigenous Disadvantage: Key Indicators 2003* by the Steering Committee for the Review of Government Service Provision 2003;
Queensland Department of Local Government and Planning: p. 63;
Risby, Dr James: p. 33 (3.2);
Smith, Carl B., Gold Coast, Qld: p. 27 (1) map adapted with permission. Source data supplied by Bureau of Meteorology;
South Pacific Applied Geoscience Commission: pp. 80–1;
Stacey, Ray: p. 75;
State of the Environment Reporting Section, Commonwealth of Australia: p. 36 (2) map adapted with permission from *Technical Papers Series II*, State of Environment 2001;
Statistics New Zealand: p. 85;
UNEP–WCMC: p. 100 (1);
UNHCR: p. 165 (1);
US Navy Bathymetry courtesy of Lamont–Doherty Earth Observatory, University of Columbia: pp. 144–5;
United Nations: p. 157 (1);
WA Office of Energy: p. 46;
WWF: p. 152 (2);
Western Australian Planning Commission: p. 71;
World Bank, World Development Indicators: pp. 154–5, 157–9, 160–2, 166, 168–75;

Pp. 20 (1), 21 (1), 32 (2), 34 (1.1 & 2), 65 source data/maps are Copyright © Commonwealth of Australia, Geoscience Australia. All rights reserved. Reproduced by permission of the Chief Executive Officer, Geoscience Australia, Canberra, ACT.
Apart from any use permitted under the *Copyright Act 1968*, no part may be reproduced by any process without prior written permission from Geoscience Australia. Requests and inquiries concerning reproduction and rights should be addressed to the Manager, Geoscience Australia, GPO Box 378, Canberra ACT 2601 or by email to copyright@ga.gov.au

Pearson Education Australia
A division of Pearson Australia Group Pty Ltd
Level 9, 5 Queens Road
Melbourne 3004 Australia

Offices in Sydney, Brisbane and Perth, and associated companies throughout the world.

Unless otherwise stated, the maps on pages 10, 11, 52, 56, 60, 64, 68, 72, 76, 80–5 inclusive, 88–167 inclusive and on the endpapers are licensed to Collins–Longman Atlases and are derived from databases © Bartholomew Ltd 2005.

Unless otherwise stated, the maps on pages 12–51 inclusive, 53–5 inclusive, 57–9 inclusive, 61–3 inclusive, 65–7 inclusive, 69–71 inclusive, 73–5 inclusive, 77–9 inclusive and 86–7 were drawn by Laurie Whiddon and Wendy Gorton. These pages were formatted by Sharon Carr.

Australian editor: Nick Tapp
Cover designed by Susannah Low
Front cover images courtesy of: photolibrary.com (main image); Jason Haack (bottom, far left); NASA/JPL–Caltech (bottom, third from left); NASA/GSFC/MITI/ERSDAC/ JAROS and US/Japan ASTER Science Team (bottom, second from right)

Set in Frutiger Roman 8/11
Produced by Pearson Education Australia
Printed in Hong Kong (SWTC/03)

National Library of Australia
Cataloguing-in-Publication data

Stacey, Malcolm.
  Longman atlas.

  5th ed.
  Includes index.
  For year 7 to 12 students.

  ISBN 0 1236 0518 0 (print).
  ISBN 0 1236 0600 4 (CD-rom).

  1. Atlases, Australian. 2. Atlases. 3. Atlases, Australian – Software. I. Ralph, Brian. II. Title.

912

1 MERCATOR

The Mercator projection, created by Flemish cartographer Gerardus Mercator in 1569, is one of the earliest world projections. It was of great value to sailors during the 'age of discovery' because direction is correct and compass bearings can be plotted as straight lines anywhere on the map. It is not a common world map in atlases because it distorts distance, shape and area above 15°N and 15°S of the equator—the 'Greenland effect' greatly exaggerates land area near the poles—but is still used at sea.

CONTINENTS

This map shows the seven continents. It follows the common practice of using the Ural Mountains as the boundary between Asia and Europe, and divides the Russian Federation into European Russia to the west of the Ural Mountains and Asian Russia to the east. The entire island of New Guinea is also usually considered to be part of Asia. New Zealand and some of the island nations of the Pacific Ocean are shown here as part of Australia, but Australia, Papua New Guinea, New Zealand and many Pacific nations are often grouped together as the region of Oceania.

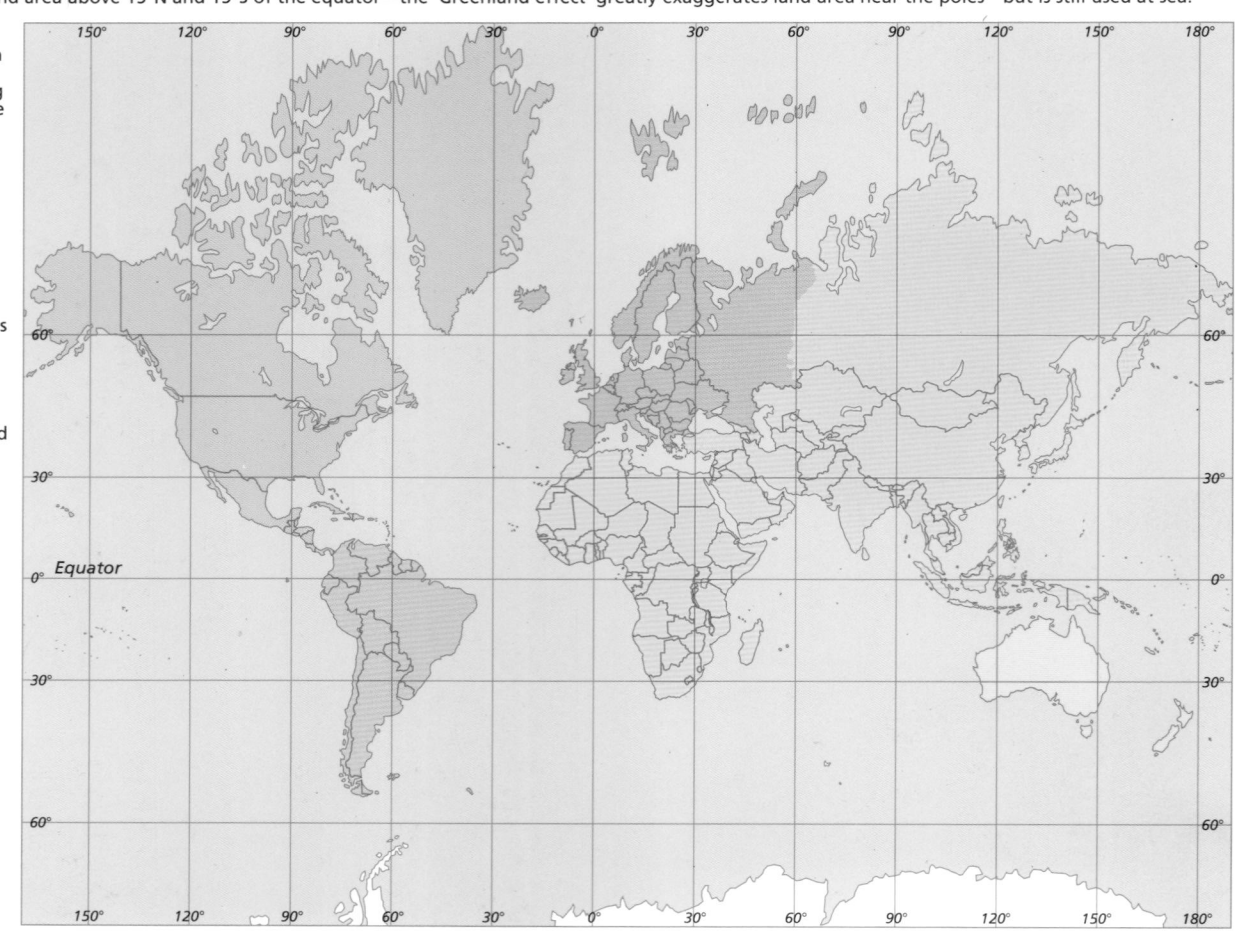

- Africa
- Antarctica
- Asia
- Australia
- Europe
- North America
- South America

2 ECKERT IV

The fourth of six projections created by German cartographer Max Eckert in 1906 is an equal-area projection, i.e. it shows the correct area of the Earth's land masses relative to each other and gives equal recognition to both tropical and higher-latitude regions. Equal-area projections are particularly useful for world thematic maps showing global distribution, where correct size/area is important to enable comparison between continents and countries. Eckert IV is the projection used for world maps in this atlas.

MAJOR GEOGRAPHICAL REGIONS

This map shows countries of the world grouped in major geographical regions, as classified by the Australian Bureau of Statistics.

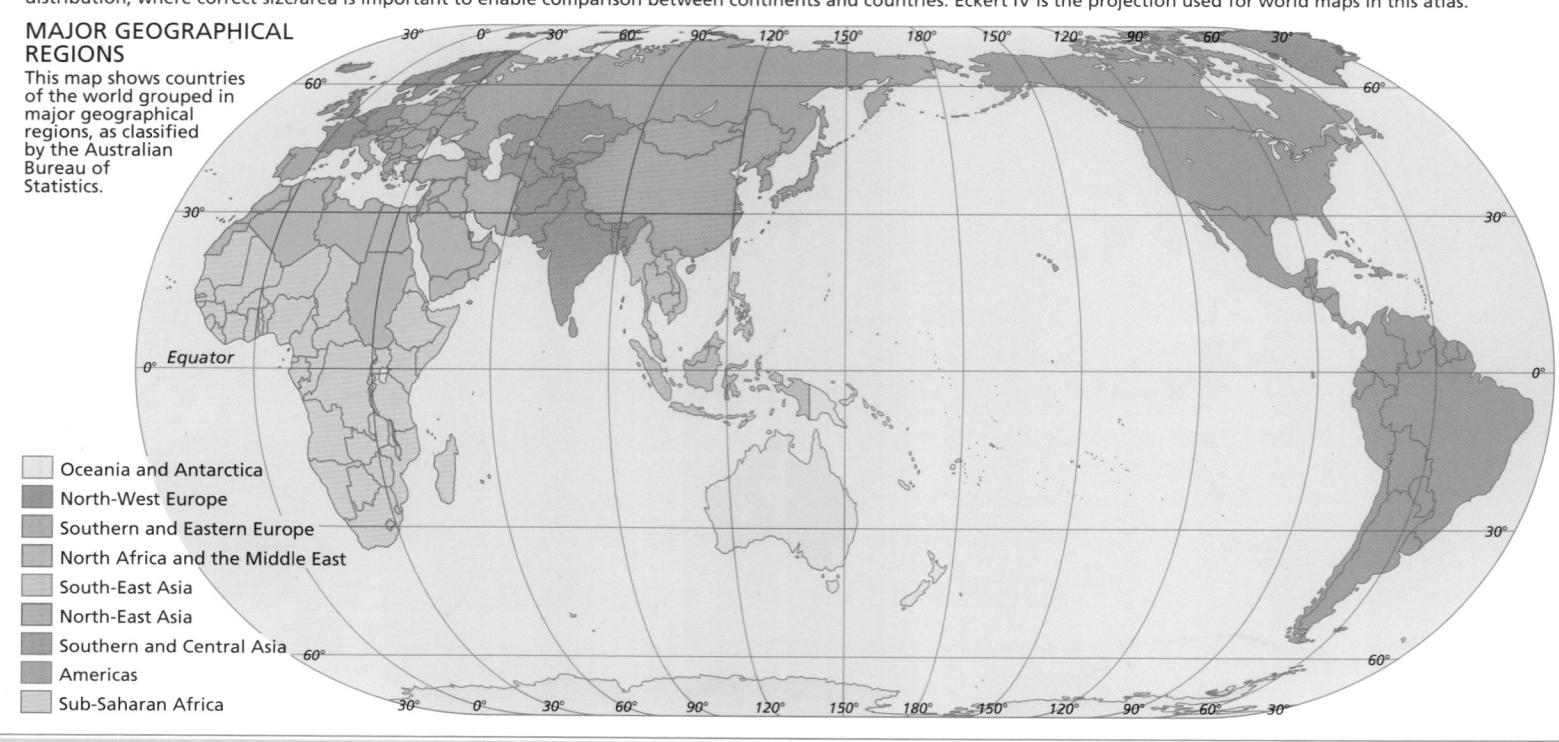

- Oceania and Antarctica
- North-West Europe
- Southern and Eastern Europe
- North Africa and the Middle East
- South-East Asia
- North-East Asia
- Southern and Central Asia
- Americas
- Sub-Saharan Africa